Emerging World Law

Volume One: Key Documents and Decisions of the Global Constituent Assemblies and the Provisional World Parliament

EDITED BY

EUGENIA ALMAND AND GLEN T. MARTIN

forthcoming

VOLUME TWO:
ORDER OF THE COURT:
GLOBAL STATUTES FOR
JUST ENFORCEMENT AND ADJUDICATION

VOLUME THREE:
EARTH LEGISLATION FOR
ECONOMY, EDUCATION,
ELECTIONS AND ENVIRONMENT

INSTITUTE FOR ECONOMIC DEMOCRACY PRESS
IED
SUN CITY, ARIZONA

Published by: the Institute for Economic Democracy Press
Sun City, Arizona, USA 888.533.1020 / www.ied.info / ied@ied.info

In cooperation with the Institute On World Problems www.worldproblems.net

Emerging World Law - Version 1.1

Cover design: Eugenia Almand. About the cover illustration:

Reproduction of the classic painting "Royal Pavilion East Front from Nash's Views" by John Nash. John Nash was both the designer for the renovation of the Roval Pavilion as well as the painter of this 1826 classic piece. The Royal Pavilion in Brighton, England, was the venue for the first session of the Provisional World Parliament in September 1982. (Reprinted by permission of the Royal Pavilion and Museums, Brighton & Hove, United Kingdom.) For more information go to: http://www.royalpavilion.org.uk/

Library of Congress Cataloging-in-Publication Data

Emerging world law / edited by Eugenia Almand and Glen T. Martin.
p. cm.

Includes bibliographical references and index.
ISBN 978-1-933567-16-7 (alk. paper) -- ISBN 978-1-933567-19-8 (trade cloth)
1. International law. 2. International organization. 3. International cooperation.
4. International relations. I. Almand, Eugenia 1955- II. Martin, Glen T. 1944-
KZ1318.E44 2009
341--dc22
2008049474

Eugenia Almand is Secretary of the Provisional World Parliament, Executive Director of the Institute On World Problems (registered 501c3 in Virginia, USA) and Deputy Secretary General of the World Constitution & Parliament Association.

Dr. Almand has had an association with the Provisional World Parliament since 1984, and as a certified delegate attended the 2nd Session of the Provisional World Parliament which met at the Vigyam Bhavan and Constitution Club in New Delhi, India, in March 1985. Dr. Almand served as Expeditor and Assistant Secretary of the 5th Session of the Provisional World Parliament at Malta in 1985. She was elected to serve as Secretary of the Parliament at the Bangkok, Sixth Session, 2003, and has served in that capacity at each parliamentary session since.

The Institute On World Problems in September 2005 awarded Dr. Almand the degree of *Juris Doctor* to reflect 13 years of international legal research work, including instruction as a seminarian for the Institute in international and world law in a half dozen countries. Dr. Almand is a bilingual teacher and also has a Masters Degree in Computer Education from California State University, Northridge, California, USA, as well as numerous bilingual/multicultural teaching certificates.

Glen T. Martin is Professor of Philosophy and Religious Studies and Chairperson of the program in Peace Studies at Radford University. He is President of International Philosophers for Peace (IPPNO) (www.radford.edu/~peace/ippno) and Secretary-General of the World Constitution and Parliament Association (WCPA) (www.wcpa.biz) – an organization that sponsors the Provisional World Parliament. Dr. Martin is also President of the Institute On World Problems (IOWP) (www.worldproblems.net) – an organization studying the solution to world problems under democratic world law.

His recent books include Millenium Dawn – The Philosophy of Planetary Crisis and Human Liberation (IED Press, 2005), World Revolution through World Law – Basic Documents of the Emerging Earth Federation (IED Press, 2005) and Ascent to Freedom – Practical & Philosophical Foundations of Democratic World Law (IED Press, 2008). Dr. Martin has given seminars, lectures, and workshops in many countries of the world and published dozens of articles on world problems, world order, democratic thought and the concept of world law. He makes his home in Radford, Virginia.

This book is dedicated to

Dr. Terence Amerasinghe
Barrister-at-law and advocate, Supreme Court of Sri Lanka
President, World Constitution and Parliament Association

The Honorable Syed Mohammed Hussein
Judge, Supreme Court of Bangladesh

Professor Philip Isely
Former Secretary-General,
World Constitution and Parliament Association
Businessman of Denver, Colorado

D. M. Spencer
Constitutional Lawyer and
Professor, Sydenham College, Bombay, India

Who together, during January and February of 1972, in Denver, Colorado
created the first draft of the
Constitution for the Federation of Earth,
according to the guidelines given them
by the first World Constituent Assembly.

And this book is dedicated to

Dr. Max Habicht
International and Constitutional Lawyer of Switzerland
President Speaker of the 1947 Montreux Conference
With whom the four consulted by telephone on a regular basis
during the winter 1972 drafting session.

And this book is dedicated to

The hundreds of World Citizens
in the four World Constituent Assemblies
of 1968, 1977, 1979, and 1991
who debated, amended, and ratified the *Earth Constitution*

The World is forever in their debt!

Acknowledgements

When a comprehensive book documenting the constitutional and legislative history of emerging world law is created, the editors owe a great deal of gratitude to the many other persons that make that creation possible. In this case, there were countless persons who made various sorts of contributions. We would like to go as far as we can to specifically name as many people and organizations as possible in the overall work, which actually stretches back beyond the beginnings of the previous century. The credits here are not exhaustive however, but are only expressed to the more recent contributors to this work.

Thousands of people contributed to and participated in the sessions of the World Constituent Assemblies and the sessions of the provisional World Parliament, including those who did tremendous organizational work to make the deliberations of the sessions possible.

The late international lawyer Dr. Terence P. Amerasinghe, long-time Speaker of the provisional World Parliament, invested much of his life work building the provisional World Parliament, as well making extensive contribution to the drafting of the *Earth Constitution*, drafting of world legislation, and writing the chapters in this book on world court development and history of world law.

Thanks to all those who helped to provide a warm and conducive environment where the editors could concentrate on the task of editing: Dr. Glen Martin's wife, Phyllis Turk, and daughters Rebekah Turk and Irayda Hicks; Al Almand, father of Eugenia Almand; Jagdish Gandhi, Founder-Manager of City Montessori School, Lucknow, also for his excellent promotion of the provisional World Parliament and leadership in world citizenship; Dr. Preeti Shankar and her family, as well as for their companionship during the writing process; the staff of the Children's International Summer Village, Lucknow, of City Montessori School; as well as the World Unity and Peace Education Department staff at CMS, Lucknow; and, not least of all, Dr. Simfei D. Balouki of Togo. We are thankful to Al Almand, father of Eugenia Almand, and to sister Dr. Sherri Almand, DVM, and family – Jamie, Dani & Dr. Steven Winokur, DVM – for providing a helpful environment for the completion of the first volume in its last stages.

We esteem Dr. Kunihiko Shimamoto and our many other colleagues of the Jinrui Aizenkai (Universal Love and Brotherhood Association) and to the Oomoto Foundation for their support, especially during the final stages of editing, but also for their long historical record of leadership for the Earth Federation. We are indebted to Bill Kovarik for his technical support; and to J.W. Smith, also for his technical support, for his world brilliant economic analysis and teachings, and for his authorship in respective bibliographic contributions to this volume. We are grateful to Garry Davis for his lifelong work in the development of world government, world law and world parliament, as well as for his authorship in respective bibliographic contributions to this book.

Thanks to Professor Errol Harris and to Dr. Roger Kotila for their own continuing support to the Institute on World Problems, helping to make the authorship possible, as well as for their cogent promotion of Earth Federation in conformance with the *Earth Constitution*.

We are grateful to Philip Isely who long insisted that the people must write the peace, and who was the foremost contributor to the drafting of the *Constitution for the Federation of Earth*, and original primary author of many of the early world legislative statutes. Thanks also to his first wife, Margaret Isely, who also participated in the process of constitutional and legislative drafting.

We are indebted to international lawyers Max Habicht, Syed Muhammed Hussein, and D. M. Spencer for their roles as the three other primary original authors of the *Earth Constitution* (along with Philip Isely and Terence Amerasinghe). Thanks to all 25 members of the 1968-1977 Constitutional Drafting Commission for making their deliberations for the development and correction of the *Earth Constitution* in preparation for the line-by-line deliberation of the second World Constituent Assembly. And special thanks to Sir Dr. Reinhart Ruge, Chair of the Constitutional Drafting Commission.

We appreciate the many other original authors of world legislation adopted to date by the Provisional World Parliament, including Dr. Nejat Veziroglu, Dr. Rashmi Mayur, Lou Kutner, Dr. Hanna Newcombe, Ian Hackett, John Stockwell, Dr. Hannan Awwad, Dick Burkhart, and Rev. Inagaki Jasuhiko. Thanks to Bill Pace and others who promoted professional drafting standards by qualified jurists and legislators in the creation of deliberative drafting groups, such as the Assembly of States Parties.

We look with great reverence and thanks to the eminent jurists Abdul Koroma, Doudou Thiam, James Crawford, Adriaan Bos, et. al., of the International Law Commission, for their work in the initial drafting of the Rome Statute for the International Criminal Court, from which much world legislation is largely derived, and for their other contributions to world jurisprudence.

Thanks to J. C. Smith with the Arizona Legislative Council, and to the Legislative Administration Committee, State of Oregon, for actually providing these professional drafting standards on-line to the worldwide public, thereby greatly increasing the quality of the world legislation being drafted, deliberated, and adopted. We are indebted to the many deliberative drafting groups that participated with the help of countless unnamed original authors of world statutes, such as the Assembly of States Parties, the International Accounting Standards Board, the 1989 session of the General Assembly of the United Nations, the Global Peoples Assembly Committee, the World Judicial Commission, the World Youth Parliament for Water. Innumerable others participated in the original drafting of various international conventions that are suitable for minor significant amendment and adoption within the framework of emerging world law.

Thanks to Hari Homaro Vacal of the Ensophion New Humanity Center, in Kalamata, Greece, for providing a place to work during the early final stages of drafting.

We are grateful to the world citizen students of City Montessori School, Lucknow, who have inspired us with their model world parliament sessions as well as with their participation in sessions of the actual provisional World Parliament, for their strength to draw youth into the process of developing world law, and for reminding us to consider the youth of the world in our deliberations. We are also thankful to our other inspiring students worldwide.

As noted above, this list of acknowledgements cannot be exhaustive, because of the many thousands of others who contributed in major or minor ways to the elaboration and deliberative adoption of the world law by the World Constituent Assemblies and the provisional World Parliament. We appreciate our good teachers. Though not all are mentioned here, we are deeply grateful.

Emerging World Law

Volume One

Key Documents and Decisions of the Global Constituent Assemblies and the Provisional World Parliament

Edited by
Eugenia Almand and Glen T. Martin

TABLE OF CONTENTS

Chapter One: Introduction (by Glen T. Martin) 1
1.1. The Greatest Gift to Humankind: the Possibility of Peace and Prosperity 1
1.2. The Structures and Functions of World Unity through World Law 5
1.3. Democratic World Law: Democracy and Private Property 11
1.4. Democratic World Law: Democracy and Sovereignty 19

Chapter Two: Conceptualizing the Earth Federation 29
2.1. Executive Summary of the *Earth Constitution* 31
2.2. Charts and diagram plates of Earth Federation 36

Chapter Three: A History of Emerging World Law: 47
the World Constitution & Parliament Association,
the Global Constituent Assemblies and Early Sessions
of the Provisional World Parliament (by Terence Amerasinghe)

3.1. The World Constitution and Parliament Association and the New Direction to Humankind's Struggle for a Better World. 47
3.2. First Sessions of World Constituent Assembly at Interlaken, Switzerland and Wolfach, Germany, 1968 52
3.3. Santa Barbara, 1972, to 2nd World Constituent Assembly, Innsbruck, Austria, 1977 55
3.4. The Ratification Campaign – Third Constituent Assembly, Colombo, Sri Lanka, 1979 ; Preparatory Conference, New Delhi, India, 1981, and First Provisional World Parliament. Brighton, U.K., 1982 58
3.5. The New Common Enemy–Accelerating Increase of Carbon Dioxide (CO_2). Second and Third Sessions of the Provisional World Parliament New Delhi, India, 1985 and Miami Beach, Florida, U.S.A., 1987 65

3.6. Fourth World Constituent Assembly, Troia, Portugal, and Fourth Session of Provisional World Parliament, Barcelona, Spain **71**
3.7. Growing Strength of W.C.P.A. Invites Superpower Opposition as Mirrored at the Fifth Session of the Provisional World Parliament, Malta, 2000 **80**
3.8. At the Millenium - NATO takes command and makes the U.N. its pawn **85**

Chapter Three: Pictorial History **91**

Chapter Three Addendum:
Recent History of the Provisional World Parliament (by Eugenia Almand) **107**

Chapter Four: Manifesto of the Earth Federation (by Glen T. Martin) **121**
Foreword 121
4.1. Prologue 123
4.2. What the Earth Federation has accomplished to date 124
4.3. Humanity poised at the crossroads between destruction and liberation 126
4.4. Failure of the United Nations 129
4.5. The dead end environmental hopes of Rio and Johannesburg 131
4.6. The condition of our world at the dawn of the twenty-first century 135
4.7. Common sense economics under democratic world government 146
4.8. Where do we go from here? A call to the people and nations of the Earth 153

Chapter Five: Analytical Commentary on World Constitution Concepts (by Eugenia Almand) **159**

Chapter Six: ***The Constitution for the Federation of Earth*** **175**
(by World Constituent Assemblies: Primary Authors Henry P. Isely, Terence P. Amerasinghe, Syed Md. Husein, D. M. Spencer & Max Habicht)

Article

1. Broad functions of Earth Federation 180
2. Basic structure of Earth Federation 180
3. Organs of the Earth Federation 181
4. Powers Granted to the Earth Federation 182
5. The World Parliament 185
6. The World Executive 189
7. The World Administration 192
8. The Integrative Complex 194
9. The World Judiciary 201
10. The Enforcement System 204
11. The World Ombudsmus 208
12. Bill of Rights 209

13. Directive Principles 211
14. Safeguards and Reservations 212
15. World Federal Zones and World Capitals 213
16. World Territories and Exterior Relations 214
17. Ratification and Implementation 215
18. Amendments 223
19. Provisional World Government 224

Chapter Seven: Clarification of the *Earth Constitution* (by Eugenia Almand) **245**

Chapter Eight: Resolutions and Memorials of the Provisional World Parliament **259**

Resolution of the Recognition of the Rights of Animals, enacted first session, Brighton 1982; 263

Peace of the Brave: Resolution for Palestinian Statehood; fifth session, Qawra, 2000; 264

Declaration of the Independence of the ***Earth Constitution*** and World Legislation, sixth session, Bangkok, 2003; 266

Rules of Procedure for the World Constituent Assembly as per *Earth Constitution*, Article 18.5., sixth session, Bangkok, 2003. 267

Resolution on the Spirit of Global Government, sixth session, Bangkok, 2003; 272

Memorial to the Assembly of States Parties, seventh session, Chennai, 2003; 273

Pledge of Allegiance to the Federation of Earth, seventh session, Chennai, 2003; 276

Recommended tax policy statement, eighth session, Lucknow, 2004; 277

Memorial to General Assembly President Jean Ping, to convene the United Nations General Review Conference in conformance with United Nations Charter Article 109, for the United Nations to consider and adopt the ***Earth Constitution*** to replace the United Nations Charter., eighth session, Lucknow, 2004; 278

Promotion of Experanto and auxiliary languages as official working languages of the Provisional World Parliament and the Earth Federation, eighth session, Lucknow, 2004. 278

Resolution on Good Government and its Essential Tasks under the Earth Federation, eighth session, Lucknow, 2004; 279

Declaration of the Rights of the People of Earth to create and ratify a World Constitution and hold sessions of the Provisional World Parliament, eighth session, Lucknow, 2004; and 284

Resolution on the Trial of War Criminals and Perpetrators of Genocide and Crimes against Humanity, tenth session, Tripoli, 2007. 287

Chapter Nine: Legislative Summaries of World Legislative Acts 1 through 42 **291**

The first session deliberated and adopted five new world legislative acts:
* World Legislative Act #1 - Weapon Prohibition 293
* World Legislative Act #2 - World Economic Development 294
* World Legislative Act #3 - World Oceans & Seabeds 295
* World Legislative Act #4 - World University System 297
* World Legislative Act #5 - Provisional District World Courts 298

The second session deliberated and adopted three new world legislative acts:
* World Legislative Act #6 - Emergency Earth Rescue Administration 299
* World Legislative Act #7 - Earth Federation Funding Corporation 300
* World Legislative Act #8 - Commission on Terrorism 301

The third session deliberated and adopted three new world legislative acts:
* World Legislative Act #9 - Ministry on Environment 302
* World Legislative Act #10 - World Hydrogen Energy System 303
* World Legislative Act #11 - Earth Financial Credit Corporation 303

The fourth & fifth session deliberated and adopted one new world legislative act: 305
* World Legislative Act #12 - The Manifesto (of 1996 & 2000) 305

The sixth session deliberated and adopted seven new world legislative acts:
* World Legislative Act #13 – The World Peace Act 307
* World Legislative Act #14 – The World Security Act 308
* World Legislative Act #15 - Enabling legislation for the World Bench for Human Rights 309
*World Legislative Act #16 - Hydrocarbon Resource Board 313
*World Legislative Act #17 - Commission for Legislative Review including professional and uniform legislative drafting guidelines 313
*World Legislative Act #18 - Provisional Office of World Revenue 314

The seventh session deliberated and adopted six new world legislative acts:
*World Legislative Act #19 - Criminal Code Penalty Classification; 315
*World Legislative Act #20 - World Bench for the Criminal Court; 317
*World Legislative Act #21 - Office of World Patents & Intellectual Property Rights; 322
*World Legislative Act #22 - The Economic Equity Act; 322
*World Legislative Act #23 - Global Accounting Standards; and 324
*World Legislative Act #24 - *Rules for Procedures and Evidence* for the Criminal Bench of the World Court. 325

The eighth session deliberated and adopted six new world legislative acts:
* World Legislative Act #25 - World Government Records Preservation; 328
* World Legislative Act #26 - Education Act; 330
* World Legislative Act #27 - Statute on the Rights of the Child (adopted with amendments from previously existing world convention format from United Nations General Assembly (1989); 331
* World Legislative Act #28 - World Bench for Juvenile Cases; 334
* World Legislative Act #29 - World Boundaries and Elections Administration Act (with provisions for a Global Peoples Assembly Movement); and 337
* World Legislative Act #30 - The Water Act. 339

The ninth session deliberated and adopted eight new world legislative acts:
* World Legislative Act #31 - World Ombudsmus; 340
* World Legislative Act #32 - Department for Conflict Resolution; 341
* World Legislative Act #33 - Fissile Production Prohibition; 342
* World Legislative Act #34 - Nuclear Weapons Elimination Protocol; 344
* World Legislative Act #35 - Nuclear Contamination Act; 347
* World Legislative Act #36 - Guantánamo Directive; 348
* World Legislative Act #37 - World Federal Privileges & Immunities 351
* World Legislative Act #38 - Public Utilities. 353

The tenth session deliberated and adopted four new world legislative acts:
* World Legislative Act #39 - Prohibition of Unauthorized Destruction of Illegal Financial Instruments; 354
* World Legislative Act #40 - Indemnity Bonds; 354
* World Legislative Act #41 - Posting the Stock Law; and 355
* World Legislative Act #42 - Universal Guaranteed Annual Income. 356

The 10th session authorized the Call to the 11th Session of the Provisional World Parliament. Parliament Call is for convening in Nainital, Uttar Anchal, India, in July 2009. 357

Chapter Ten: Legitimate World Law (by Eugenia Almand) **359**

Chapter Eleven: Conclusion – Volume 1 (by Glen T. Martin) **373**
11.1. The Problem of Origins 374
11.2. Declaration of the Rights of Peoples and the Necessity Defense 378
11.3. Interfacing with the United Nations and Existing International Law 383
11.4. A Powerful Global Democracy 384
11.5. The Roadmap 387

Bibliography for Volume 1 **391**

Index for Volume 1 **413**

Chapter One

Introduction:

Democracy, World Law, and the Promise of a Transformed Future

"*We, citizens of the world, hereby resolve to establish a world federation to be governed in accordance with this* Constitution for the Federation of Earth."

Enactment clause of the *Constitution for the Federation of Earth.*
World Constituent Assemblies, 1977 and 1991.
H. Philip Isely, Syed Md. Husain, Terence P. Amerasinghe,
D.M. Spencer and Max Habicht, principal authors.

Glen T. Martin

1.1 The Greatest Gift to Humankind: the Possibility of Peace and Prosperity

A few in every historical era have been the visionaries, the civilizers, who have brought great gifts to humankind through their lives and work. Such are the hundreds of world citizens who developed the *Constitution for the Federation of Earth*. From 1958, with the founding of the World Constitution and Parliament Association, to the Fourth Constituent Assembly in Troia, Portugal in 1991, they worked unceasingly to democratically create a document unlike any other in human history. They have given humankind perhaps the greatest gift of all: the possibility of world peace and justice with a healthy and sustainable environment for the well-being of present and future generations. What you are holding in your hands is no ordinary book.

Yet our present historical era is also different from all other eras. Great gifts now can be eschatological. They can portend the salvation and transformation of life on Earth. We are at a point in human history when we either fulfill our destiny or perish in the frenzy of unstrained egoism, immaturity, and violence that have characterized most human history to the present. Eschatology means a culmination, a fulfillment. The *Constitution for the Federation of Earth* represents the fulfillment of the agonizing struggle in human history for a just and decent world.

Eschatology can also mean a new beginning. We see for the first time the madness, the immaturity, the horror of war and weapons of war and make the decision to renounce the madness to solve our problems through democratic processes. We see for the first time the unsustainable pollution and waste of our way of life and *make the decision* to live lives of quality and dignity rather than compulsive, insatiable consumption. We see for the first time how wretched our pitiful nationalisms are: how they have ravaged the Earth and created only war and misery for humankind. We make the decision to unite under the rule of democratically legislated law. The *Earth Constitution* signals a truly new beginning for humanity: the realization of our destiny on this planet – one world, one humanity, one ecosystem, one Earth.

We are called upon today to make a decision to act for the survival of humanity and our planet. We cannot wait for someone else to do it. We cannot wait for the nations to solve our global crises, for the nations are fundamental to the crisis itself, as we shall see. We cannot wait for the mass media to "educate" people, for the mass media are integral to status quo that prevents change. We cannot wait for leaders to emerge and do it for us, for the only leaders available are you and I. If you and I cannot make the decision, why should we expect others to?

As many today understand, never before have the problems of humanity threatened our very survival on this planet. Never before has global climate change threatened to make our planetary environment uninhabitable for future generations. Never before have weapons of mass destruction given the war-makers the potential for making the human race extinct. Never before has an exploding planetary population exceeded the carrying capacity of the Earth's finite resources. Never before have the finite resources of the planet (land, forests, water, and fisheries) reached the point of exhaustion.

The root of our problems lies in the deep fragmentation of humanity. Human life is everywhere organized according to institutions centuries old that were developed long before we understood the concepts of one planet, one ecosystem, one finite resource base, and one interdependent species – and before the development of deadly, supersonic weapons systems. The modern system of sovereign nation-states, first formulated at the Peace of Westphalia in 1648, divides the people of Earth into autonomous political units, utterly divided from one another: controlling their own internal affairs to the exclusion of all other human beings and entirely independent in foreign affairs.

Under these conditions, no nation can fully trust the others. Each makes military readiness and "national defense" a priority. Power politics rule. The big nations manipulate smaller nations politically and economically. They overthrow governments they do not like, interfere in internal elections, sponsor death squads or paramilitary groups, and invade other nations with relative impunity. The rule of law does not exist in international affairs, only Machiavellian power politics, the rule of force, and gigantic systems of exploitation and domination.

Similarly, the system of corporate capitalism dominates global economics in the form of fragmentation, destructive competition, political manipulation, and exploitation of the poor (nations and peoples) worldwide by those who control corporate wealth and power. When the system of capitalism was developed, beginning with Italian merchants in the 15th and 16th centuries, the Earth seemed to be an inexhaustible wilderness of immense resources. The population of the Earth was small compared to the apparent gigantic size of the Earth.

The technology of the time and the relatively small population of the Earth were utterly incapable of cutting down the immense forests or exhausting the vast ocean fisheries. The engines of economic development, through the exploitation of these resources in combination with an ever-more efficient technology and capital investment, appeared to promise near universal prosperity for the people of Earth. 18th and 19th century theorists of capitalism like Adam Smith and John Stuart Mill predicted immense prosperity for the peoples of Earth as the fruit of the dynamics of capitalism.

But this never happened. Instead, the ruling political powers within the nation-states allied in every case with the industrial and corporate ruling classes to cause untold misery to colonized and enslaved peoples across the globe while immiserating the working classes within their own nations. The ruling elite used their political and economic power to evolve the modern system of property law giving them *exclusive titles to nature's wealth*. They took exclusive possession of nature's wealth: the mines, the forests, and the agricultural lands. The elite found immense profits in producing weapons of war for their respective nation-states and fostering the continual colonial wars that required the production of every more weapons of murder and destruction.

By ignoring the fact that neither human labor nor capital investment created the natural resources that make life possible on Earth, a global system of exclusive private property rights was developed that ensured that the stolen land, resources, and wealth of former generations remained in the hands of a tiny class of global corporate dominators and exploiters. Today, globalized poverty devastates the lives of billions of people while the dominant nations, in league with gigantic profit-making corporations, maneuver to maintain their position of disparity and to exploit the cheap labor and resources of poor countries worldwide. The immense wealth they procured through the rape and pillage of the lands of the global south is now lent back to the poor countries in the form of World Bank and IMF loans, with interest rates sucking even more wealth from the world's devastated, poor majority.

Poverty itself is a major contributor to deforestation, land degradation, over-fishing, and pollution of the environment. The life-threatening condition of our world today, created by the capitalist system of absolute property rights in conjunction with the system of sovereign nation-states, is akin to a terminal illness. The symptoms of this illness are global poverty, militarism, and environmental destruction. Unless we can address the real causes of the illness, the human project is facing imminent death.

Today, we are at the end of the line. Unless we act to protect the vital resources of the Earth (water, forests, agricultural land, and ocean fisheries), control the immense amount of pollution and toxic wastes that pour into the environment each day, vastly reduce the use of fossil fuels and other causes of global climate change, and limit the population of the Earth to sustainable levels, the Earth will soon be unable to support human or other higher forms of life. Yet the system of absolute private property rights devised by the ruling elites of the world, along with the system sovereign nation-states, makes the salvation of our planetary environment virtually impossible.

The root cause is fragmentation: lack of real unity among human beings that would allow for timely and effective action. The United Nations is a false unity and that is why it is paralyzed in the face of these global crises. The U.N. Charter creates a *voluntary association* of "sovereign" nations, which means that these nations cannot be united in principle. This is clearly shown in the failure of that organization to address all of the above named crises that are threatening the future of humankind. The Preamble of the U.N. Charter says that the organization was created to "end the scourge of war." Yet since that time of its founding there have been some 150 wars resulting in the death of some 25 million people, most of these civilians.

We must make the decision to unite, and the United Nations is a false and impotent vehicle for doing this. We do not want to abolish valuable U.N. agencies, but the Charter of the U.N. must be replaced by the *Constitution for the Federation of Earth* and the U.N. agencies integrated under non-military, democratic world government. In committing ourselves to this, we act to unite the world politically and economically. There is no other effective solution.

Similarly, mere treaties among sovereign nations create only the illusion of unity, a false hope that something might be accomplished in time. Environmental treaties such as "Agenda 21" resulting from the 1992 Rio Conference on the Environment or subsequent Kyoto Protocol on climate change (commencing in1997) have been notorious failures. Indeed, failure was a main theme of the huge 2002 U.N. Conference on Climate Change in Johannesburg, South Africa: the utter failure of the nations of the world to achieve the goals embodied in "Agenda 21." And the reason is obvious: a voluntary treaty agreement among sovereign nations existing in a competitive and conflictive world disorder can never lead to the coordination necessary to save the environment. A treaty is merely a voluntary agreement among sovereign nations. Treaties are unenforceable and nations may withdraw at any time.

This is the basic notion behind all so-called "international law." You cannot legitimately call something law that applies to absolutely "sovereign" entities that, by definition, recognize no law above themselves. Disaster threatens our planet – and the nations, with their flawed economic system representing only the rich and not all persons on the planet, and their idolatrous fantasies of absolute sovereignty, are unable and unwilling to act for the common good of humanity and our planet. The emerging world law collected in this volume is qualitatively different from presently existing "international law."

World law is enforceable over individuals, for only individuals break the law, not collectivities such as nation-states. World law applies equally to all persons, including the heads of nations who now consider themselves above both international law and the laws of their own nations. World law, enacted under the *Constitution for the Federation of Earth*, is democratically legislated by a legitimate World Parliament, unlike current, so-called international law that has no democratic basis for its enactments whatsoever and which is manifestly unable to protect human rights worldwide. World law unites the world under genuine democratic principles, under enforceable and impartially adjudicated laws legislated by a world parliament. Legitimate, enforceable world law is directed toward protecting the human rights and dignity of every person on Earth, protecting the global environment, and ending war forever. The Earth Federation Movement, represented in this volume, has given up the destructive illusion of international law and has taken its stand on authentic world law.

Genuine political and economic unity for humankind is necessary for survival and for creating a world of peace, justice, and environmental sustainability. This unity must come in the form of democratic world government under the *Constitution for the Federation of Earth*. The framers of the *Earth Constitution* created one of the finest democratic constitutions ever written. The document ingeniously creates a world law system of checks, balances, transparency, and democratic oversight that ensures the successful working of democracy at the global level. It ensures a legally enforceable principle of unity in diversity for humankind. Democratic world law is the only possible route toward a decent future for humankind, including the preservation of the Earth and its non-human creatures.

1.2 The Structures and Functions of World Unity through World Law

The autonomy and integrity of each nation is preserved and protected by the collective force of the whole even as disarmament is secured and global cooperation ensured. All nations are represented in the House of Nations. Big nations can no longer economically and politically manipulate weaker nations. Any nation can take another before the world courts for violation of its autonomy and integrity. Nations control their own internal affairs (political and economic) consistent with the rules for democracy and human rights and embodied in the Constitution. The rule of law replaces the rule of military force.

The House of Nations is only one of three houses in the World Parliament that is the ultimate authority in the world government and the direct representative of the sovereignty of the people of Earth. The World Parliament also includes a House of Peoples and a House of Counselors. The House of Peoples directly represents the people of Earth through 1000 representatives elected from 1000 electoral districts worldwide, apportioned by population and in conformity as much as possible with existing national and political boundaries. Unlike the U.N., which represents *only governments* (and not people directly) in its General Assembly, the *Earth Constitution* provides for direct representation of the people of Earth.

The House of Counsellors (200 representatives elected from 20 world regions) represents the interests of the Earth as a whole: the interests of universal human rights, universal prosperity, universal peace, and environmental integrity. Not only are nations represented in the World Parliament, and not only are people represented directly through 1000 electoral districts worldwide, but the absolutely vital interests of the planet as a whole, and of humanity as a whole, are represented in the House of Counsellors.

Not only is the House of Counsellors concerned with these global issues beyond the capacity of the nation-states or today's economic system, the *constitutional mandate* of the world government is precisely to create the political and economic unity necessary to deal with the global problems now threatening human survival on Earth. Article 1 of the *Earth Constitution* is entitled "Broad Functions of the World Government." The mandates of democratic world government are precisely those functions which the fragmented nations of the world and the present economic system of the world are incapable of addressing.

The first function of the Federation of Earth is *to prevent war, secure disarmament, and resolve territorial and other disputes which endanger peace and human rights.* The system of sovereign nations is itself by far the major cause of war. Nations militarize themselves in a perpetual arms race causing ever-greater insecurity as the speed and destructive power of modern weapons increases. Big nations use their military might in a system of power politics continually threatening or prosecuting wars to achieve their political and economic aims. Nuclear and other weapons of mass destruction remain poised to initiate global holocaust due to some horrible accident or misunderstanding. No force on Earth can "prevent war" and "secure disarmament" other than enforceable world law that makes war, preparations for war, and weapons of war, illegal.

The *second* broad function of the world government is *to protect universal human rights, including life, liberty, security, democracy, and equal opportunities in life.* Under the present system of world fragmentation, some multinational corporations have so much wealth and power that they operate nearly autonomously within poor countries. They exploit the poverty, bribe officials, pollute the environment, use child labor, extract the natural resources for pennies on the dollar, and violate the rights and dignity of their victims in the service of their insatiable drive for profits and power.

Similarly, under the system of sovereign nation-states, undemocratic nations that violate the rights of their citizens are not held accountable to any enforceable world law. Government officials often grow wealthy facilitating the exploitation of their own people by the multinational corporations. Minorities are repressed, political opponents eliminated or arrested, death squads target union organizers, government officials aid in organized crime: the sale of children, drug trafficking, or prostitution. Under today's system of absolute property rights and power given to the rich intertwined with sovereign nation-statehood, human rights are violated with impunity worldwide.

Even the condition of involuntary poverty in which more than 60% of the world's population lives constitutes a violation of their rights to health care, social security, and remuneration for work sufficient for a life of human dignity. Even the pollution of the planetary environment with toxic chemicals (now in the tissue of every human being) and the thinning of the ozone layer constitute a violation of the right of every human being to a safe and healthy environment. Only enforceable world law guaranteeing the many human rights listed in Articles 12 and 13 of the *Earth Constitution* can transform the current nightmare of world-wide human rights violations. The present world-system of *institutionalized fragmentation* can never do this. Only world political and economic unity can accomplish the protection of universal human rights.

The third and fourth functions specified in Article 1 of the *Earth Constitution* go together. The *third* function is *to obtain for all people on Earth the conditions required for equitable economic and social development and for diminishing social differences.* As with the first two duties of the Earth Federation (preventing war and protecting universal human rights), the goal of reasonable and equitable world prosperity is impossible without the authority of world government acting on behalf of the entire Earth's population. The poor, under today's world system, are marginalized, forgotten, powerless, and dispensable. The rules of world trade are formulated by the G-8: those nations with the world's largest economies. Small nations are not even invited into the discussion. The World Trade Organization is the very opposite of a democratic institution, involving secret courts, closed door decision-making, and penalties for nations that do not cooperate. Real planetary prosperity is impossible without democratic world unity.

The *fourth* broad function of the Earth Federation is *to regulate world trade, communications, transportation, currency, standards, use of world resources, and other global and international processes.* With this function (and a number of more specific ones within the body of the document), the world democratic government has the ability to make the global economy function for the benefit of all peoples, not simply powerful nations and multinational corporations. With the political and economic unity of humankind under the *Earth Constitution*, world trade is made democratic. World trade and property laws are no longer secretly formulated by the powerful and imposed on the rest of humanity. Trade and property laws are now democratically legislated to eliminate exploitation and domination and to foster rapid sustainable development for all countries and citizens of the planet.

The *fifth* broad function of the federation is *to protect the environment and ecological fabric of life from all sources of damage, and to control technological innovations whose effects transcend national boundaries, for the purpose of keeping Earth a safe, healthy, and happy home for humanity.* Just as with the elimination of war, the protection of universal human rights, the creation of global prosperity and equity, and the regulation of world trade, this fifth function cannot be achieved under the current system of world fragmentation. Many informed people identify climate change as our gravest danger, even graver than the threat of nuclear holocaust or population explosion.

Yet very little has been done despite hundreds of scientific studies and books showing the immense damage to the global climate already inflicted and the devastating global consequences that continue to mount with every year that passes without out unified dedicated action. That unified action must begin with the ratification of the *Constitution for the Federation of Earth* under the conditions set forth in Article 17. No treaties, educational initiatives, or U.N. conferences on the environment can stem the tide of global environmental destruction.

Time is rapidly running out and only unified global action by a duly elected world parliament can save the planetary environment. Global political and economic unity is the necessary and sufficient condition of such action. This unity is dependent on our *making the decision* to create this unity. It is meaningless to say that humankind is not ready yet, that we must spiritually evolve first. Our decision to create economic political institutions of unity will make possible further spiritual evolution, just as it will make possible the survival of humanity and our precious living planet.

The *sixth* and final broad function of the Federation of Earth is *to devise and implement solutions to all problems which are beyond the capacity of national governments, or which are now or may become of global or international concern or consequence.* The sixth function not only grants the world government the authority to deal with unforeseen global problems that may arise in the future, it also makes clear the rationale for all six of the basic functions of the Federation: for all of them, from the problem of war to universal human rights to the global economic problem to protection of our planetary environment, are "beyond the capacity of national governments." The system of economic and political fragmentation is helpless in the face of these problems. The solution to all of them requires genuine, enforceable economic and political unity.

Some of the authors and editors of the *Constitution* devoted many years of their lives to drafting, discussing, conferring world-wide, redrafting, editing, organizing four Constituent Assemblies, communicating by letter and fax, and democratically working out every detail of the *Constitution for the Federation of Earth.* The primary authors and leaders of this effort were H.P. Isely, S. M. Husein, T. P. Amerasinghe, M. Habicht, and D. M. Spencer. They created a document that will endure the test of time, one of the great documents of human civilization, like the Magna Carta, the French Declaration of the Rights of Man, or the U.S. Declaration of Independence.

The thinking behind the *Constitution* is astonishingly advanced. These visionaries understood, from 1958 on, what few others understood at the time: that our planet is doomed in one way or another unless we can formulate truly global democratic institutions to deal with the interconnected range of ever-mounting global problems and crises. As a philosopher myself, trained in political, social, and economic philosophies, I am continually amazed at the perceptive interconnections of the various articles of the *Constitution* creating a democratic whole that is complete, effective, as free as possible of the dangers of corruption or incompetence, and ready to be of service to humankind.

The framers understood the seriousness of the threats to humanity that today are just beginning to dawn on many thoughtful people. They understood the need to jump-start world government as rapidly as possible, even before official ratification under Article 17. For this reason, they gave world citizens, in Article 19, the authority to begin provisional world government: provisional world courts, provisional world ministries, and the Provisional World Parliament. The Earth Federation is not just a set of ideas; it has begun.

The framers realized that time is running out and that the official world parliament will need all the help it can get once it has been duly elected by the people and nations of Earth. A provisional world government will be in place to help the official world government begin once the *Constitution* is ratified. It could be that the world will have a functioning court system, some functioning ministries, a common currency, and even a world police force by the time ratification is completed. A number of initiatives have already been taken in these areas. Many ordinary citizens have already made the decision to create unity for humankind. *It is up to us to follow their example, courage, and commitment.*

The most well-known and extensive initiative taken by these citizens who have made the decision to act for a decent world order has been the creation of the Provisional World Parliament. The first session commenced in Brighton, England in 1982. In the course of its ten official sessions to date, the Parliament has produced a substantial body of high-quality provisional world law that is being published in one place for the first time in the three volume set of *Emerging World Law.*

This law will be available to the official world parliament to modify, accept, or reject as it sees fit. This body of provisional world law addresses in detail the several crises faced by humanity as well as the mechanics of activating agencies within the Earth Federation as specified by the *Constitution.* It activates detailed regulations for world criminal law that will empower both the world court system and the world enforcement system. It does this through drawing extensively on the quality work of contemporary jurists connected with the International Criminal Court in the Hague and other forms of international law. Provisional world law does not attempt to reinvent the wheel if quality work has already been done. However, it converts the unenforceable and merely voluntary character of this international law into enforceable world law under the authority of the *Earth Constitution.* It also regulates and serves as a guide (along with the *Constitution*) for the provisional world ministries and other organs of provisional world government that are being activated and advanced with each meeting of the Parliament.

The Provisional World Parliament has met ten times worldwide since 1982 in accordance with the legal requirements set out in Article 19 of the *Earth Constitution.* These meetings have taken place in Brighton, England (1982), New Delhi, India (1985), Miami Beach, Florida (1987), Barcelona, Spain (1996), Malta (2001), Bangkok, Thailand (March 2003), Chennai, India (December 2003), Lucknow, India (2004), Tripoli, Libya (2006), and Kara, Togo (2007). The Parliament is actively engaged in elaborating the democratic world law that will unite and transform the world, not just thinking about it, not just dreaming about it, not just endlessly talking about it as has been the case with most world federalists around the world. Those working to ratify the *Earth Constitution* and develop world law under its authority are not just talking the talk – they are walking the walk – taking real action for a decent world order.

The Provisional Parliament is confident that its work will be of immense value to the official World Parliament once it is activated. This body of work, as well as many other actions and accomplishments of the World Constituent Assemblies and Provisional World Parliament has been collected for *Emerging World Law*, of which the present book is the first of a three volume set. It is likely that this collection of emerging world law will be of great interest to international lawyers and all who are concerned with the future of humanity. Everyone, every citizen of Earth, is welcome to participate in sessions of the Provisional World Parliament. The parliament is held on behalf of the people of Earth. It is our parliament (as citizens of Earth) if we but make the decision to participate in his historic movement.

For three decades, the movement to ratify the *Constitution* and begin provisional world government (the Earth Federation Movement) had to struggle against the immense Cold War propaganda distortions that spewed forth from the United States and the former Soviet Union. The vigorous world federalist movement that had developed worldwide after the Second World War was seriously diminished by this East-West polarization. Many world federalist organizations lost membership and momentum, except in Japan, where the carefully preserved memory of Hiroshima and Nagasaki sustained a vigorous world federalist movement through the absurdities of the Cold War. (Today, however, younger Japanese are demanding of the Japanese World Federalists a "road map." "How is this to be done?" they ask. The *Constitution for the Federation of Earth* provides this road map in Articles 17 and 19.)

After the Cold War, the Earth Federation Movement (and other world federalist organizations) had to deal with the gigantic fabrication of a global terrorist threat and the supposed need for a global war against this threat. Both the Cold War propaganda and War on Terror propaganda constitute imperialist devices to cover the drive to global domination and hegemony, and to institutionalize the system of fragmentation and exploitation forever upon the dying Earth. If planetary democratic unity is not soon achieved, the alternative may well be planetary military tyranny and domination under the world's sole remaining superpower. A once top secret Pentagon document named "Vision 20/20," (*Joint Vision 2020*), formulated in 1996, outlines the U.S. plan to militarize space by the year 2020 and to militarily control the entire planet from that time on.

Despite these impediments, the Earth Federation Movement has grown steadily. Today the World Constitution and Parliament Association and the Earth Federation Movement have membership in 122 countries and active chapters in dozens of countries. With the dawn of the 21st century, the movement has advanced rapidly, giving many the hope and belief that they world will be free of its current institutionalized nightmare system of fragmentation within the next few years. It is not wise to try to predict the future, but the possibility is there as millions realize that that the current world-order is a dead end, *literally* a dead end for humanity, the planetary environment, and civilization itself.

The immense gift given by the framers of the *Earth Constitution* is beginning to be appreciated. Time is short and demands from us a decision. This immense gift given to humanity cannot create world unity unless we make the decision to recognize that gift and act upon it by dedicating our lives to this new *unity in diversity* for humankind.

1.3 Democratic World Law: Democracy and Private Property

Law is a fundamental expression of our humanity. In very early societies, law took the form of customs, mores, and traditional rules that were often said to help maintain the proper order and functioning of the cosmos. People took very seriously the need for cooperative behavior in conformance with cosmic and community laws. In all modern societies, by contrast, law has taken the form of written statutes, legislated by parliaments and enforceable by police and courts. Most modern societies are so immensely complex that life would be impossible without a system of rules such as property rules, tort rules, contract rules, and criminal law statutes.

The understanding of the role of law in human life has evolved over the centuries to the point where today *the concept of democratic law* emerges as fundamental. Legitimate law is democratically legislated law that protects all persons equally and makes possible their free action insofar as this is compatible with the freedom of others. Laws made by a dictatorship may have "juristic force," that is, they may be enforceable by police and courts, but they lack moral force. By nearly all accounts, such laws are said to be illegitimate and their obedience not a moral obligation of the persons subject to them.

But many factors in the modern world interfere with the process of democratically legislating laws designed to provide equality and justice for all. One of the most obvious and deleterious is the role of big money in politics. Politicians in the United States, for example, allow the big corporations to write the very legislation that is supposed to regulate these corporations. Payola, pork barreling, perks, and special interests dominate most legislative processes. The concept of "ruling class" is very much confirmed as politicians do the bidding of the wealthy and powerful to roll back the meager rights of the common people to social security, health care, occupational safety, and job security that were institutionalized in the U.S. at the end of the Great Depression of the 1930s.

Something similar is true in all the so-called Western democracies. Great wealth is won in the "disequilibrium" of capitalism's incoherent workings. Subsequently, the power and influence this generates are used to protect and augment that wealth. U.S. economist Lester C. Thurow writes the following in his 1975 book *Generating*

Inequality:

> ...At any moment in time, the highly skewed distribution of wealth is the product of two approximately equal factors – instant fortunes and inherited wealth. Inherited fortunes, however, were themselves created in a process of instant wealth in an earlier generation. These instant fortunes occur because new long-term disequilibriums in the real capital market are capitalized in the financial markets.... Those who are lucky and end up owning the stocks that are capitalized at high multiples win large fortunes in the random walk. Once fortunes are created, they are husbanded, augmented,and passed on, not because of "homo economicus" desires to store up future consumption but because of desires for power within family, economy, or society . (New York: Basic Books, 1975, p. 149)

Laws, in general, are made by the rich and for the rich. The rich clearly understand that large fortunes mean power and power translates into laws that protect and augment their wealth. Their minions in the universities and privately owned mass media translate this into the ideology of capitalism: that this system of theft, exploitation, extremes of poverty and wealth is somehow the system that provides the greatest efficiency and productivity and results in the greatest good for the greatest number of persons.

That this is not true, and never has been empirically true, is irrelevant to the ideologists. The fact that empirically this system for centuries has pillaged the planet, destroyed hundreds of millions of lives with poverty and disease, created vast systems of semi-slave sweat-shop labor, and raped the environment of the Earth, is irrelevant to the ideologues who draw their secure university or professional incomes from bowing and scraping to this immoral system in print. The politicians could not serve the rich with impunity (within so-called democracies) if they did not have the corrupt ideological support of the journalists and the academics.

Since lawmakers are lackeys of the rich (they may or may not be fully conscious of this fact), their laws also often target the poor with repressive statues that criminalize the behavior of the poor while ignoring the behavior of those wealthy and powerful who pollute the environment, rob pension funds of the poor, operate dehumanizing sweatshops, or reap millions from corrupt financial schemes. The fragmentation of our world order resulting from the nation-state system in concert with global capitalism, encourages this sort of corruption. It is not human nature that is corrupt; the fragmented system itself invites this sort of corruption. Both capitalism and the so-called sovereign nation-state invite corruption and tend to bring corrupt people into economic and political power.

It is not only lawmakers who are lackeys of the rich but the majority of professors in universities (they may or may not be conscious of this fact). It is important to remember that the dominant system in the imperial centers of law and capital organizes itself throughout these societies not only economically and politically but educationally, culturally, ideologically, etc. Persons with Ph.D.s are just as subject to the ideological framework (never transgressing beyond the perimeters of respectable, permissible debate) as taxi drivers, perhaps more so since they spend so many years of their lives studying under intellectual representatives of the system (professors, authors, and higher education administrators). The unspoken, hidden role of professors in the imperial societies is to pass along the self-justifications, the self-satisfaction, the sense of superiority, and the patriotism that every imperial society inculcates into its citizens.

The so-called social science of economics illustrates this fact. Conventional economics is at least 70% ideology and only 30% social science. Its role is to justify the system both to the victims of the system and in the minds of the educated elite of the system. It has developed a highly sophisticated, mathematically based language to justify a system whose empirical consequences (billions of persons in poverty and misery worldwide, vast destruction to the environment, etc.) are studiously ignored. In his book *Railroading Economics: The Creation of the Free Market Mythology*, economist Michael Perelman writes in his conclusion:

> I hope that this history has exposed the irrelevance of conventional economics, showing that it mostly exists as a justification for an unjust and inefficient means of organizing society. At the same time, some economists along with business leaders…have pushed for various reforms, which have also proved incapable of preventing capitalism's contradictions from showing themselves. New reforms might possibly overcome some of these problems and contradictions, but new ones will emerge in their wake. Ultimately, the basic problem is a system of intractable contradictions inherent in the market itself. In this sense, the corporatists were on the right track, but they could not take the next step and repudiate the system itself. (New York: Monthly Review Press, 2006, p. 199)

To "repudiate the system itself" means to recognize that monopoly capitalism as we know it today is incompatible with democracy. The insight of Karl Marx that genuine democracy cannot be limited to mere political democracy is dramatically illustrated by today's fragmented economics. In political democracies, our rights and dignity as citizens are said to reside in the capacity to vote, in free speech, due process, equal protection before the law, etc.

But this leaves out the entire economic sphere in which the poor are without effective rights; they are exploited, dehumanized, politically powerless, and tuned into mere commodities in the service of private profit. Those who cannot afford education, travel, publication, or leisure for organization, cannot be said to have their rights and dignity protected by living in a mere political democracy. Without a reasonable degree of economic democracy to complement political democracy, the political system is a sham, both within countries and worldwide.

Economic democracy is not necessarily identical with the communism often associated with the economics of Karl Marx. The *Constitution for the Federation of Earth* affirms private property and free enterprise. It assumes a flourishing world of private business, including large corporations. The problem is not free enterprise or even large corporations. The problem is a fragmented system that defeats the equity, peace, and prosperity for all persons that are necessary features of genuine democracy. The *Earth Constitution* places universal human rights and democratic accountability at a more fundamental level than today's system of absolute private property rights that favors the rich and necessarily corrupts democracy.

The bill of *inalienable* rights, Article 12, only mentions property in the following two items: *(1) Equal rights for all citizens of the Federation of Earth, with no discrimination on grounds of race, color, caste, nationality, sex, religion, political affiliation, property, or social status. (16) Safety of property from arbitrary seizure; protection against exercise of the power of eminent domain without reasonable compensation.* Private property is assumed but not worshipped as a god as it is under today's monopoly capitalist system.

In Article 12.1, the amount of property one holds legally cannot be the basis for discrimination. The rule of the rich over human life is ended. Today, such discrimination is built into the very laws that are framed in the service of the rich and powerful worldwide. In Article 12.16, private property is protected from arbitrary seizure by the state. Private property is protected, but now allowed to destroy democracy. The philosophy behind the *Earth Constitution* is the philosophy of *unity in diversity*, human beings as ends in themselves, and the holism of our planetary home and the human species. Nowhere does the *Constitution* support the outdated ideology of a right of private property conceived as somehow constituting the basis of human dignity or freedom as the ideology of monopoly capitalism assumes.

An unlimited right to private property is not the basis for human freedom (and dignity) as British philosopher John Locke and others asserted when they claimed inalienable rights to "life, liberty, and property." Article three of the U.N. Universal Declaration of Human Rights asserts that there is an inalienable right to "life, liberty, and security of person." This is much closer to the philosophically justified mark. Personal property is indeed a right and integral to the individual's security of person, and the *Earth Constitution* assumes this fact.

However, personal property must be distinguished from great concentrations of unearned capital that distort democracy and turn life in modern societies into what Lester Thurow, quoted above, calls a "random walk." Society has a legitimate interest in regulating these since they can be used in ways that are environmentally, economically, and socially destructive, for example, to produce weapons, to manipulate financial markets, to undemocratically influence elections, or to economically colonize poor countries. Great blocks of unearned capital or personal wealth, whether belonging to corporations or individuals (far exceeding what any individual needs for "life, liberty, and security of person") place an immense power in the hands of private individuals or enterprises, an immense power that is inherently destructive of the social good and the democratic welfare of the majority.

Any national government has the legal authority to regulate such concentrations of wealth within its borders, of course, whether of individuals or of corporations. But powerful corporations not only colonize the lawmakers within countries, they also use the present system of international fragmentation to their advantage by blackmailing countries: threatening to move elsewhere if environmental, labor, or tax laws are not tailored sufficiently to their private profit orientation. For a small country, the attempt to regulate a multinational corporation within its borders could cause even greater poverty and suffering if the multinational corporation withdraws assets, moves investment elsewhere, subverts the laws through bribery, etc. Economist David Korten's book, *When Corporations Rule the World*, documents these contentions in great detail.

Without world economic unity under democratic world law, no government has the capacity to regulate these corporations for the common welfare of humanity or the global environment. Off-shore bank accounts, currency speculation among the different currencies of the world, the transfer of assets out of countries where they might be taxed fairly, bribery and influence buying in poor countries, campaign contributions in rich countries: none of this can be controlled without the enforceable authority of unified world economic law we have seen given above by the *Earth Constitution*.

Personal property can be important for a person's sense of dignity, and the economic means to act (to travel, to dispose of one's possessions as one sees fit, to publish and communicate with others) are essential to personal freedom. However, society has the legitimate authority to democratically decide what the limits to personal property may be (for everyone equally). The ideology of an unqualified "right to private property" was developed by John Locke, among others, as a justification for the rising bourgeois class against the traditional power of the King in England. The blind allegiance to this late 17th century ideology today amounts to a subterfuge in the service of the continued domination of the ruling class under monopoly capitalism.

Nor is a right to unlimited accumulation necessary for "free enterprise investment." Capital can be held, accumulated, and used by corporations without justifying this through the ideology of human rights. Corporations need not (and should not) be treated as legally private individuals with all the rights of private persons as they are under in current monopoly capitalist law. Corporations are social organizations with immense impact on society and the environment and must be regulated as such for the common good. They can be legally treated as having only "powers" granted by society for responsible use of investment capital and production.

The right to personal property can easily be distinguished from vast accumulations of unearned capital. People can be well compensated for their creativity or their work and have the right to accumulate this personal property within limits (equally applied to all). These are socially determined legalities. Many commentators have pointed out that democracy cannot effectively function if there are vast disparities of wealth between the richest and poorest segments of a population. Good laws encourage democracy in all spheres of life and frame property law for the best interest of the majority. Bad laws serve the rich and powerful at the expense of democracy and human unity. Today, bad laws are the norm and democracy exists in name only.

Nor is one's right to property, security of person, or liberty a consequence of having "property in one's own person" as Locke claims. A person may legitimately claim inalienable human rights simply in virtue of his or her being a person. But it is bizarre to claim that one is in a property relationship to oneself. I cannot buy or sell myself as I can my automobile. The commodification of human life under capitalism makes us even treat our precious personal humanity as if it were a commodity, as if persons were their own "private property." People are ends in themselves, as the philosopher Immanuel Kant insisted, and are uniquely valuable simply in virtue of being human. They are the bearers of rights, including the right to personal property. People may be the owners of different forms of external property. They are not the owners of themselves. Their dignity is prior to all ownership relationships. They are indeed the bearers of ownership rights to personal property. However, rights derive from our inviolable humanity and are prior to property relationships.

Human rights, including security, do not include an unlimited right to personal property as integral to one's individual liberty. But an essential feature of democracy is that the liberty of one or some may not be so great as to interfere with the equal liberty of all the others. Unlimited accumulations of private wealth, whether of individuals or corporations, do exactly this. Only world economic unity under democratic world government is able to bring this essential feature of democracy to the world. Any national government democratically limiting the power of unlimited accumulation within its territory (and they all do this to a certain extent through taxes, etc.) would leave that power unchecked, and hence still destructive, within the rest of the world. It would lose business investment as corporations moved elsewhere to more "profitable" countries, that is, to countries that do not protect the environment or the democratic rights of their citizens.

The thought of Karl Marx and Friedrich Engels was limited by its reductionism. Their valid and fundamental insight that most law has been profoundly influenced by the self-interest of a ruling class (whether this was the masters in ancient Rome, the lords in feudalism, or the bourgeoisie in capitalism) does not justify the reductionist conclusion that law is nothing but the expression of class ideology. This, in turn, does not justify the utopian prediction that a free and just (classless) society would experience the "withering away" of the state and its laws as Friedrich Engels puts this in the concluding paragraphs of *Socialism: Utopian and Scientific* (1882).

Authentic democratic government is precisely the necessary mechanism for ensuring a democratic society, for protecting both capital and workers, for preserving the environment and promoting universal peace and prosperity. There is no other way to achieve these goals. And these goals cannot be achieved unless authentic democratic government is non-military world democratic government. Reasonable economic democracy is an essential component of authentic democratic government.

On the other hand, Philosophical Liberalism is also limited by reductionism. Liberal thinkers like John Stuart Mill in his essay *On Liberty* (1859) assert that the sole purpose of law and government is the enhancement and protection of the individual and his or her liberty. While it is true that the individual is the sole bearer of inalienable rights, *the social and legal matrix makes us what we are and cannot be disentangled from our identities, our individual selves.* The matrix constitutes an organic social reality that sustains, obligates, and to a large measure forms us as individuals. Government forms a large part of this matrix. We are responsible to one another and good laws reflect this responsibility on behalf of both the individual and common good.

Our rights and dignity require the *unity in diversity* of democratic government to institutionally embody them. It is not the case that the best government is the one that governs least, as American anarchist Henry David Thoreau claimed. *The best government is the one that preserves and enhances democratic freedom and equality.* Good government prevents private interests (like big money or organized religion) from interfering with the freedom and equality of all. Good government must be big enough and effective enough to democratically govern in the name of the people. A fragmented world order cannot create good government within the individual fragmented parts. Gigantic ungovernable forces disrupt any attempt to do so.

The *Earth Constitution* affirms, in numerous interconnected ways, the requirement that the Federation of Earth regulate global economics for the mutual benefit of all the Earth's citizens, something the present fragmented world system is utterly incapable of doing. Among the "Grant to Specific Powers to the World Government" in Article 2 are *(14) Regulate and supervise supra-national trade, industry, corporations, businesses, cartels, professional services, labor supply, finances, investments and insurance. (17) Establish and operate world financial, banking, credit and insurance institutions designed to serve human needs; establish, issue, and regulate world currency, credit and exchange.* The mythology and ideology of private property are abandoned by the *Earth Constitution* in favor of the proper role of government to regulate private business and property in the service of the common good of the Earth's people, environment, and future generations.

Article 13 of the *Constitution* guarantees *equal opportunity for useful employment for everyone, with wages or remuneration sufficient to assure human dignity.* With a single Earth Currency, and a single set of wage laws for the Earth, it will no longer be possible for corporations to exploit differences in currency value and to pay poverty level wages in their drive to reap extraordinary profits. The *Constitution* also guarantees the valuable social goods of *free and adequate medical care* along with free quality *public education to the pre-university level,* and *social security for everyone to relieve the hazards of unemployment, sickness, old age, family circumstances, disability, catastrophes of nature, and technological change, and to allow retirement with sufficient lifetime income for living under conditions of human dignity during older age.* Democratic economic unity will soon spell the end of involuntary global poverty.

There is plenty of wealth and capacity for productivity in the world to achieve these goals rapidly and easily. Democracy is precisely that system of governance that represents the majority of the people, and the majority of people in today's world are extremely poor. Any real democracy will regulate the economy so that the majority prosper. Any real democracy will minimize vast disparities between the rich and poor, since great wealth inevitably means great power and distorts democracy beyond recognition.

In addition, inalienable rights and liberties (including security of person and protection of personal property) require the social arrangements and guarantees provided by democratic society. Society provides the infrastructure (from clean water and sanitation to police and courts) that make possible the protection of rights and liberties. To claim that "that government is best which governs least is" to ignore the necessary role of government in the maintenance and protection of individual liberty. The social atomism of Thoreau or Mill, with its consequent fragmentation, is the legacy of a bygone era, as is Locke's attempt to justify unlimited accumulations of private property on the basis of inalienable rights.

The social matrix is not merely limited to specific cultural backgrounds or historical traditions, for, as the ancient Greek and Roman Stoics understood, it includes our very humanity that makes all persons brothers and sisters on the Earth. We all speak *some* language or languages, for example, and by this fact alone are inevitably socially connected to all other language-speaking beings. We are all rational creatures, as Immanuel Kant insisted, and by this fact alone we are in a moral relationship with all other rational creatures. We are neither beasts nor Gods, as Aristotle asserted, but by nature social and political creatures. The social matrix that forms our identities today necessarily includes the entire Earth.

Government is not a necessary evil on the prior liberty of the sovereign individual, as Mill would have it. Government and democratic law are the way that civilized beings regulate their community lives in groupings beyond the family or very small communities. Individual inalienable rights that are recognized by the *Earth Constitution* do trump government powers, but democratic government is an essential element in the protection of these rights. We require both a well-designed democratic world government directed to the common good and a substantial listing of inalienable rights that are untouchable by government. The *Constitution for the Federation of Earth* provides both within a brilliant system of checks, balances, and accountability.

In sum, neither is the individual prior to government as Mill claims, nor is unlimited private property a god-given right of people, as Locke asserts. Property is one of the legal categories by which we organize our social existence has human beings in a community. Its legal form is malleable and should be designed in the service of the common good. The concept of property can and must to reformulated from the point of view of the growing philosophical movement called "permaculture." Permaculture ultimately means "permanent culture." Just as well-designed good government is essential to both the common good and individual liberty so the regulation of private property is also essential to both the common good and individual liberty.

Human beings need to integrate with the land, water, air, and biosphere that sustains us on the Earth in such a way as to create reasonable *sustainable prosperity* for the majority of its citizens. The *Earth Constitution* ends the systems of fragmentation that are destroying the Earth. It promotes *unity in diversity*, not only in government and economics but in environmentally sustainable ways of living and working within the ecosystem of our beautiful planet.

The *Earth Constitution* constitutes a network of provisions concerning the functions of world government (the multiplicity of protections of human rights, and the variety of ways the environment is preserved and restored). It creates democratic world society through properly formed property laws must help people integrate housing, food supply, use of resources (land, water, forests, etc.), population reduction, waste considerations, and prosperity considerations so that the population of the Earth no longer lives at the expense of future generations. (See David Holmgren, *Permaculture: Principles and Pathways Beyond Sustainability*, Hepburn, Australia, 2004.) The *Earth Constitution* transforms the fragmentations of capitalism and the sovereign nation-state into the unity in diversity of perma-culture: permanent, democratic, sustainable, ecologically sound cultures living in peace and prosperity upon the Earth.

The Earth Federation has abandoned both the outdated mythologies of Mill and Locke in favor of a common sense political and economic framework consistent with our human self-understanding at the dawn of the third millennium CE of human civilization. *Unity in diversity* replaces fragmentation; democratically organized economics replaces a mythologized marketplace with absolute winners and losers; political participation and equality replaces elite manipulation of law and the political process. Finally, sustainable living replaces unrestrained consumption and debilitating waste. The *Earth Constitution* breaks free from the mythologies of both the sovereign nation-state and monopoly capitalist economics.

A new holism, embracing a genuinely respected diversity, creates a world system whose predictable consequences are peace, freedom, justice, and sustainable prosperity. The true meaning of the rule of democratically legislated law becomes a reality for the first time in human history. Human beings reach a new maturity and create a decent world order for the first time in history.

1.4 Democratic World Law: Democracy and Sovereignty

Law must therefore be in the service of the *unity in diversity* of all people. It must reflect the realities of the world we live in and democratically represent all persons. It can no longer be in the service of a ruling class. Law must protect the life, liberty, and security of person for each citizen within a democracy. However, for these very reasons, no nation on Earth today is capable of practicing genuine democracy. As mentioned above, the fragmented structure of today's world makes this impossible. If a basic function of democratic government is to protect the life, liberty, and security of citizens, then no government today is capable of doing this.

Under the system of sovereign nation-states, democracy within nations is made effectively impossible by the fragmented nature of the world as a whole in which human beings have so far refused to join together to create a system which can protect the life, liberty, and security of citizens. First, nearly every nation spends a large portion of its wealth on a military. Yet militarism in a dangerous world requires secrecy, military priorities, and undemocratic power relations, thereby both distorting democracy within each nation and making the relationship of individuals within one nation non-democratic with respect to the individuals within all other nations.

Within nations, militarism invariably creates a self-sustaining industrial-military complex in which war supplies and materials become a large portion of the economy of the nation. This in turn creates a powerful lobby for war and militarism in which the health of the economy (and the employment of many citizens) is claimed to require ever-more war supplies and materials. Militarism also creates a class of military officers who have little or no understanding of democracy: who think in strategic terms incompatible with the basic premises of democratic institutions. Militarism also requires a propaganda system within nations that justifies the immense resources spent on the military. The people must be made to think that there are enemies requiring such immense expenditure and sacrifice on their part.

Democracy is a system in which institutions function as a peaceful means for resolving human differences (through courts, elections, free communications, etc.). It requires a citizenry educated to understand and protect its institutions. It abjures propaganda in favor of the free flow of information and communications concerning issues confronting the citizens, allowing people to peacefully effect change and solve their problems. It is incompatible with militarism (the very essence of which is non-peaceful power relations between human beings: war and the threat of war).

Similarly, if I live in a militarized society (claiming to be a democracy), my relationship with my fellow human beings from other nations is not one of democratic equality (equality of political and economic rights, of freedom and liberty with respect to one another). Rather, my relationship with them is determined by an undemocratic international situation, by militarism, secrecy, treaty alliances, visa requirements, trade barriers, power relations, etc. I cannot legitimately claim that I believe in democracy and then live my life in undemocratic power relationships with the vast majority of my fellow human beings. Militarism, like the nation-state system that spawns it, is the antithesis of democracy.

To claim that it is necessary to "defend democracy" is simply a propaganda lie of every industrial-military complex justified by slogans like "freedom is not free." Such slogans are designed to suppress real thought through noble-sounding propaganda statements. A similar slogan of the Nazi propaganda machine was "the highest freedom is a noble slavery of the heart." The only way to create real democracy is *to institutionalize peace, to create a peace system on a world scale through democratic world government.* At present, we have institutionalized war and a war-system on a world scale that defeats democracy everywhere on the planet.

Finally, with today's high-tech weapons of mass destruction and super-sonic delivery systems, militarism simply *increases insecurity*, causing people to have to live their lives with the perpetual threat of nuclear holocaust or some other calamitous surprise attack. Submarines patrol the bottom of the oceans capable of wiping out dozens of cities anywhere in the world if their nuclear missiles are fired. Missiles can be launched from ships or anywhere in the world that can reach around the globe in minutes. Arms races not only drain the moral and economic resources of society, they create ever greater instability and insecurity.

Second, the disintegrating global environment takes the well-being and security of citizens of any national democracy out of the hands of the government and places them in the hands of the gigantic forces of global climate change. Governments can no longer even guarantee the right to life or security to their citizens, since environmental destruction already takes the lives of millions through cancer, unnecessary diseases, and exhaustion of resources. The protection of life, liberty, and security of person is a sham if the natural environment that makes all these possible is itself destroyed. Something similar could be said about global resource depletion and the exploding global population, both destroying the possibility of democratic living anywhere on Earth.

Third, global economics constitutes another gigantic undemocratic force that takes the possibility of democracy out of the hands of national governments. The entire economy of a country can collapse within days with the collapse of the international market anywhere in the world. This has happened repeatedly in the past several decades (Indonesia, Tanzania, Somalia, Rwanda, Bolivia, Ecuador, Argentina, etc.) with devastating consequences for citizens of many countries. Democracy within nations is only a sham under such global circumstances. Neither police, nor courts, nor lawmakers can protect citizens if the economy itself has collapsed. Neither can they be said to have institutionalized economic protection for all citizens if citizens must live with the perpetual possibility of such a collapse.

The inevitable conclusion to these reflections is that *genuine democracy is only possible on the world level.* The war system of the world (participated in by nearly every country on Earth), the disintegrating global environment (affecting every country on Earth), and the uncontrollable casino of global economics all make democracy effectively impossible at the merely national level. The only way to create a peace system that makes democracy possible, and to protect the global environment and hence the right to life, liberty and security of every citizen, and to regulate global economics for the benefit and security of all peoples is through democratic world government.

The absurdity that my constitutionally protected "human rights" end when I reach some arbitrary political boundary between countries becomes apparent here. The absurdity that I need the permission of a visa to travel where I choose on the Earth shows that democracy does not exist upon the Earth. The right to travel is among the most basic of all democratic rights, linked as it is with the right to speak, publish, communicate, and attempt to peacefully influence ones fellow human beings.

Some countries that claim to be democracies are the worst offenders of the rights of other people outside their borders. Nearly every country that today claims to be a democracy denies the right of people from other countries to travel to their so-called democracy. What a sham to claim to believe in freedom and then deny the majority of human beings on Earth the freedom to travel to "my spot" on the Earth. What a sham to claim to believe in freedom of speech but to tell people you cannot come into our country to speak to us.

Personal liberty is a sham without the freedom to travel, but under today's fragmentation, my personal liberty ends and some border that I may not cross without the permission of a foreign government. This leads to the paradox that the personal liberty of citizens from geographically large democratic countries is greater that personal liberty of small democratic countries, since citizens of small countries can only travel a few hundred miles before their "freedom" to travel ends while those in big countries can travel a few thousand miles. Every human being has the right to travel anywhere on the planet. It is our home planet, and we are all its citizens. Effective democracy can only be world democracy.

These logical contradictions inherent in the current world system of international lawlessness have led some to recognize that the nation-states, insofar as they claim to be sovereign (recognizing no enforceable democratic law above themselves), are in fact *morally illegitimate*. A nation that cannot provide security and protection of human rights for its citizens cannot be a democracy and therefore cannot be legitimate. We have seen that no nation can protect its citizens against global climate change, global weapons of mass destruction, global depletion of vital resources, possible economic collapse, or global overpopulation.

Even at the most basic level of simple respect for law, national governments are entirely hypocritical. They tell their citizens that the rule of law must be obeyed, for this is both democratic and civilized. They set up police, courts, and prisons to effectively enforce the law. Yet they are unwilling to recognize any rule of law above themselves, preferring to live in an international anarchy that is both undemocratic and uncivilized. Citizens must obey the law, but governments, insofar as they claim to be sovereign, recognize no law over themselves. Murder is outlawed within all societies, but suddenly "legitimate" when my government commands me to murder someone from another country.

Murder is considered a terrible crime, except when the government tells us to murder people who live under other governments, for "there are no world laws against murder at the command of some military, since there are no democratically legislated enforceable world laws". When I murder at the command of my country's military establishment, they pretend it is a noble act. Soldiers are decorated according to the number of people they manage to murder from other nations. The absurdity of this world system can be apparent to all who care to examine it objectively. Even if we are not the agents of this system of murder ourselves, we are all complicit in it if we do not uphold world law. Without world law, we pay taxes to support the old system, allow our children to enter it, and fail to put a stop to it within our home countries.

For these reasons many citizens who recognize the illegitimacy of their national governments are making *a pledge of civil obedience*, a pledge recognizing the *Constitution for the Federation of Earth* as the ultimate legitimate law for all citizens of Earth. They are making the decision to become world citizens within the Earth Federation. National governments can no longer satisfy my moral obligation to live under democracy, since none of them are democratic. I will not participate in this global system of murder, environmental destruction, economic chaos, and massive failure to protect my rights to life, liberty, and security.

National governments are not "sovereign" over their populations as they claim. In democracy, only the people are ultimately sovereign. But who can the people possibly be except all human beings who live upon the Earth? I sign the pledge to the *Earth Constitution* and my act of civil obedience goes a long way toward restoring my moral integrity as a citizen committed to the rule of true democratic law. The *Constitution* alone represents the sovereignty of the people of Earth. National constitutions are a sham in this respect, helpless to satisfy the moral obligation of their citizens to live under the rule of genuine democratic law.

Just as the logical implication of the development of the rule of law in human civilization is political and economic democracy (legitimate law as democratic law) so the logical implication of the development of democracy is democratic world law. Genuine and effective democracy is impossible unless it is world democracy. In addition, once world economic and political unity is created, and the dangers of climate change, militarism, economic collapse, resource depletion, and population explosion have been dealt with by world government, then the nations will be able to at last realize genuine democracy within their borders.

The Earth Federation makes possible not only world democratic unity but regional, national, and local democracy as well. It restores moral legitimacy to the nations and restores political moral integrity to citizens precisely because it takes them out of the absurd condition of the international anarchy that destroys democracy through its system of fragmentation. Once life, liberty and security are institutionalized at the planetary level through the abolition of militarism, the protection of the global environment, and the regulation of global economics for the good of all, then individual countries will be free to activate real democracy within their territories.

The *Earth Constitution*, therefore, requires our *pledge of civil obedience*. Civil disobedience to illegitimate laws is not the only way by which we can morally redeem ourselves in the face of the evils perpetuated by nation-states. We can also take a pledge of civil obedience to the sovereignty of the people of Earth under the *Earth Constitution*.

Despite its long and tortured history, the concept of the sovereignty of the people has also inexorably moved towards its rightful terminus in the sovereignty of the people of Earth. It is important to recognize the various meanings of this principle. As with inalienable human rights, the sovereignty of the people is above the institutions of positive law, including the state (on all levels) as the legitimate lawmaking body. In much democratic theory, government only legitimately exists insofar as it democratically serves the people and protects their *a priori* rights. As the U.S. Declaration of Independence puts this: "to secure these rights, Governments are instituted among Men, deriving their just powers from the consent of the governed."

The Earth Federation created by the *Constitution for the Federation of Earth* represents the sovereignty of the people of Earth, the ultimate and final form of political sovereignty. Article 2.2 states that *the world government for the Federation of Earth shall be non-military and shall be democratic in its own structure, with ultimate sovereignty residing in all the people who live on Earth.* Even in ancient times the sovereignty of the Roman emperors was said to represent that of the people. Yet where do "the people" begin and end that is represented by the authority of government? In practice the emperor did as he pleased and claimed it was in the name of the people.

Where do "the people" begin and end and how are they to be represented? All theories of human rights attribute rights to *all human beings*, not just those who live within this or that territory. The same is true of the sovereignty of the people. This notion, like that of inalienable rights, derives from the fact of our humanity, not from where we happen to be born. The sovereignty of the people means that *all the people* are sovereign. As with the concept of human rights, it does not discriminate among individuals.

We become aware here the paradox of certain limited groups of people claiming they are "sovereign" over a certain part of the Earth. If the people are sovereign, why do they stop being sovereign when I step over the invisible political line between independent nations? The government that claims to represent me in this limited territory by that very fact interferes with the sovereignty of those in some other territory. We discriminate between these individuals (within this territory) and all others (outside this territory). Neither human rights nor sovereignty can rightly be said to stop at some territorial border.

Territorial integrity should be rightly protected, but this is not the same as sovereignty. Territorial integrity can only be protected when sovereignty resides with the whole. It is protected under a federated Earth by the entire *Earth Constitution*, specifically in Article 18. Each nation is represented in the House of Nations and the world court system protects the all the nations just as it protects individuals.

However, sovereignty does not mean that people somehow "own" a certain territory: "This is my country and you cannot come into it" is an absurd idea, yet one very much in the dominant ideology of the nation-states. People cannot be sovereign within a merely limited territory. They may indeed be relatively autonomous within their territory as part of a federated Earth. They should have control over local politics and economics insofar these are consistent with the rights of everyone on Earth (under the *Earth Constitution*). But "sovereignty," like "human rights," is a political concept referring to the collective body of people in virtue of their being people. It is conceptually universal, not territorial. The only legitimate sovereignty is the sovereignty of the people of Earth.

The nation-state system distorts this truth beyond recognition. In the United States, they have even developed the concept of "superior sovereignty." Supreme court Chief Justice John Marshall formulated this doctrine in the 1830s to deal with the westward expansion of the U.S. into Indian territory. Under the world system of sovereign nations that had been formulated at the Peace of Westphalia in 1648, the Indian tribes had to be recognized as sovereign nations with whom treaties could be made (for the world, according to the Peace of Westphalia, was divided into a collection of "sovereign" nation-states). The Indians were morally expected to honor their treaties. They were also held to their treaties by the superior power of the growing U.S. military. When and if they violated treaties, this was seen as an excuse for seizing their land and wiping out their villages.

But the Marshall Doctrine held that the U.S. was not under the same obligation to honor its treaty obligations with the Indian nations. It held a "superior" form of sovereignty that allowed it to break its promises as necessary for the expansion of its superior sovereignty. Indeed, it broke nearly every treaty it ever made with the Indian nations. Finally, beginning in 1871, it dropped the pretense of dealing with sovereign Indian nations and simply swallowed the Indians whole, by 1885 extending its internal jurisdiction over the Indians. From that time on, Congress has passed more than 5000 acts regarding "Indian affairs." Indian "sovereignty" was now defined as whatever Congress did not remove through these acts. The doctrine of superior sovereignty is a key element in the ideology of imperial expansion and domination. (Ward Churchill, in Sterba, *Social and Political Philosophy*, p. 266)

Today, the same doctrine (of superior sovereignty) is apparent everywhere in U.S. foreign policy, although now clothed in more deceptive language. It is there, for example, in the mythic concept of "national interest" that operates throughout the U.S. Congress, Executive, and military institutions. Any violation of U.S. "national interest" any where in the world is considered an attack on U.S. sovereignty. It does not matter if the object of this "national interest" is the resources belonging to some other sovereign nation. National interest means securing the oil resources of the Middle East, containing the economic or political expansion of rival nations (such as China and Russia), or suppressing alternative forms of economic organization that might indicate to people that neo-liberal economics is not in the best interests of the majority of people in the world.

In any of these cases and others, the U.S. considers its right to overthrow governments, bomb other "sovereign" nations, interfere in elections, mount economic blockades, or assassinate dissident leaders in other parts of the world. Superior sovereignty today means the inviolability of U.S. interests anywhere on Earth and the right of the U.S. to interfere anywhere (especially, in practice, in countries without a capacity to defend themselves). A network of some 725 known military bases in 153 countries worldwide has been created in order to "defend" these interests. Superior sovereignty (clothed in the ideology of "national interest") remains the dominant myth of the world's superpower.

Without recognizing the sovereignty of the people of Earth, the alternative is this idolatry and mythology of unaccountable power, very much akin to the Nazi ideological concepts of *uebermensch* (German superiority) and *lebensraum* (living space for the superior nation). This alternative may mean the death of the promise of democracy for the Earth. The long development of the democratic concept to the point where world democracy is understood to be the deepest meaning of the democratic project is derailed in the military and economic domination of the entire planet by its imperial center.

Democratic world government is the only viable option. Individual nations attempting to leave the imperial system have been crushed, overthrown, and economically blockaded. A group of nations and their peoples must ally together and simultaneously sign the *Earth Constitution*. We have advised those individual nations who are interested not to separately sign the *Constitution* for this will bring down the wrath of the superpower in the form of economic blockade or worse. But a group of 25 or more nations simultaneously signing the *Constitution* would be instantly transforming the world order and realizing the true meaning of both democracy and sovereignty.

The doctrine of superior sovereignty means not only a distortion of the concept of sovereignty as it develops toward it logical terminus in the sovereignty of the people of Earth. It also means the impossibility of democracy anywhere on Earth and the loss of inalienable rights for all peoples, probably also within the United States. The U.S. government and the Pentagon, in concert with gigantic multinational corporations, have no intention of bringing democracy to any country on Earth, let alone within the imperial center itself.

Superior sovereignty suits them just fine, as it did the superiority myths that drove the Nazis in their attempt at world conquest. The "manifest destiny" of the 19th century that resulted in the genocide of the native-American population has become the doctrine of economic globalization and imposing pseudo-democracy (U.S. style) on the rest of humankind through the use of economic and military force. Behold: the "Project for the New American Century" (www.newamericancentury.org). Read it and see for yourself.

One of the ways the sovereignty of the people of Earth is manifested is in their authority to designate certain rights as "inalienable." The authority of the people is, of course, invested in law and government. But law and government are not the absolute arbiters of which laws can be made. For the people, in founding a government (in their founding constitution), may designate certain rights as inalienable, that is, beyond the authority of the government to alter.

A doctrine of these rights without democratic government to institutionalize them in dozens of laws and due process procedures is relatively useless, just as the U.N. Universal Declaration of Human Rights is effectively useless. The *Earth Constitution* embodies these rights in enforceable world law. Articles 12 and 13 detail the rights of all citizens of Earth that are beyond the authority of the Earth Federation to interfere with. Equality is institutionalized, carefully designed into the *Constitution*. All mythologies of superiority are exposed as an ideological cover for exploitation and domination, that is, for stealing the wealth of others and militarily repressing them when the poor rebel against their degradation and dehumanization.

Everyone on Earth has the same rights, everyone benefits from the same unification, everyone may participate equally in government; everyone is protected. The great statements of human rights in the past stated this *universality*. The U.S. Declaration of Independence asserts that "all men are created equal and endowed by their creator with certain inalienable rights." Yet this "all" can never be embodied in the fragmented nation-state system. "All" means all, every human being equal to every other and protected by the political unity of democratic world government that binds them all together while at the same time protecting their individual identities and diversity. Otherwise, this "all" without concrete embodiment is nothing but empty rhetoric.

We must make every effort to rapidly ratify the *Constitution for the Federation of Earth*, not only because the world is at the end of the line with the global crises outlined above. We must also ratify the *Earth Constitution* because it represents the genuine fulfillment of the human civilizational project. It represents the culmination of both democratic thought and the concept of the sovereignty of the people. The alternative is clear: either death (military or environmental) under the present international anarchy, or a temporary tyranny inevitably leading toward that same death.

Climate change, militarization, and today's neo-liberal economics are the great common enemies of humankind. They are very real threats to our existence and we can only meet them through uniting together in a world system of *unity in diversity*. Only world economic and political unity can salvage the future of civilization. The *Earth Constitution* represents the fulfillment of the long development of the civilized rule of law on Earth to the point where we realize that the only legitimate democracy is the democratic unity of all the people who live on Earth.

Finally, the *Constitution* represents the fulfillment of the true meaning of the sovereignty of people on Earth for the only legitimate sovereignty is the sovereignty of all the people who live on Earth. Democratic world government will not only save us from impending disaster and death. It will usher in a new era of fulfillment for human beings, and era of peace, prosperity, and justice the like of which the world has never seen. Just as the historical development of the concept of democracy leads to world democracy so the historical development of the concept of sovereignty leads to the sovereignty of all the people on Earth.

Institutional arrangements have real human consequences. The consequences of the world's fragmentation are everywhere to be seen in the nightmare of today's world disorder, war, insecurity, environmental disintegration, poverty, and disease. The highly probable consequences of world economic and political unity must surely also be apparent to all reasonable persons. The root cause we have seen is fragmentation: the nation-state and monopoly capitalism as we know them today have institutionalized fragmentation. On the other hand, the institutionalization of the true meaning of law, democracy, and the sovereignty of the people will mean real civilizational fulfillment for human beings and our precious planet Earth.

We are all connected to one another as human beings and as citizens of planet Earth. We are all bearers of inalienable rights and participants in the sovereignty of the people. Yet our dominant institutions (sovereign nation-states and monopoly capitalism) keep us from living according to these realities. They keep us fragmented, divided, incapable of reaching our true potential as human beings and as a civilization.

These volumes of *Emerging World Law* bring together for the first time in history the most fundamental work that has been done to bring the world out of its conditions of fragmentation and war into a transformed world of peace, prosperity, and freedom for our entire planet. Just as today's fragmented system of sovereign nation-states in league with monopoly capitalism is inherently a war system so a peace system is established by the *Earth Constitution* and the provisional world laws passed subsequently under its authority. Peace is not an empty ideal of starry-eyed utopians. Peace is a consequence of the way we organize our political and economic lives, not a result of some imagined good or bad human nature. Peace can and must be established, and the *Earth Constitution* is the most practical, realistic, and immediately possible way of doing this.

We are called upon to act, to make a decision, in the face of this immoral situation threatening our very existence on this planet. Time is rapidly running out and the demand that we act intensifying each day. Recognition and affirmation of the emerging world law collected in these volumes are the practical and moral duty of each person on Earth. Tomorrow may be too late. Each nation, and each person, is called upon (morally and pragmatically) to take the pledge of civil obedience to the *Constitution for the Federation of Earth*.

Chapter Two

Conceptualizing the Earth Federation

with the Executive Summary of the ***Earth Constitution*** and with Initial Charts and Diagrams of the Earth Federation

based on the *Earth Constitution* and on the World Legislation of the Provisional World Parliament

"A goal without a plan is just a wish." Antoine de Saint-Exupery (1900 - 1944)

"Make no little plans; they have no magic to stir men's blood...Make big plans, aim high in hope and work."

Daniel H. Burnham (1846 - 1912)

Eugenia Almand, Editor

On the following pages is the Executive Summary of the Earth Constitution. This is a summary that includes the basic features of the Earth Constitution, but omits details, so that a literate person would be able to grasp an overview of the Earth Constitution in fifteen minutes or less. Then there are the basic provisional World Region maps for the Earth Federation in conformance with the August 2004 adoption of the Hanna Newcombe Plan (first drafted by Ian Hackett), as a starting point for drawing the regional and district boundaries. These maps are based upon the provisions of the Earth Constitution regarding regional electoral and administrative structure. The maps are provisional in that the Provisional World Parliament is open to receive commentary, suggestions for improvement and even comprehensive plebiscites by initiative from the people of Earth, the world citizens themselves.

It is likely that with time the regional lines and name designations will undergo adjustment. The names of regions are and should be open to determination by any plebiscites conducted in the general elections for the residents of the respective regions, within the limits of avoiding conflict with other regions.

Following the World Region maps are diagrams of the Earth Federation structure, and diagrams of systemic structures within the Earth Federation: the Earth Federation Funding Corporation, and the Enforcement System. The Earth Federation Funding Corporation serves as a provisional government corporation within the World Financial Administration.

The Enforcement System serves integrating actions for the World Attorneys General Office, the World Police, the World Disarmament Agency, the World Commission on Terrorism, and significant parts of the Emergency Earth Rescue Administration and other agencies of the Earth Federation.

There are various ways to depict the structure of the Earth Federation in accordance with the *Constitution for the Federation of Earth*. One such manner is a text summary. The text summary portrays in an abbreviated but accurate form the primary features of the *Earth Constitution*. This makes it possible to convey the structural essence of the *Constitution* in about four pages.

Other means of depicting the structure of the Earth Federation as defined in the *Earth Constitution* are the Diagram of the Earth Federation and the diagram Transfer, Reconstitution and Integration of the United Nations System. Since the Earth Federation Diagram shows listed agencies of the Earth Federation as named in the *Earth Constitution*, a small type size was required for fitting it cohesively onto a single page of this book. The Summary of the *Constitution for the Federation of Earth* printed below faithfully reproduces most of the information of the diagram. This can be read first for greater ease of comprehension.

Following the overall structural diagrams are two other structural diagrams. One depicts the structure of the Earth Federation Funding Corporation, from *Earth Constitution* Articles 8.7., and 17.6 (World Government Funding Corporation), and from World Legislative Act #7. The other diagram depicts the structure of the Enforcement System, from *Earth Constitution*, Article 10.2. and from World Legislative Act #14.

There are charts and diagrams not in this chapter. Originally, Aake Anker Ording drew three diagrams depicting the transition from the United Nations Regime to Earth Federation. This are in the *World Encyclopedia of Peace* (McGraw-Hill).
There are charts detailing the world regions and world districts. These will be published in one of the subsequent volumes of *Emerging World Law*. Due to the comprehensive and cumulative nature of the work being done. it is likely that many additional supplementary diagrams will be developed to show the organizational structure of many other agencies of the Earth Federation.

Executive Summary of the

Constitution for the Federation of Earth

(Earth Constitution)

1. Broad functions of Earth Federation are the following:
1.1. to prevent war; 1.2. to protect universal human rights; 1.3. to end poverty; 1.4. to regulate international processes; 1.5. to protect the environment and ecological fabric of life, that is, the biosphere; and 1.6. to devise solutions to world problems beyond the capacity of national governments.

2. Basic structure of Earth Federation is the following:
2.1. People and nations organize as a universal federation, to include all people, all nations, and all oceans, seas and lands of Earth, including atmosphere and space.
2.2. Earth Federation is non-military and democratic, with ultimate sovereignty of the people of Earth.
2.3. Powers of Earth Federation apply to problems that transcend national boundaries.
2.4. For world elections and administration, Earth is united into 1000 World Districts total, within +/-10% limits equal in population, of 20 World Regions, combining to 10 Magna-Regions in 5 Continental Divisions.

3. Organs of the Earth Federation are the following:
3.1. The World Parliament;
3.2. The World Executive;
3.3. The World Administration;
3.4. The Integrative Complex;
3.5. The World Judiciary;
3.6. The Enforcement System; and
3.7. The World Ombudsmus.

4. This *Earth Constitution* grants Earth Federation the jurisdiction and powers necessary to ensure the effective broad functions of the Earth Federation. Earth Federation must have no military power, but may use world legislation, administration, education, finance, civil police enforcement system, world court system, ombudsmus, public defense and other regulatory powers to ensure effective enforcement of world law.

5. World Parliament composes of three legislative houses, to consider, adopt, amend and repeal World Legislation.

* People of Earth directly elect **House of Peoples**, with one delegate from each of 1000 World Electoral and Administrative Districts. Term of office is 5 years, with no re-election limits. Minimum age is 21.

* Nations appoint or elect **House of Nations**. Term of office is 5 years, with no re-election limits. Minimum age is 21.

* University students and faculty of World Regions nominate regional candidates from anywhere for **House of Counsellors**. From nominations, Regional Members of both House of Peoples and House of Nations elect 10 Counsellors for Region to total 200, 10 from each of 20 Regions; House of Counsellors has nominative, consultative, initiative and referral functions. Term of office is 10 years, with no re-election limits. Minimum age is 25. People of Earth may launch initiatives for world legislation, and may vote on referendums submitted from World Parliament.

6. World Parliament elects and supervises a **World Executive**. House of Counsellors nominates and World Parliament elects Presidium of an annually rotating president and 4 vice-presidents, all current Members of World Parliament (MPs), and an Executive Cabinet of 30 ministers, all MPs. The World Executive must neither veto nor suspend the World Parliament nor the *Earth Constitution*. The World Executive has no military power.

7. The 30 Cabinet Ministers and Vice Presidents head the **World Administration**, of about 30 ministries. The Presidium nominates and Cabinet elects a **Secretary General** to coordinate the ministries.

8. Broad functions that naturally duplicate within each ministry integrate in agencies of the **Integrative Complex**: World Civil Service Administration; World Boundaries and Elections Administration; Institute on Governmental Procedures and World Problems; Agency for Research and Planning; Agency for Technological and Environmental Assessment; World Financial Administration; and Commission for Legislative Review. World Parliament with variable organs of the Earth Federation elect 12-member commissions to head each agency. All agencies except Commission for Legislative Review include a Cabinet Minister or Vice President of the Executive, plus a Senior Administrator from civil service lists.

9. Benches form a **World Judiciary**, including **World Supreme Court, Regional World Courts and District World Courts**, having mandatory jurisdiction over different kinds of issues:
Human Rights, Criminal Cases, Civil Cases, Constitutional Cases, International Conflicts, Public Cases, Appelate Bench, Advisory Bench, and Superior Tribunal for cases of extra-ordinary public importance. World Judiciary has 5 continental seats. House of Counsellors nominates and World Parliament elects a Collegium of World Judges of 20 to 60 Members, headed by a Presiding Council of 5 members which assigns judges to the several Benches. Judge minimum age is 30. Judge minimum juristic or legal experience is 10 years.

10. The Enforcement System
World Parliament elects an Office of World Attorneys General with 5 World Attorneys General and commission of 20 Regional World Attorneys, to head non-military Enforcement System. Earth Federation neither retains nor uses weapons of mass destruction. World Attorney minimum age is 30. World Attorney minimum legal experience is 7 years. Term limit is 3 consecutive 5-year terms. World Parliament may remove World Attorneys. World Attorneys appoint a World Police Supervisor and 20 Regional World Police Captains, all removable by Parliament, with 10-year employment limit. World Police apprehend individual suspected lawbreakers. World Parliament regulates World Police, which shall follow due process, and obtain warrants for search & arrests.

11. House of Counsellors nominates and World Parliament elects a **World Ombudsmus** Council of 5 World Ombudsen and Commission of 20 Regional World Advocates protect human rights and ensure proper government functioning. Limits are two 10-year terms. Ombudsan minimum age is 30. Ombudsan minimum legal experience is 5 years.

12. Bill of Rights guarantees inalienable human rights, including all those customarily guaranteed by civil nations: equal rights, equal protection, freedom of expression, association & religion, *habeas corpus* rights, universal suffrage, property, privacy, & other prohibitions against government intrusions.

13. Directive Principles of 19 sections list additional civil rights and benefits to be guaranteed and implemented over time for all people.

14.1. Earth Federation guarantees the following: full faith and credit to public acts, records, legislation and judicial proceedings of member nations; nations retain jurisdiction over internal affairs; asylum for refuge seekers from nations not in Earth Federation;

14.2. *Earth Constitution* reserves non-delegated powers to Earth Federation member nations and to the people of Earth.

15. World Parliament establishes five world capitals in 5 Continental Divisions: 1 Primary Capital and 4 Secondary Capitals. World Parliament establishes 20 World Federal Zones in 20 World Regions.

16.1. The people of Earth have ownership and Earth Federation has jurisdiction of all oceans from 20 kilometers offshore, the seabeds, vital straits, channels, canals, the Moon and the atmosphere from 1 km. above the general surface of the land.

16.2. Earth Federation shall establish peaceful external relations. The Presidium negotiates external relations and treaties, subject to approval by the World Parliament.

17. Earth Constitution implements by stages:
Provisional Earth Federation, before 25 countries or before World Districts including 10% of world population have ratified.
First Operative Stage, when 25 countries or World Districts including 10% of world population have ratified, or equivalent mix.
Second Operative Stage, when 50% of countries and World Districts including 50% of world population have ratified, or equivalent mix.
Full Operative Stage, when 80% of countries, comprising 90% of world population, have ratified.

Nations may give preliminary ratification. Preliminary ratification is subject to final ratification of people at least 18 years of age, by simple majority of votes cast in popular referendum, with at least 25% of electorate casting votes within any respective world district. Viable agencies of the United Nations Organization integrate into the Earth Federation.

18. People may initiate amendment procedures to the *Earth Constitution* by 200,000 signatures from each of 20 world districts and submission to vote of World Parliament. Additionally, World Constitutional Convention shall convene not less that every 20 years. Amendments are subject to absolute 2/3 majority vote of 3 Houses of World Parliament voting separately.

19. Provisional World Parliament may adopt world legislation prior to first operative stage, subject to re-confirmation by World Parliament.

⊕

The *Constitution for the Federation of Earth* was developed and adopted by 4 sessions of World Constituent Assembly meeting around the world in 1968, 1977, 1979 & 1991.

The World Districting Plan was originally prepared by eminent world federalist Ian Hackett in *The Spring of Civilization,* first published in 1973. This plan was then revised somewhat by Dr. Hanna Newcombe.

The Hackett World District Plan as revised by Dr. Newcombe was adopted as part of world legislative Act #29 for the World Boundaries and Elections Administration, August 2004, meeting at City Montessori School, Lucknow, in Uttar Pradesh, India, at the eighth session of the provisional World Parliament, convened in conformance with Article 19 of the *Earth Constitution*.

We are aware that many of the listed world districts are somewhat outside the 10% limits for equality of population, as defined in the *Earth Constitution*, Article 2.4. The table of World Districts continues to be a work in progress. The World Boundaries and Elections Commission, as well as the Commission for Legislative Review welcome the public to help with updating population reports and district line recommendations for presentation to the provisional World Parliament. Recommendations are particularly encouraged when it is apparent that world district lines will not easily conform to existing national, state, province or county lines. The Commissions are currently receiving updated population reports for the defined World Districts. The World Boundaries and Elections Commission will retabulate with new census figures as soon as feasible.

All of the World Region lines are drawn on a provisional basis and are subject to further deliberation and decision by the operative World Parliament when that forms, as well as subject to comprehensive plebiscites as might be required in cases by the *Earth Constitution* (Article 4, Item 5).

On the following two pages is a table of the World Regions according to the districting plan adopted. Then, the next four pages comprise world region maps to better visualize the geographic structure of the Earth Federation's World Regions.

It might be helpful to note here that World Districts and World Regions do not and are not intended to replace national borders. World Districts and World Regions are for affairs at the world federal level of jurisdiction, such as for world federal elections and world federal administration. The federal principle of subsidiarity protects the constituent nations and other constituent governments of the Earth Federation from incursion by the Earth Federation.

Table of World Regions

Region number	Listing of included district names or districted countries	World District Numbers	Number Quantity of districts	Total districts for region
01	Ethiopia, Somalia, Kenya	920-930	11	39
	Uganda, Tanzania, Rwanda, Burundi,	931-939	9	
	Angola, Zambia, Malawi, Mozambique	948-953	6	
	Zimbabwe, Namibia, Botswana, and any others in this geographical area	954-957	4	
	South Africa	958-963	6	
	Madagascar	964-966	3	
02	West Africa small states	881-894	14	44
	Nigeria	895-914	20	
	Cameroon, Central African Republic	915-916	2	
	Congo, Democratic Republic of Congo	940-947	8	
03	Brazil	840-868	29	42
	Bolivia, Chile, Argentina, Uruguay, Paraguay	827-839	13	
04	Mexico	785-799	15	42
	Cuba, Haiti, Domincan Republic, Puerto Rico	800-804	5	
	Caribbean small islands, Jamaica, Guatemala, El Salvador, Honduras, Nicaragua, Costa Rica	805-810	6	
	Panama, Colombia, Venezuela, Guyana, Surinam, Guyane	811-820	10	
	Ecuador, Peru	821-826	6	
05	Fukien, Kwantung	597-613	17	57
	Kwansi Chuang, Kweichow	614-625	12	
	Szechuan, Yunnan	626-653	28	
06	Anhwei, Chekiang	549-566	18	48
	Hunan, Kiangsu, Kiangsi	567-596	30	
07	Shansi, Shensi	497-507	11	52
	Honan	508-522	15	
	Shantung	523-538	16	
	Hupeh	539-548	10	
08	Tibet, Sinkiang-Uighur, Chinghai, Kansu, Ningsia Hui	453-461	9	44
	Inner Mongolia, Heilungkiang	462-470	9	
	Kirin, Liaoning, Hopei	471-496	26	
09	Japan,	667-694	28	48
	South Korea	659-666	8	
	Taiwan, Hong Kong	695-699	5	
	Australia, New Zealand	778-782	5	
	Papua-New Guinea, Pacific Islands	783-784	2	
10	Thailand	713-722	10	58
	Malaysia, Singapore	730-733	4	
	Philippines	734-743	10	
	Indonesia	744-777	34	

Region number	Listing of included district names or districted countries	World District Numbers	Number Quantity of districts
11	West Bengal, Assam, Nagaland, other India panhandle states, Nepal, Bhutan Bangladesh Burma (Myanmar) Vietnam, Laos, Cambodia	339-354 450-452 432-449 723-729 700-712	16 3 18 7 13
12	Andhra Pradesh Kerala Tamil Nadu Haryana Sri Lanka Orissa, Chhattisgarh Bihar, Jharkhand	401-411 412-416 417-426 427-428 429-431 371-375 325-338	11 5 10 2 3 5 14
13	Uttar Pradesh, Uttaranchal Madhya Pradesh Maharashtra Mysore (Karnataka)	303-324 361-370 382-393 394-400	22 10 12 7
14	Iran Afghanistan Pakistan Kashmir, Himachal, Punjab Rajasthan Gujarat	266-273 274-278 279-296 297-302 355-360 376-381	8 5 18 6 6 6
15	Turkey, Syria, Lebanon, Palestine, Israel, Jordan Egypt, Yemen, Saudi Arabia, Gulf states Iraq, Kurdistan Morocco, Algeria, Tunisia, Libya Sudan	235-249 250-262 263-265 869-880 917-919	15 13 3 12 3
16	All states of the Russian Federation Asian states of former Soviet Republics Mongolia North Korea	12-41 63-72 654 655-658	30 10 1 4
17	Poland, Czechoslovakia Albania, Hungary, Romania, Bulgaria Lithuania, Latvia, Estonia, Byelorussia, Ukraine, Moldavia, Georgia, Armenia, Azerbaijan	189-199 222-232 42-62	11 11 21
18	France, Spain, Portugal Austria, Switzerlan, Italy, former Yugoslavia states Greece	139-162 200-221 233-234	24 22 2
19	Contiguous 48 States of USA	073-125	53
20	Canada, Alaska, Greenland, Iceland, Faeroes Scandinavia Denmark Ireland, and U.K. Benelux, Germany	001-007 008-011 188 126-138 163-187	7 4 1 13 21

20 World Regions

in conformance with World Legislative Act #29 for the World Boundaries and Elections Administration (Elections Act) and in conformance with the *Constitution for the Federation of Earth*

World Region lines on map are approximate and not exactly to scale.

Ian Hackett developed proposals based on the *Earth Constitution* which were then further elaborated by Dr. Hanna Newcombe. The Provisional World Parliament adopted the proposals as an initial framework from which the world constitutional ratification program and initial administration of Earth Federation can emerge.

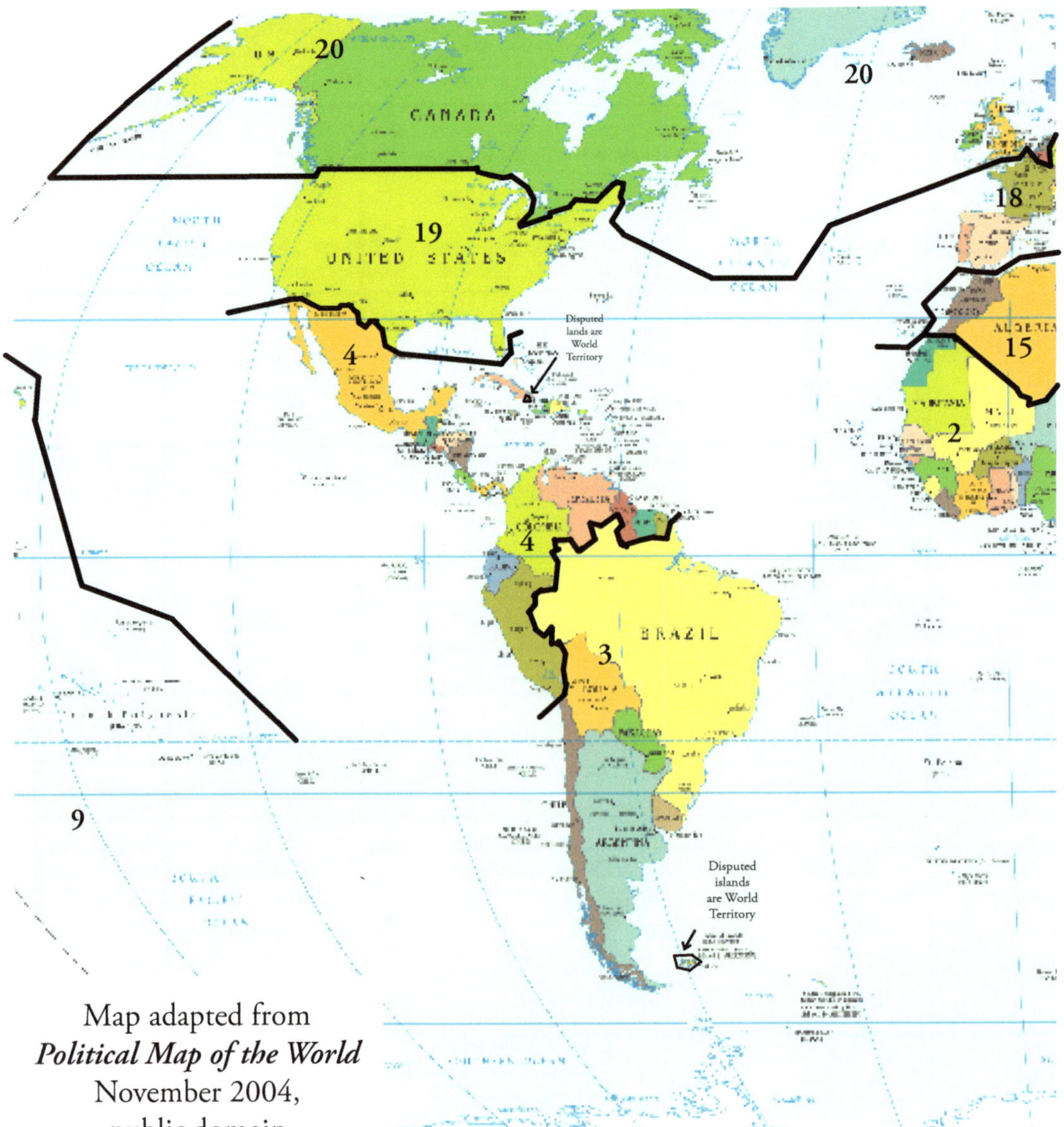

Map adapted from
Political Map of the World
November 2004,
public domain
map from CIA Factbook.

Regions	Magna-Regions	Continent	Description
1, 2, 15 & 18	1 & 8	1	Africa & Mediterranean
5, 6, 7 & 8	3 & 4	2	Mainland China
9, 10, 11, & 12	5 & 6	3	South Asia, East and Southeast Asia, Australia, and Pacific
13, 14 , 16 & 17	7 & 9	4	South Central Asia, North Asia, and East Europe
3, 4, 19 & 20	2 & 10	5	North & South America, Caribbean, and Northern Europe

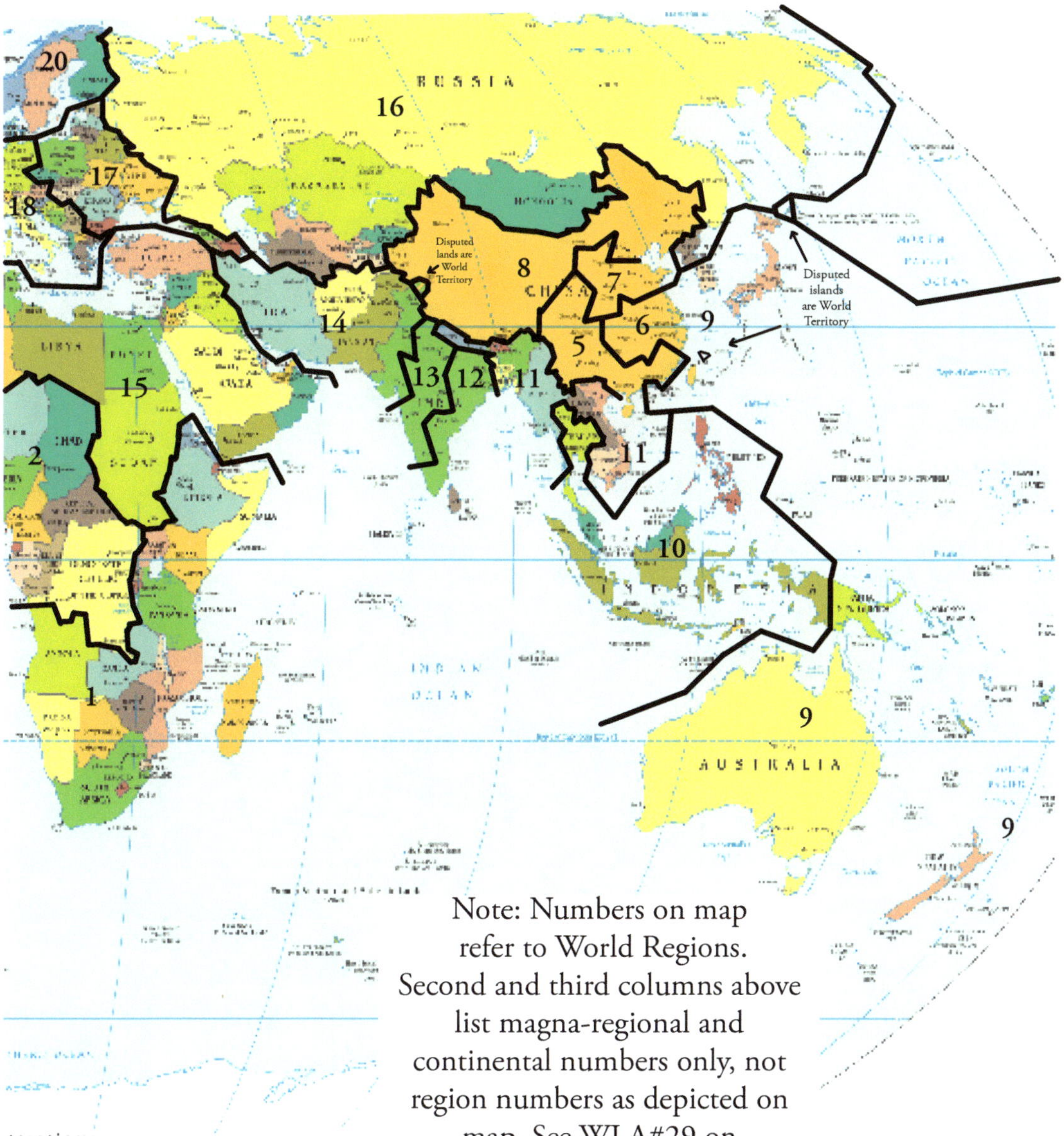

Note: Numbers on map refer to World Regions. Second and third columns above list magna-regional and continental numbers only, not region numbers as depicted on map. See WLA#29 on elections for details.

China and India Provisional Detail Maps

The Continents of the Earth Federation do not strictly adhere to pure geographical areas, such as the Earth's tectonic plates. Instead, the continents are formed of areas designated on grounds of population, for efficiency of administration, as well as for popular support. For these reasons, China measures as slightly more than one continent in 5 World Regions under the adopted Hackett-Newcombe Plan, as shown below. The provisional plan is subject to change based largely on plebiscites and national input.

For the same reasons, India, though not taking up an entire continent on its own, comprises 4 World Regions, spanning parts of two continents, as shown in the provisional detail map on the facing page.

Map adapted from Nations Online Project
http://www.nationsonline.org/oneworld/index.html?china.htm&2

It is important to recognize that the heavy black lines on these maps show the Region boundaries, and not boundaries where the laws are significantly different on either side of the boundary for the boundary level of jurisdiction. For instance, during the 1947 Partition of India, families and property rights were terribly disturbed by the partition into India and Pakistan, because laws and rights to either side of the line were competing and anyone who lived on the line tended to lose all, or at least whatever property or family that was on the far side of the line. Region boundaries of world federation are entirely different. This is because Region boundaries are for electoral and administrative purposes at world federal level only, and not for establishing contrary or competing legal systems. World federal law is the same on both sides of the line, so there is protection. Placements of lines are subject to re-determination by World Parliament and also can be overruled by plebiscite.

Map adapted from Nations Online Project
http://www.nationsonline.org/oneworld/index.html?india.htm&2

DIAGRAM OF EARTH FEDERATION IN CONFORMANCE WITH THE
CONSTITUTION FOR THE FEDERATION OF EARTH

THE PEOPLE OF THE WORLD GOVERN THEMSELVES

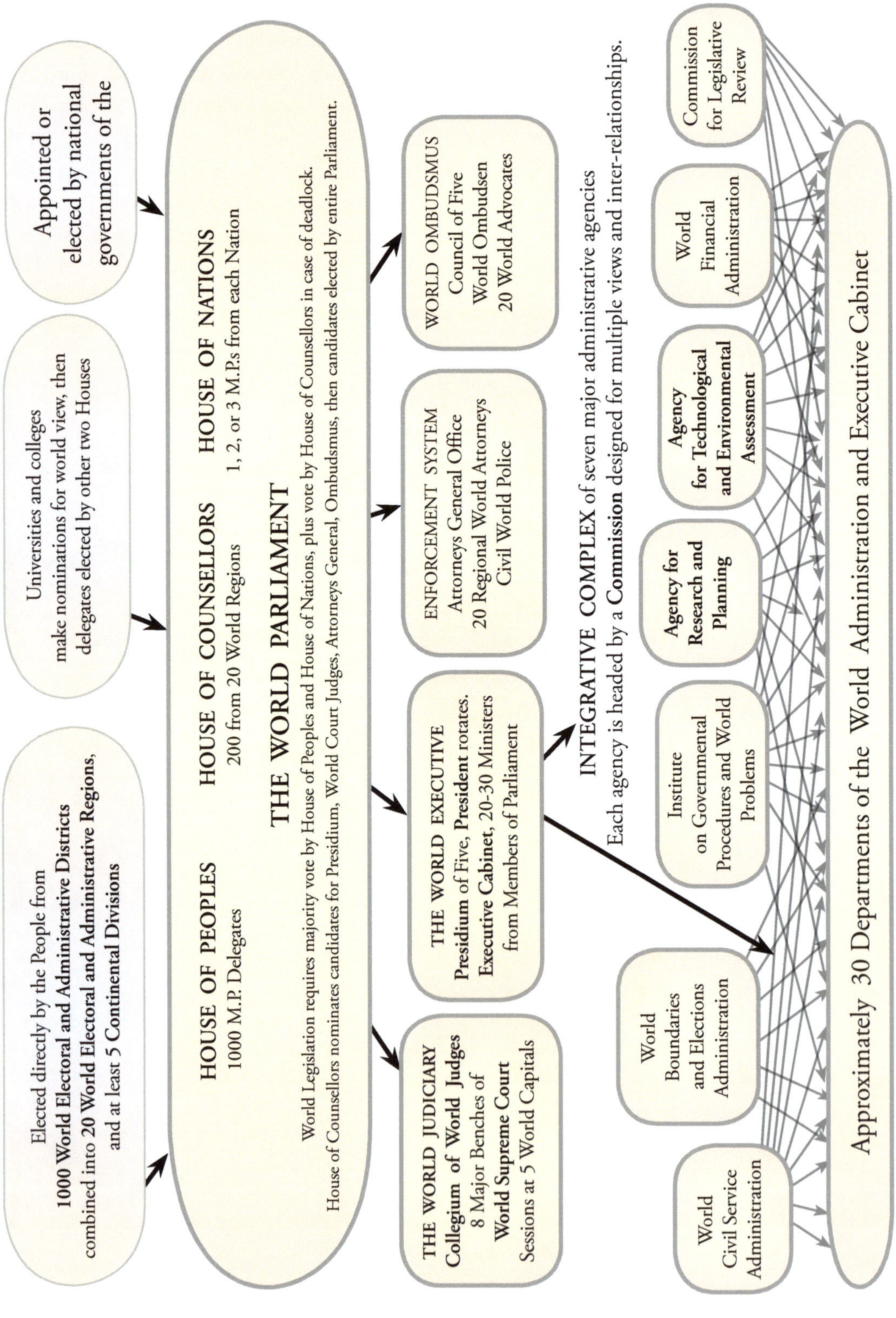

Transfer, Reconstitution & Integration of the United Nations System

according to the *Constitution for the Federation of Earth* (Article 17)

The people of the world are sovereign.

Earth Federation gives Security Council advisory status only, stripping Security Council's former and repeatedly abused war powers.

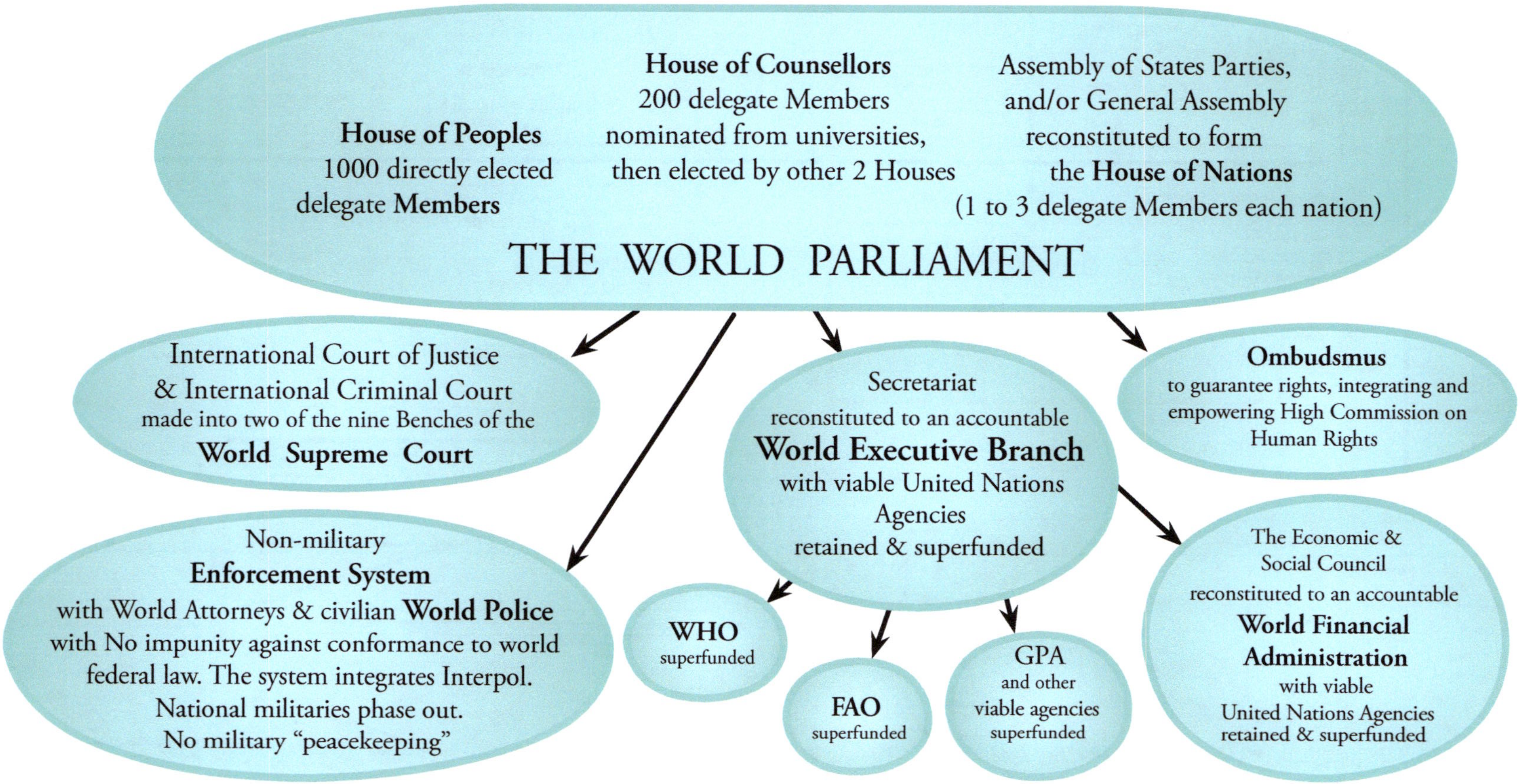

From World Legislative Act #7 - Diagram of the

Earth Federation Funding Corporation

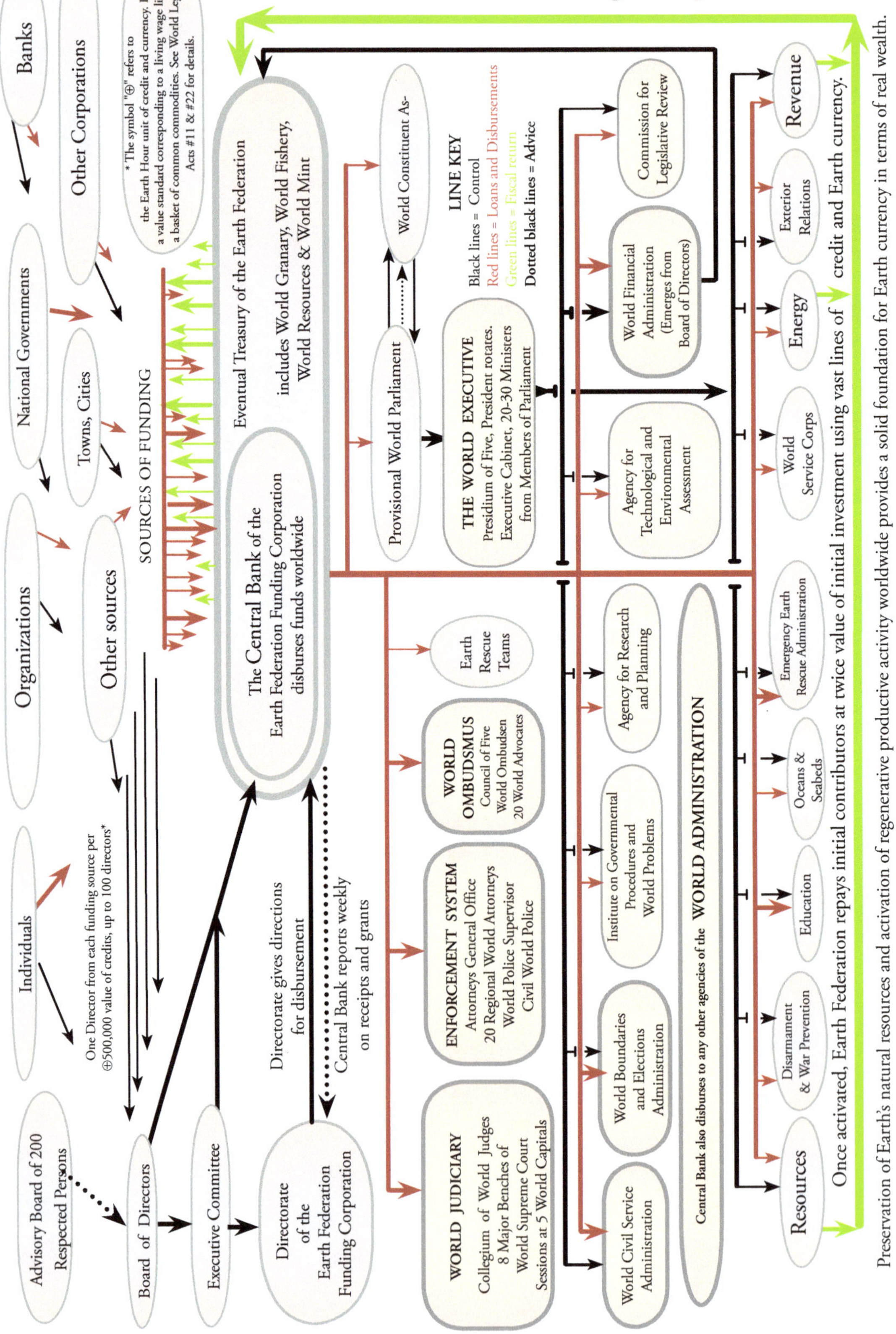

World Disarmament Agency and Enforcement System, as per *Earth Constitution*, Article #10, and World Legislative Acts #1 and #14

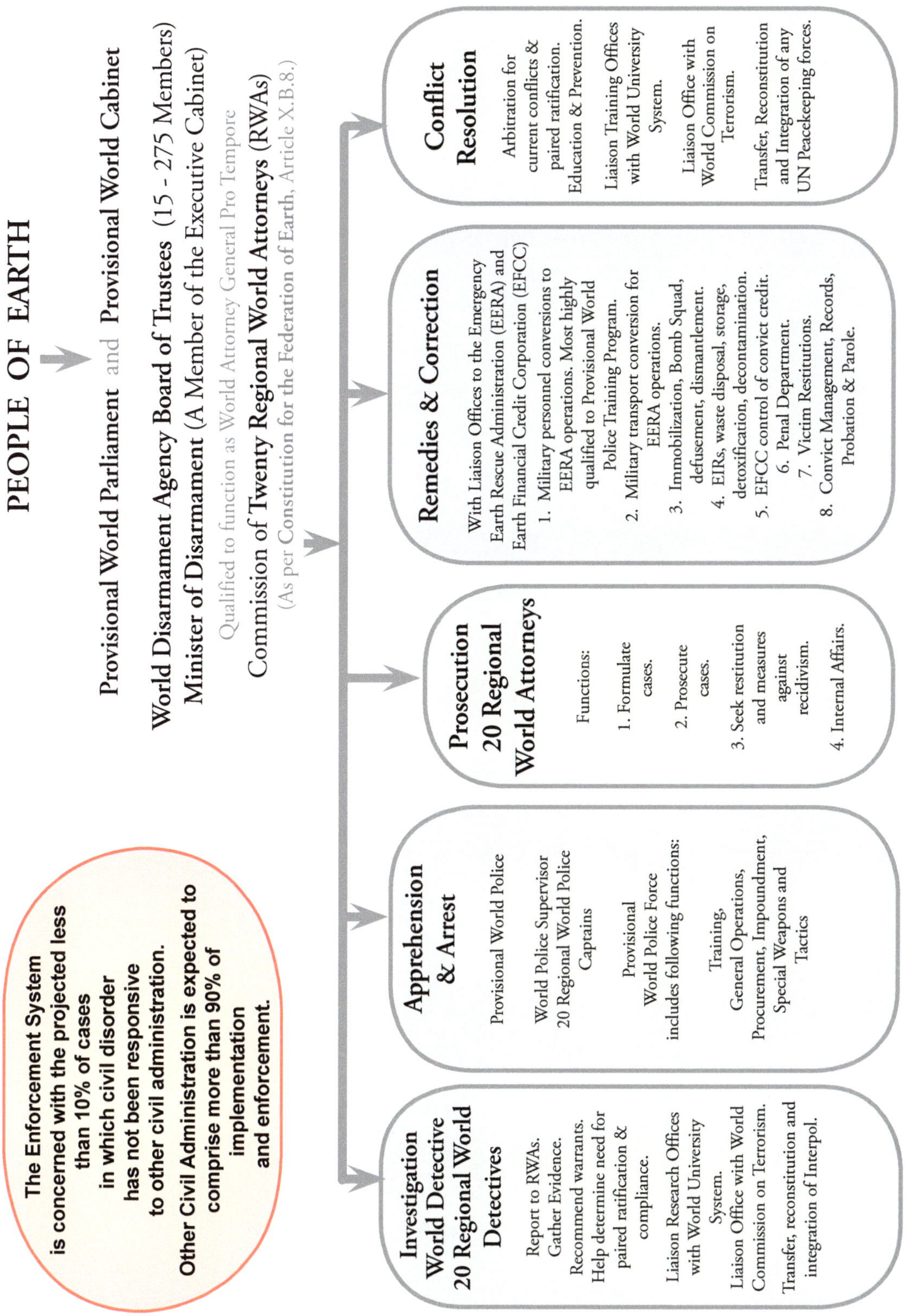

Chapter Three

A History of Emerging World Law

The World Constitution and Parliament Association, Global Constituent Assemblies and Early Sessions of the Provisional World Parliament

"For I dipt into the future, far as human eye could see,
Saw the Vision of the world, and all the wonder that would be;
Saw the heavens fill with commerce, argosies of magic sails,
Pilots of the purple twilight dropping down with costly bales;
Heard the heavens fill with shouting, and there rain'd a ghastly dew
From the nations' airy navies grappling in the central blue;
Far along the world-wide whisper of the south-wind rushing warm,
With the standards of the peoples plunging thro' the thunder-storm;
Till the war-drum throbb'd no longer, and the battle-flags were furl'd
In the Parliament of man, the Federation of the world.
There the common sense of most shall hold a fretful realm in awe,
And the kindly earth shall slumber, lapt in universal law."

Alfred Lord Tennyson (1809-1892)

Terence P. Amerasinghe

Section 1. The World Constitution and Parliament Association and the New Direction to Humankind's Struggle for a Better World.

The terms "World Government" and "World Parliament" before World War II were at best nebulous conceptions. These conceptions date back to Vedic and Puranic times. In the Rig Veda (before 5000 B.C.) calls that "Vasudhaiv Kutumbakum," that is, that "Mankind must live as one family." The Buddha reiterated this 4 centuries later. Christ in the first millennium called for a Kingdom of God on Earth. Socrates, the Greek Philosopher declared: "Say not I am a Citizen of Athens, but a Citizen of the World." Between then and now many others have spoken in a similar vein. Alfred Lord Tennyson crystallized this manner of thinking in his poem Locksley Hall: "The Parliament of Man and the Federation of the World."

Before World War II and even after, men of vision and learning expressed these sentiments . Albert Einstein urged national governments to create a World Government: "There is no salvation for civilization or even the human race," without it. Mahatma Gandhi in his very simple style wrote: "Our objective is One World. We have to work for it and the brotherhood of humanity." Emery Reeves wrote his well-known *Anatomy for Peace*. In U.K., Henry Usborne, M. P. and

Gilbert McAllister were foremost not only in promoting the idea but even formed groups to work for world government. In France Jacques Savery and Guy Marchand acted as apostles for world government. In U.S.A., Mary Georgia Lloyd set up an office in Chicago under the name of "The Campaign for World Government." She was joined by Henry Philip Isely and Margaret Sheesley (later Margaret Isely) and Thane Read. It was then and only then that the four answered the question as to how World Government can be achieved. Together they called for a World Constitutional Convention for World Government. National Governments were ruled by Constitutions under which the Rule of Law was enforced on their citizens. The World has been, and even today, devoid of a Constitution to which the nations of the World can adhere and regard as strictly binding. The Concert of Europe, after the Napoleonic Wars; the League of Nations, after World War I; and the United Nations, after World War II were merely based on treaty obligations and as history tells were broken by nations as their exigencies demanded.

The Chicago Campaign for World Government chalked out a new direction for Humankind's struggle for a better world. It petitioned National Governments to convene a World Constitutional Convention for World Government. The petition began with "We the People" and promised popular action if the National Governments failed to respond. It should be noted that the U. N. Charter began with "We the People" and quickly forgot "the People." It thereafter enthroned the sovereignty of national governments. This Campaign for World Government which later developed into the World Constitution and Parliament Association has never forgotten or failed "the People". It chartered a course in human history to form a Democratic Federal World Government that sets it apart from such ineffectual bodies as the League of Nations and the United Nations.

From 1949 to 1950, Philip Isely along with James Freutal and Fred Carmey made a theoretical study of the basis for popular action to organise a World Constitutional Convention. In 1950 Philip Isely published his pamphlet; "The People Must Write the Peace." World Government hitherto conceived as a dream of ages was seen as a practical reality. The World needs a Constitution. Such a Constitution must be federal in nature. It cannot be otherwise. National governments must submit to enforceable world laws legislated by a world parliament under a *Constitution for the Federation of Earth*. Anything short of it, like the U.N. Charter based on sovereignty of national governments subject only to laws called "international laws" based on the treaty system, only spells disaster.

The Manifesto for a Peoples World Convention prepared by Philip Isely was adopted by the North American Council at its convention held in Colorado Springs. It immediately drew a group of world-wide contacts. The seed for the future World Constitution and Parliament Association began to germinate. Among the number of persons who agreed to serve as delegates for the Peoples World Convention a divergence of views as to who should be delegates threatened to halt progress. Gerry Kraus, Henry Usborne and Gilbert MacAllister wanted only delegates from national governments to attend. Others like Jacques Savery and Guy Marchand wanted only people's delegates. It was Philip Isely's great and unique contribution that with Thane

Read, Margaret Isely and Marie Philips Scot, he formulated a plan that would seek to admit delegates from both national governments and delegates from peoples of all countries. The form of agreement was drafted by Thane Read and revised by Philip Isely. Together they travelled in Europe and other parts of the world seeking support. By 1960 delegates from 50 countries agreed to attend. Endorsements for the Agreement were received from several heads of state and Governments. An U.S. Committee for a World Constitutional Convention was formed. A World Committee with Philip Isely as Secretary met in Vienna. In 1961 the headquarters of the World Committee was established in Denver, Colorado. The first Call was issued in 1962. Over one thousand invitations were sent out along with it. A second Call went out with many signers from around the world.

Surprisingly, there were no signers from the leading World Governmentalists in the U.S.A. They simply refused. Mary Georgia Lloyd and her family, the World Association for World Federalists and Norman Cousins, from whom much was expected, failed to oblige. In England, Philip met Gilbert MacAllister. He declined to sign giving as the reason that National Governments should sign first. Arnold Toynbee, the celebrated historian, refused on the grounds that it would not work. On the plus side was the philosopher Bertrand Russel of U.K., Queen Elizabeth of Belgium, Lord Boyd Orr, Nobel Laureate and former head of F.A.O., Lady Boyd Orr, Lord Silkin P.C., head of the World Parliament Association, U.K., *On. Dottora* Mary Tibaldi Chiesa, Vice President of the Council of the World Parliament Association, Pastor Martin Niemoller (Germany) Co-President, World Council of Churches, Van de Capello (Netherlands) Treasurer, World Association U.N. Associations, I. K. Gujral, later Prime Minister of India, Goday Murahari (India) Member of Parliament and later Deputy Speaker of the Lok Sabha, Dr. T. P. Amerasinghe (Ceylon, now Sri Lanka), Co-President, WCPA, W. A. Falaiye (Nigeria) Member of Parliament, Dr. Juliyano Kyane, then Minister of Commerce, Kenya, Mrs. Helen Tucker, Canada, Past President, Voice of Women.

The list of signers is large and replete with world figures. It was in marked contrast to the inexplicable stand of those who refrained and the hollowness of their pretence to champion the cause of world government.

The Call to all Peoples and all National Governments of the Earth referred to above is definitive.

> "Independent National Governments, pressing their competing interests, have been unable to agree upon disarmament. Repeatedly they endanger the safety of their own citizens and every one else by testing and threatening. Even if one crisis passes, there are endless possibilities for potentially fatal crises, unless a new way is found to handle World Problems. Life cannot go on like this: a breaking point could come at anytime and then destruction.
>
> "To us it is clear; the point has been reached in the evolution of human Society where the rule of law must be established at the world level to replace international anarchy which threatens our daily lives. But what does World Law mean? It is simply commonsense to recognise that World Law if it is to be democratic and just, requires a democratic World Legislature to make the Law and executive with power to enforce the law and courts to which any international dispute must be submitted. This means a Federal

> World Government. Nothing less can provide the kind of World Law under which free men will be happy and safe.
>
> "It is also commonsense to recognise that a starting point for democratic federal world government is the drafting of its Constitution to define what powers shall be given to the World Government, what powers shall be kept by National Governments and to reach agreement on all other aspects of the World Government; and welfare of the people of Earth. We do hereby join in issuing this call for a World Constitutional Convention to Convene..."

It is significant that heads of Five National Governments were signatories to this call: Field Marshal Mohamed Ayub Khan, President of Pakistan; Dr. Francisco J. Orlich, President of Costa Rica, The Right Honourable Sir Milton Margoi, Prime Minister of Sierra Leone; The Hon. Leopold Senghor, President of Senegal; and The Hon. Julius Nyere, Prime Minister of Tanzania.

To further the convening of the World Constitutional Convention the First Preparatory Congress was held in Denver, Colorado, U.S.A. from Sept. 3rd to 8th 1963. Delegates from five continents participated. Lord and Lady Boyd Orr issued a stirring dedication:

> "There is no doubt about what the vast majority of people want. They want freedom from the fear of war. They want the full life, the just and true inheritance of the common man. They want friendship and security in the common brotherhood of all men. The people of the world can get all this by joining in the work of bringing about a World Constitutional convention where delegates from the National Governments together with delegates representing the people of various countries can provide a World Federal Government dedicated to serve the needs of mankind."

The Organisers of this First Preparatory Congress were the World Committee for a World Constitutional Convention, headquartered at Denver, Colorado, U.S.A., the Executive Cabinet of which consisted of Victor W. Haflich, then Member of the State Legislature, Kansas, President Dr. Neal Bishop, Vice President, Professor Agnes B. Hatfield, Secretary, T. E. Robertson Jr., Treasurer and Philip Isely, Executive Director. The congress met at the Denver Hilton Hotel. Dr. Josué de Castro, then Ambassador of Brazil in Geneva, Switzerland, chaired the meeting.

Dr. de Castro set the tone for a successful preparatory Congress in his keynote address. "A total revision of world political relations is now imperative: a revision which will make it possible to abolish definitively all risks of war and to consolidate definitively, through world security, the world peace. The real road to the building of a lasting peace--not a fictitious peace, synonymous today with cold war-- is through the creation of a world federation..... The instrumentality or the authority capable of realising this vital objective in our day will be a world constitution ratified by the World Constitutional Convention. [We] will issue a call to all nations of the world to request them to get ready to send delegates to a world constitutional convention." There were 126 participants from 15 countries. The call which was issued defined the terms forming the basis of the campaign for the ensuing years. It had signatories numbering 1000 from 55 countries. The Preparatory Congress elected Dr. Josue de Castro to be President of the World Committee for a World Constitutional Convention, and elected Philip Isely to be Secretary General.

Philip Isely outlined some of the next steps to be taken at the conclusion of the Congress:

(1) To move rapidly as possible to obtain a quorum of delegates to begin the World Constitutional Convention as specified in the call;
(2) To circulate the call and statements of support to acquire millions of signers in as many countries as possible and to publicize the call throughout the world;
(3) To continue the work of the Preparatory Commissions established at the congress;
(4) To help develop a strong Worldwide movement in which all groups and organisations working for peace, world federation and welfare of man may join to promote the rapid success of the World Constitutional Convention.

The conference ended with a passionate plea: "The High Vision, Faith and Courage together with the dedicated effort and personal sacrifice that have made the first step possible must now be aroused and mobilized on a much larger scale, in order to take the next steps without faltering."

In 1964 a meeting of the World Committee for a World Constitutional Convention was held in San Francisco. It was followed by Philip Isely's visit to Latin America with the aim of increasing support there. On his return, the Second Preparatory Congress was held in Milan, Italy, in 1965, with the co-operation of Dr. Mary Tibaldi Chiesa, a signer of the call and a dedicated worker for world government. Although much progress was not made, a very important move, fundamental to future work, was promoted by Madame Chiesa, Dr. Max Habicht and Philip Isely. This was the compromise reached in the debate which had broken out anew as to which should prevail at a World Constituent Convention or Assembly—delegates from national governments only or delegates of the peoples of the world.

A decision to hold Peoples World Parliaments concurrently with preparatory congresses of delegates from national governments temporarily laid to rest this ghost which had bedevilled work since the initial attempts to hold a world constitutional convention. Dr Max Habicht voted for conformity. Time and again the ghost would resurrect as in the interesting debates --in the eighties between Dr .T. P. Amerasinghe and Dr. Max Habicht printed verbatim in "Across Frontiers". The former opted for people power as against the power of the representatives of national governments, should they refuse to cooperate.

The year 1966 is significant. Since 1958, the WCPA had been called "the World Committee for a World Constitutional Convention. A decision was taken to change the name to World Constitution and Parliament Association. In the meanwhile a Third Preparatory Congress met in Geneva in 1967 at which the name change was reaffirmed. The Geneva Congress took a firm decision to hold the World Constitutional Convention in 1968 even if there was no participation from delegates of national governments. The road before us seemed sure and certain: With or without the participation of national governments, a world government under a *Constitution for the Federation of Earth* was a vital necessity if Planet Earth was to be reclaimed for humanity.

Section 2. First Sessions of World Constituent Assembly at Interlaken, Switzerland and Wolfach, Germany, 1968

What the English Poet Wordsworth called "the glory and the freshness of a dream" was translated into reality. The World Constitution and Parliament Association was in 1966 poised to make the great leap forward. Those who worked for this, all encompassing project were voluntary personnel. Time, money, labour were to them mere bagatelle.

"Friends and loves had we none
Nor wealth nor blessed abode
But the hope of the City of God
At the other end of the road."

"*De Civitatis Dei*" was St. Augustine's great work. To him the City of God was where peace and prosperity was attainable. Philip Isely produced a booklet (1966) several centuries after St. Augustine, more practical and immediate: "Reclaiming Planet Earth for Humanity". It was as immediate as that of St. Augustine in the days when the Roman Empire was falling in universal ruin. Many centuries removed and yet so urgent! Then it was a call for a Kingdom of God on Earth, after the ruin and desolation of Rome. "Reclaiming Planet Earth" was written in 1966 when the Cold War was at its height and nuclear arms stood poised for destruction. Philip Isely's strategy was practical not visionary. The 40 page booklet has had a wide and continuous circulation. The bedrock of an organisation is an efficient staff and a sound treasury. The World Constitution and Parliament Association established its office in Lakewood, Colorado with a staff of five. Determined search for funds began. The group appealed for legacies, bequests, and donations. The team regularized membership fees. Philip and Margaret Isely's flourishing Vitamin Cottage business pledged considerable funds. The important bequest of Mrs. Murial Kruliak (U.S. Dollars 43,400) deserves mention because it came at a time when the situation was perilous in the extreme.

The confrontation between the United States and the Soviet Union in October,1962, brought the world to the brink of disaster. The Secretary of Defence Robert S. McNamara has since written: "The World was faced with what many of us felt then and what since has been generally agreed as the greatest danger of a catastrophic war since the advent of the Nuclear Age."

Though legal wrangling over the Kruliak Legacy made the movement wait for some time the buoyancy that was felt enabled 200 persons from 27 countries from five continents to assemble at World Constitutional Convention and a Peoples World Parliament from 27th August to September 12, 1968 first at Interlaken, Switzerland and later at Wolfach, Germany.

At this point there occurred an important meeting between Philip lsely and Reinhart Ruge of Mexico. Schooled in the same line of thought, working in the same direction for democratic federal world government, they met at Wolfach to begin an association that has lasted to this day. Reinhart Ruge was a good complement to Philip lsely. An extrovert with remarkable capacity to make friends and reconcile people with divergent views, he soon became an asset to the movement and on the retirement of Dr. Josué de Castro, succeeded him as President of the World Constitution and Parliament Association.

Another meeting with another useful personality in the World Constitution and Parliament Association, Dr. T. P. Amerasinghe however proved a non event. Dr. Amerasinghe was kicking his heels in London, U.K. waiting for a Visa to attend the Interlaken and Wolfach World Constitutional Convention and Peoples World Parliament. Dr. Amerasinghe had been working in similar fields in different countries, Ceylon (later re-named *Sri Lanka*), U. K. & U. S. A. His work for World Government was markedly similar to what Philip Isely had developed in U. S. A. A graduate of universities of three countries, Ceylon (Sri Lanka), London and U.S.A., another of Philip's fellow workers at the International Centre, Washington, D. C., U. S. A., had informed Dr. Amerasinghe of Philip Isely's work as far back as 1954. What strange meetings in fortuitous circumstances! Though the physical meeting was to be two years later [in 1970], contact by correspondence had continued since 1954. Dr. Amerasinghe was to join Dr. Reinhart Ruge as Co-President of the World Constitution and Parliament Association.

Interlaken, Switzerland, the beautiful Alpine Town, was the venue of the Main Sessions of the World Constitutional Convention and the Peoples World Parliament. The date was August, 27, 1968. Delegates met in the Theatre Hall of the Kursall. Philip Isely made it clear that this was the first working sessions - "not another preparatory conference, not a model, not a preview, but the real thing." It was the first working session to draft a constitution for a federal world government with the concurrent organisation of a peoples world parliament. This event was, it is important to note preceded by three preparatory Congresses. The first, in 1963, in Denver, Colorado, U.S.A. when a call was issued defining basic terms for the Convention and inviting people and governments of all countries to send delegates. 4 years had passed since its launch in 1958. A second Preparatory Conference at Milan in 1965 and a third in Geneva in 1966 fixed terms for beginning the Convention and Parliament now at Interlaken.

Six days at Interlaken, and then on September 2nd 1968, sessions moved to Wolfach, Germany, a world-minded town in the Black Forest close to the Swiss border. A tremendous welcome was accorded to the delegates. The city decided to co-operate fully in the W.C.C. Programme. Here a decision was taken to establish a commission to draft a democratic federal world constitution, under the chairmanship of Philip Isely. His commission prepared the "Declaration of Wolfach." This document deserves a page or two in our history. It states:

> "Twenty three years have passed since the most destructive war in history, but the arms race is continuing with mounting burdens on the people and more nations have got equipped with nuclear and chemical - biochemical weapons. There is an increasing disparity between rich and poor people within these nations. There is a revolution of rising expectations as a result of the failure to make available to the great masses of people the economic and scientific developments of the modern world....

> ”We instruct the World Constitution and Parliament Association to ensure the completion of a draft or drafts of a World Constitution for preliminary debate during 1970 and for submission to the World Constitutional Convention in 1971. We also charge the WCPA with the task of arousing popular forces around the world as well as national governments and national legislatures, for participation in 1971 and working out details”.

At Interlaken, WCPA had speakers on subjects of importance relating to World Government. Some of them were the following: Abbe Piere, Dr. Martin Niemoller. Elizabeth Mann Borgese and Dr. Max Habicht. Help came from different directions. For example translation facilities were personally provided by Prof. Theo Pontzen and Ms. Althya Youngman. They deserve not merely a passing mention but homage for their selfless endeavours. Althya Youngman was later prominent in movements like “Artists Embassy” and “One World in Art” and in cooperation with Dr. T. P. Amerasinghe helped complement the work of the WCPA.

At Interlaken and Wolfach the largest delegations to the Convention and Peoples Parliament were from U.S.A., France, India, United Kingdom, Switzerland and West Germany. There were participants from Argentina, Belgium, Brazil, Denmark, Canada, Ceylon (Sri Lanka), Colombia, Finland, Ghana, Israel, Italy, Japan, Kenya, Mexico, Netherlands, Nigeria, Norway, Pakistan, Peru, Senegal and Thailand. Delegates from Czechoslovokia and East Europe could not participate due to the sudden political turmoil that occurred there. On August 20th 1968, Soviet Troops suddenly invaded Czechoslovokia. The U.N. Security Council to which the Czech delegation at the U. N. appealed failed to take action.

Many worthwhile contributions were made by delegates. Chief W. J. Falaiye, Former Member of Parliament of Nigeria concerned himself with the creation of revenue earning projects for WCPA. Dr. Max Habicht, leading International Lawyer and a legal adviser to the league of Nations, suggested and launched “The Institution for Documentation and Research for the creation of a World Federal Authority” with the double aim convincing governments to spend money for such a purpose and to appoint an official to sit on the board. He thought this would open a direct channel to governments for future World Constitutional Convention, He continued to work on this project with Aake Anker Ording of Norway, one of the originators of U.N.I.C.E.F. Their efforts strengthened the work of WCPA. Dr. Max Habicht gave yeoman service to our movement as Legal Adviser until the time of his death.

Onkar Nath, former Member of Parliament and Organiser of the delegation from India contributed in no small measure to the success of the Convention at Interlaken and Wolfach. He later helped the strong WCPA Indian Branch and became its Secretary with R. K. Nehru as President.

Others made contributions of no less importance. Omissions are not intended in any way to downgrade their importance. To sum it all, the 1968 Convention marks a great divide. It was in a sense a beacon because it led in the intervening years to WCPA’s crucial work for the *Constitution for the Federation of Earth*.

Section 3. Santa Barbara, 1972, to 2nd World Constituent Assembly, Innsbruck, 1977

The deepening world crises (political, economic and social) of the 1970's called for urgent action. The World Constitution and Parliament Association worked in organising an Emergency Council of World Trustees during 1969 and 1971. A 10-page "Proposal for Immediate Action by an Emergency Council of World Trustees" was drawn up by Philip Isely as secretary of E.C.W.T. in consultation with Thane Read and Lloyd Oxley. The plan was adopted in 1971. The Emergency Council met at Santa Barbara, California, U.S.A. from December 28th, 1971 to January 2nd, 1972. The 1967 Egypt – Israel Conflict, so disastrous to Egypt, was yet another proof of the U.N's impotency in the face of World Crisis. Secretary General, U Thant agreed to Nasser's demand to "withdraw U. N. Forces." Israel's stunning victory in 1967 made the Fourth Arab Israel war in 1973 virtually inevitable. The Emergency Council issued the First Decree for the Protection of Life: "When life is seriously threatened and existing governments are either unable or unwilling to take the action if needed to protect life and improve the world situation, then it becomes necessary for responsible citizens to proceed with remedies which seem appropriate. Citizens acting under such circumstances may be described as Trustees acting for the common good..."

Hence the Decree for the Protection of Life. The first includes the outlawing of nuclear and biochemical weapons and other weapons of mass destruction. The second decree was to assist in convening a peoples world parliament and a call was issued to this effect. The third was to prepare a draft of a *Constitution for the Federation of Earth*, which could be implemented in stages and then submitted to the Peoples World Parliament as soon as it convenes. The Emergency Council also requested national governments to send delegates to meet concurrently when the Peoples World Parliament convenes for the purpose of reaching agreement on a world constitution.

The Council of Santa Barbara adopted a fourth task to appoint and activate planetary legislative commissions on several major problems for the purpose of preparing global legislative measures to have ready for submission to the parliament when it convenes. Other possible actions covering environmental problems, pressing social and economical issues were also adopted. The Council terminated deliberations on January 2nd 1972 with a call to immediate action: "The time is at hand for action by those who are ready and capable opening the way for support and participation by the millions who will quickly see the potentiality of the action once it is under way."

At Santa Barbara there were many dedicated delegates from over 25 countries. The delegates from India included such distinguished figures like R. K. Nehr, who had served in the Foreign Office of the Government of India, Goday Murahari, later Speaker of the Raja Sabha, D. H. Spencer, a leading constitutional Lawyer, Dr. T. P. Amerasinghe, Barrister-at-law from Sri Lanka, Reinhart Ruge, Mexico, Dr. Lucile Green, Calif., U.S.A. Mrs. Helen Tucker, Canada, Thane Read, Arizona, U.S.A., Archie Casely-Hayford, Ghana, Hon. Syed Mohamed Husain, Bangladesh, Dr. Charles Mercieca, Malta and U.S.A. , Jorgen Laursen Vig, Denmark. 225 Representatives from 53 countries signed "The First Decree for the Protection of Life".

In January and February, 1972, D. M. Spencer, Constitutional Lawyer and Professor from Sydenham College, Bombay, Hon. Syed Mohammed Husain, Advocate, later Judge of the Supreme Court of Bangladesh, Dr. T. P. Amerasinghe, Barrister-at-law and Advocate, Supreme Court of Sri Lanka with Philip Isely, Secretary General, WCPA all from the Drafting Commission, met in Lakewood, Colorado. U.S.A. for intensive work. The World Constitutional Convention and Peoples World Parliament in Interlaken and Wolfach in 1968 had commenced this work. Philip Isely had then drawn up a 19 page "Outline for the Debate and Drafting of a World Constitution" which the World Constitutional Convention had endorsed unanimously. He had also already prepared the first Chapter. The Commission of Lawyers aforementioned reviewed this and continued with the rest of the work.

The first draft was finally completed and printed in November 1974, titled "*A Constitution for the Federation of Earth.*"

A number of draft constitutions for world government or World Authority have been written. As Philip Isely has pointed out in his article in Humanist July/August, 1975, the features which distinguish this draft were the following:

1. Provision is made for adequate powers and means to cope with the multitude of interrelated world problems that must be solved to serve the needs of humanity today and in years to come, not merely "to keep the peace" of a status quo.

2. The World Government is specifically empowered and equipped to deal with all of the most urgent supranational problems that have come to the forefront in recent years.

3. Both world elections and world administration are based upon "World Electoral and Administrative Districts" which emphasize world citizenship and equal rights for everybody, but do not interfere with the concurrent jurisdiction over the internal affairs of nations reserved to national Governments.

4. The World Parliament consists of House of Peoples, A House of Nations, and a House of Councilors for particular purposes.

5. The World Executive, with five Member rotating Presidium is at all times responsible to the World Parliament.

6. The Federation of Earth is non military.

7. The concept and procedures for distributive justice are given emphasis.

8. The specific provisions are made for Research and Planning, an Institute for Governmental Procedures and World Problems; an Agency for Technological and Environmental Assessment and a World Ombudsmus.

9. Other unique features are incorporated in the several organs of the world government not as a replica of national governments but for the particular purposes of a universal democratic government for Earth.

10. The World Constitution is designed so that it can be implemented in stages -- beginning with a provisional World Government and proceeding with a built-in constitutional provision from stage to stage to full World Government.

The WCPA circulated worldwide this first draft finished in 1974 for assessment together with the Call to the second session, in 1977, now defined as World Constituent Assembly. Throughout 1974 and 1975, the WCPA received comments. The drafting commission met again in 1976 and completed a second draft, which the WCPA circulated.

Innsbruck, Austria was the venue of the second session of the World Constituent Assembly, held at Kongresshaus from the 16th - 29th June, 1977. The drafting commission presented the *Constitution for the Federation of Earth*, sometimes referred to as the *Earth Constitution*, for debate and adoption. 138 delegates from 25 countries in six continents participated. The constitution was examined clause by clause and amendments were made. Foremost in the debate was the leader of the Indian Delegation, A. B. Patel, Former Member of the Kenya Legislature, Dr. S. Kaiser from the Netherlands, Dr. Carmel Kussman, New York, Mrs. Mia Lord, London, U.K., Dr. Helen Tucker, Canada, Dr. Hanna Newcombe, Canada, Kenneth Komo, Botswana, Foster Parmalee, U.S.A., Margaret Isely, U.S.A. Dr. Ahmed Subandjo, Indonesia. After sometimes acrimonius, sometimes prolonged debate, the Assembly adopted the draft constitution unanimously. A. B. Patel from the rostrum described the occasion "as the day of a new age". Dr. T. P. Amerasinghe who acted as facilitator quoted the poet Milton's famous lines:

"Well have ye judged, well-ended long debate synod of Gods." Rapturous applause greeted Dr. Patel as he rose to call for all those present to come up to the stage and affix their signatures to the Constitution. Emotion was so high that tears were in the eyes of many; some openly wept for joy. It was an unprecedented event in human history and a triumph for 20 years of unremitting toil by the World Constitution and Parliament Association.

The Assembly issued a call for Ratification, by the nations and peoples of Earth. The WCPA sent the Constitution to the United Nations, to the Members of the General Assembly, requesting them to have the Constitution transmitted to their national Governments. Later, the WCPA sent a copy to all national Governments. The call requested (a) people of Earth to ratify the Constitution by direct referendum and by an initiative petition followed by election of delegates to the House of Peoples; (b) the national governments and legislatures of the world to ratify the Constitution and elect delegates to the House of Nations; and (c) the universities, Colleges, Churches, Scientific Academies and Institutes to ratify the Constitution and nominate delegates with a world view as candidates for election to the House of Councillors. The call ended: "So let us build on this solid base which has been prepared over the last 25 years and unite our energies in achieving ratification and implementation."

Section 4. The Ratification Campaign – Third Constituent Assembly, Colombo, Sri Lanka, 1979 ; Preparatory Conference, New Delhi, India, 1981, and First Provisional World Parliament. Brighton, U.K., 1982

The World Constitution and Parliament Association, in view of the seemingly intransigent insistence upon National Sovereignty by Governments, altered its strategy and moved towards mobilising the people to pressurise their Governments to ratify the constitution. As the horrible memories of World War II began to fade, Governments took a more lackadaisical view of the threat of the nuclear menace and the equally looming threat of Hunger, Pollution, Mounting National Debts, more especially in the third world. All major high level conferences among national Governments on the solution of world problems floundered on the principle that each nation has the sovereign and exclusive right to determine the development and exploitation of natural resources within its borders, with no interference. This was evident at the Natural Resources Conference in Dakar. The Caracas Conference on the Law of the Sea only opened the door for all nations with the sea coasts to grab the adjoining two hundred miles offshore for exclusive economic development, rather than the three miles that was the previously recognised territorial limit. The Population Conference in Bucharest, ended with the insistence that population control was the exclusive province of each individual nation. The concept of a global granary never got to first base at the Food Conference in Rome. The Stockholm World Congress on the Environment ended only by agreeing to set up a monitoring system to detect early warnings of danger to the environment. The message is clear that so called functional approach does not provide stepping stones to World Federation.

The Third Session of the World Constituent Assembly was held at Ranmuthu Hotel, Colombo, Sri Lanka in January 1979. Delegates from many countries in Asia, Africa, Europe and Latin America participated. The Speaker of the Sri Lanka Parliament, the Hon. Mohammed Bakeer Markar, presided. The local and foreign press reported the deliberations. The then President J. R. Jayawardene sent his representative, the Hon. Gamini Dissanayake, a Cabinet Minister. Philip Isely presented "the Rationale for a World Constitutent Assembly," defining the right of the people to convene the Assembly, present the draft constitution and obtain ratification. There was an animated debate. The opposition was led by the distinguished Indian M. P. Hari Vishnu Kamath, former secretary of the Forward Bloc of Subhas Chandra Bose, the venerated Socialist from Bengal and one time Indian Congress President. Speakers in support of Philip Isely were, among others, Shri A. B. Patel, the Hon. Goday Murahari, Puran Singh Azad, Mrs. Helen Tucker. Dr. T. P. Amerasinghe, President of W. P. C. A. Sri Lanka, Organiser of the Third Constitutent Assembly, reminded the Assembly that it was the gathering of the people in the Tennis Court outside the National Assembly in Paris, France in 1789 that sparked the French Revolution. He cited many other examples from history. The assembly understood Philip Isely's Rationale. Since it is valid today, as in 1979, a few extracts are printed below:

> "In the course of history, particularly during the past several hundred years, the Technique of a Constitutional Assembly has been developed and used under

various circumstances as a means to devise the constitution for democratic Governments, either to create new Governments where none existed before or to replace old or crumbling Governments under both peaceful and revolutionary situations... Sometimes only a small minority might actually participate during the time when a new democratic Government is emerging under conditions of revolution from tyranny or peaceful political turmoil or urgent crisis, or in the absence of any organised political system which was willing or able to supervise a vote of the total potential electorate for such an assembly or newly emerging democratic Government.

"It is under the latter kind of circumstances that the move has gone forward during the years since World War II for the organization of a World Constitutent Assembly to devise the Constitution for a democratic form of Federal Government.

"Under the existing circumstances of global Anarchy, of political turmoil in many parts of the world as well as of the unprecedented urgencies of many growing world wide crises requiring extra ordinary measures if humanity is to survive, action has been organised by the World Constitution and Parliament Association... as well as by other organisations and groups since 1945... to attempt to convene World Constitutent Assemblies for the purpose of a constitution for democratic federal world government and of securing the acceptance and ratification of such a world constitution.

"Those sessions of a World Constituent Assembly are fully conversant with the respected theory that democratic government, arises from the initiative and consent of the people who will be citizens under that Government, that people at all times have the democratic right and prerogative to discharge or change Governments which do not adequately serve their welfare and to initiate new Government when urgently required for their safety and welfare. No superior authority exists any time to this basic right of people to initiate such actions; and in particular, no authority superior to the action by people exists for the organisation and functioning of a World Constituent Assembly or a democratic World Parliament."

The Rationale was in direct confrontation with the approach in most current proposals for dealing with World problems: Create special international agencies to deal with each particular problem.

Usually the method is through negotiation among sovereign nations or through the United Nations–which is equal to the same thing. The Rationale called for global action leading to global solutions. Sovereign nations will not discuss because they refuse to submit their sovereignty to world authority. A similar situation confronts the problem of the death of oceans by oil, and also a list of other problems. So the people of Earth cannot expect national governments to initiate any move for a democratic world government, although some members of national governments are willing to assist. They cannot expect to achieve world government devoted to the cause of human welfare and social justice by amendment of the U .N. Charter for the U. N. is only the voice of the foreign policies of sovereign national governments. Each permanent member of the Security Council holds veto power over any proposed amendment.

The session of the Third Constituent Assembly ended with a call to national parliaments to ratify the *Earth Constitution*. To intensify this work, the World Constitution and Parliament Association met in New Delhi, India, in 1981. The organising work was done by Shri Puran Singh Azad, then Editor "National Solidarity" and one time leader of the Congress Student movement. He was also the General Secretary of the WCPA in India and prominent in Indian National Congress circles. Several Members of the parliament of India attended the meeting, including Smt. Savitri Nigam, former M. P. and then President of the All India House Wives Association. The wife of Shri B. P. Nigam, she was foremost in winning support for the ratification campaign. The role of women was emphasized at the meeting. Hon. Smt. Margaret Alva who was a Minister of the Cabinet and Smt. Heptullah, later a deputy Speaker of the Raj Sabha presided at some of the sessions. At the New Delhi Meeting many new Branches of WCPA in Asia and Africa were recognised. Chief among these was the branch in Bangkok, Thailand. Its leader Dr. Suchart Kosokitiworg was elected as World Peace Envoy of WCPA in recognition of his work for Human Rights and World Federation of Religions.

Dr. Suchart was revered in Thailand for establishing the Hoopha Sawan Religious Land. He was also instrumental in translating the *Constitution for the Federation of Earth* into Thai and actively campaigning for its ratification. For this he earned the displeasure of the Thai Government. He had to face many civil and criminal charges and his Religious Land, Hoopha Sawan in Ratcburi province was seized by the Government under Court Order. The WCPA set up a committee for the defence of its activists under the Joint Chairmanship of Rev. Dr. Toshio Miyake of Japan, a Vice President of WCPA World Body, and Reinhart Ruge, President of WCPA. Rev. Dr. Toshio Miyake, was head of the Konko Kyo Church of Isuo, Osaka, Japan until his death at the ripe age of ninety. For the promotion of World Government, Dr. Miyake set up the Asian Youth Federation, now administrated by his grandson Rev. Mitsuo Miyake.

Dr. T. P. Amerasinghe, Commonwealth Barrister-at-law from Sri Lanka and then Executive Vice President of WCPA, accepted to be Secretary General of the defence committee. Dr. Amerasinghe took a leading part in Dr. Kosolkitwong's defence, and with the aid of Thai Lawyers obtained acquittal in nine of the ten cases. Dr. Suchart however was found guilty for setting up on archaeological reserve the Religious Land of Hoopha Sawan. He was forced to seek religious exile by getting ordained as Bhikku Ariyawanso. Today he has built a new Religious Land –a focal point for thousands who love peace and tranquility - and the work for World Government continues in his well ordered office of World Peace Envoy. [Ed. note: Dr. Suchart Kosolkitiwong, the Bhikku Ariyawanso, passed away in 2003, but his World Peace Envoy office continues under the leadership of Dr. Phichai Tovivich.]

During the New Delhi Meeting interviews with Shrimati Indira Gandhi, India Prime Minister, and Shri Venkata Raman, Vice President of India took place. Margaret and Philip Isely, Reinhart Ruge and Dr. T. P. Amerasinghe participated. They had favourable response and every encouragement to carry forward the work. Members of the Parliament of India both in the Lokh Sabha and Raja Sabha agreed to introduce resolutions to a directive principle under Article 51 of the Constitution of India that would enable the government and people of India to work for a world federation.

The resolution of Hari Vishnu Kamath, M.P., was debated at length and achieved near unanimity. It would have been passed but for the prorogation of Parliament.

The New Delhi Meeting terminated with a call for a Provisional World Parliament to convene in 1982, under terms of Article 19 of the *Earth Constitution*:

> "At this moment, all people on Earth are confronted with imminent growing threats of universal catastrophe in nuclear war. At the same time, many other problems also urgently require solutions on a planetary scale if the people in any locality are to survive and prosper... Action is needed immediately to establish a Provisional World Parliament which can take steps to halt the arms race and go to work constructively on other urgent problems. In this way, a Provisional World Parliament can gain strength as an effective rallying ground for humanity, which demonstrates in practice constructive approach towards solving world problems."

On the initiative of Philip Isely, Secretary General, WCPA, an honorary sponsor list of 150 prominent persons were enrolled. The list included Nobel Laureates, men and women well-known in the fields of Science, Philosphy and Arts, renowned statesman and politicians. To name a few: Tony Benn, then Cabinet Minister of the Government of the United Kingdom; Hon. Ramsey Clark, J. D., U. S. A. Attorney General 1967-69; Dr. Alexander Dubček, Czechoslovakia, President Federal Assembly 1969 and again 1999; Dr. Taslim Elias, Nigeria, President World Court 1981-85; Hon. Balram Jakhar, India, Speaker of Lok Sabha 1980-89; Hon. Justice Michael Kirby CMG, Australia, President Court of Appeal; Kapasa Makasa, Zambia, M.P. and Cabinet Minister; Hon. Kéba M'Baye, Senegal Judge at the World Court, 1987; Lord Philip Noel Baker, U.K. Nobel Laureate; Dr. Linus Pauling, U.S.A., Nobel Laureate; Dr. Alex Quainson-Sackey, Ghana, President, U. N. General Assembly 1964-65; Hon. Jose Sette-Camara, Brazil Judge, World Court 1979-88; and the Most Rev. Desmond M. B. Tutu, South Africa, Nobel Laureate 1984.

The first ever Provisional World Parliament met in Brighton, U.K. at the Royal Pavilion in 1982. Delegates from over 25 countries representing all 6 continents attended. The colourful inauguration was presided over by Sir Chaudhry Mohammad Zafrullah Khan, Pakistan. His doughty deeds as former President of the General Assembly at the U.N. and as Foreign Minister of his country were recalled. Though feeble in body, his voice was still resonant, "The only solution to solve world' s ills is a democratic federal world government". He recalled the poet Tennyson lines: - "And then the kindly Earth shall slumber wrapped in universal law."

On this high note, Parliament proceeded to elect the Speaker. Dr. Max Habicht as Legal Advisor to the World Constitution and Parliament Association presided. Interest among the delegates was so high that a contest ensued. Shri Puran Singh Azad of India proposed the name of Shri A. B. Patel, then Secretary General of the Sri Aurobindo Ashram and World Union and veteran legislator. Dr. Karmel Kussman proposed Dr. Lucile Green, Professor and Educator, later President of the World Citizens Assembly, California, U. S. A. After a ballot Dr. Max Habicht declared Shri Patel the elected Speaker. The Parliament elected Reinhart Ruge, Mexico, and Dr. T. P. Amerasinghe, Sri Lanka, as Deputy Speakers. Much work was done both in Parliament and in the Parliamentary Commissions and several World Legislative enactments were adopted.

These enactments are of such wide import that the author is compelled to deal with them in detail. World Legislative Bill No.1 to outlaw nuclear weapons and weapons of mass destruction and to create a World Disarmament Agency was enacted as World Law on 11th September, 1982 by unanimous vote. The preamble reads:

> "Recognising that the abolition of war requires complete nuclear disarmament and the elimination of all weapons of mass death and destruction as the first priority for survival of humanity on Earth;
>
> "Recognising that any arms limitation or disarmament schemes or proposals which do not immediately provide for complete and universal disarmamant are inadequate, and that life on Earth is not safe so long as any nuclear weapons or facilities for producing nuclear weapons remain; Recognising that disarmament negotiations among nations, together with protests against armaments by people, have continued for decades, while wars have followed one after another and armaments have greatly increased and continue to increase;
>
> "Recognising further the immediate and extreme dangers of nuclear war, and that as a consequence immediate action by an agency representing the welfare of humanity as a whole is required to take actions to secure complete and universal nuclear disarmament and elimination of all weapons of mass death and destruction."

World Legislative Bill No. 2 was to inaugurate a World Economic Development Organisation. Its preamble was:

> "Adequate and equitable and sustainable world economic development is the other half of the disarmament equation, since adequate economic development can provide the conditions required to apply resources for evelopment. The World is on the verge of extreme financial crisis, which greatly affects the lives and livelihood of everybody, requiring new approaches to financing procedures which are designed to serve maximum human welfare. The conditions of economic development are also related to protection of the environment, renewable energy supplies, human equity and democracy. The World Parliament and the Provisional World Parliament are specifically authorized to proceed with a World Economic Development Organisation and related financial institutions under the *Constitution for the Federation of Earth*, specifically pursuant to Article XIX Sec B5 and Sec. E5 and to Article XVI Sec C 9 and Sec C 10 E."

Enacted on 12th September 1982, the bill was unanimously adopted as World Law.

The Third World Legislative Bill was on the Ownership, Administration and Development of the Oceans and Seabeds of Earth as the common heritage of the peoples of Earth. Unanimously adopted as world Law at the afternoon session of September 12, 1982, Article 16, section 1.2. of the *Constitution for the Federation of Earth* makes all oceans and seabeds from 20 kilometers offshore World Territory. The

Act declares,"The recently drafted *Law of the Sea* treaty among nations is contrary to and in violation of important provisions of Article XVI of the *Constitution for the Federation of Earth,"* as well as "The environmental health and equitable economic development of Earth depend in large measure upon the conditions of ownership, administration and development of oceans and seabeds." The Act requested the nations of the world not to ratify the so-called "Law of the Seas" and to accept instead the jurisdiction of the World Oceans and Seabeds Authority which is to be established by the World Parliament or by the Provisional World Parliament under the terms of the *Constitution for the Federation of Earth.* [Editors' note: Subsequent amendment and other legislation of the Provisional World Parliament prohibits the military activities that were allowed under the nations' ratified version of the Law of the Sea. The world legislation declares the military provisions of the "Law of the Sea" unlawful and therefore null.]

World Legislative Bill No. Four for inaugurating a World University System with a Graduate School of World Problems was also adopted at the Brighten sessions of the Provisional World Parliament, September 12, 1982. Since there is a great, and immediate need for persons who are trained and competent to work on world problems from a global and human point of view and since it is feasible for the Provisional World Parliament to inaugurate a Graduate School of World Problems as a first part of a World University System, the Act directs the first session of the Provisional World Parliament to grant the charter to the Graduate School of World Problems.

The Fifth World Legislative Bill was for the Establishment of Provisional District World Courts and Provisional Regional World Courts of the World. World Supreme Court System in accordance with Article XIX, Section E. 2. and with Article IX of the *Constitution for the Federation of Earth* was adopted on 16th September 1982. An extract from the preamble to the act reads:

> "Whereas international law and world law and article 1, 2, 34, 39 and 40 of the *Earth Constitution* together with Legislative Bill Number One outlawing nuclear weapons and other weapons of mass destruction which has been adopted by the Provisional World Parliament in its first session now comprises a body of world law appropriate for adjudication and enforcement under a world court system", a Provisional District World Court (hereinafter called P. D.W.C.) shall be established in Los Angeles, California U.S.A., and a P. D.W.C. shall also be established in New York City, New York, U.S.A. As needed and as possible, additional Provisional District World Courts may be established in London, England, Paris, France, Tokyo, Japan, New Delhi, India, and in other appropriate locations in any part of the world. We deem the Brighton session to be epoch making. We now see an emerging World Law as opposed to International Law which depends on treaties between nations and therefore ineffective and at most times unenforceable due to the sovereignty of individual nations."

In 1983 the First Provisional District World Court organized in Los Angeles under the direction of Leon Vickman. Three eminent legal personalities sat this court: California Supreme Court Judge Hon. Justice Professor Frank Newman, Justice

Professor Covey Oliver and Justice Professor Richard B. Lillich. Alternate Justices were Professor Burns H. Weston and Professor Francis A. Boyle. The Court arraigned nuclear powers and national governments engaged in research, testing, designing, production, transportation, deployment, purchase, sale, storage, threatened use or actual use of any nuclear weapons of any size in any delivery system below or above the surface of the Earth, oceans or anywhere in the atmosphere or outer space. For further detail of the World Court System development, we direct readers to World Legislative Acts Numbers 5, 15, 20, 24, 28 and 37. World legislative summaries of these statutes are in Chapter 9 of this volume.

Section 5. The New Common Enemy–Accelerating Increase of Carbon Dioxide (CO_2). 2nd and 3rd Sessions of the Provisional World Parliament, New Delhi, India, 1985 and Miami Beach, Florida, U.S.A., 1987

In 1984, the World Constitution and Parliament Association planned to hold a second session of the Provisional World Parliament in the Sudan. With the outbreak of Civil War in that country, the WCPA chose Nigeria as the venue. This too was thwartered by a sudden coup. The then Chairman of the Foreign Relations Committee who was fully committed to help work to hold the second sessions in Lagos was a victim of the Military and subsequently jailed. In this prevailing uncertainty, the WCPA, which had always held the view that its work should extend to Africa, decided on India.

In 1985, the Second Session of the Provisional World Parliament was held in New Delhi at the prestigious Vigyan Bhawan. The All India WCPA, led by Shri Puran Singh Azad, Savitri and Brij Nigam, Goday Murahari, Ratna Singh Rajda amongst other devoted workers helped in its organisation. Delegates from all parts of the world with a number of Parliamentarians assembled. His Excellency Zail Singh, then President of India, inaugurated the sessions. The Parliament elected Hon. Balram Jakhar, then Speaker of the Lok Sabha, to be Speaker for the second session of the Provisional World Parliament. He said this was one of his proudest moments. From being Speaker of perhaps the largest Parliament in any country, he was now the Speaker of the Provisional World Parliament, representing the peoples of the World.

The New Delhi Sessions 15th to 25th March 1985 adopted three more world legislative acts. World Legislative Bill No. 6 for the Emergency Earth Rescue Administration was the first bill in the agenda. The preamble points out that "the people of the Earth have a new common enemy, which requires an Emergency World Wide campaign in which both East and West, North and South, must abandon armaments and join in a common cause for survival. The New Common Enemy is the rapidly accelerating increase of carbon dioxide (CO_2) in the atmosphere which will result in cataclysmic climate changes unless overcome soon". The preamble listed these changes: widespread drought, rapidly spreading desert and forest dieouts; erratic weather extremes; crop failures in the temperate zone "bread baskets" of the world; massive starvation for hundreds of millions of people; excessive evaporation from oceans in lower latitudes; the rapid on-set of an ice age; attempted mass migration of people from vast areas increasingly becoming uninhabitable, increasing volcanic eruptions due to pressure of growing ice-fields on Earth.

The Act legislates for an Emergency Earth Rescue Administration to be established (E.E.R.A). Its task is to carry out a coordinated worldwide emergency campaign on several major fronts concurrently to overcome the increase of CO_2 before climatic and geological changes become irreversible. The Act outlines the ways and means; 1. massive re-forestation; 2. massive remineralisation of forest lands and crop lands; 3. massive mineralisation and remineralisation in selected areas of the oceans of Earth and in man-made lakes (This third means was adopted as an amendment at the 4th Sessions of the Provisional World Parliament on 17th September 1996); and 4. expedited transition from fossil fuels to safe and sustainable energy supplies and technology.

In moving this landmark bill, Philip Isely outlined the benefits of the Emergency Earth Rescue Administration Plan. Among the 35 benefits he pointed out which would accrue to humanity were the following: agricultural stability; prevention of impending starvation of several billion inhabitants; conservation of the soil; increase of the Earth's oxygen supply; and salvation and revival of the rain forests. He ended on the forceful note that disarmament will no longer be a problem when all expenditures, resources, manpower and scientific talent now squandered in military programs can be immediately used to fighting the new common enemy of mankind, which is the rapid increase of CO_2 in the atmosphere.

The session then took up for consideration World Legislative Bill Number 7 for a World Government Funding Corporation [Ed. note: now Earth Federation Funding Corporation]. The then Speaker of Parliament, Balram Jakhar remarked that in a sense it was the mother of the preceding bills enacted as World Law both at Brighton and now in New Delhi. The preamble to the bill makes this clear." To obtain acceptance and implementation of all parts of the comprehensive plan of action outlined above, requires a very massive global campaign. To carry out such a campaign requires adequate funding in terms of hundreds of million dollars, far beyond the financial capacity o£ those persons who have envisioned and initiated this course of action". The bill proposed creation of a World Government Funding corporation. The bill provided for loans to the corporation, to be called Earth Rescue Loans to be sought from national governments, cities, private corporations, non-governmental organisations, and individuals, to be sought as lump sums or as annual subscriptions over a period of years. The Funding Corporation (WGFC) would be empowered to make grants and disbursements in such manner and in the judgment of the Directors and Officers of the (WGFC) as to best serve and help to achieve the purposes of the WGFC. The bill provided for the repayment o£ the loans made to the WGFC. It also provided for the establishment of a Central Bank for the WGFC in a country most suitable for the receipts of loans and funds world-wide and the disbursement of grants and payments under conditions of minimum difficulties in respect to regulations, taxes, currency conversions and political freedom.

After much discussion the Bill Number 7 was unanimously adopted as an act on 17th March 1985.

Terrorism which was a growing feature in the years preceding the second session of the Provisional World Parliament flared up in new and dangerous proportions in 1985. In a world already plagued by many global crises and difficult problems the situation was made more complicated by the remarkable rise in terrorist activities. National governments were seeking remedies within their own borders and by treaties with neighbouring countries. Attempts to stamp out terrorism made situations worse. State terrorism compounded the problem. The World Constitution and Parliament Association had long since been of the view that the terrorist menace had to be resolved globally.

World Legislative Bill Number 8 –World Commission on Terrorism was moved by Dr. T. P. Amerasinghe, Sri Lanka, Co-President, WCPA. The Bill defined terrorism "as the use of violence against lives or property or threat to use such violence without a formal declaration of war for the purpose of trying to achieve objectives which may appear difficult to achieve by peaceful means". The preamble makes it clear: "Both organised terrorism and random terrorist acts serve to confuse issues, inflame passions, exaggerate problems and make peaceful and reasonable solutions more difficult... Sometimes terrorism is organised by states against citizens, sometimes terrorism is organised by people against states or against other people".

The bill laid down the objectives and functions of the World Commission on Terrorism (W.C.T.):

1. To investigate and clarify the views and circumstances of any particular situation in which terrorism is involved and in particular any situation in which terrorism appears to be organised on a transnational or world-wide level;
2. To discover, uncover, clarify and define any just grievances or partly just grievances which may be involved;
3. To discover, uncover, clarify and define any extraneous, hidden, manipulative, devious or false issues or reasons for terrorist activities; and
4. To uncover and clarify the true facts and nature of situations where terrorist activities may be used to inflame or confuse and utilize local or transnational situations e.g., ethnic conflicts, for the achievement of objectives pursued by third parties.

The Bill would empower the Commission: (a) To expose and seek an end to all transnational shipment or trade in arms and terrorist supplies of all kinds; (b) To expose and seek an end to all training for purposes to engage in terrorist activities, particularly where terrorist are trained in one country for terrorist activities in another country; (c) To publicise the true nature of situations where violations of human rights may be involved, and to have such problems taken up for a peaceful solutions by the World Economic Development Organisation with adequate resources applied to implement peaceful solutions; and (d) To expose and seek the apprehension of any terrorist agents or individuals engaged in transnational terrorist activities without just cause, and to seek to bring such agents or individuals before World Courts of Justice.

The New Delhi session unanimously adopted the bill as an act without prolonged debate, sensing the urgency of the prevailing dangerous terrorist situation. The subsequent history of terrorism in the world and the sad and fruitless attempts of nations to solve the problem within the context of national sovereignty only emphasised the contribution of the Provincial World Parliament not only on this particular question but in all problems confronting humankind. Global problems must be solved globally not within the context of national sovereignty but with a democratic federal government. In 1981, Prime Minister Smt. Indira Gandhi, before her sad and tragic demise, had said to the WCPA Convention in New Delhi , "It is time nations learnt to cede a part of their sovereignty to a world organisation to build a safer world".

The Second Session of the Provisional World Parliament ended with a grand reception at Lodhi Gardens, New Delhi; the Chief Guest was the Prime Minister of India, the Honourable Rajiv Gandhi. Dr. Reinhart Ruge, WCPA Co-President presented the Hon. Rajiv Gandhi with the *Constitution for the Federation of Earth*. Hon. Rajiv Gandhi asked many constructive questions. His untimely death by a female terrorist suicide bomber proved an obstacle for India' s ratification of the *Constitution* which then seemed imminent.

In 1987, the Campaign for Ratification of the *Constitution for the Federation of Earth* was intensified. Voluntary effort with help of leaders of WCPA from India, Italy, France and Germany translated the *Earth Constitution* into Hindi, Italian, French and German. Dr. Edvige Bestazzi, Professor of Humanities brought out an Italian translation. Shri Puran Singh Azad secured the services of English/Hindi translation to bring out a Hindi version. An abridged Sinhalese version circulated in Sri Lanka. Today the WCPA is using machine translation software for perfecting the translations and printing German, Italian, Portugese, Korean and Japanese translations of the *Constitution*. An Arabic translation is due to be released shortly [Ed. note: available now in .pdf].

The third session of the Provisional World Parliament met from 18 to 28 June 1987, Miami Beach Florida, U.S.A. at Fontainbleau Hilton Hotel, then reputed to be the largest in the Hilton Group. It worked on the implementation of World Legislation previously adopted by the Parliament as well as the ratification campaign. In addition, a limited number of new world legislative bills were presented and a Provisional World Cabinet established. The elected Speakers were Reinhart Ruge and Dr. T. P. Amerasinghe, Co-presidents of WCPA. The Parliament accommodated others on the dais: Philip Isely, WCPA Secretary-General, Mrs. Margaret Isely, WCPA Treasurer, Mrs. Helen Tucker, WCPA Vice President, and Ratansingh Rajda, former M.P., Bombay, India.

A feature of this Provisional World Parliament session was an exhibition and sale of locally produced articles from different countries in the world. It was not merely an attempt to hold a World's Fair for profit but to uplift the economic and social condition of the developing countries by displaying the economic potential these countries.

The third session at Miami Beach discussed and enacted World Law Bill Number Nine to Protect Life and Nature on Planet Earth and to create a Global Ministry of Environment, on 25th June 1987. Emil E. O. Peter, Wolfach, Germany, later elected Assistant Chairman of the Commission on Environment, Provisional World Parliament, presented the preamble to the bill which stated:

> "Seventeen years after the first United Nations Conference on the environment held at Stockholm, Sweden, many global environmental problems are evident and some of them are worsening There are many problems in our World in terms of:
>
> a) lack of industrial safety;
> b) pollution;
> c) improper use of technology; and
> d) unequal distribution of the benefits of technological development.

> "Many problems of the environment affect humanity as a whole. The Earth is the only world we have and environmental problems disregard boundaries...Most problems are supra-national, and therefore require a global or transnational approach. To identify and find solutions to those problems of the environment, a Global Ministry of Environment is needed for which there may be no substitutes."
>
> "The combustion products of fossil fuels are causing growing damage to our biosphere (the only known domain in the universe to be supportive life) and especially to its living components through pollution, and rain, CO_2, and carcinogens. The combustion products and their harmful effects do not stop at natural boundaries. It is of utmost importance to keep the biosphere clean and fit for life. There exists clean primary sources, which, however, are not as convenient to utilize as fossil fuels in general (e.g., in transportation). There is a need for two types of energy carriers (meeting about one quarter of the demand at the consumer end) and fuel (meeting about three quarters of the demand). There exists technology for the production (by any and all primary energy sources) and utilization of the environmentally compatible and efficient fuel energy carrier, i. e., hydrogen. Hydrogen would enable all new primary energy sources to be presented to the consumer in the best utilizable form. The resulting energy system "the hydrogen energy system" would save the biosphere and life from ruin, would be universal and permanent, and would provide humankind with abundant energy for economic progress and higher quality of life.

Dr. Veziroglu's clear concise statement made the preamble to the Bill which created the World Hydrogen Energy Systems Authority (WHESA). The Parliament adopted the Bill as an act unanimously on 24th June 1987.

The Third Session also considered World Legislative Bill Number Eleven - An Act for the Earth Financial Credit Corporation. Philip Isely tabled [introduced] the bill. The preamble outlined the need for such a corporation. Adequate financing is a prerequisite for the success of the movement to establish a federal world government under the *Constitution for the Federation of Earth* and to implement the world legislative measures enacted by the Provisional World Parliament. Repeated devolutions, inflations and manipulations of monetary values, exchange rates and interest rates are disrupting the economies and livelihoods of the peoples of the world. To free the people from this, the financial credit, money and banking systems under the Federation of Earth must be based on virtually unlimited financial credit, which can be extended wherever there are people to work, resources available, technology available, and viable plans for the use of credit, without being dependent on or limited by prior savings or prior capital formation. The *Constitution for the Federation of Earth* under Article VIII, Section G.1. sub-item (e) and (f) specifies a new Planetary Monetary and Credit System based on useful productive capacity and performance. To launch such a system it is desirable that the national governments of a sufficient number of countries (sufficient to establish full credibility and operative acceptance of the new global financial system) ratify or give preliminary ratification to the *Constitution for the Federation of Earth* and use and make the transition to the new global financial system.

The Act was adopted unanimously on 27th June 1987.

It is necessary to note that Section 7 of the Earth Financial Credit Corporation approved the creation of the Earth Dollar: "The line of credit will be accounted in Earth dollars, which shall at no time have a lower value than U.S.A. Dollars or international S.D.R's (Special Drawing Rights) whichever is higher in value at the time of exchange." [Ed. note: This was amended at subsequent sessions 6, 8 and 10 of the provisional World Parliament, to establish the *Earth Hour*, with an assigned value entirely independent from whatever value a U.S.A. Dollar or Special Drawing Right might have.]

To educate its members on matters relating to the Earth Dollar, the World Constitution and Parliament Association issued specimen Earth Dollars. It was clearly indicated in these that they will become encashable only when one or more national governments have given preliminary ratification to the *Constitution for the Federation of Earth* and have also ratified World Legislative Bills 1, 2, 6, 7, and 11, the eleventh being the act for the Earth Financial Credit Corporation. [Ed. note: The legislative ratification requirements to these acts were repealed at the sixth session of the provisional World Parliament.] To date, there has been much discussion on the importance of the Earth Dollar in the context of the emerging new global finance and credit system. Dr. Roger Kotila, Earth-Star Radio, California, U.S.A. and a delegate to sessions of the World Parliament strongly supports it. He points out some interesting restrictions on what type of Earth Dollar lines of credit could not be issued; "No Military or military related proposals on projects will be accepted." Projects and proposals must serve peaceful human needs, must meet "specified human values of decent working conditions, adequate living wages, no excessive salaries or profits to owners, administrators or managers, and must meet specified ecological and environmental standards."

The Miami Beach, Florida session of the Provisional World Parliament laid the foundations for the Provisional World Cabinet, under Article VI, Section D. of the *Constitution for the Federation of Earth*. Ministries were identified and the chair persons of the Parliamentary Commissions who had been working in those areas requested to continue. Some of the ministries were Disarmament, World Economic Development, Emergency Earth Rescue, Environment protection, Human Rights, Graduate School and World University System. With this the session ended on 28th June 1987, after eleven days of exhausting work.

Section 6. Fourth World Constituent Assembly, Troia, Portugal, and Fourth Session of Provisional World Parliament, Barcelona, Spain

While the United Nations Organisation was adding new countries to its membership without consulting the peoples of those countries and engaging in futile debates in its assembly, world problems kept mounting to unbelievable proportions. Disillusionment with its pious platitudes was becoming widespread. U. N. Reform became the hot topic of the day. Despite the impressive practical record of the WCPA, despite its campaign for ratification of the *Constitution for the Federation of Earth* and the eleven World Legislative Acts offering global solutions to the world's ills, talks of adding a second Chamber of Peoples Representatives to the General Assembly and increasing the number of members in the Security Council blurred the main issues. These were encouraged by those with vested interests in the United Nations. The United Nations world body remained weak and spineless. More debate and less solutions was the order of the day.

The World Constitution and Parliament Association, while countering this campaign for U.N. Reform, called for its immediate replacement. In 1988, it launched a plan of collobaration by many organisations to prepare the Fourth Session of the World Constitutent Assembly. The political, social, economic and technological changes since 1977 necessitated some amendments to the *Constitution for the Federation of Earth*. Over 150 organisations joined in preparatory committee. Two meetings were held in New York focusing on the futility of U.N. Reform and the need for a democratic federal world government. The first was in St. Moritz Hotel, New York. It was a luncheon meeting. 25 Ambassadors and many Deputy Ambassadors were present. The Speakers from the WCPA were Philip Isely, Reinhart Ruge, Dr. T. P. Amerasinghe and Dr. Rashmi Mayur. There were good responses from the diplomatic group. The *Constitution* and the Legislative Acts of the Provisional World Parliament were presented to the Ambassadors with a request that they be sent to their national governments.

Encouraged by this, the WCPA held a second Luncheon Meeting at the Roosevelt Hotel in New York. Only a very few Ambassadors graced the occasion. The reason for this failure was obvious. The powers that pull the strings in the U.N.O. had been at work. Long years ago, 1963 to be exact, Dr. Josué de Castro, Brazil's Ambassador to the Disarmament Commission of the U.N. confided to us, that super powers used a technique whenever a national government made a move against a super power interest. They would indicate to that government that they would consider it an "unfriendly act." The "unfriendly act" business was worked with a vengeance ever since the Second Luncheon meeting held by the WCPA in 1989. It has spiralled and bedeviled our activities as we moved from strength to strength.

A WCPA delegation visited Egypt in 1990, with a view to holding the Fourth World Constituent Assembly there. Two successful preparatory meetings were held, and the delegation was asked to return the next day to sign the agreement. When the delegation called at the Foreign Office there was a wall of silence. We are left with conjecture. The Gulf War shattered the peace of the world. The U.N. was ignored.

U.S. Forces with Britain left Iraq "bloodied but unbowed". Saddam Hussain was the culprit, not the Iraqi people. The embargo, however, continued to make innocent women, children and the aged suffer and die so that super power will could prevail!

Left to its own resources the World Constitution and Parliament Association held the Fourth World Constitutent Assembly in Troia, Portugal, in May 1991. The Portuguese Immigration gave assurances that there would be no problems with visas for delegates. The hand was the hand of Esau, but the voice was the voice of Jacob. Those transiting through Italy, France, London and Spain were refused transit visas. Dr. Amerasinghe and party could not get Visa to Portugal and were left stranded in Madrid. Even an Honorary Consul, Abdul W. M. Ameer, could not get a visa. The Nigerian delegation consisting Dr. Atiku Abubakar, Ali Monguno and Bernard Shaw Mazi, after many travels, got to Troia, on the penultimate day! In spite of these difficulties there were many delegates from Europe and the U.S.A. who needed no visas. Fortresses cannot be built everywhere. Perhaps this is the motivation for the U.S. plans to militarise space!

At Troia, the World Constitutuent Assembly voted 59 amendments to the *Constitution for the Federation of Earth*. A new ratification campaign was launched. Many honorary sponsors inaugurated the World Constituent Assembly with their personal ratification.

The future held promise for the Nigerian Delegation. Dr. Abubakar is now Vice President of the Republic of Nigeria and committed member of WCPA.
[Ed. note: Dr. Abubakar stepped down from Vice-Presidency of WCPA to concentrate on the 2007 Nigeria re-election bid, which was lost.] Ali Monguno became a Cabinet Minister with Oil Portfolio and Co-President of WCPA. Bernard Shaw Mazi continues to be Secretary General of the Nigeria Branch of WCPA.

Opposition from vested interests both covert and overt, silent diplomacy from the new emergent single super power and its allies made the World Constitution and Parliament Association to work all the harder. In 1992, the Global Ratification and Elections Network (GREN) organised. Its instant success showed that millions in the developing world and elsewhere, particularly in Africa, were deeply dissatisfied with the way governments both within and outside the United Nations were handling the affairs of their countries. The demand for a radical change was mirrored in the numerous applications for GREN membership and the formation of branches:

A World Charter established GREN. The Charter clearly laid down the purposes:

1. To work for Ratification of the *Constitution* by national governments, Parliaments and by people of the Earth;
2. To help organise sessions of the Provisional World Parliament in collaboration with the World Constitution and Parliament Association;
3. To elect or appoint and send delegates to the Provisional World Parliament on a representative basis as defined in Article 19 of the *Constitution*;
4. To help organize elections to the World Parliament after the *Constitution for the Federation of Earth* is ratified; and

5. To help where possible in achieving implementation of the World Legislation adopted by the Provisional World Parliament, and of the Manifesto for the beginning of World Government, as adopted by the Provisional World Parliament.

The Charter continues thus:

> "The members of GREN shall be organizations that adhere to the purposes of GREN and which confirm their adherence and participation by adopting the resolution provided by GREN for participation in GREN. To join GREN, an organisation must have a minimum of 15 individual members. - The number of organisations joining GREN shall be unlimited. A wide variety of organisations are invited to join GREN, including peace, disarmament, world government, the environment, the climate crisis, human rights, economic development, global finance, non-polluting energy, the oceans, the atmosphere, world resources, food supplies, water supplies, transportation, communication, labour, women, students, business, agriculture, fishing, forestry, public administration, lawyers, scientists, professors, professional groups, education, health, housing, community and regional planning, political parties, democracy, race relations, technological development, comprehensive reforms, all causes for human welfare, etc.

The Charter describes the relationship between GREN and WCPA. GREN was initiated and developed by WCPA and shares certain defined purposes. However GREN was defined as a separate organisation and was not controlled by WCPA GREN was composed of organisations, whereas WCPA is composed of individuals as members. The objective of GREN was to obtain the aid, strength and participation of many millions of people in thousands of organisations in most countries of the world to achieve the common purposes and objectives defined in Article 1 of the *Earth Constitution* as compared with the relatively small membership of WCPA itself.

The organisation was described in the Charter as follows: A World Co-ordinating Council with National Co-ordinating Councils and Regional Co-ordinating Councils. The overall and worldwide functioning of GREN was managed by the World Co-ordinating Council (W.C.C.)

The World Headquarters was at the same location as the World Headquarters of WCPA.

As for budgets and Finance, the sources for funding at the present time was from membership fees, solicitations for large and small contributions, contributions from money earned by the sale of goods or services, by member organisations or individuals and benefit concerts.

GREN was WCPA's answer to the continued monopoly of power by the remaining super power. GREN's immediate success, particularly, in Africa in 1992, provoked reprisals in the nature of "unfriendly Act", to prevent national governments from ratifying the *Constitution for the Federation of Earth* and the denial of visas to impede the progress of the Provisional World Parliaments. Despite this, Alexander Dubček, President-Chair of Czechoslovakia General Assembly personally ratified the *Earth Constitution* and helped in its translation into the Czech [Slovak] language.

So also Sam Nujoma, then President of Namibia, personally ratified. We hope their actions will blaze the trail for other heads of National Governments, especially in the developing world.

[Editors' note: The Global Ratification and Elections Network transformed into the Earth Federation Movement, comprised of both organizations and people who are taking the initiative on the task of obtaining ratification of the *Earth Constitution*.]

Meanwhile, the world situation took a dramatic turn in the collapse of the Soviet Union and its replacement by the Commonwealth of States. It led to free movement of an hitherto imprisoned people. To us it was noticeable in the presence of delegates from the Ukraine, Russia and Uzbekistan at the 4th session of the Provisional World Parliament in Barcelona, Spain.

The single super power, the U.S.A., and its allies moved to reduce whatever prestige the United Nations had left. The world stood aghast at the manner in which it was knocked about. The loans from the International Monetary Fund and the World, Bank was U.S.A.'s bait to entrap developing countries. Like the Gadarene swine, they rushed headlong into disaster. The walking skeletons in Ethiopia, the disaster of Sierra Leone, the horrors of the Congo were echoed in the mounting criticism of the U.N.O.

The cover-up was the 50th Anniversary of the U.N. To mark the occasion, Shridath Ramphal and Ingvar Carlsson were commissioned to publish their report *Our Global Neighbourhood*. The World Constitution and Parliament Association countered it, through the Emergency Earth Rescue Administration, working with other authors to produce the book *Toward Genuine Global Governance*.

Articles and analyses were contributed by Keith Beggs of the World Government Organisations Coalition [Ed. note: now Coalition for Democratic World Government], Professor Ronald J. Glossop, Professor Errol Harris, [Emeritus] Professor Northwestern University and author of *One World or None*, Professor Philip Isely, then Secretary General, WCPA, Dr. Glen Martin, current Secretary General of WCPA, and Dr. James B. Thring, President of Planning for Peace, London, England. It was a devastating exposure of the hypocrisy of the Authors of *Our Global Neighbourhood*. Dr. Glossop states that it would be unethical to confuse "International Governance" with "Global Governance." There can be no such thing as "Global Governance."

Dr. Glossop uses Harlan Cleveland's definition of "Governance" in his book "Birth of a New World", published two years before "Our Global Neighbourhood". The "World Governance," says Dr. Cleveland, "was never intended to imply global *government* but rather the aggregate of institutions of co-operation, co-ordination and communications among sovereign states and non-governmental organisations that constitute the management of Peace." Prof. Glossop comments: "It means managing the Planet with same kinds of international institutions we already have, but with more of them... Governance can only be used with 'International' never "Global." By using the word "Global" before the word "Governance," the authors of *Our Global Neighbourhood* tried to cover U.N. nakedness–which for fifty years had left humanity rudderless–with a new dress to continue to confuse the peoples of the world.

The book *Toward Genuine Global Governance* further exposes Ingvar Carlsson and Shridath Ramphal. Prof. Harris refers to the statement in the report: "We are not proposing movement towards world government, for were we to travel in that direction we could find ourselves in an even less democratic world than we have –one more accommodating to power, more hospitable to hegemonic ambition, and more reinforcing of the roles of states and Governments rather than the rights of people." Prof. Harris comments: "Nothing could be further from the truth. It is astonishing that the Co-Chairman of the Commission could have written what is quoted above, when they already had in their hands the *Constitution for the Federation of Earth*, drafted by the World Constituent Assembly over forty years in four separate meetings, by which democratic elections are prescribed, individual and national rights explicitly protected and a World Ombudsmus is established to prevent corrupt or arbitrary exercise of authority by individuals or organisations." Prof. Harris calls "Global Governance" a weasel-word to disguise a situation in which genuine government is rendered impossible by the claim to, and exercise of national sovereignty. Further exposing the hollowness of the Carlsson-Ramphal Report, Prof. Harris points out that the Co-Chairman could not avoid facing stark facts: "The United Nations was there to be used," says the Report, "and not infrequently abused; to be an instrument of national interest where it could be; and to be by-passed where it could not be made to serve that interest." The Co-Chairman dared not give examples because the frequent violators were the super power and its allies, stating them would risk the fall of the guilotine on their comfortable necks! So Carlsson and Ramphal complains that the U.N. Charter was drafted fifty years ago, when the international scene was very different from the present. They consider the time is ripe for reform. Prof Harris agrees that "the international situation has changed significantly," but he also says that, "in one respect it remains the same. It is still that of an assemblage of sovereign states, mutually recognized as such and negotiating in terms of treaty. In these circumstances reform of the U.N. Charter, less drastic than transforming it into a federal world constitution, will be of no avail."

Prof. Philip Isely in his contribution puts the lid on the pious platitudes in the Carlsson-Ramphal Report:

> "When the camouflage of nice sounding administrations and verbiage is removed, the specifics of the report are mainly for further concentration of power in the hands of those national governments and economic interests which are now dominant. Instead of empowering the people, the exact opposite would be accomplished if the recommendations of the Commission on Global Governance are carried out, as shown in this critique.
>
> "The kind of action which is truly needed is for people to set aside this Report as entirely misleading and to proceed with the task of instituting a democratic federal government, to which the people can directly elect their representatives to a world legislative parliament. ...For this the *Constitution for the Federation of Earth* is ready for immediate ratification and implementation and is designed in every respect to serve the peaceful needs of humanity."

The Carlsson–Ramphal Report had some influence on people, organisations and institutions that believed or wished to believe that U.N. Reform was still possible. Chief among these were the World Association of World Federalists (W.A.W.F.) and the World Citizens Assembly (W.C.A.). The former was hoary with age and still wearing the halo of the famous 1947 Montreaux Declaration that pointed out frailties of the United Nations Charter and declared for a federal world. The W.A.W.F., waiting to celebrate its Fiftieth Anniversary, changed its name to World Federalist Movement (W.F.M.)–a watered-down version of the original. The Japanese World World Federalists continue in their determined stand for World Government. This was clear at the 25th Anniversary Celebrations of W.F.M. in New Delhi and Madras. In Shakespearean words: "Oh! what a fall was there my countrymen. Then I and you and all of us fell down."

There was no meeting at the previously announced Vigyan Bhawan, no reception at the Rashtrapathi Bhawan with the President of India but a hastily got up meeting in Y.M.C.A. Hall in New Delhi. There were distinguished personalities who had come with great expectation. The move to Chennai (Madras) to the resplendent hall of the Taj Coromandel Hotel, was both refreshing and heartening. It was, however, a predominantly declaration for world government, not "global governance."

The World Constitution and Parliament Association in spite of obstacles and continuous overtures to adopt the U.N. Reform road has marched steadily forward "in no way doubting clouds would break."In the belief that "though right were worsted, wrong would never triumph," it issued a clear, uncompromising booklet "A Bill of Particulars: Why the U.N. Must Be Replaced." It was more a call to genuine doubters, than to the faithful. The U.N's failures to solve global problems, defects in its Organisation, why it cannot be amended; why the proposed amendments are delusions, then the practical alternative. Replace the U.N.Charter immediately with the *Constitution for the Federation of Earth*. There is an old saying that, "None are as blind as those who will not see." With the issue of the booklet we can well condemn the ditherers. "Having eyes you see not. Having ears you hear not."

With this the WCPA began to search for a venue for the 4th sessions of the Provisional World Parliament. Innsbruck, Austria, the scene of the second Constitutional Assembly, was investigated. The managers of Kongresshaus assured us that they thought there would be no visa problems for the 2,000 delegates registered to attend. Conference rents and Hotels were booked. Reports from intending delegates were that impossible demands were made by local Austrian Embassies for grants of visas. The writer and his fellow delegates were requested to obtain sponsorship from an Austrian national ready to guarantee their stay with accident and sick insurance included. The document must be authorized in German. Was it another example of the "unfriendly act"? Appeals to Kongresshaus to intervene with the Austrian Foreign Office and live up to their original promise fell on deaf ears. The paid-for advances amounted to 25,000 U.S. Dollars. Subsequent attempts were made to recover this sum, through legal process at the Court of Human Rights in Strasbourg by Dr. T. P. Amerasinghe. The Strasbourg Court, ruled that before they could intervene legal process in the country where the breach took place must be exhausted first. It was a merry-go-round: we go to the Court of Human Rights because Kongresshaus broke its promise we would not be denied visas. We were now asked to enter Austria, exhaust legal remedies before filing legal process in Strasbourg!

The World Constitution and Parliament Association chose Andorra as the alternate venue. The beautiful independent principality in the high Pyrenees was said to need no visas. Its hotel managers gave assurances that there was no question of visas. On this understanding WCPA booked hotels. Hotel Panorama with its breathtaking view of the mountains which inspired the song of Roland echoing an united, peaceful world, seemed an adequate setting. WCPA booked rooms and conference halls to house the 2,000 delegates. However, countries through which delegates had to transit–Italy, France, and Spain–denied transit visas. Some held up the passports and visa applications for several days, as did the French Embassy in Colombo until the initial date of the Parliament was passed. There is a mass of evidence that this was a clear act of sabotage on the part of or at the instigation of the dominant super power. The growing forces behind the cry for the replacement of the U.N. with a Democratic Federal World Government would be blunted.

The delegates who trickled down to Barcelona, Spain, 14th September 1996, were made of sterner stuff. The fourth session was memorable in many ways. Members of Parliament from Togo, West Africa, from Uzbekistan, Ukraine and Russia were accredited delegates. On 15th September the directive Amendment to World Lesislative Act Number 11 was unanimously adopted. It outlined the method for beginning and operating the new global finance and credit system, as originally defined in World Legislative Act No.11. The basic process was to be a new global credit card system in which all credit advances and all payments can be instantly accounted worldwide by modern electronic technology, measured in terms of Earth Dollars (later renamed as "Earth Hours"):

> "The system employing credit cards may be used for Government and public purposes, for private corporations, businesses and associations and for individual persons as employees and consumers.Where credit card systems are not yet installed, credit advances and payments of all kinds may be done by cheques and other paper accounting as presently customary, until the Universal Card System is available."

The fourth session approved the Manifesto for beginning world government with the ownership and management of all the oceans and sea beds of Earth. It declared "Federal world government is already 48 years overdue, since it should have been established at the end of World War II instead of the delusionary United Nations Organisation. Because of this delay a multi-million dollar arms race has ensued resulting in extreme insecurity for all inhabitants of Earth, and the radio-active poisoning of the environment spreading for thousands of years, when hundreds of wars have raged and dozens continue at this moment..... into this scene because of continued lack of direction for human civilization on Earth, thousands of protest movements and hundreds of proposals to remedy the situation have multiplied over the years resulting in great confusion as to be what can be done. Therefore we believe the time has come for very decisive action to cut through the confusion and delay and establish positive direction to get the common affairs of the inhabitants of Earth under responsible and democratic controls for the mutual and equitable benefit of everybody. This requires democratic federal world government. For this purpose a *Constitution for the Federation of Earth* has already been prepared by delegates from all continents and is ready for ratification and implementation, to replace the grossly defective U.N. Charter.

The Manifesto declared:

> " We who are delegates meeting together in the fourth session, organised under Article 19 of the *Earth Constitution*, do hereby proclaim and take the following action:
> 1. On behalf of all mankind, inhabitants of Earth, we take possession of all oceans and seabeds of Earth from 20 kilometers offshore comprising 70 percent of Earth for the beginning of World Government but reserving the first 200 miles offshore for the priority of fishing rights of adjoining countries;
> 2. We invite and urge all nations and national governments to share the benefits derived from their administration by quickly joining the World Federation by ratification of the *Earth Constitution*. Until 25 nations have ratified the delegates of this fourth session shall serve as the Provisional World Parliament of a Provisional World Government and shall expeditiously begin the administration of Oceans and seabeds and all other world territory claimed under the Manifesto;
> 3. As a first act of Administration in order to help to rid the Earth of nuclear weapons and weapons of mass destruction we outlaw and forbid them as required by World Legislative Act No One;
> 4. As a second act the Manifesto declares that we activate World Legislative Act Number Two to obtain ample financial credit for development;
> 5. World Legislative Act Number Six (as amended) is activated to cope with the on-rushing climate crisis;
> 6. As delegates of this fourth session we reconfirm a standing parliamentary Committee on Disarmament as specified in World Legislative Act No. One;
> 7. As delegates we are enacting World Legislation for a comprehensive Global Energy Administration;
> 8. We as delegates are establishing a continuing Provisional World Cabinet to serve until replacement after 25 countries ratify the *Constitution for the Federation of Earth;*
> 9. As a seventh act of the manifesto, we as delegates are electing a continuing President for the Provisional World Parliament and ensuing World Government until replacement when 25 countries ratify.

The Manifesto is of importance in the history of the World Constitution and Parliament Association and is dealt with in some detail because it indicates both the urgency of the world problems and the way out for humanity.

All this was done in the gathering gloom that hung over the delegates at the fourth session in Barcelona. At the news that Margaret Isely was critically ill in Lakewood, Colorado, U.S.A., "If you have tears, prepare to shed them now," was echoed by every one in the assembly. For this gracious Lady was the very life and soul of the World Constitution and Parliament Association since its inception and before. Single handedly she built the financial structure which till her death remained the main source of funding for this gigantic enterprise to save the world from the horrors of war and usher in an era of happy living for humanity. Years of hard work, with a family of six children, she kept not only a decent hearth and home but worked to achieve the same for the millions of the Earth's people. No resounding word could compensate for her devotion to the work of the WCPA. Some families build marble monuments to commemorate their dead, but the Isely family will do well to build a monument more lasting than bronze and loftier than the Pyramids of Kings.

As the English poet Matthew Arnold said of another Margaret:

> "Call her once before she goes
> In a voice that she might know,
> Margaret, Margaret."

Section 7. Growing Strength of WCPA Invites Superpower Opposition as Mirrored at the Fifth Session of the Provisional World Parliament, Malta, 2000

Through the years 1997 to 2000 the Global Ratification and Elections Network Organisations increased in such numbers that WCPA believes warning signals went out to those nations which presently dominate the world both technologically and financially. The pages of the WCPA bulletin *Across Frontiers* were replete with the news that branches were being registered in the developing world. In the eight years since GREN was formed, organisations and members spiralled. For example in May 1999 there were 1,396 branches in 121 countries, with reputedly many million members. GREN Youth Organisations stood at 486. Within two months GREN Organisations soared to 1,578 in 124 countries. These were not merely in Africa and Asia but also in Europe, Latin America and the islands of the Pacific. WCPA publications called for more organisations by the millennium. It would mean that WCPA/GREN would have many millions in 130 countries pushing for the replacement of the U.N. by a democratic federal world government under the *Constitution for the Federation of Earth*. By a silent revolution it was thought possible that the machinations of the few industrialised nations led by the Super Power would cease and the developing nations would free themselves from the bondage of the I.M.F., the World Bank and the World Trade Organization.

[Editors' note: The editors have the GREN database. Many of the registered organizations lack significant funding. Furthermore, over five years have passed without significant follow-up and contact renewals. We cannot verify the millions of members cited above. Nevertheless, the strong positive response does seem typical of people and groups in countries of the Global South regarding the *Earth Constitution*, the Provisional World Parliament and the Earth Federation Movement.]

This growing strength naturally attracted growing opposition. The WCPA/GREN plan has great appeal to countries which have little or no technological and political clout. It does not probably have so much appeal to countries technologically and financially advanced which are nevertheless very few. This probability has already been demonstrated. When examined, their interests are primarily security and otherwise maintaining their exalted position. The fall of the Soviet Union and the emergence of the Superpower has certainly not changed their outlook.

The World Constitution and Parliament Association has always been confronted with this problem, more especially in the years 1997-2000. Any developing country daring to even seriously consider ratification of the *Constitution for the Federation of Earth* would be threatened with non-renewal or cancellation of loans from the International Monetary Fund and denial of financial credit, even if these were miserly. In spite of pressure from the common people of their countries, leaders of developing countries continued to make annual pilgrimages to the I.M.F. and the World Bank to beg for pittances–crumbs–when abundance is at the door through the process of ratification of the *Constitution for the Federation of Earth*. Denial of credit proved to the Superpower and its allies a more effective way of deterring ratification than dropping bombs. During the course of this history we have pointed out many instances. There are signs that they are ready to strike. The Meeting of the Group of 77 (now expanding) in April 2000 was the latest example. Leader after leader referred to the plight of their people. They called for "reform", for a "human order". Belize's Prime Minister stated, "Nothing we say or do will have any true meaning for our people unless we can significantly and quickly reduce the shameful number of those who live in poverty, even as more people than ever become millionaires. One day, humankind will be called to account: How come you never made any connection between growing poverty for the many and booming wealth for a few?"

Dozens of Presidents and Prime Ministers at this Havana Conference would go no further than call for a new Global Order. Not a word about the *Constitution for the Federation of Earth* and the immediate economic benefits of world government.

The World Constitution and Parliament Association addressed its mind and planned to meet this new situation. WCPA worked unceasingly to resolve this dilemma. It made four suggestions:

1) to implement the New Global Finance and Credit system concurrent with ratification of the *Constitution* by the first 25 countries or possibly as few as the first ten;

2) to appeal newly and strongly to the technologically and financially developed countries on the basis of security related to the two issues: climate security and military security. These two issues are common to all countries and might force a consensus;

3) to convene a Founding Ratification Convention for those national governments that might be ready for life-saving action of ratifying the *Constitution for the Federation of Earth*; and

4) to convene another session of the Provisional World Parliament.

Subsequently the WCPA issued the booklet "Immediate Economic Benefits of World Government." It showed the developing countries and their national governments how to break out of the net of new loans, cancellation of old debts, servicing etc. which is strangling their economies and promising no hope of economic uplift.

A new ratification resolution was proposed. This resolution included both ratification of the *Constitution for the Federation of Earth* and Ratification of World Legislative Act Number Eleven with immediate implementation. Preparations began for a 5th session of the Provisional World Parliament. Throughout 1999 a search was made for a venue. Iraq offered its Parliament Building and generous facilities despite being under seige. A WCPA Delegation visited Iraq and documents were exchanged. The Provisional World Parliament was set to meet 11th to 24th September, 2000. An estimated 2,000 delegates registered to attend. U. S. bombings on Iraq resumed. There were no flights to Bagdad nor was there a likehood of termination of the no-fly decree. Only road access was possible; a convoy of buses carrying the large number of delegates over a 15 hour journey. A strategy meeting of WCPA and GREN decided reluctantly to inform Iraq that a change of Venue was called for. The Revolutionary Committees Movement (R.C.M.) of Libya offered to host. Dr. Salem Elzubedi of R.C.M. declared: "Irrespective of political pressure, we stand by R.C.M. principles of supporting grass root movements and non-governmental organisations".

A WCPA delegation composed of Philip Isely, Secretary General, Dr.Reinhart Ruge, Co-President and Sarwar Alam visited Libya 5-10 July, 1999. Ideas and information were exchanged at several sessions with the R.C.M. leaders Dr. Husbafa Zaidi, Co-ordinator of Foreign Affairs Department, R.C.M., Dr. Salem Elzubedi, Dr. Ali Godban, Dr. Salem Bedi Amer and Dr. Ramadan Breki. The R.C.M. agreed within its capacity to invite its members and friendly organisers to join GREN. A Libyan National Preparatory Committee was set up. The convention hall was booked. The 5th session of the Provisional World Parliament was to be under the patronage of Brother Muammar Al-Quadaffi, the Leader of the Revolution. Many facilities were to be provided by R. C. M. October 21 to November 2, 2000 was confirmed. However as late as March 2000, R. C. M.'s arrangements appeared to have slowed down. There was much talk of restoration of friendly relations with the U.S. Brother Muammar Al-Quadaffi would not inaugurate the 5th session of the P.W.P. but could attend the closing sessions. These concerns were made known to the R.C.M. Since it was imperative that the PWP should meet before the end of 2000, the World Constitution and Parliament Association and GREN at its strategy meeting held at Hotel Roosevelt, New York on March 18th 2000 decided to cancel the arrangements and informed R.C.M. that Libya may be considered a venue for a later Provisional World Parliament. Good relations continue to prevail between R.C.M. and WCPA-GREN and it was heartening to have a sizeable Libyan delegation when the 5th session of P.W.P. was finally held in Malta.

Alongside preparations for the 5th Session of the Provisional World Parliament, the WCPA expanded its activities in Southern India where there was a growing demand for a branch in Chennai (Madras). North India had a Branch in New Delhi since 1970 and an All India WCPA headed by Shri B. P. Nigam. Dr. T. P. Amerasinghe Co-President visited Madras in January, 2000. The inauguration took place on 11th January, 2000 at Palmgrove Hotel, Chennai. Addressing the large gathering al1 of whom had signed as members he said, "Although New Delhi is the nerve centre of India, representation there is not enough. A vast and growing power like India must have centres in its big cities with teeming populations to take up the challenge to ratify the *Constitution for the Federation of Earth*. After Chennai branches would follow in Bangalore, Mysore, Calcutta and Bombay". Mr. Karikar Vaitha, a federalist for 50 years, a friend of Lord Atlee who was one of the original signer's for the call for a World Constitutional Convention in 1961, was elected President and Subramaniam Aiyar as Secretary-General. A twenty five member Committee which included Professor S.Varadaraju, a long standing WCPA member and Justice S. K. Ram agreed to press for Ratification of the *Earth Constitution* by the important Tamil Nadu Legislature and its Chief Minister.

Philip Isely, the Secretary-General visited Malta with others from the WCPA Office in Lakewood to make arrangements for the 5th session of the Provisional World Parliament. Malta with its central position in the Mediterranean between Italy and Tunisia, and having close relations with Libya appeared a suitable venue. Malta is a country which issues on the spot visas to citizens of countries which are exempt. However for purposes of travel for citizens of those countries requiring Visas, the Malta Immigration is required to issue the necessary document. The WCPA delegation having discussed all these requirements and been assured by Immigration that they see no obstacles, booked the Oracle Conference Center for the Parliament and rooms in the

New Dolman Hotel and huge Topaz Hotel in Qawra and Buggibba tourist resorts on the sea coast. 22nd to 27th November, 2000 were the dates for the session. Registration for delegations began. A WCPA-GREN Office was opened in Malta at Number 1, Gozo Street and Sawar Alam, WCPA Youth Co-ordinator and later Eugenia Almand, WCPA Executive Director of Education, and Paula Grima were appointed to help Malta Immigration to expedite visa applications and get the visa confirm action letters to delegates. Computer and Fax Machines were installed in the office. About this time the number of Global Ratification and Elections Network (GREN) Organisations had swelled to 2000 in 142 countries with a membership of many millions. These details are necessary to understand the chaos that followed.

It is best described in, the Secretary-General's "Report and Call to action, to all delegates and GREN Organisations" dated 12th December, 2000: "Sabotaged Again". That is the most astounding negative description of what happened to the Malta Session of the Provisional World Parliament scheduled for 22 -27 November, 2000.

Of the more than 1,400 registered delegates, only 49 straggled in from 23 countries over the period of 5 days. Some of those attending were identified as probably CIA agents or informers. Of 401 visa applications taken in a bunch late on November 3rd (none were permitted earlier) to Malta Visa police, only 41 were granted, 10 days later on November 13th, too late for most of those approved to attend. Instead of expediting visas, the slowness of the procedure pointed to deliberate obstruction. Since the visa police operate on instructions from their Government, the blame is easy to identify. Many delegates from Africa were denied passage on Airlines.

But what pressure may have been brought against the government of Malta by a higher power is difficult to prove, although previous history indicates who and why. Our programe of action, if successful, will replace the United Nations and NATO and subordinate the government of the U.S.A. which now virtually rules the world, to the rule of law under the *Constitution for the Federation of Earth*. Thus any country hosting the provisional World Parliament is committing "an unfriendly act", against the ruling power and subject to reprisal – especially economic reprisals of which many are possible.

To the above report the author must add that he received his visa confirmation letter in Sri Lanka only, hours before his E. K. Flight was due to leave Katunayake Airport, Colombo, for Dubai and Malta. Further, Uganda, for example, is a country which is listed under "No Visa Required", had one of its citizens strip-searched on arrival, kept in the Airport without food and sanitary facilities. Finally he was given a three day visa. By this time the Parliament was in its penultimate day.

Despite these drawbacks the 5th Session was able to do some work of reaching importance. It approved the Five Year Plan to prepare and carry out the series of Five Global Expositions, primarily for developing countries as the basic course of action which could do much to solve the visa problem and the financial problem: A beginning was made to establish a world committee to organise the global expositions. The session also approved the plan to prepare for the next five sessions of the Provisional World Parliament. Locations for the global expositions and the parliament sessions were discussed and likely locations identified. India was the first choice at the Malta parliament. The Republic of South Africa where strong support was expected from the World Solidarity Movement and the Bhava Jahan Society was to follow. Other identified locations were Cuba for the Western Hemisphere; The Phillipines and a country in Eastern Europe.

Eugenia Almand, as Executive Director of the Graduate School of World Problems was commended by the Malta Parliament for the extensive work so far done in working out its details. Dr. Amerasinghe moved that it was time the G. S. W. P. took off ground because WCPA-GREN needed, informed and dedicated leaders for our global movement. The question of Palestine was debated at length when Dr. Hanan Awwad, Palestinian delegate to Parliament and President Palestine Council for GREN presented a resolution. A parliamentary committee was appointed under the Chairmanship of Dr. Amerasinghe to consider it and Dr. Hanan Awwad's resolution expressing the Provisional World Parliament's support for the aspirations of Palestine to be a separate state within the Earth Federation, was adopted.

The Parliament ended on 27th November on the affirmation of delegates "that despite the infliction of financial loss the attempts to suppress our Parliament and our movement are in a sense a recognition of our strength. The movement to achieve Federal World Government under the *Constitution for the Federation of Earth*, presents a strong and growing threat to the continued monopoly of militarism by the remaining Superpower". What is need by us all, the Provisional World Parliament's concluding statement asserted is : "Courage not to submit or yield, and what is more, not to be overcome".

Section 8. At the millennium – NATO takes command and makes the U. N. its pawn.

The Millennium Assembly in New York to celebrate the entry of the U. N. into the new Millennium of the 21st century was perhaps the saddest spectacle of modern times. In the face of facts flying in the face of national governments, world leaders gathered in strength to pay tribute to an organisation which for 55 years failed to eliminate war or solve the pressing problems of the world. The World Constitution and Parliament Association statement of August 1999 had pointed out that the last vestiges of U.N. independence had vanished with North Atlantic Treaty Organization's new strategic concept. The statement was entitled "Move over U.N.–NATO is, now in command." In April 1999, 19 NATO Member nations met in Washington D.C. and approved the NATO concept. From being limited to defence against attacks which might be made in Europe or North America, NATO is now authorized, not merely to defend, but to intervene and take the offensive anywhere in the world where "peace, security and stability" of NATO members may be considered threatened. Action can be taken by economic, political and military means, by economic blockades, by a change of governments, by any military actions deemed helpful to carry out "the full range of alliance missions." Under the guise of "crisis management operations" or "crisis response operations," NATO can achieve its end without declaration of war. "Peace, Security and Stability" can be broadly interpreted. Under the "New Strategic Concept" NATO takes the entire world. The "WCPA statement pointed out that the two and a half months of intensive bombing in Yugoslavia was not war but a "crisis management operation." The U.S. now need not go to the Security Council of the U.N. and canvass votes. Not that the former method was very difficult, but this new method is easier!

Despite this statement and the new imbecility of the U. N., Leaders of National Governments queued up at the Millennium Assembly in an act of hypocrisy, or fear of losing the crumbs that fall from the International Monetary Fund!

Meanwhile people's pressure continued to mount from the remarkable increase of GREN Organisations throughout the World. From November 2000, when the Provisional World Parliament met in Malta, the number of GREN organisations rose from 2000 to 2222. An increase of 222 within the short period of six months. These organisations are not merely from the developing world. The total membership of these organisations stand at millions. Student organizations agree that world government is the only real answer to global chaos. H. E. Sarwar Alam, WCPA World Student Co-ordinator, in his recent report to the Strategy Committee of the World Constitution and Parliament Association listed some of these organisations:

> "The Indian Youth Congress, (youth wing of the Indian Congress party) with its strong commitment of co-operation. The National Union of Eritrea (Youth and Students) Youth Morocco; V.J.S.A.R.I.O. (Union de la Juventud de Saguiat et Hamra y Rio de Oro) from Sahara also joined with GREN GREN has good relations with ANC Youth League (South Africa), Southern Africa Youth Forum. Young Communists in U.S.A., Youth Communists in U.K., Communist Youth union of the Russian Federation (S.K.M.R.F), Communist Youth Union of Vietnam, Democratic Youth

League of Japan, General Union of Arab Students, Union de la Jeunesse Democratique Lebanaise, Kim Il Sung Socialist Youth League, Union de Jovenes Communistas (Cuba); U. C. L. A. E. (Organisation Continental Latin Americana y Caribeana de Estudiantes)".

Sarwar Alam met with Dr. Belaïd Abrika, President of National Union of Algerian Youth at the 15th World Festival of Youth and Students, where they discussed bilateral cooperation between WCPA/GREN and the N.U.A.Y. It is of great significance that WCPA/GREN was invited to actually participate and send a delegation to World Festival in Algiers, 8th to 16th August 2001. The Conference program was most interesting. All the problems confronting humanity today were listed for discussion. They are all global problems which need to be solved globally.

They cannot be solved within the present system of sovereign states as mentioned in the U.N. Charter. The WCPA/GREN delegation presents the only reasonable alternative–democratic federal world government under a *Constitution for the Federation of Earth*–and called upon the 30,000 participants to immediate action to ratify the *Constitution* and pressurize their governments to do so. "No more protests" the World Constitution and Parliament Association has said. "Youth leaders (with some elders) could in fact establish world government by composing the first 15 or 20 world ministries and act as coordinators in working out details to get them into functional operation".

[Editors' note: As previously noted, the editors have the GREN database. We have seen the list of 2222 organizations, including the organizations listed just above. However, we cannot verify the millions of members cited. We include this notation not to contradict Dr. Amerasinghe, but to qualify this book for editorial objectivity. We simply are not certain of the actual size and strength of organizations subscribing to GREN.]

With the peoples and students pressure on the national governments to ratify, the WCPA issued another letter to the Group of 77 (now 130). It is entitled CRASH! and is reproduced here:

"During the next few years, from whom do you expect to get money for investments, loans and markets to develop the economy of your country?

"Money to employ the large number of citizens of your country and who are now unemployed or who are barely employed living at near starvation or miserly incomes!

"Money from the U.S.A.? where investors have recently lost more than 4 Trillion Dollars in stock market and other crashes and more trillions in business bankruptcies and liquidation? Or from any other sources more solvent than in the U.S.A.

"Do you think you can be saved by debt forgiveness by current crash victims, and then obtain more loans under the same rules and disastrous finances that have led to the present situation -where most countries of the group of 77 (now 130) as well as other developing countries suffer with 20 to 50 percent unemployment?

"A TURNING POINT IS AT HAND!

"The opportune time has come, we believe, for you, together with leaders of other countries of the Group of 77 to cut loose from the Crash-Structure exploitive global economy featuring massive unemployment, and create a New Global Economy of Abundance- which is designed to serve the needs of the vast majority of people and nations of Earth, instead of the greedy acquisitiveness of present rulers?

"How can this be done without dependence on investment and loans from those now afflicted by economic crash?

"WE POINT TO A PRACTICAL WAY

"1. Build a new global economy based on the design and principles defined by World Legislative Act Number Eleven, which is set forth in the booklet: Immediate Economic Benefits of World Government was providentially written before the current crash, and is based on the commonsense proposition of extending financial credit wherever people are available to work.

"2. Develop the new global economy in the essential framework of a democratic world federation, with a Federal World Government which can be organised rapidly by adoption of the *Constitution for the Federation of Earth.* A copy of this modern World Constitution which was drafted with 21st Century vision at several sessions of a World Constitutent Assembly is enclosed.

"3. Introduce this practical course of action at a series of 5 Global Exhibitions where the potentials of all participating countries can be dramatically presented–particularly the potentials of developing countries.

"4. At the first Global Exposition, introduce for immediate implementation the New Global Finance, Credit and Accounting System, by which virtually unlimited financial credits can be advanced sufficiently to employ everybody at fair incomes to produce the goods and services which people need for happy living on Planet Earth. No past savings are needed as fully explained in the booklet: "Immediate Economic Benefits of World Government."

"5. By the time of the Second Global Exposition, make sure that the *Constitution for the Federation of Earth* is ratified by a sufficient number of countries to go into full force and effect–together with financial credits already advanced so as to demonstrate the opportunities and practicability of the New Global Finance and Accounting System.

"6. IT IS WITHIN YOUR POWER

"Acting together with other leaders of the Group of 77 (now 133) to do all that is briefly outlined above. You do not need to ask the permission of any present day Global power. Financial assistance from them is no longer needed.

"By this letter and enclosures, we have outlined a positive course of action by which Earth can be made into a good home for everybody. But the authors of this letter, and the NGO's represented, cannot issue the financial credits which are possible. It is necessary for you, together with other leaders of the Group of 77 to break away from dependence on present Global rulers, and replace the present Financial System of scarcity with the World Political and Financial Structure which we describe.

"Action by you is now required. We can then mobilize the support of thousands of NGO's worldwide, and growing hundreds of millions of members as represented in the Global Ratification and Elections Network.

"The choice is between Crumbs and Abundance. When shall we meet?

"For adequate action for the happy survival of humanity on Earth"

The letter was sent under the signatures of Dr. Terence Amerasinghe, Co-President, and Philip Isely, then Secretary-General of WCPA.

The letter went at a time when the prevailing market, the crash and the pressure exerted by peoples and student movements on national governments in developing countries was to move away from servility to the I.M.F. and World Bank and move towards the WCPA alternative. Abundance not crumbs. In the few technologically and financially advanced countries led by the U.S.A. dwindling reserves are even sizably reducing the crumbs offered to developing countries. The I.M.F. and World Bank repeat demands to national governments in the developing world to "tighten their belts" by cutting social welfare programs. These signs are reflected in the recent speeches of some of the leaders of the Group of 77. Calls are being made for "outright cancellation of unsustainable debts," for increased aid and for measures to ensure that the developing nations receive new technologies and "freer movement of workers." The World Bank stabilised poverty. Fidel Castro castigated the United States and charged that the 727 billion dollars from World Bank reserves are in the United States, leading to the paradox that the poor countries are offering cheap long term financing to the wealthiest and most powerful country in the world with the reserves.

All this high falutin' talk of Fidel Castro and others will lead to nothing unless the Group of 77 get down to practicalities. Dr. Glen Martin, Member of W.C.P.A's World Strategy Committee pointed this out to leaders in the Cuban Government and Cuban NGO's in an open letter in June 2001. He urged:

"...Cuba to take the lead among the Governments in the Group of 77 to free the world from its present nightmare of poverty, misery, disease, exploitation and environmental destruction. Indeed Cuba has called for unity among the debtor nations of the World. Article 17 of the *Constitution for the*

> *Federation of Earth* specifies a minimum of 25 nations acting together to change the present World Order. No nation can do this alone. This can be done soon and needs to be done soon...A true revolutionary is not only a person in solidarity with all oppressed people everywhere. A true revolutionary is someone who thinks outside the ideological box imposed by the old oppressive order. At WCPA-GREN, we do not accept either the economic or political assumptions of the current world order of exploitation and dominance. We are thinking creatively for a truly revolutionary future for human kind."

Dr. Glen Martin deserves an extended notice in this history. He is Professor of Philosophy and Religious Studies at Radford University in southwest Virginia. He is President of International Philosophers for Peace, an international association which issues documents concerning peace related matters and actively campaigns for the elimination of nuclear and other threats to global existence. The World Constitution and Parliament Association is indebted to him for bringing his wealth of learning in a voluntary capacity to further its aims and objectives. He takes an active part on WCPA's Strategy Committee and is a delegate to the Provisional World Parliament. He has spared time to promote the activities of the Global Ratification and Elections Network and serves on its World Co-ordinating Council. He also actively participated in the Graduate School of World Problems and the Institute On World Problems.

The World Office of the World Constitution and Parliament Association and the General Ratification and Elections Network, the nerve centre for all the activities described in this chapter during a period of forty-two years, was originally housed at 1480 Hoyt Street, Lakewood, Colorado, and later shifted to the more spacious building at 8800 West 14th Avenue in the same neighbourhood. Fully computerised with a well-ordered website and a competent staff, the headquarters was home to oppressed peoples and distraught national governments seeking humankind's release from poverty and want in a new age of Peace and Plenty.

The WCPA had planned to hold a Ratification Convention and Five Provisional World Parliaments alongside five Global Expositions during a 5 year period. This was explained to the leaders of the Group of 77 in June 2001. The plan was designed to build the new global economy within the essential framework of a democratic world federation with a federal world government. The concept was explained further. World fairs to date have been held in the so-called "first world", in economically and technologically developed countries. The Global Expositions planned by the World Constitution and Parliament Association are to feature primarily the potential of developing countries where most of the people of the Earth live. Simultaneously to feature the emergence of world federalism because it is clear that without world federation solutions to world problems cannot be realised. Exhibits will be called for from national governments and the private sector; N.G.O.'s; innovators with innovations; youth organisations. Exhibits to be featured on How Federal World Government will function: how each ministry of world government will help solve global problems: how the new global finance and credit system will work with the Earth Hour as common global currency. At the time of this writing, the WCPA is working on two venues –Libya and South Africa. [Editors' note: The ninth sessioon of Provisional World Parliament was successfully convened in

Libya, April 2006.] The Plan is being once again circulated to national governments, exhibitors in general and attendees. Acting together with leaders of the Group of 77, supported by the vast number of GREN organisations, WCPA is convinced that the New Global Finance System can replace the prevailing chaotic world order based on exploitation of the many to the advantage of the few.

Conscious that it should build leadership skills for the emerging Earth Federation, the first session of the Provisional World Parliament held in Brighton, U.K. had legislated for the establishment, of a Graduate School of World Problems and a World University System. At the fifth session of the Provisional World Parliament held in Malta in 2000, the importance of a crash programme designed to train cadres for the future world civil service and to develop the ministries of world government, was considered. Besides having a permanent world campus, the Graduate School was directed to hold a series of 4 to 6 week seminars on understanding global problems and administering world affairs towards their solution in Asia, Africa, the Near and Middle East and the Americas. A beginning was made in Takoradi, Ghana (West Africa) and Chennai, Tamil Nadu (India). A flourishing Campus is now in existence in Lucknow, Uttar Pradesh (India). Eugenia Almand, JD, Executive Director of the Institute On World Problems, needs to be commended for her work in researching and expanding the scope of the Institute On World Problems and the Graduate School of World Problems (G.S.W.P.). Alongside this work, she produced a thesis on the same subject and won a Master's Degree from California State University, Northridge. Eugenia writes: "Graduates of the School of World Problems will be expected to have mastered the understanding and vision necessary to function in a truly integrated, federal democratic world order". This writer, who amongst his other work is President of the Institute On World Problems, has found it rewarding to work with Eugenia, Dr. Glen Martin and others on the board.

Earth Federation Pictorial History

featuring photographs from sessions of the Provisional World Parliament held at venues around the world

Introduction

Part of the story of the World Constituent Assemblies should be told in pictures. Unfortunately, many of the pictures from the world constituent assemblies are few and scattered. Some of those held at the archives of the World Constitution and Parliament Association seem to have been lost after break-ins at the Lakewood, Colorado office during which various records were stolen. Some pictures are on hand but are not verified as to the venue they represent. For others we are awaiting permissions for reproduction, as they have been published elsewhere. As of publication of the first volume of Emerging World Law, the editors are working to compile a photographic section from the World Constituent Assemblies for the second or third volume of Emerging World Law.

There are more photographs available from the sessions of the Provisional World Parliament. Many of the photographs available may be thought of as plain and uninspiring. We have provided some photos from several of the sessions, as well as some photos taken during intersession activities, such as seminars of the Graduate School of World Problems. It should be kept in mind that these provide only glimpses of the various meetings that have been held.

This is one of the last photos of the late Dr. Terence Amerasinghe, longtime Co-President of the World Constitution & Parliament Association. Dr. Amerasinghe also served for many sessions as the principal Co-Speaker for the Provisional World Parliament. Here, Dr. Amerasinghe is receiving the Visionaries for Peace Award shortly before giving the closing keynote address at the 7th International Conference of Chief Justices of the World at the World Unity Conference Center, City Montessori School, Lucknow, Uttar Pradesh, India. December 2006.

Reproduction of the classic painting "Royal Pavilion East Front from Nash's Views" by John Nash. John Nash was both the designer for the renovation of the Roval Pavilion as well as the painter of this 1826 masterpiece. The Royal Pavilion in Brighton, England, was the venue for the first session of the Provisional World Parliament in September 1982. (Reprinted by permission of the Royal Pavilion and Museums, Brighton & Hove, United Kingdom. www.royalpavilion.org.uk/)

Left to right: Ram Niwas Mirdha, MP; unidentified member, Sir Dr. Reinhart Ruge, Dr. Terence Amerasinghe, Dr. Bal Ram Jakhar, Lok Sabha; security guard; India President Zail Singh; 2 unidentified members; then WCPA President N. S. Rao; Margaret Isely, then WCPA Secretary; H. Philip Isely, then WCPA Secretary General. (March 1985.)

Roy Johnstone, Member of the Provisional World Parliament from Jamaica, addresses the third session. Others left to right: Yogi Shantiswaroop, India; Margaret Isely, USA; Sir Dr. Reinhart Ruge, Mexico, H.P. Isely, USA, and Dr. Terence P. Amerasinghe.

One of several committee meetings held at the third session of the Provisional World Parliament, Fontainebleau Hilton, Miami Beach, Florida, June 1987.

Facing the adversity of visa denials, the fourth session of the Provisional World Parliament found its venue in a conference room at the Alpha Aeropuerto Hotel, Barcelona, 1996.

Some Members of the 5th Session of Provisional World Parliament gather for a photograph. Qawra, Malta, 2000.

The late Dr. Rashmi Mayur, Chair of the Commission for the Environment for the Provisional World Parliament, addresses the Parliamentary Committee on the Environment. Qawra, Malta, 2000.

Dr. Hanan Awwad and Co-Speaker Dr. Terence Amerasinghe discuss legal points during the Committee meeting on Palestine and the Middle East. Qawra, Malta, 2000

Students of City Montessori School, Lucknow, perform classical Indian dances for chief justices, international jurists and the World Constitution and Parliament Association at the 2nd International Conference of Chief Justices of the World, December 2001, at Lucknow, India.

Chief justices, international jurists and executive members of the World Constitution and Parliament Association held panel discussions at the 2nd International Conference of Chief Justices of the World, December 2001, at Lucknow, India.

The Graduate School of World Problems held its first international seminar with participants from Ghana, Togo, Nigeria, Cote d'Ivoire, Sri Lanka and United States. Takoradi, Ghana, May 2002.

Top: His Excellency President Gnassingbe Eyadema and Cabinet of Togo
Bottom, from left: Dr. Eugenia Almand, Dr. Terence Amerasinghe and Dr. Simfei Balouki met with President Eyadema and the Togolese Cabinet on 2 consecutive days to discuss the holding of Provisional World Parliament meetings in Togo, including the concept of the Founding Ratification Conventions. Presidential Palace. Lomé, May 2002.
(Photos courtesy of His Excellency Gnassingbe Eyadema, late President of the Republic of Togo, West Africa.

Teachers and students of the *Institut Scholaire d'Application de Kara* (INSAK) welcomed the Institute On World Problems to hold seminar at INSAK campus in Kara, Togo, which was then held in May 2003. (Photo April 2002.)

Dr. Preeti Shankar of City Montessori School, Lucknow (front second from left), coordinated and convened the Seminar on World Problems for World Parliament in June 2002 at the Gompti Nagar campus of City Montessori School, Lucknow. CMS received the 2002 UNESCO Prize for Peace Education.

The Graduate School of World Problems held a world problems and world law seminar at Gompti Nagar Campus of City Montessori School, Lucknow.

At sixth session of Provisional World Parliament, Bangkok, Thailand, March 2003. Left to right: Sir Dr. Reinhart Ruge, the Venerable Bhikku Ariyawansu Dr. Suchart Kosolkitiwong as Convenor of the Sixth Session, Yogi Shantiswaroop, and Mr. Surinder Singh Machanda.

The conservative Thai military had observers attend to ensure security for participation of Thai government and parliamentary officials.

The sixth session of the Provisional World Parliament adopted the pioneering principle that the world legislation depends on world parliamentary participation. World legislation is not subject to ratification or veto by any national government, but only to the vote of the world parliament itself, with national participation open.

The ceremony lighting the candle of world law and world peace. former India Supreme Court Justice Sawant, on the left, was the keynote speaker for the 7th Session of the Parliament, in Chennai, 2003. Mr. Ananthanaryanan, second from the right, was and is a chief local organizer for the Parliament in south India.

Dr. L. M. Singhvi, Chief Advocate of the Permanent Court of Arbitration at The Hague lit the lamp and gave keynote address at the 8th session at City Montessori School, Lucknow, Uttar Pradesh, India, August 2004. Dr. Singhvi has also been a member of both the Lok Sabha and the Raja Sabha, the lower and upper houses of India's national parliament.

At the eighth session, the Provisional World Parliament deliberated on the creation of a world juvenile justice system, on the structure of the world electoral system, and on water resources. City Montessori School, Lucknow, Uttar Pradesh, India. August 2004.

Japanese Esperantists from the Jinrui Aizenkai (Universal Love & Brotherhood Association) and Esperanto-Populariga Asocio (EPA) successfully moved the adoption of Esperanto as a world auxiliary language. 8th session of Parliament. Lucknow, U.P., August 2004.

About 400 lawyers and judges from various states of India attended the 8th session of Provisional World Parliament. Lucknow, U.P., August 2004.

Each year in December, Chief Justices of Nations, eminent jurists and international lawyers convene in Lucknow at City Montessori School Lucknow for the International Conference of Chief Justices of the World. This is a photo taken from the 7th Conference in 2006. 19 national chief justices attended and 18 supreme court justices and other judges came in representation of their respective chief justices.

Dr. Amerasinghe presented Dr. Suleiman Shahumi, Foreign Secretary of Libya, to give the keynote speech at the ninth session of the Provisional World Parliament. Tripoli, Libya, April 2006.

Senator Samuel Oyatolu Oyebisi of Nigeria (Former Senator NCP) coordinated the Founding Committee for the African Children's Parliament, which here petitioned the ninth session of the Provisional World Parliament for assistance in combatting malaria. The Parliament subsequently allocated for a diseases fund. The session convened in the Grand Hall of the El Kabir Grand Hotel, Tripoli, Libya, April 2006.

Dr. Simfei Balouki addresses the tenth session of the Provisional World Parliament at the Congressional Palace, Kara, Togo, West Africa, June 2007.

Youth from the Univesity of Kara and from other schools performed in a cultural performance at the closing ceremonies of the 10th session of the Provisional World Parliament, Kara, Togo, West Africa, June 2007.

Many additional photos of the sixth, seventh, eighth, ninth and tenth sessions of the Provisional World Parliament are available at the photo gallery of the editor Dr. Glen Martin, available at www.radford.edu/~gmartin.

Chapter Three Addendum

Recent History of the Provisional World Parliament

The Provisional World Parliament matures by passing from its original international convention law framework to the more appropriate parliamentary law format

"History seems to us an arena of instincts and fashions, of appetite, avarice, and craving for power, of blood lust, violence, destruction, and wars, of ambitious ministers, venal generals, bombarded cities, and we too easily forget that this is only one of its many aspects. Above all we forget that we ourselves are a part of history, that we are the product of growth and are condemned to perish if we lose the capacity for further growth and change. We are ourselves history and share the responsibility for world history and our position in it. But we gravely lack awareness of this responsibility."

Hermann Hesse (1877–1962)

Eugenia Almand

As Herman Hesse pointed out, we share the responsibility for world history. Hopefully, the human awareness of this responsibility will grow strong with widespread roots to create a triumphant further growth and change.

After the fifth session of Provisional World Parliament in Malta, Philip Isely became seriously ill for several weeks. His recovery was uncertain. Many members of the executive cabinet of WCPA met in Lakewood, Colorado for discussions.

Over several months, Philip Isely slowly recovered. Then he announced engagement with Eli Kungulovska of Macedonia, whom he had met at the Malta session of the Parliament (Margaret Isely had passed away three years before.) In the late spring of 2001 they were married.

In December of 2001, the WCPA cabinet met in Lucknow, India, during the 2nd International Conference of Chief Justices of the World (on Article 51 of the India Constitution), where the Chief Justices declared for a World Parliament for deliberating and adopting enforceable world law for the operation of the world judiciary. The cabinet sought to outline plans for a session of the Provisional World Parliament, but was not able to come to agreement.

During the months that followed, the WCPA cabinet continued to be eager to hold a new session of the Provisional World Parliament. However, plans and reports were not forthcoming from the Lakewood Office. Philip Isely called a WCPA cabinet meeting on short notice (in violation of WCPA by-laws) in late summer of 2002. Because notice was so short, Dr. Amerasinghe and Dr. Rashmi Mayur had no way of participating. Only five people attended the meeting, one of whom was Philip Isely's new wife and another his paid clerical secretary. At this meeting Philip Isely attempted to change WCPA by-laws and to make his new wife both Deputy Secretary-General and Treasurer. Many members of the WCPA cabinet questioned the validity of the meeting and its decisions. Meanwhile, plans were in development for the sixth session of Provisional World Parliament to meet, not in India, but in Thailand.

From the time of his new marriage in the spring of 2001, all six paid workers at World Headquarters in Denver, Colorado were, one by one, laid off until there finally was only the clerical secretary left and, eventually, she too, was laid off and the formerly active offices there were, for all practical purposes, closed. Over the next several years the once vibrant worldwide magazine of WCPA, *Across Frontiers*, came out less and less frequently, with less and less content since very little was happening at World Headquarters.

A Session of Parliament in India would have to wait until after a session in Thailand. The World Peace Envoy, that is, the Reverend Bhikku Ariyawanso (Dr. Suchart Kosolkitiwong), together with the World Peace Envoy Office, was interested to host a session at an early date.

However, Philip Isely, now 86 years of age, was not able to keep the pace of the others who were arranging for the session. Philip Isely, after leadership for so many years, declined to assist in the preparations and declined to come.

Since he also declined to contribute any money for organizing the parliament, members of the Executive Cabinet contributed their own funds for the development of the Parliament. It was the first session of Provisional World Parliament done entirely without the participation of Philip Isely. Dr. Amerasinghe had called a meeting of the Executive Cabinet in connection with the Bangkok Parliament, with more than 30 days advance notice to all members (including Philip Isely) as the by-laws require. Isely declined to respond, still insisting that his new wife was now Treasurer and Deputy Secretary-General of WCPA and that his changes in the by-laws were valid, even though none of these things were ever validated by the Executive Cabinet.

For months, Dr. Amerasinghe, Co-President of WCPA, and other members of the Executive Cabinet, tried to reason with Philip Isely concerning these issues. Finally, at the Cabinet meeting in Bangkok, which included a quorum consisting of Mr. Sarwar Alam, Dr. Eugenia Almand, Dr. Amerasinghe, Dr. Dauji Gupta, Dr. Glen Martin, and Dr. Reinhart Ruge, the decision was made to remove Isely as Secretary-General. When this announcement was officially sent to Mr. Isely, he refused to accept it and proceeded to arbitrarily state that Dr. Amerasinghe was "fired" appoint a new "President" for WCPA, a poet who until only recently had very little to do with our movement.

Subsequently, all the officers and membership of WCPA went with the legitimate decisions of the Executive Cabinet in Chennai and Philip Isely was left virtually alone, with his new wife and his new "President," and a closed down former "World Headquarters." A new World Headquarters was set up in Radford, Virginia, under Dr. Glen T. Martin as Secretary-General, with Asia Offices under WCPA President Dr. Amerasinghe in Colombo, Sri Lanka, and Africa Offices under Dr. Simfei Balouki in Kara, Togo.

Dr. Phichai Tovivich, President of the Office of the World Peace Envoy, was Chair of the Local Organizing Committee for the Parliament. Mr. Dhanabhumi Pabhassarakul helped greatly to coordinate the arrangements. The Parliament was held at the Bangkok Centre Hotel in late March of 2003 in Bangkok. Colonel Dr. Somkid Risangkom, Member of Thai Parliament and Representative of the President of the Senate, participated and gave the opening keynote address. Associate Professor Yandej Thongsima, Member of Thai Parliament and Chief Advisor to the Prime Minister of Thailand, participated and gave the closing keynote address.

Up until this time, the Provisional World Parliament had convened, deliberated and adopted world legislation according to the old school style of convention law format. This is to say that the wording of five of the first twelve world legislative acts of the Provisional World Parliament had included provisions that the acts not be in effect until the acts had also passed through the legislatures of the national governments of the world. This requirement was in addition to the requirement for preliminary ratification of the *Earth Constitution*. So if we do the math – the *Earth Constitution* plus five statutes – that makes six documents in need of ratification. Six documents times some 200 national governments makes 1200 non-integrated national ratifications, to be accomplished on little or no budget. This was clearly not a practical avenue for moving forward, especially since the Provisional World Parliament had a full legislative agenda but was so far batting zero on legislative ratifications.

So the Provisional World Parliament had to consider its true role. Was it to be another mere advisory world parliament? In the course of the past century, the world has seen about ten advisory world parliaments of various names. These bodies would recommend, petition and cajole national governments. Wars would continue, one after another, overlapping and engulfing nations without any end to it. Advice to be "peaceful" is of little value when there is no over-arching protection of enforceable world law. So if the Provisional World Parliament were now to continue on this path as a mere advisory body, its true destiny could never blossom.

There is an essential distinction between international conventions and a true world parliament. That distinction is that the world parliament transcends the shirking of responsibility that avoids framing its work in terms of a binding social contract applicable to everyone. The World Parliament is open to democratic participation. If a country so wishes, the country can participate in the deliberations of the world parliament and vote for or against any particular world legislative measure, fulfilling the true destiny of democracy. However, if a country is unable or unwilling to participate in a democratic world parliamentary process, how could we expect that country to make a responsible decision on world affairs through self-enclosed national deliberations? Do not the national governments have enough on their national agendas without vainly attempting in isolation to address world problems, too? So, it was never the rightful place, and there was never the capacity for national governments to address these issues at a national level. Hence the inefficacy of international conventions.

To address this world legislative crisis, the sixth session of the Provisional World Parliament took up the challenge to never again accept new world legislative proposals that would require national ratifications. The formerly adopted world legislative acts were amended to remove the corresponding provisions requiring national ratifications. This affected the following world legislative acts: WLA#1 for disarmament; WLA#2 for the World Economic Development Organization; WLA#6 for an Emergency Earth Rescue Administration; WLA#7 for a World Government Funding Corporation (now Earth Federation Funding Corporation); and WLA#11 for the Earth Financial Credit Corporation.

The removal of these encumbrances was a revolutionary conceptual breakthrough. No longer would the Parliament think of itself as petitioning the nations or needing to placate the Machiavellian politics of the nations. For the nations were now understood to be illegitimate as autonomous, sovereign states. Their legitimacy could only be restored if they became part of the emerging Earth Federation under the authority of the *Earth Constitution*. Now, the Provisional World Parliament had established a precedent by which further integrating world legislation could be developed, adopted and implemented.

This precedent also helped create a template for review of the entire body of international convention law for conversion–for transfer, re-constitution and integration into world parliamentary law format. Hence, the very format by which the world legislative acts debated and passed by the Parliament was transformed. The Parliament began using the highest quality rules for legislative drafting, widely recognized for drafting binding legislation.

At the sixth session, there was landmark legislation, the World Legislative Act #13 – The World Peace Act – for recognizing and responding to a wide variety of crimes against humanity and war crimes that were listed neither in the *Elements of Crimes* nor in the *Rome Statute*. For instance, the primary economic impetus of multi-trillion dollar investment in bomb production corporations is prohibited under the legislation, with prohibition against purchase, sale or brokerage of stock in companies that build bombs or conveyances of bombs. In subsequent sessions of the Provisional World Parliament, the World Penal Code was adopted to specify the sentencing parameters for individuals convicted of violating these laws. Also, a means of legal divestment was initiated, so that persons who were already engaged in the illegal activities during the period before a legal divestment was possible would be able to legally extricate themselves and agree to no longer violate these world laws. (The Parliament further delineated these provisions in 2007 by World Legislative Act #40.)

In addition to the adoption of the World Peace Act, the Provisional World Parliament deliberated and adopted World Legislative Act #14 – the World Security Act. The World Security Act is enabling legislation to further define and regulate the Enforcement System of the Earth Federation as defined in the *Earth Constitution*, Article 10. The Enforcement System is a civilian (that is, non-military) system for the vigorous and effective enforcement of the world legislation and the *Earth Constitution*. This is not a so-called peace-keeping force comprised of units from national militaries such as the U.N. possesses. Rather it is a civil law enforcement system for the wide variety of functions necessary for just and effective enforcement: forensic investigation, apprehension & arrest, prosecution, remedies & correction and conflict resolution. These functions are empowered on a global level within a tightly regulated regime that requires recognition of principles of *habeas corpus*. The overall program is scheduled to be super-funded for an adequate dedicated civilian force to apply and ensure compliance with the democratically created laws of the Earth Federation.

Additional world legislation was adopted, including the following:

World Legislative Act #15 - enabling legislation for the World Bench for Human Rights enabling the people to directly seek redress beyond the Enforcement System;
World Legislative Act #16 - creating a Hydrocarbon Resource Board to manage world hydrocarbons as part of the heritage of humanity, rather than permitting ownership under any particular corporation or national government;
World Legislative Act #17 - enabling legislation for the Commission for Legislative Review, including professional and uniform legislative drafting guidelines; and
World Legislative Act #18 - for a Provisional Office of World Revenue.

After the sixth session, the delegate Members attended the 60th birthday celebration for the Bhikku Ariyawanso (Dr. Suchart Kosolkitiwong) at the Kuan Yin Inter-religious Park south of Bangkok. Kuan Yin Inter-religious Park is a Buddhist yet ecumenical park which celebrates and honors cultures from all around the world, encouraging people to understand the beauty of diversity within human religious cultures without fomenting conflict.

At the fifth session of Provisional World Parliament there had been a decision to return to India for a session. Preparation was postponed while legislative agenda was developing. By the time of the Bangkok session, additional necessary world legislative bills were undergoing rapid revisions. The seventh session of Provisional World Parliament could be held soon after the sixth. The eighth session could be held soon after the seventh.

The sixth session had adopted dozens of prohibitions associated with war activity or with preparations for war. There was an urgency for penal provisions to correspond with the many prohibitions. Parliamentary custom is to provide the judiciary with sentencing parameters for crimes, so that there can be an approach to equal protection, and also to be able to state to the public what the legal consequences are for specific illegal behaviors. So a World Penal Code was on the agenda for the seventh session.

Also, Members of the Provisional World Parliament had noted that there was a somewhat parallel development of world legislative code in the Assembly of States Parties to the Rome Statute for the International Criminal Court. A highly comprehensive body of statutory code, albeit confederal, was developing from the Assembly. With some review and modification, the Provisional World Parliament would be able to consider and adopt versions of the Assembly of States Parties' statutes that would be fully federal in format, and that would also honor the principle of equal protection (U.D.H.R. Article 7.), and the principle that the will of the people is the basis for the authority of government (U.D.H.R. Article 21.3.)

Originally, the steering committee for the session had planned on holding the seventh session at Pune. However, preparations were going too slow. Sri Karikar Vaitha, the eldest known world federalist in South Asia, recommended Chennai (also known as Madras) for the seventh session of the Parliament. After the steering committee discussed this for some weeks, Sri Karikar Vaitha was made Chair of the local steering committee and the preparations shifted to Chennai. Professor Ramajunam Ananthanarayanan of Chennai coordinated the local endeavor.

The Seventh Session of the Provisional World Parliament convened as planned on 26th December 2003, at the Palmgrove Hotel, Chennai (Madras), India, inaugurated by former India Supreme Court Justice P. B. Sawant, and presided by Dr. Terence P. Amerasinghe and by Sir Dr. Reinhart Ruge.

The Session deliberated and adopted six new legislative statutes:

World Legislative Act #19 - Criminal Code Penalty Classification;
World Legislative Act #20 - World Bench for the Criminal Court;
World Legislative Act #21 - Office of World Patents & Intellectual Property Rights;
World Legislative Act #22 - The Economic Equity Act;
World Legislative Act #23 - Global Accounting Standards; and
World Legislative Act #24 - *Rules for Procedures and Evidence* for the Criminal Court.

Additionally, a bill for an Act for a Global Peoples Assembly Movement was introduced, deliberated and sent to a standing parliamentary committee for report at the Eighth Session of the Provisional World Parliament. Major legislative amendments to World Legislative Act #9, for the Ministry of the Environment was introduced, deliberated and tabled to the next Session, and one resolution on citizen responsibilities was introduced, deliberated and tabled to the next Session.

The Session deliberated and adopted four new resolutions and one memorial: A resolution adopting "Manifesto of the Earth Federation" as an official policy statement of the Provisional World Parliament; a Pledge of Allegiance to the Earth Federation; the Chennai Declaration; a resolution adopting "Subverting the Coming Totalitarianism" as an official policy statement of the Provisional World Parliament; and a "Memorial to the Assembly of States Parties". The Session formed a judicial committee for the purpose of elaborating a legislative draft for a World Bench for Juvenile Cases, as indicated by the Criminal Court Statute. Additional information on the bills presented at the Seventh Session of the Provisional World Parliament is accessible at www.worldproblems.net. The legislative work, as amended and adopted by the Provisional World Parliament is regularly posted at this web site.

The Seventh Session of the Provisional World Parliament deliberated and adopted a revised version of the *Rome Statute of the International Criminal Court* as the *World Bench for Criminal Cases.*

The *Rome Statute* was well drafted by professional jurists (A. Koroma, D. Thiam, J. Crawford, A. Bos, et. al.), and at the time had been ratified by 92 national governments (now 108) that have declared the Statute to be conditionally supreme world law applicable to individuals for world crimes. These governments have also convened the Assembly of States Parties, which has authority, albeit under instruction, to draft, deliberate and adopt world statutory law. In a limited, confederal and *ad hoc* sense, the Assembly of States Parties functions as a legislative body to the World.

With these limitations, some great difficulties existed for the *Rome Statute,* and for the citizens of Earth affected by the *Rome Statute* as accepted by the Assembly. For one, the *Rome Statute* was originally drafted and adopted as a confederal court process, without true, full compulsory jurisdiction, that is, without benefit of the knowledge of the *Constitution for the Federation of Earth*:

* Articles 2 and 16 allowed the United Nations Security Council to override decisions of the World Criminal Court.

* Article 72 allowed confederal military circumvention of the World Court.

* Part 9, from Article 86 to Article 98, dozens of provisions granted the World Court mere powers to request that were obviously unbecoming of a World Court, which requires the power of *mandamus*, the court order, in all the respective provisions.

* Articles 100, 109, and 112 through 118 had fiscal provisions that were merely confederal and therefore inadequate.

* Articles 124 and 127 allowed non-acceptance of jurisdiction and withdrawal, respectively, which created yet more unnecessary weakness in the World Court Statute.

The legislative bill of the World Bench for Criminal Cases was introduced to re-consider the *Rome Statute of the International Criminal Court*. The purpose was to deliberate and adopt improvements to give the Statute true character as global, just, world legislation, amenable by the World Parliament. The Seventh Session of the Provisional World Parliament considered the weaknesses and loopholes of the original *Rome Statute*. After deliberation, these significant proposed changes were adopted to greatly strengthen the Statute. In the view of the Provisional World Parliament, the Statute, as amended, stands as supreme statutory law. It is a legislative act. As such, it is not subject to ratification by national governments. However, the Provisional World Parliament did enact a separate Memorial to the Assembly of States Parties, urging the Assembly to adopt the amended version of the Statute, as well as two other related statutory acts of the Provisional World Parliament: *Rules of Procedure and Evidence*, and the Criminal Code Penalty Classification (Penal Code). These final two acts were largely based on the work of the Assembly of States Parties and on features of the criminal justice system in the State of Arizona, in the United States.

It is noteworthy that from *Rules of Procedure and Evidence*, only about one page was amended out of the original document of 97 pages. The new *Rules of Procedure and Evidence* includes provisions for jury process. Lack of jury provisions had been a major objection to the original statutes for the world criminal justice system, but now the Provisional World Parliament is further addressing this concern with its newly forming World Jury Commission.

The Global Accounting Standards that were adopted by the Session were based on the standards of the International Accounting Standards Board. It is hoped that by adopting these rigorous and professionally developed standards, the Provisional World Parliament is constructing a stronger fiscal base for its operations.

A motion was made by the City Montessori School delegation to reconvene as the eighth session of the Provisional World Parliament in August 2004 in Lucknow, Uttar Pradesh, India. This proposal was unanimously adopted. As both Speakers, Dr. Terence Amerisinghe, as well as Sir Dr. Reinhart Ruge, were faced with personal emergencies, Provisional World Parliament Vice-President and Treasurer, Dr. Glen T. Martin, presided on the final day of deliberations. As most of the deliberative agenda of the Provisional World Parliament had been addressed before the end of the day on 29th December, the seventh session adjourned one day early.

Mr. Jagdish Gandhi, Founder Manager of City Montessori School, Lucknow, served as Chair of the local organizing Committee for the eighth session of the Provisional World Parliament. Mr. Raj Chandola, then Head of City Montessori School's World Unity and Peace Education Department, coordinated for the session.

The eighth session of the Provisional World Parliament convened as planned on 10th August 2004, at the City Montessori School, Lucknow, Uttar Pradesh, India, inaugurated by His Honor L. M. Singhvi of the Permanent Court of Arbitration (this is a civil and public bench of the World Court with seat at The Hague). His Honor L. M. Singhvi is also both a former Member of Indian lower house (Lok Sabha) and former Member of the Indian upper house (Raja Sabha). The eighth session was presided over by Dr. Terence P. Amerasinghe. Attendence varied with the functional proceedings.

During L. M. Singhvi's keynote address, the Provisional World Parliament had over 400 lawyers and judges in attendance. That at least half of these were women lawyers and women judges was refreshing and perhaps can be partly attributed to conditions of better gender equity in at least part of India's higher education system.

His Excellency Singhe Yadav, Chief Minister of Uttar Pradesh was Chief Guest at the closing ceremonies on the final day, 14th August 2004.

The Session deliberated and adopted six new legislative statutes:

* World Legislative Act #25 - World Government Records Preservation;
* World Legislative Act #26 - Education Act;
* World Legislative Act #27 - Statute on the Rights of the Child (adopted with amendments from previously existing world convention format from United Nations General Assembly (1989);
* World Legislative Act #28 - World Bench for Juvenile Cases;
* World Legislative Act #29 - World Boundaries and Elections Administration Act (with provisions for a Global Peoples Assembly Movement); and
* World Legislative Act #30 - the Water Act.

Major legislative amendments to World Legislative Act #9, for the Ministry of the Environment were adopted. Major legislative amendments to World Legislative Act #7 were adopted, notably the recognition of the sunset of the provisions for original incorporators, and a name change from World Government Funding Corporation to Earth Federation Funding Corporation. Major legislative amendments to World Legislative Act #11 were adopted, notably an entire transition to the Earth credit and currency system, including the establishment of value of the Earth unit of credit and currency, based on time of labor pegged to a basket of commodities, and linked to the Economic Equity Act.

The general legislative amendments made earlier at the sixth and seventh session of the Parliament were reconfirmed, regarding the independence of the *Earth Constitution*, the lack of necessity for national level ratification of World Legislation (no world legislation requires national ratification for full force and effect). Also by general consent, amendment was adopted to World Legislative Act #17, the Commission for Legislative Review, regarding the full numeric codification of the legislation of the Provisional World Parliament. All world legislation and world legislative bills are now to be presented in full numeric form, unless prior international convention requires a supplemental codification, as for instance in *Elements of Crimes*. Adoption of amendments to the World Legislative Act #18 were made, including a name change to the Provisional Office of World Revenue.

The Eighth Session deliberated and adopted six new resolutions and one memorial:

* A Declaration on the Rights of People of Earth to Create and Ratify a World Constitution;
* A Statement on Emerging World Law (Statement on the World Court);

* A Resolution on Good Government;
* A Resolution on the promotion of Esperanto and auxiliary languages;
* A Policy Statement on Taxation;
* The Lucknow Declaration of 2004; and
* A Memorial Directive to the President of the United Nations General Assembly, M. Jean Ping, to call the General Assembly to vote for a General Review Conference in conformance with United Nations Charter Article 109, for considering and adopting the *Constitution for the Federation of Earth* to replace the United Nations Charter.

A delegation from Jinrui Aizenkai of Japan motioned to support the study and promotion of the designed language Esperanto for use by the Earth Federation, including use by the World Parliament. The Parliament discussed this proposal and adopted Esperanto as a working and official language of the Earth Federation. The Parliament resolved to facilitate and promote the learning of Esperanto and communication in Esperanto to delegates from a wide variety of linguistic backgrounds. The adopted resolution also provisions for instantaneous interpreters, translators, accessibility options, other auxiliary languages and computer translation programs.

The Global Tax Accounting Standards that were adopted by the Session were based on the recommended policy of the International Chamber of Commerce. It is hoped that by adopting these professionally developed policies, the Provisional World Parliament is constructing a stronger fiscal base for its operations.

Several venues were recommended for reconvening as the Ninth Session of the Provisional World Parliament: Togo, Libya, Greece and other locations. However, since there was not adequate substantiation of strength at any of the proposed venues, the Provisional World Parliament delegated the determination of the venue for the Ninth Session of the Provisional World Parliament to the Standing Parliamentary Commission for subsequent intersession decision.

After the eighth session, Dr. Glen Martin had the opportunity for meetings with the Revolutionary Committees Movement of Libya, which had long expressed interest in the Provisional World Parliament and the *Earth Constitution*. During the meetings, Dr. Martin had the opportunity to have audience with Brother Moammar Khadaffi, Leader of Libya and of the Revolutionary Committees Movement.

The Parliament was invited to hold its ninth session in Libya. Dr. Ramadan Breki, a Vice-President of the World Constitution and Parliament Association served as Chair of the local organizing committee. Mr. Rajab Sheha coordinated for the preparations and holding of the session.

The ninth session of the Provisional World Parliament convened at the famous El Kabir Hotel in Tripoli, from 11th through 15th of April 2006. Mr Suleiman Shahumi,

Secretary, Committee for Foreign Liaison, of the Peoples' National Congress of Libya delivered the keynote address as Guest of Honor for the session of Parliament.

The ninth session deliberated and adopted eight new world legislative acts:

* World Legislative Act #31 - the World Ombudsmus;
* World Legislative Act #32 - the Department for Conflict Resolution;
* World Legislative Act #33 - the Fissile Production Prohibition;
* World Legislative Act #34 - the Nuclear Weapons Elimination Protocol;
* World Legislative Act #35 - the Nuclear Contamination Act;
* World Legislative Act #36 - the Guantánamo Directive;
* World Legislative Act #37 - Public Utilities; and
* World Legislative Act #38 - World Federal Privileges & Immunities.

Children delegates of a Committee for African Children's Parliament had an audience to present Memorial Bill for provision of treated mosquito nets to all schoolchildren in malarial endemic regions of Africa, beginning with pilot programs in association with the African Children's Parliament. Commission for Legislative Review moved for consideration of Memorial Bill & funding. Dr. Dauji Gupta, who is a Vice-President of the World Constitution & Parliament Association and is a long-time Member from the India legislature of Uttar Pradesh, assisted with the drafting and revision for the Public Utilities Act. For the first time in any session of Provisional World Parliament, the funding was drawn up as a direct action of the Parliament, rather than legislatively basing the financial resources on loans or on tributes from any national governments. This simple short act of the Parliament marked a significant advance in the fiscal policies and principles of world parliamentary law.

The deliberations for the ninth session were broadcast live by Radio for Peace International. Ms. Jean Parker operated the radio broadcast and recording. The Parliament had 58 delegates from 29 different countries. Dr. Simfei Balouki, World Constitution & Parliament Association Coordinator for Africa, motioned that the next session for the Provisional World Parliament be held in Togo, West Africa.

The last night of the Parliament, the Government of Libya gave us a special invitation to all delegate Members of the Provisional World Parliament to come to the national palace to attend the 20th anniversary commemorative service of the United States bombing attack on Libya which killed 500 civilians including the Leader Moammar Khadaffi's 1 year old stepdaughter, who was sleeping in the national palace bedrooms when the attack came. Though of course parts of the service were very solemn, there was also a sense of expression of forgiveness and also celebration that relations with the United States were improving. At the service, José Carreras sang accompanied by the Vienna Symphony Orchestra. Also during the performance, Dr. Simfei Balouki came upon the stage to dance while Lionel Richie sang "All Night Long".

In April of 2007, during the planning for the 10th session of Provisional World Parliament, the Executive Cabinet was unsettled by news from Dr. Terence Amerasinghe that he was suffering from some ailment that caused severe loss of appetite. Specialists in Sri Lanka were uncertain of the cause, so in May Dr. Amerasinghe flew to his second home in Toronto, Canada, for diagnostics there. Dr. Amerasinghe phoned to tell us that due to his illness it was unlikely that he would be able to participate in the 10th session, but that each of us should not hesitate on his account. The last week of May, he informed us that surgery might be required. Dr. Amerasinghe made us each promise that no matter what happened in the surgery or afterward, we would persevere and move forward with the session of Parliament on schedule.

Dr. Amerasinghe died in surgery on 1st June 2007. There was funeral held in Toronto. Memorial service was held again on 15th July in his native city of Colombo, Sri Lanka, with his family and friends in attendance, and with condolences from the many people who could not make the distant trip into the war-torn country. A friend and former law student of Dr. Amerasinghe, the former Vice-President of the International Court of Justice, His Honour Christopher Weeramantry, gave eulogy at the ceremony. Also friend and former law student of Dr. Amerasinghe, WCPA Deputy Secretary-General Eugenia Almand, J.D., also gave eulogy at the memorial service. Dr. Amerasinghe's ashes were interred at the gravesite together with the ashes of his late wife.

In keeping with the final wishes of our President Speaker Dr. Amerasinghe, the 10th session of Provisional World Parliament convened at the Palais du Congrès, in Kara, Togo, West Africa, from 21 to 24 June 2007. The Parliament made Parliament former Vice-President Dr. Glen T. Martin to be Speaker and President of the Parliament.

Numerous world legislative amendments were adopted:

*An amendment to WLA#35 annulled the 1959 letter of understanding between WHO and IAEA. (This letter had blocked WHO from warning public of radiological dangers.) Parliament annulled the letter with stipulation that copy of the annulled letter would be presented to Provisional World Parliament at the next session of parliament for refinement or other reconsideration.

*Amendments to WLA#11, WLA#23 and other world legislation, the symbol for Earth credit and currency unit was changed from "θ"to "⊕" [circle with cross or x inside] and "&". (θ was too easily confused for an eight at the beginning of a string of numbers. "⊕" is the more customary symbol for Earth, and also is iconic for an analog clockface.) An amendment designated the credit and currency unit name as the "Earth Hour".

*An amendment to WLA#22 adjusted the minimum wage to ½ Earth Hour per hour and maximum wage to 2 Earth Hours per hour.

*Amendments to WLA#36 withdrew amnesty at the Guantánamo Base from Base Commander level on up, except for replacement commanders. The amendments declared the prisoners as kidnap victims, canceling the previous order to remand to the World Court, and ordering the immediate unconditional release of all victims, with compensation and follow-up. Further amendments extended the area of the world eminent domain to include a five kilometer perimeter of the entire Guantánamo Bay, including the North Bay and Ensenada de Joa, with the border coordinates of North boundary at 20°06' North latitude. West boundary at 75°17' West longitude; East boundary at 75° 02' West longitude, and South boundary at 19°42' North latitude.

Four world legislative acts were deliberated and adopted:

*World Legislative Act #39 - Prohibition of Unauthorized Destruction of Illegal Financial Instruments;
* World Legislative Act #40 - Indemnity Bonds;
*World Legislative Act #41 - Posting the Stock Law; and
*World Legislative Act #42 - Universal Guaranteed Annual Income.

World Legislative Act #39 involved the Prohibition of Unauthorized Destruction of Illegal Financial Instruments with comprehensive prohibition against unauthorized destruction of illegal financial instruments for preservation of evidence and assured disinvestment from illegal weapons manufacture. To assure accountable retirement of illegal stocks (divestment) and for due process of the World Court, Act #39 prohibits unauthorized destruction of illegal financial instruments and records: bomb corporation stock certificates, holding certificates, bank liens on illegal stock and related documents. Refer to WLA#13.1.2.1.

World Legislative Act #40 creates Indemnity Bonds to catalyze a system of divestment from illegal weapons corporation stocks. Act #40 introduces a comprehensive program for Earth Federation issue of indemnity bonds with conditional amnesties and conservation of resources for early and registered divestment.

World Legislative Act #41 for Posting of the Stock Law defines comprehensive guidelines for posting the world stock law at stock exchanges around the world. Act #41 requires public posting of world law regarding brokerage and trade of illegal financial instruments.

World Legislative Act #42 for a Universal Guaranteed Annual Income defines a system for a comprehensive guaranteed annual income for all adults of the Earth Federation, including provisions to recognize domestic and agricultural work as well as to provide social security pensioning. The universal guaranteed annual income becomes effective at first operative stage of Earth Federation.

The Session adopted a Resolution, drafted by the Democratic Social Forum of Bangladesh, on the Trial of War Criminals and Perpetrators of Genocide and Crimes Against Humanity.

The 10th session of the Provisional World Parliament also conditionally adopted Rules of Procedure for a Founding Ratification Convention with the direction for the agencies of the Provisional World Parliament to emit a Call to a Founding Ratification Convention for the simultaneous ratification of the *Constitution for the Federation of Earth* by about 25 national governments worldwide. The Parliament decided that the adopted Rules of Procedure will only be published in French and English or other languages after further proofreading and formatting in French, and release by the Standing Parliamentary Commission on Translations, or otherwise further decision by the Provisional World Parliament.

The 10th session authorized the Call to the 11th Session of the Provisional World Parliament. Parliament was originally to convene in Kolkata, India, in January 2009. Dr. Santi Nath Chattopadhyay, Executive Director of the International Society for Intercultural Study and Research and Programme Director of the World Peace Congress, Member of the Provisional World Parliament, was serving as as the Chair of the Local Organizing Committee. Unfortunately, Dr. Chattopdhyay became ill and the local organizing committee was faltering. The Executive Cabinet began search for alternative venue. Auroville in Pondicherry was discussed, but there was not time for a January venue, and in summer Auroville would be too hot. The Auroville committee suggested Van Niwas Ashram Complex in Nainital, in the Himalayas of Uttar Anchal, India. This happened to be a site previously examined as a possible venue. In October 2008, the Aurobindo group approved the site. The Call to the 11th Session of the Provisional World Parliament is for 1rst through 10th July, 2008, in Nainital.

Among agenda items are environmental legislation and elaboration of provisions for jury process in court trials. Since the *Rome Statute* is coming due for general review conference by the Assembly of States Parties by July of 2009, one might expect that directives or recommendations regarding that review will also be discussed. After the April 2006 adoption of the Nuclear Weapons Elimination Protocol by the Provisional World Parliament, Costa Rica and Malaysia together have redacted and in January 2008 submitted their revised version to the General Assembly of the United Nations (UNGA document #A/62/650.) The Provisional World Parliament will consider an updated revision of this extremely important document for universal nuclear disarmament. The Parliament is scheduled to reconsider the letter of understanding between the World Health Organization and the International Atomic Energy Agency which the Parliament conditionally voided in June of 2007 because of unsafe public conditions created by the letter, which had illegally prohibited WHO from warning the world public about any radiological dangers. The Parliament will be deliberating strategies for building general administration as well as for recruiting, managing and remunerating staff. Some of these agenda items have been long in development. Further details of agenda will develop between now and the 11th session of Parliament. There will likely be more legislative material than can be deliberated during the session. The Parliament itself prioritizes, finalizes and decides the agenda items, so we will see what happens in the next session of Parliament as the time comes.

Chapter Four

Century Twenty-One: Humanity at the Crossroads

Manifesto of the Earth Federation

Unanimously ratified as an official statement
of the Provisional World Parliament
at its Seventh Session,
Chennai, India, December 2003

"Men speak of natural rights, but I challenge any one to show where in nature any rights existed or were recognized until there was established for their declaration and protection a duly promulgated body of corresponding laws."

Calvin Coolidge (1872–1933)

Glen T. Martin

Foreword

This manifesto summarizes, as briefly as possible, the multiple crises our world is facing and the kind of response necessary if we are to survive the twenty-first century. It demonstrates on every page why federal world government under the *Constitution for the Federation of Earth* is necessary in the very near future. In 1995, the report of the blue ribbon "Commission on Global Governance" outlined many of the global crises we confront today and stated that "the present generation knows how close it stands to cataclysms." This manifesto shows this claim to be false.

The present generation insists on remaining in denial and willful ignorance. Yet the arguments for federal world government are compelling and decisive. They are presented on nearly every page of this manifesto. Those who have ears to hear and eyes to see, need to listen and look. This manifesto is intentionally as short as possible so that it may be easily read and understood. It deals with the issues of terrorism, war, the environment, social movements, the U.N., the system of nations, and global economics. It may well be one of the most significant documents you will ever read.

The Prologue below describes the final crossroads that human beings face today. We can reap the insights of twentieth-century science showing the holism and interdependency of every aspect of our universe. Or we can continue in fragmentation, division, and mutual destruction. Our world of war, terror, massive poverty and misery, and environmental destruction cannot endure much longer. Human beings must become politically and economically whole or we will perish. The choice is clear and simple, and the momentous consequences at stake are not difficult to discern.

Part Two, what the Earth Federation has accomplished to date, reviews the momentous legacy that we inherit from the generations who created the *Constitution* and the Provisional World Parliaments. A tremendous movement has emerged around the *Constitution for the Federation of Earth*. It has been translated into many languages and people in nearly every country are beginning to rally around the banner of the Earth Federation. Much excellent work is already accomplished. We do not have to invent the wheel. We are in a position today to set the wheel in motion.

Part Three, humanity poised at the crossroads between destruction and liberation, expresses the reasons we are at a crossroads for human existence on this planet. It considers global economics, the nation-state system, the United Nations, and global social movements. It shows the interdependence of all these movements in the nexus of crises that we face on Earth. It shows the role of our major world institutions in creating and deepening these crises. We must choose for a civilized world order today, with a clear choice and decisive action, or we will surely destroy the Earth for ourselves and for all future generations.

Part Four, failure of the United Nations, considers the United Nations, its history, its structure, and its failure to transform our world into a world of peace with justice. It lays out the facts for all who are willing to see and hear, and shows clearly why the U.N. has failed. It details how the many worthwhile agencies of the U.N. could really do their job if they were incorporated into the Earth Federation and, for the first time, had adequate funding and authority.

Part Five, the dead end environmental hopes of Rio and Johannesburg, looks at the Environmental Summits at Rio de Janeiro in 1992, at Johannesburg in 2002, and other treaties such as the Kyoto Protocol. It documents the failure of the nations to live up to their environmental agreements (leading to ever greater planetary catastrophe) and why they do not and cannot act to save the global environment. It shows that the very structure of our world system, which is historically outdated and manifestly unjust, is preventing humanity from saving the planetary environment.

Part Six, the condition of our world at the dawn of the twenty-first century, considers the nexus of global crises that we confront at the outset of our new century. It provides the latest scientific facts documenting all these crises: the crisis of fresh water, the crisis of poverty, the crisis of arable land and viable fisheries to feed the people of Earth, the environmental crisis, the population crisis, the crisis of sickness and disease, the crisis of education, the crisis of global economics, and the crisis of global militarism.

It demonstrates in what ways these crises are all interdependent and interrelated and underlines how they all stem from the fragmented world system of so-called sovereign nation-states and global monopoly capitalism. It makes clear for each crisis why federal world government is the only viable solution. It specifies exactly how these problems are addressed by the *Constitution for the Federation of Earth*, including how the *Constitution* specifically addresses the problems of militarism, terrorism, and war.

Part Seven, common sense economics under democratic world government, outlines the intelligent and fair economics that are being developed by the Earth Federation to create a world of prosperity and equity rather than one of scarcity and misery. The seven economic innovations outlined in Part Seven are readily understood and easily implemented. It makes clear that a world of plenty and justice is not merely a utopian dream but a very real possibility under the *Constitution for the Federation of Earth*. All reasonable people can understand the rationality and simplicity of these options. Another world is truly possible.

Finally, Part Eight, where do we go from here? addresses the actions we must take at this historical crossroads to create a sustainable, just, and prosperous world order. These actions are common sense and based on clear, compelling arguments, and extensive factual evidence. Part Eight appeals to the poor majority of people on Earth to act on their own behalf and on behalf of a future for their children.

But it points out that we are all made poor by the present world order of injustice, misery, and war. We are all citizens of the Earth under the *Constitution*, and today we are all made poor by the wretched conditions that the old rotten system perpetuates into the future. It calls for all citizens of the world to unite under the Earth Federation. If many citizens of the Earth were to stand up on behalf of a decent world order at this crossroads of history, a world of sanity, peace, and prosperity would be just around the corner.

1. Prologue

1.1. Human history on planet Earth has reached its final crossroads. Human beings can continue on the road to imminent perdition, or we can rise to a new level of civilization for the Earth. This manifesto clearly describes that crossroads for all who care to see and hear. Our message is not a confused and sentimental longing for a better world as is so often heard today from groups seeking to protect human rights, or advance democracy, promote peace, or address poverty and disease. Our message is clear, precise, and specific. The reasons we are on the road to imminent perdition can be easily understood. And the reasons for the Earth Federation are clear, compelling, and decisive. This manifesto is about that choice. Time is running out when this choice will be available to us. The time for firm decision is now. There is no other time.

1.2. This choice is not an arbitrary or irrational one. For the concept of holism (unity) emerges as the fundamental insight of every twentieth-century revolution in science. The Einstein revolution showed that nature and the cosmos must now be understood holistically. And Quantum physics has shown this to be true on the sub-atomic level. On both the macro and micro levels, our universe exhibits unity as a seamless, interdependent field of space/time/energy/matter. Ecology and the biological sciences have also demonstrated holism at every level of living nature, including the encompassing ecosystem of the Earth.

1.3. The major sphere where fragmentation, division, and reductionism remain is the sphere of human social life in the system of territorial nation-states and the global economic system of violence, greed, and non-cooperation. It is no accident that Einstein was an outspoken advocate of planetary federal government. He understood the inescapable holism of the world we live in. The choice before us is to convert our thinking to holism (the unity and interrelatedness of all persons on the Earth) or to continue into destruction with our fragmentation and violence. This holism is embodied in the *Constitution for the Federation of Earth* through a dynamic and comprehensive relationship of unity-in-diversity. We must immediately choose the holism of federal world government or we may soon perish from the Earth.

1.4. Today, a creative groundswell in the movement for a sane federal world order is making the current lords of the Earth tremble in their corruption and fragmentation. The people of the world are awakening to the lies and distortions of the media, their subservience to power, and the corrupt interests defending the old rotten order while destroying the Earth for future generations. We citizens of the Earth Federation are spokespersons of this new world order predicated on wholeness, democratic values, and the common good of all persons on Earth. They may imprison or kill us as individuals, but the groundswell of awakening among the people of the Earth is unstoppable. We are poised at a crossroads for humanity. We must choose wisely – for humanity – or we may perish from the Earth.

2. What the Earth Federation has accomplished to date

2.1. We citizens of the Earth Federation, gathered at this historic Seventh Session of the Provisional World Parliament, recognize that we are building on the collective efforts of thousands of world citizens who worked tirelessly since 1958 (and throughout the twentieth century) to bring us the great legacy that we inherit today. They are to be honored and revered as prophets and designers of the Earth Federation that is destined to create truly civilized life on planet Earth for the first time in human history.

2.2. Our predecessors, some of whom are among our leaders yet today, gave humanity, first and foremost, the *Constitution for the Federation of Earth*. This document, one of the great milestone documents of human history, was forged to the finest quality by the effort of hundreds of world citizens in four Constituent Assemblies from Wolfach, Germany in 1968 to Troia, Portugal in 1991. Today, it has been distributed worldwide and translated into twenty-two languages.

2.3. The *Constitution* is recognized by many people around the world as the supreme law for Planet Earth, superseding all laws passed by the approximately 190 territorial entities that today call themselves "nation-states" and claim the false right to pass laws for their territories not accountable to the rest of humankind. We understand today that no merely territorial entity has the right to claim absolute sovereignty for its laws unaccountable to the universal principles of equity, justice, freedom, and peace embodied in the *Earth Constitution* and widely endorsed universal declarations of rights and responsibilities, including the Earth Charter. True sovereignty resides with all the citizens who live on Earth, not within limited territorial entities.

2.4. The *Constitution* creates a parliamentary system that will not be subject to subversion and corruption as has turned the so-called liberal democracies into "national security states" dominated by executive branch secrecy and arbitrary power. There will be no need for executive secrecy and arbitrary power when all nations are demilitarized under the rule of democratically legislated laws. The world parliament has three houses (a House of Counselors representing all humanity, a House of Nations representing every nation on Earth, and a House of Peoples with proportional representation from 1000 electoral districts worldwide). The main branches of government under this Parliament (the World Judiciary, the World Executive, the World Police and Attorneys General, and the World Ombudsmus) are all directly accountable to the Parliament and have no power to suspend the *Constitution*, withhold spending of the budget, violate human rights, create a military apparatus, or otherwise subvert the universal guarantees given to all nations and peoples by the *Constitution*.

2.5. By recognizing the sovereignty of the people of Earth and universal economic and political rights for all citizens, the *Constitution* ends once and for all the power-politics of nation-states that struggle for economic advantage, control of resources, military hegemony, and spheres of influence. This struggle continues to destroy the rights and the lives of millions around the globe, as it has for centuries. It mandates equitable use of the Earth's essential resources for all people, making possible a truly civilized world order under the rule of democratically legislated law for the first time in history.

2.6. Will there be "opposition parties" within the Earth Federation? Of course. Unlike the pseudo-diversity of today's two party systems, a genuine diversity of voices is the heart and soul of democracy. Under today's common one or two party systems, the group in power attempts to suppress, silence, co-opt, or eliminate its opposition. There is a lack of that mutual respect and unity necessary to legitimate the diversity of genders, cultures, religions, ethnicities, or political viewpoints.

2.7. Sheer diversity without authentic unity results in conflict, violence, and the rule of the most powerful. The Earth Federation is predicated on "unity in diversity." Diversity is protected and encouraged precisely because it is encompassed by the unity of the universal rule of law and universal citizenship. Everybody has a voice and a stake in the welfare of the whole and of everyone else. A genuine plurality of voices listening to one another (rather than trying to suppress and drown one another out) is here made possible for the entire Earth.

2.8. The second great accomplishment of our predecessors was to take many active steps to actually initiate democratic world government under the *Constitution*. They have given us a body of provisional world law that has been carefully developed since the first Provisional World Parliament met in 1982, and they have begun elaborating the ministries necessary for the functioning of world government. Since 1982, the Provisional World Parliament has met in six different locations around the world, the Sixth in Bangkok, Thailand in March 2003, the Seventh in Chennai, India in December 2003, and the Eighth in Lucknow, India in August 2004.

2.9. Today, the world inherits from our predecessors a body of quality planetary law that serves as a model and a beacon for all humanity lighting the path by which we can move from a world of chaos, war, and imminent disaster to a world of peace, freedom, equity, and justice. The Sixth Provisional World Parliament established a Commission for Legislative Review to codify and professionalize this body of world law. When the first operative stage of World Government has begun, and the official World Parliament has been constituted, this body of law will serve as a tremendous gift to humankind, and available to the Parliament for review, modification, or immediate ratification.

2.10. Those of us worldwide who have personally ratified the *Earth Constitution* are now ambassadors and spokespersons for the Earth Federation, voices crying in the wilderness of global chaos, violence, and fragmentation, but also prophets speaking for the future of civilization and the greatest hope for humanity. The Earth Federation lives at the moment through us until the day when it will become recognized and embraced by all of humanity. On that day we will be honored and revered as courageous pioneers who selflessly struggled against tremendous odds on behalf of our precious planet Earth, universal justice, and a decent life for future generations.

3. Humanity poised at the crossroads between destruction and liberation

3.1. Recognition of our great movement is happening everywhere among the poor and dispossessed majority of the world. Recognition that all the tired options of the past have long been exhausted and that the present world order is kept in place not by hope and vision for a better future but by institutionalized force and violence. This poor and dispossessed majority are the great hope for humanity and the Earth Federation.

3.2. Monopoly conditions dominated by global corporations and imperial governments enforce upon the world's poor majority a global system of economic exploitation and domination. The World Trade Organization, the International Monetary Fund, the World Bank, imperial governments, and the heads of multinational corporations work in secret forums to effectively eliminate all opposition to their criminal pillage of the planet and its resources. This system is one of planetary institutionalized violence, forcing unnecessary death and disease on untold millions who are victims of the rape of the planet by the rich and powerful. This system is enforced by the overt violence of strategically placed global weapons sales, counter-insurgency military training provided to dominant elites in poor countries, political manipulation, threats of economic sanctions or punishment, and outright invasions or bombings of countries that attempt to take an independent course.

3.3. Yet with the failure of the United Nations to prevent genocide against the Iraqi people culminating in the 2003 invasion of their country, and the total failure of the U.N. to prevent the complete devastation of Afghanistan over the past twenty years, it has become clear to the poor nations and peoples of the world that the U.N. is a false prophet and an ideological cover for the preservation of the system of global exploitation and domination. The recently created "International Coalition Against Terror," illustrates the impotence and irrelevancy of the U.N. This coalition creates a permanent, global war system largely comprised of the wealthiest nations, most of whom have a history of colonial domination of other countries, who today produce most of the world's weapons, including weapons of mass destruction.

3.4. Independent people's movements, like the World Social Forum, have sprung up globally, determined to create a more just and equitable world order. There are also many non-governmental organizations working to protect human rights, relieve poverty, preserve the environment, or promote health-care throughout the world. They speak of "resistance" to the dominant order, of restoring "living democracy" to the planet, empowering the poor, canceling international debt, or "food first" for the world. Yet they offer no clear means for achieving these goals within a world system predicated on war, national imperialism, and power politics, only vague ideas about making economics and politics more democratic, more just, or more responsive to the needs of the poor.

3.5. The Earth Federation does not want to be "more responsive to the needs of the poor." The Federation provides the means for eradicating poverty from the Earth. We do not work to make the existing institutions of power, domination, and exploitation (the "sovereign" nation-state and global capitalism) "more democratic." There is no way to make the flawed and fragmented power-based institutions of today's world "more democratic." They are inherently totalitarian and undemocratic, whatever their ideologies may claim, and have produced a living hell for those unfortunate enough to be their victims.

3.6. The metaphor of hell is apt, for the institutions of the "sovereign" nation-state and their global economic system have created a living hell on Earth for the past five centuries through their policies of merciless conquest, genocides of indigenous peoples, brutal systems of slavery, vicious colonialism, endless colonial wars, world wars, and militarized neocolonial domination of today. Presently, for at least 1.5 billion citizens on this planet, and for the poor majority of the world, they truly represent the rule of hell on Earth. We understand that these institutions must be replaced by genuine federal world government and by an economic system premised on rapid sustainable development and the welfare of all the Earth's citizens.

3.7. The key to solving the terrible global crises confronting humanity is the creation of global institutions capable of planetary action and premised on creating a world of equity, freedom, justice, and peace. There are no such institutions in the world today. Only democratic world government is capable of dealing with global crises on a planetary level. Gradual modification of the present flawed institutions of the world is a prescription for planetary suicide.

3.8. Approximately 150 years ago, another manifesto announced that a "specter was haunting Europe," the specter of violent revolution and expropriation of the stolen wealth of the rich. We announce that a peaceful revolution is at hand, more far reaching than that earlier manifesto could have imagined. We announce that there is no need to expropriate the wealth of the rich to create global equity, freedom, justice, peace, and prosperity.

3.9. Our revolution is more far reaching because it is planetary in scope and because humanity is at the final crossroads. The earlier revolution was premature, for humanity had not yet reached its final crossroads. Our revolution for the first time in history creates planetary institutions that represent all the world's people based on the principle of unity-in-diversity. No one is excluded. For the first time in history, the needs, rights, and interests of the whole of humanity are taken into account by democratic, truly planetary institutions.

3.10. The choice today is between certain chaos, barbarism, and destruction or democratic world government under the *Earth Constitution*. Our revolution abolishes not only the worst features of capitalism and monopoly corporate pillage as did that earlier manifesto. It also abolishes that other demon from hell that has wreaked havoc on the Earth for the past five centuries: the absolute "sovereignty" of nation-states. The so-called "sovereign" nation-state is a fragmented, irrational, and dangerous institution that has divided the Earth into approximately 190 competing territorial entities. Its very existence denies the sovereignty of the people of Earth. We must not only eliminate the worst features of capitalism. We must also eliminate the warring, imperialistic, and greedy institution of the absolute sovereignty of nation-states.

3.11. Since nation-states call themselves "sovereign," and recognize no authority of law above themselves, they are always in a relation of chaos, struggle, and *defacto* war with one another. This fact was pointed out by Thomas Hobbes, Baruch Spinoza, Immanuel Kant, G. W. F. Hegel, and many other political thinkers. In this situation, action for the common good of humanity and the Earth is in principle impossible. The only authentic and legitimate sovereignty is that of all the people who reside on Earth. And the

Earth Constitution embodies that sovereignty in effective world government in which all people and nations live under the rule of democratically legislated law for the first time in history. The holism of nature and the ecosystem of Earth is for the first time realized also in human affairs. The common good of the Earth and future generations can for the first time be effectively addressed.

3.12. The old order is dead and dying. The world is at its final crossroad. We can sink further toward imminent destruction of the Earth and its inhabitants led by the rich and powerful corporations, governments, and financial institutions concerned only to preserve their system of exploitation and domination as long as possible into the ever darkening future. Or we can move to a higher level of human dignity and civilization on planet Earth by uniting in one world under the *Constitution for the Federation of Earth.*

4. Failure of the United Nations

4.1. Many nations and many well-meaning people in the world, however, have not embraced a truly new world order under the *Earth Constitution* but have followed the U.N. system based on the failed institutions of the past five centuries of the modern era. The United Nations was created by the victors of the Second World War in order to ensure their continued dominance in the affairs of the world. This has been illustrated in its sad history of veto upon veto, preventing the majority of nations in the world, representing the majority of the people of the world, from altering the world order in the direction of equity, freedom, justice, or peace.

4.2. The ideals embodied within the U.N. Charter, such as preventing "the scourge of war" are belied by its undemocratic organizational structure and its underlying assumptions. According to the U.N. Charter, the "scourge of war" is to be prevented in the last resort by the Security Council going to war. Such absurdities of our present world order permeate the document. The U.N. Charter is based on "the sovereign independence" of its member states, reaffirming the flawed and false principle of territorial sovereignty. For this reason also imperial nations can ignore the U.N. when they choose, and go to war at will entirely outside of the U.N. system.

4.3. In practice, for the past five centuries, this doctrine of "sovereign independence" has meant that the powerful nations dominate and exploit the weaker nations. It has meant that the global north has become rich through exploiting the global south. Today, this system continues through the GATT system of the U.N., the World Bank, International Monetary Fund, and the World Trade Organization. The global south (Africa, Latin America, South Asia) is poorer, more exploited, and more miserable today than ever before in history. The wealthy elite in the global north is richer today than ever before in history.

4.4. The United Nations has failed to prevent war. There have been some 130 wars since the advent of the U.N. resulting in some 25 million war-related deaths, most of them civilians. The U.N. has failed to create security for the people of the world. It has allowed rampant world militarism with ever faster and more destructive weapons created and deployed at the staggering figure of approximately 850 billion U.S. dollars per year. Not only has military insecurity increased worldwide, the people of the world are today faced with an every growing number of insecurities connected directly with the failure of the United Nations.

4.5. Food insecurity has increased worldwide, as has water insecurity, insecurity with respect to health care, and insecurity of educational opportunities. Under the U.N., millions have been displaced from their rural lands and been forced into horrible slums in gigantic third world cities to be faced with community chaos and insecurity in the form of drugs, prostitution, violence, and crime.

4.6. The U.N. has failed to eradicate poverty. Global poverty is significantly greater today than when the U.N. was created. Today, largely under domination by the United States with its shameless promotion of multinational corporations dedicated to pillaging the planet of its resources and cheap labor in the service of private profit, the U.N. is turning more and more to "private solutions," making deals with private, profit making corporations to supply education, water, electricity, health care, vital drugs, farming, or transportation to so-called developing countries.

4.7. Dozens of countries around the world have seen their essential infrastructures and services that served the people privatized and destroyed by employee cutbacks, profit gouging, and holding poor populations hostage to their monopoly control of essential services. The bottom line is that the concept of "developing countries" is a misnomer, for most of the world remains merely a colonial service area to supply cheap resources, labor, and quick profits for the wealthy corporations and their sponsor governments. Under the present system, there is no hope and no real intention of these countries ever "developing."

4.8. In addition, the U.N. has failed to limit the exploding global population that today is in excess of six billion persons and growing by eighty million new persons each year, numbers of people that the finite resources of the Earth cannot possibly support. Finally, it failed to protect the disintegrating environmental integrity of our planet despite holding huge conferences on the environmental crisis in Rio de Janeiro in 1992 and Johannesburg in 2002.

5. The dead-end environmental hopes of Rio and Johannesburg

5.1. The June 1992 Earth Summit at Rio de Janeiro was a milestone in a clear understanding of our human condition on planet Earth. The documents produced at Rio show the understanding that the global crises are all interconnected and interrelated. We cannot protect the environment without simultaneously eliminating poverty, eradicating war and militarism, controlling population growth, and restricting the drive for economic gain through acting on universal principles of what sustains and protects the common good of the planet and its future.

5.2. By the time the 35,000 delegates met at the Earth Summit in Rio, it was clear that all development on the Earth must be "sustainable," for the planet could not much longer survive a model of development treating the finite resources of the Earth as an unlimited cornucopia for exploitation. Nor could the limited ability of the planet to absorb waste materials and pollution be treated any longer as an infinite cesspool, where industrial development indiscriminately externalized its costs and its wastes into the water, air, and soil. The people at the Rio Summit understood that sustainable development means meeting the needs and improving the quality of life in the present without sacrificing the ability of future generations to meet their own needs while living lives of quality and dignity.

5.3. The delegates at Rio created one of the great documents of the twentieth century: "Agenda 21." This document understood that workers and farmers in developing countries had to be empowered and protected, that protections and opportunities for women and children worldwide had to be strengthened, that education had to be disseminated to all peoples of the developing world. In short, sustainable development must necessarily mean reducing population growth, eliminating poverty, providing the education necessary for development. Agenda 21 also made it clear that definite, rigorous goals had to be set for the reduction of greenhouse gasses and ozone depleting gasses by nations and their industries, and that global fisheries, farmlands, grazing lands, and forests had to be preserved and restored. Many nations signed Agenda 21 and promised to achieve the goals set for them by the document.

5.4. The subsequent Earth Summit at Johannesburg, South Africa in August-September 2002 represented a widespread recognition of the failure of Agenda 21 and the hopes of Rio for bringing the world back from the brink of disaster. There was nothing wrong with the Agenda 21 plan itself. The nations of the world simply did not honor the commitment and demand to reduce greenhouse and ozone depleting emissions, to empower the developing world in ways that provided education, eliminated poverty, and reduced population growth, and to create a sustainable and integrated world economy and more equitable world order.

5.5. Why should any one of the 190 competing territorial units, each with its own internal problems and self-interest in mind, act for the common good of the Earth and future generations? The very assumption that they might do this was hopelessly naive. Why should any of the multi-billion dollar corporations now pillaging the Earth act for the common good of humanity and future generations? Familiarity with their actions around the world demonstrates that these organizations are often criminal in nature and run by criminals. Several of the books in the bibliography to this manifesto document in detail the worldwide criminal interrelationships between multinational corporations, banking institutions, governments, and even global terrorism. How naive for the people at Rio to believe that any hope for the environment was possible under the current world system!

5.6. Many at Johannesburg recognized that governments alone (of which the U.N. is officially comprised) cannot save the world from disaster. Many governments are not representative of their own people: many are dominated by big business interests, some are dominated by religious extremists or criminal thugs (dictators), many are under the thumb of the big imperial powers or the structural adjustment programs of the World Bank. For this reason, many world citizens struggled at the Johannesburg conference to get a voice for the non-governmental organizations at the decision-making tables.

5.7. They argued that governments (and their corporate partners) alone are not capable of representing the interests of the future, the people of the world, or the planet itself. Some progress was made in getting NGOs recognized as a voice in the dialogue about the future of the world, and some people, sadly, believe this represents a success of Johannesburg. But in reality it only illustrates the complete failure and hopelessness of the U.N. process.

5.8. Agenda 21 failed not because its goals were incorrect or unrealistic, but because it was a product of a United Nations Conference recognizing the "sovereign independence" of each of the 190 territorial entities on the planet and affirming a global economic system of crass greed and pillage. Agenda 21 was merely a treaty, like the subsequent Kyoto Protocol on the environment, like the United Nations Millennium Declaration of the year 2000, and like whatever agreements emerged from Johannesburg. Subsequently, corporations and imperial nations acted to destroy the Kyoto Protocol from within by creating a system for "pollution credits" or, as they call it, or "global emissions trading." This system has allowed them to continue trashing the environment while claiming that they are conforming to "free market" environmentalism.

5.9. The structure of the world system is deeply flawed and absolutely inadequate to the vital needs of the world to end poverty, war, population growth, environmental degradation, and social chaos. A system of 190 territorial entities all claiming sovereignty over some piece of land cannot possibly produce universal equity, freedom, justice, or peace in the world. A world economic system based upon the unbridled greed and self-interest of nations and corporations cannot possibility create sustainable development and save the planet from impending disaster.

5.10. 'To bring new voices of NGOs to the discussion table may push governments and public opinion towards recognizing existing injustices. International groups of doctors and others have prompted resolutions about land mines, an international criminal court, and the environment. However, naively assuming that this produces adequate and responsible remedies is a recipe for total disaster. NGOs, like world citizens, have a healthy democratic function but not a right to speak for all humanity apart from world government. The nations of the U.N. do not speak for all humanity but only for themselves and their sovereign interests. Neither are such NGOs elected by the people of the Earth to represent their interests.

5.11. The U.N. system is as undemocratic and unjust as any set of institutions could possibly be. The U.N. failure to protect the global environment and create sustainable development is not the result of a lack of understanding of the problems we face. It is a result of an organization premised on the particularized and inadequate institutions nearly five centuries old (the nation-state and global capitalism) and entirely inadequate to address universal needs and interests.

5.12. To add a powerless "peoples' assembly" to the already powerless General Assembly of the U.N., or to add the voices of a few NGOs to the dialogue about the world's future, may seem to some a giant step, but it is a feeble gesture towards a democratic rule of law among nations. It is to ignore the living hell that is the world we live in for a good portion of humanity. It is to ignore the impending cataclysms nearly upon us of global population increase, global epidemics, global water shortage, global starvation, global collapse of fisheries and farmlands, global warming, global flooding of coastal lands, global ozone depletion, global war, and global social chaos.

5.13. Democratic world government is the only rational option, the only possible vehicle that can represent universal and global needs and interests. The *Constitution for the Federation of Earth* is directed explicitly to the global crises faced by our planet: population, poverty, militarism, health care, education, and environment. It gives the elected representatives of the sovereign people of Earth the legal authority and the mandate to create sustainable development for the entire Earth and to transform the world to one of equity, freedom, justice, and peace. No other force on Earth can accomplish this task within the limited time available to us.

5.14. Replacing the U.N. Charter with the *Earth Constitution* does not mean dismantling many excellent U.N. organizations and their worthwhile infrastructure that can be used as a basis for the agencies of world government concerned with health care, the welfare of children, the rights of women, sustainable development, education and cultural exchange, labor standards, international shipping, postal regulations, meteorology, environmental standards, and other important fields. Many U.N. agencies do excellent work in all these areas despite the impediments placed in their way by sovereign nations and global economics. The Earth Federation will immediately increase the funding and global scope of all worthwhile U.N. agencies, converting them to ministries of the Federation. Many agencies of the U.N. are valuable and should be preserved. It is the U.N. Charter with its flawed assumptions that must be replaced.

5.15. The failed United Nations system is bringing the world ever nearer to complete disaster, as was recognized by many at Johannesburg. To invest more time and energy into that system is mad and even suicidal. We are one world, one humanity, one global ecosystem, one system of information and communication. We are deeply interdependent and interrelated with every other person on the planet. Yet we have failed to create any global institutions based on this truth. The *Constitution for the Federation of Earth* is the only viable document based on this understanding. Its Preamble states that "Humanity is One," and that the principle of "unity in diversity is the basis for a new age when war shall be outlawed and peace prevail," and "when the Earth's total resources shall be equitably used for human welfare."

5.16. The *Earth Constitution* represents, for the first time in human history, planetary institutions, planetary vision, planetary responsibility, and democratically guided planetary planning for sustainable development and the welfare of future generations. This is the only truly viable, widely publicized option presently available as we face the crossroads of the early twenty-first century. Shall we continue on our disastrous course of attempting to deal with planetary crises through fragmented and divisive institutions nearly five centuries old?

5.17. Or shall we move to a new level of existence on this planet, perhaps fulfilling the very meaning of our historical pilgrimage on Earth? Shall we at last create planetary institutions representing all the people of Earth, all the living creatures of Earth, and the welfare of future generations? The Seventh Provisional World Parliament (who ratified this Manifesto), along with the many thousands of planetary citizens who have ratified the *Earth Constitution* worldwide, recognize that we are the prophets and harbingers of a truly new world order premised on the universal principles of equity, freedom, justice, and peace. Our responsibility is correspondingly great. We must continue activating a global movement among the peoples and nations of Earth to ratify the *Constitution* and initiate truly democratic, federal world government before it is too late.

6. Condition of our world of at the dawn of the twenty-first century

6.1. The crisis of fresh water. There is a growing shortage of fresh water worldwide. Every person living needs approximately thirty gallons of clean water daily. Yet hundreds of millions of people live on less than ten gallons daily. As the population of the planet continues to increase by eighty million persons per year, so does the need for water. Yet underground aquifers from which most water comes are receding at an alarming rate. Four decades ago groundwater levels could be found a few meters below ground. Today in many places special wells and pumping systems are required to access water 180 meters or more beneath the Earth.

6.1.1. The size of the giant underground aquifers on which people depend for irrigation and to supply cities with water are steadily shrinking. The aquifer under the Midwest of the United States is half the size it was less than one hundred years ago. In addition, unsustainable industrial development has poisoned water systems around the world so that many groundwater systems are polluted with heavy metals and other toxins from mining, oil drilling, or manufacturing.

6.1.2. Governments of the world have also not acted to preserve the water that falls in the form of rain. They have not acted to preserve the forests that retain fresh water over the land and serve as a conduit to move the water inland from the sea. Irrigation systems, accounting for seventy percent of the world's fresh water use, irresponsibly waste immense amounts of water, often because of the drive to maximize profit rather than preserve the Earth for future generations. Meanwhile, drip irrigation systems are available that could conserve a tremendous volume of fresh water.

6.1.3. How is the global water crisis to be handled if not by democratic world government? Nation-states alone have no ability to deal with this global phenomena. Water patterns are global. Global warming is changing these patterns worldwide, creating droughts in some places and floods and hurricanes in others. Sources of water cross borders, as for example the sources of water in Bangladesh, with its immense problems of flooding, lie largely in India. Currently, water systems in many nations have been privatized, placed in the hands of global corporate criminals. Water prices have skyrocketed, while purity and protection of clean water supplies have evaporated. Only the World Parliament operating under the *Earth Constitution* can create a workable water policy for the entire planet.

6.2. The crisis of poverty. Poverty is greater and far more extensive today that ever before on Earth. 1.5 billion people, or close to twenty percent of the Earth's population, live on less than one U.S. dollar per day. This means a large portion of the Earth's population go to bed hungry each night. It means millions of malnourished children and immense human potential for creativity and development lost because malnourishment often leads to retardation or diminished intellectual capacity.

6.2.1. It is often truly said that there is enough food grown globally to feed all people currently on the Earth. But the global economic system distributes that food to those who can pay, to the wealthy first world nations, leaving hundreds of millions of people in the developing world hungry. Poverty cannot be eliminated through giving resources directly to hungry people. Charity is not development.

6.2.2. Poverty can only be eliminated through extensive programs of education, health care to eliminate the many diseases and diminished potential that go with poverty, non-exploitative finance capital to activate local and regional economies, and infrastructure development to enhance the economic multiplier effect that can come from widespread circulation of money between producers and consumers throughout the developing world.

6.2.3. There are no Earthly institutions that can accomplish all these goals in an effective and timely manner. To accomplish these tasks would take immense resources, planning, coordination, and oversight to provide education, health care, nonexploitative finance capital, and a high quality infrastructure throughout the developing world. Only world government representing the Earth Federation could do this. Without effective world government, there is no hope of eliminating poverty and misery from the Earth.

6.3. The crisis of resources for feeding the people of Earth. There are at least four features of the Earth that humans and animals depend on for food and survival: farmlands, grazing lands, ocean fisheries, and forests. All of these resources are being degraded and destroyed at alarming rates.

6.3.1. Farmlands lose many billions of tons of topsoil every year to wind and water erosion because of unsustainable farming methods. Farmlands worldwide are also being over-planted, leading to soil exhaustion and deterioration. Every year millions of acres of agricultural land are become unusable and are lost to human food production.

6.3.2. Grazing lands, where herds of goats, cows, sheep or other animals are pastured, are becoming degraded and diminished through overgrazing. Overgrazing eventually destroys the land itself, leading to growing desertification worldwide. Deserts, increasing in size worldwide, are largely waste that cannot support human or animal life. By some estimates, fifty percent of the land in Asia and Africa is now useless for supporting life.

6.3.3. Third, ocean fisheries are dying due to over-fishing and perhaps to the rise of ocean temperatures from global warming. The tonnage in fish harvests is diminishing each year. In some cases, such as the once rich North Atlantic fishery, the entire fishery has collapsed, costing the world millions of tons of protein once supplied by those fish each year.

6.3.4. Finally, we are losing the forests of the world. Forests hold the soil from eroding, store fresh water and move it inland, moderate the climate, provide a habitat for the Earth's wild creatures, and provide a wealth of biological materials for medicine and human well-being. They are also "the lungs of the Earth," since they bind the carbon dioxide given off by most human industrial processes and give off oxygen to replenish the atmosphere. As with agricultural lands, grazing lands, and fisheries, forests are disappearing from our planet at an alarming rate. The world loses approximately thirty million acres of rain forest per year.

6.3.5. As with the other crises listed here, the causes of this are well-known and understood. And as with the other crises, the factors are intertwined with the factors causing all these crises. Global militarism at 850 billion U.S. dollars per year obviously wastes immense resources that should be used for education and development. Global militarism produces immense amounts of toxic wastes, and war itself creates environmental havoc. Global poverty contributes to the destruction of forests since most people in the developing world use wood for cooking.

6.3.6. In addition, the global economic system of unregulated greed and self-interest unsustainably logs these forests for private profit. Global population pressures lead to over-farming, over-grazing, and overfishing, and hence destruction of the very basis for feeding future generations on this planet. Industrial pollution and the continued production of greenhouse and ozone depleting gases daily diminish the planet's ability to support life in the future.

6.3.7. What institutions in our world possess the ability to mount a coordinated, carefully thought-out, well-financed, and strategically designed plan for dealing simultaneously with all these interdependent and interrelated crises? There are none, least of all the United Nations which we have seen is predicated on the fragmented institutions of the past and committed to the barbaric and outmoded systems of "sovereign nation-states" and corporate pillage.

6.3.8. What is needed is not merely a coordinated policy of conservation, what is needed is a dynamic policy directed toward reversing the tremendous damage already done and restoring the Earth to ecological health. Only a World Parliament, representing all the people of Earth as well as future generations, with the authority and resources to carry humanity over the crossroad from possible extinction to a new world order of equity, freedom, justice, and peace, can provide the solution to these otherwise insurmountable problems.

6.4. ***The environmental crisis.*** The crisis of resources for feeding the people of Earth, like the water crisis, are part of a multi-dimensional breakdown of the planetary ecological systems. Depletion of the ozone layer that protects living things from the deadly ultraviolet radiation of the sun, destruction of the forests and phytoplankton in the oceans, exhaustion of fresh water supplies, and dumping of millions of tons annually of toxic wastes into the air, water, and soil, all constitute substantial disruptions of the health of the planetary ecosystem and portend eventual environmental collapse.

6.4.1. Global warming is a widely recognized scientific fact that has already resulted in massive weather pattern changes, increased melting of the polar caps, and unprecedented "superstorms." And it is widely recognized that global warming will inevitably bring rising oceans and flooding of the coastal lands of Earth, displacing more than a billion people and submerging a good portion of the Earth's remaining farmland. Yet little is being done to change this nightmare scenario. We are told that the demand for oil (a chief cause of global warming) will increase by thirty percent in the next ten years. And today the nations and multinational corporations of the world are fighting (economically, politically, and militarily) to ensure the "stability" of countries housing old oil reserves and to control vast regions of Asia in the light of the new reserves soon to be available from the Caspian Sea basin.

6.4.2. Under the current world system such madness (with the power and profit that the control of oil brings) is inevitable. Only a federation representing the entire Earth could have the political will and authority to convert the world to solar, wind, water, and hydrogen power, find ways of recycling and minimizing toxic waste, really protect the ozone layer, and restore the other essential features of Earth necessary for a quality human life for all persons.

6.5. The population crisis. The teeming slums and social chaos of Mumbai, Dhaka, Mexico City, or Rio de Janeiro spread diseases like Malaria, Cholera, Tuberculosis, and AIDS. They create pollution from cooking on innumerable charcoal fires, and they crowd more people into tiny areas than can possibly live on the resources available there. Such teeming slums in hundreds of cities around the world, create immense sanitation and water problems. They create social chaos, crime, drug and alcohol addiction, and they damage the environment simply because there are too many human beings in too small a space.

6.5.1. All over the world, overpopulation is causing havoc. It is crowding more and more people onto agricultural lands and villages that cannot support them. Desperate for income and work, millions are being driven into the vast slums of monstrous cities where a nightmarish life of suffering and deprivation await.

6.5.2. Eighty million persons per year are added to the population of the Earth. Many scientists estimate eight or nine billion persons on our planet by the year 2025. Yet even the current population cannot be sustained by the finite and diminishing resources of Earth. Ninety percent of the eighty million children born into the world each year are born into extreme poverty. Every new person requires another thirty gallons per day of potable water. Every person requires food, educational, health care, and infrastructural resources. Every person produces waste and pollution that must be absorbed by the environment.

6.5.3. While some governments have had limited success in reducing population, the problem is global, not territorial. Reducing population growth in Kenya will little affect the world's bleak future if the planet continues to add eighty million new persons each year to its limited carrying capacity. Only democratic world government has the authority and resources to promote the health of the whole planet.

6.5.4. The remedies are as simple as they are impossible under the system of territorial nation-states. Elimination of poverty, education, support for family planning programs, if done on a global scale with adequate resources and organization, can quickly reduce the birth rate on the planet. Some estimate that the Earth can only sustain reasonably well about 2.5 billion persons. Under the present world system, the goal of reducing the Earth's population to this level is a mere chimera. Under the Earth Federation, a significant reduction in the planetary birth rate is a sensible and rational possibility and can be achieved within fifteen to twenty years of the inception of world government.

6.5.5. The net result will not be costly for the people of Earth. Population reduction through education, family planning programs, and the elimination of poverty will add to the world's human resource potential, eliminate the cost of rampant diseases and the spread of AIDS, eliminate the costly effects of pollution generated by an unsustainable population, and free up the resources of the Earth for the prosperity of future generations.

6.6. The crisis of sickness and disease. Overcrowding, lack of basic sanitation, poor water quality, shortage of fertile land, inadequate nutritious food, environmental pollution all are causes of disease and crippling health limitations among the poor of the world. Fifty percent of the population of the world lack adequate sewage and sanitation systems. The sewage runs into local streams and rivers, and into the puddles in the dirt roads where children play and adults walk. Poor sewage systems threaten sources of clean water, compounding the risks and sources of possible disease.

6.6.1. Waterborne diseases like cholera and typhoid are common. These diseases have been eliminated in developed countries because we understand their causes and how to eliminate them through sanitation and clean water systems. The problem is not lack of knowledge and understanding. The problem is today's world system that makes providing clean water and sanitation to the poor countries of the world a virtual impossibility.

6.6.2. Anyone traveling in South Asia, South America or Africa is struck by the number of crippled and maimed people living in every city, town, and village. Polio and other preventable crippling diseases are common. People unnecessarily crippled by these diseases often become less productive and less useful to the economic potential of their societies. Early death and a drain on the health care systems of poor countries also comes from such common diseases as tuberculosis, malaria, or AIDS. Tuberculosis is on the increase worldwide as is AIDS. Yet dealing with these diseases requires dealing with all the other global crises outlined in this manifesto. It requires effective sanitation systems for all, clean and adequate supplies of water for all, education and adequate health care systems for all, and nutritious, adequate food supplies for all.

6.6.3. The transformation to a decent world order required is not a luxury or a utopian dream. It is an absolute necessity if the world is to have a future at all. More than a century after microbiology discovered the causes of most disease, many decades after the development of the technologies of water purification and sanitation, many decades after the development of antibiotics and drugs adequate to control most diseases, unnecessary sickness and disease are still increasing worldwide.

6.6.4. This epidemic of preventable sickness and disease among the world's poor is a shame upon the humanity of us all. It cannot be dealt with apart from democratic world government under the Earth Federation. The *Earth Constitution* mandates health care for everyone, education for everyone, clean and sanitary environment for everyone, not just for those who can pay, not just for those who now dominate and exploit the rest for their own benefit.

6.6.5. The AIDS epidemic alone requires vast resources and coordinated efforts across the world. Yet these are not forthcoming under the present world system. The entire continent of Africa is being ravaged by AIDS, with an estimated 28 million cases in this year, 2003, as well as the other diseases mentioned here. Only the Earth Federation with the resources, authority, and coordinated planning to deal with simultaneously with global sanitation, poverty, disease, pollution, militarism, land degradation, global warming, human rights protections, and universal education can adequately address the AIDS epidemic or the problems of preventable sickness and disease.

6.7. The crisis of education. Universal quality education is absolutely fundamental to sustainable development, just as it is to the elimination of poverty, the prevention of disease, and the control of population growth. In the developing world, some 120 million children do not even go to elementary school. Even where schooling is available, many millions of poor children throughout the world must go to work at an early age to help themselves and their families survive.

6.7.1. Eight and nine year old children in bare feet, with no parents anywhere to be seen, beg pennies from automobiles at stoplights in Managua and Mumbai. The AIDS epidemic in Africa alone may leave twenty million children orphans within the next few years. These children, and others in similar desperate poverty throughout the developing world, have little chance of becoming literate, let alone gaining enough education to become effective agents in the transformation of global society towards equity, freedom, justice, and peace.

6.7.2. Poor nations, strangled by international debt to the World Bank and wealthy First World financial institutions, are being forced through structural adjustment programs to sell off public educational systems, transportation systems, water systems, health care, and other systems to private, profit making enterprises. As a result education is becoming ever more elitist in the developing world as those who can afford to pay for private schooling get the tools necessary for success or escape from their native country to the first world, while the vast majority who are extremely poor are deprived of any opportunity for a decent education. Those who can afford an education often immigrate and this "brain drain" diminishes the number of skilled and educated people necessary for sustainable development.

6.7.3. Education, while absolutely essential to development, is not a priority for those remaining who struggle simply to survive from day to day. As with the other features of our planetary crises, education is not possible without eliminating poverty, without developing sanitation and clean water systems, without developed infrastructure from roads to computer terminals and telephone lines. Education is not possible while poor countries waste their resources on purchasing ever more sophisticated weapons from the first world arms merchants. Education is not possible when the Earth is adding eighty million new persons to its population each year. Education is not possible in the face of ever increasing food shortages and water shortages.

6.7.4. To create an educated population capable of energetic and creative solutions for sustainable development requires the complete transformation of our present institutions and an integrated solution to the interrelated nexus of global crises. Only federal world government under the *Earth Constitution* would have the resources, universal vision, and integrated, global approach necessary to solve the world's problems through putting education at the center of a global policy of sustainable development. Educated and energetic people can solve their own local sanitation and water problems, address the waste of their own governmental bureaucracies, initiate development projects, and control population growth.

6.7.5. The airwave communications spectrum supporting radio, television, telephone, and Internet must be used by the people of developing nations for free education of their populations concerning sanitation, family planning, agricultural methods, control of disease, and development projects. There is tremendous potential for real institutional transformation through education that is next to impossible under present global institutions.

6.7.6. Corporations are interested in private profit, not education for fundamental change. Governments are often interested in militarism and staying in power rather than in fundamental change. Only world government under the *Earth Constitution* can solve the crisis of education and make possible a quality education for every citizen of Earth. Only world government under the *Constitution* is unafraid of fundamental social change, since its mandate is precisely fundamental change to a world of equity, freedom, justice, and peace.

6.8. The crisis of global economics. The vocal protests at World Bank meetings and meetings of the World Trade Organization (WTO) around the world emphasize the elitist nature of the global economic system, controlled by multinational corporations, First World financial institutions, and powerful First World governments. This economic system, despite the rhetoric of "free trade" or "development" is designed, as were its colonial predecessors, to benefit the powerful financial players of the world and to ignore the consequences for the rest of humanity and future generations.

6.8.1. Corporations have gained extraordinary power in the last few decades. Even to the limited extent that territorial governments can deal with multinational corporations with more assets than many governments themselves, the corporations have taken steps to ever more exempt themselves from the environmental or social consequences of their practices. Corporations can now sue governments before secret WTO tribunals if, for example, environmental laws interfere with the profit margin of corporations doing business in those countries. Global economic regulations are formulated in secret by the powerful and imposed upon the weaker majority of the nations of the world. They are not formulated with the common good of human beings or the planet in mind, but for the prosperity and profit of private financial institutions.

6.8.2. Who is to regulate corporations and the powerful governments that support them? Who is to speak for a rational, democratically planned, and equitably designed economic system directed toward universal sustainable development? Clearly the U.N. has been colonized by these very multinational corporations as well as dominated by the powerful governments that represent these corporations, primarily the United States. Clearly the World Bank and the IMF serve these same interests.

6.8.3. The present global economic system has destroyed jobs in mass on the local level worldwide. It has created a race to the bottom where many poor countries compete to sell off their precious natural resources or other export products to the lowest bidder. It has destroyed effective environmental regulations everywhere. It has led the economies of entire nations to crash and burn in a chaos of poverty, social disintegration, and unemployment. Some examples of this (out of many) are the destruction of the economies of Somalia, Rwanda, Tanzania, Indonesia, Bolivia, Ecuador, and Argentina, with the ensuing horrific violence and social disintegration in each case.

6.8.4. A decent economic system for the world promoting universal prosperity and ending exploitation and domination in the service of private interests is impossible without federal world government under the *Constitution for the Federation of Earth.* Only enforceable world laws, applicable to all individuals (whether heads of corporations or heads of governments), can give us sufficient democratically guided economic regulation and activation to eliminate poverty and create genuine sustainable development worldwide.

6.8.5. The principles of a decent global economic system are rational, common sense, and easily attainable. Some of these will be described below. At this point we wish to make clear that there can be no dealing with the numerous global crises outlined here without an equitable and thriving planetary economic system. Only democratically legislated and enforceable world law can create such a system.

6.9. The crisis of global militarism. Global militarism has not decreased with the end of the Cold War. Weapons sales worldwide have only increased, as has the amount most nations of the world spend upon their military establishments. Neither has the world been able to create effective treaty bans on land minds, antipersonnel weapons, depleted uranium weapons, nuclear weapons, intercontinental missiles, or space-based weapons. Chemical and biological weapons are still being researched and developed by many nations.

6.9.1. Powerful forces have tremendous economic and imperial interests in preventing any progress towards arms control or demilitarization. We have seen that the world currently spends approximately 850 billion U.S. dollars per year on militarism and war. It is sometimes said that only half this amount spent annually for the next two decades could transform the world into one of equity, prosperity, and environmental integrity.

6.9.2. Yet to make this claim is to say little or nothing in the face of the immense forces of the world arrayed against arms limitations or demilitarization. To make this claim without challenging the global institutions promoting war – the system of so-called sovereign nations and the global economic system that makes war and militarism extremely profitable for a few powerful corporations – is to state a merely utopian dream.

6.9.3. Nothing can control the militarism of the world under the present world system, not NGOs, not the U.N., not individual nation-states. Under the present system of militarized "sovereign" nation-states, there is a nearly inevitable temptation, within both large and small nations, to try to impose military solutions on what are essentially economic, social, and political problems. The result is inevitably disaster, spawning immense human rights abuses, devastation of civilian infrastructures, environmental destruction, rebellion and social unrest, radical terrorist groups, religious fundamentalism, and a host of other problems. The result of thinking in terms of violence and coercion (which is what all military thinking does) is that nations are involved in a complex and corrupt global power game that even leads them to arm and support some terrorist groups while trying to suppress others.

6.9.4. Extremist terrorist movements flourish under the conditions of a militarized, violent, warring world order. Such terrorist movements are an inevitable response to state terrorism. And nearly every military action by nations amounts to exactly this: state terrorism. The standard definition of terrorism (the illegal use of violence and coercion to achieve social or political goals) fits the military actions of nations as well as those of extremist groups. The solution to both extremist group terrorism and state terrorism is to legally abolish all terrorist and military activities worldwide. They are two sides of the same coin.

6.9.5. World government under the *Earth Constitution* abolishes all military and concentrates on the economic, social, and political problems that breed extremism and social unrest. It encourages political, religious, and cultural pluralism so that all groups feel their voices are heard rather than suppressed. It addresses the roots of terrorism which involve the suppression of political participation, poverty, exploitation, and domination of the many by the few. By doing so it will break the cycle of violence forever.

6.9.6. Without effective world government under the *Earth Constitution*, there is no possibility of reaping the almost unimaginable benefits of converting the nearly one trillion dollars per year now wasted on world militarism to sustainable development and human welfare. The *Constitution* prohibits the world government from having a military of its own in any form. Therefore, no resources of the Federation will be wasted on militarism.

Under the *Earth Constitution*, nations joining the Federation (and they will join in droves once they see the incredible benefits of uniting) are required by law to demilitarize under the careful supervision of the World Disarmament Agency.

6.9.7. Each nation joining the Federation is required to give half its last year's military budget to the Federal Government and may keep the other half of this amount for its own purposes. Nations joining the Federation would immediately have not only innumerable benefits from a federal world government now very well funded with former wasted military money, but would reap the benefits of retaining for useful purposes half their own funds formerly wasted on militarism.

6.9.8. Here is the key to creating a decent and civilized world order and addressing all the crises outlined in this manifesto. The money for transforming the world order to one of equity, freedom, justice, and peace is readily available. This one source alone can provide 850 billion dollars per year. But there is no way to tap this cornucopia of now wasted wealth without the authority and legitimacy of democratic world government. The U.N. has failed miserably in this regard, for one cannot defend the integrity of the nation-state system, base global economics on the Western model of greed, financial exploitation, and corporate self-interest, claim that peace can be preserved by going to war, create U.N. armies called "peacekeeping" forces, and expect at the same time to diminish the insane militarism of the world.

6.9.9. Under the *Earth Constitution* all nations are disarmed and the world federal government itself is nonmilitary. All weapons of war and of mass destruction are carefully and systematically destroyed. Disarmed governments without armies and weapons do not invade one another or attack one another. Extremist groups do not emerge as "blowback" against military suppression. Disputes are handled by the World Court system designed to create a just and equitable world order and through political participation of everyone in the World Parliament. An independent branch of government is created (the World Ombudsmus) to represent those who believe their rights under the *Constitution* have been violated. The world police possess only weapons necessary to apprehend individuals, for only individuals (and not entire nations) commit crimes.

6.9.10. Crimes (whether in the form of manufacturing weapons, human rights violations by heads of state, or environmentally destructive policies by corporations) are committed by individuals, and a global society under the rule of law has the authority and means to arrest and prosecute individuals. The madness of attacking the people of an entire nation for the supposed crimes of a few is ended forever under the *Earth Constitution*. There will be no more bombings of the good people of Yugoslavia because their President is suspected of crimes, no more bombings of the good people of Afghanistan because it is suspected there are terrorists in their midst, no more invasions of the innocent people of Iraq because their leader is suspected of crimes.

6.9.11. The madness of the current world system of sovereign nation-states where an entire nation must be militarily attacked or economically punished because of the suspected crimes of a few must be abolished forever. The only way to abolish this mad system is to create a demilitarized Earth Federation where all individuals on the planet are equally subject to the rule of democratically legislated law. The powerful heads of corporations or imperial nations will no longer be exempt from arrest and prosecution as they currently are. Terrorists and violators of human rights will no longer be able to hide behind the borders of so-called sovereign nations as they often do today. For the first time in human history, universal justice and equity will be possible on our planet.

7. Common sense economics under democratic world government

The economics of a decent world order under the Earth Federation can be summarized in seven simple, yet fundamental principles. Once the official World Parliament is elected, it will have the authority to implement a global economic policy based on these principles.

7.1. First, extensive lines of credit in Earth Currency and nonexploitative loans will be made immediately available to individuals, businesses, and governments for purposes of sustainable development. The great lie of the present world order is that only those who possess wealth can loan money or create lines of credit. But real wealth is a product of natural resources, capital, and human labor. The world government can create immense lines of credit in Earth Currency to be used for rapid, sustainable economic development wherever this is needed within the Federation.

7.1.1. With the creation of real wealth from development, these lines of credit can be repaid for only an additional small accounting fee. There will be no exploitative interest rates. And the value of Earth Currency will not be predicated on the global financial institutions that now devalue currencies of poor countries and manipulate the "convertible currencies" to continue to enrich themselves.

7.1.2. The first twenty-five nations to ratify the *Constitution* (comprising a large portion of the Earth's population, resources, and collective technological know-how) will form a substantially autonomous economic unit. The Federal government will immediately begin extending lines of credit for development, not merely to the already wealthy elites within these countries but to the poor or whoever has a sustainable, nonmilitary project in mind that would create wealth as well as benefit society. Individuals, businesses, and governments will have ample lines of credit available to them for only the cost of an accounting fee. Governments could reasonably focus on rapid development of infrastructure (roads, schools, hospitals, sanitation, communications), while businesses focused on goods and services.

7.1.3. Every poor nation knows that it is watched carefully by the imperial powers to ensure that it does not deviate from its subordinate role within the global system of domination and exploitation. Every nation knows that if it ratified the *Constitution for the Federation of Earth* alone, it would be economically punished for this by withdrawal of investments, recall of loans, or economic sanctions. Witness the forty-three years of suffering that has been imposed on the Cuban people because their government attempted to take an independent course that cared about its own poor and dispossessed citizens.

7.1.4. For this reason, a number of governments in the developing world must coordinate their efforts and plan to simultaneously ratify the *Constitution*. World government can easily begin with perhaps twenty-five nations simultaneously joining together to create the initial Earth Federation. Immediately such a group of nations ratifying the *Constitution* would become a substantially autonomous economic unit, using Earth Currency and receiving extensive lines of credit for development from the newly created federal government. Withdrawal of investments, recall of loans, or threat of sanctions would not matter. The federal government would assume all international debt of these nations to be paid back in a reasonable manner at nonexploitative interest rates.

7.1.5. Approximately twenty-five nations would immediately enter into dynamic cooperation in the use of their resources, technologies, educated leaders, and development initiatives. Their debts would be removed under the current world order and they would receive extensive lines of credit for sustainable development based on the ability of their people to produce real wealth using finance capital, labor, and natural resources. Corporations or industries within these nations that refuse to cooperate in the conversion to Earth Currency would be nationalized or mundialized, whichever is most appropriate. The simple but liberating economic principles outlined in this manifesto would immediately take effect. The increase in prosperity, creative energy, and hope would be immediately evident and contagious.

7.1.6. There is no mystery about how to create prosperity. Place a great deal of money in the hands of people who wish to develop projects, employ workers, procure the necessary natural resources, and buy and sell locally and regionally. Money gets into the hands of ordinary people who then recirculate it through increased consumption and the purchase of services. There is no reason to take anything away from the already rich or oppose the policies of the World Bank or corporations operating outside the initial Federation.

7.1.7. Those who are rich may retain their wealth. What is eliminated is their ability to exploit others to make themselves richer. The World Bank may continue to offer its development loans to poor countries of the world. But who will want these loans when immense lines of credit are available to individuals, nations, and businesses at the cost of only an accounting fee? Exploitative interest rates are eliminated and with it the ability of those already rich to exploit and dominate the poor who need money for development purposes.

7.2. Second, large scale technology transfer and infusion of fertile ideas and techniques for sustainable development can be activated through common sense revisions of current intellectual property rights laws. As the writings of economists Michael Chossudovsky, David Korten, Vandana Siva, J. W. Smith and others have shown, one of the ways the wealthy world retains neo-colonial monopoly control on the global economy is through intellectual property rights, which have become a fundamental tenant in WTO regulations. The simple device of allowing any patented idea to be used for the payment of a reasonable royalty fee would make all ideas and techniques available to humankind for sustainable development purposes.

7.2.1. Through its system of absolute intellectual property rights, the current world system keeps the developing world in a low tech condition, forcing them to sell their natural resources to the wealthy world to be there manufactured and sold back to the developing countries at a profit. It keeps monopoly control over marketable ideas and innovations, thereby belying its ideology of "free trade." Versions of this policy have been going on since the advent of colonialism. They keep life saving drugs from reaching the AIDS stricken countries of Africa. They keep seeds and key agricultural necessities profitably expensive while poor farmers starve worldwide.

7.2.2. The simple change of allowing any idea to be used if a reasonable royalty is paid, eradicates these intellectual property rights monopolies and liberates the poor of the world for efficient, rapid development. This modified system of intellectual property rights would also activate the regional economies of the world with a tremendous influx of new techniques and ideas. Scarcity would be ended and prosperity rapidly created.

7.3. The third simple principle for rapidly creating global equity and prosperity involves massive programs of education and empowerment of populations throughout the world through use of airwaves and other forms of communication for free global education on behalf of rapid sustainable development. Just as the present world system involves a monopoly on money creation and lending, and a monopoly on advanced technologies and techniques, so the present world order involves a monopoly on media and communications. The governments of the world have given away the airways and media for communication to private, profit-making interests. The electromagnetic spectrum from TV to radio to satellite communications is largely used for commercial purposes, for enrichment of private, profit making corporations, and for propaganda on behalf of the current world system. These should be used for sustainable development and global free education that this requires.

7.3.1. We have seen that a massive worldwide educational effort is essential to rapid sustainable development and the elimination of poverty and unsupportable population growth. The technologies and means of communication are available to achieve this. All that is required is government that serves the needs and interests of all the world's citizens and not government, as in the United States, that serves the needs and interests of the big corporations.

7.3.2. Use of the available technologies and means of communication for rapid sustainable development would activate regional and local economies. People would learn sanitation techniques, family planning techniques, literacy, foreign languages, water purification techniques, techniques for generating nonpolluting forms of energy, techniques for increasing their income and quality of life. This simple change in the use of the world's airways and means of communication would serve as a third major step for creating universal prosperity and sustainable development.

7.4. Fourth, simple legal steps would be taken fostering the empowerment of regional and local economies where money is retained within the locality and not siphoned off to foreign banks or corporations. Regions would produce as many goods and services for themselves as reasonably possible and economically feasible, and import only what is necessary to complement the local economies. The amazing waste of energy and resources that now occurs in transporting goods around the world that could just as well be produced locally would cease. Regions would employ many at good wages creating a population capable of buying good and services and businesses would develop in response to these demands.

7.4.1. In the United States, when a multinational "superstore" moves into a town, many local businesses begin to fold. They cannot compete with the ability of the superstore to procure cheap clothing, food, drugs, shoes, housewares, furniture, sporting goods, hardware and nearly everything else. The superstore may employ a few people at low wage jobs, but its profits do not remain in the community. They are sent back to corporate headquarters and to distant investors. The economy of the local community begins to die. Small businesses close up and unemployment increases.

7.4.2. This same phenomena also happens on a global scale. A soft drink or medical drug from a multinational corporation in a developing country may be able to undersell a domestically produced soft drink or drug. But the profits from the multinational soft drink or medical drug return to wealthy first world investors and are not recirculated within the local or regional economy. Very often, the developing country is even prevented from producing its own drink or medical drug by intellectual property rights regulations. These global monopolies strangle regional economies.

7.4.3. The principle of health for economies, and for sustainable development of prosperity in developing countries, is to activate regional and local markets. This includes raising wages, producing locally whatever can be produced to supply the needs of the population, and creating a healthy interchange of supply and demand that keeps money circulating within the region.

7.4.4. The Earth Federation is not opposed in principle to "globalization." Converting the world system to democratic federal world government is maximal globalization.

But globalization of economics without the globalization of democratic world law has simply extended the current system of chaos and violence worldwide. Without world law, imperial nations and gigantic corporations exploit and dominate the poor of the world in their own self-interest. We need global planning for the future, global monitoring of the environment, and global trade where appropriate for the benefit of everyone involved. Globalization without democratic planning, regulation, or concern for the common good will necessarily result in the viciousness and corruption that we see everywhere in today's "globalized" economy.

7.4.5. Today, the "anti-globalization movement" is providing vital resistance to this world system of economic domination and exploitation. Many of the individuals and organizations that participate in this movement are committed to democracy, justice, the ending of poverty, environmental protection, and human rights. They play a vital role in exposing the terrible legacy of economic globalization with respect to all these issues. However, the central focus of this movement is that it is against globalization.

7.4.6. To be against all "globalization" is to be against planning for the future of the Earth. It is to be against the universal rule of law on Earth. They are "anti," without having a clear vision of how the world can be transformed into a civilized world order. Vague notions of justice, democracy, or protecting human rights without a global, democratic, legal mechanism for achieving these are futile. The *Earth Constitution* gives humanity the specific political and economic means to achieve these goals.

7.5. Fifth, the market may be an efficient way of determining prices for many things, but certainly not for wages. There must be equal pay for equal work at good wages throughout the Earth Federation. Economist J. W. Smith points out that the rate of advantage of equally productive but unequally paid workers doing the same work is exponential, not arithmetical. Take the example of a worker in the developing world paid one U.S. dollar an hour for producing an item that is identical to the item produced by a first world worker making ten dollars per hour. Since the cost of labor largely determines the prices of these items, the developing world item sells for one dollar while the first world item for ten dollars. How many of the developing world items can the first world worker buy after working ten hours? How many items of the first world worker can the developing world worker buy after working ten hours? The rate of advantage in this simple example is 100 to 1 (Smith 2005a, Chapter One).

7.5.1. Under this rate of advantage there is no possibility of the developing world ever catching up with the first world through activation of its economies or sale of natural resources. The exponential rate of advantage ensures what has in fact been the case for decades: billions of dollars in wealth are transferred annually from the poorest segment of humanity to the wealthiest segment of humanity. The poor under our current world order are getting poorer and the rich are getting richer.

7.5.2. Markets have a useful but limited role in human economies. They are not and cannot be the solution to all problems as the imperial economic ideology has it. Markets can produce many (not all) goods and services efficiently. But essential services like water, electricity, and health care are much better served by good government. Nor can markets ensure just or equitable distribution of services or wealth. And they cannot ensure sustainable development that involves conceptions of the common good and the welfare of future generations.

7.5.3. Markets are blind to all noncommercial values such as community, human rights, sustainability, equity, justice, and peace. Markets, as we know so well, will produce weapons of war if there is a profit to be made from this, or weapons of mass destruction. Markets (like big business) are morally blind and must be tempered by democratic, non-commercial values that are necessarily built into good government. Markets are not based on the moral principle of unity-in-diversity.

7.5.4. The principle of equal pay for equal work at decent, living wages will place cash in the hands of the poor in the developing counties and will produce an activated local economy while at the same time increasing global equity. As we said earlier, there is no need to appropriate the accumulated wealth of the rich to solve the global crises facing humanity. All that is necessary is to eliminate the means for the rich to continue to accumulate more wealth through exploiting those already poor. The exploitative, monopoly features of the current system listed here perpetuate both the wealth of the rich and the poverty of the poor and make global equity and sustainable development an impossibility.

7.6. Sixth, economically stable and equitable laws will be enacted to promote worldwide land reform so that the land and its wealth can be returned to the people of Earth. The exploitation of the poor by the few who now control the quality land and resources of the world will rapidly come to an end. In general, land and resources will be recognized as belonging to the people of the Earth and need to be legally protected for the common good. Land and resources will be seen as the global commons and private property will be recognized for land use by individuals, governments, and businesses. That is, property rights will be converted from "absolute rights" to "conditional rights."

7.6.1. Land is provided by nature, not built by labor, thus all natural resources are nature's heritage for all. Applying Henry George's concept of exclusive title to nature's wealth restructured to conditional title (society collecting the landrent) instantly collapses those exclusive (monopoly) values to zero. The price of homes are the cost of building a house and the price of businesses will be the facilities themselves. Monopoly values have been converted to use-values owned by true producers. Just as with land, today's technology, money, and communications monopolies are subject to the same efficiency gains.

7.6.2. The effectiveness of careful organic farming, with composting, crop rotation, and ecologically sound planting and harvesting has been repeatedly demonstrated. These farming methods produce many times the food per acre now produced by commercial agribusiness while conserving the soil and eliminating the pollution cased by chemical fertilizers. They are best done by small farmers who own and care about their own land and have a stake in its preservation. Even with the diminished quality farm land in the world today, a global program of population reduction, effective farming methods, and activated local economies can easily end hunger and create a world sufficient for all.

7.6.3. Such programs of land reform have been attempted in individual countries such as Guatemala in the early 1950s, Chile in the early 1970s, Nicaragua in the 1980s, Cuba in the 1970s, 80s, and 90s, and Venezuela at the beginning of this century. In every case the United States has destroyed or attempted to destroy the government promoting the land reform. This has been a global policy of the imperial center since the Second World War.

7.6.4. All good examples of economic health and common sense must be destroyed so that the world believes there is no alternative to global economic monopolies dominated by multi-billion dollar corporations and protected by the military might of First World nations. The lethal combination of the our present world system of sovereign nation-states (dominated as always by the imperial centers) and ruthless global corporations cannot but act to enforce a regime of global domination and exploitation. These consequences are built into these global institutions of the past five centuries.

7.6.5. Only democratically legislated law, enacted by a World Parliament representing all the people and nations of Earth, can formulate and effectively carry out a planetary policy of land reform. Such reform is badly needed not only to activate the local and regional economies of the world, but to end exploitation of the poor by the rich, to conserve the soil while reducing erosion and pollution, and to increase food production, rapidly ending hunger on Earth.

7.7. Seventh, the federal world government will engage in large-scale employment of the unemployed or underemployed millions in developing counties in a multitude of projects directed toward sustainable development and the activating of regional and local economies. These projects will certainly include replanting the depleted forests of the Earth, restoring the soil and grazing lands to integrity, building schools and health care centers, creating efficient, low cost sanitation and water systems, converting military installations and weapons factories to the production of peaceful goods and services, and converting the energy sources of the world to sustainable, non-polluting forms of water, wind, solar, and hydrogen energy.

7.7.1. The condition of the developing world today is similar to that of the United States during the great depression of the 1930s. There is massive unemployment and hence no money to circulate within economies. The U.S. government had the vision to create vast public works projects and put hungry people back to work.

7.7.2. The Earth Federation will undertake similar initiatives, thereby not only putting people to work and activating their economies, but creating the infrastructure necessary to a prosperous sustainable development. The nexus of global crises are too advanced and the threat to the future of the world too extreme to sit passively by and hope for private development efforts alone to succeed. The world needs sanitation and water systems now. It needs to restore the damaged environment now. It needs to deal with the crisis of sickness and disease now. It needs to restore soil, grazing land, fisheries, and forests now. It needs family planning and population reduction efforts now. It needs education for the masses now. It needs to employ the unemployed millions now.

7.7.3. As one of the great speeches before the 1992 Rio Environmental Summit expressed this principle: "tomorrow is too late." The global crises outlined here are upon us and action must be taken immediately to create a decent, prosperous, and equitable world order. We are at the crossroads of human existence. One road leads to certain disaster. The other to an equitable, free, just, and peaceful world order.

8. Where do we go from here? A call to the people and nations of the Earth

8.1. That earlier manifesto of 150 years ago demanded that "workers of the world unite!" The manifesto of the Earth Federation demands that the poor, the disenfranchised, and all decent people of the world unite. The problem is not simply exploitation and dehumanization of workers, although today this continues in sweat shops, extensive use of child labor, and starvation wage employment practices worldwide. The problem is the nexus of global economics and sovereign nation-states that continues the global system of domination and exploitation from generation to generation.

8.2. At least a billion human beings fall outside this system of worker exploitation. They are not "workers" needed by the profit-seeking institutions, and are of no use to the imperial nation-states, and therefore are considered extraneous, useless, mere surplus to be allowed to rot and die in their hell of poverty or to be slaughtered as acceptable "collateral damage" through carpet bombings of their countries. The poorest of the world are of no concern to the world order as it now exists. It is they who are uniting for a new world order. It is the poor majority who are the hope of the world.

8.3. The poor majority who are the central hope for the world -- and those caring and awakened people and nations who act in solidarity with them in their struggle to create a decent world order for themselves and their children. We are all made "poor" by the current world order. We are all degraded, manipulated, and shamed through our complicity with the rule of corrupt wealth and power. We are all faced with the historical, practical, and moral demand to save the Earth from further destruction and create a decent, sustainable world order before it is too late.

8.4. Why do the wealthy of the world and their minions in government fear us so much? They know we are not interested in taking their wealth from them. We are only interested in simple changes that remove global monopolies and eliminate the ability of private organizations and nations to continue to enrich themselves at the expense of the poor. Yet this very fact fills them with dread.

8.5. The thought of a world of equity and justice, where the few have lost their ability to dominate and exploit the rest, terrifies those who have never worked for a living but have only ruled, dominated, and exploited. They are mortified by the thought of civilized world order where the rich actually have to live in equity and justice with the poor, where special privileges have been abolished, where freedom and peace mean there can be no more military domination of the powerful over the rest, where no more profits can be reaped from selling weapons, pillaging, or defrauding the poor in a world of chaos and violence.

8.6. It is difficult for the average decent person to imagine how corrupt are most of the captains of industry, military, and government in today's world. The ruling elite in business, military, and government know only power relations, influence pedaling, and corrupt deals with super-rich corporate executives, arms merchants, drug kingpins, regional warlords, dictators, torturers, shady financial investors, or slimy politicians. They have only contempt for the poor or ordinary decent people. The chaos of the political and economic worlds is so deep under global capitalism and the nation-state system that any talk of a decent world order based on universal values sounds like naive gibberish to their ears. Yet they fear us because they know that decent people everywhere respond positively to the *Earth Constitution* designed to create planetary justice, peace, and prosperity.

8.7. Is "human nature" so corrupt that government, military, or business will always attract to themselves twisted people who without remorse are willing to destroy human beings, our environment, and the welfare of future generations in their lust for wealth and power? Most ordinary human beings are honest and decent. The corruption is fostered by the institutions dominating our world. Fragmented institutions often attract fragmented and corrupt human beings to positions of power. Both the system of territorial nation-states and the global economic system are founded on immoral self-interest, the drive for domination, and structures of greed and exploitation. They cannot in principle be reformed to create a decent world order for they are fragments predicated on naked power, chaos, and violence.

8.8. Fragments result in unredeemed conflict and power relationships. The *Constitution for the Federation of Earth* is founded on the fundamentally different principle of unity-in-diversity. Diversity (of interests, races, ethnicities, religions, nations, cultures, and individuals) is protected and legitimated through the moral unity recognizing all equally as citizens and members of the Earth Federation. Diversity within the moral unity created by the Earth Federation does not corrupt persons into violence and greed as does fragmentation.

8.9. We are all one as citizens of the Earth Federation and members of the human race. We have historical, practical, and moral obligations to one another, to our Earth, and to future generations. Under the Earth Federation, this unity-in-diversity is both a moral and a legal category creating, for the first time in history, government and business operating according to morally legitimate principles. Who will lead humanity into a new, morally decent world order premised on the principle of unity-in-diversity?

8.10. Solidarity with the Earth Federation is not likely to come from the comfortable classes of the First World nations who are conditioned to be passive, self-interested consumers and without compassion or concern for their fellow human beings around the planet. Solidarity with the Earth Federation will not come from the imperial nations or the multinational corporations who now dominate the world in their ignorance and corruption. Unity with the Federation can only come from the poor, those in solidarity with the poor, and those rare governments who have some concern for their own people and the future of the Earth.

8.11. The poor of the world must organize under the banner of the Earth Federation! They must educate themselves, raise funds for educating others, send delegations to their leaders, write editorials, get on radio shows, hold town meetings, and hold ratification campaigns. Localities, villages, towns and cities may commit to the Earth Federation. There must be active pressure placed upon the governments of poor countries, and upon all decent governments. Chapters of the World Constitution and Parliament Association must be organized and members must join the rapidly growing Earth Federation. The *Constitution for the Federation of Earth* must be studied and translated into ever more languages.

8.12. We must urge poor nations and their populations (and those nations and world citizens in solidarity with them) to work together and coordinate a simultaneous ratification of the *Constitution* by many nations. The effect on the world would be electrifying. Before the imperial powers and the multinational corporate criminals could even think in terms of blockades or sanctions, other poor nations would be clamoring to join the Federation. A truly new world order recognizing the equality and right to prosperity of all human beings would be unmistakable and irresistible.

8.13. The majority of countries would immediately see that they have nothing to lose and everything to gain from joining the Earth Federation. Soon the entire world would perceive that at last true liberation for humanity and the Earth was at hand. The tiny minority of powerful imperial leaders, bankers, and corporate executives who oppose this order would be overwhelmed by public pressure and before long the final operative stage of the Earth Federation would be reached and there would be peace, prosperity, freedom, and justice on the Earth. We do not mean a "utopia." We mean a practical, workable, decent world order for the first time in history.

8.14. It is important to see that the first twenty-five nations ratifying the *Constitution* would not be forming another power block like North America or the European Union. If there were to be an African Union within the current world order, this would change nothing. It would simply create another military and economic block to struggle with Europe, Japan, China, the U.S. or other power centers. The world would remain in fragmentation and chaos. However, an African Union, or a Latin American Union, could easily be magna-regions within the Federation of Earth.

8.15. The initial Earth Federation is something truly new in human history, for it invites in all and excludes no one. It recognizes every human being as a citizen of the Earth Federation, and invites every nation to be a member of the Federation with all the rights, privileges, and benefits that apply under the *Constitution*. It would take nothing from those already rich and oppose no one militarily or economically. It would end exploitation of nation by nation and person by person. And it would be clear to the world that the Earth Federation was the only institution that could address the nexus of global crises that threaten our extinction on Earth.

8.16. Our task is to communicate this message to the world. Our task is for the poor nations and peoples of the world to unite and organize behind the Earth Federation. The Federation is not an ideal we are promoting but a dynamic reality from which we live. Our every thought, breath, and movement must emanate from the living reality of the Earth Federation. Every human being must know and ratify the *Constitution*.

8.17. The poor majority of our planet must take the initiative to liberate themselves and their world. They must ratify the *Constitution* personally and collectively. The poor nations of the world (and those nations in solidarity with them) must act in unison and ratify the *Constitution* collectively. The Earth Federation will grow like wildfire until there is one citizenship, one system of justice, one World Parliament, one bill of rights, and one world order of peace with justice. Then, and only then, can the religious or the nonreligious affirm the final meaning of history as one world under God, Allah, Brahman, the holy cosmos, this sacred Earth, or this just world order.

8.18. All people on Earth are already citizens of the Earth Federation. For the only sovereignty is that of the people of Earth. We are already members of the new world order of equity, freedom, justice, and peace. If we act from this living reality, we will successfully pass the crossroads of imminent death and destruction. To unite under the banner of the Earth Federation is to act for the liberation of humanity, this precious Earth, and future generations.

8.19. The poor, the dispossessed, and all decent people of the world must unite! We have nothing to lose but our misery, our chains of economic and political domination! For we are all victims in this present world of injustice and violence. We are all made poor and disenfranchised by this current world order. We are all already citizens of the Earth Federation! In the darkness of these times, we know that tomorrow is too late, and the time is now. A new dawn is rising for the world. Liberation for humanity is at hand. Citizens of the world unite!

Long Live the Earth Federation!!!

Chapter Five

A Comparative Critique of World Constitutions, World Constitutional Concepts and UN Charter Reform Proposals

Constitution for the Federation of Earth
(***Earth Constitution***, Isely et al., World Constitutent Assembly)
Binding Triad (Hudson, R. & Szasz, P.)
Constitution of the Earth Federation (Rausher, S.)
New United Nations Charter (Musslewhite, B.)
The Old *United Nations Charter* (with Article 22 Consultative World Parliament, under numerous proposals & authors)

"Certain great fundamental ideas of right are common to the world, and ... all laws of man's making which trample on these ideas, are null and void—wrong to obey, right to disobey."

Anna Elizabeth Dickenson, US Abolitionist and Suffragist (1842-1932)

Eugenia Almand

World constitutions, world constitutional concepts, and United Nations Charter Article 22 implementation are under consideration in this chapter. Definite strengths or weaknesses are inherent in each of the projects under consideration. Some world constitutions or concepts share the same strengths; some share the same weaknesses. Each has noteworthy differences. In the event of United Nations Charter Article 109 convocation of a General Charter Review Conference, an intense review of each of the five proposals is strongly recommended, and cosmetic reforms, such as Permanent Security Council Member enlargements, are discouraged. The *Earth Constitution* as a founded document for civil democratic Earth Federation bypasses conventional strategies, and can be instituted by the people and nations whether or not any Charter Review Conference is held.

Global government is an extremely complex process. There are many aspects and layers to this endeavour. This critique analyses only constitutional bases of world federation. A few lines need to be posited regarding what this paper does not thoroughly address, because these aspects and layers of the process are not the focus of this paper. This will help clarify the focus.

This comparative critique does not thoroughly consider mere sets of statements of governing principles, howsoever well stated. For instance, the ***Earth Charter*** was initiated in 1994 by Maurice Strong, Mikhail Gorbachev and the government of the Netherlands, at the suggestion of the United Nations Environmental Council. The Earth Charter is extremely well stated. However, it is merely a statement of principles rather than a constitution defining a governing structure ***per se.*** Likewise, the World Government of World Citizens is developing principles for a dynamic world constitution based upon a World Syntegrity Project, but these are not published in the form of a definitive structure for world governing. Each of the above subtitled five world constitutions or world constitution concepts has its own respective auxiliary writings of principles. These writings on principles are not under review here, but rather the prescribed or defined governing structures themselves. The comparative critique here is to elucidate both strengths and weaknesses of five currently proposed world constitutions or world constitution concepts.

This is not a review of non-governmental world federalist organizations or of other non-governmental organizations in the world government movement. There are many such organizations, but these do not necessarily have their own world constitutions. Many of these organizations are taking a "wait and see" position regarding specific ideas for world governing structures, rather than elaborating specific proposals for a world constitution.

Also, this briefly refers to the isolated world parliament formative strategies that have been proposed. There may be a dozen or more strategies for world parliament formation. Since many of these are without a strong context of an overall constitutional structure, these many strategies will not be individually reviewed here. These strategies are worthy of rigorous analyses, however. When considering these strategies, it is important to distinguish between those parliamentary assemblies that are intended to be consultative and assemblies that are intended for actual legislation. There might be a strategic intent where consultative assembly proposals are intended to lead to assemblies with binding legislative powers. In this article, parliamentary assemblies without further constitution will be briefly addressed as a whole under the category of an old ***United Nations Charter*** with the addition of an Article 22 consultative world parliament.

Also, there are historic world constitutions, such as the *Constitution for the World* (1948, by the Chicago Committee to Frame a World Constitution). The Clark and Sohn proposal, *World Peace through World Law*, is another such world constitutional concept proposal. These constitutions and structural proposals have historical significance, and certainly played a role in the development of the above world constitutions under consideration. However, since these earlier world constitutions are not currently under promotion, they also are not going to be considered, at least in depth, within the present analysis. It is worth mentioning that some of the promoting members of these two mentioned early constitutional proposals, the late Louis Sohn and the late Elizabeth Mann Borgese, and perhaps others, had been involved in the promotion of one of the constitutional proposals to be discussed here, that is, the Binding Triad proposal.

There are derivative world constitutional structures, such as the Revolutionary Committees Movement Amendment proposal to the ***Earth Constitution***, and the Schwartzberg Weighting proposal to the *United Nations Charter*. These will be addressed only briefly during the consideration of the closest respective world constitution.

There are other specific currently proposed world constitutions. The omission of other current proposals for world constitutions is not intended to disparage other constitutions. It will be good to receive and study any other current proposals, so that interested persons may continue to elaborate the analysis.

This essay addresses world constitutional properties of current leading world constitutions. Leading world constitutions means specific and comprehensive plans for a fundamentally new system for making global decisions. The essay also generally addresses one popular *United Nations Charter* proposal—that of a non-binding world parliamentary assembly based on ***United Nations Charter*** Article 22, although that does not constitute a comprehensive plan for a fundamentally new system.
The constitutions and forms themselves may be abbreviated:

F.E.C. - *Constitution for the Federation of Earth* or *Earth Constitution*
B.T. - *Binding Triad*
C.E.F. – *Constitution of the Earth Federation*
U.N.Ch.A.-109 – New *United Nations Charter*; and the U.N. Charter proposal
U.N.Ch.A.-22 – Old *United Nations Charter with an advisory world parliamentary assembly.*

The following characteristics will be noted in this essay:

1. The Structure of the Parliament
2. Parliamentary weakness
3. Political strength of the Parliament
4. Potential popularity
5. Essential strength of Parliament
6. Currently civil or military
7. Dispositions for implementation
8. Nature of the Rights Declaration
9. Jury Process
10. Right to Keep and Bear Arms (R.K.B.A.)
11. Amendment process to the constitution.

A comparison chart (q.v.) at the end of this chapter contrasts most of these characteristics in a graphic form. The chart does not entirely reflect the list.

Constitution for the Federation of Earth or Earth Constitution (F.E.C.)

The *Earth Constitution*, was adopted by a series of World Constituent Assemblies. The document was primarily drafted by a U.S. businessman and four international lawyers, over a period of about thirty years (Isely, H. P., Husein S. M., Amerasinghe, T. P., Habicht, M., & Spencer, D. M.), from the early 1960's until 1991. Its tri-cameral legislature is fairly simple, though it has been criticized for its inequitable weighting in its upper house, the House of Nations. Habicht (1987) pointed out this difficulty. Continental mega-states such as China, India and the USA would be greatly underrepresented in the House of Nations if they were to be considered member nations of the Earth Federation. However, this has a fairly simple resolution by interpretation relating to the spirit of the *Earth Constitution*. Since the *Earth Constitution* does not define what comprises a nation other than the requirement of ratification of the *Constitution* by a government, in principle, cantons, pradesh and component states of otherwise nuclear powers would be able to ratify to join and have representation as member nations. On careful reading of the requirements for the creation of the World Cabinet and appointment of Commissioners to the Integrative Complex, it becomes clear that this component-state interpretation of the *Earth Constitution* is a strong way or the only way for there to be compliance with the *Constitution*. This interpretation resolves the objection and the weighting becomes normal and representative. Since there is reasonably imminent danger under the old system that will not admit delay, and since federation is an internal question and not an external question, there are no reasonable grounds under, for instance, U.S. Constitution Article 1, Section 10, to refrain from this arrangement. In fact, this strategy extends more power to the participating states, so eventual accession by cantons, pradesh and component states of continental federations is likely.

The *Earth Constitution* has also been criticized on the grounds that there is only a 1 delegate to 6 million voter ratio in its lower house, the House of Peoples. The Libyan Revolutionary Committees Movement (R.C.M.) says in effect that the *Earth Constitution* is basically sound, but that the representation ratio does not allow for a popular representation and necessarily results in the representatives being distanced from their constituents. R.C.M. proposes the addition of councils with legislative power of proposition and revision, which seems to be at least somewhat akin to the proposal of Global Peoples Assembly and Regional Peoples' Assemblies, to draw much more public participation into the process. (This process of popularizing the constitution by large representative bodies is also an approach of Musslewhite in the New ***United Nations Charter*** by Article 109.) It should be noted that in August 2004, the Provisional World Parliament defined in Article 19 of the F.E.C. took legislative measures to incorporate and fund the Global Peoples Assembly with councils and committees that have certain legislative power of proposition and revision. The constitutional grounds for this legislative measure are in Article 8, Section C. of the F.E.C.

Because of the clear assignment of powers, the tri-cameral World Parliament under the *Earth Constitution* will function strongly. Only the voice of the people serves as protective barrier to the legislative force the World Parliament will wield. Because the *Earth Constitution* comprises a whole systems approach to world problems, its World Parliament begins with the integration of the World Court system and integration of a civil Enforcement System, to ensure the implementation of legislative decisions. Additionally, the *Earth Constitution* provides for the organ of the World Ombudsmus, to help ensure that the enforcement is done while respecting human rights worldwide. For instance of the effect of the *Earth Constitution*, the Provisional World Parliament, operating in conformance with Article 19 of the *Earth Constitution,* has already repeatedly deliberated the *Rome Statute* family of world legislation, to identify strengths and weaknesses, and to adopt polished, strengthened versions of the Assembly of States Parties' versions. These actions are part of what in necessary for the World Court itself to function in conformance with Article 7 (equal protection clause) and Article 21.3 (authority of government clause) of the *Universal Declaration of Human Rights.*

The *Earth Constitution* itself is civil rather than military, meaning that there is not a world military, not even on a transitional basis. There are however national militaries in transition during the period of implementation of the *Earth Constitution*, and this process could conceivably last many years, though it is also conceivable that it might be implemented rather quickly, perhaps in a period of less than two years. States acceding to the *Earth Constitution* promise not to engage with one another militarily, but to address conflicts via the World Court system and other agencies of the Earth Federation. Under legislation of the World Parliament, national militaries will be financed for learning powerful civil enforcement procedures to systematically replace military procedures. Eventually, the civil enforcement capacity of the Earth Federation excedes the military power, including military power that might remain outside the Earth Federation. Then, it will be safe for the militaries of the world to cease all military operations and procedures, because the civil enforcement power will be more effective and secure than the military power.

The dispositions for implementation of the *Earth Constitution* are the most elaborated of any of the constitutions. These comprise about eleven pages of thoughtful steps that make smooth implementation more likely. It is unlikely that the actual implementation will conform to the plan entirely, but to a great degree, the steps appear plausible and necessary.

The *Earth Constitution* includes a Bill of Rights (Article 12) and a declaration of Directive Principles (Article 13) for those economic rights that cannot be immediately implemented. The guarantee of recognition of these rights is enabled by the World Ombudsmus, a branch of government financially independent from both the World Judiciary and the Enforcement System (The World Ombudsmus is responsible directly to the World Parliament.) The World Ombudsmus is empowered to initiate cases in the

Human Rights Bench of the World Court System. Furthermore, the *Earth Constitution* provides for not only the World Supreme Court, but also for Regional World Courts and District World Courts. In 2006, the Provisional World Parliament adopted enabling legislation for the World Ombudsmus, making provision for District World Ombudsen and Deputy District World Ombudsen to be directly elected from the constituencies of their respective World Districts, with operations financed federally, rather than from state tributes, as in the old international system. Basically, this signifies that the United Nations High Commissioner for Human Rights will be superfunded from the world federal system, and that salaries and overhead will provide for operations of the world federal government to ensure the protection of rights down from world level to the local level, in any cases where local or state governments have not been able to ensure human rights protection. This protection upholds the principles of subsidiarity and local autonomy.

The Directive Principles are fairly thorough and read somewhat like the Universal Declaration of Human Rights (UDHR). However, the ***Earth Constitution*** Bill of Rights is rated in the comparative chart as moderate (though not inadequate), in that it includes only seven of the first eleven amendments of the ***United States Constitution***. The missing recognition of rights include the right to self protection (***United States Constitution***, U.S.C. amendment 2), the right to jury in criminal (U.S.C. 6) and civil (U.S.C. 7) cases, the retention of unnamed rights (U.S.C. 9), and the restriction of judicial process to plaintiffs subject to the jurisdiction of the Court (U.S.C. 11)

Noting these omissions, the Provisional World Parliament took legislative measures in March of 2003 to recognize the right to self protection in its World Legislative Acts numbers 13 and 14. Many additional rights were specified for due process of law in World Legislative Act number 15. Also, in December 2003, the Provisional World Parliament recognized the right of jury trial in criminal cases in its World Legislative Act number 24. These legislative actions demonstrate that a world constitution can work in conjunction with world legislation to lay foundation for effective protection of human rights.

Finally, the amendment process to the *Earth Constitution* is clear. In fact, the F.E.C., in 4 world constituent assemblies convened over a thirty year period, has already undergone major transformation with numerous substantive amendments. 59 amendments were made in the most recent session of the World Constituent Assembly meeting in Troia, Portugal, in 1991. The *Earth Constitution* in its Article 18 suggests that if the *Earth Constitution* were not implemented by 1995, that a new session of the World Constituent Assembly may be necessary and proper. In March 2003, in conformance with F.E.C. Article 18, Section 5., the Provisional World Parliament established procedures for any upcoming World Constituent Assembly for the *Earth Constitution*. World Constituent Assembly was not actually called, however, as the Provisional World Parliament did not strongly sense a constituent call to be timely, and there was little popular clamour for any world constituent assembly.

One of the principles of the World Constituent Assemblies was that the Assembly would consider whether certain provisions of the *Earth Constitution* were or were not working. If any provisions were clearly not working, or if provisions were widely unpopular, then amendments were made in the interest of practicality. In order for the world to have a realistic and practical world constitution, amendment process was necessary. This process progressively excludes romantic and sentimental notions from the operating document. A world constitution does not work by luck or mere political will. The design of the constitution has to fit the actual world in which the constitution operates. When the world constitution reflects the actual world system, yet provides additional strength to its constituents that was not there without the world constitution, the world constitution applies. One can observe this application in the workaday development of the legislative process of the Provisional World Parliament.

The *Earth Constitution* is a founded document, elaborated under rules established for its purpose. *Founded* means that the *Constitution* has been deliberated and adopted as the supreme law of Earth by the participating members of the World Constituent Assemblies, and by a large number of other people. This is to say that the *Earth Constitution* is not considered a proposal as possible supreme world law, but rather that it *is* the supreme world law. The ***Earth Constitution*** and its derivative world legislation is in effect for those who give their affirmation to the ***Constitution***. In this sense it is a living document and not merely a proposal. In conformance with the *Earth Constitution*, neither the *Constitution* itself nor its derivative world legislation is subject to the veto of the United Nations Security Council. Nor is the *Earth Constitution* subject to national level veto, as there are no such provisions within it. Since national political decision making is mystical at the world level and out of touch with the world reality, sense requires this higher order. The document itself does however have provisions for preliminary ratification by nations and its own cumulative ratification by peoples, as well as for its own amendment. If the people do not accept the *Earth Constitution*, then the world constituent process resumes. The people participate in this process. Therefore, the question of democratic legitimacy is fully addressed by the *Earth Constitution*, in spite of the fact that the ratification process is not yet complete.

Although the ratification process has not reached a stage where there can be claimed fully operative legitimacy based on enforcement praxis, this question is logically a matter of time. Provisions in the *Earth Constitution* itself, together with the world legislation of the Provisional World Parliament, address the questions of operative enforcement legitimacy in a manner that is both practical and truly civil, constituting a world legal revolution. This body of world law strengthens the best parts of enforceable international law, and especially recognizes, reconstitutes and integrates international criminal law.

Binding Triad (B.T.)

The Binding Triad was first proposed by Richard Hudson and the Center for War / Peace Studies. The premise of the Binding Triad is that there would be an adequate basis for world legislative action by amendment to a single article, Article 13, of the *United Nations Charter*. The amendment, if adopted, would allow the General Assembly to make legislation and binding decisions on selected issues that are agreed to be world issues. The General Assembly would decide as a uni-cameral legislature based on weighted voting that considers the three factors of number of states, respective population, and respective financial contributions.

The Center for War/Peace Studies submits the Binding Triad is democratic, since the B.T. considers the population of a country in its weighting. However, that perspective and weighting does not account for whether the respective people of those countries actually have voice in the governing decisions that affect their lives.

A critique of the Binding Triad has been that it is unfair that the money leg of the triad decision making would have as much weight as the population criteria and the fact of being a U.N. member state. If the Binding Triad is instituted so that it would include the necessity of an integrating world monetary system, the rules of a global system would tend to level the financial field. Accounting and auditing are stronger when universal standards are adopted, and these function within a system that can manage a world currency. The world currency makes it easier to create equitable working conditions for all human beings around the world. At that point there would be neither hard currencies nor soft currencies, but only the world currency and no country could be starved out for lack of exchange.

Among other problems with the Binding Triad is that it is limited to changing the voting system in the U.N. General Assembly and does not address other issues such as the dominance of military power and the issue of Human Rights with any declaration of rights other than the Universal Declaration of Human Rights and the other international human rights instruments, which are widely criticised as defective regarding political rights, especially in that national governments–the primary violators–can override the protections. There is no recognised right to self-protection. The Binding Triad does not meet the UDHR Article 21.3. standard of universal suffrage as the basis for authority of government.

The Binding Triad proposal is dependent on the *United Nations Charter* amendment process, and so would be subject to veto by any one of the five Permanent Security Council Members. As such, it is a proposal and not a founded document. At the same time, Binding Triad supporters point out that other changes have been made in the Charter when there was overwhelming support for change in the General Assembly and when, one-by-one, the P-5 states decided to not block the broad consensus.

Constitution of the Earth Federation (C.E.F.)

The proposed *Constitution of the Earth Federation* by Scott Rausher and promoted by Mark Foster, is perhaps the most obscure and unstudied of any of the world constitution proposals. However, upon examination, one can see that it is a legitimate proposal and among the strongest of all the world constitutions. The 25-page document provides for a uni-cameral legislature of persons directly elected by the people. A notable feature of this world constitution is that 15 of the 25 pages comprise a well-worded bill of rights, which is stronger than any other world constitutional bill of rights. The explicit recognition of rights includes all of those in the *U.S. Constitution*, all of those in the Universal Declaration of Human Rights and more besides. The constitution includes the affirmation that not to mention rights is not to disparage those not named. It does not use the same nation-centric phraseology as in conventional bills of rights, but a more precise language—very clear. For lack of publicity only, the Rauscher C.E.F. is obscure. As the people learn of it, then it is likely to get more promotion. The C.E.F. is a civil world constitution, like the F.E.C. There is no world military, even from the inception, only civil police forces bound to adhere to the regulations of civil enforcement.

Problems of the *Constitution of the Earth Federation* include the provision that the Prime Minister can dissolve the World Parliament and call for new elections. This has been shown to be extremely disruptive to progressive legislation, and could cause adoption of good legislation and implementation of necessary programs to be stymied. Also, the right to self protection is recognized, but qualified. The recognition of this particular right needs a wording that will be strong beyond qualification, as it can be demonstrated that recognition of all the other rights survive based on the strength of this one.

As it stands, the *Constitution of the Earth Federation*, though strong in rights recognition, is still only a constitutional proposal, and not a founded document.

New United Nations Charter (U.N.Ch.A-109)

Benton Musslewhite, an international lawyer, and President of One World Now, has drafted a proposal for a New *United Nations Charter*. This proposal would be implemented through a United Nations General Review Conference as defined in Article 109 of the *United Nations Charter*. The General Review Conference can deliberate fundamental changes to the *U.N. Charter*, and the convening of the Conference is not dependent on the Security Council assent or veto. As with the other proposals, the draft has strengths and weaknesses. There is ample representation, including a legislative body, the Duma, which has a 1 delegate per 40,000 voters, and which is strong for gathering popular support and interest. The Congress would have 1000 men and 1000 women elected from each of 1000 Administrative Districts. Also, the proposal includes a guarantee of gender equity for both of these legislatures.

In addition to the above two assemblies, there are five other houses of the world legislature, including a world senate, representing the national governments, a house of deputies representing local governments, a people's assembly, representing civil society organizations, a youth assembly and an electronic parliament of professional parliamentarians from national and local governments.

The representation is thorough. However, we might argue that a legislature of seven houses will be encumbered. When and how can legislation get through so many houses? Perhaps this is not really a problem. Indeed, when considering both the *Constitution for the Federation of Earth* as well as the deliberative bodies of its derivative world legislation, particularly the World Elections Act (World Legislative Act #29), there are specific provisions for a separate well-funded Global Peoples Assembly, for youth participation and for electronic deliberations. In this respect, the New United Nations Charter and the *Constitution for the Federation of Earth* are convergent.

One difficulty of the New *U.N. Charter* proposal is that the system retains a global military, and the global legislature retains the power to engage in war.

The New *United Nations Charter* proposal has a set of principles recognizing all of the U.S. Bill of Rights and all of the Universal Declaration of Human Rights. However, it is not clear whether this is part of the constitution itself, or is just a promotion. The strong rights stance is not so clear as that of Rausher's C.E.F., in which the rights recognition is obviously intended as an integral part of the world constitution.

The original adoption and the amendment process of the New *United Nations Charter* proposal are dependent upon an Article 109 General Review Conference. According to the *United Nations Charter*, any changes made in a review conference would be subject to the unanimous confirmation of the Permanent Members of the Security Council. (It is not entirely certain that this original U.N.Ch. provision would stand, were there to be a general review conference. The potential demise of the veto power may be why there has not been a review conference since the inception of the United Nations Organization.) For these reasons, the U.N.Ch.A-109 remains only a proposal and not a founded document.

Subsidiary Assembly Under the Old United Nations Charter (U.N.Ch.A.-22)

Article 22 of the *United Nations Charter* states that the General Assembly can establish any needed subsidiary bodies. Based upon this provision, many groups argue that a second assembly can be established without any amendment to the *United Nations Charter*. An assembly based upon Article 22 does not require affirmation of the Security Council. It could simply be formed by vote of the General Assembly.

It is true that this would create a bi-cameral assembly. It also appears to be, at least for present, the most popular of the proposals, at least in the New York area. This proposal has medium political strength and more political strength in North America than any of the other four proposals here under consideration. This might be a proposal that will get funding and this might be a proposal that will get published in refereed journals. However, it is expected that the political strength of this proposal will wane, because both of the houses, whether the General Assembly, or its Peoples' Assembly, or a World Parliament of the U.N., would be merely straw parliaments without binding effect. The political will is overshadowed by the current Security Council System, which can veto or ignore any recommendation coming from either of the two deliberative houses.

Although the dispositions for implementation are simple, the proposal depends on moral authority alone, which may postpone forceful legal authority into the indefinite future, allowing tremendous loss of life and endangerment to the Earth.

The rights provisions here are weak, based solely on the Universal Declaration of Human Rights and the conventional rights instruments, and there is no recognition of the right to self protection. Prospects for significant amendment are poor, as these would be dependent upon the Security Council assent or veto. Although the Article 22 strategy might be considered as based on a founded document, the *United Nations Charter*, upon which it is based, is not a world constitution for democratic, non-military world federation. The creation of an elected assembly subordinate to the General Assembly can not establish such federation.

Projection

A Second Assembly, based upon Article 22 and the old ***United Nations Charter***, will probably emerge, with its acclaimed moral force, because this is a primary means by which the conventional system can most durably resist the convergence toward significant change. However, the moral force of the General Assembly was a distraction for over sixty years. It is unclear how the moral force of a subsidiary body to the General Assembly will make much difference. It could cause harm, by leading concerned citizens away from approaches of significant action. Significant change is much more likely either outside of the United Nations System, or through the General Review Conference, as defined by *United Nations Charter* Article 109. World conditions will deteriorate, and any second assembly will not be able to effect change, except perhaps indirectly through an insistence on the General Review Conference. There is little point in resisting the formation of the Second Assembly, because additional proof of its futility would be in its formation. There are already many people working toward the Article 22 Second Assembly. We recommend to let those people do that work and to not spend too much energy in coaching them away. The Second Assembly movement is apparently an integral part of the current efforts to transform the U.N. process to be either more effective to address security matters, to be more democratic, or both. When formed, the Second Assembly, in displaying impotence as a consultative body, might give impetus to action that greatly matters. Furthermore, a Second Assembly itself may have some recommendations worth considering.

Unlike the Second Assembly to the United Nations under U.N.Ch.A. 22., the Elections Act of the Provisional World Parliament, in conformance with the *Earth*

Constitution, defined the Global Peoples Assembly with significant power in terms of determining its own venues as well as a significant role in the world's direct democracy processes, initiatives and other powers. Elected representatives of the Global Peoples Assembly might convene themselves at the United Nations Headquarters in New York City, by arrangement with the appropriate United Nations authorities, as there is no respective prohibition or discouragement from doing so. It is important to distinguish between the functions of a U.N.Ch.A.-22. Assembly and a Global Peoples Assembly established under the Elections Act that might convene in United Nations facilities, as the functions and powers of the two bodies are distinct.

Recommendations

In this essay, strengths and weaknesses of four current world constitutional proposals have been examined. There is little point in allowing pride to deter us from reconsideration when we examine multiple proposals and find provisions in the unfamiliar proposals that have more strength than the proposal with which we are most familiar.

There are four conceivable broad strategies for moving forward. If we seriously examine multiple proposals for world constitution and world constitution concepts, and there are outstanding strengths and outstanding weaknesses in each of the proposals, it is not reasonable to simply drop our original proposal and wander over to another, which we see has certain weaknesses. However, we can communicate with the proponents of the other proposals, for the purpose of strength through convergent elaboration. The four strategies of constitutional development are these:

1) An independent World Constituent Assembly, to consider proposals, at which all the world constitutional proposals are considered in full;

2) A coalition of world constitutional proposal organizations, together with world federalist organizations and other organizations of civil society, might coordinate action for the purpose of promoting, and ultimately legally forcing a convention of the United Nations Charter Article 109 General Review Conference;

3) An independent World Constituent Assembly, in which one's own world constitution is protected in its perceived strengths, but open to adjustments in its perceived weaknesses. For example, in March 2003, the Provisional World Parliament of the ***Earth Constitution*** (F.E.C.) completed the elaboration of its Rules of Procedure for such a process, as permitted by the *Earth Constitution* itself in Article 18., Section 5. Though the Provisional World Parliament has prepared in case of the upcoming necessity of such a world constituent assembly, the Parliament organizing agencies have not yet called any new Session of the World Constituent Assembly, because there has not been the required quorum of perceived necessity as defined by the Parliament; or

4) Strict adherence and promotion of the *Earth Constitution* during which its programs coordinate a Founding Ratification Convention and the first operative stage

of Earth Federation with approximately two dozen national governments participating. A Founding Ratification Convention would not be a world constitutional convention, but would only be a special first session of operative World Parliament in which substantive enabling world legislation would be deliberated and hopefully adopted. Then, after no more than an additional time period of 10 years, as required by the *Earth Constitution* Article 18., Section 4., a world constitutional convention would be convened according to the guidelines defined in the *Earth Constitution.*

The first strategy is probably most likely to encounter debilitating conflict, because of the risks involved in offering one's world constitution to the decision of others who have come with a different constitution. Reasonable persons will look askance at why excellent constituent deliberation already done would be disregarded in favor of starting all over, a process sometimes humorously referred to as "NIH" for "Not Invented Here."

In addition to the first strategy, the possibility of the General Review Conference is unlikely to produce a civil world federation of nations, because the people themselves would not be the stakeholders and participants in its process. Only delegates assigned by national powers would be able to vote, or national cronies appointed by those national powers from non-governmental bodies that happen to be in favor at the time of any general review conference. No electoral process provisions are in effect to ensure even the eventual enforcement of the UDHR Article 7 guarantee for equal protecion and UDHR Article 21.3 guarantee for universal suffrage. The people of Earth might be even further disempowered after the conclusion of such a conference

The adjustment of the Security Council is an often recounted purpose of an Article 109 Conference. Some such proposals would not necessarily be bad, if it is taken that the Security Council is to be an advisory body only and no longer authorized to carry out or permit war. For instance, applying the weighted voting proposal of Professor Joseph Schwartzberg to the Security Council might be helpful, if it is clearly directed that the Security Council has advisory power only and no executive power.

The Security Council might be expanded by two or five members, but to what end? The addition of Permanent Security Council Members and expansion of the Security Council are mere cosmetic reforms. We rightly discourage Permanent Security Council Member enlargements for the purpose of expanding the veto. We remember that under the Covenant of the League of Nations, each nation had the veto. To expand the veto power is to head in that archaic direction, which as we know, leads to paralysis, and likely war.

Well-regulated civil police, together with a just and empowered world court system, and legislation comprehensively criminalizing specific war activities are the road of peace. To do a good job, civil society and the proponents of world constitutions must have a strong voice. Any General Review Conference cannot do a good job unless it has the best world constitutional proposals on hand while making its deliberations. It must also have the best minds available, to defend and promote the specifics of the world constitutional proposals. The likelihood of the best proposals and best minds would be reduced by the selection process that would be based on the United Nations Charter original flaws.

So what would one recommend to the General Review Conference if one were to insist on the very best from each of the five world constitutional concepts considered in this paper? How would one support views for the best constitutional structure?

The General Review Conference would need to deliberate to create an integrated and integrating document that puts all of the powers—legislative, judicial, and executive—into a global system that is humane and responsive to individual citizens. We believe that the best constitutional framework for that is the *Constitution for the Federation of Earth*.

A general review conference would undoubtedly have its own priorities and agenda. Some changes from the *Earth Constitution* would be acceptable to the people, but a mere re-wording of the United Nations Charter would not work for creating world federation. One possibly workable integration might be comprised by adopting the ***Binding Triad***, as developed by Richard Hudson and the Center for War /Peace Studies, and placing it into the position of the House of Nations defined in the *Earth Constitution*. This might help correct the *Earth Constitution*'s problem of relatively weak clarity of weighting in its House of Nations. However, a legislative interpretation for the basis of nationhood by the Provisional World Parliament and World Parliament might be even more effective. This could be done even without any General Review Conference.

The thorough bill of rights found in the Rausher *Constitution of the Earth Federation* could be integrated fully into the rights recognized in the *Earth Constitution*. This would help correct the deficiencies in political rights recognitions noted in the *Earth Constitution,* and the nation-centric, conditional conventional rights declarations of the other world constitutions. Principles of gender equity and popular participation of Musslewhite's ***New U.N. Charter*** could likewise be integrated into the provisions of the ***Earth Constitution*** (The 200-Member House of Counsellors is ideally suited for this gender equity provision.) The proposal for a Global Peoples Assembly or Provisional Peoples' Assembly can be promoted and funded even before any further constitutional elaboration, since there is already a near-consensus recognized need for this within the world government and world governance communities. These final steps would reflect the needs for ensured gender equity in government and also the need for a Peoples Assembly and Duma to reflect popular participation.

Such a document would take best features from each of the reviewed world constitutions and concepts. It is a radical approach and would not be guaranteed. However, it might be strong as well as concise. A world constitution synthesizing the best features of each of the first four structures or concepts reviewed in this article might be easier to promote than each of the world constitutions alone, because it would integrate these best features together in a common document, and because a general review conference might be seen by the people as authoritative.

However, it is entirely possible that no Article 109 conference will ever be forthcoming. Furthermore, even if there were eventually an Article 109 conference, what would keep the nuclear force from imposing itself? What safeguards would ensure that the general review conference would faithfully address the real human problems in the world and the democratic deficit of the conventional United Nations system? Finally, under the old *United Nations Charter*, though the General Review Conference ostensibly can convene without Security Council approval, the decisions of the Conference are subject to approval or disapproval of unanimous affirmation by the five Permanent Members of the Security Council. Subjecting the fate of the Earth and the well-being of humanity to such tenuous terms would be a desperate long shot.

A stronger approach is that of operating from a founded document that is already operating, such as the *Constitution for the Federation of Earth* (*F.E.C. or Earth Constitution)*. The use of a founded universal civil constitution allows the immediate participation of others who have honest drive for the necessary change. This founded world constitution has provisions for its own amendment, as well as adequate provisions defining the manner in which the world constitution will be implemented. The *Earth Constitution* has clear provisions for universal suffrage as the basis for the authority of government. Being founded, the *Earth Constitution* does not subject itself to conventional powers or to nuclear powers. Instead, its implementation emerges in provisional operation, and through that provisional operation, a network for world electoral process is created without waiting for the conventional system to initiate it. Then through the electoral process, the world constitution itself can be tested. Part of the legitimacy of the the *Earth Constitution* is that it can move us forward, protecting the people of the Earth. Part of its legitimacy is that the *Earth Constitution* already has the provision and operation of a Provisional World Parliament that is deliberating and adopting world legislation with a comprehensive systems approach to all world problems, and as a viable means to integrate previously fragmented international laws within an operating world federal system.

If there are provisions of this *Earth Constitution* that are not adequate, or that are objectionable to the people, then these provisions will become apparent in the ratification process. World constitutional refinement is merely a matter of further world constituent assemblies, and resubmission of the world constitution until the objections have been adequately addressed in the world constitutional revisions. In the meanwhile, the people of the world can immediately take self-governing action by implementation of the system of multi-cameral world legislation that proves the efficacy of the *Earth Constitution.*

A Comparison Chart of Current World Constitution Proposals and Concepts, including the Proposal for an Article 22 UN Assembly

World Constitution Properties	***Earth Constitution* (FEC)**	**Binding Triad (BT)**	***Constitution of Earth Federation* (CEF)**	**New *UN Charter* (U.N.Ch. Article -109)**	**Old *UN Charter* (U.N.Ch. Article 22)**
Parliamentary Structure?	Tri-cameral	Uni-cameral or bi-cameral	Uni-cameral (lower)	Multi-Cameral (7)	Bi-cameral
Parliamentary weakness?	Upper house nationhood not clearly defined	Not directly elected	PM can dissolve WP	Cumbersome number of chambers may bog legislation	Straw Parliaments
Currently Civil or Military?	Civil	Military	Civil	Civil / Military	Military
Dispositions for implementation	complex (maximalist)	simple	medium	complex (maximalist)	simple
Rights Declaration?	Modest, but in two parts, as E. Roosevelt suggested (political & economic).	Weak, UDHR and conventional guarantees only. UDHR Article 21.3 is not protected.	Strongest. 15 pages clearly enumerated.	Strong in statement of principles only. Rights Bill not part of world constitution ***per se***.	Weak, UDHR and conventional guarantees only
Right to keep and bear arms? (RKBA?)	Not in *Constitution*, but right to self protection guaranteed in derivative world legislation.	No RKBA	Yes, but qualified.	RKBA in principles only.	No RKBA
Amendment process?	Defined & tenable independent of 109 General Review Conference	Requires Security Council assent, but 109 Conference might bypass.	Defined & Tenable Independent of 109	Partially Defined. 109 Conference to set.	United Nations Charter Chapter 18, Articles 108 & 109
Essential strength? (Probability it would promptly do the needful, if adopted) [author's opinion]	high	medium (Lacks civil architecture, but that might be provided by BT vote.)	medium (Dangerous, excessive executive power)	medium (Strength: guarantee of gender equity in one of the world legislative chambers)	low (Civil architecture cannot be provided by vote.)

Chapter Six

The Constitution for the Federation of Earth

As amended at the fourth session of the World Constituent Assembly, Troia, Portugal, May 1991

"A constitution is the arrangement of magistracies in a state." Aristotle (384–323 B.C.)

World Constitution Drafting Committee of 25 members
Drafting Committee Chair: Sir Dr. Reinhart Ruge
Primary authors: H. Philip Isely, Terence P. Amerasinghe, Syed Md. Husain, D. M. Spencer, and Max Habicht

Foreword

The *Constitution for the Federation of Earth* is a document that was worked out by successive world constituent assemblies meeting in countries around the world over the course of about 23 years, from 1968 to 1991. The *Earth Constitution* was elaborated with input from people from numerous countries and all continents, including eminent international lawyers. People have translated it into 20 major world languages. It is the most important and strongest of all the non-military world constitutions for parliamentary Earth Federation. To date, thousands of individual citizens have ratified the *Earth Constitution.*

The editors believe that this *Constitution for the Federation of Earth*, adopted by the Members of the 4th World Constituent Assembly, convened in Troia, Portugal, in 1991, is an adequate founded world constitution for the successful Federation of Earth. We hope that the reader will study the document with care to see its intrinsic value.

The editors have placed the *Earth Constitution* into full numeric codification. This is intended to simplify the codification, since not all readers are familiar with roman numerals. It also standardized the codification. Eventually, the *Earth Constitution* needs translation into all active written human languages. Since by their very nature, alphabets do not have one-to-one correspondence between languages, full numeric codification makes accurate and standard translation possible.

Additional Editors' Note: Examples of how to read numeric codification "1.2.03." is read "Article One, Section Two Point Zero Three" "4.05.12.10." is read "Article Four, Section Five Point Twelve Point Ten". "Point" need not be called out for the section heading, that is, second set of digits from left, nor after the final digit.

Reading out the zero is perhaps optional, but it should be in written form if there are 10 or more sections in an Article or in any subsection. This cues the reader that there are at least 10 items at that level. The zero also allows orderly columnar stacking of section headings for analytical tasks and government documents. The zero thereby eases reading and reduces likelihood of errors.

A CONSTITUTION FOR THE FEDERATION OF EARTH

Contents 177

Preamble 179

Article 1 - Broad Functions of the Earth Federation 180

Article 2 - Basic Structure of World Federation 180
Article 3 - Organs of the Earth Federation 181

Article 4 - Grant of Specific Powers to the Earth Federation 182

Article 5 - The World Parliament 185
5.1. - Functions and Powers of the World Parliament
5.2. - Composition of the World Parliament
5.3. - The House of Peoples
5.4. - The House of Nations
5.5. - The House of Counsellors
5.6. - Procedures of the World Parliament

Article 6 - The World Executive 189
6.1. - Functions and Powers of the World Executive
6.2. - Composition of the World Executive
6.3. - The Presidium
6.4. - The Executive Cabinet
6.5. - Procedures of the World Executive
6.6. - Limitations on the World Executive

Article 7 - The World Administration 192
7.1. - Functions of the World Administration
7.2. - Structure and Procedures of the World Administration
7.2.5. and 7.2.6.: Secretary General of the Administration
7.3. - Departments of the World Adminstration

Article 8 - The Integrative Complex 194
8.1. - Definition
8.2. - The World Civil Service Administration
8.3. - The World Boundaries and Elections Administration
8.4. - Institute on Governmental Procedures and World Problems
8.5. - The Agency for Research and Planning
8.6. - The Agency for Technological and Environmental Assessment
8.7. - The World Financial Administration
8.8. - Commission for Legislative Review

Article 9 - The World Judiciary 201
9.1. - Jurisdiction of the World Supreme Court
9.2. - Benches of the World Supreme Court
9.3. - Seats of the World Supreme Court
9.4. - The Collegium of World Judges
9.5. - The Superior Tribunal of the World Supreme Court

Article 10 - The Enforcement System 204
10.1. - Basic Principles
10.2. - The Structure for Enforcement
10.3. - The World Police
10.4. - The Means of Enforcement

Article 11 - The World Ombudsmus 208
11.1. - Functions and Powers of the World Ombudsmus
11.2. - Composition of the World Ombudsmus

Article 12 - Bill of Rights for the Citizens of Earth 209

Article 13 - Directive Principles for the Earth Federation 211

Article 14 - Safeguards and Reservations 212

Article 15 - World Federal Zones and the World Capitals 213

Article 16 - World Territories and Exterior Relations 214

Article 17 - Ratification and Implementation 215
17.1. - Ratification of the World Constitution
17.2. - Stages of Implementation
17.3. - First Operative Stage of Earth Federation
17.4. - Second Operative Stage of Earth Federation
17.5. - Full Operative Stage of Earth Federation
17.6. - Costs of Ratification

Article 18 - Amendments 223

Article 19 - Provisional Earth Federation 224
19.1. - Actions to be Taken by the World Constituent Assembly
19.2. - Work of the Preparatory Commissions
19.3. - Composition of the Provisional World Parliament
19.4. - Formation of the Provisional World Executive
19.5. - First Actions of the Provisional Earth Federation

PREAMBLE

Realizing that Humanity today has come to a turning point in history and that we are on the threshold of an just, humane order that promises to usher in an era of peace, prosperity, justice and harmony;

Aware of the interdependence of people, nations and all life;

Aware that man's abuse of science and technology has brought Humanity to the brink of disaster through the production of horrendous weaponry of mass destruction and to the brink of ecological and social catastrophe;

Aware that the traditional concept of security through military defense is a total illusion both for the present and for the future;

Aware of the misery and conflicts caused by ever increasing disparity between rich and poor;

Conscious of our obligation to posterity to save Humanity from imminent and total annihilation;

Conscious that Humanity is One despite the existence of diverse nations, races, creeds, ideologies and cultures and that the principle of unity in diversity is the basis for a new age when war shall be outlawed and peace prevail; when the Earth's total resources shall be equitably used for human welfare; and when basic human rights and responsibilities shall be shared by all without discrimination;

Conscious of the inescapable reality that the greatest hope for the survival of life on Earth is the establishment of a democratic world federation;

We, citizens of the world, hereby resolve to establish a world federation to be governed in accordance with this *Constitution for the Federation of Earth*.

A CONSTITUTION FOR THE FEDERATION OF EARTH

Article 1 - Broad Functions of the Earth Federation

The broad functions of the Federation of Earth shall be:

1.1. To prevent war, secure disarmament, and resolve territorial and other disputes which endanger peace and human rights.

1.2. To protect universal human rights, including life, liberty, security, democracy, and equal opportunities in life.

1.3. To obtain for all people on earth the conditions required for equitable economic and social development and for diminishing social differences.

1.4. To regulate world trade, communications, transportation, currency, standards, use of world resources, and other global and international processes.

1.5. To protect the environment and the ecological fabric of life from all sources of damage, and to control technological innovations whose effects transcend national boundaries, for the purpose of keeping Earth a safe, healthy and happy home for humanity.

1.6. To devise and implement solutions to all problems which are beyond the capacity of national governments, or which are now or may become of global or international concern or consequence.

Article 2 - Basic Structure of Earth Federation

2.1. The Federation of Earth shall be organized as a universal federation, to include all nations and all people, and to encompass all oceans, seas and lands of Earth, inclusive of non-self governing territories, together with the surrounding atmosphere.

2.2. The World Government for the Federation of Earth shall be non-military and shall be democratic in its own structure, with ultimate sovereignty residing in all the people who live on Earth.

2.3. The authority and powers granted to the World Government shall be limited to those defined in this Constitution for the Federation of Earth, applicable to problems and affairs which transcend national boundaries, leaving to national governments jurisdiction over the internal affairs of the respective nations but consistent with the authority of the World Government to protect universal human rights as defined in this World Constitution.

2.4. The basic direct electoral and administrative units of the World Government shall be World Electoral and Administrative Districts. A total of not more than 1000 World

Electoral and Administrative Districts shall be defined, and shall be nearly equal in population, within the limits of plus or minus ten percent.

2.5. Contiguous World Electoral and Administrative Districts shall be combined as may be appropriate to compose a total of twenty World Electoral and Administrative Regions for the following purposes, but not limited thereto: for the election or appointment of certain world government officials; for administrative purposes; for composing various organs of the world government as enumerated in Article 4; for the functioning of the Judiciary, the Enforcement System, and the Ombudsmus, as well as for the functioning of any other organ or agency of the World Government.

2.6. The World Electoral and Administrative Regions may be composed of a variable number of World Electoral and Administrative Districts, taking into consideration geographic, cultural, ecological and other factors as well as population.

2.7. Contiguous World Electoral and Administrative Regions shall be grouped together in pairs to compose Magna-Regions.

2.8. The boundaries for World Electoral and Administrative Regions shall not cross the boundaries of the World Electoral and Administrative Districts, and shall be common insofar as feasible for the various administrative departments and for the several organs and agencies of the World Government. Boundaries for the World Electoral and Administrative Districts as well as for the Regions need not conform to existing national boundaries, but shall conform as far as practicable.

2.9. The World Electoral and Administrative Regions shall be grouped to compose at least five Continental Divisions of the Earth, for the election or appointment of certain world government officials, and for certain aspects of the composition and functioning of the several organs and agencies of the World Government as specified hereinafter. The boundaries of Continental Divisions shall not cross existing national boundaries as far as practicable. Continental Divisions may be composed of a variable number of World Electoral and Administrative Regions.

Article 3 - Organs of the Earth Federation

The organs of the World Government shall be:

3.1. The World Parliament.
3.2. The World Executive.
3.3. The World Administration.
3.4. The Integrative Complex.
3.5. The World Judiciary.
3.6. The Enforcement System.
3.7. The World Ombudsmus.

Article 4 - Grant of Specific Powers to the Earth Federation

The powers of the World government to be exercised through its several organs and agencies shall comprise the following:

4.1. Prevent wars and armed conflicts among the nations, regions, districts, parts and peoples of Earth.

4.2. Supervise disarmament and prevent re-armament; prohibit and eliminate the design, testing, manufacture, sale, purchase, use and possession of weapons of mass destruction, and prohibit or regulate all lethal weapons which the World Parliament may decide.

4.3. Prohibit incitement to war, and discrimination against or defamation of conscientious objectors.

4.4. Provide the means for peaceful and just solutions of disputes and conflicts among or between nations, peoples, and/or other components within the Federation of Earth.

4.5. Supervise boundary settlements and conduct plebiscites as needed.

4.6. Define the boundaries for the districts, regions and divisions which are established for electoral, administrative, judicial and other purposes of the World Government.

4.7. Define and regulate procedures for the nomination and election of the members of each House of the World Parliament, and for the nomination, election, appointment and employment of all World Government officials and personnel.

4.8. Codify world laws, including the body of international law developed prior to adoption of the world constitution, but not inconsistent therewith, and which is approved by the World Parliament.

4.9. Establish universal standards for weights, measurements, accounting and records.

4.10. Provide assistance in the event of large scale calamities, including drouth, famine, pestilence, flood, earthquake, hurricane, ecological disruptions and other disasters.

4.11. Guarantee and enforce the civil liberties and the basic human rights which are defined in the Bill of Rights for the Citizens of Earth which is made a part of this World Constitution under Article 12.

4.12. Define standards and promote the worldwide improvement in working conditions, nutrition, health, housing, human settlements, environmental conditions, education, economic security, and other conditions defined under Article 13 of this World Constitution.

4.13. Regulate and supervise international transportation, communications, postal services, and migrations of people.

4.14. Regulate and supervise supra-national trade, industry, corporations, businesses, cartels, professional services, labor supply, finances, investments and insurance.

4.15. Secure and supervise the elimination of tariffs and other trade barriers among nations, but with provisions to prevent or minimize hardship for those previously protected by tariffs.

4.16. Raise the revenues and funds, by direct and/or indirect means, which are necessary for the purposes and activities of the World Government.

4.17. Establish and operate world financial, banking, credit and insurance institutions designed to serve human needs; establish, issue and regulate world currency, credit and exchange.

4.18. Plan for and regulate the development, use, conservation and re-cycling of the natural resources of Earth as the common heritage of Humanity; protect the environment in every way for the benefit of both present and future generations.

4.19. Create and operate a World Economic Development Organization to serve equitably the needs of all nations and people included within the World Federation.

4.20. Develop and implement solutions to transnational problems of food supply, agricultural production, soil fertility, soil conservation, pest control, diet, nutrition, drugs and poisons, and the disposal of toxic wastes.

4.21. Develop and implement means to control population growth in relation to the life-support capacities of Earth, and solve problems of population distribution.

4.22. Develop, protect, regulate and conserve the water supplies of Earth; develop, operate and/or coordinate transnational irrigation and other water supply and control projects; assure equitable allocation of trans-national water supplies, and protect against adverse trans-national effects of water or moisture diversion or weather control projects within national boundaries.

4.23. Own, administer and supervise the development and conservation of the oceans and sea-beds of Earth and all resources thereof, and protect from damage.

4.24. Protect from damage, and control and supervise the uses of the atmosphere of Earth.

4.25. Conduct inter-planetary and cosmic explorations and research; have exclusive jurisdiction over the Moon and over all satellites launched from Earth.

4.26. Establish, operate and/or coordinate global air lines, ocean transport systems, international railways and highways, global communication systems, and means for interplanetary travel and communications; control and administer vital waterways.

4.27. Develop, operate and/or coordinate transnational power systems, or networks of small units, integrating into the systems or networks power derived from the sun, wind, water, tides, heat differentials, magnetic forces, and any other source of safe, ecologically sound and continuing energy supply.

4.28. Control the mining, production, transportation and use of fossil sources of energy to the extent necessary to reduce and prevent damages to the environment and the ecology, as well as to prevent conflicts and conserve supplies for sustained use by succeeding generations.

4.29. Exercise exclusive jurisdiction and control over nuclear energy research and testing and nuclear power production, including the right to prohibit any form of testing or production considered hazardous.

4.30. Place under world controls essential natural resources which may be limited or unevenly distributed about the Earth. Find and implement ways to reduce wastes and find ways to minimize disparities when development or production is insufficient to supply everybody with all that may be needed.

4.31. Provide for the examination and assessment of technological innovations which are or may be of supranational consequence, to determine possible hazards or perils to humanity or the environment; institute such controls and regulations of technology as may be found necessary to prevent or correct widespread hazards or perils to human health and welfare.

4.32. Carry out intensive programs to develop safe alternatives to any technology or technological processes which may be hazardous to the environment, the ecological system, or human health and welfare.

4.33. Resolve supra-national problems caused by gross disparities in technological development or capability, capital formation, availability of natural resources, educational opportunity, economic opportunity, and wage and price differentials. Assist the processes of technology transfer under conditions which safeguard human welfare and the environment and contribute to minimizing disparities.

4.34. Intervene under procedures to be defined by the World Parliament in cases of either intra-state violence and intra-state problems which seriously affect world peace or universal human rights.

4.35. Develop a world university system. Obtain the correction of prejudicial communicative materials which cause misunderstandings or conflicts due to differences of race, religion, sex, national origin or affiliation.

4.36. Organize, coordinate and/or administer a voluntary, non-military World Service Corps, to carry out a wide variety of projects designed to serve human welfare.

4.37. Designate as may be found desirable an official world language or official world languages.

4.38. Establish and operate a system of world parks, wild life preserves, natural places, and wilderness areas.

4.39. Define and establish procedures for initiative and referendum by the Citizens of Earth on matters of supra-national legislation not prohibited by this World Constitution.

4.40. Establish such departments, bureaus, commissions, institutes, corporations, administrations, or agencies as may by needed to carry out any and all of the functions and powers of the World Government.

4.41. Serve the needs of humanity in any and all ways which are now, or may prove in the future to be, beyond the capacity of national and local governments.

Article 5 - The World Parliament

Sec. 5.1. - Functions and Powers of the World Parliament

The functions and powers of the World Parliament shall comprise the following:
5.1.01. To prepare and enact detailed legislation in all areas of authority and jurisdiction granted to the World Government under Article 4 of this World Constitution.
5.1.02. To amend or repeal world laws as may be found necessary or desirable.
5.1.03. To approve, amend or reject the international laws developed prior to the advent of World Government, and to codify and integrate the system of world law and world legislation under the World Government.
5.1.04. To establish such regulations and directions as may be needed, consistent with this world constitution, for the proper functioning of all organs, branches, departments, bureaus, commissions, institutes, agencies or parts of the World Government.
5.1.05. To review, amend and give final approval to each budget for the World Government, as submitted by the World Executive; to devise the specific means for directly raising funds needed to fulfill the budget, including taxes, licenses, fees, globally accounted social and public costs which must be added into the prices for goods and services, loans and credit advances, and any other appropriate means; and to appropriate and allocate funds for all operations and functions of the World Government in

accordance with approved budgets, but subject to the right of the Parliament to revise any appropriation not yet spent or contractually committed.

5.1.06. To create, alter, abolish or consolidate the departments, bureaus, commissions, institutes, agencies or other parts of the World Government as may be needed for the best functioning of the several organs of the World Government, subject to the specific provisions of this World Constitution.

5.1.07. To approve the appointments of the heads of all major departments, commissions, offices, agencies and other parts of the several organs of the World Government, except those chosen by electoral or civil service procedures.

5.1.08. To remove from office for cause any member of the World Executive, and any elective or appointive head of any organ, department, office, agency or other part of the World Government, subject to the specific provisions in this World Constitution concerning specific offices.

5.1.09. To define and revise the boundaries of the World Electoral and Administrative Districts, the World Electoral and Administrative Regions and Magna Regions, and the Continental Divisions.

5.1.10. To schedule the implementation of those provisions of the World Constitution which require implementation by stages during the several stages of Provisional World Government, First Operative Stage of World Government, Second Operative Stage of World Government, and Full Operative Stage of World Government, as defined in Articles 17 and 19 of this World Constitution.

5.1.11. To plan and schedule the implementation of those provisions of the World Constitution which may require a period of years to be accomplished.

Sec. 5.2. - Composition of the World Parliament

5.2.1. The World Parliament shall be composed of three houses, designated as follows:

o The House of Peoples, to represent the people of Earth directly and equally;

o The House of Nations, to represent the nations which are joined together in the Federation of Earth; and a

o House of Counsellors with particular functions to represent the highest good and best interests of humanity as a whole.

5.2.2. All members of the World Parliament, regardless of House, shall be designated as Members of the World Parliament.

Sec. 5.3. - The House of Peoples

5.3.1. The House of Peoples shall be composed of the peoples delegates directly elected in proportion to population from the World Electoral and Administrative Districts, as defined in Article 2.4.

5.3.2. Peoples delegates shall be elected by universal adult suffrage, open to all persons of age 18 and above.

5.3.3. One peoples delegate shall be elected from each World Electoral and Administrative District to serve a five year term in the House of Peoples. Peoples delegates may be elected to serve successive terms without limit. Each peoples delegate shall have one vote.

5.3.4. A candidate for election to serve as a peoples delegate must be at least 21 years of age, a resident for at least one year of the electoral district from which the candidate is seeking election, and shall take a pledge of service to humanity.

Sec. 5.4. - The House of Nations

5.4.1. The House of Nations shall be composed of national delegates elected or appointed by procedures to be determined by each national government on the following basis:

5.4.1.1. One national delegate from each nation of at least 100,000 population, but less than 10,000,000 population.

5.4.1.2. Two national delegates from each nation of at least 10,000,000 population, but less than 100,000,000 population.

5.4.1.3. Three national delegates from each nation of 100,000,000 population or more.

5.4.2. Nations of less than 100,000 population may join in groups with other nations for purposes of representation in the House of Nations.

5.4.3. National delegates shall be elected or appointed to serve for terms of five years, and may be elected or appointed to serve successive terms without limit. Each national delegate shall have one vote.

5.4.4. Any person to serve as a national delegate shall be a citizen for at least two years of the nation to be represented, must be at least 21 years of age, and shall take a pledge of service to humanity.

Sec. 5.5. - The House of Counsellors

5.5.1. The House of Counsellors shall be composed of 200 counsellors chosen in equal numbers from nominations submitted from the twenty World Electoral and Administrative Regions, as defined in Article 2.5. and 2.6., ten from each Region.

5.5.2. Nominations for members of the House of Counsellors shall be made by the teachers and students of universities and colleges and of scientific academies and institutes within each world electoral and administrative region. Nominees may be persons who are off campus in any walk of life as well as on campus.

5.5.3. Nominees to the House of Counsellors from each World Electoral and Administrative Region shall, by vote taken among themselves, reduce the number of nominees to no less than two times and no more than three times the number to be elected.

5.5.4. Nominees to serve as members of the House of Counsellors must be at least 25 years of age, and shall take a pledge of service to humanity. There shall be no residence requirement, and a nominee need not be a resident of the region from which nominated or elected.

5.5.5. The members of the House of Counsellors from each region shall be elected by the members of the other two houses of the World Parliament from the particular region.

5.5.6. Counsellors shall be elected to serve terms of ten years. One-half of the members of the House of Counsellors shall be elected every five years. Counsellors may serve successive terms without limit. Each Counsellor shall have one vote.

Sec. 5.6. - Procedures of the World Parliament

5.6.01. Each house of the World Parliament during its first session after general elections shall elect a panel of five chairpersons from among its own members, one from each of five Continental Divisions. The chairpersons shall rotate annually so that each will serve for one year as chief presiding officer, while the other four serve as vice-chairpersons.

5.6.02. The panels of Chairpersons from each House shall meet together, as needed, for the purpose of coordinating the work of the Houses of the World Parliament, both severally and jointly.

5.6.03. Any legislative measure or action may be initiated in either House of Peoples or House of Nations or both concurrently, and shall become effective when passed by a simple majority vote of both the House of Peoples and of the House of Nations, except in those cases where an absolute majority vote or other voting majority is specified in this World Constitution.

5.6.04. In case of deadlock on a measure initiated in either the House of Peoples or House of Nations, the measure shall then automatically go to the House of Counsellors for decision by simple majority vote of the House of Counsellors, except in the cases where other majority vote is required in this World Constitution. Any measure may be referred for decision to the House of Counsellors by a concurrent vote of the other two houses.

5.6.05. The House of Counsellors may initiate any legislative measure, which shall then be submitted to the other two houses and must be passed by simple majority vote of both the House of Peoples and House of Nations to become effective, unless other voting majority is required by some provision of this World Constitution.

5.6.06. The House of Counsellors may introduce an opinion or resolution on any measure pending before either of the other two houses; either of the other houses may request the opinion of the House of Counsellors before acting upon a measure.

5.6.07. Each house of the World Parliament shall adopt its own detailed rules of procedure, which shall by consistent with the procedures set forth in this World Constitution, and which shall be designed to facilitate coordinated functioning of the three houses.

5.6.08. Approval of appointments by the World Parliament or any house thereof shall require simple majority votes, while removals for cause shall require absolute majority votes.

5.6.09. After the full operative stage of World Government is declared, general elections for members of the World Parliament to the House of Peoples shall be held every five years. The first general elections shall be held within the first two years following the declaration of the full operative stage of World Government.

5.6.10. Until the full operative stage of World Government is declared, elections for members of the World Parliament to the House of Peoples may be conducted whenever feasible in relation to the campaign for ratification of this World Constitution.

5.6.11. Regular sessions of the House of Peoples and House of Nations of the World Parliament shall convene on the second Monday of January of each and every Year.

5.6.12. Each nation, according to its own procedures, shall appoint or elect members of the World Parliament to the House of Nations at least thirty days prior to the date for convening the World Parliament in January.

5.6.13. The House of Peoples together with the House of Nations shall elect the members of the World Parliament to the House of Counsellors during the month of January after the general elections. For its first session after general elections, the House of Counsellors shall convene on the second Monday of March, and thereafter concurrently with the other two houses.
5.6.14. Bi-elections to fill vacancies shall be held within three months from occurrence of the vacancy or vacancies.
5.6.15. The World Parliament shall remain in session for a minimum of nine months of each year. One or two breaks may be taken during each year, at times and for durations to be decided by simple majority vote of the House of Peoples and House of Nations sitting jointly.
5.6.16. Annual salaries for members of the World Parliament of all three houses shall be the same, except for those who serve also as members of the Presidium and of the Executive Cabinet.
5.6.17. Salary schedules for members of the World Parliament and for members of the Presidium and of the Executive Cabinet shall be determined by the World Parliament.

Article 6 - The World Executive

Sec. 6.1. Functions and Powers of the World Executive

6.1.1. To implement the basic system of world law as defined in the World Constitution and in the codified system of world law after approval by the World Parliament.
6.1.2. To implement legislation enacted by the World Parliament.
6.1.3. To propose and recommend legislation for enactment by the World Parliament.
6.1.4. To convene the World Parliament in special sessions when necessary.
6.1.5. To supervise the World Administration and the Integrative Complex and all of the departments, bureaus, offices, institutes and agencies thereof.
6.1.6. To nominate, select and remove the heads of various organs, branches, departments, bureaus, offices, commissions, institutes, agencies and other parts of the World Government, in accordance with the provisions of this World Constitution and as specified in measures enacted by the World Parliament.
6.1.7. To prepare and submit annually to the World Parliament a comprehensive budget for the operations of the World Government, and to prepare and submit periodically budget projections over periods of several years.
6.1.8. To define and propose priorities for world legislation and budgetary allocations.
6.1.9. To be held accountable to the World Parliament for the expenditures of appropriations made by the World Parliament in accordance with approved and longer term budgets, subject to revisions approved by the World Parliament.

Sec. 6.2. Composition of the World Executive

The World Executive shall consist of a Presidium of five members, and of an Executive Cabinet of from twenty to thirty members, all of whom shall be members of the World Parliament.

Sec. 6.3. The Presidium

6.3.1. The Presidium shall be composed of five members, one to be designated as President and the other four to be designated as Vice Presidents. Each member of the Presidium shall be from a different Continental Division.

6.3.2. The Presidency of the Presidium shall rotate each year, with each member in turn to serve as President, while the other four serve as Vice Presidents. The order of rotation shall be decided by the Presidium.

6.3.3. The decisions of the Presidium shall be taken collectively, on the basis of majority decisions.

6.3.4. Each member of the Presidium shall be a member of the World Parliament, either elected to the House of Peoples or to the House of Counsellors, or appointed or elected to the House of Nations.

6.3.5. Nominations for the Presidium shall be made by the House of Counsellors. The number of nominees shall be from two to three times the number to be elected. No more than one-third of the nominees shall be from the House of Counsellors or from the House of Nations, and nominees must be included from all Continental Divisions.

6.3.6. From among the nominees submitted by the House of Counsellors, the Presidium shall be elected by vote of the combined membership of all three houses of the World Parliament in joint session. A plurality vote equal to at least 40 percent of the total membership of the World Parliament shall be required for the election of each member to the Presidium, with successive elimination votes taken as necessary until the required plurality is achieved.

6.3.7. Members of the Presidium may be removed for cause, either individually or collectively, by an absolute majority vote of the combined membership of the three houses of the World Parliament in joint session.

6.3.8. The term of office for the Presidium shall be five years and shall run concurrently with the terms of office for the members as Members of the World Parliament, except that at the end of each five year period, the Presidium members in office shall continue to serve until the new Presidium for the succeeding term is elected. Membership in the Presidium shall be limited to two consecutive terms.

Sec. 6.4. The Executive Cabinet

6.4.1. The Executive Cabinet shall be composed of from twenty to thirty members, with at least one member from each of the ten World Electoral and Administrative Magna Regions of the world.

6.4.2. All members of the Executive Cabinet shall be Members of the World Parliament.

6.4.3. There shall be no more than two members of the Executive Cabinet from any single nation of the World Federation. There may be only one member of the Executive Cabinet from a nation from which a Member of the World Parliament is serving as a member of the Presidium.

6.4.4. Each member of the Executive Cabinet shall serve as the head of a department or agency of the World Administration or Integrative Complex, and in this capacity shall be designated as Minister of the particular department or agency.

6.4.5. Nominations for members of the Executive Cabinet shall be made by the Presidium, taking into consideration the various functions which Executive Cabinets members are to perform. The Presidium shall nominate no more than two times the number to be elected.

6.4.6. The Executive Cabinet shall be elected by simple majority vote of the combined membership of all three houses of the World Parliament in joint session.

6.4.7. Members of the Executive Cabinet either individually or collectively may be removed for cause by an absolute majority vote of the combined membership of all three houses of the World Parliament sitting in joint session.

6.4.8. The term of office in the Executive Cabinet shall be five years, and shall run concurrently with the terms of office for the members as Members of the World Parliament, except that at the end of each five year period, the Cabinet members in office shall continue to serve until the new Executive Cabinet for the succeeding term is elected. Membership in the Executive Cabinet shall be limited to three consecutive terms, regardless of change in ministerial position.

Sec. 6.5. Procedures of the World Executive

6.5.1. The Presidium shall assign the ministerial positions among the Cabinet members to head the several administrative departments and major agencies of the Administration and of the Integrative Complex. Each Vice President may also serve as a Minister to head an administrative department, but not the President. Ministerial positions may be changed at the discretion of the Presidium. A Cabinet member or Vice President may hold more than one ministerial post, but no more than three, providing that no Cabinet member is without a Ministerial post.

6.5.2. The Presidium, in consultation with the Executive Cabinet, shall prepare and present to the World Parliament near the beginning of each year a proposed program of world legislation. The Presidium may propose other legislation during the year.

6.5.3. The Presidium, in consultation with the Executive Cabinet, and in consultation with the World Financial Administration, (see Article 8, Sec. 7.1.9.) shall be responsible for preparing and submitting to the World Parliament the proposed annual budget, and budgetary projections over periods of years.

6.5.4. Each Cabinet Member and Vice President as Minister of a particular department or agency shall prepare an annual report for the particular department or agency, to be submitted both to the Presidium and to the World Parliament.

6.5.5. The members of the Presidium and of the Executive Cabinet at all times shall be responsible both individually and collectively to the World Parliament.

6.5.6. Vacancies occurring at any time in the World Executive shall be filled within sixty days by nomination and election in the same manner as specified for filling the offices originally.

Sec. 6.6. Limitations on the World Executive

6.6.1. The World Executive shall not at any time alter, suspend, abridge, infringe or otherwise violate any provision of this World Constitution or any legislation or world law enacted or approved by the World Parliament in accordance with the provisions of this World Constitution.
6.6.2. The World Executive shall not have veto power over any legislation passed by the World Parliament.
6.6.3. The World Executive may not dissolve the World Parliament or any House of the World Parliament.
6.6.4. The World Executive may not act contrary to decisions of the World Courts.
6.6.5. The World Executive shall be bound to faithfully execute all legislation passed by the World Parliament in accordance with the provisions of this World Constitution, and may not impound or refuse to spend funds appropriated by the World Parliament, nor spend more funds than are appropriated by the World Parliament.
6.6.6. The World Executive may not transcend or contradict the decisions or controls of the World Parliament, the World Judiciary or the Provisions of this World Constitution by any device of executive order or executive privelege or emergency declaration or decree.

Article 7 - The World Administration

Sec. 7.1. - Functions of the World Administration

7.1.1. The World Administration shall be organized to carry out the detailed and continuous administration and implementation of world legislation and world law.
7.1.2. The World Administration shall be under the direction of the World Executive, and shall at all times be responsible to the World Executive.
7.1.3. The World Administration shall be organized so as to give professional continuity to the work of administration and implementation.

Sec. 7.2. - Structure and Procedures of the World Administration

7.2.01. The World Administration shall be composed of professionally organized departments and other agencies in all areas of activity requiring continuity of administration and implementation by the World Government.
7.2.02. Each Department or major agency of the World Administration shall be headed by a Minister who shall be either a member of the Executive Cabinet or a Vice President of the Presidium.
7.2.03. Each Department or major agency of the World Administration shall have as chief of staff a Senior Administrator, who shall assist the Minister and supervise the detailed work of the Department or agency.

7.2.04. Each Senior Administrator shall be nominated by the Minister of the particular Department or agency from among persons in the senior lists of the World Civil Service Administration, as soon as senior lists have been established by the World Civil Service Administration, and shall be confirmed by the Presidium. Temporary qualified appointments shall be made by the Ministers, with confirmation by the Presidium, pending establishment of the senior lists.

7.2.05. There shall be a Secretary General of the World Administration, who shall be nominated by the Presidium and confirmed by absolute majority vote of the entire Executive Cabinet.

7.2.06. The functions and responsibilities of the Secretary General of the World Administration shall be to assist in coordinating the work of the Senior Administrators of the several Departments and agencies of the World Administration. The Secretary General shall at all times be subject to the direction of the Presidium, and shall be directly responsible to the Presidium.

7.2.07. The employment of any Senior Administrator and of the Secretary General may be terminated for cause by absolute majority vote of both the Executive Cabinet and Presidium combined, but not contrary to civil service rules which protect tenure on grounds of competence.

7.2.08. Each Minister of a Department or agency of the World Administration, being also a Member of the World Parliament, shall provide continuous liaison between the particular Department or agency and the World Parliament, shall respond at any time to any questions or requests for information from the Parliament, including committees of any House of the World Parliament.

7.2.09. The Presidium, in cooperation with the particular Ministers in each case, shall be responsible for the original organization of each of the Departments and major agencies of the World Administration.

7.2.10. The assignment of legislative measures, constitutional provisions and areas of world law to particular Departments and agencies for administration and implementation shall be done by the Presidium in consultation with the Executive Cabinet and Secretary General, unless specifically provided in legislation passed by the World Parliament.

7.2.11. The Presidium, in consultation with the Executive Cabinet, may propose the creation of other departments and agencies to have ministerial status; and may propose the alteration, combination or termination of existing Departments and agencies of ministerial status as may seem necessary or desirable. Any such creation, alteration, combination or termination shall require a simple majority vote of approval of the three houses of the World Parliament in joint session.

7.2.12. The World Parliament by absolute majority vote of the three houses in joint session may specify the creation of new departments or agencies of ministerial status in the World Administration, or may direct the World Executive to alter, combine, or terminate existing departments or agencies of ministerial status.

7.2.13. The Presidium and the World Executive may not create, establish or maintain any administrative or executive department or agency for the purpose of circumventing control by the World Parliament.

Sec. 7.3. - Departments of the World Administration

Among the Departments and agencies of the World Administration of ministerial status, but not limited thereto and subject to combinations and to changes in descriptive terminology, shall be those listed under this Section. Each major area of administration shall be headed by a Cabinet Minister and a Senior Administrator, or by a Vice President and a Senior Administrator.

7.3.01. Disarmament & War Prevention.
7.3.02. Population.
7.3.03. Food and Agriculture.
7.3.04. Water Supplies and Waterways.
7.3.05. Health and Nutrition.
7.3.06. Education.
7.3.07. Cultural Diversity and the Arts.
7.3.08. Habitat and Settlements.
7.3.09. Environment and Ecology.
7.3.10. World Resources.
7.3.11. Oceans and Seabeds.
7.3.12. Atmosphere and Space.
7.3.13. Energy.
7.3.14. Science and Technology.
7.3.15. Genetic Research & Engineering.
7.3.16. Labor and Income.
7.3.17. Economic & Social Development.
7.3.18. Commerce & Industry
7.3.19. Transportation and Travel.
7.3.20. Multi-National Corporations.
7.3.21. Communications & Information.
7.3.22. Human Rights.
7.3.23. Distributive Justice.
7.3.24. World Service Corps.
7.3.25. World Territories, Capitals & Parks.
7.3.26. Exterior Relations.
7.3.27. Democratic Procedures.
7.3.28. Revenue.

Article 8 - The Integrative Complex

Sec. 8.1. - Definition

8.1.1. Certain administrative, research, planning and facilitative agencies of the World Government which are particularly essential for the satisfactory functioning of all or most aspects of the World Government, shall be designated as the Integrative Complex. The Integrative Complex shall include the agencies listed under this Section, with the proviso that other such agencies may be added upon recommendation of the Presidium followed by decision of the World Parliament.

8.1.1.1. The World Civil Service Administration.
8.1.1.2. The World Boundaries and Elections Administration.
8.1.1.3. The Institute on Governmental Procedures and World Problems.
8.1.1.4. The Agency for Research and Planning.
8.1.1.5. The Agency for Technological and Environmental Assessment.
8.1.1.6. The World Financial Administration.
8.1.1.7. Commission for Legislative Review.

8.1.2. Each agency of the Integrative Complex shall be headed by a Cabinet Minister and a Senior Administrator, or by a Vice President and a Senior Administrator, together with a Commission as provided hereunder. The rules of procedure for each agency shall be decided by majority decision of the Commission members together with the Administrator and the Minister or Vice President.

8.1.3. The World Parliament may at any time define further the responsibilities, functioning and organization of the several agencies of the Integrative Complex, consistent with the provisions of Article 8 and other provisions of the World Constitution.

8.1.4. Each agency of the Integrative Complex shall make an annual report to the World Parliament and to the Presidium.

Sec. 8.2. - The World Civil Service Administration

8.2.1. The functions of the World Civil Service Administration shall be the following, but not limited thereto:

8.2.1.1. To formulate and define standards, qualifications, tests, examinations and salary scales for the personnel of all organs, departments, bureaus, offices, commissions and agencies of the World Government, in conformity with the provisions of this World Constitution and requiring approval by the Presidium and Executive Cabinet, subject to review and approval by the World Parliament.

8.2.1.2. To establish rosters or lists of competent personnel for all categories of personnel to be appointed or employed in the service of the World Government.

8.2.1.3. To select and employ upon request by any government organ, department, bureau, office, institute, commission, agency or authorized official, such competent personnel as may be needed and authorized, except for those positions which are made elective or appointive under provisions of the World Constitution or by specific legislation of the World Parliament.

8.2.2. The World Civil Service Administration shall be headed by a ten member commission in addition to the Cabinet Minister or Vice President and Senior Administrator. The Commission shall be composed of one commissioner from each of ten World Electoral and Administrative Magna-Regions. The persons to serve as Commissioners shall be nominated by the House of Counsellors and then appointed by the Presidium for five year terms. Commissioners may serve consecutive terms.

Sec. 8.3. - The World Boundaries and Elections Administration

8.3.1. The functions of the World Boundaries and Elections Administration shall include the following, but not limited thereto:

8.3.1.1. To define the boundaries for the basic World Electoral and Administrative Districts, the World Electoral and Administrative Regions and Magna-Regions, and the Continental Divisions, for submission to the World Parliament for approval by legislative action.

8.3.1.2. To make periodic adjustments every ten or five years, as needed, of the boundaries for the World Electoral and Administrative Districts, the World Electoral and Administrative Regions and Magna-Regions, and of the Continental Divisions, subject to approval by the World Parliament.

8.3.1.3. To define the detailed procedures for the nomination and election of Members of the World Parliament to the House of Peoples and to the House of Counsellors, subject to approval by the World Parliament.

8.3.1.4 To conduct the elections for Members of the World Parliament to the House of Peoples and to the House of Counsellors.

8.3.1.5 Before each World Parliamentary Election, to prepare Voters' Information Booklets which shall summarize major current public issues, and shall list each candidate for elective office together with standard information about each candidate, and give space for each candidate to state his or her views on the defined major issues as well as on any other major issue of choice; to include information on any initiatives or referendums which are to be voted upon; to distribute the Voter's Information Booklets for each World Electoral District, or suitable group of Districts; and to obtain the advice of the Institute on Governmental Procedures and World Problems, the Agency for Research and Planning, and the Agency for Technological and Environmental Assessment in preparing the booklets.

8.3.1.6. To define the rules for world political parties, subject to approval by the World Parliament, and subject to review and recommendations of the World Ombudsmus.

8.3.1.7. To define the detailed procedures for legislative initiative and referendum by the Citizens of Earth, and to conduct voting on supra- national or global initiatives and referendums in conjuction with world parliamentary elections.

8.3.1.8. To conduct plebiscites when requested by other Organs of the World Government, and to make recommendations for the settlement of boundary disputes.

8.3.1.9. To conduct a global census every five years, and to prepare and maintain complete demographic analyses for Earth.

8.3.2. The World Boundaries and Elections Administration shall be headed by a ten member commission in addition to the Senior Administrator and the Cabinet Minister or Vice President. The commission shall be composed of one commissioner each from ten World Electoral and Administrative Magna-Regions. The persons to serve as commissioners shall be nominated by the House of Counsellors and then appointed by the World Presidium for five year terms. Commissioners may serve consecutive terms.

Sec. 8.4. - Institute on Governmental Procedures and World Problems

8.4.1. The functions of the Institute on Governmental Procedures and World Problems shall be as follows, but not limited thereto:

8.4.1.1. To prepare and conduct courses of information, education and training for all personnel in the service of the World Government, including Members of the World Parliament and of all other elective, appointive and civil service personnel, so that every person in the service of the World Government may have a better understanding of the functions, structure, procedures and inter-relationships of the various organs, departments, bureaus, offices, institutes, commissions, agencies and other parts of the World Government.

8.4.1.2. To prepare and conduct courses and seminars for information, education, discussion, updating and new ideas in all areas of world problems, particularly for Members of the World Parliament and of the World Executive, and for the chief personnel of all organs, departments and agencies of the World Government, but open to all in the service of the World Government.

8.4.1.3. To bring in qualified persons from private and public universities, colleges and research and action organizations of many countries, as well as other qualified persons, to lecture and to be resource persons for the courses and seminars organized by the Institute on Governmental Procedures and World Problems.

8.4.1.4. To contract with private or public universities and colleges or other agencies to conduct courses and seminars for the Institute.

8.4.2. The Institute on Governmental Procedures and World Problems shall be supervised by a ten member commission in addition to the Senior Administrator and Cabinet Minister or Vice President. The commission shall be composed of one commissioner each to be named by the House of Peoples, the House of Nations, the House of Counsellors, the Presidium, the Collegium of World Judges, The World Ombudsmus, The World Attorneys General Office, the Agency for Research and Planning, the Agency for Technological and Environmental Assessment, and the World Financial Administration. Commissioners shall serve five year terms, and may serve consecutive terms.

Sec. 8.5. - The Agency for Research and Planning

8.5.1. The functions of the Agency for Research and Planning shall be as follows, but not limited thereto:

8.5.1.01. To serve the World Parliament, the World Executive, the World Administration, and other organs, departments and agencies of the World Government in any matter requiring research and planning within the competence of the agency.

8.5.1.02. To prepare and maintain a comprehensive inventory of world resources.

8.5.1.03. To prepare comprehensive long-range plans for the development, conservation, re-cycling and equitable sharing of the resources of Earth for the benefit of all people on Earth, subject to legislative action by the World Parliament.

8.5.1.04. To prepare and maintain a comprehensive list and description of all world problems, including their inter-relationships, impact time projections and proposed solutions, together with bibliographies.
8.5.1.05. To do research and help prepare legislative measures at the request of any Member of the World Parliament or of any committee of any House of the World Parliament.
8.5.1.06. To do research and help prepare proposed legislation or proposed legislative programs and schedules at the request of the Presidium or Executive Cabinet or of any Cabinet Minister.
8.5.1.07. To do research and prepare reports at the request of any other organ, department or agency of the World Government.
8.5.1.08. To enlist the help of public and private universities, colleges, research agencies, and other associations and organizations for various research and planning projects.
8.5.1.09. To contract with public and private universities, colleges, research agencies and other organizations for the preparation of specific reports, studies and proposals.
8.5.1.10. To maintain a comprehensive World Library for the use of all Members of the World Parliament, and for the use of all other officials and persons in the service of the World Government, as well as for public information.
8.5.2. The Agency for Research and Planning shall be supervised by a ten member commission in addition to the Senior Administrator and Cabinet Minister or Vice President. The commission shall be composed of one commissioner each to be named by the House of Peoples, the House of Nations, the House of Counsellors, the Presidium, the Collegium of World Judges, the Office of World Attorneys General, World Ombudsmus, the Agency for Technological and Environmental Assessment, the Institute on Governmental Procedures and World Problems, and the World Financial Administration. Commissioners shall serve five year terms, and may serve consecutive terms.

Sec. 8.6. - The Agency for Technological and Environmental Assessment

8.6.1. The functions of the agency for Technological and Environmental Assessment shall include the following, but not limited thereto:
8.6.1.1. To establish and maintain a registration and description of all significant technological innovations, together with impact projections.
8.6.1.2. To examine, analyze and assess the impacts and consequences of technological innovations which may have either significant beneficial or significant harmful or dangerous consequences for human life or for the ecology of life on Earth, or which may require particular regulations or prohibitions to prevent or eliminate dangers or to assure benefits.
8.6.1.3. To examine, analyze and assess environmental and ecological problems, in particular the environmental and ecological problems which may result from any intrusions or changes of the environment or ecological relationships which may be caused by technological innovations, processes of resource development, patterns of human settlements, the production of energy, patterns of economic and industrial de-

velopment, or other man-made intrusions and changes of the environment, or which may result from natural causes.
8.6.1.4. To maintain a global monitoring network to measure possible harmful effects of technological innovations and environmental disturbances so that corrective measures can be designed.
8.6.1.5. To prepare recommendations based on technological and environmental analyses and assessments, which can serve as guides to the World Parliament, the World Executive, the World Administration, the Agency for Research and Planning, and to the other organs, departments and agencies of the World Government, as well as to individuals in the service of the World Government and to national and local governments and legislative bodies.
8.6.1.6. To enlist the voluntary or contractual aid and participation of private and public universities, colleges, research institutions and other associations and organizations in the work of technological and environmental assessment.
8.6.1.7. To enlist the voluntary or contractual aid and participation of private and public universities and colleges, research institutions and other organizations in devising and developing alternatives to harmful or dangerous technologies and environmentall y disruptive activities, and in devising controls to assure beneficial results from technological innovations or to prevent harmful results from either technological innovations or environmental changes, all subject to legislation for implementation by the World Parliament.
8.6.2. The Agency for Technological and Environmental Assessment shall be supervised by a ten member commission in addition to the Senior Administrator and Cabinet Minister or Vice President. The commission shall be composed of one commissioner from each of ten World Electoral and Administrative Magna-Regions. The persons to serve as commissioners shall be nominated by the House of Counsellors, and then appointed by the World Presidium for five year terms. Commissioners may serve consecutive terms.

Sec. 8.7. - The World Financial Administration

8.7.1. The functions of the World Financial Administration shall include the following, but not limited thereto:
8.7.1.1. To establish and operate the procedures for the collection of revenues for the World Government, pursuant to legislation by the World Parliament, inclusive of taxes, globally accounted social and public costs, licenses, fees, revenue sharing arrangements, income derived from supra-national public enterprises or projects or resource developments, and all other sources.
8.7.1.2. To operate a Planetary Accounting Office, and thereunder to make cost/benefit studies and reports of the functioning and activities of the World Government and of its several organs, departments, branches, bureaus, offices, commissions, institutes, agencies and other parts or projects. In making such studies and reports, account shall be taken not only of direct financial costs and benefits, but also of human, social, environmental, indirect, long-term and other costs and benefits, and of actual or possible

hazards and damages. Such studies and reports shall also be designed to uncover any wastes, inefficiencies, misapplications, corruptions, diversions, unnecessary costs, and other possible irregularities.
8.7.1.3. To make cost/benefit studies and reports at the request of any House or committee of the World Parliament, and of the Presidium, the Executive Cabinet, the World Ombudsmus, the Office of World Attorneys General, the World Supreme Court, or of any admi nistrative department or any agency of the Integrative Complex, as well as upon its own initiative.
8.7.1.4. To operate a Planetary Comptrollers Office and thereunder to supervise the disbursement of the funds of the World Government for all purposes, projects and activities duly authorized by this World Constitution, the World Parliament, the World Executive, and other organs, departments and agencies of the World Government.
8.7.1.5. To establish and operate a Planetary Banking System, making the transition to a common global currency, under the terms of specific legislation passed by the World Parliament.
8.7.1.6. Pursuant to specific legislation enacted by the World Parliament, and in conjunction with the Planetary Banking System, to establish and implement the procedures of a Planetary Monetary and Credit System based upon useful productive capacity and perfo rmance, both in goods and services. Such a monetary and credit system shall be designed for use within the Planetary Banking System for the financing of the activities and projects of the World Government, and for all other financial purposes approved by the World Parliament, without requiring the payment of interest on bonds, investments or other claims of financial ownership or debt.
8.7.1.7. To establish criteria for the extension of financial credit based upon such considerations as people available to work, usefulness, cost/benefit accounting, human and social values, environmental health and esthetics, minimizing disparities, integrity, competent management, appropriate technology, potential production and performance.
8.7.1.8. To establish and operate a Planetary Insurance System in areas of world need which transcend national boundaries and in accordance with legislation passed by the World Parliament.
8.7.1.9. To assist the Presidium as may be requested in the technical preparation of budgets for the operation of the World Government.
8.7.2. The World Financial Administration shall be supervised by a commission of ten members, together with a Senior Administrator and a Cabinet Minister or Vice President. The commission shall be composed of one commissioner each to be named by the House of Peoples, the House of Nations, the House of Counsellors, the Presidium, the Collegium of World Judges, the Office of Attorneys General, the World Ombudsmus, the Agency for Research and Planning, the Agency for Technological and Environmental Assessment, and the Institute on Governmental Procedures and World Problems. Commissioners shall serve terms of five years, and may serve consecutive terms.

Sec. 8.8. - Commission for Legislative Review

8.8.1. The functions of the Commission for Legislative Review shall be to examine World Legislation and World Laws which the World Parliament enacts or adopts from the previous Body of International Law for the purpose of analyzing whether any particular legislation or law has become obsolete or obstructive or defective in serving the purposes intended; and to make recommendations to the World Parliament accordingly for repeal or amendment or replacement.
8.8.2. The Commission for Legislative Review shall be composed of twelve members, including two each to be elected by the House of Peoples, the House of Nations, the House of Counsellors, the Collegium of World Judges, the World Ombudsmus and the Presidium. Members of the Commission shall serve terms of ten years, and may be re-elected to serve consecutive terms. One half of the Commission members after the Commission is first formed shall be elected every five years, with the first terms for one half of the members to be only five years.

Article 9 - The World Judiciary

Sec. 9.1. - Jurisdiction of the World Supreme Court

9.1.1. A World Supreme Court shall be established, together with such regional and district World Courts as may subsequently be found necessary. The World Supreme Court shall comprise a number of benches.
9.1.2. The World Supreme Court, together with such regional and district World Courts as may be established, shall have mandatory jurisdiction in all cases, actions, disputes, conflicts, violations of law, civil suits, guarantees of civil and human rights, constitutional interpretations, and other litigations arising under the provisions of this World Constitution, world legislation, and the body of world law approved by the World Parliament.
9.1.3. Decisions of the World Supreme Court shall be binding on all parties involved in all cases, actions and litigations brought before any bench of the World Supreme Court for settlement. Each bench of the World Supreme Court shall constitute a court of highest appeal, except when matters of extra-ordinary public importance are assigned or transferred to the Superior Tribunal of the World Supreme Court, as provided in Section 5 of Article 9.

Sec. 9.2. - Benches of the World Supreme Court

The benches of the World Supreme Court and their respective jurisdictions shall be as follows:

9.2.1. Bench for Human Rights: To deal with issues of human rights arising under the guarantee of civil and human rights provided by Article 12 of this World Constitution, and arising in pursuance of the provisions of Article 13 of this World Constitution, and arising otherwise under world legislation and the body of world law approved by the World Parliament.

9.2.2. Bench for Criminal Cases: To deal with issues arising from the violation of world laws and world legislation by individuals, corporations, groups and associations, but not issues primarily concerned with human rights.

9.2.3. Bench for Civil Cases: To deal with issues involving civil law suits and disputes between individuals, corporations, groups and associations arising under world legislation and world law and the administration thereof.

9.2.4. Bench for Constitutional Cases: To deal with the interpretation of the World Constitution and with issues and actions arising in connection with the interpretation of the World Constitution.

9.2.5. Bench for International Conflicts: To deal with disputes, conflicts and legal contest arising between or among the nations which have joined in the Federation of Earth.

9.2.6. Bench for Public Cases: To deal with issues not under the jurisdiction of another bench arising from conflicts, disputes, civil suits or other legal contests between the World Government and corporations, groups or individuals, or between national gov ernments and corporations, groups or individuals in cases involving world legislation and world law.

9.2.7. Appellate Bench: To deal with issues involving world legislation and world law which may be appealed from national courts; and to decide which bench to assign a case or action or litigation when a question or disagreement arises over the proper jurisdiction.

9.2.8. Advisory Bench: To give opinions upon request on any legal question arising under world law or world legislation, exclusive of contests or actions involving interpretation of the World Constitution. Advisory opinions may be requested by any House or committee of the World Parliament, by the Presidium, any Administrative Department, the Office of World Attorneys General, the World Ombudsmus, or by any agency of the Integrative Complex.

9.2.9. Other benches may be established, combined or terminated upon recommendation of the Collegium of World Judges with approval by the World Parliament; but benches number one through eight may not be combined nor terminated except by amendment of this World Constitution.

Sec. 9.3. - Seats of the World Supreme Court

9.3.1. The primary seat of the World Supreme Court and all benches shall be the same as for the location of the Primary World Capital and for the location of the World Parliament and the World Executive.

9.3.2. Continental seats of the World Supreme Court shall be established in the four secondary capitals of the World Government located in four different Continental Divisions of Earth, as provided in Article 15.

9.3.3. The following permanent benches of the World Supreme Court shall be established both at the primary seat and at each of the continental seats: Human Rights, Criminal Cases, Civil Cases, and Public Cases.

9.3.4. The following permanent benches of the World Supreme Court shall be located only at the primary seat of the World Supreme Court: Constitutional Cases, International Conflicts, Appellate Bench, and Advisory Bench.

9.3.5. Benches which are located permanently only at the primary seat of the World Supreme Court may hold special sessions at the other continental seats of the World Supreme Court when necessary, or may establish continental circuits if needed.
9.3.6. Benches of the World Supreme Court which have permanent continental locations may hold special sessions at other locations when needed, or may establish regional circuits if needed.

Sec. 9.4. - The Collegium of World Judges

9.4.01. A Collegium of World Judges shall be established by the World Parliament. The Collegium shall consist of a minimum of twenty member judges, and may be expanded as needed but not to exceed sixty members.
9.4.02. The World Judges to compose the Collegium of World Judges shall be nominated by the House of Counsellors and shall be elected by plurality vote of the three Houses of the World Parliament in joint session. The House of Counsellors shall nominate between two and three times the number of world judges to be elected at any one time. An equal number of World Judges shall be elected from each of ten World Electoral and Administrative Magna-Regions, if not immediately then by rotation.
9.4.03. The term of office for a World Judge shall be ten years. Successive terms may be served without limit.
9.4.04. The Collegium of World Judges shall elect a Presiding Council of World Judges, consisting of a Chief Justice and four Associate Chief Justices. One member of the Presiding Council of World Judges shall be elected from each of five Continental Divisions of Earth. Members of the Presiding Council of World Judges shall serve five year terms on the Presiding Council, and may serve two successive terms, but not two successive terms as Chief Justice.
9.4.05. The Presiding Council of World Judges shall assign all World Judges, including themselves, to the several benches of the World Supreme Court. Each bench for a sitting at each location shall have a minimum of three World Judges, except that the number of World Judges for benches on Continental Cases and International Conflicts, and the Appellate Bench, shall be no less than five.
9.4.06. The member judges of each bench at each location shall choose annually a Presiding Judge, who may serve two successive terms.
9.4.07. The members of the several benches may be reconstituted from time to time as may seem desirable or necessary upon the decision of the Presiding Council of World Judges. Any decision to re-constitute a bench shall be referred to a vote of the entire Collegium of World Judges by request of any World Judge.
9.4.08. Any World Judge may be removed from office for cause by an absolute two-thirds majority vote of the three Houses of the World Parliament in joint session.
9.4.09. Qualifications for Judges of the World Supreme Court shall be at least ten years of legal or juristic experience, minimum age of thirty years, and evident competence in world law and the humanities.
9.4.10. The salaries, expenses, remunerations and prerogatives of the World Judges shall be determined by the World Parliament, and shall be reviewed every five years, but shall not be changed to the disadvantage of any World Judge during a term of office. All

members of the Collegium of World Judges shall receive the same salaries, except that additional compensation may be given to the Presiding Council of World Judges.

9.4.11. Upon recommendation by the Collegium of World Judges, the World Parliament shall have the authority to establish regional and district world courts below the World Supreme Court, and to establish the jurisdictions thereof, and the procedures for appeal to the World Supreme Court or to the several benches thereof.

9.4.12. The detailed rules of procedure for the functioning of the World Supreme Court, the Collegium of World Judges, and for each bench of the World Supreme Court, shall be decided and amended by absolute majority vote of the Collegium of World Judges.

Sec. 9.5. - The Superior Tribunal of the World Supreme Court

9.5.1. A Superior Tribunal of the World Supreme Court shall be established to take cases which are considered to be of extra-ordinary public importance. The Superior Tribunal for any calendar year shall consist of the Presiding Council of World Judges together with one World Judge named by the Presiding Judge of each bench of the World Court sitting at the primary seat of the World Supreme Court. The composition of the Superior Tribunal may be continued unchanged for a second year by decision of the Presiding Council of World Judges.

9.5.2. Any party to any dispute, issue, case or litigation coming under the jurisdiction of the World Supreme Court, may apply to any particular bench of the World Supreme Court or to the Presiding Council of World Judges for the assignment or transfer of the case to the Superior Tribunal on the grounds of extra-ordinary public importance. If the application is granted, the case shall be heard and disposed of by the Superior Tribunal. Also, any bench taking any particular case, if satisfied that the case is of extra-ordinary public importance, may of its own discretion transfer the case to the Superior Tribunal.

Article 10 - The Enforcement System

Sec. 10.1. - Basic Principles

10.1.1. The enforcement of world law and world legislation shall apply directly to individual, and individuals shall be held responsible for compliance with world law and world legislation regardless of whether the individuals are acting in their own capacity or as agents or officials of governments at any level or of the institutions of governments, or as agents or officials of corporations, organizations, associations or groups of any kind.

10.1.2. When world law or world legislation or decisions of the world courts are violated, the Enforcement System shall operate to identify and apprehend the individuals responsible for violations.

10.1.3. Any enforcement action shall not violate the civil and human rights guaranteed under this World Constitution.

10.1.4. The enforcement of world law and world legislation shall be carried out in the context of a non-military world federation wherein all member nations shall disarm as a condition for joining and benefiting from the world federation, subject to Article 17, Sec. 3.8., and 4.6. The Federation of Earth and World Government under this World Constitution shall neither keep nor use weapons of mass destruction.

10.1.5. Those agents of the enforcement system whose function shall be to apprehend and bring to court violators of world law and world legislation shall be equipped only with such weapons as are appropriate for the apprehension of the individuals responsible for violations.

10.1.6. The enforcement of world law and world legislation under this World Constitution shall be conceived and developed primarily as the processes of effective design and administration of world law and world legislation to serve the welfare of all people on Earth, with equity and justice for all, in which the resources of Earth and the funds and the credits of the World Government are used only to serve peaceful human needs, and none used for weapons of mass destruction or for war making capabilities.

Sec. 10.2. - The Structure for Enforcement: World Attorneys General

10.2.01. The Enforcement System shall be headed by an Office of World Attorneys General and a Commission of Regional World Attorneys.

10.2.02. The Office of World Attorneys General shall be comprised of five members, one of whom shall be designated as the World Attorney General and the other four shall each be designated an Associate World Attorney General.

10.2.03. The Commission of Regional World Attorneys shall consist of twenty Regional World Attorneys.

10.2.04. The members to compse the Office of World Attorneys General shall be nominated by the House of Counsellors, with three nominees from each Continental Division of Earth. One member of the Office shall be elected from each of five Continental Divisions by plurality vote of the three houses of the World Parliament in joint session.

10.2.05. The term of office for a member of the Office of World Attorneys General shall be ten years. A member may serve two consecutive terms. The position of World Attorney General shall rotate every two years among the five members of the Office. The order of rotation shall be decided among the five members of the Office.

10.2.06. The Office of World Attorneys General shall nominate members for the Commission of twenty Regional World Attorneys from the twenty World Electoral and Administrative Regions, with between two and three nominees submitted for each Region. From these nominations, the three Houses of the World Parliament in joint session shall elect one Regional World Attorney from each of the twenty Regions. Regional World Attorneys shall serve terms of five years, and may serve three consecutive terms.

10.2.07. Each Regional World Attorney shall organize and be in charge of an Office of Regional World Attorney. Each Associate World Attorney General shall supervise five Offices of Regional World Attorneys.

10.2.08. The staff to carry out the work of enforcement, in addition to the five members of the Office of World Attorneys General and the twenty Regional World Attorneys, shall be selected from civil service lists, and shall be organized for the following functions:

10.2.08.1. Investigation.

10.2.08.2. Apprehension and arrest.

10.2.08.3. Prosecution.

10.2.08.4. Remedies and correction.

10.2.08.5. Conflict resolution.

10.2.09. Qualifications for a member of the Office of World Attorneys General and for the Regional World Attorneys shall be at least thirty years of age, at least seven years legal experience, and education in law and the humanities.

10.2.10. The World Attorney General, the Associate World Attorneys General, and the Regional World Attorneys shall at all times be responsible to the World Parliament. Any member of the Office of World Attorneys General and any Regional World Attorney can be removed from office for cause by a simple majority vote of the three Houses of the World Parliament in joint session.

Sec. 10.3. - The World Police

10.3.1. That section of the staff of the Office of World Attorneys General and of the Offices of Regional World Attorneys responsible for the apprehension and arrest of violators of world law and world legislation, shall be designated as World Police.

10.3.2. Each regional staff of the World Police shall be headed by a Regional World Police Captain, who shall be appointed by the Regional World Attorney.

10.3.3. The Office of World Attorneys General shall appoint a World Police Supervisor, to be in charge of those activities which transcend regional boundaries. The World Police Supervisor shall direct the Regional World Police Captains in any actions which require coordinated or joint action transcending regional boundaries, and shall direct any action which requires initiation or direction from the Office of World Attorneys General.

10.3.4. Searches and arrests to be made by World Police shall be made only upon warrants issued by the Office of World Attorneys General or by a Regional World Attorney.

10.3.5. World Police shall be armed only with weapons appropriate for the apprehension of the individuals responsible for violation of world law.

10.3.6. Employment in the capacity of World Police Captain and World Police Supervisor shall be limited to ten years.

10.3.7. The World Police Supervisor and any Regional World Police Captain may be removed from office for cause by decision of the Office of World Attorneys General or by absolute majority vote of the three Houses of the World Parliament in joint session.

Sec. 10.4. - The Means of Enforcement

10.4.1. Non-military means of enforcement of world law and world legislation shall be developed by the World Parliament and by the Office of World Attorneys General in consultation with the Commission of Regional World Attorneys, the Collegium of World Judges, the World Presidium, and the World Ombudsmus. The actual means of enforcement shall require legislation by the World Parliament.

10.4.2. Non-military means of enforcement which can be developed may include: Denial of financial credit; denial of material resources and personnel; revocation of licenses, charters, or corporate rights; impounding of equipment; fines and damage payments; performance of work to rectify damages; imprisonment or isolation; and other means appropriate to the specific situations.

10.4.3. To cope with situations of potential or actual riots, insurrection and resort to armed violence, particular strategies and methods shall be developed by the World Parliament and by the Office of World Attorneys General in consultation with the Commission of Regional World Attorneys, the collegium of World Judges, the Presidium and the World Ombudsmus. Such strategies and methods shall require enabling legislation by the World Parliament where required in addition to the specific provisions of this World Constitution.

10.4.4. A basic condition for preventing outbreaks of violence which the Enforcement System shall facilitate in every way possible, shall be to assure a fair hearing under non-violent circumstances for any person or group having a grievance, and likewise to assure a fair opportunity for a just settlement of any grievance with due regard for the rights and welfare of all concerned.

Article 11 - The World Ombudsmus

Sec. 11.1 - Functions and Powers of the World Ombudsmus

The functions and powers of the World Ombudsmus, as public defender, shall include the following:

11.1.01. To protect the People of Earth and all individuals against violations or neglect of universal human and civil rights which are stipulated in Article 12 and other sections of this World Constitution.

11.1.02. To protect the People of Earth against violations of this World Constitution by any official or agency of the World Government, including both elected and appointed officials or public employees regardless of organ, department, office, agency or rank.

11.1.03. To press for the implementation of the Directive Principles for the World Government as defined in Article 13 of this World Constitution.

11.1.04. To promote the welfare of the people of Earth by seeking to assure that conditions of social justice and of minimizing disparities are achieved in the implementation and administration of world legislation and world law.

11.1.05. To keep on the alert for perils to humanity arising from technological innovations, environmental disruptions and other diverse sources, and to launch initiatives for correction or prevention of such perils.

11.1.06. To ascertain that the administration of otherwise proper laws, ordinances and procedures of the World Government do not result in unforseen injustices or inequities, or become stultified in bureaucracy or the details of administration.

11.1.07. To receive and hear complaints, grievances or requests for aid from any person, group, organization, association, body politic or agency concerning any matter which comes within the purview of the World Ombudsmus.

11.1.08. To request the Office of World Attorneys General or any Regional World Attorney to initiate legal actions or court proceedings whenever and wherever considered necessary or desirable in the view of the World Ombudsmus.

11.1.09. To directly initiate legal actions and court proceedings whenever the World Ombudsmus deems necessary.

11.1.10. To review the functioning of the departments, bureaus, offices, commissions, institutes, organs and agencies of the World Government to ascertain whether the procedures of the World government are adequately fulfilling their purposes and serving the welfare of humanity in optimum fashion, and to make recommendations for improvements.

11.1.11. To present an annual report to the World Parliament and to the Presidium on the activities of the World Ombudsmus, together with any recommendations for legislative measures to improve the functioning of the World Government for the purpose of better serving the welfare of the People of Earth.

Sec. 11.2. - Composition of the World Ombudsmus

11.2.1. The World Ombudsmus shall be headed by a Council of World Ombudsen of five members, one of whom shall be designated as Principal World Ombudsan, while the other four shall each be designated as an Associate World Ombudsan.

11.2.2. Members to compose the Council of World Ombudsen shall be nominated by the House of Counsellors, with three nominees from each Continental Division of Earth. One member of the Council shall be elected from each of five Continental Divisions by plurality vote of the three Houses of the World Parliament in joint session.

11.2.3. The term of office for a World Ombudsan shall be ten years. A World Ombudsan may serve two successive terms. The position of Principal World Ombudsan shall be rotated every two years. The order of rotation shall be determined by the Council of World Ombudsen.

11.2.4. The Council of World Ombudsen shall be assisted by a Commission of World Advocates of twenty members. Members for the Commission of World Advocates shall be nominated by the Council of World Ombudsen from twenty World Electoral and Administrative Regions, with between two and three nominees submitted for each Region. One World Advocate shall be elected from each of the twenty World Electoral and Administrative Regions by the three Houses of the World Parliament in joint session. World Advocates shall serve terms of five years, and may serve a maximum of four successive terms.

11.2.5. The Council of World Ombudsen shall establish twenty regional offices, in addition to the principal world office at the primary seat of the World Government. The twenty regional offices of the World Ombudsmus shall parallel the organization of the twenty Offices of Regional World Attorney.

11.2.6. Each regional office of the World Ombudsmus shall be headed by a World Advocate. Each five regional offices of the World Ombudmus shall be supervised by an Associate World Ombudsan.

11.2.7. Any World Ombudsan and any World Advocate may be removed from office for cause by an absolute majority vote of the three Houses of the World Parliament in joint session.

11.2.8. Staff members for the World Ombudsmus and for each regional office of the World Ombudsmus shall be selected and employed from civil service lists.

11.2.9. Qualifications for World Ombudsan and for World Advocate shall be at least thirty years of age, at least five years legal experience, and education in law and other relevant education.

Article 12 - Bill of Rights for the Citizens of Earth

The inhabitants and citizens of Earth who are within the Federation of Earth shall have certain inalienable rights defined hereunder. It shall be mandatory for the World Parliament, the World Executive, and all organs and agencies of the World Government to honor, implement and enforce these rights, as well as for the national governments of all member nations in the Federation of Earth to do likewise. Individuals or groups suffering violation or neglect of such rights shall have full recourse through the World Ombudsmus, the Enforcement System and the World Courts for redress of grievances. The inalienable rights shall include the following:

12.01. Equal rights for all citizens of the Federation of Earth, with no discrimination on grounds of race, color, caste, nationality, sex, religion, political affiliation, property, or social status.

12.02. Equal protection and application of world legislation and world laws for all citizens of the Federation of Earth.

12.03. Freedom of thought and conscience, speech, press, writing, communication, expression, publication, broadcasting, telecasting, and cinema, except as an overt part of or incitement to violence, armed riot or insurrection.

12.04. Freedom of assembly, association, organization, petition and peaceful demonstration.

12.05. Freedom to vote without duress, and freedom for political organization and campaigning without censorship or recrimination.

12.06. Freedom to profess, practice and promote religious or religious beliefs or no religion or religious belief.

12.07. Freedom to profess and promote political beliefs or no political beliefs.

12.08. Freedom for investigation, research and reporting.

12.09. Freedom to travel without passport or visas or other forms of registration used to limit travel between, among or within nations.

12.10. Prohibition against slavery, peonage, involuntary servitude, and conscription of labor.

12.11. Prohibition against military conscription.

12.12. Safety of person from arbitrary or unreasonable arrest, detention, exile, search or seizure; requirement of warrants for searches and arrests.

12.13. Prohibition against physical or psychological duress or torture during any period of investigation, arrest, detention or imprisonment, and against cruel or unusual punishment.

12.14. Right of habeous corpus; no ex-post-facto laws; no double jeopardy; right to refuse self-incrimination or the incrimination of another.

12.15. Prohibition against private armies and paramilitary organizations as being threats to the common peace and safety.

12.16. Safety of property from arbitrary seizure; protection against exercise of the power of eminent domain without reasonable compensation.

12.17. Right to family planning and free public assistance to achieve family planning objectives.

12.18. Right of privacy of person, family and association; prohibition against surveillance as a means of political control.

Article 13 - Directive Principles for the Earth Federation

It shall be the aim of the World Government to secure certain other rights for all inhabitants within the Federation of Earth, but without immediate guarantee of universal achievement and enforcement. These rights are defined as Directive Principles, obligating the World Government to pursue every reasonable means for universal realization and implementation, and shall include the following:

13.01. Equal opportunity for useful employment for everyone, with wages or remuneration sufficient to assure human dignity.
13.02. Freedom of choice in work, occupation, employment or profession.
13.03. Full access to information and to the accumulated knowledge of the human race.
13.04. Free and adequate public education available to everyone, extending to the pre-university level; Equal opportunities for elementary and higher education for all persons; equal opportunity for continued education for all persons throughout life; the right of any person or parent to choose a private educational institution at any time.
13.05. Free and adequate public health services and medical care available to everyone throughout life under conditions of free choice.
13.06. Equal opportunity for leisure time for everyone; better distribution of the work load of society so that every person may have equitable leisure time opportunities.
13.07. Equal opportunity for everyone to enjoy the benefits of scientific and technological discoveries and developments.
13.08. Protection for everyone against the hazards and perils of technological innovations and developments.
13.09. Protection of the natural environment which is the common heritage of humanity against pollution, ecological disruption or damage which could imperil life or lower the quality of life.
13.10. Conservation of those natural resources of Earth which are limited so that present and future generations may continue to enjoy life on the planet Earth.
13.11. Assurance for everyone of adequate housing, of adequate and nutritious food supplies, of safe and adequate water supplies, of pure air with protection of oxygen supplies and the ozone layer, and in general for the continuance of an environment which c an sustain healthy living for all.
13.12. Assure to each child the right to the full realization of his or her potential.
13.13. Social Security for everyone to relieve the hazards of unemployment, sickness, old age, family circumstances, disability, catastrophies of nature, and technological change, and to allow retirement with sufficient lifetime income for living under condi tions of human dignity during older age.
13.14. Rapid elimination of and prohibitions against technological hazards and man-made environmental disturbances which are found to create dangers to life on Earth.
13.15. Implementation of intensive programs to discover, develop and institute safe

alternatives and practical substitutions for technologies which must be eliminated and prohibited because of hazards and dangers to life.
13.16. Encouragement for cultural diversity; encouragement for decentralized administration.
13.17. Freedom for peaceful self-determination for minorities, refugees and dissenters.
13.18. Freedom for change of residence to anywhere on Earth conditioned by provisions for temporary sanctuaries in events of large numbers of refugees, stateless persons, or mass migrations.
13.19. Prohibition against the death penalty.

Article 14 - Safeguards and Reservations

Sec. 14.1.- Certain Safeguards

The World Government shall operate to secure for all nations and peoples within the Federation of Earth the safeguards which are defined hereunder:

14.1.1. Guarantee that full faith and credit shall be given to the public acts, records, legislation and judicial proceedings of the member nations within the Federation of Earth, consistent with the several provisions of this World Constitution.
14.1.2. Assure freedom of choice within the member nations and countries of the Federation of Earth to determine their internal political, economic and social systems, consistent with the guarantees and protections given under this World Constitution to assure civil liberties and human rights and a safe environment for life, and otherwise consistent with the several provisions of this World Constitution.
14.1.3. Grant the right of asylum within the Federation of Earth for persons who may seek refuge from countries or nations which are not yet included within the Federation of Earth.
14.1.4. Grant the right of individuals and groups, after the Federation of Earth includes 90 percent of the territory of Earth, to peacefully leave the hegemony of the Federation of Earth and to live in suitable territory set aside by the Federation neither restricted nor protected by the World Government, provided that such territory does not extend beyond five percent of Earth's habitable territory, is kept completely disarmed and not used as a base for inciting violence or insurrection within or against the Federation of Earth or any member nation, and is kept free of acts of environmental or technological damage which seriously affect Earth outside such territory.

Sec. 14.2.- Reservation of Powers

The powers not delegated to the World Government by this World Constitution shall be reserved to the nations of the Federation of Earth and to the people of Earth.

Article 15 - World Federal Zones and the World Capitals

Sec. 15.1. - World Federal Zones

15.1.1. Twenty World Federal Zones shall be established within the twenty World Electoral and Administrative Regions, for the purposes of the location of the several organs of the World Government and of the administrative departments, the world courts, the o ffices of the Regional World Attorneys, the offices of the World Advocates, and for the location of other branches, departments, institutes, offices, bureaus, commissions, agencies and parts of the World Government.

15.1.2. The World Federal Zones shall be established as the needs and resources of the World Government develop and expand. World Federal Zones shall be established first within each of five Continental Divisions.

15.1.3. The location and administration of the World Federal Zones, including the first five, shall be determined by the World Parliament.

Sec. 15.2. - The World Capitals

15.2.1. Five World Capitals shall be established in each of five Continental Divisions of Earth, to be located in each of the five World Federal Zones which are established first as provided in Article 15 of this World Constitution.

15.2.2. One of the World Capitals shall be designated by the World Parliament as the Primary World Capital, and the other four shall be designated as Secondary World Capitals.

15.2.3. The primary seats of all organs of the World Government shall be located in the Primary World Capital, and other major seats of the several organs of the World Government shall be located in the Secondary World Capitals.

Sec. 15.3. - Locational Procedures

15.3.1. Choices for location of the twenty World Federal Zones and for the five World Capitals shall be proposed by the Presidium, and then shall be decided by a simple majority vote of the three Houses of the World Parliament in joint session. The Presidium shall offer choices of two or three locations in each of the twenty World Electoral and Administrative Regions to be World Federal Zones, and shall offer two alternative choices for each of the five World Capitals.

15.3.2. The Presidium in consultation with the Executive Cabinet shall then propose which of the five World Capitals shall be the Primary World Capital, to be decided by a simply majority vote of the three Houses of the World Parliament in joint session.

15.3.3. Each organ of the World Government shall decide how best to apportion and organize its functions and activities among the five World Capitals, and among the twenty World Federal Zones, subject to specific directions from the World Parliament.

15.3.4. The World Parliament may decide to rotate its sessions among the five World Capitals, and if so, to decide the procedure for rotation.

15.3.5. For the first two operative stages of World Government as defined in Article 17, and for the Provisional World Government as defined in Article 19, a provisional location may be selected for the Primary World Capital. The provisional location need no t be continued as a permanent location.
15.3.6. Any World Capital or World Federal Zone may be relocated by an absolute two-thirds majority vote of the three Houses of the World Parliament in joint session.
15.3.7. Additional World Federal Zones may be designated if found necessary by proposal of the Presidium and approval by an absolute majority vote of the three Houses of the World Parliament in joint session.

Article 16 - World Territories and Exterior Relations

Sec. 16.1. - World Territory

16.1.1. Those areas of the Earth and Earth's moon which are not under the jurisdiction of existing nations at the time of forming the Federation of Earth, or which are not reasonably within the province of national ownership and administration, or which are declared to be World Territory subsequent to establishment of the Federation of Earth, shall be designated as World Territory and shall belong to all of the people of Earth.
16.1.2. The administration of World Territory shall be determined by the World Parliament and implemented by the World Executive, and shall apply to the following areas:
16.1.2.1. All oceans and seas having an international or supra-national character, together with the seabeds and resources thereof, beginning at a distance of twenty kilometers offshore, excluding inland seas of traditional national ownership.
16.1.2.2. Vital straits, channels, and canals.
16.1.2.3. The atmosphere enveloping Earth, beginning at an elevation of one kilometer above the general surface of the land, excluding the depressions in areas of much variation in elevation.
16.1.2.4. Man-made satellites and Earth's moon.
16.1.2.5. Colonies which may choose the status of World Territory; non-independent territories under the trust administration of nations or of the United Nations; any islands or atolls which are unclaimed by any nation; independent lands or countries which choo se the status of World Territory; and disputed lands which choose the status of World Territory.
16.1.3. The residents of any World Territory, except designated World Federal Zones, shall have the right within reason to decide by plebiscite to become a self-governing nation within the Federation of Earth, either singly or in combination with other World Territories, or to unite with an existing nation with the Federation of Earth.

Sec. 16.2. - Exterior Relations

16.2.1. The World Government shall maintain exterior relations with those nations of Earth which have not joined the Federation of Earth. Exterior relations shall be under the administration of the Presidium, subject at all times to specific instructions and approval by the World Parliament.

16.2.2. All treaties and agreements with nations remaining outside the Federation of Earth shall be negotiated by the Presidium and must be ratified by a simple majority vote of the three Houses of the World Parliament.

16.2.3. The World Government for the Federation of Earth shall establish and maintain peaceful relations with other planets and celestial bodies where and when it may become possible to establish communications with the possible inhabitants thereof.

16.2.4. All explorations into outer space, both within and beyond the solar system in which Planet Earth is located, shall be under the exclusive direction and control of the World Government, and shall be conducted in such manner as shall be determined by the World Parliament.

Article 17 - Ratification and Implementation

Sec. 17.1. - Ratification of the World Constitution

This World Constitution shall be submitted to the nations and people of Earth for ratification by the following procedures:

17.1.01. The World Constitution shall be transmitted to the General Assembly of the United Nations Organization and to each national government on Earth, with the request that the World Constitution be submitted to the national legislature of each nation for preliminary ratification and to the people of each nation for final ratification by popular referendum.

17.1.02. Preliminary ratification by a national legislature shall be accomplished by simple majority vote of the national legislature.

17.1.03. Final ratification by the people shall be accomplished by a simple majority of votes cast in a popular referendum, provided that a minimum of twenty-five percent of eligible voters of age eighteen years and over have cast ballots within the nation or country or within World Electoral and Administrative Districts.

17.1.04. In the case of a nation without a national legislature, the head of the national government shall be requested to give preliminary ratification and to submit the World Constitution for final ratification by popular referendum.

17.1.05. In the event that a national government, after six months, fails to submit the World Constitution for ratification as requested, then the global agency assuming responsibility for the worldwide ratification campaign may proceed to conduct a direct ref erendum for ratification of the World Constitution by the people. Direct referendums may be organized on the basis of entire nations or countries, or on the basis of existing defined communities within nations.

17.1.06. In the event of a direct ratification referendum, final ratification shall be accomplished by a majority of the votes cast whether for an entire nation or for a World Electoral and Administrative District, provided that ballots are cast by a minimum of twenty-five percent of eligible voters of the area who are over eighteen years of age.

7.1.07. For ratification by existing communities within a nation, the procedure shall be to request local communities, cities, counties, states, provinces, cantons, prefectures, tribal jurisdictions, or other defined political units within a nation to ratify the World Constitution, and to submit the World Constitution for a referendum vote by the citizens of the community or political unit. Ratification may be accomplished by proceeding in this way until all eligible voters of age eighteen and above within the nation or World Electoral and Administrative District have had the opportunity to vote, provided that ballots are cast by a minimum of twenty-five percent of those eligible to vote.

17.1.08. Prior to the Full Operative Stage of World Government, as defined under Section 5 of Article 17, the universities, colleges and scientific academies and institutes in any country may ratify the World Constitution, thus qualifying them for participation in the nomination of Members of the World Parliament to the House of Counsellors.

17.1.09. In the case of those nations currently involved in serious international disputes or where traditional enmities and chronic disputes may exist among two or more nations, a procedure for concurrent paired ratification shall be instituted whereby the nations which are parties to a current or chronic international dispute or conflict may simultaneously ratify the World Constitution. In such cases, the paired nations shall be admitted into the Federation of Earth simultaneously, with the obligation for each such nation to immediately turn over all weapons of mass destruction to the World Government, and to turn over the conflict or dispute for mandatory peaceful settlement by the World Government.

17.1.10. Each nation or political unit which ratifies this World Constitution, either by preliminary ratification or final ratification, shall be bound never to use any armed forces or weapons of mass destruction against another member or unit of the Federatio n of Earth, regardless of how long it may take to achieve full disarmament of all the nations and political units which ratify this World Constitution.

17.1.11. When ratified, the Constitution for the Federation of Earth becomes the supreme law of Earth. By the act of ratifying this Earth Constitution, any provision in the Constitution or Legislation of any country so ratifying, which is contrary to this Earth Constitution, is either repealed or amended to conform with the Constitution for the Federation of Earth, effective as soon as 25 countries have so ratified. The amendment of National or State Constitutions to allow entry into World Federation is not necessary prior to ratification of the Constitution for the Federation of Earth.

Sec. 17.2. - Stages of Implementation

17.2.1. Implementation of this World Constitution and the establishment of World Government pursuant to the terms of this World Constitution, may be accomplished in three stages, as follows, in addition to the stage of a Provisional World Government as provided under Article 19:

17.2.1.1. First Operative Stage of World Government.

17.2.1.2. Second Operative Stage of World Government.

17.2.1.3. Full Operative Stage of World Government.

17.2.2. At the beginning and during each stage, the World Parliament and the World Executive together shall establish goals and develop means for the progressive implementation of the World Constitution, and for the implementation of legislation enacted by the World Parliament.

Sec. 17.3. - First Operative Stage of World Government

17.3.01. The first operative stage of World Government under this World Constitution shall be implemented when the World Constitution is ratified by a sufficient number of nations and/or people to meet one or the other of the following conditions or equivalent :

17.3.01.1. Preliminary or final ratification by a minimum of twenty-five nations, each having a population of more than 100,000.

17.3.01.2. Preliminary or final ratification by a minimum of ten nations above 100,000 population, together with ratification by direct referendum within a minimum of fifty additional World Electoral and Administrative Districts.

17.3.01.3. Ratification by direct referendum within a minimum of 100 World Electoral and Administrative Districts, even though no nation as such has ratified.

17.3.02. The election of Members of the World Parliament to the House of Peoples shall be conducted in all World Electoral and Administrative Districts where ratification has been accomplished by popular referendum.

17.3.03. The Election of Members of the World Parliament to the House of Peoples may proceed concurrently with direct popular referendums both prior to and after the First Operative Stage of World Government is reached.

17.3.04. The appointment or election of Members of the World Parliament to the House of Nations shall proceed in all nations where preliminary ratification has been accomplished.

17.3.05. One-fourth of the Members of the World Parliament to the House of Counsellors may be elected from nominees submitted by universities and colleges which have ratified the World Constitution.

17.3.06. The World Presidium and the Executive Cabinet shall be elected according to the provisions in Article 6, except that in the absence of a House of Counsellors, the nominations shall be made by the members of the House of Peoples and of the House of Nations in joint session. Until this is accomplished, the Presidium and Executive Cabinet of the Provisional World Government as provided in Article 19, shall continue to serve.

17.3.07. When composed, the Presidium for the first operative stage of World Government shall assign or re-assign Ministerial posts among Cabinet and Presidium members, and shall immediately establish or confirm a World Disarmament Agency and a World Economic and Development Organization.

17.3.08. Those nations which ratify this World Constitution and thereby join the Federation of Earth, shall immediately transfer all weapons of mass destruction as defined and designated by the World Disarmament Agency to that Agency. (See Article

19, Sections A-2-d, B-6 and E-5). The World Disarmament Agency shall immediately immobilize all such weapons and shall proceed with dispatch to dismantle, convert to peacetime use, re-cycle the materials thereof or otherwise destroy all such weapons. During the fir st operative stage of World Government, the ratifying nations may retain armed forces equipped with weapons other than weapons of mass destruction as defined and designated by the World Disarmament Agency.

17.3.09. Concurrently with the reduction or elimination of such weapons of mass destruction and other military expenditures as can be accomplished during the first operative stage of World Government, the member nations of the Federation of Earth shall pay ann ually to the Treasury of the World Government amounts equal to one-half the amounts saved from their respective national military budgets during the last year before joining the Federation, and shall continue such payments until the full operative stage of World Government is reached. The World Government shall use fifty percent of the funds thus received to finance the work and projects of the World Economic Development Organization.

17.3.10. The World Parliament and the World Executive shall continue to develop the organs, departments, agencies and activities originated under the Provisional World Government, with such amendments as deemed necessary; and shall proceed to establish and beg in the following organs, departments and agencies of the World Government, if not already underway, together with such other departments, and agencies as are considered desirable and feasible during the first operative stage of World Government:

17.3.10.01. The World Supreme Court;
17.3.10.02. The Enforcement System;
17.3.10.03. The World Ombudsmus;
17.3.10.04. The World Civil Service Administration;
17.3.10.05. The World Financial Administration;
17.3.10.06. The Agency for Research and Planning;
17.3.10.07. The Agency for Technological and Environmental Assessment;
17.3.10.08. An Emergency Earth Rescue Administration, concerned with all aspects of climate change and related factors;
17.3.10.09. An Integrated Global Energy System, based on environmentally safe sources;
17.3.10.10. A World University System, under the Department of Education;
17.3.10.11. A World Corporations Office, under the Department of Commerce and Industry;
17.3.10.12. The World Service Corps;
17.3.10.13. A World Oceans and Seabeds Administration.

17.3.11. At the beginning of the first operative stage, the Presidium in consultation with the Executive Cabinet shall formulate and put forward a proposed program for solving the most urgent world problems currently confronting humanity.

17.3.12. The World Parliament shall proceed to work upon solutions to world problems. The World Parliament and the World Executive working together shall institute through the several organs, departments and agencies of the World Government whatever means shall seem appropriate and feasible to accomplish the implementation and enforcement of world legislation, world law and the World Constitution; and in particular shall take certain decisive actions for the welfare of all people on Earth, applicable throughout the world, including but not limited to the following:

17.3.12.01. Expedite the organization and work of an Emergency Earth Rescue Administration, concerned with all aspects of climate change and climate crises;

17.3.12.02. Expedite the new finance, credit and monetary system, to serve human needs;

17.3.12.03. Expedite an integrated global energy system, utilizing solar energy, hydrogen energy, and other safe and sustainable sources of energy;

17.3.12.04. Push forward a global program for agricultural production to achieve maximum sustained yield under conditions which are ecologically sound;

17.3.12.05. Establish conditions for free trade within the Federation of Earth;

17.3.12.06. Call for and find ways to implement a moratorium on nuclear energy projects until all problems are solved concerning safety, disposal of toxic wastes and the dangers of use or diversion of materials for the production of nuclear weapons;

17.3.12.07. Outlaw and find ways to completely terminate the production of nuclear weapons and all weapons of mass destruction;

17.3.12.08. Push forward programs to assure adequate and non-polluted water supplies and clean air supplies for everybody on Earth;

17.3.12.09. Push forward a global program to conserve and re-cycle the resources of Earth.

17.3.12.10. Develop an acceptable program to bring population growth under control, especially by raising standards of living.

Sec. 17.4. - Second Operative Stage of World Government

17.4.01. The second operative stage of World Government shall be implemented when fifty percent or more of the nations of Earth have given either preliminary or final ratification to this World Constitution, provided that fifty percent of the total population of Earth is included either within the ratifying nations or within the ratifying nations together with additional World Electoral and Administrative Districts where people have ratified the World Constitution by direct referendum.

17.4.02. The election and appointment of Members of the World Parliament to the several Houses of the World Parliament shall proceed in the same manner as specified for the first operative stage in Section 3.2, 3.3, 3.4 and 3.5 of Article 17.

17.4.03. The terms of office of the Members of the World Parliament elected or appointed for the first operative stage of World Government, shall be extended into the second operative stage unless they have already served five year terms, in which case new elections or appointments shall be arranged. The terms of holdover Members of the World Parliament into the second operative stage shall be adjusted to run concurrently with the terms of those who are newly elected at the beginning of the second operative stage.

17.4.04. The World Presidium and the Executive Cabinet shall be re-constituted or reconfirmed, as needed, at the beginning of the second operative stage of World Government.

17.4.05. The World Parliament and the World Executive shall continue to develop the organs, departments, agencies and activities which are already underway from the first operative stage of World Government, with such amendments as deemed necessary; and shall proceed to establish and develop all other organs and major departments and agencies of the World Government to the extent deemed feasible during the second operative stage.

17.4.06. All nations joining the Federation of Earth to compose the second operative stage of World Government, shall immediately transfer all weapons of mass destruction and all other military weapons and equipment to the World Disarmament Agency, which shall immediately immobilize such weapons and equipment and shall proceed forthwith to dismantle, convert to peacetime uses, recycle the materials thereof, or otherwise destroy such weapons and equipment. During the second operative stage, all armed forces and para-military forces of the nations which have joined the Federation of Earth shall be completely disarmed and either disbanded or converted on a voluntary basis into elements of the non-military World Service Corps.

17.4.07. Concurrently with the reduction or elimination of such weapons, equipment and other military expenditures as can be accomplished during the second operative stage of World Government, the member nations of the Federation of Earth shall pay annually to the Treasury of the World Government amounts equal to one-half of the amounts saved from their national military budgets during the last year before joining the Federation and shall continue such payments until the full operative stage of World Government is reached. The World Government shall use fifty percent of the funds thus received to finance the work and projects of the World Economic Development Organization.

17.4.08. Upon formation of the Executive Cabinet for the second operative stage, the Presidium shall issue an invitation to the General Assembly of the United Nations Organization and to each of the specialized agencies of the United Nations, as well as to other useful international agencies, to transfer personnel, facilities, equipment, resources and allegiance to the Federation of Earth and to the World Government thereof. The agencies and functions of the United Nations Organization and of its specialized agencies and of other international agencies which may be thus transferred, shall be reconstituted as needed and integrated into the several organs, departments, offices and agencies of the World Government.

17.4.09. Near the beginning of the second operative stage, the Presidium in consultation with the Executive cabinet, shall formulate and put forward a proposed program for solving the most urgent world problems currently confronting the people of Earth.

17.4.10. The World Parliament shall proceed with legislation necessary for implementing a complete program for solving the current urgent world problems.
17.4.11. The World Parliament and the World Executive working together shall develop through the several organs, departments and agencies of the World Government whatever means shall seem appropriate and feasible to implement legislation for solving world problems; and in particular shall take certain decisive actions for the welfare of all people on Earth, including but not limited to the following:
17.4.11.1. Declaring all oceans, seas and canals having supra-national character (but not including inland seas traditionally belonging to particular nations) from twenty kilometers offshore, and all the seabeds thereof, to be under the ownership of the Federati on of Earth as the common heritage of humanity, and subject to the control and management of the World Government.
17.4.11.2. Declare the polar caps and surrounding polar areas, including the continent of Antartica but not areas which are traditionally a part of particular nations, to be world territory owned by the Federation of Earth as the common heritage of humanity, and subject to control and management by the World Government.
17.4.11.3. Outlaw the possession, stockpiling, sale and use of all nuclear weapons, all weapons of mass destruction, and all other military weapons and equipment.
17.4.11.4. Establish an ever-normal grainery and food supply system for the people of Earth.
17.4.11.5. Develop and carry forward insofar as feasible all actions defined under Sec. 3.10., and 3.12. of the First Operative Stage.

Sec. 17.5. - Full Operative Stage of World Government

17.5.1. The full operative stage of World Government shall be implemented when this World Constitution is given either preliminary or final ratification by meeting either condition (17.5.1.1.) or (17.5.1.2.):
17.5.1.1. Ratification by eighty percent or more of the nations of Earth comprising at least ninety percent of the population of Earth; or
17.5.1.2. Ratification which includes ninety percent of Earth's total population, either within ratifying nations or within ratifying nations together with additional World Electoral and Administrative Districts where ratification by direct referendum has been accomplished, as provided in Article 17, Section 1.
17.5.2. When the full operative stage of World Government is reached, the following conditions shall be implemented:
17.5.2.01. Elections for Members of the House of Peoples shall be conducted in all World Electoral and Administrative Districts where elections have not already taken place; and Members of the House of Nations shall be elected or appointed by the national legisl atures or national governments in all nations where this has not already been accomplished.
17.5.2.02. The terms of office for Members of the House of Peoples and of the House of Nations serving during the second operative stage, shall be continued into the full

operative stage, except for those who have already served five years, in which case elections shall be held or appointments made as required.

17.5.2.03. The terms of office for all holdover Members of the House of Peoples and of the House of Nations who have served less than five years, shall be adjusted to run concurrently with those Members of the World Parliament whose terms are beginning with the full operative stage.

17.5.2.04. The second 100 Members of the House of Counsellors shall be elected according to the procedure specified in Section 5 of Article 5. The terms of office for holdover Members of the House of Counsellors shall run five more years after the beginning of the full operative stage, while those beginning their terms with the full operative stage shall serve ten years.

17.5.2.05. The Presidium and the Executive Cabinet shall be reconstituted in accordance with the provisions of Article 6.

17.5.2.06. All organs of the World Government shall be made fully operative, and shall be fully developed for the effective administration and implementation of world legislation, world law and the provisions of this World Constitution.

17.5.2.07. All nations which have not already done so shall immediately transfer all military weapons and equipment to the World Disarmament Agency, which shall immediately immobilize all such weapons and shall proceed forthwith to dismantle, convert to peaceful usage, recycle the materials thereof, or otherwise to destroy such weapons and equipment.

17.5.2.08. All armies and military forces of every kind shall be completely disarmed, and either disbanded or converted and integrated on a voluntary basis into the non-military World Service Corps.

17.5.2.09. All viable agencies of the United Nations Organization and other viable international agencies established among national governments, together with their personnel, facilities and resources, shall be transferred to the World Government and reconstituted and integrated as may be useful into the organs, departments, offices, institutes, commissions, bureaus and agencies of the World Government.

17.5.2.10. The World Parliament and the World Executive shall continue to develop the activities and projects which are already underway from the second operative stage of World Government, with such amendments as deemed necessary; and shall proceed with a complete and full scale program to solve world problems and serve the welfare of all people on Earth, in accordance with the provisions of this World Constitution.

Sec. 17.6. - Costs of Ratification

The work and costs of private Citizens of Earth for the achievement of a ratified Constitution for the Federation of Earth, are recognized as legitimate costs for the establishment of constitutional world government by which present and future generations will benefit, and shall be repaid double the original amount by the World Financial Administration of the World Government when it becomes operational after 25 countries have ratified this Constitution for the Federation of Earth. Repayment specifically includes contributions to the World Government Funding Corporation and other costs and expenses recognized by standards and procedures to be established by the World Financial Administration.

Article 18 - Amendments

18.1. Following completion of the first operative stage of World Government, amendments to this World Constitution may be proposed for consideration in two ways:

18.1.1. By a simple majority vote of any House of the World Parliament.

18.1.2. By petitions signed by a total of 200,000 persons eligible to vote in world elections from a total of at least twenty World Electoral and Administrative Districts where the World Constitution has received final ratification.

18.2. Passage of any amendment proposed by a House of the World Parliament shall require an absolute two-thirds majority vote of each of the three Houses of the World Parliament voting separately.

18.3. An amendment proposed by popular petition shall first require a simple majority vote of the House of Peoples, which shall be obliged to take a vote upon the proposed amendment. Passage of the amendment shall then require an absolute two-thirds majority vote of each of the three Houses of the World Parliament voting separately.

18.4. Periodically, but no later than ten years after first convening the World Parliament for the First Operative Stage of World Government, and every 20 years thereafter, the Members of the World Parliament shall meet in special session comprising a Constitutional Convention to conduct a review of this World Constitution to consider and propose possible amendments, which shall then require action as specified in Clause 2 of Article 18 for passage.

18.5. If the First Operative Stage of World Government is not reached by the year 1995, then the Provisional World Parliament, as provided under Article 19, may convene another session of the World Constituent Assembly to review the Constitution for the Federation of Earth and consider possible amendments according to procedure established by the Provisional World Parliament.

18.6. Except by following the amendment procedures specified herein, no part of this World Constitution may be set aside, suspended or subverted, neither for emergencies nor caprice nor convenience.

Article 19 - Provisional Earth Federation

Sec. 19.1. - Actions to be Taken by the World Constituent Assembly

Upon adoption of the World Constitution by the World Constituent Assembly, the Assembly and such continuing agency or agencies as it shall designate shall do the following, without being limited thereto:

19.1.1. Issue a Call to all Nations, communities and people of Earth to ratify this World Constitution for World Government.
19.1.2. Establish the following preparatory commissions:
19.1.2.01. Ratification Commission.
19.1.2.02. World Elections Commission.
19.1.2.03. World Development Commission.
19.1.2.04. World Disarmament Commission.
19.1.2.05. World Problems Commission.
19.1.2.06. Nominating Commission.
19.1.2.07. Finance Commission.
19.1.2.08. Peace Research and Education Commission.
19.1.2.09. Special commissions on each of several of the most urgent world problems.
19.1.2.10. Such other commissions as may be deemed desirable in order to proceed with the Provisional World Government.
19.1.3. Convene Sessions of a Provisional World Parliament when feasible under the following conditions:
19.1.3.1. Seek the commitment of 500 or more delegates to attend, representing people in 20 countries from five continents, and having credentials defined by Article 19, Section 3;
19.1.3.2. The minimum funds necessary to organize the sessions of the Provisional World Parliament are either on hand or firmly pledged.
19.1.3.3. Suitable locations are confirmed at least nine months in advance, unless emergency conditions justify shorter advance notice.

Sec. 19.2. - Work of the Preparatory Commissions

19.2.01. The Ratification Commission shall carry out a worldwide campaign for the ratification of the World Constitution, both to obtain preliminary ratification by national governments, including national legislatures, and to obtain final ratification by people, including communities. The ratification commission shall continue its work until the full operative stage of World Government is reached.
19.2.02. The World Elections Commission shall prepare a provisional global map of World Electoral and Administrative Districts and Regions which may be revised during the first or second operative stage of World Government, and shall prepare and proceed with p lans to obtain the election of Members of the World Parliament to the House of

Peoples and to the House of Counsellors. The World Elections Commission shall in due course be converted into the World Boundaries and Elections Administration.

19.2.03. After six months, in those countries where national governments have not responded favorable to the ratification call, the Ratification Commission and the World Elections Commission may proceed jointly to accomplish both the ratification of the World Constitution by direct popular referendum and concurrently the election of Members of the World Parliament.

19.2.04. The Ratification Commission may also submit the World Constitution for ratification by universities and colleges throughout the world.

19.2.05. The World Development Commission shall prepare plans for the creation of a World Economic Development Organization to serve all nations and people ratifying the World Constitution, and in particular less developed countries, to begin functioning when the Provisional World Government is established.

19.2.06. The World Disarmament Commission shall prepare plans for the organization of a World Disarmament Agency, to begin functioning when the Provisional World Government is established.

19.2.07. The World Problems Commission shall prepare an agenda of urgent world problems, with documentation, for possible action by the Provisional World Parliament and Provisional World Government.

19.2.08. The Nominating Commission shall prepare, in advance of convening the Provisional World Parliament, a list of nominees to compose the Presidium and the Executive Cabinet for the Provisional World Government.

19.2.09. The Finance Commission shall work on ways and means for financing the Provisional World Government.

19.2.10. The several commissions on particular world problems shall work on the preparation of proposed world legislation and action on each problem, to present to the Provisional World Parliament when it convenes.

Sec. 19.3. - Composition of the Provisional World Parliament

19.3.1. The Provisional World Parliament shall be composed of the following members:

19.3.1.1. All those who were accredited as delegates to the 1977 and 1991 Sessions of the World Constituent Assembly, as well as to any previous Session of the Provisional World Parliament, and who re-confirm their support for the Constitution for the Federation of Earth, as amended.

19.3.1.2. Persons who obtain the required number of signatures on election petitions, or who are designated by Non-Governmental Organizations which adopt approved resolutions for this purpose, or who are otherwise accredited according to terms specified in Calls which may be issued to convene particular sessions of the Provisional World Parliament.

19.3.1.3. Members of the World Parliament to the House of Peoples who are elected from World Electoral and Administrative Districts up to the time of convening the

Provisional World Parliament. Members of the World Parliament elected to the House of Peoples may continue to be added to the Provisional World Parliament until the first operative stage of World Government is reached.
19.3.1.4. Members of the World Parliament to the House of Nations who are elected by national legislatures or appointed by national governments up to the time of convening the Provisional World Parliament. Members of the World Parliament to the House of Nations may continue to be added to the Provisional World Parliament until the first operative stage of World Government is reached.
19.3.1.5. Those universities and colleges which have ratified the World Constitution may nominate persons to serve as Members of the World Parliament to the House of Counsellors. The House of Peoples and House of Nations together may then elect from such nominees up to fifty Members of the World Parliament to serve in the House of Counsellors of the Provisional World Government.
19.3.2. Members of the Provisional World Parliament in categories (1) and (2) as defined above, shall serve only until the first operative stage of World Government is declared, but may be duly elected to continue as Members of the World Parliament during the first operative stage.

Sec. 19.4. - Formation of the Provisional World Executive

19.4.1. As soon as the Provisional World Parliament next convenes, it will elect a new Presidium for the Provisional World Parliament and Provisional World Government from among the nominees submitted by the Nominating Commission.
19.4.2. Members of the Provisional World Presidium shall serve terms of three years, and may be re-elected by the Provisional World Parliament, but in any case shall serve only until the Presidium is elected under the First Operative Stage of World Government .
19.4.3. The Presidium may make additional nominations for the Executive Cabinet.
19.4.4. The Provisional World Parliament shall then elect the members of the Executive Cabinet.
19.4.5. The Presidium shall then assign ministerial posts among the members of the Executive Cabinet and of the Presidium.
19.4.6. When steps (1) through (4) of section 19.4. are completed, the Provisional World Government shall be declared in operation to serve the welfare of humanity.

Sec. 19.5. - First Actions of the Provisional World Government

19.5.1. The Presidium, in consultation with the Executive Cabinet, the commissions on particular world problems and the World Parliament, shall define a program for action on urgent world problems.
19.5.2. The Provisional World Parliament shall go to work on the agenda of world problems, and shall take any and all actions it considers appropriate and feasible, in accordance with the provisions of this World Constitution.

19.5.3. Implementation of and compliance with the legislation enacted by the Provisional World Parliament shall be sought on a voluntary basis in return for the benefits to be realized, while strength of the Provisional World Government is being increased by the progressive ratification of the World Constitution.
19.5.4. Insofar as considered appropriate and feasible, the Provisional World Parliament and Provisional World Executive may undertake some of the actions specified under Section 3.12.of Article 17 for the first operative stage of World Government.
19.5.5. The World Economic Development Organization and the World Disarmament Agency shall be established, for correlated actions.
19.5.6. The World Parliament and the Executive Cabinet of the Provisional World Government shall proceed with the organization of other organs and agencies of the World Government on a provisional basis, insofar as considered desirable and feasible, in partic ular those specified under Section 3.10. of Article 17.
19.5.7. The several preparatory commissions on urgent world problems may be reconstituted as Administrative Departments of the Provisional World Government.
19.5.8. In all of its work and activities, the Provisional World Government shall function in accordance with the provisions of this Constitution for the Federation of Earth.

(The Constitution for the Federation of Earth was originally ratified at the second session of the World Constituent Assembly held at Innsbruck, Austria in June, 1977; and was amended and ratified at the fourth session of the World Constituent Assembly held at Troia, Portugal in May 1991. The Amended Constitution is being personally ratified by outstanding personalities throughout the world as the campaign for ratification by the people and governments of the world gets underway.)

Signatures of participants in the World Constituent Assemblies are on following pages.

After the signature pages, the next chapter addresses points of interpretation of the *Earth Constitution*, based on cross-referenced provisions of the *Earth Constitution*, based on decisions of the sessions of the provisional World Parliament, or, in a very few cases, based on interpretation by the Editors.

Chapter Six Addendum

Original Signatories to the *Earth Constitution*

"We have been here over forty years, a longer period than the children of Israel wandered through the wilderness, coming to this Capitol pleading for this recognition of the principle that the Government derives its just powers from the consent of the governed. Mr. Chairman, we ask that you report our resolution favorably if you can but unfavorably if you must; that you report one way or the other, so that the Senate may have the chance to consider it."

Anna Howard Shaw (1847–1919), U.S. minister, suffragist, and speaker.
April 19, 1910, before a hearing of the United States Senate Judiciary Committee

It has been now fifty years since Mary Georgia Lloyd and her colleagues called out for there to convene a World Constituent Assembly to draft and adopt a non-military *Constitution for the Federation of Earth*. Since the first session of World Constituent Assembly in 1968, forty years have passed. Since the initial signing in 1977, signaling the readiness of the *Earth Constitution* for adoption, more than thirty years have transpired. Nearly eighteen years have come and gone since the last review and signing of the *Constitution*. In terms of the human need for self government at a global level, very little has changed qualitatively since 1991. We strongly believe that the *Earth Constitution* is adequate as it is for the global legal renaissance of emerging world law.

In the quote above, Anna Howard Shaw pled with the United States Senate Judiciary Committee on this matter of self-government, which was timely for that period.

Now we, those citizens of the world who have participated in the creation of the *Earth Constitution*, and those who have thereafter come across this marvelous document, urge the rest of the citizens and civilians of the world to seriously consider the value of the *Constitution*'s rapid adoption, so that there is the elevation of self-government to the planetary level.

On the following pages are the signatures of persons from every walk of life who attended the second and fourth sessions of the World Constituent Assembly, where there were official signing ceremonies, together with a list of persons on the last page who had wanted to attend and who agreed to support the *Earth Constitution*. Since the time of the official ceremonies, thousands more people have signed their support for the document.

Our initial goal is to get both the joint ratification of a large number of national governments (about 25, perhaps) and also the measured direct ratification by the people of the world adequate to initiate the first operative stage as defined in the *Earth Constitution*.

Participants in the World Constituent Assembly, 16 to 29 of June, 1977, have affixed their signatures to the draft of the CONSTITUTION FOR THE FEDERATION OF EARTH herewith:

A. Patel	India
[illegible]	MEXICO
Philip Isely	EARTH, USA
Lucile W. Green	Earth, USA
Max Habicht	Hon. Legal Advisor
Hanna Newcombe	Canada
T.P. Amerasinghe	Sri Lanka.
[illegible]	Israel
Archie Casely Hayford	Ghana.
K. Koma	Botswana
Helen Tucker (Canada) Women's Universal Movement	
[illegible]	Fed. Rep. of Germany
Thane Read	U.S.A.
[illegible]	India.
[illegible]	Thailand.
Rose J. Cheney,	Australia.
[illegible]	Germany
[illegible]	Netherlands
[illegible]	JAPAN

Name	Country
ANDREA von SCHINCY	GERMANY
Edith Farovich	Germany
Gisela Gintzel	Germany
Klaus Flakus-Schlichtmann	Germany
Ann Mische	World, U.S.A
Gerald Mische	U.S.A.
Dr. Ludwig C. [illegible]	W. Germany
Dr. Fred Karl Scheile	U.S.A.
Max Jaeger	Germany
Olga Jaeger	Germany
Beatrice Meyers	U.S.A.
Elisabeth [illegible]	INNSBRUCK
Theo [illegible]	Switzerland
Dr Helen K Billings	U.S.A
Magister Kirsti Balthasar	Finland live in Mexico
Robert Rosamond	United Peoples Federation of Earth
Valerie Hagenhuber	Austria
Herbert Groder	~
[illegible]	"

Name	Country
Louis R. Gomberg	U.S.A
P. C. Malhotra	India
Hildegard Heuer	Schweiz
PURAN SINGH AZAD.	(INDIA)
Dr Miss. Geeta Shah	INDIA.
Maria Iseli	Schweiz
Karl Krentz	[illegible]
Bonnie Allen	U.S.A
Rustom M. Bharucha	India.
William Bryant	USA
Jeanne C. Burrows	USA. World
Leo J. Murray sa (Pax Christi USA)	
Simon R. [illegible]	Botswana
Mrs. Renée Dangoor	United Kingdom
MR. J. Lelaka	Botswana
[illegible] Coleman	Australia
Donald L. Coleman	Australia
[illegible]	AUSTRIA

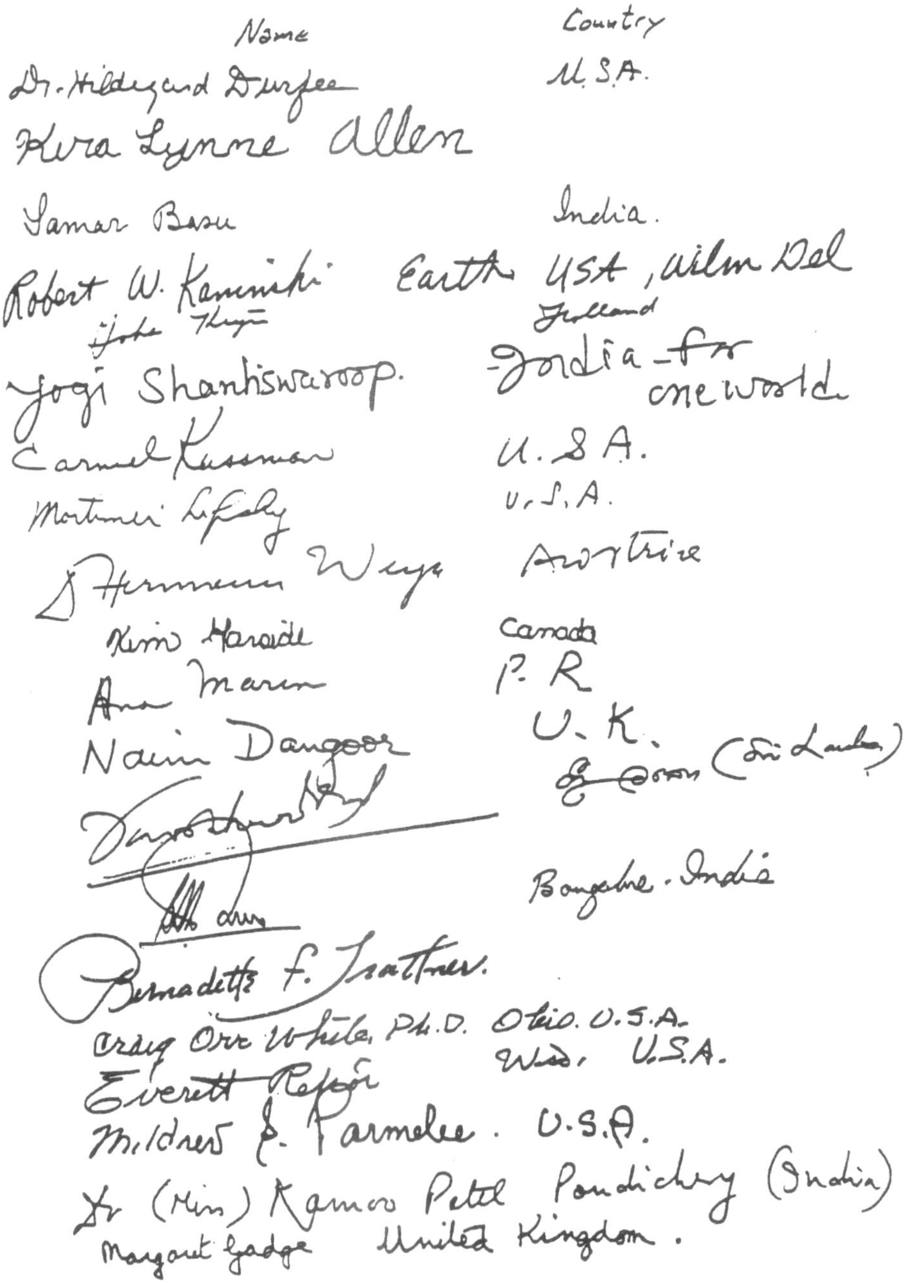
Name Country
Dr. Hildegard Durfee U.S.A.
Kira Lynne Allen
Samar Basu India.
Robert W. Kaminski Earth USA, Wilm Del
John Thijn Holland
Yogi Shantiswaroop. India – for oneworld
Carmel Kussman U.S.A.
Mortimer Lipsky U.S.A.
Hermann Weyr Austria
Kim Haraide Canada
Ana Marin P. R
Naim Dangoor U.K.
(Sri Lanka)
Bangalore. India
Bernadette F. Trattner.
Craig Orr White, Ph.D. Ohio. U.S.A.
Everett Refior Wis. U.S.A.
Mildred S. Parmelee. U.S.A.
Dr (Miss) Kamini Patel Pondichery (India)
Margaret Gadge United Kingdom.

Name	Country
Bandula Sri Gunawardhana	Sri Lanka
Margaret Isely	U.S.A.
Maitzenberger Elisabeth	Austria
[illegible]	PUERTO RICO
Gregory Alexander	U.S.A.
Edward R. Leader	Puerto Rico
[illegible]	India.
Dorothy Gillam Baker	U.S.A.
Carl F. Cattarin	Earth!
[illegible]	Denmark
Heather Isely	U.S.A.
Foster Parmelee	U.S.A.
Ogola Justus	Kenya
H.A. Hacinsing	W-Germany
Kemper Isely	U.S.A.
Bernard Shaw Mazi	Nigeria.
Mitsuo Miyazaki	JAPAN
Johanna Materhelle	Netherlands
[illegible]	Botswana

Name	Address
Eggert, Charlotte Luise	[illegible]
Josephine [illegible]	N.Y.-C. [illegible]
Martha [illegible]	USA
[illegible] Kurt	Innsbruck Austria
Suzanne [illegible]	San Francisco USA
Holzapfel Heiner	Innsbruck
[illegible]	Innsbruck
Vera C. Herold	Mexico [illegible]
Hurel Ingeborg	Germany
Schmeding, Hans-Friedrich	Germany
[illegible]	Germany
B. Molnar	World Citizen
Leland P. Stewart	Los Angeles
John Stockwell	San Francisco
Guido Graziani	Rome, Italy
Dorothea [illegible]	Hannover, WOMAN

Name	Country
[illegible]	Holla
William [illegible]	[illegible]
Raphie [illegible]	U.S.A.
Carmel Painter	USA
Janet [illegible]	USA
Stephen Sipho Moncube	stateless
Ahmed [illegible] Jaffer	Pakistan
Bruno [illegible]	Italy
	México

Por el mundo espiritual
[illegible] José M. Ortega

Por la unión en el arte en el espíritu (México)
[illegible] Elsa [illegible]

Rev. GAGPA Maria Carlota [illegible] Estrada (México)

"Por el mundo Espiritual"
Rev. GagPa [illegible] (México)

"Por el mundo Espiritual"
[illegible] Adolfo Olivera (México)

Name	Country
Tiakoga Ruge	Mexico
Stefanie Gollinger	Austria
[illegible]	Austria
Herbert [illegible]	Deutschland (BRD)
Siddhartha I. Patel	Kenya.
Kalaben Patel.	India
Umesh A Patel	Great Britain.
Kumud I. Patel	Great Britain.
Ahmad Soebandjo [illegible]	Indonesia
Setyobudiarti	Indonesia
Sylvia Stickel	New Zealand + USA
Alice Stephens	England.
Elizabeth E. Stewart	United States
[illegible]	Bangladesh
Harbhajan Singh Khalsa / HARBHAJAN SINGH Yogiji / Sikh Dharma Western Hemisphere	USA

Note: This list of initial signers of the CONSTITUTION FOR THE FEDERATION OF EARTH would include several hundred more persons from fifty countries, prevented only by the cost of travel to attend the Assembly at Innsbruck, Austria.

PERSONAL RATIFIERS OF THE CONSTITUTION FOR THE FEDERATION OF EARTH AS AMENDED AT THE 4th SESSION OF THE WORLD CONSTITUENT ASSEMBLY HELD AT TROIA, PORTUGAL, 29th APRIL, to 9th MAY, 1991

Prof. Dr. Kalman Abraham, Hungary

Atiku Abubakar, Nigeria

Dr. Ebenezer Ade. Adenekan, Nigeria

Malcolm S. Adiseshiah, India

Abdur Rahim Ahamed, Bangladesh

Shahzada Kabir Ahmed

MOHSIN A. ALAINI

Mohsin A. Alaini, Yemen

MD. Nural Alam, U.S.A.

MD. Maser Ali, Bangladesh

Dr. Terence P. Amerasinghe, Sri Lanka

Samir Amin, Senegal

Benjamin K. Amonoo, Ghana

George Anca, Romania

Mauricio Andres-Ribeiro, Brazil

Dr. Munawar A. Anees, U.S.A.

Rev. Ebenezer Annan, Ivory Coast

Jose Ayala-Lasso, Ecuador

Ir. Hasan Basri, Indonesia

Samar Basu, India

Tony Benn, United Kingdom

PERSONAL RATIFIERS - page 2

Prof. Mrs. Edvige Bestazzi, Italy

Petter Jakob Bjerve, Norway

Goran von Bonsdorff, Finland

Selma Brackman, U.S.A.

Jean-Marie Breton, Int. Regis. World Citizens

Tomas Bruckman, Germany (East)

Dennis Brutus, South Africa (U.S.A.)

Dr. Mihai Titus Carapancea, Romania

Prof. Henri Cartan, France

Amb. Khub Chand, India

Dr. Sripati Chandrasekhar, India

Most Rev. French Chang-Him, Seychelles

Munyaradzi Chiwashira, Zimbabwe

Dr. Pratap Chandra Chunder, India

Prof. Dr. Rodney Daniel, France

Daniel G. De Culla, Spain

Dr. Dimitrios J. Delivanis, Greece

Prof. Dr. Francis Dessart, Belgium

Raymond F. Douw, Germany

Prof. Hans-Peter Duerr, Germany

Kennedy Emekan, Nigeria

M. Necati Munir Ertekun, Cyprus

Douglas Nixon Everingham, Australia

John R. Ewbank, U.S.A.

PERSONAL RATIFIERS - page 3

Marjorie Ewbank, U.S.A.

Miss Lianmangi Fanai, India

Dr. Mark Farber, U.S.A.

Feng Ping-Chung, China

Prof. Dr. Mihnea Georghiu, Romania

Lucile W. Green, U.S.A.

Dr. Dauji Gupta, India

Kisholoy Gupta, India

Takeshi Haruki, Japan

Dr. Gerhard Herzberg, Canada

Jozsef Holp, Hungary

A. K. Fazlul Hogue, Bangladesh

Chowdhury Anwar Husain, Bangladesh

Margaret Isely, U.S.A. (Earth)

Philip Isely, U.S.A. (Earth)

Ram K. Jiwanmitra, Nepal

Roy E. Johnstone, Jamaica

Mohammed Kamaluddin, Bangladesh

Mohammad Rezaul Karim, Bangladesh

Rev. George Karunakeran, India

Dr. Inamullah Khan, Pakistan

Johnson S. Khan, Pakistan

Roger Kotila, Ph.D., U.S.A.

PERSONAL RATIFIERS - page 4

David M. Krieger, U.S.A.

Diemuth Kuebart, Germany

Jul Lag, Norway

Ben M. Leito, Netherlands Antilles

Thomas Lim, East Malaysia

Adam Lopatka, Poland

Anwarul Majid, Bangladesh

Dr. M. Sadiq Malik, Pakistan

Guy Marchand, France

Alvin M. Marks, U.S.A.

BERNARDSHAW MAZI

Bernardshaw Mazi, Nigeria

Dr. Zhores A. Medvedev, U. K. (USSR)

Anna Medvegey, Hungary

R. C. Mehrotra, India

Charles Mercieca, U.S.A.

Lt. Col. Pedro B. Merida, Philippines

Yerucham Meshel, Israel

Sheta Mikayele, Zaire

PERSONAL RATIFIERS - page 5

Mohamed Ezzedine Mili, Switzerland

Rev. Toshic Miyake, Japan

Shettima Ali Monguno, Nigeria

Swapan Mukherjee, India

Hanna Newcombe, Canada

Brij P. Nigam, India

Josephine Okafor, Nigeria

Johnson Olatunde, Sierre Leone

Rev. Nelson Onono-Onweng, Uganda

Umit Ozturk, Turkey

Yasar Ozturk, Turkey

Linus Pauling, U.S.A.

Fernando Perez Tella, Spain

Emil Otto Peter, Austria

Dr. Alex Quaison-Sackey, Ghana

Soili Raikkonen, Finland

Sudhir Kumar Rangh, India

Thane Read, U.S.A.

Dr. Sayed Qassem Reshtia, Switzerland

Erzebet Rethy, Hungary

Miguel B. Ricardo, Portugal

G. Rivas Mijares, Venezuela

Reinhart Ruge, Mexico

PERSONAL RATIFIERS - page 6

Prof. Sir A. M. Sadek, South Africa

Abdus Salam, Italy

Akbar Ali Saleh, Comoros Islands

Blagovest Sendov, Bulgaria

Indira Shrestha, Nepal

Rabi Charan Shrestha, Nepal

Jon Silkin, United Kingdom

Jozef Simuth, Slovak Republic

Dr. Kewal Singh, India

Blaine Sloan, U.S.A.

Ross Smyth, Canada

Lord Donald Soper, United Kingdom

Scott Jefferson Starquester, U.S.A.

Homi J. H. Taleyarkhan, India

Rev. Yoshiaki Toeda, Japan

Dr. Duja K. Torki, Tunisia

Helen Tucker, Canada

Evelyn Utulu, Nigeria

Mrs. Justina N. Uwechue, Nigeria

Ogieva O. Uwuigbe, Nigeria

Ann Valentin, U.S.A.

T. Nejat Veziroglu, U.S.A.

Jorgen Laursen Vig, Denmark

George Wald, U.S.A.

Prof. D. A. Walker, United Kingdom

Additional Original Ratifiers:

Kenneth B. Clark, U.S.A.

David Daube, U.S.A.

Nzo Ekangaki, Cameroon

Richard W. Wilbur, U.S.A.

Dr. Sylwester Zawadzki, Poland

Prof. Chief J.O. Agboye, Nigeria
Dr.Francis Alexis, Grenada
Sir Abdul W.M.Ameer, Sri Lanka
Hanan Awwad, Palestine
Hon. Lukasz Balcer, Poland
Chief Dr. Kolawole Balogun, Nigeria
Dr.Saburi O. Biobaku, Nigeria
Dr. Jur. Jan Carnogursky, Slovakia
Dr. Gouin Cedieu, Cote D'Ivorie
Amarsinh Chaudhary, India
Mdm. Justice L. P. Chibesakunda, Zambia
Ashis Kumar De, India
Dr. Mostafa El Desouky, Kuwait
Dr. Rolf Edberg, Sweden
Dr. Benjamin B. Ferencz, U.S.A.
Prof. Vitalii I.Goldanskii, Russia
Prof. Dr. Zbigniew Gertych, Poland
Prof. Errol E. Harris, U.S.A./U.K.
LIC Juan Horacio S., Argentina
Sir Dr. Akanu Ibiam, Nigeria
K. Jeevagathas, Sri Lanka
R. B. Junoo, India
Dr. Jan Kleinert, Slovakia
Dr. Yuri A. Kosygin, Russia
Adv. Ranjan Lakhanpal, India
Adv. Aqil Lodhi, Pakistan
Dr. Nikolai A. Logatchev, Russia
Mochtar Lubis, Indonesia
Perry Maison, Ghana
Kapasa Makasa, Zambia
Dr. Ignacy Malecki, Poland
Prof. Ivan Malek, Czechoslovakia
Dr. Mrs. Alla G. Massevitch, Russia
Mhlagano S. Maatsebula, Switzerland

Dr. Mihajlo Mihajlov, Yogoslavia
Hon. Ram Niwas Mirdha, India
Dr. Robert Muller, Costa Rica
Justice M. A. Muttalib, Bangladesh
Dr. Siteke G. Mwale, Zambia
Dr. Rashmi Mayur, India
Dr. Jayant V. Narlikar, India
Paul Nkadi, Nigeria
Osman N. Orek, Turkish Rep. N. Cyprus
Prof. Lenard Pal, Poland
Prof. Jean-Claude Pecker, France
Prof. Gamini L. Peiris, Sri Lanka
Gerard Piel, U.S.A.
Rev. Daniel O. Peprah, Cote D'Ivoire
Prof. M. S. Rajan, India
Prof. C. N. R. Rao, India
Sri N. S. Rao, India
Michal Rusinek, Poland
Dr. Frederick Sanger, U.K.
Sir Ainsworth D. Scott, Jamaica
David Shahar, Israel
Toma Sik, Israel
Chandan Som, India
Hon. Robert D. G. Stanbury, Canada
Dr. Bogdan Suchodolski, Poland
Abdul Hathy Sulaiman, Sri Lanka
Dr. Sol Tax, U.S.A.
Millicent Obenewaa Terry, Ghana
Dr. Walter E. Thirring, Austria
Most Rev. Desmond M. Tutu, South Africa
Kenji Urata, Japan
Dr. Pieter Van Dijk, Netherlands
Carlos Warter, M.D., U.S.A.
Rod Welford, M.L.A., Australia

Chapter Seven

Clarification of the *Earth Constitution* by the Provisional World Parliament and Subsequent Editorial Review

"I doubt, too, whether any other Convention we can obtain may be able to make a better constitution. For when you assemble a number of men to have the advantage of their joint wisdom, you inevitably assemble with those men all their prejudices, their passions, their errors of opinion, their local interests and their selfish views. From such an assembly can a perfect production be expected? It therefore astonishes our enemies, who are waiting with confidence to hear that our councils are confounded, like those of the builders of Babel... Thus I consent to this constitution, because I expect no better, and because I am not sure that it is not the best. The opinions I have had of its errors I sacrifice to the public good... I hope therefore, that for our own sakes, as a part of the people, and for the sake of posterity, we shall act heartily and unanimously in recommending this Constitution wherever our influence may extend, and turn our future thoughts and endeavors to the means of having it well administered."

Quote from Benjamin Franklin at the close of the U.S. Constitutional Convention in 1787.

Eugenia Almand

Since the *Earth Constitution* reached its present form in the Fourth Constituent Assembly in Troia, Portugal, in 1991, it has been subject to on-going careful scrutiny by the Provisional World Parliament and the Committee for Legislative Review, which includes the present editors of this volume. This chapter examines a variety of provisions within the Constitution for the purposes of interpretative clarification. Of course, some ambiguity will be found in any constitution because of the nature of language. And some ambiguities can be clarified through subsequent legislation, or by later proofreaders and grammarians. It is also true that rapidly changing historical conditions necessitate a process of on-going interpretative clarification.

Linguists who work to correct, spelling, grammar and other possible form & style errors of the *Earth Constitution* do not change the original substance of the *Constitution*.

While this chapter does not suggest that the *Earth Constitution* is perfect, the chapter's author is a subsequent signatory to the *Earth Constitution* and holds to the provisions and supreme law of the *Earth Constitution*. Therefore, these suggestions of interpretation, most officialized by the Provisional World Parliament, should not be construed as disparagement of the *Earth Constitution*, nor as disparagement of world law, the World Constituent Assemblies or the world constitutive process.

Here are comments on correct interpretation of the *Earth Constitution*, on a sequential basis, with paragraphs numbered by *Earth Constitution* article, section and item:

2.6. To help form the World Regions and World Districts, the World Boundaries & Elections Administration consults with the people and holds not just "yes or no" plebiscites, but comprehensive plebiscites in which the people can fully qualify their positions to integrate direct democracy and grassroots into the process. (Requirement for comprehensive plebicites was first pointed out to Provisional World Parliament by its Members from the Revolutionary Committees Movement, Libya. Provisional World Parliament, 2000. Interpretive decision, Provisional World Parliament, 2004, Act #29.2., Act #29.3.)

2.9. There are basically 5 largely populated Continental Divisions, plus Antarctica. This interpretation forestalls conflict with the several other provisions of the *Earth Constitution* that require 5 Continental Divisions. (*Earth Constitution* Article 2. Section 5 and Article 2, Section 7. Provisional World Parliament, 2004, Act #29.3.)

4.5. The power of Earth Federation to conduct plebiscites is tempered by the requirement that these plebiscites be comprehensive and meaningful. (See paragraph number 2.6., above.)

5.4.1. Nations were not defined in the *Earth Constitution*. It was generally assumed that India, China and the United States were nations, but that the European Union was not a nation. Would the European Union be restricted to 3 national votes in the House of Nations simply because there was now a continental federation? Of course not. Then how could China, India and United States be restricted to 3 votes in the House of Nations, since they are no more and no less than continental federations? Logically, then, upon preliminary or final ratification, cantons, pradesh and states, or some combinations thereof would be counted as nations under the *Earth Constitution*, not the continental federations themselves. Although under the United Nations Charter, continental federations were presumed to be nations, there are no provisions in the Earth Constitution that bind anyone to sustain such presumptions. Indeed, there are explicit restrictions in the *Earth Constitution* regarding the World Executive Cabinet that implicitly prevent the interpretation of continental federations as nations under the *Earth Constitution*: (Article 6.4.1. & 6.4.3.)

5.5.3. Universal vote helps prevent runoff elections, which tend to poorly represent a group and often place a less competent person into the leadership. (Provisional World Parliament, 2004. Act #29, Section 14.4.2.)

5.6.17. How would the World Parliament decide salaries for its own representative member delegates? If World Parliament is to work, the salary has to have the people's support. Popular control is the only responsible intelligent way. To this end, the Provisional World Parliament deliberated and adopted world legislative provisions to restrict parliamentary salaries according to this principle. (Provisional World Parliament, 2004. Act #22, Article 12.)

6.3.1. For eligibility to be candidates for the Presidium, members have to come from a respective Continental Division. Members would have to be *residents* of the respective continent for Peoples Members, *national citizens* of a Earth Federation member nation on that continent for Nations Members, or *sourced* from an included Region of Member nomination of the respective continent for Counsellors. According to the *Earth Constitution*, teachers and students of universities, colleges, scientific academies and institutes within each world electoral and administrative region participate in the nomination of candidates to serve in the House of Counsellors. Then non-Counsellor Members from the respective region elect a candidate to serve as Counsellor. Nominees need neither be residents of the respective region nor citizens of a Federation member nation of the region. However, if a Counsellor is to be elected to the Presidium, the counsellor is eligible only from the region or regions from which the counsellor election was made, regardless of residency or nationality. This interpretation is a just basis for determination of eligibility for Presidium candidacy from the three houses (Editors' interpretation).

8.1.2. Many of the rules of agencies of the Integrative Complex are of necessity legislative, so agency rule-setting authority is qualified and limited by world legislation of the World Parliament. Each agency establishes rules of procedure in conformance with world legislation, as well as the *Earth Constitution*, which is supreme. (*Earth Constitution*, Article 8.1.3.).

8.7.1.6. Although the Earth Federation cannot charge interest against citizens, corporations, nations or other organizations, the Earth Federation has extensive revenue generating powers. However, the qualification that the Earth Federation can offer simple interest in its ratification and initial implementation efforts is necessary to reconfirm the provisions of *Earth Constitution*, Article 17.6. that guarantee up to double value return for costs and work, and World Legislative Act #7 provisions that provide for issuance of funding corporation bonds of the Earth Federation. This is a form of interest paid from the Earth Federation, for which the Earth Federation is solvent, with claims to the various commons of Earth. (*Earth Constitution*, Article 4.16., 4.17., 4.23., 4.28., 4.30., Article 16.1.1., Article 16.1.2., Article 17.6. WLA#7).

9.1. The Provisional World Parliament conserves to the Earth Federation the tremendous energy vested in the international court system, and appreciates the value of previous judicial development. (Provisional World Parliament, 1982, Act #5, conserving common law principles and principles of district courts; 2003, Act #15, further and comprehensively specifying *habeas corpus* guarantees; 2003, Act #20, Integrating the International Criminal Court; 2003, Act #24, integrating the *Rules of Evidence and Procedure* of the International Criminal Court; 2004, Act #28, creating integrative structure for the World Juvenile Bench that is in parallel and in harmony with the adult Criminal Bench, yet fully in conformance with well-developed principles of international juvenile law; and neither last nor least, 2006, Act #37, further specifying world federal privileges and immunities, strengthening the spirit of the *Immunities and Privileges of the World Court*, so that the world federal system operates harmoniously and seamlessly with the principles of federal subsidiarity among the nations and local communities of the world.)

9.1.1. An extremely important aspect of the world court system that has conventionally been disregarded is the urgent necessity for establishing Regional World Courts and District World Courts. It would be ridiculous to think that a single hall at the Hague will be adequate to adjudicate all of the disputes that might and do arise worldwide among billions of people. Though not yet convicted, there is strong probable cause to suspect many tens of thousands of perpetrators of world crime around the world: crimes of genocide, crimes against humanity, war crimes, environmental crimes and crimes of governmental corruption at international and world level. To adequately adjudicate this global crisis, it is reasonable to expect that we might need for most benches at least one chamber of District World Court within each of the 1000 world districts. Considering that each world district has approximately 6 million inhabitants, to project that even one-hundredth of one percent of inhabitants might violate world law would generate a projection of about 6000 cases--enough to keep a single chamber of the District World Court occupied with dockets for a long time. When one considers the number of people worldwide involved in bomb production, bomb company investment and related activities, that are illegal not only under international law (ICJ, 1996), but also under World Legislative Acts #1, 13 and #39, to name only a small sector of the crimes against humanity, one can surmise that these cases alone could easily entail up to one-hundredth of one percent of the world population. This need to respond wholly to the necessity of world law enforcement with decentralized regional and district world courts, rather than exclusively a single-chamber, relatively small, centralized world court, is recognized by the *Earth Constitution*, as well as by world legislation of the Provisional World Parliament. (Provisional World Parliament, 1982, Act #5; 2003, Act #13, Act #14; 2007, Act #39).

9.2.09. A significant part of the world's problems are associated with young people, and young people need protection as well as guidance. Young people have additional needs and rights, so the Juvenile Bench is to distinguish and respond for the need for a good world juvenile justice system. The Juvenile Bench does not only address criminal cases, but also civil, public, and other types of cases in which juveniles have to be associated with the world court system. (Provisional World Parliament, 2004, Act #28)

9.4.02. The Collegium of World Judges comprises the World Supreme Court. As described above in paragraph 9.1.1., there are overall many more world federal judges. Counsellors may select from world federal judges already serving in the lower courts of Earth Federation. After the House of Counsellors nominates two to three times the number of judges to be elected to the Collegium of World Judges, the joint session of World Parliament elects the judges via a universal vote in which each Member of Parliament delivers a rating from among all the nominees. This process, also called Borda count, as well as by other names, best assures competent election when selections are made. (Provisional World Parliament, 2004. Act #29, Section 14.4.2.)

9.4.03. and **9.4.04.** Unless removed from office for cause, world justices continue any particular cases for which they are serving without any interruption based on expiry of terms. (Provisional World Parliament, 2003. Act #15, Article 6.2; 2003. Act #20, Part 4., Articles 35, 36, 37 & 41.)

9.4.12. *The Rome Statute of the International Criminal Court*, the *Rules of Procedure and Evidence*, Act #20 for the Criminal Bench, and the *Earth Constitution* all give professional procedural parameters to the World Courts. However, each of these four documents also recognizes that participation of the World Judges themselves in the development and refinement of rules of procedure is necessary to further professionalize the extremely comprehensive rules of procedure of the world judiciary.

10.1.5. and **10.4.1.** In keeping with the principle of limiting law enforcement agents to enforcement tools appropriate to the task, and assigning that determination to the World Parliament, the sixth session of provisional World Parliament limited world law enforcement officers to only such enforcement instruments as are not prohibited to the general public and that do not require public registration, permit or display. This helps prevent the emergence of an armed caste or state class. It also increases the ability of the people to assure self-government and to uphold the *Earth Constitution*. This also deters official corruption and governmental intrusion. Furthermore, upon full operative stage of the Earth Federation, officers themselves and the corporate (private) security sector may only use less lethal munitions, which should increase the protection of the right to fair trial and right to testify, helping to create a more peaceful and free world society (Provisional World Parliament, 2003. Act #14).

10.2.08. This organization of the Enforcement System into five major departments enables *Earth Constitution* Articles 19.2.06.; 19.5.3.; 19.5.4; 17.3.07.; and 17.3.08.

The World Disarmament Agency, designed to prohibit and dismantle weapons of mass destruction, integrates with and is dependent upon the Enforcement System (Provisional World Parliament, 2003, Act #1, Act #14, Act #34 and other acts).

10.4.2.6. Power to require performance of work to rectify damage is conditional and limited by constitutional principle to prohibit penal slavery (*Earth Constitution*, Article 12, Item 10).

10.4.4. The World Judiciary and World Ombudsmus also have key roles in the assurance of fair hearing. (*Earth Constitution*, Article 9, Section A, and Article 11, Section A).

11.1.09. The World Ombudsmus has power to initiate legal action and court proceedings in the Human Rights Bench (Provisional World Parliament, 2006. Act #31).

11.2. In conformance with the spirit of these provisions, staffed elective offices of District Ombudsen and Deputy District Ombudsen were created to help assure that there will be a participative voice from the people in human rights protection. This also helps assure that the World Ombudsmus has adequate staffing to fulfill its mission of human rights protection (Provisional World Parliament, 2006. Act #31).

Article 12 - In the general introduction to this article the terms "inhabitants" and "citizens" are intended as appositives so that there is clarity that the citizens (people, residents, etc.) are not simply a caste or privileged class among the inhabitants of Earth. The phrase "Within the Earth Federation" here does not refer to whether any particular nation has ratified, but rather is inclusive for human rights of all human beings everywhere. Human rights are inalienable and and are not a revocable grant or privilege of the Earth Federation or of some national or other government. In the case of civil rights, the rights are inclusive of anyone who affirms the *Earth Constitution*, irrespective of nationality. (Editors' interpretation)

12.15. The corporate (private) security sector has similar world legislative restrictions regarding tools of enforcement as that of the Earth Federation enforcement officers, as previously mentioned in paragraph 10.1.05 and 10.4.1. of this chapter. Since the implication of the respective world legislation is that civilians will be reasonably armed for the purposes of upholding government and their rights, there is less pressure for the formation of private armies and para-militaries. (Provisional World Parliament, 2003. Act #14).

12.13. Excessive force is not civil. Death penalty is not civil. (Provisional World Parliament, 2003. Act #14).

12.14. *Habeas corpus* includes a broad number of rights not all specified here in the *Earth Constitution.* For instance, *bill of attainder* means a warrant issued by the legislature. Allowance of bills of attainder lend toward political persecutions. Warrants are properly issued by the World Attorney General, not the Parliament. Protection from bill of attainder, the right to redress of grievances, right to trial by jury in criminal cases, right to refuse jury and other related rights are further and explicitly recognized in acts of world legislation. (Provisional World Parliament, 2003, Act #14, #15, #24).

12.17. This provision for family planning prohibits the Earth Federation from interfering against family planning. Although family planning is technically an economic right and civil right, the *Earth Constitution* guarantees free public assistance in this because of the extreme urgency worldwide for adequate family planning services. The implication here is that the Earth Federation subsidizes the cost of public assistance at the world federal level, rather than require national or local governments to shoulder the cost (Editors' interpretation).

13.19. Prohibition against the death penalty is clearly a political right and so in spirit, this provision comes from *Earth Constitution,* Article 12. To affirm the value of life, the Provisional World Parliament has excluded the death penalty from its penal code (Provisional World Parliament, 2003, Act #19).

16.2. Although not specifically mentioned in the list of world territories, under principles of *Earth Constitution* Article 2, Section 1, and Article 16, Section 1., Antarctica would reasonably be included within the jurisdiction of the Earth Federation as part of the heritage of humanity. (Provisional World Parliament, 1996, 2000. Act #12).

17. Ratification of the *Earth Constitution* - 17.1.01; 17.1.04.; and **17.1.07.** Although the term used in the *Earth Constitution* is "*request* preliminary ratification", reasonable interpretation of a world constitutive document allows people to politely *direct* the United Nations Organization, national heads, and other governing units to ratify. Polite directives are probably more effective than petitions. Along these lines, when the children of City Montessori School, Lucknow, presented an initiative to the Provisional World Parliament that the Parliament seek the United Nations Review Conference of United Nations Charter Article 109 to examine the *Earth Constitution,* the Parliament took up the proposal, and sent it to General Assembly President Jean Ping as a polite directive. (Provisional World Parliament, 2004. Unnumbered session memorial.)

17.1.04. In the case where there is a national legislature, but the legislature does not respond to any request or polite directive to preliminarily ratify the *Earth Constitution,* the effect is as if the national legislature were the straw legislature of a failed state. In these cases, howsoever many, the head of the national government can respond directly by joining a simultaneous multi-national assent to the *Earth Constitution*. If it is not feasible to personally attend a meeting where this assent is formally granted, the special non-treaty nature of the *Earth Constitution* can be invoked. The *Earth Constitution* is a founded document and full non-military social contract–not a treaty. Not being a treaty or ordinary convention, the head of state can assign plenipotentiary authority for any formal meeting for expressing assent by definitive signature, without requiring any explicit provision for definitive signature in the constitutive document. The power of definitive signature to the *Earth Constitution* can be expressed as a special kind of reservation of power that is positive, rather than a negative reservation of power as is found in treaties. (*Earth Constitution*, Article 14.2.) No amendment is needed to any national constitution before state recognition of this power. (*Earth Constitution*, Article 17.1.11.)

17.1.05. Any *Earth Constitution* ratification campaign has to emerge from the people themselves, who then employ agencies to help do the work. Among agencies that have worked to sponsor or otherwise take responsibility for the ratification campaign are the World Constitution & Parliament Association (originally assigned at the World Constituent Assemblies), the Global Ratification & Elections Network, Earth Rescue Corps, the Institute On World Problems and the World Boundaries and Elections Administration (WBEA). Other agencies may emerge as time goes on. However, the WBEA has final responsibility regarding ratification affairs, and is responsible to the World Parliament (*Earth Constitution*, Article 8.3., Provisional World Parliament, 2004. Act #29).

17.1.08.; **17.1.11.**; "Political" units here means *governing* units, not political parties, which have no governing authority (Editors' interpretation).

17.1.09. Regarding illegal weapons, jurisdiction by the Earth Federation emerges. The term "turn over weapons of mass destruction" does not mean that Earth Federation has ownership or maintains these weapons. Rather, whatever persons that have allegiance to the Earth Federation and ability to begin the dismantlement process begin that process. This clarifies the action and non-military nature of Earth Federation. (Provisional World Parliament, 1982, Act #1; 2003, Act #13; 2006, Act #34, Act #36; 2007, Act #39, Act #40.)

17.3. The *Earth Constitution* is generally 30 to 60 pages long, depending on type size. In an ideal world everyone would be literate in Esperanto and eager to read the 60 pages to quickly give their assent. In fact, however, life and politics don't work that way. Further, because of logistical impossibility of printing and distributing 4 billion sets of the *Earth Constitution* full text in the some 700 major languages of the world, the ratification campaign is primarily depending on an *Executive Summary and Diagram* of the *Earth Federation* to be circulated in perhaps only about two dozen languages. It is this official summary and diagram that people generally are voting on, not the full text. Concerned and interested world citizens would be able to reference the full text of the *Earth Constitution* at libraries, community centers or on-line, and communicate their concerns about any technical details of the *Earth Constitution* to the world constituency. The framers of the *Earth Constitution* had faith that the comprehensive *Earth Constitution* would be highly preferable to the out-dated international military system. The use of Executive Summary and Diagram in the ratification process, together with the participation of concerned and interested world citizens, greatly increases the feasibility of the overall ratification campaign. (Editors' interpretation)

17.3.02. The World Boundaries and Elections Administration (WBEA) conducts these elections with the help of additional agencies. Among agencies who are authorized to conduct these elections, are the people themselves as they coordinate and organize. However, additionally specific agencies are involved in electoral campaigns. The Control Commission of Elections to the Peoples Congress associated with the Registry of World Citizens can manage these elections at least during the formative period. It is hoped that the World Service Authority will participate in the electoral management. The World Federalist Movement, its constituent organizations, and other organizations of the Coalition for Democratic World Government are also vital agencies. The Global Peoples Assembly and the Revolutionary Committees Movement, and the Office of the World Peace Envoy are additional agencies whose task is to manage certain appointive posts, commissions and committees that are working to build the Earth Federation. This is not an exhaustive listing. Responsibility and credit go to many other agencies as well. (Provisional World Parliament, 2004, Act #29).

17.3.08. & 17.4.06. & 17.5.2.07. This clarifies that the jurisdiction is transferred to the World Disarmament Agency of the Earth Federation. The World Disarmament Agency is a sub-Department of the Enforcement System. Because of its importance, it additionally has its own ministerial status. In the vast majority of cases, weapons of mass destruction are to be de-activated on-site where they are stored or deployed, not transported as live weapons.

The World Disarmament Agency under the regulations enacted by the World Parliament dismantles weapons of mass destruction and regulates kinds of instruments of defense available to nations or persons. The World Disarmament Agency does not use weapons but uses instruments of defense suitable for law enforcement purposes, listed in world legislation. World legislation guarantees the right to self-protection. The World Disarmament Agency and Enforcement System does not aim to disarm civilians from vital tools suitable for upholding the Earth Federation.

The Earth Federation and the World Disarmament Agency devise guidelines to dismantle and make harmless illegal and inappropriate weapons. Some technical difficulties might be encountered in the process of disarming the world war system. In some cases, chemical explosives will be unstable, and cannot be readily stabilized by chemical or mechanical means. In other cases, chemical explosives may be useful for quarrying purposes, or for other useful demolitions work, such as preparations for quarries, sea dikes or other large scale projects of the Earth Federation. For such projects, the chemical explosive materials left over from weapons dismantlement is under the civil jurisdiction of the Emergency Earth Rescue Administration, also working in association with the Enforcement System. (Provisional World Parliament, 1982, Act #1; 2003, Act #13; 2006, Act #34.)

17.3.09. In principle and practice, there is no tribute to the Earth Federation in the sense that there was to the United Nations Organization. Contributions to the U.N.O. were never expected to be repaid. However, under the *Earth Constitution*, member nations that are paying in are actually loaning national currency to the Earth Federation to be paid back to the respective national government at simple interest. This arrangement faces economic realities of nations' needs, and clarify means of meeting economic needs in a manner that integrates with the rest of the *Earth Constitution* and with world legislation. (*Earth Constitution*, Article 1.3.; Article 1.4.; Article Sections 4.14., 4.16., 4.17., 4.19., 4.33., and 4.40.; Article 17.6.; Provisional World Parliament, 1982, Act #2; 1985, Act #7).

17.3.10.08. Climate change is a system and must be addressed as a system (Ecimovic, T. et. al. 2005).

17.3.12.01. Climate change is a system and must be addressed as a system (Ecimovic, T. et. al. 2005).

17.3.12.04. "*Maximum sustained*" here actually means "*Optimum regenerative*". The intent of the World Constituent Assembly was not to reinforce monocultures that damage ecosystems, nor to overcultivate. *Optimum regenerative* agriculture encourages moderation. (Provisional World Parliament, 1985. Act #6).

17.3.12.10. Earth Federation does not control population, nor does an increase in living standard control population, though growth rates of course decline with higher living standards. For protection of the Earth, however, the Earth Federation does encourage regenerative stasis, and plans to do this by equitably raising standards of living worldwide and by other non-coercive measures.

17.4.06. (Please refer to 17.3.08 commentary, above.)

17.4.07. (Please refer to 17.3.09. commentary, above.)

17.4.08. As in paragraph 17.1.01; 17.1.04.; and 17.1.07, above, although the term used in the *Earth Constitution* is "issue an *invitation*" to the General Assembly of the United Nations and specialized agencies, reasonable interpretation of the world constitutive document allows the Presidium to politely *direct* the United Nations General Assembly and agencies to transfer allegiance to the Earth Federation. Polite directives are probably more effective than petitions or invitations. People are ordinarily responsive to clear direction. Therefore, it is correct that the Presidium issues the UN a *directive* rather than a literal invitation.

Jurisdiction transfers. This avoids the image of persons physically having to quit offices or otherwise ship out. Furthermore, this direction is a larger process for people generally, not just the Presidium. For illustrations, the Fissile Production Prohibition of the provisional World Parliament directs compliance to the International Atomic Energy Agency, and the Contamination Act directs compliance to the World Health Organization and the International Atomic Energy Agency. (Provisional World Parliament, 2006, Act #33, Article 4; Act #5).

17.5.2.07. (Please refer to 17.3.08. & 17.3.09. commentaries, above.)

17.5.2.08. Some former military persons might be of suitable skills and disposition to serve well in a law enforcement capacity, in which case the Enforcement System may commission them to keep and bear such arms as are appropriate for law enforcement purposes. Otherwise, world citizens may continue to keep and bear arms that are appropriate for upholding the Earth Federation and for self-protection, not to include any weapons classified as weapons of mass destruction, or weapons of war that transcend the capacity for individual self-defense, which even Earth Federation officials must not maintain or possess. (Provisional World Parliament, 2003, Act #13; Act #14).

17.6. The costs, accounting, finance and entitlements of the world federative process are perhaps the least elaborated of all the aspects of effective formation of Earth Federation. The costs of ratification are addressed briefly in *Earth Constitution* Article 17, Section 6.

The *Earth Constitution* recognizes the work and costs of private Citizens of Earth (inhabitants, civilians, natural persons, people) for the achievement of a ratified *Constitution for the Federation of Earth*, as legitimate costs for the establishment of constitutional parliamentary Earth Federation by which present and future generations will benefit. The World Financial Administration shall repay double the original amount of value by installments beginning when Earth Federation becomes operational after 25 countries have ratified this *Constitution for the Federation of Earth*. Repayment specifically includes contributions to the World Government Funding Corporation (Earth Federation Funding Corporation) and other costs and expenses recognized by standards and procedures the World Financial Administration establishes. Accountable costs also specifically include labor and services, and other in-kind contributions, not only direct cash investments. Note that the *Earth Constitution* explicitly states, "The work *and* costs..." (Editor's italics)

The *Earth Constitution* recognizes the work and costs of groups for establishing the Earth Federation and achievement of a ratified *Constitution for the Federation of Earth*. This would include the following: national governments, municipal governments, other governing units, not-for-profit organizations, international agencies, corporations and other organizations. The World Financial Administration would repay up to double the original amount of value by installments beginning when Earth Federation becomes operational after 25 countries have ratified the *Constitution for the Federation of Earth*. Repayment specifically includes contributions to the Earth Federation Funding Corporation and other costs and expenses recognized by standards and procedures the World Financial Administration establishes. Earth Federation Funding Corporation will draw up contracts for the exact values to be repaid. Reimbursements to individuals are constitutionally guaranteed.

Though not specified in the *Earth Constitution* or in World Legislative Act #7, Earth Federation Funding Corporation accounts survive and are transferable. Survivability and transferability of accounts are specified in the World Legislative Act #40, for Indemnity Bonds. Survivability and transferability of accounts are also specified for retirement accounts in the World Legislative Act #36, the Guantanamo Directive. It is expected that this principle will be included in further world legislation as the provisional World Parliament addresses enabling legislation for the World Civil Service Administration.

The Earth Federation Funding Corporation together with the World Financial Administration is developing repayment schedules to be applied in the cases of various types and sources of funding:

1. World Financial Administration will likely schedule natural persons' provisional or first operative stage accounts for completion of repayment installments within ten years of the beginning of second operative stage of Earth Federation;
2. World Financial Administration will likely schedule natural person's second operative stage accounts for completion of repayment installments within five years of the beginning of the full operative stage of Earth Federation;
3. World Financial Administration will likely schedule provisional or first operative stage group accounts for completion of repayment within fifteen years of the beginning of second operative stage of Earth Federation; and
4. World Financial Administration will likely schedule second operative stage group accounts for completion of repayment within ten years of the beginning of full operative stage of Earth Federation.

The Earth Federation Funding Corporation distinguishes between individual and group accounts to prevent overpayment liability. For instance, if a group takes the responsibility for particular costs, the World Financial Administration does not double the credit to the group account and also double the credit to the accounts of individuals that make up the group. However, and this is extremely important, if a group (nation, municipality, corporation or other group) elects to create individual accounts for the individuals that comprise its constituency, the Earth Federation is then constitutionally bound to make repayment in double directly to the individual constituents of the group. This obligation of *Earth Constitution* Article 17.6 is the exception clause clarifying the interpretation of *Earth Constitution* Article 8.7.1.6., that addresses debt financing of the Earth Federation.

The World Financial Administration makes repayment in the world federation's Earth Hour unit of credit or currency, not in any national or continental unit of credit or currency. The Provisional World Parliament has authorized other financing arrangements that guarantee a repayment amount less than double, such as indemnity bonds for divestment from weapons of mass destruction. Earth Federation Funding Corporation may contract variable repayment ratios, but not to exceed double the original investment in the Earth Federation, and may contract fractional repayment at the time of issuance of the indemnity bonds.

Please refer to World Legislative Acts 7, 11, 18, 22, 23, 38 and other world legislative acts to reach a better comprehension of the processes and dynamics of the financial process. World Legislative Act 7 is most critically important for understanding how this process works. Available: www.wcpa.biz, www.worldproblems.net.)

19.1.3.1. The question of quorum and numbers of delegates committed to attend was raised at the first session of the Provisional World Parliament. There had been a commitment by the prescribed number of delegates (500 commitments required), but all of these were not able to attend, based on visa restrictions, apparent political interventions and for other reasons. The Provisional World Parliament decided that the commitment was based on the original word and intention of the certified delegates, and that as this number was not specified as quorum, that it would be inappropriate to interpret this number as a designated quorum requirement, but that this number would be rather the initial planning requirement. The view of the Parliament was that it would be grossly unjust and self-defeating if the old system were to be allowed to smother the new. Hence, at that time and since, the operating number in the sessions of the Provisional World Parliament has always been less that the number originally committing to attend. (Provisional World Parliament, 1982.)

19.2.06. (Please refer to 17.3.08. commentaries, above.)

19.5.3. "Implementation of and compliance with the legislation enacted by the Provisional World Parliament shall be sought on a voluntary basis in return for the benefits to be realized, while strength of the Provisional World Government is being increased by the progressive ratification of the World Constitution." For lack of initial subject, there were at least two interpretations of this provision:
1) "While the progressive ratification of the World Constitution increases strength of

the Provisional Earth Federation, the people may volunteer to seek implementation of and compliance with the world legislation enacted by the Provisional World Parliament in return for the benefits to be realized," or
2) "The people cannot be serious to propose to govern themselves, so whoever wishes may violate the world legislation until the ratification campaign is overpowering."

During the ninth session of the Provisional World Parliament the subject of this provision came up for discussion. It was argued that the latter interpretation would be illogical, because to interpret in that manner would defeat the purpose of holding a world constituent assembly for a basic self-governing document for the world, and would defeat the purpose of a Provisional World Parliament. Therefore, appeal to this second interpretation could not have been the intent of the framers of the *Earth Constitution.* Based upon reason and also upon the prior implicit interpretation of this provision by at least the last 4 sessions of the Provisional World Parliament, there was general consensus that the first interpretation was the only suitable, just and civil interpretation.

19.5.5. (Please refer to 17.3.08. commentaries, above.)

Conclusion

Part of the process of implementation and administration of a constitution is the interpretation of the document. The *Earth Constitution* has been interpreted repeatedly during many sessions of the provisional World Parliament. The *Earth Constitution* also has been interpreted during its promotion. Interpretations might arise at different levels of implementation and administration, as well as in promotion or analytical reviews of the *Earth Constitution*, such as the review by this chapter. The *Earth Constitution* wisely recognized the inevitability of interpretation, and provided for addressing and adjudicating any conflicts based on interpretation by its Article 9.2.04., the *Bench for Constitutional Cases of the World Supreme Court.* Further interpretation is likely to arise in the future. Interpretational disputes are the jurisdiction of this World Supreme Court bench.

Eventually, sessions of World Constitutional Convention will likely review any passages of the *Earth Constitution* that have been particularly contentious based on interpretations. However, most persons studying the *Earth Constitution* have not proposed any changes, and there is virtually no world movement for any world constitutional convention to review the *Earth Constitution* or to independently hold any world constitutional convention whatsoever, though there are clear rules of procedure for convoking world constituent assembly. Therefore, the current opinion of the editors of this book is that the process of interpretation of the *Earth Constitution* up to the present date has been adequate to converge world federation strategies and otherwise accommodate all movements for world federation.

Chapter Eight:

Resolutions, Memorials and Other Non-statutory World Legislation of the Provisional World Parliament

Expression Strengthened by Statutory Framework

"Some hours seem not to be occasion for any deed, but for resolves to draw breath in. We do not directly go about the execution of the purpose that thrills us, but shut our doors behind us and ramble with prepared mind, as if the half were already done. Our resolution is taking root or hold on the earth then, as seeds first send a shoot downward which is fed by their own albumen, ere they send one upward to the light."

Henry David Thoreau (1817–1862)

Eugenia Almand, Editor

Introduction

There are various types of parliamentary decisions: statute, resolution, memorial, and other legislation. Statutes form the primary body of law that directly affects the the world citizens as the general public. For this reason, a large part of this three volume set is devoted to the statutes. Factors that differentiate the statutes from other types of parliamentary actions include that statutes define directives to either agencies of the government or to the general public. These directives will often carry provisions of force, such as penal classification for non-compliance, or provisions for reprimand, censure or destitution in the case of government positions. Statutes stand as law for an indefinite period of time.

On the other hand, there are forms of decision that do not necessarily carry penal clauses. When a parliament expresses its stance on a matter, or its intention to do something, this is a resolution. It is expected that government officials and the public will consider the expression in their respective actions, though the parliament declines to attach penal provisions to the expression. A resolution can be commemorative or an expression of condolence, for example.

Memorial is a type of parliamentary decision that is not expression of condolences or commemorations. (Those are better termed as resolutions of condolence or commemoration.) Instead, memorials are directives made to specific recipients, urging them to take or not to take specific actions. Memorial may be particularly necessary in cases where there is clearly no enforcement authority to take or not take action in response to non-compliance. When the Provisional World Parliament has appealed (on several occasions) to the Non-Aligned Movement to consider and adopt the ***Earth Constitution***, these were clear cases of memorials. Similarly, Provisional World Parliament directives to the Assembly of States Parties of the International Criminal Court are likewise memorials.

Other legislation has various forms. This includes largely budgetary decisions, nominations and elections of government officers within and beyond parliament, decisions of venues, and decisions upon rules of procedure to be used within Parliament and within World Constituent Assembly.

Legislation of the Provisional World Parliament is considerable, and is not as thoroughly documented in these volumes as the statutory decisions of the Parliament. We believe that resolutions memorials and other legislation tends to be perceived as of less import and less interest to the general public than statutory code which carries a penal provision or which otherwise more directly affects us all in day to day living. However, to have a complete understanding of the Provisional World Parliament, one should also have some good idea of the workings of parliament other than only the statutes. With this in mind, we are presenting in this chapter the full-texts of adopted non-statutory world legislation, including memorials and resolutions. The chapter includes most principle non-statutory decisions, yet is not exhaustive. Additionally, projects, protocols and public utilities will be addressed in the following two volumes of *Emerging World Law*, as these are classified as enumerated acts, and fit better in their order with world statutes.

Most are probably familiar with the international convention forms of assembly decision, making proclamations that apparently were never intended to have any binding effect. In actual proper parliamentary practice, however, resolutions do have a role as binding legislation. Unlike the relation of the people to the United Nations General Assembly, if the Provisional World Parliament commits to a stance with a resolution, the people are empowered to seek the Parliament's performance through the World Ombudsmus and the World Courts, by filing suit to seek restitution or other redress of grievance from the parliament.

A non-exhaustive list and then full texts of non-statutory legislation of the Provisional World Parliament are given below. This current amended version of this legislation, as presented here, varies only slightly from the original texts. Differences are primarily the adoption of full numeric codification at the eighth session of the Provisional World Parliament in 2008. For original texts, refer to the bibliographical references in volume three of *Emerging World Law*. The legislative decisions in this chapter are the following:

Resolution of the Recognition of the Rights of Animals, enacted first session, Brighton 1982;
Peace of the Brave: Resolution for Palestinian Statehood; fifth session, Qawra, 2000;
Independence of the Ratification of the ***Constitution for the Federation of Earth*** and Provisional World Parliament Legislation, sixth session, Bangkok, 2003;
Rules of Procedure for the World Constituent Assembly as per *Earth Constitution*, Article 18.5., sixth session, Bangkok, 2003.
Resolution on the Spirit of Global Government, sixth session, Bangkok, 2003;
Memorial to the Assembly of States Parties, seventh session, Chennai, 2003;
Pledge of Allegiance to the Federation of Earth, seventh session, Chennai, 2003;
Recommended tax policy statement, eighth session, Lucknow, 2004;
Memorial to General Assembly President Jean Ping, to convene the United Nations General Review Conference for the United Nations to consider and adopt the ***Earth Constitution***, eighth session, Lucknow, 2004;
Promotion of Experanto and auxiliary languages as official working languages of the Provisional World Parliament and the Earth Federation, eighth session, Lucknow, 2004.
Resolution on Good Government and its Essential Tasks under the Earth Federation, eighth session, Lucknow, 2004;
Declaration of the Rights of the People of Earth to create and ratify a World Constitution and hold sessions of the Provisional World Parliament, eighth session, Lucknow, 2004; and
Resolution on the Trial of War Criminals and Perpetrators of Genocide and Crimes Against Humanity, tenth session, Tripoli, 2007.

As mentioned above, this is a non-exhaustive report of most resolutions, memorials and non-statutory world legislation of the Provisional World Parliament. The Parliament has adopted numerous resolutions and memorials in its sessions to date. All of these have not been disseminated, and it is imposssible here to include them all.

However, this is not to imply that these non-statutory decisions of the Parliament are insignificant. In fact, some of these hold revolutionary significance and impart to the Parliament a highly degree of legitimacy by their universal character. For instance, the *Declaration of the Independence of the Ratification of the* ***Constitution for the Federation of Earth*** *and Provisional World Parliament Legislation* marked a historic milestone in the parliamentary development of human society on Earth. Until that declaration, the principles of distinction of world constitution and world legislation had not yet become completely drawn. The Provisional World Parliament had operated until that declaration as a dependency on customary international convention law, which required petitioning the national governments' legislatures for ratification of each of the more urgent world statutes.

However, there was never any world constitutional provision that required that subordinate stance, and the decisions of the world legislation are clearly outside and above the jurisdictions of the national governments. Not having world jurisdiction, the national governments would have no grounds or ability to consider the world legislation. So it had been improper and immature to originally seek national accessions to the legislation. The Provisional World Parliament in sixth session then recognized the respective provisions for national legislative ratifications of world legislation as self-defeating. The significance of this resolution was the sweeping amendment to half of the legislative statutes that had been enacted to date, striking out all clauses pertaining to national level ratification of world legislation. The resolution cleared the path for the correction of viable international conventions through world parliamentary deliberation. This also made it possible to direct the Assembly of States Parties to consider the ***Earth Constitution*** and to ponder their role in the emergence of the eventual tricameral character of the World Parliament. (The Assembly of States Parties is the internationally created and recognized body that initially developed and deliberated the Rome Statute family of world legislation. The 108-member-nation Assembly has a deliberative freedom, power and responsibility beyond that of the United Nations General Assembly, and so far is proving more capable than the General Assembly in helping coordinate the initiation of a functioning House of Nations, with full legislative competence and authority shared in conformance with the ***Earth Constitution***.)

The world resolutions, memorials and other world legislation follow.

Recognition of the Rights of Animals and Nature in the Federation of Earth

Recognizing that, in the words of Sir Muhammad Zafrulla Khan, the human being must be a source of bliss for every being; recognizing also that the human being is not the only source of bliss;

Recognizing that, in the words of Sri Krishna, all are one–and that, in the words of Albert Schweitzer, the way back to civilization lies through the reverence for life;

Aware, as stated in the Preamble to the *Constitution for the Federation of Earth*, of the interdependence of people, nations and all life–and aware that man's abuse of science and technology has brought humanity also to the brink of ecological catastrophe;

Recognizing that, as described in the Global 2000 Report to the President of the United States, the destruction of the natural world has progressed to an advanced stage, to a stage where, many authorities agree, within 30 to 50 years perhaps 50% or more of the world's animal species will have become extinct–unless the prevalent attitude of humanity toward the status of animals changes radically;

Recognizing that, at least since the time of Darwin, it has been scientifically established that humankind shares in significant degree a common origin with the rest of the natural world and especially with its animal species;

Recognizing that, with few exceptions, under present law the inhumane treatment of animals is common practice in scientific laboratories, factory farms, and at the hands of hunters and trappers–and that present national basic laws do little to implement an ethic of the protection of nature;

Recognizing that we need to be concerned not only with the future of humanity, but also, under the *Constitution for the Federation of Earth*, with the fate of the planet;

Recognizing, finally, that under the Call to the Provisional World Parliament, the business of the Parliament includes a concern with global environmental protection;

And as an expression of love;

THEREFORE, be it enacted by this Provisional World Parliament in first session, 1982:

1. From the date of adoption of this resolution by the Provisional World Parliament, in all considerations and decisions bearing upon the present conditions and future of humanity, the Earth Federation shall consider the interests of other species.

2. From the date of adoption of this resolution by the Provisional World Parliamen, the following activities are

strongly discouraged or prohibited:
2.1. All practices of factory farming involving animals;
2.2. Research using animals as experimental subjects, of the trapping and hunting of animals except by peoples for their own subsistence use, and not including for cash sales or trade;
2.3. Employment of animals in cruel sport;
2.4. Removal of species from native habitat, in disregard of protective standards for removals;
2.5. Production of so-called animal "products" for profit.

3. The Provisional World Parliament and Provisional World Government shall establish a World Environmental Protection Agency, which shall include in the scope of its responsibilities the implementation of this resolution and the supervision of the establishment of the recognition of animal rights throughout the world. (see WLA#9, 3rd session, 1987, eds.)

4. Until a more fully operative democratic world federation is established, the World Environmental Protection Agency is responsible to the Provisional World Parliament, and to any Provisional World Cabinet that is created by the Provisional World Parliament. The World Environmental Protection Agency shall have a Board of Trustees of twenty-five members, to be appointed by the Provisional World Cabinet, to be drawn from all parts of the Earth, and to include no fewer than five well-known advocates of animal rights. The Board of Trustees shall determine the organization and functioning of the World Environmental Protection Agency in accordance with the terms of this resolution and in conformance with the ***Constitution for the Federation of Earth***, while at all times responsible to the Cabinet and Parliament. No nation may have veto powers in the decisions of the World Environmental Protection Agency.

5. At subsequent sessions of the Provisional World Parliament, the implementation of this resolution shall be reviewed, and further appropriate action shall be taken.

⊕⊕⊕⊕⊕⊕⊕⊕⊕⊕

The first session of the Provisional World Parliament adopted the above resolution 6th September 1982, at Brighton, England, .

Peace of the Brave Statement: Declaration of Statehood

This fifth session of the Provisional World Parliament reaffirms its position of recognizing and supporting the right of the Palestinian people to establish the State of Palestine in its national soil, with Al Quds Al Sherif (East Jerusalem) as its capital, on the border of 1967. (UN 242-November 1967, UN 338 –September 1969).
It is the resolution of this fifth session of the Provisional World Parliament to recognize Palestine as a nation within the World Federation upon ratification

of the ***Constitution for the Federation of Earth*** and agreement to abide by the World Law established under the ***Earth Constitution.*** Upon preliminary ratification of the ***Earth Constitution*** by the official authority of Palestine, Palestine will be recognized as an equal member among the Nations of the Earth Federation. Confirmation by an additional decision by future Sessions of the Provisional World Parliament are not necessary.

It should be noted that with Preliminary Ratification, the people of Palestine reserve the right for final ratification, as specified by Article XVII Section A of the ***Constitution for the Federation of Earth.*** This is the assurance of popular sovereignty within the context of independent World Government.

We direct Israel, and all nations, to abide by the ***Constitution for the Federation of Earth*** and World Legislative Bill #1, to outlaw all nuclear weapons and other weapons of mass destruction.

The Provisional World Parliament urges Israel to adhere to the principle of land for peace. Israel must end the occupation of Palestine land. Israel must comply with the prior agreements and United Nations resolutions regarding the right of return of refugees, Israeli withdrawal to pre-1967 borders with Al Quds Al Sharif (East Jerusalem).

We specifically express the following:

We condemn the atrocities against the Palestinian population committed by Israeli administrations, especially the 'shoot to kill' of civilians, including children, by military forces and settler militias; helicopter gunfire and air to ground rockets.

We deplore the current siege of Palestinian towns, villages and roads, which severely curtails the movement of people to their homes, places of work, access to essential services, and the closure of sea and airports. Such actions are an affront upon Palestinian dignity and the dignity of human beings everywhere.

We fully support the right of return for Palestinian refugees to return to their homes if they wish, to receive compensation. (UN 194 – December 1948)

We reaffirm and defend the territorial integrity of the Palestinian land; Al Quds Al Sharif (East Jerusalem) is indivisible from the Palestinian lands of 1967.

And finally, but not least, the World Parliament extends its regards to His Excellency Yasser Arafat for his endless efforts to achieve a just and durable peace in the region and for his initiatives to defend the supreme norms and values for Humanity. A statesperson with these qualities will surely win freedom.

⊕⊕⊕⊕⊕⊕⊕⊕⊕⊕

The fifth session of the Provisional World Parliament Network adopted the above resolution, November 2000, at Qawra, Malta.

Resolution: Independence of the Ratification of the *Constitution for the Federation of Earth* and Provisional World Parliament Legislation

WHEREAS, the *Constitution for the Federation of Earth* (FEC) was created through four separate Constituent Assemblies independently of the existence of any Provisional World Parliaments;

WHEREAS, there is nothing in the FEC requiring the World Parliament under the FEC to accept legislation adopted by Provisional World Parliaments;

WHEREAS, the most important objective of all Provisional Parliament delegates and the organizations supporting the *Earth Constitution* is world-wide ratification of the Constitution;

WHEREAS, we have no wish to encumber the ratification process of the FEC with a collection of legislation inseparable from the FEC, that may reduce its appeal or popularity with people or nations or Earth;

WHEREAS, the six Provisional World Parliaments to date have certified their delegates in a variety of ad hoc ways that do not resemble the criteria for legitimate membership in the operative World Parliament of the FEC;

WHEREAS, the main thrust of the Provisional World Parliaments has been to begin elaboration of world law as a model and incentive for people and nations to ratify the *Constitution for the Federation of Earth* and undertake the legitimate elaboration of effective world law under the authority of the Constitution;

WE, THE DELEGATES of the sixth Provisional World Parliament, resolve that the *Constitution for the Federation of Earth* be ratified independently of any legislation adopted by Provisional World Parliaments.

ONCE THE *Constitution for the Federation of Earth* is ratified, we strongly recommend that the newly organized World Parliament consider the legislation adopted in Provisional World Parliaments as a model and sample of legislation vital to the future of the planet and humanity.

LEGISLATION adopted by Provisional World Parliaments is not intended to be considered by legislatures of individual nation-states. We strongly recommend that it be considered by the newly organized World Parliament of the Earth Federation.

WE RECOMMEND that this legislation be studied, modified as needed, discarded if necessary, and used in all ways helpful to the newly formed Earth Federation. But the legislation adopted by Provisional World Parliaments must not be construed as linked to the ratification process of the *Constitution for the Federation of Earth.* Nor can it be construed as binding upon the newly formed Earth Federation and the people of Earth, against the decisions of the World Parliament.

⊕⊕⊕⊕⊕⊕⊕⊕⊕⊕

Above resolution introduced by Dr. Glen T. Martin. Resolved unanimously 5:15 p.m., 24th March 2003, in Bangkok, Thailand, by the sixth session of the Provisional World Parliament

Rules of Procedure for the World Constituent Assembly

(Deliberated and adopted under the authority of Article 18, Item 5, of the *Constitution for the Federation of Earth*, by the Sixth Session of the Provisional World Parliament, meeting in Thailand in 2003)

1. Purposes of the Fifth Session of the World Constituent Assembly, shall be as defined in the Call to the Fifth Session of the World Constituent Assembly, subject to the Call being made by either the Provisional World Parliament, in accordance with Article XVIII, Item 5 of the *Constitution for the Federation of Earth*, or by the Standing Steering Committee for the World Constituent Assembly that the Provisional World Parliament shall designate. Purposes shall not supercede these Rules of Procedure.

2. The Provisional World Parliament shall elect five chairpersons, a secretary and a treasurer to serve as the Standing Executive Cabinet of the Provisional World Parliament. These seven members of the Standing Executive Cabinet of the Provisional World Parliament shall comprise the initial Steering Committee for the administration of the World Constituent Assembly (as the organizing agent for the World Constituent Assembly), together with seven members elected by in Plenary Session on the 2nd day of the World Constituent Assembly. All members of the Steering Committee must be accredited delegates to the World Constituent Assembly, which includes the requirement of prior personal ratification of the *Constitution for the Federation of Earth* in its 1991 edition. The Steering Committee shall elect its own Chairperson and Secretary. Until the World Constituent Assembly has its own permanent financing, the Standing Executive Cabinet of the Provisional World Parliament (organizing agent) of the World Constituent Assembly shall supervise any staff personnel for the Assembly, both paid and volunteer. The Steering Committee shall invite suggestions for proposed amendments. If there is a significant request, the Steering Committee shall recommend to the Provisional World Parliament to call the World Constituent Assembly.

3. The Steering Committee shall nominate accredited delegates to serve official roles for the World Constituent Assembly, including Chair, Vice Chair, and Secretary. These delegates must be confirmed by simple majority vote of the World Constituent Assembly. If simple majority confirmation is not forthcoming, the Steering Committee may make new nominations based upon nominations made from the floor of the World Constituent Assembly, subject to simple majority confirmation of the Assembly. The World Constituent Assembly shall hold elections no later than the third day of the particular full session of the World Constituent Assembly. Until the officers are determined, the original nominees of the Steering Committee shall serve. The term of office for World Constituent Assembly officers shall be for only one full session, with re-election permitted for any subsequent sessions.

One hundred (100) accredited delegates, paid and present, constitute a quorum to convene the World Constituent Assembly.

4. The business of the World Constituent Assembly shall be limited to consideration, deliberation and action on constructive amendment to the *Constitution for the Federation of Earth.* Sole consideration shall be for amendments which conserve the basic non-military, federal and parliamentary attributes of the Provisional World Government and World Government, and which strengthen the overall program for non-military, federal, democratic world government. Likewise, only proposals that conserve all of the seven major branches of the World Government shall be considered: the tri-cameral World Parliament, the World Judiciary, the World Executive, the Enforcement System, the World Ombudsmus, the Integrative Complex and the World Administration. The Steering Committee and the Chair of the World Constituent Assembly shall give special consideration to strengthening of the Bill of Rights of the *Constitution for the Federation of Earth*, to strengthening of the World Parliament by increasing its accountability, and to the clarification of the relationship of the World Government to the United Nations Organization and related agencies, which are to undergo transfer, reconstitution and integration by the World Government in conformance with the *Constitution for the Federation of Earth.* The Steering Committee and the Chair shall also give special consideration to amendment proposals to improve the implementation and ratification process.

5. The Chair of the World Constituent Assembly shall rule as out of order any speeches or discussions during sessions of the World Constituent Assembly not clearly relevant to the business defined under #4 above, except for short greetings or presentations by Honorary Sponsors or by honorary invitees.

6. Proposals for constitutional amendments are not be limited to those mentioned in the Call to the World Constituent Assembly. However, the Assembly, by simple majority vote, may require deliberative priorities. Any accredited delegate may submit an amendment proposal, which must receive simple majority vote for consideration, as defined by the *Constitution for the Federation of Earth*, Article XVIII Section 1.a., or by petitions signed by a total of 200,000 persons eligible to vote in world elections from a total or at least 20 World Electoral and Administrative Districts where the *Earth Constitution* has received final ratification, as defined by the *Constitution for the Federation of Earth*, Article 18. Section 1.2.

7. Persons may submit proposals for constitutional amendment by writing to the organizing agent, to be received at least 90 days in advance of the Assembly, so that the preliminary agenda may be adapted and printed for the Assembly. However, in any case, all proposals of over thirty-five words in length must be submitted in written form by the end of the first day of the World Constituent Assembly, with individual copies to each member of the Steering Committee and to each accredited delegate in attendance, at the expense of the delegate making the submission. Delegates making

proposals have the sole responsibility for printing arrangements, not the Steering Committee for the Assembly, nor the organizing agent. Written proposals must also meet the qualifications of item 3 and 7 of the Rules of Procedure for the World Constituent Assembly, pertaining to the reservation of the non-military, federal, and tri-cameral parliamentary structure of the World Government, and reserving the sovereignty of the people of Earth through the *Constitution for the Federation of Earth.*

8. At the time that the Agenda designates, proposals may be introduced. Seconded proposals shall be given one reading in the Session. After reading, the delegate submitting a proposed amendment may have up to three minutes to present attributed merits of the proposal before the vote on deliberation. After this eulogy, questions for clarification are in order, but no judgmental statements. Answers to questions for clarification shall be limited to seven minutes total time per proposed amendment, which shall be monitored electronically by the Secretary of the Assembly, giving the presenter one-minute's notice to conclude each response for clarification. Any debate on the merits of any proposal shall not take place until after the Assembly has decided whether to accept the proposal for deliberation by its simple majority vote. Reading of individual amendments are limited to a reading time of ten minutes.

9. Any deliberative priorities on proposed amendments shall be voted upon after the conclusion of the initial readings of the written proposals for amendment, and after the adoption for deliberation of written proposals for possible amendment. After any simple majority decision to require deliberative priorities, these shall be established by a signed rating sheet ballot (universal ballot), which shall include all written proposals which have been accepted for deliberation by the Assembly. After the ballot but before beginning deliberations, the Steering Committee shall publish a spreadsheet for the Assembly, to audit the rating sheet results (Abstentions in the rating sheet shall be permitted, but duplicate ratings in the sheet from any one delegate shall be discarded for the respective ratings in question).

10. Any measure to amend the *Constitution for the Federation of Earth* must be consistent with the principle of non-military, federal, democratic world government. Amendments to establish a military, to abolish the Parliament, or any of its three Houses, or to reduce the legislative power, other than proposals which thereby clearly increase overall legislative accountability, are out of order and shall not be deliberated. Likewise, any proposal to eliminate any of the seven major branches of the World Government are out of order. These may be screened out by the Steering Committee after written submission, to preclude their coming to the Assembly floor.

11. Any amendment shall require the simple two thirds majority of delegates actually attending the Assembly, unless 25 national governments have given preliminary or final ratification to the *Constitution for the Federation of Earth* by the time that the 5th Session of the World Constituent Assembly convenes, in which case, an absolute two-thirds majority of delegates shall be required for passing an amendment.

12. No world legislation under the *Constitution for the Federation of Earth* may be debated at sessions of the World Constituent Assembly. At any session of the World Constituent Assembly, during recess, proposed legislation or legislative amendments may be caucused, without comment on the floor of the Assembly. The Steering Committee may then refer any legislative proposals to any respective Standing Parliamentary Commission of the Parliament. Legislative proposals may only be officially deliberated and voted upon at a session of the Provisional World Parliament or World Parliament.

13. All delegates to the World Constituent Assembly must register on approved registration forms, which include a pledge of support for the World Constituent Assembly, the Provisional World Parliament, and World Legislation enacted to date by the Provisional World Parliament, as well as pledge support to the principle of non-military federal, democratic world government. Delegates must pay the designated registration fees to the organizing agent for the World Constituent Assembly, unless the Steering Committee waives this as may be provided in the Call to the World Constituent Assembly.

14. All observers at the World Constituent Assembly must register on observer registration forms, which shall include a pledge not to obstruct the work of the Assembly, and must pay registration fees for observers. Observers shall have neither vote nor voice on the floor of the Assembly.

15. The Steering Committee shall use registration fees only to finance the World Constituent Assembly and its related work, such as following reports. Before the next to the last day of the World Constituent Assembly, the Treasurer shall make a report of income and expenses. The Steering Committee shall publish the budget of the World Constituent Assembly by the next to last day of the particular full session of the World Constituent Assembly. If any expenses remain unpaid due to insufficient funds, the treasurer shall take a collection. The World Constituent Assembly may not adjourn until all legitimate expense bills have been paid.

16. The Steering Committee, by a two-thirds majority vote, may expel any participant from the World Constituent Assembly, whether a delegate or an observer, if found to be acting in a manner obstructive to the purposes of the World Constituent Assembly. A simple two thirds majority vote of the World Constituent Assembly may also expel any participant found to be acting in an obstructive manner.

17. The organizing agent, as well as those members of the Steering Committee who are retained by the organizing agent at the conclusion of each full session of the World Constituent Assembly, shall comprise the Continuation Steering Committee, to serve between sessions of the World Constituent Assembly. However, the World Parliament can reconstitute the Continuation Steering Committee upon the commencement of the First Operative Stage of World Government under the *Constitution for the Federation of Earth.*

18. During sessions of the World Constituent Assembly, the Steering Committee shall meet daily to take care of any necessary business, and may make changes to the Agenda of the World Constituent Assembly, if found necessary. Such meetings of the Steering Committee shall require a quorum of seven members after the third day of the Assembly.

19. The Steering Committee shall publish a daily report of World Constituent Assembly proceedings. The Steering Committee shall publish a list of all World Constituent Assembly participants by the third day of the Assembly. The Steering Committee shall publish a final list of participants with home addresses upon the end of the World Constituent Assembly.

20. Except where otherwise specified, simple majority vote of those present and qualified to vote shall decide all questions of the Steering Committee, of other Commissions or Committees of the World Constituent Assembly, and of meetings of the Assembly itself.

21. Proxy voting is prohibited and each delegate shall have only one vote. One hundred (100) accredited delegates, paid and present, constitute a quorum to convene the World Constituent Assembly. Thereafter, quorum for each day's session shall require the attendance of at least 60% of the registered accredited delegates who have shown up for the particular full session.

22. Procedural matters, including these Rules of Procedure (after original adoption by the Provisional World Parliament), shall not be debated in the sessions of the World Constituent Assembly. During the sessions of the Assembly, the rulings of the Speaker shall be final on procedural conduct of the Assembly. Any questions concerning Rules of Procedure or the Agenda must be referred to the Steering Committee for decision. After original adoption by the Parliament, the Rules of Procedure can be amended during sessions of the Provisional World Parliament only by a two thirds absolute majority vote of the Parliament in Plenary Session.

23. Robert's Rules of Order and Erskine May Code shall supplement these Rules of Procedure, but not supersede at any point of possible variance. Robert's Rules of Order shall be the standard guide for meetings of the World Constituent Assembly, of the Steering Committee and of the Continuation Steering Committee on points not covered therein.

24. If any Founding Ratification Convention including representation from national governments determines that adjustment must be made to the *Constitution for the Federation of Earth*, the Founding Ratification Convention shall conform to these Rules of Procedure for the World Constituent Assembly.

⊕⊕⊕⊕⊕⊕⊕⊕⊕⊕

The sixth session Provisional World Parliament adopted Rules of Procedure for World Constituent Assembly, March 2003, Bangkok, Thailand

Resolution on the Spirit of Global Government under the *Constitution for the Federation of Earth*

We, the delegates of the sixth Provisional World Parliament at Bangkok, meeting under the auspices of the *Constitution for the Federation of Earth* in March 2003, do hereby affirm the following resolution:

In the light of the fact that many people today express a fear of what they call "big government", a sentiment that makes them hesitate before the idea of world government out of concern that local autonomy and individuality may be diminished,

In the light of the fact that many people today express a fear of what they call "bureaucracy", a sentiment that individual freedoms may be curtailed under a global federal bureaucracy that might require permits for everything and anything that people wish to do,

In the light of the fact that some nation-states today express a fear that world government might diminish their integrity and autonomy as individual nations, which they now claim is defended under the concept of "national sovereignty",

WE WISH TO EMPHASIZE that the *Constitution for the Federation of Earth* is carefully written to eliminate these potential dangers of world government. The Preamble of the Constitution asserts that "the principle of unity in diversity is the basis for a new age when war shall be outlawed and peace prevail; and when basic human rights and responsibilities shall be shared by all without discrimination." The Constitution is written with the protection of individuals and the integrity of nations in mind, and creates a separate branch of government known as the World Ombudsmus to explicitly prevent world government from violating the rights and freedoms of individuals, groups and nations.

At this Provisional World Parliament, we assembled delegates wish to emphasize these principles embodied in the world constitution by formulating a guideline for future legislation:

The foundation of a secure future for humanity and our natural environment is genuine democracy for all citizens of the planet. This means the empowerment of citizens from the local level to the global level through a social infrastructure providing education and other institutions aimed at making possible effective participation of citizens in democratic decision making.

We wish to emphasize that world government must be a federal system that preserves sufficient local autonomy for citizens to concretely work for justice and the redress of grievances on all levels from local, to national, to global. They must be free to pass local laws to address their particular concerns within the larger democratic framework of a world government that ensures universal political, economic and social rights to all.

Citizens must be encouraged by world government to recognize and challenge undemocratic institutions and practices at every level. The Constitution as quoted above emphasizes responsibilities as well as rights. World government must encourage a broad range of active citizen involvement in democratic processes. Active citizenship and taking responsibility is not fully accomplished through periodic voting, but through attending public forums, organizing, signing petitions, protesting, street theatre, civil disobedience, writing articles and editorials, contributing money, teaching, supporting and establishing alternative media, and many other ways. The active involvement and critical questioning upon which the democratic process depends both permits and encourages each citizen to take active responsibility for good government.

Similarly, nation-states must be protected from unwanted imperialism by other nations-states, or by world government itself, whether this takes the forms of cultural, economic or power based attempts at coercion. The integrity and autonomy of individual nation-states can only be effectively protected by the democratic authority of the whole of humanity, which is the only legitimate sovereign on Earth. Under the principle of unity in diversity, a truly federal system emphasizing the diversity of individuals, peoples, and nations is to be promoted and protected. This resolution emphatically states that future legislation enacted under the *Constitution for the Federation of Earth* should conform to the principles outlined herein.

⊕⊕⊕⊕⊕⊕⊕⊕⊕⊕

The sixth session of Provisional World Parliament adopted the above Spirit of Global Government resolution 3 p.m., 25th March 2003, Bangkok, Thailand.

A Memorial

To direct the Assembly of States Parties to enhance its legislative function by adopting the *Earth Constitution* and by deliberating world legislation

Commending the Assembly of States Parties for the good legislative work already initiated for the creation of a world criminal court with full compulsory jurisdiction;
Reminding the Assembly of States Parties regarding the role of deliberative assemblies in global statutory legislative development, and the fact that the Assembly of States Parties has taken a *de facto*, if not also *de jure,* role as upper house to a world legislature;

Prompting the Assembly of States Parties to consider the absolute necessity for a constitutional ground for the work of the world deliberative assemblies;

Asserting to the Assembly of States Parties that the *Constitution for the Federation of Earth* (*Earth Constitution* and *FEC*) provides an adequate framework that facilitates integration of the world criminal court with other agencies of emerging world government, especially for integration with the other necessary benches of the world judiciary, of which there are at least seven, such as Bench for Civil Cases and Bench for Juvenile Cases, etc. However, the world court also requires integration into a comprehensive and constitutionally based world government for other purposes as well, such as for providing adequate financing for prosecuting all the pending cases, which cannot be adequately done through mere confederal financing. Also, for the purpose of the popular mandate, it is necessary that the world legislative process include representatives of the people, not merely representatives of the peoples' national rulers.

Therefore, in representation of the People of Earth, this seventh session of the Provisional World Parliament, functioning in conformance with the *Earth Constitution*, meeting in Chennai, India, 26 to 30 December 2003, gives direction to the Assembly of States Parties, to consider and adopt the world legislation of the Provisional World Parliament, and in particular to consider and adopt the legislative adjustments that the Provisional World Parliament has made regarding the *Rome Statute for the Criminal Court*, the *Rules of Procedure and Evidence*, and the *Criminal Code Penalty Classification*.
Adoption of the Criminal Code Penalty Classification by the Assembly of States Parties is especially urged, as around the world it has usually been the customary practice of legislatures to determine penalties through legislative deliberation, rather than to leave the penalty designations up to the pleasure of the judiciaries.

⊕⊕⊕⊕⊕⊕⊕⊕⊕⊕

Memorial to Assembly of States Parties adopted 28 December 2003 at seventh session Provisional World Parliament, Chennai, India

Chennai Declaration

Global Problems at our Doorstep – Human Liberation in the Palm of our Hand

We delegates of the seventh Provisional World Parliament here assembled at Chennai, India, December 2003, affirm the *Constitution for the Federation of Earth* as the key to human liberation. We hold in the palm of our hand a blue print for a just, sustainable, and peaceful world order.

* The horrible problems daily faced by human beings all over planet Earth are simultaneously global problems devastating our planet. The nightmare of our unjust and divided world order is at the doorstep of every citizen of the planet. It is time we honestly face this horror and create a liberating world order.

* The invasion and destruction of Iraq and Afghanistan is directly connected with the suppression of civil liberties in our home countries as the forces of global domination increase their stranglehold over the individual lives of each of us. The spectre of global domination has perched on our doorsteps.

* The weapons used by terror groups worldwide are weapons produced by the multinational corporations in their greed and callousness. They are everywhere at our doorsteps. Bombs strapped to persons full of anger and hatred are equally as criminal as bombs dropped from the air without feeling by trained military personnel.

* The small farmer driven out of business to become a slave on his own fields, is a victim of the same corporate system that builds the bombs and promotes globalized economic exploitation. The problem of world militarism and greed has perched on the doorstep of the starving farmer.

* The roadblocks, police searches, airport inspections, and intimidation of our free speech and travel that we experience daily are direct consequences of global corporate militarism and the war economy. This world order of chaos and violence has perched on the doorstep of our freedoms and security.

* Several billion poor of the world lack nutritious food. Their hunger is directly related to the production of weapons of mass destruction supplying both the corporate dominators and the militarized resisters in nearly every country on Earth. Global militarism has perched like a vulture at the doorsteps of the poor.

* When water is privatized, and people in Latin America struggle over the right to water against the corporate predators, their lack of water is at the doorstep of hundreds of millions of the Earth's citizens who daily live without adequate water for a decent life. Global corporate greed and domination has perched at their doorstep.

* When bad sanitation causes disease, and the people of Africa contract cholera or typhoid because they lack adequate sanitation systems, their lack of sanitation and the crippling diseases are identical to those of fifty percent of the Earth's citizens. The dying children in Togo experience in their misery the same global problem as the dying children of Nicaragua. At the doorstep of each is the spectre of a global system predicated on death, not life.

* When a village in Bangladesh is flooded by rising ocean tides, downing their children and destroying the homes of villagers, the fumes from millions of cars racing the streets of Hong Kong and Mumbai have come to sit on their doorstep in the form of global warming. The global rule of corporate greed is at their doorstep.

* When cancer strikes the wealthy middle class woman in the United States in the prime of her life because she has eaten vegetables poisoned with the rocket fuel used to bomb Vietnam, Cambodia, Laos, Yugoslavia, Afghanistan, and Iraq.

Her horrible suffering reveals the spectre of global imperialism at her doorstep.

No one escapes the consequences of this world of chaos, greed, and violence. No one escapes the spectre of more than 190 "sovereign" nations competing with one another for wealth, resources, and corrupt power.Yet we hold in our hands the design for a new world based on planetary democratic equality, not power and privilege for the few. We hold in our hands the simple, noble design for a global peace system, not a global war system, for a global system of prosperity and sustainable development, not global poverty and environmental destruction.

We affirm with the *Earth Constitution* that Humanity is One despite the existence of diverse nations, races, creeds, ideologies and cultures and that the principle of unity in diversity is the basis for a new age when war shall be outlawed and peace prevail; when the earth's total resources shall be equitably be used for human welfare... We hold in the palms of our hands the blue print for a new world order. We call out this day to people of good will everywhere. Tomorrow is too late! The time is now to unite for human liberation under the *Constitution for the Federation of Earth*!

⊕⊕⊕⊕⊕⊕⊕⊕⊕⊕

Above Chennai Declaration adopted by the Provisional World Parliament in seventh session, Chennai, India, 28 December 2005.

A Pledge of Allegiance to the Federation of Earth

I pledge allegiance to the *Constitution for the Federation of Earth*,
And to the Republic of free world citizens for which it stands,
One Earth Federation, protecting by law the rich diversity of the Earth's citizens,
One Earth Federation, protecting the precious ecology of our planet.

I pledge allegiance to the World Parliament representing all nations and peoples,
And to the democratic processes by which it proceeds,

One law for the Earth, with freedom and equality for all,
One standard of justice, with a bill of rights protecting each.

I pledge allegiance to the future generations protected by the *Earth Constitution*,
And to the unity, integrity, and beauty of humankind, living in harmony on the Earth,

One Earth Federation, conceived in love, truth, and hope, with peace and prosperity for all.

⊕⊕⊕⊕⊕⊕⊕⊕⊕⊕

Note: This pledge was ratified as the official pledge of the Earth Federation at the seventh session of Provisional World Parliament in Chennai, India, 26-30 December 2003.

Resolution of
Tax and Accounting Policy Statement

Important Differences between Taxation and Accounting Rules*

Countries may retain the power to follow different approaches with respect to the relationship between commercial and tax accounting (dependence/ independence). Both approaches have advantages and shortcomings. However, in both cases, well-established principles of taxation must not be disregarded.

Specific accounting and reporting standards for listed companies increase transparency and comparability, mainly for investors. A convergence of the principles governing existing accounting and reporting standards is desirable in order to increase comparability and to facilitate multiple listings. However, possible tax implications for companies, especially in countries relying on commercial accounts as primary basis for tax assessment, have to be kept in mind, and the convergence should not deteriorate the tax position of enterprises.

Tax authorities and policy makers should accept that the underlying principles of financial accounting are not always compatible with basic principles and practices used in the field of taxation. From a tax policy perspective, it is important that taxation rules are not undermined by an inappropriate extension of financial reporting requirements (e.g. fair value accounting or disregard of realisation).

Taxation and financial accounting rules serve different purposes, have different objectives and are based on different principles. Although both sets of rules are used to measure the annual results of an enterprise, differences in the results (profits) or in the methods applied (e.g. valuation) have to be accepted. Financial accounting looks at the enterprise as an economic entity (group), whereas taxation is normally based on a separate entity approach.

Because of the speed and the direction of developments in financial accounting and reporting (transparency, market valuation, single performance statement, convergence of standards), existing differences will become even more important in the future. Policy makers in the fields of taxation and accounting must be aware of these differences. Tax authorities must respect them and refrain from using companies' financial results for tax adjustments.

⊕⊕⊕⊕⊕⊕⊕⊕⊕⊕

The seventh session of Provisional World Parliament adopted the above Taxation and Accounting policy in December 2003 at Chennai, Tamil Nadu, India.

* From the Memorial of the World Chamber of Commerce.

Memorial to President Jean Ping to call General Review Conference

Below is the memorial sent to Jean Ping, then President of the General Assembly of the United Nations. The letter in French with cover letter and other Earth Federation documentation was sent by USPS certified mail on 23 October 2004:

"This eighth session of the Provisional World Parliament hereby directs the President of the General Assembly of the United Nations, His Excellency M. Jean Ping, to call a vote of the General Assembly for a general review conference in conformance with Article 109 of the United Nations Charter, to deliberate on the adoption of the *Constitution for the Federation of Earth* to replace the original *United Nations Charter.*"

⊕⊕⊕⊕⊕⊕⊕⊕⊕⊕

The Eighth Session of Provisional World Parliament adopted this above memorial at Lucknow, Uttar Pradesh, India in August 2004

Adoption and Promotion of Esperanto as a World Auxiliary Language

As, in the words of Onisaburo Deguchi, "to bring about everlasting world peace, first tangible and intangible barriers between nations and peoples must be removed";

As these barriers must be removed while respecting inherent cultures and linguistic diversity;

As it is indispensable for human beings to speak an international and neutral supplemental language, to maintain and develop the diverse cultures along with deepening mutual relationship among different cultures and races;

As Esperanto has been designed by Dr. Ludoviko Zamenhof, and further developed by linguistic scholars and enthusiasts, so that ordinary people can speak, study and understand, as well as have excellent expression and abundant vocabulary of special terminology in a fully regular language;

As the World Parliament intends to encourage an extremely high degree of linguistic competence within its own ranks, as well as within the personnel of the Earth Federation and among the general public;

As the World Parliament intends to promote full linguistic equity among human beings everywhere;

This eighth session of the Provisional World Parliament hereby adopts Esperanto as a working and official language of the Earth Federation. The Parliament resolves to facilitate and promote the learning of Esperanto and communication in Esperanto to delegates from a wide variety of linguistic backgrounds.

Furthermore, the World Parliament pledges to do its best to encourage the use of whatever other auxiliary means as may be necessary to make the work of the World Parliament available to persons of every linguistic background, and to facilitate communication among all delegate Members of the World Parliament, among all officials and all employees of the Earth Federation. These means may include instantaneous interpreters, translators, accessibility options, other auxiliary languages and computer translation programs.

⊕⊕⊕⊕⊕⊕⊕⊕⊕⊕

The eighth session of Provisional World Parliament adopted the above resolution, meeting at City Montessori School, Lucknow, India, 10 -14 August 2005.

Resolution on Good Government and its Essential Tasks under the Earth Federation

We delegates of the Eighth Session of the Provisional World Parliament affirm that one of the functions of the Provisional World Parliament is to outline, on behalf of the emerging Earth Federation, the characteristics of good government and the essential role of the Federation under the concept of good government. The *Constitution for the Federation of Earth* provides a brilliantly conceived and carefully thought out framework for non-military democratic world government. It is up to the Provisional Parliament to articulate further the spirit of that government so the peoples and nations of the world will see the wisdom of ratifying the *Constitution* and moving the world forward to a world of prosperity, law, freedom, and justice.

We hope that the outline of good government that we present here will be further developed in scholarly books, essays, and articles by members of the emerging Earth Federation. This resolution asserts four fundamental characteristics of good federal world government: (1) human rights are protected equally for all citizens great and small, rich or poor, no matter what their race, religion, gender, or ideology, (2) prosperity for all is promoted and a general economic equality and security for all is encouraged by government policies, (3) freedom for citizens is maximized insofar as this is compatible with the equal freedom of all others, and (4) individual, local, and regional autonomy is promoted insofar as this is compatible with the autonomy of other persons, localities, and regions.

We maintain that good government does not merely give citizens what political philosophers have called "negative freedom" by reducing its activities to a minimum required for regulation of trade, prevention of crime, protecting the environment, etc. Rather, good government has the duty to promote "positive freedom" by encouraging education, prosperity, mutual understanding among peoples, world peace, and environmental awareness. The Earth Federation has a duty to be proactive in developing people's understanding of the global crises faced by citizens and nations of our planet, to promote educational study of the similarities and differences between cultures, religions, and ideologies with the view to encouraging peace, tolerance, and mutual understanding, and to encourage the development of world citizenship and a sense of world community.

We recognize that the *Constitution for the Federation of Earth* gives the federal world government significant authority to regulate world trade, protect essential resources of the planet, protect and restore the planetary environment to health, prevent war, and to establish a federal bureaucracy necessary to implement these broad powers. Even if the laws deriving from these powers were legislated by the representatives of the people and nations in the World Parliament, the resulting laws and their enforcement could result in the people of Earth feeling that there were alien restrictions imposed upon them by distant legislators who knew nothing of their local problems or issues.

Good government will find ways to involve individuals, communities, and regions in discussion and decision making of the issues affecting their lives without, at the same time, compromising the effectiveness of government (see, for example, the Bill on Education before this Eighth Session of the Provisional Parliament). For example, true protection of human rights worldwide requires that people and communities internalize the standards of human rights outlined in Articles 12 and 13 of the *Constitution* and routinely act according to these standards. True protection of these rights cannot and should not be enforced from the top down through a system of monitoring or policing that might defeat the very freedoms that are at stake. A commonly understood role of government involves defining standards by which people can transmit information, do business, and trade, such as by official recognition of the metric system for standard weights and measures. The same applies to human rights and the other universal standards embedded in the *Constitution for the Federation of Earth.*

The Earth Federation needs to perform this common standards-defining function for the peoples and nations of Earth, for example, by defining shipping, communications, and mailing codes, defining the value of currency (see the Bill on Economic Equality before this Parliament), and defining environmental standards (For example, what constitutes safe emissions into the soil, air, and water from an industry or what constitutes safe drinking water?) In addition, good government must also define standards for protection of human rights, humane treatment of prisoners, due process of law, safe working conditions, and other conditions specified in Articles 12 and 13 of the *Earth Constitution*.

The Earth Federation must also be proactive in addressing the problems faced by the citizens of Earth and proactive in making possible lives of security, quality, prosperity, and dignity for all its citizens. It must help transform a disparate and fragmented world population into a conscious political and cultural world community. World peace is not likely to occur, nor the Federation be ultimately successful, unless that task can be accomplished is a relatively short period of time. Such a task cannot be accomplished from the top down without the active cooperation and support of the diverse citizens and peoples of Earth.

The difficulty is to promote realization of this human potential of the peoples, nations, and cultures of the Earth without imposing on people any preconceived notion of what constitutes "the good life" and without generating the perception among people that such a preconceived conception of the good life is being imposed. Such a perception would be particularly onerous to certain cultures and religions that rightly wish autonomy for themselves and their adherents. As the Preamble to the *Constitution* states, the goal of the Federation is to promote genuine "unity in diversity" on Earth whereas at present there is much that is simply unredeemed diversity and fragmentation. To do this the emerging Earth Federation must develop non-coercive, voluntary mechanisms that encourage the participation and cooperation of the peoples of Earth in this process.

The key to success in this difficult task is to set up the conditions for realization of world citizenship among citizens and the conditions for the development of individual, local, and regional autonomy. This task must also include developing the framework of good law in such a way as to prevent commercial interests or other major special interest power groupings from preventing or colonizing the these conditions in their own interests. This task is of utmost importance if the planet under the Earth Federation is to become a genuine community with genuine protection of human rights for all, rapid elimination of poverty and creation of prosperity for all, with genuine freedom and individual, local, and regional autonomy as much as is feasible within the framework of the rights of all peoples and nations and protecting the Earth for future generations.

To this end we urge the emerging Earth Federation to develop as rapidly as possible the following seven aspects of global federal infrastructure that we believe necessary to promote local and regional autonomy, rapid development of prosperity, and the sense of being part of a world community with corresponding loyalty to the Earth Federation.

1. Foster development of a planetary system of quality, well-equipped schools, staffed by highly trained teachers. Local communities need to control their schools as much as possible without compromising the standards of quality learning and scientific integrity that highly trained teachers will bring to the schools. Such schools would not only fulfill the mandate of Article 13 of the *Constitution* for free, universal education, they would give people training for good jobs and prosperous lives while simultaneously creating consciousness of being part of a world community.

2. Emphasize both within and outside these schools (for example, on public radio and television) the teaching of whatever universal language or languages the World Parliament has determined as a second language (see the resolution on Esperanto and other artificial languages before this session of the Provisional Parliament). Teaching of the universal language or languages should not be to the exclusion of a primary language or languages.

3. Begin an extensive system of public education through public radio and television systems. Such systems have tremendous potential for teaching primary literacy, second languages, special work skills, conditions for sanitation, prevention of disease, cure of common health problems, how to protect the environment on a local level, sustainable agricultural methods, and efficient use of resources. Such programs would also have the secondary but extremely important effect of developing consciousness of being part of the world community under the Earth Federation.

4. Develop an extensive system of libraries throughout the world. These libraries would not only house books and journals necessary for people seeking information on technical, scientific, business, or literary concerns, they would give people free access to the world wide web, email communications, and the developing world community through these mediums. As with the above items (1-3), these libraries should be under local control to the extent that they do not violate the guarantees in the *Earth Constitution* of freedom for information, and access to the inherited scientific and cultural wealth of humanity to which every citizen has a right. Local citizens or governments controlling these libraries could adapt their content and programs to local needs and sustainable development as much as possible.

5. Develop a system of community recreation and meeting centers for the world. Citizens need public places where they can meet that are controlled locally open equally to everyone. If local autonomy is to be encouraged along with political participation in the Federation itself, then such meeting places will be invaluable for both purposes. Communities can define their specific needs, invite wide participation of their citizens, and communicate with representatives of the Earth Federation invited to meetings or events. Such community centers can be important places of recreation providing forms of recreation valued by the local community, bringing people together for political and other forms of discussion, and creating a sense of participation in the Earth Federation.

6. Develop a system of community meditation and interdenominational religious centers. Such centers might be part of the community recreation and meeting centers specified in number 5. They also might be part of the library system specified in number 4. Their purpose, absolutely vital in a world of religious intolerance, narrowness, and fragmentation, should be to allow the free development of spirituality independently of particular religious doctrines or dogmas, to allow interaction among adherents of various religions on neutral (yet religiously serious) ground, to promote study of the world's religions and hence mutual understanding and interaction among followers of these religions, and to create a sense of participation in the Earth Federation on behalf of world unity, toleration, understanding, and peace. While the Earth Federation is non-religious and stands for both freedom of religion and freedom from religion for citizens, the function of good government to provide the conditions necessary for people to realize their potential for unity in diversity makes the development of such centers essential at this point in history.

7. Develop mechanisms by which local citizens and communities can politically participate directly in the Earth Federation. Under the *Constitution for the Federation of Earth,* the House of Peoples has 1000 representatives from 1000 federal electoral districts arranged by population worldwide. At the current population of the Earth, this would equal only one representative for every six million persons. While the size of Parliament needs to be small enough to remain effective (under the *Constitution* it will be about 1600 persons among the three houses), the representation of the peoples of Earth must be encouraged through additional mechanisms that personalize the Federation through more direct methods of political participation for ordinary citizens.

This might take the form of a "Global Peoples Assembly" currently being developed by some members of the emerging Earth Federation or such mechanisms might be developed by the offices of each representative to the House of Peoples. Extensive mechanisms supporting the democratic spirit of the *Constitution* must be developed by which each representative's six million constituents can make their voices heard and participate effectively in influencing the decision making process that affects their lives. Much thought and hard work still needs to go into developing such mechanisms for local participation in the world government. However, this is absolutely essential if the emerging Earth Federation is to truly promote local freedom and autonomy while simultaneously activating peoples potential for mutual understanding, mutual respect and toleration, and world peace.

We the delegates at the historic Eighth Session of the Provisional World Parliament do hereby affirm these principles and urge the emerging Earth Federation to act upon them as rapidly and efficiently as possible.

⊕⊕⊕⊕⊕⊕⊕⊕⊕⊕

The eighth session of the Provisional World Parliament adopted the above resolution, meeting in August 2004, at City Montessori School, Lucknow, Uttar Pradesh, India.

Declaration of the Rights of the People of Earth to create and ratify a World Constitution and hold sessions of the Provisional World Parliament

We, the citizens of the Earth, have the right and duty to establish a viable world government capable of maintaining the Rule of Law among all nations in place of the disastrous anarchy now prevailing among sovereign states, to abolish massively destructive armaments and end all wars, to protect the global environment for future generations, and to create economic justice and prosperity for all the citizens of our planet.

1. These are the times the world will not soon forget. Future historians will wonder how a few of us maintained our sanity and dignity in the face of the global breakdown of world order. Never in history have so many people been starving to death on Earth. Never have so many people lacked clean water or sanitation. Never has there been so much poverty and misery.

Never in history have so many people possessed so many weapons and engaged in continuous mutual slaughter of one another, in Columbia, Afghanistan, Sudan, Uganda, Chechnya, Iraq and elsewhere. Never have human beings everywhere on Earth been so insecure. Never has the average person anywhere on Earth felt so afraid and the future seemed so hopeless. Fifteen years after the collapse of the USSR, the threat of a global nuclear holocaust remains in place, while the superpower continues to develop space-based and tactical nuclear weapons.

Nowhere in previous history has the world faced a possible breakdown of its planetary ecosystem. Never has the ozone layer that protects the Earth from the sun's deadly radiation been threatened. Never have the ocean fisheries been collapsing from over-fishing, never before has grazing land been turning to desert on a global scale from overgrazing, never has agricultural land disappeared at the astonishing rates that we see today. Never before has the world's fresh water supply been endangered.

2. Some people in every age of historical crisis have been the visionaries, the civilizers, the advanced thinkers, who see the way forward beyond the narrow assumptions and petty issues of their day. Some people in every age have spoken for universal principles, for justice and human dignity, for equality and freedom among nations, peoples, and individuals of the Earth. These are the civilizers; these are the voice of legitimate creativity. These are the ones who establish new institutions and give renewed hope for the future.

The legitimacy of an action is not always whether it is approved by some majority. Very often in history the majority have represented reaction, intolerance, and injustice. The legitimacy of an action is whether it moves history forward toward greater universality. The innovators within history, like the writers of the French Declaration of the Rights of Man or the U.N. Universal Declaration of Human Rights, have always been a tiny minority.

the legitimacy of their work derives from its universality. The movement of history, the extension of rights, is from the tribe to the clan to the territory to the nation to the entire planet. The ultimate universality is the sovereignty of the people of Earth. New eras of legitimacy in history have been initiated by those who extended human rights and freedom to ever greater numbers of people and to those who promoted the just rule of law in human affairs.

The criterion of legitimacy in human affairs is moral universality. The core of democracy is not majority rule but the protection of minorities from both majorities and tyrants. It is equal rights for all under just laws. Nor is legitimacy derived from either power or existing institutions by themselves. Gigantic systems of power have existed historically from the Roman Empire to the many European Empires, to the present American Empire. The fact of military, bureaucratic, or institutional power does not lend legitimacy.

The only criterion is whether human rights, dignity, freedom, and justice prevail because of these institutions. This is why democracy is the ultimate criterion of legitimacy, democracy defined as any system that promotes rights, dignity, freedom, and justice in human affairs. Only global democracy represents the sovereignty of the people of Earth.

3. The present institutions of the world are failed institutions. The global economic system has not led to prosperity for most of the Earth's citizens, but to starvation, poverty, disease, and misery for the majority. The present global political systems of the world, called territorial nation-states, have not led to a just or peaceful world order, but to endless wars, destruction of peoples and cultures, imperial domination and conquest, and global systems of exploitation of the weaker by the stronger.

The United Nations has not led to a world where the many rights listed in its Universal Declaration of Human Rights have been extended to the Earth's citizens, but to denial of those rights for the majority and continuous increase in war, poverty, social chaos, and environmental destruction. By the criterion of legitimacy set forth in this document, these institutions have made themselves illegitimate. Citizens of Earth have the right and duty to create new institutions that represent the people of Earth.

4. The sovereignty of the people of Earth is represented in those who seek universal human political, social, and economic rights. The sovereignty of the people of Earth is represented in those who seek universal economic justice and the common good of all who live on Earth. The sovereignty of the people of Earth is represented by those who promote the rule of law on Earth and an end to the barbaric rule of militarized force and violence. The sovereignty of the people of Earth is represented by those who seek global democracy in the form of federal world government.

It is irrelevant whether the people of Earth elected representatives to write the *Constitution for the Federation of*

Earth. What matters is that the people of Earth have the opportunity to ratify the *Constitution* and begin the rule of just law in the world. It is irrelevant whether delegates to the Provisional World Parliament were elected by their countries as representatives to the Parliament. What matters is that the delegates promote universal human rights, justice, freedom, and prosperity.

Those who represent the people of Earth in this quest are not self-appointed partisans of special interests. Such self-appointed demagogues are easily identifiable by their programs that always deny rights and dignity to those they oppose. Delegates to the Provisional World Parliament are appointed, under Article 19 of the *Constitution*, by the universal principle of morality on which the *Constitution* is based that is the criterion of legitimacy in human political and economic affairs. Their work includes all persons on Earth, and excludes none.

5. At this juncture of world history, no nation can have a fully legitimate democracy. For the very existence of "sovereign" nations means that the rights of those outside its borders are ignored or betrayed. At this junction of world history, no nation can protect the environment for future generations. For the destruction of the planetary ecosystem is beyond the scope and effectiveness of any nation-state.

At this juncture of world history, no nation can create economic justice. For in today's globalized economy, prosperity for individual nations always involves exploitation and poverty for other nations. The nation-state system is dead. Only those representing global democracy through federal world government can possibly represent legitimacy in human affairs.

The present world-system not only embodies failed institutions but it is also built on morally illegitimate institutions. Every human being is morally required to live under democratically legislated universal laws. Without the rule of law, human affairs are always in a defacto state of war in which the stronger or more clever will be able to take advantage of the weaker.

Genuine law legislates equality, freedom, and the principle of justice for all. Yet in the world-system today there is no genuine law, for nations are all victims to the social, military, and economic chaos that characterizes international affairs and afflicts all persons living within particular nation-states. The unenforceable pronouncements of the treaty-system that constitutes the United Nations is a travesty of genuine "international law." We are morally required to live under universal democracy and federal world government representing all persons on Earth equally and creating the just rule of enforceable law on Earth.

6. In the face of our world condition in the past five decades, world citizens had every right to create the *Constitution for the Federation of Earth*. In the face of the global chaos resulting from monopoly capitalism and the system of sovereign nation-states, these world citizens also had a duty to write a *Constitution* *for the Federation of Earth*. We do not characterize these acts as the noble actions of do-gooders contributing to the human project. We describe here the universal duty of every person on Earth to live under the rule of enforceable world law.

Our work is not only more legitimate than that of politicians within nations who pass legislation excluding the majority of humanity from the laws they write. Our work is absolutely obligated by the demand for universality in human affairs and by the need to protect future generations from the lethal consequences of present institutions. It is with this understanding that we affirm our right and duty to hold future sessions of the Provisional World Parliament, to work unceasingly to activate the fledgling institutions of democratic world government, and to communicate to every citizen on Earth the absolute need to ratify the *Constitution for the Federation of Earth*.

⊕⊕⊕⊕⊕⊕⊕⊕⊕⊕

The eighth session of Provisional World Parliament deliberated and adopted the above declaration, meeting in August 2004, at City Montessori School, Lucknow, Uttar Pradesh, India

Resolution on the Trial of War Criminals and Perpetrators of Genocide and Crimes Against Humanity

This Provisional World Parliament, at its Tenth Session in Kara, Togo, June 21-24, 2007, affirms the principles set forth in the Nuremburg Accords, in the "international law" of the U.N., and in the common law of humankind that individual persons be held responsible for atrocities, torture, genocides, war crimes, or crimes against humanity committed during war. War, itself a barbaric activity in contradiction to the rule of law, cannot and must not be used as a cover for even greater barbaric actions such as genocide and crimes against humanity.

The Provisional World Parliament recalls specifically the historic and heroic war of liberation of Bangladesh in 1971 through which the people of Bangladesh achieved their independence on 16 December 1971. The territory that now comprises Bangladesh was the eastern part of Pakistan. Since the establishment of Pakistan through the British partitioning of India in 1947, the people of the eastern wing were subjugated like a colony by the Pakistani rulers who were primarily from the western part.

The people of eastern Pakistan had to fight for establishing their mother language, Bangla, as the state language, and for regional autonomy. They also had to struggle for their due share in governance, the economy, social, and cultural life. However, the Pakistani rulers (mainly from the western wing and from the province of Punjab) denied these rights.

In 1970, the first ever national general election since independence from India took place on the basis of adult franchise. The political party Awami League obtained the majority of seats in the national parliament. But this party was denied the opportunity to form the government.

As a result, mass upsurge took place in the eastern wing during the months of January to March 1971, and the Pakistani army junta, in order to suppress the public unrest, launched an all out attack on the unarmed people of then east Pakistan in the night of 25 March 1971. Immediately, the national leader Sheikh Mujibur Rahman declared independence for Bangladesh on 26th March. The people were compelled to start their war of liberation from this date.

This Parliament also recalls that, according to the testimony of freedom fighters still living, the Pakistani army started with an unprecedented genocide mercilessly killing an estimated 3,000,000 people, including women and children. According to some estimates, the Pakistani army burned millions of houses and also committed mass rape upon 20,000 women. More than an estimated 10,000,000 people fled the country and took refuge in neighboring India. Youths, peasants, workers, and people from all walks of life participated in the liberation war by forming Mukti Bahini (Liberation Army) and fought in the war of liberation. Ultimately, the 95,000 Pakistani occupation army surrendered to the joint command of Mukti Bahini and the Indian army in Dhaka on 16 December 1971, and Bangladesh was freed on that date with the victory of the freedom fighters.

This Parliament understands that the surrendered Pakistani army generals were taken to India where the understanding of the Bangladeshi people was that they were to be tried for committing genocide and other war crimes. However, ultimately the India government appears to have freed them and no trials have yet taken place. What happened in India that allowed due process of law not to take place needs to be investigated and brought to light.

This Parliament considers the commission of such war crimes as crimes against humanity. The perpetrators of such heinous crimes should be brought to justice, face properly constituted trials, and be dealt with appropriately. The Provisional World's Parliament's own World Legislative Acts antedate the commission of these alleged crimes by the Pakistani army in Bangladesh and, therefore (under the principle in the *Earth Constitution* of no *ex post facto* application of laws), these crimes must be tried under earlier laws against genocide and war crimes, such as U.N. international law, or the traditional common laws of humanity against such heinous actions as murder, torture, and rape.

Therefore, this Parliament resolves that the army personnel of the Pakistan army who were allegedly responsible for committing war crimes in Bangladesh during the War of Liberation of 1971, and their associates who helped them in furtherance of the above mentioned heinous crimes, be brought to trial by due process of law and ultimately be brought to justice.

This Parliament urges the world community to come forward to form world-wide opinion in favor of immediately bringing the suspects of these crimes to justice under due process of law.

⊕⊕⊕⊕⊕⊕⊕⊕⊕⊕

The tenth session of the Provisional World Parliament adopted the above resolution, 24th June 2007, at Kara, Togo.

The Provisional World Parliament resolutions, memorials and other decisions printed in this chapter are accurate and complete insofar as practicable and known by the editors. However, due to some dispersions of records over time, some resolutions and memorials are thought to be perhaps missing. That is, this record is not guaranteed as an exhaustive record. Furthermore, this record in *Emerging World Law* does not include parliament decisions regarding elections of officers, creation of parliamentary committees, unengrossed decisions other than main motions, decisions on parliament procedure or decisions on the order of the day.

Attested by Eugenia Almand, JD, Parliament Secretary, Provisional World Parliament

Chapter Nine

World Legislative Summaries

"No measure shall be accepted at the Desk for introduction unless it is accompanied by an impartial summary of the measure's content...The measure summary should present a brief and impartial statement of the essential features of the measure (a summary is not an analysis)."

Legislative Administration Committee
Oregon Form and Style Manual for Legislative Measures (1997)

Eugenia Almand, Editor

Introduction

After a world legislative bill has been drafted, it has to undergo a process in which people become familiar with the bill, just as with any legislative act at any other level of jurisdiction. As legislation is often comprehensive and lengthy, and as members of a legislature have to wisely allocate their limited time to the examination of legislative proposals, it is customary to summarize legislation to a length which all members of the legislature can read and understand within the limits of time that may be available. Therefore, when a bill is brought before the Provisional World Parliament, the Parliament expects that drafters will include a summary with each bill presented. The legislative summary should be an honest reflection of the full-length legislation in question. Because of a necessity to portray the comprehensive, integrating quality of world legislation, world legislative summary is unlike that of some lower jurisdictions, such as State of Oregon, in that the world legislative summary does inventory the articles.

There are a number of stylistic differences between full-length legislation and legislative summary. For one, legislative summaries are not written with complete sentences but rather, correctly, are incomplete sentences wherein each general provision of the summary begins with a verb. Articles (as the part of speech, i.e. a, an and the) are omitted from the summary. The general action of the legislation is portrayed, but details may be omitted from the summary.

Once the legislative bill is under deliberation, the Parliament may decide on an amendment to the full text, or on an amendment to the summary. In either case, a substantial amendment adopted to one is an amendment adopted to the other, as well, and the particular wording is worked out there in session.

The Provisional World Parliament has to date enacted forty-two world legislative acts. Some of the legislative acts were drafted outside and beyond international convention law. Other world legislative acts are based on the previously existing body of international legal convention, but with the important difference of being submitted, deliberated and adopted according to parliamentary law, procedures and drafting guidelines. One of those guidelines is the requirement for legislative summary. (Summary was not required within international law and diplomacy.) So some statutes of international convention are now converted by parliamentary law into statutes that have the parliamentary form. Therefore, for these statutes, legislative summaries are available. One example of this is the summary of the World Bench for Criminal Cases which derived from the *Rome Statute for the International Criminal Court.*

This chapter summarizes the 42 ennumerated world legislative acts of the Provisional World Parliament. The summaries are up-to-date in their most recent versions, including world legislative amendments up through the most recent session of the Provisional World Parliament (Kara, Togo. June 2007). For comprehending the legislation within its legislative context, we recommend that one read the legislative summaries before reading the statutes in full text. Most of the world legislation in full text form follows in Volumes 2 and 3 of this set of *Emerging World Law.*

These world legislative acts and any subsequent world legislative acts can be found on-line at www.worldproblems.net.

First Session of the Provisional World Parliament, Royal Pavilion, Brighton, England, September 1982,

adopted World Legislative Acts #1 through #5.

World Legislative Act #1 Summary

To Prohibit Weapons of Mass Destruction, Including Nuclear Weapons, and to Create a World Disarmament Agency

Short title: **Disarmament Act**

Enacted by this Provisional World Parliament in first session, September, 1982:

1. Prohibits all weapons of mass destruction (WMDs) and related activities:

- **1.1.** design, engage in research thereon, or test (class 6 felony)
- **1.2.** produce, manufacture, fabricate (class 1 felony)
- **1.3.** transport, deploy, install (class 1 felony)
- **1.4.** maintain, store, stockpile (class 1 felony)
- **1.5.** sell (class 5 felony)
- **1.6.** buy (class 6 felony) or
- **1.7.** detonate (class 7 felony)
- **1.8.** direct, request or command violation (one felony level above violation requested, unless class 7 felony)

2. Establishes World Disarmament Agency (WDA) to supervise military disarmament throughout world.

3. Assigns *pro tempore* responsibility of World Disarmament Agency to Provisional World Parliament, and to Provisional World Cabinet.

4. Designates Board of Trustees of World Disarmament Agency (WDA) to have from 15 to 275 members. Defines sources for Member composition to Board of Trustees. Directs Board of Trustees to determine organization and functioning of World Disarmament Agency in accordance with terms of World Legislation. Prohibits national or international veto in decisions of World Disarmament Agency.

5. Requires Cabinet of Provisional World Parliament to submit Act for compliance by all national governments and by all national parliaments.

5.1. Prohibits work related to weapons of mass destruction, except work of dismantlement or conversion under supervision of World Disarmament Agency.

5.2. Conditionally requires governing units within nations to immediately render inoperable WMDs. within their boundaries. Directs governing units to require cessation of WMD activities. Requires governing units to recognize supervision by World Disarmament Agency.

5.3. Requires educational institutions to comply.

5.4. Requires other organizations to comply.

5.5. Directs national governments, national parliaments, and national courts to recognize the World Disarmament Agency. Directs compliance. Encourages conditional recognition of enforcement jurisdiction at Earth Federation level.

6. Declares entry into force six months from adoption of this Act by Provisional World Parliament.

7. Directs Earth Federation Funding Corporation (EFFC), to request at least 1% from each entity ratifying *Earth Constitution.* Directs EFFC to request country subscription of 5% of last respective military budget, or 1% of respective annual budget, whichever is greater.

8. Directs Provisional World Parliament to elect standing Parliamentary Commission on Disarmament (PCD), to elaborate necessary details for inauguration of World Disarmament Agency. Defines composition of PCD.

Includes as Appendix – Non-exhaustive list of Weapons of Mass Destruction.

⊕⊕⊕⊕⊕⊕⊕⊕⊕⊕⊕

The first session of Provisional World Parliament, meeting at Brighton, England, adopted the Disarmament Act on 11 September 1982. Entry into force was 11 March 1983. Parliament amended the act at sixth session of Provisional World Parliament, meeting at Bangkok, Thailand, March 2003. Parliament adopted sentencing parameters at Seventh Session, Chennai, India, December 2003. Parliament adopted formatting amendments at eighth session of Parliament, Lucknow, India, August 2004.

World Legislative Act # 2
Summary

Act to Inaugurate a World Economic Development Organization

Adopts Act to inaugurate World Economic Development Organization (WEDO) under following conditions:

1. Requires WEDO to administrate adequate program of world economic development to meet peaceful human needs, with development budget in Earth credits or Earth currency for countries and people that ratify or preliminarily ratify *Earth Constitution* (Article 19, Sec. B-5, FEC).

2. Seeks capital funds for operation of WEDO from public and private sources, basing finance on potential productive capacity in both goods and services, rather than on past savings.

3. Establishes Planetary Banking and Credit system to receive, manage, create and disburse funds and credit, in conjunction with WEDO. Requires WEDO to extend lines of credit to countries making subscription to

Earth Federation Funding Corporation on basis of productivity potential of approved projects.

4. Composes WEDO Board of Directors of up to 33 members to develop and supervise WEDO. Defines sources, terms, removal and replacements for Board members.

5. Requires Board of Directors to define and select Administration for WEDO.

6. Defines Subscribers Council to elect replacements of Subscriber Members of Board of Directors, after first terms are served.

7. Permits WEDO to establish roster of consultants and to retain outside agencies on consulting basis.
Requires WEDO to utilize services of Earth Federation agencies.

8. Defines conditions for projects.

9. Requires WEDO to use designated criteria in evaluating projects.

10. Requires WEDO to employ secretariat and start preparatory work as soon as 10 countries have subscribed or as soon as Provisional world government has created Earth credit or Earth currency.

11. Assigns tasks to Continuation Steering Committee for Provisional World Parliament to appoint WEDO Parliamentary Preparatory Commission with authorization to prepare further details for organization and operation of WEDO.

⊕⊕⊕⊕⊕⊕⊕⊕⊕⊕⊕

The first session of Provisional World Parliament adopted Act #2 on 12 September 1982. Parliament amended the Act during sixth session Provisional World Parliament, meeting at Bangkok, Thailand, December 2003. Parliament adopted formatting amendments during eighth session of Parliament, Lucknow, India, August 2004.

World Legislative Act # 3
Summary

Act for Ownership, Administration and Development of Oceans and Seabeds of Earth as Common Heritage of People of Earth

1. Declares oceans and seabeds from 20 km. offshore from all countries as Common Heritage of People of Earth, and as World Territory. Declares that Earth Federation owns, administers and develops all oceans and seabeds as World Territory for benefit of Humanity.

2. Declares development and exploitation of ocean resources beyond 20 km. offshore to be under jurisdiction, supervision and administration of World Oceans and Seabeds Authority (WOSA), responsible to Earth Federation under *Earth Constitution*.

3. Declares invalid any claims to any Exclusive Economic Zones or to any ownership of oceans or seabeds or resources thereof beyond 20 km. offshore.

4. Requires Commission for Legislative Review or World Oceans and Seabeds Commission to study Law of the Seas convention to determine provisions in violation of principle of oceans and seabeds as common heritage of humanity, or unconstitutional provisions or provisions in violation of world legislation. Strikes legal validity of unconstitutional provisions of Law of the Sea, and provisions in violation of world legislation.

5. Requires World Oceans and Seabeds Authority to manage, supervise, directly operate or require world licensing for development of mineral, oil, food and other resources of oceans and seabeds from 20 km. offshore.

6. Recognizes that in some provisions, Law of the Sea convention violates principle of oceans and seabeds as common heritage of humanity; specifically prohibits Weapons of Mass Destruction (WMDs), from transit on or within oceans (class 1 felony).

7. Requires World Oceans and Seabeds Authority (WOSA) to develop licensing requirements and require world licenses from 20 km. offshore. Permits WOSA to adopt regulations of International Seabed Authority and Law of the Sea not inconsistent with *Earth Constitution* and world legislation.

8. Creates World Oceans and Seabeds Commission (WOSC) to prepare details for World Oceans and Seabeds Authority. Requires WOSC to report back to subsequent sessions of Provisional World Parliament recommendations regarding conditional adoption of Law of the Sea as world legislation, with repeal of unconstitutional provisions or provisions that violate World Law. Requires WOSC to make recommendations consistent with *Earth Constitution.* Requires recommendations to include listing of recommended repeal of original provisions in Law of the Sea that are inconsistent with *Earth Constitution* or in violation of world legislation. Requires Steering Committee of Provisional World Parliament to appoint five members to compose WOSC. Assigns authority to WOSC to co-opt additional members and consultants.

⊕⊕⊕⊕⊕⊕⊕⊕⊕⊕

The first session of Provisional World Parliament adopted Act #3 on 12 September 1982. Parliament amended the Act during sixth session Provisional World Parliament, meeting at Bangkok, Thailand, December 2003. Parliament adopted formatting amendments during eighth session of Parliament, Lucknow, India, August 2004.

World Legislative Act # 4
Summary

Act for Inaugurating a World University System with a Graduate School of World Problems

Grants Charter for Graduate School of World Problems as part of World University System, under following conditions:

1. Declares purposes of World University System, and of Graduate School of World Problems.

2. Permits national and state level incorporation.

3. Assigns sources for Board of Trustees of nineteen members. Requires Board of Trustees to employ administration for Graduate School and to oversee entire functioning of Graduate School. The Board of Trustees shall elect its own Chairperson and other officers. Requires Board of Trustees to meet at least twice annually.

4. Requires Chancellor to head Graduate School administration. Requires Board of Trustees to elect Chancellor, responsible to Board of Trustees.

5. Assigns sources for Advisory Council of neither less than 24 nor more than 48 members, so as to represent all parts of Earth.

6. Assigns Location for the primary campus of Graduate School to be Radford, Virginia, U.S.A. Assigns locations for other campuses: Institute of Mundialist Studies in France; City Montessori School, Lucknow, India; Ensophion of Humanity in Kalamata, Greece; World Government Institutes (separate entities) in Japan and in USA; Kara, Togo; Toronto, Canada; Colombo, Sri Lanka or Clarkesville, Georgia, USA. Permits Board of Trustees to decide other locations for other campuses.

7. Conditionally permits Board to withdraw local charters.

8. Requires Chancellor to prepare annual budgets for operation of Graduate School, together with annual financial campaigns. Assigns Parliamentary Trustees to prepare initial budget and finance campaign. Requires Board of Trustees and Administration to work together to develop and obtain sources of financing for Graduate School. Assigns non-exclusive sources.

9. Assigns Board of Trustees to be responsible to Provisional World Parliament or World Parliament until more complete World University System is established.

10. Requires Board of Trustees and School Administration to develop and refine further details for Graduate School by working in collaboration.

⊕⊕⊕⊕⊕⊕⊕⊕⊕⊕

The first session of Provisional World Parliament adopted Act #4 on 12 September 1982. Parliament amended the Act during sixth session Provisional World Parliament, meeting at Bangkok, Thailand, December 2003. Parliament adopted formatting amendments during eighth session of Parliament, Lucknow, India, August 2004.

World Legislative Act # 5
Summary

Act for the Establishment of Provisional District World Courts

and Provisional Regional World Courts of the World Supreme Court System, in accordance with Article 19, Sec. E-2, and with Article 4, of the *Constitution for the Federation of Earth*, hereinafter referred to as "*Earth Constitution.*"

Short title: **World Court Act**

1. Establishes Provisional District World Court (PDWC) in Los Angeles, California, U.S.A., and New York City, New York, U.S.A. Permits establishment of additional Provisional District World Courts.

2. Requires PDWCs to operate in conformance with *Earth Constitution*. Requires PDWCs to utilize as Rules those Rules presently in force in highest courts of host country or countries, except when national high court Rules are in contradiction with said *Earth Constitution* or of subsequent resolutions or legislation of Provisional World Parliament or World Parliament or World Supreme Court established under *Earth Constitution*. Declares World Legislative Act Number 24, for Rules of Procedure and Evidence as subsequent legislation.

3. Establishes first Provisional Regional World Court (PRWC) in Los Angeles, California, U.S.A. Permits Provisional World Parliament, or World Supreme Court or Provisional World Supreme Court to establish additional PRWCs in countries and cities. Declares same rules for PRWCs as for PDWCs.

4. Permits World Citizen appeals from any judgment of any PDWC or from any judgment of any PRWC, directly to appropriate Bench of World Supreme Court or Provisional World Supreme Court or to Superior Tribunal of World Supreme Court.

5. Recognizes no necessity for district or regional origin and progression of appeal process.

6. Locates primary seat of Provisional World Supreme Court in Primary World Capital or Los Angeles, California, U.S.A., if primary capital not yet established.

7. Declares judgments of world courts to full force under World Law and International Law, have complete stare decisis effect and are res judicata in World Law and International Law on all issues adjudicated. Empowers PDWCs to fully function.

8. Assigns rules to World Court regarding Service of Process.

9. Declares general boundaries for indefinite terms or periods of operation for Provisional World Courts.

10. Defines juridical competence. Requires three competent Judges to preside World Court.

11. Permits Courts power to adopt local Rules consistent with high court rules and with *Earth Constitution*, and world legislation.

12. Establishes Standing Parliamentary Judicial Commission. Grants authority to implement provisions of Act. Requires standing commission to further carry on work in ways not contrary to provisions of *Earth Constitution.*

⊕⊕⊕⊕⊕⊕⊕⊕⊕⊕

The first session of Provisional World Parliament adopted Act #5 on 16 September 1982. Parliament adopted formatting amendments during eighth session of Parliament, Lucknow, India, August 2004.

Second Session of the Provisional World Parliament, Vigyan Bhavan and Constitution Club, New Delhi, March 1985,

adopted World Legislative Acts #6 through #8.

World Legislative Act # 6 Summary

Emergency Earth Rescue Administration

Lists in preamble 9 systemic climatic and resulting catastrophes. Describes in preamble several concurrent reasons for rapid increase of CO_2 in atmosphere.

1. Creates Emergency Earth Rescue Administration.

2. Requires Emergency Earth Rescue Administration (EERA) to carry out coordinated worldwide emergency campaign on several major fronts concurrently, to overcome increase of CO_2 .

3. Requires EERA to conduct reforestation.

4. Requires EERA to conduct re-mineralization of forest lands, crop lands, selected areas of oceans of Earth, and in man-made lakes.

5. Requires EERA to expedite the transition from fossil fuels to safe and sustainable energy supplies and technology.

6. Requires EERA to conduct publicity.

7. Requires EERA to encourage, foster and coordinate participation of concerned agencies, both public and private, both local, regional, national and international, in common campaign for re-forestation, re-mineralization, and transition to safe and sustainable energy supplies.

8. Declares fronts of the emergency campaign as not limited to those defined herein, and other fronts may be defined and developed by EERA.

9. Assigns sources to create and compose Board of Trustees of up to 200 members, serving terms of five years, to direct and administer the EERA, within the framework and specifications of this World Legislation. Assigns responsibilities and regulations to Board of Trustees. Permits Board of Trustees to establish its own rules of procedure and operating structure within framework and terms of World Legislation and *Earth Constitution.* Requires Board of Trustees to make annual reports to Provisional World Parliament, together with interim reports as necessary.

10. Requires Board of Trustees to elect an Earth Rescue Executive Council (EREC) of 21-33 members to employ key personnel and manage the daily operations of EERA between meetings of the full Board of Trustees. Included ex-officio on the EREC are the three Co-Chairpersons and the Executive Director. The EREC is responsible for preparing the operating budgets for EERA, subject to approval by the Board of Trustees.

11. Requires appropriate salaries payable in Earth credits or Earth currency, amounting to Earth credit or Earth currency equivalent of three million annual equity salaries per year, or more. Designates sources of funding, including sale of Earth Bonds (WLA#7).

12. Assigns structure, purpose and terms for Original Executive Committee.

13. Requires Original Executive Committee to create Global Rescue Teams to seek ratification by national parliaments and national governments, by communities, states and other sub-national political entities, and by corporations and other organizations.

14. Requires election and operation of Parliamentary Commission for EERA of 9 members.

⊕⊕⊕⊕⊕⊕⊕⊕⊕⊕

(Addendum) Specifies non-exhaustively 35 benefits of Emergency Earth Rescue Administration.

⊕⊕⊕⊕⊕⊕⊕⊕⊕⊕

The second session of Provisional World Parliament adopted Act #6 in March 1985. Parliament amended the Act during fourth session (Barcelona, 1996), sixth session (Bangkok, 2003), and eighth session (Lucknow, 2004).

World Legislative Act # 7 Summary

Earth Federation Funding Corporation

Short title: **Funding Act**

Article 1. Creates Earth Federation Funding Corporation (EFFC). Lists purposes: to obtain loans and contributions from both public and private sources; to disburse grants and payments to various agencies that will work to achieve democratic non-military, world federation; to arrange for repayment of loans by Treasury of World Government. Limits loan aggregate.

Article 2. Permits Earth Federation Funding Corporation to contract loans as lump sums, or as annual subscriptions over a period of years. Lists permitted sources for Earth Rescue Loans.

Article 3. Requires Directors and Officers of Earth Federation Funding Corporation (EFFC) to determine approval or declinations of grants and disbursements of loans to best serve and help to achieve purposes of EFFC. Lists Earth Federation agencies to receive loans. Lists Activities for which loans can be put to use: Ratification of *Earth Constitution* and implementation of world legislation.

Article 4. Requires repayment of Earth Rescue Loans according to specified conditions, including repayment schedule, interest to loan creditors, notification of conditions for repayment, and bonus interest for early investors,

Article 5. Defines organizational and operating structure of Earth Federation Funding Corporation to include Board of Directors, Officers, and Executive Committee, Directorate, and Central Bank. Defines composition, terms, and responsibilities of EFFC organizational members. Requires grant applicants to submit applications to Directorate with copies to Central Bank. Requires audit process.

Article 6. Requires Parliamentary Directors to invite up to 300 respected persons from many countries to form prestigious Advisory Board, and/or Board of Honorary Financial Sponsors, to give credibility, status and stability to Earth Federation Funding Corporation.

Article 7. Defines and requires first steps of Earth Federation Funding Corporation:

⊕⊕⊕⊕⊕⊕⊕⊕⊕⊕⊕

The second session of Provisional World Parliament adopted Act #7 in March 1985. Parliament amended the Act during sixth session Provisional World Parliament, meeting at Bangkok, Thailand, December 2003. Parliament adopted formatting amendments during eighth session of Parliament, Lucknow, India, August 2004.

World Legislative Act Number 8
Summary
World Commission on Terrorism

Article 1. Creates World Commission on Terrorism.

Article 2. Defines Terrorism as use of violence against lives or property, or threat to use violence against lives of property, without formal declaration of war, for purpose of trying to achieve objectives that may appear difficult to achieve by peaceful means. Defines violence as use of force or coercion that is unlawful under world legislation and world law.

Article 3. Declares objectives and functions of World Commission on Terrorism (WCT):

Article 4. Composes nucleus of WCT from members of Provisional World Parliament, at minimum of one from each country.

Article 5. Authorizes WCT to invite each country affected by activities of terrorists to send both government and people's representatives to serve on World Commission on Terrorism.

Article 6. Directs WCT to function with liaison to Office of World Attorney General, and in particular, with Investigations Department of Enforcement System.

Article 7. Authorizes WCT to begin work.

Article 8. Directs Earth Federation Funding Corporation to fund WCT.

⊕⊕⊕⊕⊕⊕⊕⊕⊕⊕

The second session of Provisional World Parliament adopted Act #8 in March 1985. Parliament adopted formatting amendments during eighth session of Parliament, Lucknow, India, August 2004.

Third Session of the Provisional World Parliament, Fontainbleau Hilton, Miami Beach, Florida, June 1987

adopted World Legislative Acts #9 through #11.

World Legislative Act # 9 Summary

Global Ministry of Environment

Article 1. Specifies authorizations of Global Ministry of Environment (GME), as follows: Identify major issues of environmental problems; Monitor environmental dangers; Solve world environmental problems on global or transnational scale; and
Implement remedies and prevention of extinctions.

Article 2. Requires Global Ministry of Environment to work with Integrative Complex to solve global environmental problems according to specified directives.

Article 3. Requires Global Ministry of Environment to protect endangered animals and plants. Requires Ministry to review international convention law for integration and codification into World Law, submitting proposals to Commission for Legislative Review:

Article 4. Details further responsibi lities,particularly regarding military, agricultural, transportation and energy industries. Prohibits intentional destruction of surplus food stocks without permit (class 3 felony).
Requires world legislation to prevent food surplus distributions from disrupting local economies.

Article 5. Sets guidelines for developmental projects. Prohibits utilization of public or private funds for any major project without environmental assessment (class 3 felony). Requires permits from GME for major projects. Prohibits beginning or continuing of major project without GME permit (class 3 felony).

Article 6. Creates of Global Ministry of Environment. (GME) Directs Global Ministry of Environment to begin operation. Assigns accountability of Environment Ministry to Provisional World Parliament and Provisional World Cabinet. Directs GME to receive assessments from agencies of Integrative Complex.

Article 7. Defines composition, terms, sources, conditions and responsibilities of Governing Council with 15 to 95 Trusteeship Council Members.

⊕⊕⊕⊕⊕⊕⊕⊕⊕⊕

The third session of Provisional World Parliament adopted Act #9 in June 1987. Parliament amended the act during eighth session of Parliament, Lucknow, India, August 2004.

World Legislative Act # 10
Summary

World Hydrogen Energy System Authority

1. Creates World Hydrogen Energy System Authority (WHESA).

2. Directs WHESA to administrate various tasks to replace existing fossil fuel system with Hydrogen Energy System, including research, education and implementation of technologies, with assistance to each country to convert from present hydrocarbon/carbon fuel system to hydrogen energy system.

3. Composes WHESA administration to include a Minister and General Directors for tasks listing in Article 2. Defines procedure for employing technical and administrative personnel.

4. Assigns conditions for activation of WHESA, including budgetary provisions.

⊕⊕⊕⊕⊕⊕⊕⊕⊕⊕

The third session of Provisional World Parliament adopted Act #10 in June 1987. Parliament amended the Act during sixth session Provisional World Parliament, meeting at Bangkok, Thailand, December 2003. Parliament adopted formatting amendments during eighth session of Parliament, Lucknow, India, August 2004.

World Legislative Act # 11
Summary

Earth Financial Credit Corporation

Article 1. Defines condition of Provisional ratification of *Earth Constitution* by ten national governments for activating Earth Financial Credit Corporation as division of World Economic Development Organization, to introduce new Earth finance, credit, money and banking system.

Article 2. Defines method of introducing and making transition to new Earth finance, credit, money and banking system, by extending multi-billion unit revolving lines of credit in Earth credits or Earth currency to all countries willing to accept terms.

Article 3. [Repealed and reserved. PWP, session 10]

Article 4. Bases the capacity and ability of Earth Financial Credit Corporation to extend lines of credit simply on facts of people available to work, resources available, and technology available, whether within country or by transfer, and not dependent on nor limited by prior savings. Lists further values for extension of financial credit by the EFCC.

Article 5. Lists terms and criteria for extending revolving lines of credit, and for repayment. Requires Provisional ratification of *Earth Constitution* as prerequisite to activating line of credit to nations.

Prohibits misappropriation, theft or unauthorized transfer of world federal property. (class 3 felony)
Prohibits fiscal tampering with records of Provisional World Government – Class 1 felony (WLA#13. 2.22.1.), or tampering with records of World Government – Class 3 felony (WLA#13. 2.22.2.).

Article 6. Composes EFCC Board of Directors to include up to 25 national participant directors or more and 30 world federal directors.

Article 7. Requires EFCC Board of Directors to elect EFCC Board officers from among own number, to include Executive Director and administrative personnel.

Article 8. Requires EFCC Board of Directors to formulate and adopt rules and regulations necessary for operation of EFCC, subject to Executive Cabinet approval.

Article 9. Sets conditions for Procurement Department under separate legislation.

Article 10. Specifies circumstances to initiate Earth Financial Credit Corporation without participation of national governments.

Article 11. Empowers EFCC Board of Directors to introduce and develop Earth Hour credits and currency as global legal tender from a global financial base in offshore World Territory or in zone of existing country where country grants legal extra-territorial status.

Article 12. Requires EFCC to develop more fundamental changes defined by World Legislative Act #11, in conjunction with transitional financial procedures defined in World Legislative Acts #2, #7 and #23.

Article 13. Defines terms to recognize net cash assets of cooperating banks and financial institutions.

Article 14. Establishes Basket of 16 Commodities linked to value of an hour of labor as basis for determining the value of Earth Hour credit or Earth Hour currency: 1 unit of Earth Hour credit or Earth Hour currency = 2 hours labor at minimum wage (@ ⊕0.50 units per hour minimum) = 1/2 hours labor at maximum wage (@⊕2.0 units per hour maximum) [Ed.: where "⊕" is the symbol for the Earth Hour, the standard monetary unit of the Earth Federation. See World Legislative Act #23 or summary thereof.]

Prohibits attempt to adversely influence the value of the Earth credit or Earth currency (class 3 felony).

⊕⊕⊕⊕⊕⊕⊕⊕⊕⊕⊕

The third session of Provisional World Parliament adopted Act #11 in June 1987. Parliament amended the Act during fourth session (Barcelona, 1996),
sixth session (Bangkok, 2003), eighth session (Lucknow, 2004), and 10th session (Kara, 2007).

Fourth Session of the Provisional World Parliament, Barcelona, Spain, 1996

At the fourth session of the Provisional World Parliament, the Parliament adopted amendments to World Legislative Acts #6 and #11. Also, the Parliament declared the Manifesto (of 1996).

The Manifesto (proclamation) of the 4th session of the Provisional World Parliament (Barcelona, 1996), was reconfirmed and ennumerated at the 5th session of the Provisional World Parliament (Qawra, 2000). The proclamation comprises the first world legislative attempt at legislative summary of previously adopted world legislation, together with some modification. As such, the Manifesto of 1996 and 2000 was numbered as an omnibus bill and adopted as World Legislative Act #12 in 2000.

Fifth Session of the Provisional World Parliament, Qawra, Malta, November 2000

adopted World Legislative Act #12.

At the fifth session of the Provisional World Parliament, the Parliament gave the Manifesto (of 1996) enumerated status as an Act of the Parliament.

World Legislative Act #12
Summary
Manifesto (of 1996)

1. Reconfirms possession of all oceans and seabeds of Earth from 20 kilometers offshore of all land masses and island territories of existing nation-states, reserving first 200 miles offshore for priority fishing rights of adjoining countries.
Claims possession of Antarctica, together with all territories and islands that are not already claimed under recognized ownership of nations; Claims airspace above oceans and Antarctica, and stratospheric space of Earth. Claims possession of Earth's moon.

2. Invites and urges participation by nations and national governments. Declares beginning of World Administration.

3. Reconfirms provisions of World Legislative Act #1, to prohibit weapons of mass destruction worldwide, particularly noting prohibition of weapons of mass destruction by sea and air. Assigns penalty for prohibited movements or transport (Class 1 felony); directing violation (Class 2 felony).

4. Activates World Legislative Act Number 11 for an Earth Financial Credit Corporation (EFFC), by pledging total wealth of oceans and seabeds, Antarctica, Earth's Moon and solar system space behind all creation of financial credit per World Legislative Act #11. Declares no requirement or priority for privatization. Grants public sector full access to financial credit for legitimate purposes and to guarantee

full employment for all. Prohibits EFFC credit to be used for military purposes, for nuclear energy production or for burning of hydrocarbons.

5. Activates World Legislative Act Number 6 for Emergency Earth Rescue Administration, to cope with global environmental crisis. Requires annual fiscal allocation for next 50 years, employing all available personnel. Directs that national governments of all countries immediately join Earth Federation by ratifying *Earth Constitution*, to implement world legislation.

6. Requires Standing Parliamentary Commission on Disarmament and World Disarmament Agency to proceed as rapidly as possible to establish full institutional machinery to implement World Legislative Act Number One (de-nuclearization and de-militarization).

7. Enacts provisions for Global Energy Administration, to substitute fossil fuels and nuclear energy by solar energy, hydrogen power, magnetic power, and other sure sources of energy; to build super grid of electric power connecting most of Earth and to decommission all nuclear plants and all oil wells in sea.

8. Reconfirms or recomposes standing Provisional Worldwide Cabinet, to serve three year terms until replacement after 25 countries have ratified *Earth Constitution*, in accordance with Article 19 of the *Earth Constitution*. Lists positions for Provisional Ministers (Commission Chairs), ministries (Standing Commissions), services and agencies for initial election and selection.

9. Elects continuing Provisional Presidium for Provisional World Parliament, and ensuing Provisional Earth Federation, to serve until replacement under provisions of *Earth Constitution*, and to continue until 25 countries have ratified *Earth Constitution*, as defined under Article 19, Section D. of *Earth Constitution*.

10. Directs Presidium to designate locations with five continental areas of Earth as first five World Federal Zones.

⊕⊕⊕⊕⊕⊕⊕⊕⊕⊕⊕

The fourth session of the Provisional World Parliament declared the Manifesto, meeting 1996 at Barcelona, Spain. The fifth session of the Provisional World Parliament reconfirmed the Manifesto as World legislative act #12, meeting 2000 at Qawra, Malta. Parliament amended the Act during sixth session Provisional World Parliament, meeting at Bangkok, Thailand, December 2003. Parliament adopted formatting amendments during eighth session of Parliament, Lucknow, India, August 2004.

Sixth Session of the Provisional World Parliament, Bangkok, Thailand, March 2003,

adopted World Legislative Acts #13 through #18.

World Legislative Act #13 Summary

World Peace Act

Article 1. Abbreviates term "Weapons of Mass Death and Destruction" as "WMDs".

Article 2. Prescribes immediate effective date. Prohibits activities related to WMDs: finance, brokerage, representation, funding, threats, advertisement, bunkers, accidents, intellectual property recognition, borrowing, lending, design or production of exclusive identifiable portions, software programming. Prohibits activities causing social disorder: directing other people to violate World Legislation; military assistance to violators of World Legislation; impeding enforcement or implementation of World Legislation; impeding World Legislatures; use of arms suitable for law enforcement to violate World Legislation; transfer of arms suitable for law enforcement to entities not ratifying the *Earth Constitution*; military blockades; using intelligent animals to violate World Legislation; disrupting telecommunications; designing machine viruses; conscription; tampering with records of World Government. Prohibits bids for war damage, unless bid is to Earth Federation after damage has already taken place. Strikes down Geneva Convention exceptions that permit targeting of civilians and civilian structures. Prohibits targeting of civilians on absolute basis.

Article 3. Prohibits United Nations Security Council veto power or unanimous assent as grounds for initiating acts of war. Permits Security Council recommendation if respective Members ratify *Earth Constitution*.

Article 4. Permits World Attorney General to issue warrants. Confers restriction of enforcement to established World Federal areas. Declares purpose of enforcement as for public protection and restitution. Lists possible enforcements. Imposes civil and criminal penalties, in criminal cases up to life imprisonment with possibility of parole, in civil cases up to loss of all assets excluding minimum necessary for reasonable decent living. Permits conditions for leniency or stringency. Considers complexity of financial instruments. Permits supervised community service at standard minimum living wage to de-mine, decontaminate, disassemble military hardware or perform other work. Imposes progressive enforcement penalties. Permits compilation of credit files on convicts. Upholds suffrage rights of individuals in penal system. Confers civil jurisdiction to World Court. Exempts necessity for criminal code penalty classification until 180 days after commencing first operative stage of World Government. Permits conditional confiscation of property of violators. Permits conditional conversion of munitions plants.

Article 5. Directs universal compliance. Specifies direction to United Nations Center for Disarmament. Requests Provisional World Government to provide public notices.

Article 6. Establishes minesweeping program. Permits deactivation of nuclear weapons. Administrates disbanding of military forces. Permits local defusing of bombs. Confers chemical explosives to Emergency Earth Rescue Administration quarry operations. Establishes missile research program for sodium seeding of ozonosphere.

Article 7. Protects law-abiding veterans and law-abiding retirees, including benefits.

Article 8. Defines less lethal munitions. Restricts government and corporations to less lethal munitions by full operative stage of World Government.

Article 9. Establishes incentives for conversion to less lethal munitions.

Article 10. Declares no statute of limitations for violation of World Legislation.

⊕⊕⊕⊕⊕⊕⊕⊕⊕⊕

The sixth session of Provisional World Parliament adopted the World Peace Act as World Legislative Act #13, in morning session, 26 March 2003, Bangkok, Thailand. The Parliament adopted formatting amendments at the eighth session, August 2004, in Lucknow, Uttar Pradesh, India.

World Legislative Act # 14
Summary

To Create an Office of the World Attorneys General Pro Tempore including Major Departments of the Enforcement System

Short title: **World Security Act**

Article 1. Creates an Office of the World Attorneys General Pro Tempore including Major Departments of the Enforcement System.

Article 2. Calls nomination of World Attorneys General Pro Tempore and Provisional Regional World Attorneys.

Article 3. Integrates Office of World Attorneys General and World Disarmament Agency. Requires World Attorneys General Pro Tempore to hold qualification as Minister of Disarmament. Permits World Disarmament Agency Board of Trustees to set policy regarding disarmament processes of Enforcement System.

Article 4. Defines structure of Enforcement System, including five major departments: Department of Investigation; Department of Apprehension & Arrest; Department of Prosecution; Department of Remedies & Correction; and Department for Conflict Resolution. Lists respective functions for each major department.

Article 5. Permits Offices of World Attorneys General to determine location of first office quarters.

Article 6. Allocates 5% of annual world federal budget to World Attorneys General Office.

Article 7. Permits agents of Provisional World Attorneys General Office to hold two employments to obtain supplemental income, if jurisdictions are represented only at respective levels.

Article 8. Directs reporting procedures for Agencies and Departments.

Article 9. Requires World Police Officers to make an affirmation of loyalty to people of Earth. Subjects World Police Officers to public surveillance and public scrutiny.

Article 10. Mandates World Police Officers to report knowledge or suspicion of official corruption to Internal Affairs.

Article 11. Subjects World Police Officers to registration of weapons possessed while on duty.

Article 12. Subjects World Police Officers to Grand Jury in cases of deaths or permanent injuries associated with performance of duties.

Article 13. Requires Department of Apprehension and Arrest to provide training to World Police.

Article 14. Requires World Police Officers to use the least force necessary. Defines least force necessary. Declares least force necessary as guiding principle of world law enforcement. Subjects World Police Officers to suspension or expulsion for brutality or unnecessary force. Lists unsuitable equipment. Recommends and lists suitable equipment for World Police.

Article 15. Creates structure for World Police, including air, sea, land and space corps. Creates command hierarchy of World Police. Requires periodic rotation of officer assignments.

Article 16. Defines legal requirements of warrants.

Article 17. Permits World Disarmament Agency to determine further organization and functioning of the Office of World Attorneys General.

⊕⊕⊕⊕⊕⊕⊕⊕⊕⊕

The sixth session of Provisional World Parliament adopted the World Security Act as World Legislative Act #14, at 10:30 a.m., 26 March 2003, Bangkok, Thailand.

World Legislative Act # 15
Summary

Statute of the World Court of Human Rights

Declares and lists basis in preamble for Human Rights Bench of World Court. Recounts origin of Human Rights Bench in *Earth Constitution* and in Convention of World Government of World Citizens.

CHAPTER 1

Article 1 STRUCTURE
Comprises World Court of Human Rights as Bench for Human Rights as defined in Article 9, Section B1 of *Earth Constitution*.

Article 2 REMEDIES
Empowers Court to process petitions for writ of World Habeas Corpus and other complaints or communications by and on behalf of individuals if individual security or other human rights are violated without due process of law.

Article 3 THE JURISTS
Composes Regional Courts with Juris-Consults of recognized competence in World Law.

Article 4 JURISDICTION
Defines jurisdiction of Court of Human Rights

Article 5 ASSOCIATE JUSTICES
Requires Presiding Council of World Judges to assign Associate Justices from nominations to preside Regional Courts.

Article 6 TENURE
Defines term of office for judges.

Article 7 REPLACEMENT
Specifies conditions for replacement of judges.

Article 8 INDEPENDENCE
Requires judicial independence with no other professional function.

Article 9 INTEGRITY
Prohibits participation as an agent, counsel or advocate, or in cases if Member judge has previously taken part as agent, counsel or advocate.

Article 10 DISMISSAL
Prohibits dismissal without cause.

Article 11 OATH
Requires oath of every member of Court.

Article 12 REGISTRÁRS, CLERKS, CONSENT
Specifies qualifications for appointment of registrars and clerks without requirement of consent by parties involved or counsels of record.

Article 13 PRESIDING OFFICERS
Defines Chief Justice and Associate Justices as Presiding Officers of respective Tribunals.

Article 14 COURT OF REVIEW
Presiding Judge to designate Associate Justices to accommodate all parties in interest without preventing Court of Review from sitting and exercising functions elsewhere if desirable.

Article 15 PERMANENT SESSION
Requires permanent session of Court of Human Rights.

Article 16 ALTERNATES
Specifies conditions for Alternate Members of Court.

Article 17 FULL COURT
Requires full Court to sit in all judicial venues except when Chief Justice expressly determines otherwise.

Article 18 JUDGMENT
Specifies Circuit Tribunals judgment as subject to review only by Chief Justice and two designated Associate Justices.

Article 19 APPEALS
Specifies conditions for appeals from decision of Regional Tribunals.

Article 20 RULES
Requires Court to occasionally determine Rules of Procedure for carrying out functions.

Article 21 EMOLUMENTS
Provides emoluments for members of Court.

Article 22 COURT EXPENSE
Requires Tribunal to bear the expense of each Regional Court.

CHAPTER 2

Article 23 COMPETENCE
Permits only individuals (natural persons) or groups of individuals to be parties in cases before Court to seek redress for deprivation of any human right.

Article 24 ACCESS TO COURT
Provides access to World Court

Article 25 WORLD BILL OF RIGHTS
Lists and specifies 15 additional rights not necessarily listed in Articles 12 and 13 of *Earth Constitution.*

Article 26 WORLD *HABEAS CORPUS*
Includes those rights designated in Article 25 as types of rights for which violations may result in writ of world *habeas corpus.*

Article 27 SANCTIONS
Empowers sanctions by World Court, World Ombudsmus and Enforcement Department of Earth Federation.

CHAPTER 3

Article 28 SPECIAL COMPETENCE OF CHIEF JUSTICE
Specifies further provisions for appeal from decisions of Circuit Tribunals.

CHAPTER 4

Article 29 VENUE
Requires party to make any petition for Writ of World *Habeas Corpus* to Circuit Tribunal having jurisdiction over place where person is detained, imprisoned or deprived of any other human rights.

Article 30 ALLEGATIONS
Requires specified allegations.

Article 31 *PRIMA FACE* RELIEF
Permits conditionally Associate Justice to find, *prima facie*, that petition is legally sufficient, and, empowers Associate Justice to issue show cause order upon respondent state as to why writ of world habeas corpus should not issue or relief sought should not be granted.

Article 32 SHOW CAUSE
Requires time sensitive show cause order from Court.

Article 33 RETURN TO SHOW CAUSE ORDER
Requires specification in return to show cause order.

Article 34 MOTION TO DISMISS
Allows petitioner time to challenge motion to dismiss.

Article 35 FAILURE TO SHOW CAUSE
Empowers Court to issue writ of world *habeas corpus* and set early date for hearing on relief sought.

Article 36 *SUBPOENAS*
Empowers Court to issue *subpoenas* and *subpoenas duces tecum.*

Article 37 SERVICE
Requires service of process.

Article 38 PRODUCTION OF BODY
Requires production of body as disclosure of custody.

Article 39 INFIRMITY OF PETITIONER
Requires consideration in case of infirmity of petitioner.

Article 40 CUSTODY
Permits direct or supervisory custody by World Court.

Article 41 PROCEEDINGS WITHOUT DELAY
Requires Court to proceed without delay upon respondent's return or answer, to examine cause of imprisonment or restraint, but examination may be adjourned from time to time as circumstances and substantive justice requires.

Article 42 DEFENSE TO RETURN
Permits party imprisoned or restrained to traverse respondent's return or answer.

Article 43 HEARINGS
Provides for alternate Justice in hearings.

Article 44 PUBLIC HEARING
Requires hearing in Court to be public.

Article 45 MINUTES
1) Requires Registrar or Registrar's Assistant to make Minutes of each hearing. Registrar or Assistant appointed for Circuit Tribunals who attends hearing shall sign Minutes, affirming validity; Court minutes are permanent record. Requires Court to make all Minutes publicly available.
2) Requires Court Reporter or Rapporteur to authenticate minutes by oath.

Article 46 FLEXIBILITY OF PROCEDURE
Grants flexibility of procedure to Court for conduct of each case. Requires Court to decide form and time in which each party must conclude presentation of evidence and arguments and make all arrangements connected with presenting or taking of evidence, including deposition form, if necessary.

Article 47 JUDGMENT ON FACT
Declares necessity for judgment on integrity and independence of appropriate, competent, material, relevant and ascertainable fact. Requires Court to proceed exparte if declination persists. Declares unchallenged or unrebutted evidence as *pro confesso* and final.

Article 48 LEGISLATIVE REVIEW
Requires Commission for Legislative Review to review functions of Presiding Judge of this Statute to help determine original intent of World Judicial Commission, which drafted most of this legislative Act.

⊕⊕⊕⊕⊕⊕⊕⊕⊕⊕

The sixth session of the Provisional World Parliament adopted the World Bench for Human Rights Cases as World Legislative Act #15, at 9:50 a.m., 27 March 2003, Bangkok, Thailand.

World Legislative Act #16

Summary

World Hydrocarbon Resource Act

Mundializes all as yet unmined natural hydrocarbon resources on Earth, creating World Hydrocarbon Reserve Board for proper regulation of use of this common heritage of humanity.

1. Accountability - Defines World Hydrocarbon Reserve Board accountable to World Executive.

2. Minister of World Resources - Permits World Parliament to nominate Minister or Commission Chair of World Resources to head World Hydrocarbon Reserve Board. Prohibits Minister of Energy from heading World Hydrocarbon Reserve Board. Declares world hydrocarbons not viable fuel available for unregulated combustion by world public, but instead source for durable, recyclable plastics and lubricants for now and for generations to come. Lists responsibilities and powers of Minister or Commission Chair of World Resources, including consideration for licenses, issuance of licenses, fines, other penalties and tax assessments.

3. Advisory Board - Creates and defines functions of Advisory Board of World Hydrocarbon Reserve Board.

4. Composition of the Advisory Board - Defines Composition of Advisory Board, with membership from specified agencies of Earth Federation and from specified existing international agencies that ratify *Earth Constitution*. Defines rules for suspension or expulsion.

5. Licensees - Permits license requirements of persons and organizations that work with hydrocarbon resources.

6. Authority of License - Disavows authority of national level licenses without world license.

⊕⊕⊕⊕⊕⊕⊕⊕⊕⊕

The sixth session of Provisional World Parliament unanimously adopted the World Hydrocarbon Resource Act as World Legislative Act #16 at 5:10 p.m., 26 March 2003, Bangkok, Thailand.

World Legislative Act #17

Summary

To Implement the Commission for Legislative Review

1. Inaugurates Commission for Legislative Review to function on Provisional basis. Guides Provisional World Parliament to elect up to twelve of its members to serve on Provisional Commission. Requires World Parliament to reconstitute Commission for Legislative Review according to guidelines of *Earth Constitution*, Article VIII. Sec. H – 2, upon commencement of first operative stage of World Government.

2. Lists complementary roles of Commission for Legislative Review.

3. Requires Members of World Parliament to abide by form, style and codification regulations of Commission for Legislative Review, subject to

regulation by World Parliament, by simple majority vote in joint session.

4. Permits World Court process for suspected unconstitutional legislative provision. Permits publication of world legislation in a labeled recommended form.

5. Permits Commission for Legislative Review to compile, codify and publish a list of suggested amendments to *Earth Constitution*. Permits Commission for Legislative Review to recommend to World Constituent Assembly.

6. Establishes basic guidelines for legislative drafting.

⊕⊕⊕⊕⊕⊕⊕⊕⊕⊕⊕

The sixth session of Provisional World Parliament adopted the Commission for Legislative Review, March 2003, at Bangkok, Thailand.

World Legislative Act #18 Summary

Provisional Office of World Revenue

Establishes Provisional Office of World Revenue.

1. Authorizes Provisional Office of World Revenue to collect taxes forthwith. Authorizes tax collection primarily from rents on use of world commons, including following:
1.1. Land rents;
1.2. Mining surcharges;
1.3. Resource utilization fees, including sales taxes on hydrocarbon resources and carbon resources;
1.4. Technology rents;
1.5. Currency transactions; and
1.6. Electromagnetic spectrum rents;

2. Requires Provisional Office of World Revenue (POWR) to draft, recommend and submit to Parliament franchise tax schedule against sales of recreational drugs, including alcohol and tobacco.

3. Permits Provisional Office of World Revenue to collect annual poor tax at rate of 1/100th of 1% of net worth of every person. Lists taxable persons to include individuals, corporations and governments

4. Requires Provisional Office of World Revenue to operate collections department to encourage tax payment. Permits Provisional Office of World Revenue to report failure to pay rents or other taxes to Earth Financial Credit Corporation for enforcement. Defines tax evasion as intentional refusal or neglect to pay taxes owed to government.
Permits tax avoidance. Prohibits global tax evasion (class 3 misdemeanour).

5. Requires Provisional Office of World Revenue (POWR) to operate standards department to create tax schedule proposals and other tax proposals. Requires POWR to coordinate with agencies of Integrative Complex. Requires POWR to submit tax schedule proposals and other tax proposals at least annually to Provisional World Parliament.

6. Requires Provisional Office of World Revenue (POWR) to coordinate with lower levels of jurisdiction that have ratified *Earth Constitution*, to track cases of tax evasion at every level.

7. Permits Provisional Office of World Revenue (POWR) to operate exchange offices, receiving national currencies, Special Drawing Rights (SDRs), or Local Economic Trading Systems (LETS) until transition to Earth monetary system is complete. Requires POWR to endeavour to collect taxes in Earth credits or Earth currency. Requires POWR to reimburse overpayment of taxes exclusively in terms of Earth credits or Earth currency.

8. Schedules Provisional Office of World Revenue to begin operations in most suitable location or locations for beginning tax collection. Requires Members of Provisional World Parliament able and willing to begin this work to report at successive sessions of Provisional World Parliament.

⊕⊕⊕⊕⊕⊕⊕⊕⊕⊕⊕

The sixth session of Provisional World Parliament adopted the Provisional Office of World Revenue 27 March 2003. Parliament adopted amendments at seventh session, December 2003 and at eighth session in August 2004.

Seventh Session of the Provisional World Parliament, Chennai, Tamil Nadu, India, December 2003

adopted World Legislative Acts #19 through #25.

World Legislative Act #19 Summary

Criminal Code Penalty Classification

Short Title: **World Penal Code**

Adopts Act for Criminal Code Penalty Classification.

1. Defines criminal offences as divided into seven felony classifications, three misdemeanour classifications and petty offences.

1.1. Presumes term of imprisonment for each felony, except for class 1 felonies. This term may be increased or decreased depending on the nature of offence, defendant's criminal history and existence of any mitigating or aggravating circumstances.

1.2. Requires Penal Department to work together with Department of Convict Management, Probation & Parole to design less disruptive and more humane measures for managing penal system, to include electronically supervised house arrest or electronically supervised internal exile within Earth Federation.

1.3. Requires World Ombudsmus to monitor criminal justice system and to take legal action if system or parts of system are in violation of basic human

rights, as listed in *Earth Constitution*, Article 12, in Statute of World Court of Human Rights (World Legislative Act #15) or in other generally recognized Bills of Rights.
1.4. Permits imposition of fines.

2. Requires draft proposals for new world legislation or amendments containing penal provisions to previously existing world legislation or to generally accepted international law, to state criminal penalty as classified offence, at end of any section or provision defining prohibited activity. Directs Commission for Legislative Review to insert respective penalty classifications defined in addendum into respective sections or provisions of previously adopted world legislation of Provisional World Parliament.

3. Schedules jail and prison terms according to classification of offence.

4. Schedules payment of fines by individual convicts according to classification of offence and projected income of convict.

5. Schedules payment of fines for enterprises according to classification of offence and projected income of enterprise, except in cases of license revocation, in which case convicted enterprise may forfeit all assets.

6. Defines Petty offences as all lesser offences with no imprisonment authorized.

7. Defines mitigating and aggravating circumstances.

8. Defines extenuating circumstances for reducing penalties or dropping criminal charges, or otherwise dismissing case.

9. Recommends World Court to investigate causes of offence, if Court convicts person for third or further offense.

Includes Addendum cross-referencing list of penalty classifications applied to world legislation. Lists additional crimes with respective classifications. Lists penalty classifications to *Elements of Crimes*.
Requires Enforcement System and World Courts to consider constitutionality in any cases resulting from violations defined in *Elements of Crimes*.
Requires more severe sentencing in cases where violator directs another to commit world crime, applicable in cases resulting from violations listed in *Elements of Crimes* as well as within all world legislative acts.

⊕⊕⊕⊕⊕⊕⊕⊕⊕⊕

The seventh session of the Provisional World Parliament adopted the World Penal Code as World Legislative Act #19,
on 28 December 2003, Chennai, Tamil Nadu, India. The Parliament adopted formatting amendments at the eighth session (Lucknow, 2004).

World Legislative Act #20
Summary
World Bench for Criminal Cases

(Underlined sections amended to original International Criminal Court Statute during act adoption by the Provisional World Parliament, in Seventh Session at Chennai (Madras), India, December 2003)

Adopts Act to establish World Bench for Criminal Cases.

PART 1. ESTABLISHMENT OF THE COURT

Article 1 (A-1) Establishes World Bench for Criminal Cases ("the Court") as permanent institution with power to exercise its jurisdiction over persons for most serious crimes of world concern, complementary to national criminal jurisdictions.

A-2 Establishes mandatory jurisdiction judicial relationship of World Court to United Nations.

A-3 Establishes seats of World Court.

A-4 Defines Legal status and powers of World Court.

PART 2. JURISDICTION, ADMISSIBILITY AND APPLICABLE LAW

A-5 Lists Crimes within jurisdiction of World Court, extending from original Rome Statute to also include environmental crimes, world federal corruption and interference in world government.

A-6,7,8 Defines world crimes: crime of genocide, crimes against humanity, war crimes, crime of aggression, environmental crimes, world federal corruption and interference in world government.

A-9 Outlines purpose of *Elements of Crimes*.

A-10 Permits independent development of binding world law.

A-11 Declares immediate date of entry into force.

A-12,13 Defines jurisdiction of World Court.

A-14,15 Defines roles of World Attorneys General, Presidium and World Ombudsmus with respect to World Court.

A-16 Prohibits Security Council representatives to deny or defer jurisdiction (class 3 felony).

A-17,18,19 Defines issues of admissibility. Grants jurisdiction to World Court in event of national judicial incapacity.

A-20 Reconfirms human right of freedom from double jeopardy within World Court (*Ne bis in idem.*) Prohibits secret trials and binding mock trials, (*ad hoc* tribunals or kangaroo courts) (class 3 to 6 felony).

A-21. Cites applicable law.

PART 3. GENERAL PRINCIPLES OF CRIMINAL LAW

A-22 *Nullum crimen sine lege.* Reconfirms principle of no ex-post-facto prosecution.

A-23 *Nulla poena sine lege.* Declares World Legislative criminal classification necessary for penal sentences.

A-24 Reconfirms that criminal responsibility is not retroactive (*ratione personae*)

A-25 Confirms that individuals are liable for crimes. Defines criminal responsibility.
A-26 Excludes juvenile jurisdiction from Criminal Bench. Refers to world legislation for juvenile bench [Ed. note: 2004 amendment. WLA#28 was adopted at 8th session in Lucknow, August 2004].
A-27 Declares irrelevance of official capacity. Declares all officials fully liable to prosecution and sentencing.
A-28 Declares all commanders and other superiors fully liable to prosecution and sentencing.
A-29 Re-confirms world crimes as not subject to any statute of limitations.
A-30 Considers mental element.
A-31 Defines grounds for excluding criminal responsibility based on mental disease or defect.
A-32 Considers instance of mistake of fact or mistake of law.
A-33 Considers exceptions regarding superior orders and prescription of law, with orders to commit genocide, crimes against humanity, war crimes or to otherwise violate world legislation manifestly unlawful.

PART 4. COMPOSITION AND ADMINISTRATION OF THE COURT

A-34 Establishes organs of World Court: Presidency (Presiding Council); Appeals Division, Trial Division, & Pre-Trial Division; Registry; Prosecutor (World Attorneys General)
A-35 Defines service of judges.
A-36 Defines qualifications, nomination and election of judges.
A-37 Defines procedure in event of judicial vacancies.
A-38 Defines Presidency with Chief Justice and Associate Chief Justices.
A-39 Defines Chambers.
A-40 Requires independence of judges.
A-41 Defines conditions for excusing and disqualification of judges.
A-42 Defines & reconfirms Office of Prosecutor (World Attorney General)
A-43 Defines and establishes Registry and functions of Registrar.
A-44 Defines and establishes Staff for Registry and World Attorneys General.
A-45 Requires solemn undertaking by judges, attorneys, & registrars to affirm and uphold *Earth Constitution*.
A-46 Defines conditions for removal from office of judges, prosecutors or registrars.
A-47 Allows disciplinary measures for less serious misconduct.
A-48 Defines privileges and immunities regarding World Court over national jurisdictions.
A-49 Defines process for salaries, allowances and expenses.
A-50 Establishes Arabic, Chinese, English, French, Russian, Spanish and Esperanto as official languages of Court. Establishes French and English as working languages.
A-51 Declares role and conditions for Rules of Procedure and Evidence.
A-52 Grants Judges authority to adopt conditional Regulations of the Court.

PART 5. INVESTIGATION AND PROSECUTION

A-53 Defines conditions for initiation of investigation.

A-54 Defines duties and powers of Prosecutor with respect to investigations.
A-55 Re-confirms rights of persons during an investigation, including right to competent interpretation & right to own counsel.
A-56 Defines role of Pre-Trial Chamber in relation to unique investigative opportunities.
A-57 Defines functions and powers of the Pre-Trial Chamber.
A-58 Defines issuance by Pre-Trial Chamber of warrants of arrest or summons to appear.
A-59 Defines arrest proceedings in the custodial State during Provisional World Government and first operative stage of World Government.
A-60 Defines initial proceedings before World Court.
A-61 Requires confirmation of charges before trial.

PART 6. THE TRIAL

A-62 Establishes conditionally Court Seat as place of trial.
A-63 Requires conditionally presence of accused in trial.
A-64 Defines functions and powers of Trial Chamber.
A-65 Prescribes proceedings on admission of guilt.
A-66 Requires presumption of innocence until conviction.
A-67 Defines and re-confirms rights of accused.
A-68 Requires protection of victims and witnesses and their participation in proceedings.
A-69 Defines procedure for submission of evidence.
A-70 Defines offences against administration of justice.
A-71 Permits Court sanctions for misconduct before World Court.
A-72 Allows conditional protection of national security information only for world citizens and states Members of Earth Federation.
A-73 Establishes procedure regarding third-party information or documents.
A-74 Defines requirements for decision.
A-75 Considers reparations to victims.
A-76 Establishes procedure for sentencing.

PART 7. PENALTIES

A-77 Defines generally applicable penalties, in terms of imprisonment, fines and forfeiture of benefits derived from the crime. Refers to Criminal Code Penalty Classification (Penal Code).
A-78 Defines guidelines for determination of sentence.
A-79 Directs Assembly of States Parties to Establish Trust Fund for victims.
A-80 Declares non-prejudice to national application of penalties and national laws.

PART 8. APPEAL AND REVISION

A-81 Defines grounds & procedure for appeal against decision of acquittal, or conviction or against sentence. Permits Court to suspend execution of decision or sentence during period allowed for appeal and for duration of appeal proceedings.
A-82 Defines Appeal conditions.
A-83 Defines appeal powers & proceedings.

A-84 Defines grounds for revision of conviction or sentence.
A-85 Recognizes right to compensation of wrongly arrested or convicted person.

PART 9. INTERNATIONAL COOPERATION AND JUDICIAL ASSISTANCE

A-86 Declares general obligation to cooperate with Court.
A-87 Establishes role of Court orders for cooperation with general provisions.
A-88 Requires availability of procedures under national law.
A-89 Defines procedure for surrender of persons to World Court.
A-90 Declares World Court precedence in cases of requests competing to court orders.
A-91 Defines contents of order for arrest and surrender.
A-92 Defines orders for Provisional arrest.
A-93 Defines and prescribes other forms of cooperation.
Prohibits World Court assistance to States attacking, Earth Federation or Earth Federation member states.
A-94 Permits conditionally postponement of execution of order in respect of ongoing investigation or prosecution.
A-95 Permits conditionally postponement of execution of order in respect of admissibility challenge.
A-96 Defines contents of order for other forms of assistance under article 93.
A-97 Requires States to consult with World Court in case of conflict, uncertainty or confusion.
A-98 Prohibits refusal to cooperate with world federal court on grounds of immunity (Class 3 felony).
A-99 Clarifies requirement for execution of orders under articles 93 and 96.
A-100 Requires cost accounting. Allocates installments of reimbursement in Earth Credits of court costs to States Party to *Earth Constitution.*
A-101 Requires specialty of charges.
A-102 Defines terms:
(1) "Surrender" means delivering up of person by State to World Court, pursuant to this Statute.
(2) "Extradition" means delivering up of person by one State to another as provided by treaty, convention or national legislation.
(3) "Request" means petition from one State to another, or from one state to World Court.
(4) "Order" means binding directive from World Court.
(5) "Consultation" means two-way communication that is not merely report.

PART 10. ENFORCEMENT

A-103 Defines role of States and Earth Federation in enforcement of sentences of imprisonment.
A-104 Permits World Court change in designation of State of enforcement.
A-105 Requires enforcement of sentence, subject to World Court.
A-106 Defines supervision of enforcement of sentences and conditions of imprisonment.
A-107 Defines conditions for transfer of person upon completion of sentence.
A-108 Limits conditionally prosecution or punishment of other offences.

A-109 Requires enforcement of fines and forfeiture measures. Requires fines to be in Earth Hour credits or Earth Hour currency.

A-110 Permits review by World Court concerning reduction of sentence.

A-111 Permits response to escape.

PART 11. ASSEMBLY OF STATES PARTIES

A-112 Defines functions & powers of Assembly of States Parties in relation to *Earth Constitution*. Permits State Party to pay financial contribution in terms of Earth credits.

PART 12. FINANCING

A-113 Establishes financial regulations for Assembly of States Parties.

A-114 Requires payment of expenses in standard unit of Earth Hour credit or currency.

A-115 Permits conditionally revenues of other types.

A-116 Permits voluntary contributions. Declares voluntary contributions conditionally eligible for reimbursement (FEC, Article 17., Section 6.)

A-117 Directs assessment of contributions to be determined in Earth Hour credit or currency.

A-118 Requires independent annual audit.

PART 13. FINAL CLAUSES

A-119 Defines conditions for settlement of disputes concerning judicial functions, to include primarily World Court, but also Assembly of States Parties, World Parliament, World Ombudsmus or International Bench, when formed.

A-120 Prohibits national reservations to this Statute.

A-121 Defines process for amendments to the Statute.

A-122 Defines process for amendments to provisions of institutional nature.

A-123 Defines procedure for review of World Court Statute within seven years of entry into force.

A-124 Reserved by the Parliament (Strikes seven year allowance to renege & deny compulsory jurisdiction of World Court.)

A-125 Defines conditions for signature, ratification, acceptance, approval or accession. Prohibits direct national signature or approval of revised Statute for World Bench of Criminal Court. Recommends simultaneous accession to *Earth Constitution* by minimum of approximately two dozen national governments, World Parliament of which can confirm, amend or strike down this Statute, in joint session, or severally.

A-126 Declares immediate entry into force for operations of World Bench of Criminal Court, binding upon individuals and States Parties, upon adoption by Provisional World Parliament. Declares Court itself bound by this Statute upon deposit of 25th instrument of national ratification, or by conditions defined in *Earth Constitution*, Article 17, Section C-1.

A-127 Reserved by the Parliament (Strikes original allowance for national withdrawal from Statute.)

A-128 Requires deposit of authentic texts, as soon as feasible, with Presidium of Earth Federation.

⊕⊕⊕⊕⊕⊕⊕⊕⊕⊕

The seventh session of the Provisional World Parliament adopted the World Bench for Criminal Cases at Chennai, Tamil Nadu, India, 27th day of December 2003. The Parliament adopted formatting amendments at the eighth session of the Provisional World Parliament (Lucknow, 2004).

World Legislative Act #21 Summary

Department of World Patents and Intellectual Property Rights

Explains rationale for act in preamble

1. Creates Department of World Patents and Intellectual Property Rights as a ministry of the World Administration.

2. Describes functions of the Department of World Patents and Intellectual Property Rights:

2.1. To categorize IPRS into generas and types as appropriate for systematic registry and regulation worldwide.

2.2. To standardize IPRS into fair and equitable system inexpensively and easily available to all worlds citizens and businesses.

2.3. To devise system of royalties on patents and property rights that rewards and protects innovators while simultaneously maximizing technology transfer for rapid sustainable development worldwide.

2.4. To protect traditional cultures and indigenous peoples from intellectual piracy through unjustifiable use of patent powers.

2.5. To work closely with Agency for Technological and Environmental Assessment and other relevant agencies to monitor genetic engineering and other possibly dangerous technologies and regulate permits for development of technologies for protection of people of Earth.

2.6. To present Department's research and conclusions on above items to World Parliament for possible enactment into law.

⊕⊕⊕⊕⊕⊕⊕⊕⊕⊕

The Provisional World Parliament adopted the Patents Act as World Legislative Act #21 in Chennai, Tamil Nadu, India, 28 December 2003.

World Legislative Act #22 Summary

Act for Promotion of Economic Equity within the Earth Federation with global standards for wages and salaries

Short title: **Economic Equity Act**

Adopts Act for Promotion of Economic Equity through Global Living Wage with global standards for wages and salaries.

1. Requires Earth Federation to calculate gross domestic product. Defines gross economic product (GEP) of Earth Federation as sum total of productive and service activities that serve actual production of wealth within Earth Federation, excluding factors that actually detract from increased wealth.

2. Requires Earth Federation to calculate number of hours worked by all workers within Earth Federation and divide GEP by total work hours spent to produce that GEP to get average wage per hour worked. Defines this figure as Federal Wage and Price Standard. Defines Earth Currency value to tie to Federal Wage and Price Standard so that Earth currency value does not fluctuate through speculation, inflation, or manipulation. Universally defines standards.

3. Requires annual review of maximum and minimum wage or basket of commodities.

4. Requires annual recalculation of definition of "full time work" as average hours worked per worker-week to produce the GEP minus percentage rate of unemployment within Earth Federation.

5. Sets highest legal limit of personal income, including investment income as no more than four times that of minimum wage.

6. Requires excess income to be either taxed off or delivered to business or non-profit organization.

7. Permits salary differentials only on experience, competency and merit.

8. Declares aim of living wage.

9. Defines Salary Scales for personnel of all organs, departments, bureaus, offices, commissions and agencies of Earth Federation. Minimum wage is set at ⊕0.50 Earth Hours per hour and maximum wage is set at ⊕2.00 Earth Hours per hour.
[Ed.: where "⊕" is the symbol for the Earth Hour, the standard monetary unit of the Earth Federation. See World Legislative Act #23 or summary thereof.]

10. Requires maximum and minimum wage compliance in acceptance of private contractors' bids.

11. Requires Earth Federation agency promotion to persons and groups that are seeking global standards and world currency, to build network for launching new currency system.

12. Defines process for determination of World Parliament salaries within limits of minimum and maximum wage, and under popular electoral control by plebiscite.

⊕⊕⊕⊕⊕⊕⊕⊕⊕⊕

The seventh session of the Provisional World Parliament adopted the Equity Act at Chennai, Tamil Nadu in December 2003. The Parliament adopted amendments during eighth session, 11 August 2004 at Lucknow, Uttar Pradesh, India, and during tenth session at Kara, Togo, West Africa (2007).

World Legislative Act #23
Summary

Global Accounting and Auditing Standards using the work of the International Accounting Standards Board as the rational basis

Short Title: **Account Standards Act**

Commends the International Accounting Standards Board.

Adopts Global Accounting Standards for all world federal economic activities.

Article 1 - Defines Basis for Global standards currently set by International Accounting Standards Board as standards of the Provisional World Government and World Government, to be used in all internal and external operations.

Article 2 - Implementation

2.1. Requires major offices of Earth Federation to acquire and maintain a copy of International Accounting Standards in paper form or on electronic disk. Requires economic supervisory and regulatory officers of Earth Federation to read to understand International Accounting Standards.

2.2. Requires accountants of the Earth Federation to provide proof of certification in International Accounting Standards, or to take a competency exam to demonstrate familiarity with Standards. Assigns responsibility to World Economic Development Organization to develop and provide exam, if no standards exam is available from International Accounting Standards Board. Permits World Financial Administration or World Economic Development Organization to approve or require adjustments to certification process.

2.3. Permits World Economic Development Organization to cooperate with International Accounting Standards Board, and permits advice of the International Accounting Standards Board before taking economic decisions.

2.4. Requires corporations, institutions, groups or individuals contracting privately to Earth Federation to keep records according to Global Accounting Standards. Requires economic reports and projections to conform to Global Accounting Standards.

2.5. Requires Earth Federation to use global unit of credit in fiscal operations, rather than any particular national unit. Permits Earth Federation agencies and offices to supplementarily convert records, reports and projections to particular national unit, but not to use solely national unit as basic unit of accounting in records and computations.

2.6. Requires any corporation, institution, group or individual contracting privately to Earth Federation to keep records, and to submit records, projections or proposals using global unit of credit in fiscal operations, and permits supplementary conversion of records, reports and projections to and from particular national unit.

Article 3 - Name of Unit

3.1. Amends all reference to Earth Dollar in previous world legislation. Names "Earth Hour" unit of Earth Federation credit and currency.

3.2. [Reserved.]

3.3. Requires agencies and offices of Provisional Earth Federation to use term "Hour" or "Earth Hour" to refer to unit of Earth Federation credit or currency in all of recordkeeping, reports, budgets, projections, proposals and other official communications.

3.4. Defines Earth Hour as divisible.

Article 4 - Symbol of Unit

Assigns the symbol designation of Earth Hour units as the astronomical symbol for Earth (⊕). Explains rationale for ⊕ symbol. Allows alternate symbols (⊗) and (&).

Article 5 - Promotion of the Global Accounting Standards

Directs offices and agencies of Provisional Earth Federation to take proactive stance to promote of Global Accounting Standards, together with International Accounting Standards of International Accounting Standards Board. Explains rationale. Requires offices and agencies of the Provisional Earth Federation to consider advice and directives of International Accounting Standards in financial operations.

Article 6 - Sovereignty over the International Accounting Standards

Declares sovereignty of Earth Federation for adjustments in global standards as necessary. Defines requirements for amendment.

⊕⊕⊕⊕⊕⊕⊕⊕⊕⊕⊕

The seventh session of the Provisional World Parliament adopted the Account Standards Act, Chennai, Tamil Nadu India, December 2003. The Parliament adopted amendments at the tenth session, meeting in Kara, Togo, West Africa, in June 2007.

World Legislative Act #24

Summary

*Rules of Procedure and Evidence**

* Editor's explanatory note: *The Rules of Procedure and Evidence* are an instrument for the application of the World Bench for Criminal Cases (World Legislative Act #20, originally the *Rome Statute of the International Criminal Court*), to which the *Rules* are subordinate in all cases. The original *Rules of Procedure and Evidence* were drafted by jurists and deliberated by the Assembly of States Parties. The Provisional World Parliament version of the *Rules of Procedure and Evidence* vary from the Assembly of States Parties version in only a little more than one page of changes in about 100 pages of text. Much of this change was the requirement for the *Rules*

to accommodate a world jury system, the former lack of which was one of the true reasons that many nations have not been willing to accede to the World Court jurisdiction. Additionally, the changes were to bring certain provisions of the *Rules* into conformance with the *Earth Constitution.* From the world parliamentary perspective, the World Court has mandatory jurisdiction and the power of *mandamus,* that is, the power of the court order, not in the original ICC Rome Statute.

In elaborating the *Rules of Procedure and Evidence,* care has been taken to avoid rephrasing and, to the extent possible, repeating the provisions of Act #20. Direct references to the Statute have been included in the *Rules,* where appropriate, to emphasize the relationship between the *Rules* and the Statute, as provided for in article 51, in particular, paragraphs 4 and 5. In all cases, the *Rules of Procedure and Evidence* should be read in conjunction with and subject to the provisions of the Statute (#20). The *Rules of Procedure and Evidence* of the International Criminal Court do not affect the procedural rules for any national court or legal system for the purpose of national proceedings.

The *Rules* are subdivided into 226 specific rules, which are not reflected in the summary codification below, and are only partly reflected in the Summary Memorandum in the second volume of *Emerging World Law.* The editors recommend the reading of the full text of the Assembly of States Parties' version, which is available at www.icc-cpi.int and at www.iccnow.org. The Summary Memorandum gives a clear picture of how the two versions differ.

Short Title: ***The Rules***

Chapter 1. Defines general provisions
1.1. Refers to use of terms. Refers to Chief Justice as President. Refers to World Attorneys General as Prosecutor. Refers to Regional World Attorneys as Deputy Prosecutor.
1.2. Declares authentic texts.
1.3. Defines procedure for Rules amendments.

Chapter 2. Defines composition and administration of the Court
2.1. Defines general provisions relating to the composition and administration of the Court.
2.2. Defines Office of Prosecutor.
2.3. Defines Registry.
2.3.1. Provides general provisions relating to the Registry.
2.3.2. Defines Victims and Witnesses Unit.
2.3.3. Defines counsel for the defence.
2.4. Addresses situations that may affect the functioning of the Court.
2.4.1. Defines procedures for removal from office and disciplinary measures.
2.4.2. Defines procedure for excusing, disqualification, death and resignation of judge.
2.4.3. Permits replacements and alternate judges.
2.4.5. Directs and requires publication, languages and translation.

Chapter 3. Jurisdiction and admissibility
3.1. Defines declarations and referrals relating to articles 11, 12, 13 and 14.

3.2. Defines and requires initiation of investigations under article 15.
3.3. Defines challenges and preliminary rulings under articles 17, 18 and 19.

Chapter 4. Defines provisions relating to various stages of the proceedings
4.1. Defines procedures with evidence.
4.2. Defines rules for disclosure.
4.3. Defines victims and witnesses.
4.3.1. Defines general principle relating to victims.
4.3.2. Requires protection of victims and witnesses.
4.3.3. Permits participation of victims in the proceedings.
4.4. Defines miscellaneous provisions.

Chapter 5. Investigation and prosecution
5.1. Defines decision of the Prosecutor regarding the initiation of an investigation under article 53, paragraphs 1 and 2.
5.2. Defines procedure under article 53, paragraph 3.
5.3. Defines rules for collection of evidence.
5.4. Defines procedures in respect of restriction and deprivation of liberty.
5.5. Defines proceedings with regard to the confirmation of charges under article 61.

Chapter 6. Defines trial procedure

Chapter 7. Defines penalties

Chapter 8. Provides for appeal and revision.
8.1. Defines general provisions.
8.2. Defines procedure for appeals against convictions, acquittals, sentencces and reparation orders.
8.3. Defines conditions and procedure for appeals against other decisions.
8.4. Defines procedure for revision of conviction or sentence.

Chapter 9. Offences and misconduct against the Court
Section 1. Defines offences against the administration of justice under article 70.

Section 2. Defines misconduct before the Court under article 71.

Chapter 10. Defines conditions for compensation to an arrested or convicted person.

Chapter 11. International cooperation and judicial assistance.
Section 1. Defines orders and requests for cooperation under article 87.
Section 2. Defines surrender, transit and competing requests under articles 89 and 90.
Section 3. Defines rules for documents of arrest and surrender under articles 91 and 92.
Section 4. Requires cooperation under article 93
Section 5. Requires cooperation under article 98
Section 6. Defines rule of speciality under article 101 .

Chapter 12. Defines Enforcement
Section 1. Defines role of States in enforcement of sentences of imprisonment and change in designation of State of enforcement under articles 103 and 104.

Section 2. Defines enforcement, supervision and transfer under articles 105, 106 and 107.
Section 3. Limits prosecution or punishment of other offences under article 108.
Section 4. Defines enforcement of fines, forfeiture measures and reparation orders.
Section 5. Permits measures under article 111 in event of escape.

Chapter 13. Permits Jury Process

Nominates a Jury Development Commission, to begin with four members, but to extend to 10 members of World Parliament, to elaborate propositions for Criminal Bench to be tempered by benefit of regulated jury process. Directs Jury Development Commission to elaborate rules to integrate well regulated and just world jury system within context of Earth Federation and *Rules of Procedure and Evidence.* Directs World Jury Commission to report back to World Parliament with bill proposal for adjustment of *Rules of Procedure and Evidence* to accommodate jury process. Requires simple majority approval of World Parliament for adoption of jury process provisions. Directs that jury process at world federal level is under jurisdiction of World Ombudsmus. Separates funding of jury process from budget of World Attorneys General Office and from budget of Benches of World Judiciary, except in matters regarding facilities management and integration of various primary branches of world government. Exempts Assembly of States Parties and World Bench of Criminal Court from covering costs of jury process, except regarding facilities management (reasonable accommodation costs for juror participation and sequesters, which World Treasury shall reimburse). Exempts Assembly of States Parties and World Bench from costs for juror selection and juror compensation, which costs are part of budget of World Ombudsmus.

⊕⊕⊕⊕⊕⊕⊕⊕⊕⊕

The Seventh Session of the Provisional World Parliament adopted *The Rules of Procedure and Evidence* as World Legislative Act #24, Chennai, Tamil Nadu, India, December 2003.

Eighth Session of the Provisional World Parliament, City Montessori School, Lucknow, Uttar Pradesh, India, August 2004

adopted World Legislative Acts #25 through #30.

World Legislative Act #25 Summary

Standards of Preservation of World Government Records

Short Title: **Records Act**

Creates standards of care for records of Provisional World Government and world government.

1. Defines World Government Records.

2. Defines stewarding agency.

3. Permits assignment of original records to stewarding agencies, with power to require original copies delivered to Earth Federation agencies at cost.

4. Permits conditional private retention of documents, if documents are made available for viewing and copy on demand.

5. Permits conditional availability to public.

6. Prohibits removal of original world government records from secured stewarding agency facilities (unauthorized misappropriation, theft or transfer of world federal property – Class 3 felony).

7., 8. 9., & 10. Specify storage condition requirements.

11. Requires stewarding agency to preserve each record. If particular record seems worthless, stewarding agency may notify the Institute on Governmental Procedures and World Problems. Prohibits stewarding agency from destruction of any record, or part of any record, unless Institute on Governmental Procedures and World Problems determines that record is not valuable testimony.

11.1. Prohibits unauthorized intentional destruction of world government record (class 4 felony).

11.2. Prohibits unintentional destruction of world government records (class 2 misdemeanour).

11.3. Permits stewarding agency curation of records. Prohibits obfuscation.

12. Requires retention of envelopes and stamps to be safeguarded together and intact with important paper letters.

13. Requires use of acid-free paper. Requires Secretariat record of official proceedings.

14. Requires stewarding agency to make electronic back-ups of electronic media. Requires stewarding agency to protect electronic records from magnetic and digital viral damage.

15. Permits stewarding agencies to request financial assistance for meeting care standards of care for world government records. Assigns to stewarding agencies responsibility to comply with the standards.

16. Permits Institute on Governmental Procedures and World Problems to directly enforce act with civil procedures. Permits Institute on Governmental Procedures and World Problems to seek further enforcement through World Courts and **World Enforcement System.**

17. Assigns discretion to Institute on Governmental Procedures and World Problems.

18. Requires Institute on Governmental Procedures and World Problems to meet preservation standards for records, if stewarding agency assigns or forfeits stewardship.

19. Permits compliance period of 30 days.

20. Permits search and seizure warrants in case of non-compliance.

21. Due to critical importance of this Act, this world legislation is effective immediately.

⊕⊕⊕⊕⊕⊕⊕⊕⊕⊕

The eighth session of the Provisional World Parliament adopted the Records Act as World Legislative Act #25, August 2004, in Lucknow, Uttar Pradesh, India.

World Legislative Act #26 Summary

Education within the Earth Federation

Recognizes need for public education; Recognizes rights to education; Recognizes deficiency of education in world, and global education crisis; Recognizes the need for immediate serious measures to create a quality world educational system to create universal prosperity, save the planetary environment, eradicate poverty, and activate world democracy.

Adopts this Act for Global Education.

1. Requires Earth Federation to develop schools, training of teachers, and integration of all children into educational process (whether in public or private schools) as basic priority of government.

2. Financing

2.1. Requires operating agencies of the Integrative Complex to create education budget. Lists programs, projects and agencies scheduled for budgeting and allocations.

2.2. Loans -
Requires Earth Financial Credit Corporation (EFCC) to give substantial lines of credit to both existing public and private schools worldwide, to meet additional needs perceived by respective school systems and by credit determining process of EFCC. Requires EFCC to consider legislatively mandated conditions for extension of credit.

2.3. Requires conditional distribution of allocated World Treasury subventions and distribution of Earth Financial Credit Corporation loans. Requires next session of Provisional World Parliament to set Provisional educational standards, to expedite allocations and loans.

2.4. Requires recipient public and private schools to submit and implement plans for quality education. Lists specified requirements, including pedagogies of human development, self-realization, and empowerment. Defines and gives examples of appropriate pedagogies, including global issues, study within academic subjects, study of *Earth Constitution*, peace studies, unity in diversity indices and good government indices. Encourages open-ended pedagogies.

3. - **Ministry and Administration**. Directs reconfirmation or re-election of Provisional Education Minister or Education Commission Chairperson to nominate Provisional Senior Administrator and begin implementation. Directs Education Ministry to employ staff, and allows five year budget plan.

4. **Advisory Council** - Allows interlock of Earth Federation Educational Advisory Councils.

5. **Location** - Permits Education Ministry headquarters Permits Education Minister and Senior Administrator to determine own residency.

⊕⊕⊕⊕⊕⊕⊕⊕⊕⊕⊕

The eighth session of the Provisional World Parliament adopted the Education Act as World Legislative Act #26, 12 August 2004, in Lucknow, Uttar Pradesh, India.

World Legislative Act #27
Summary

Statute on the Rights of the Child

Part 1

Article 1. Defines «child». Defines «custodian». Assigns custodian accountability to Statute.

Article 2. Assigns custodian responsibility.

Article 3. Proclaims best interests of child as primary consideration.

Article 4. Directs custodians to undertake all appropriate legislative, administrative and other measures for the protection and implementation of recognized rights

Article 5. Directs custodians to respect the responsibilities, rights and duties of parents or, where applicable, the members of the extended family.

Article 6. Proclaims every child to have inherent right to life. Directs custodians to ensure child survival and development.

Article 7. Requires primary custodian to register birth and to name child.

Article 8. Protects child identity.

Article 9. Requires custodians to keep child with family, unless competent authorities determine this to be against child interest. Requires custodians to notify family if separation occurs.

Article 10. Recognizes right to family reunification and child right to change residence anywhere in world.

Article 11. Prohibits illicit transfer and non-return of children abroad. Criminalizes child slavery (class 5 felony) and child prostitution (consummated, class 7 felony).

Article 12. Guarantees freedom of expression and freedom to hearing.

Article 13. Defines further child freedom of expression.

Article 14. Guarantees child right to freedom of thought, conscience and religion.

Article 15. Guarantees child right to freedom of association and to freedom of peaceful assembly.

Article 16. Protects child privacy.

Article 17. Encourages wholesome media worldwide.

Article 18. Recognizes responsibility of both parents. Requires world federal assistance, if necessary.

Article 19. Directs Earth Federation and States Parties to provide child protection.

Article 20. Entitles child to special protection and assistance provided by Earth Federation or child's national state. Permits foster care, kafalah or adoption.

Article 21. Requires permit of competent placement authority if special protection and assistance is necessary.

Article 22. Protects refugee child or internationally lost child.

Article 23. Protects mentally or physically disabled child.

Article 24. Recognizes child right to health care, preventative care, and also pre-natal and post-natal health care for mothers.

Article 25. Recognizes right to periodic review of treatment.

Article 26. Recognizes child right to regulated social security benefits.

Article 27. Recognizes right to adequate living standard.

Article 28. Recognizes right to education. Requires at least minimum standards in education. Includes supportive provisions for both public and private schools, to include home schooling programs.

Article 29. Defines principles of basic education standards.

Article 30. Protects child's maintenance of own culture, religion, and language.

Article 31. Recognizes child right to rest and leisure. participation in child's cultural and artistic life, and recreational activity.

Article 32. Recognizes right of protection from economic exploitation.

Article 33. Prohibits administering or supplying narcotic drug or psychotropic substance to child (class 4 felony). Prohibits use of children in production and trafficking of illicit substances. (class 3 felony).

Article 34. Directs Earth Federation and States Parties to take measures to prevent sexual abuse. Prohibits coercion, inducement or exploitative use of children in prostitution or other unlawful sexual practices (class 7 felony). Prohibits child pornography (class 6 felony).

Article 35. Prohibits abduction of, sale of or traffic in children (class 4 felony).

Article 36. Directs Earth Federation and States Parties to otherwise protect child.

Article 37. Recognizes prohibitions of penal code as applicable to children. Prohibits child torture (class 7 felony). Prohibits cruel, inhumane or degrading treatment or punishment (class 5 felony). Prohibits genital mutilation. Prohibits capital punishment and life imprisonment without possibility of release (execution: class 7 felony). Requires conformity to law in child arrest, detention or imprisonment. Directs Earth Federation and States

Parties to separate incarcerated children from incarcerated adults. Guarantees right to prompt legal assistance.

Article 38. Guarantees rights in case of armed conflicts. Sets recruitment age limits for the transitional national militaries and for the Enforcement System. Prohibits conscription (resulting in child death or permanent injury - class 4 felony; no permanent injury – class 3 felony).

Article 39. Requires measures for recovery and reintegration.

Article 40. Recognizes child legal rights if alleged as, accused of, or recognized as having infringed penal law.

Article 41. Recognizes jurisdiction of respective most conducive legal provision.

Article 42. This Statute recognizes the right of children and right of future generations of children, to inherit a safe and healthy ecology.

(**Editor's Note:** Here the Juvenile Bench varies substantially from the original Rome Statute. Articles 42 through 45 have been re-numbered Articles 43 through 46, to accommodate the addition of new Article 42. Old Articles 46 through 48 were before introduction stricken from the bill as unconstitutional, that is, they are now *reserved*. Hence the change of enumeration from the original statute in following articles.)

Part 2

Article 43. Proclaims undertaking to disseminate Statute to adults and children worldwide.

Article 44. Recognizes Committee on the Rights of the Child. Defines Committee formation.

Article 45. Defines Committee work and report timetables.

Article 46. Defines and permits Committee function. Integrates Committee between United Nations and Earth Federation agencies. Otherwise reserved.

Article 47. Reserved.

Article 48. Reserved.

Part 3

Article 49. Declares Statute as reconstitution, integration and adoption of the Convention on the Rights of the Child.

Article 50. Defines amendment process.

Article 51. Reserved.

Article 52. Reserved.

Article 53. Assigns World Problems Institute as repository.

Article 54. Directs World Problems Institute to translate.

⊕⊕⊕⊕⊕⊕⊕⊕⊕⊕

The eighth session of the Provisional World Parliament adopted the Rights of the Child as World Legislative Act #27, August 2004, in Lucknow, Uttar Pradesh, India.

World Legislative Act #28
Summary

World Bench for Juvenile Cases

Short Title: **World Juvenile Bench**

Part 1. Establishes Juvenile Court

Article 1. Establishes a World Bench for Juvenile Cases (Juvenile Court). as a permanent institution with the power to exercise jurisdiction over persons for most serious crimes of world concern. Complements national juvenile criminal jurisdictions. Supplements other benches of the World Court System. Governs jurisdiction and functioning of Juvenile Court. Lists purposes of the Juvenile Bench.

Article 2. Designates first Seats of the Juvenile Bench.

Article 3. Legal status and Powers of the Juvenile Bench - Assigns Juvenile Bench global legal personality. Assigns Juvenile Bench legal capacity for exercise of Juvenile Bench functions and fulfilment of Juvenile Bench purposes. Permits Court to exercise functions and powers anywhere on Earth.

Part 2. Jurisdiction, Admissibility and Applicable Law

Article 4. Crimes within the Jurisdiction of the Court - Defines jurisdiction. Limits jurisdiction of the Juvenile Court to cases involving juveniles, or persons who were juvenile at time of alleged crime. Assigns Court jurisdiction with respect to following crimes:
4.1.1. Crime of genocide;
4.1.2. Crimes against humanity;
4.1.3. War crimes;
4.1.4. Crime of aggression;
4.1.5. Environmental crimes;
4.1.6. World federal corruption;
4.1.7. Interference in world government.

Article 5. Recognizes Elements of Crimes in effect for Juvenile Bench. Declares crimes defined in world legislation as also crimes for juveniles. Declares adult penal code sentencing parameters not in effect for children. Directs the World Judicial Commission to draft provisions for a juvenile penal code. Directs Provisional World Parliament to nominate Juvenile Advisory Committee, composed of juvenile members, to give recommendations to World Judicial Commission.

Article 6. Jurisdiction *ratione temporis* Declares jurisdiction only with respect to crimes committed after entry into force of respective world statutes. Declares entry into force upon adoption by Provisional World Parliament.

Article 7. Describes preconditions and exercise of jurisdiction.

Article 8. Establishes office of Juvenile Case Prosecutor within the Office of World Attorneys General.

Article 9. Declares Admissibility same as for respective adult benches, whether case is civil or criminal.

Article 10. Declares Challenges – same as for adult cases.

Article 11. Declares *Ne bis in idem* same as for adult cases.

Article 12. Declares Applicable Law same as for adult cases, except age is determining factor.

Part 3. General Principles of Juvenile Law

Article 13. Declares *Nullem crimen sine lege* also applicable for Juvenile Bench.

Article 14. Declares *Nulla poena sine lege* also applicable for Juvenile Bench.

Article 15. Declares non-retroactivity *ratione personae* also applicable for Juvenile Bench.

Article 16. Limits jurisdiction of Juvenile Bench to cases where juvenile has reached at least the age of 14 at the time alleged crime is committed. Permits prosecution of adult by Juvenile Bench, if accused adult was juvenile at time of alleged crime.

Article 17. Declares mental element same as for adult cases.

Article 18. Grounds for excluding criminal responsibility, except that in cases where commission of crime takes place before defendant's 14th birthday, in which case, criminal responsibility is excluded. Juvenile Bench may determine conditions for treatment or care of juveniles for whom age excludes criminal responsibility. However, Juvenile Court must not subject underage juveniles to trial, nor juveniles or adults who were underage at time of commission of crime.

Article 19. Declares Mistake of fact or mistake of law same as for adult cases.

Part 4. Composition and Administration of the Court

Article 20. Defines Organs of the Court

Article 21. Defines Service of Judges

Article 22. Defines qualifications, nomination and election of judges.

Article 23. Directs Presiding Council of World Judges to fill juvenile judicial vacancies giving preference to Judges with expertise in Juvenile Law or with significant juvenile case experience.

Article 24. Defines Chambers.

Article 25. Declares Independence of Judges.

Article 26. Defines regulations for excusing and disqualification of judges.

Article 27. Defines Office of the Prosecutor.

Article 28. Defines Registry.

Article 29. Defines Staff.

Article 30. Defines Solemn undertaking.

Article 31. Defines removal from office.

Article 32. Sets disciplinary measures.

Article 33. Declares Privileges and Immunities.

Article 34. Defines salaries, allowances and expenses. Salaries, allowances and expenses of Juvenile Court are same as for other benches of World Court System.

Article 35. Declares official and working languages.

Article 36. Defines special Rules of Juvenile Procedure and Evidence requiring Juvenile Court to consider best interest of child under all circumstances. Defines conditions for parental or guardian participation in Court process. Defines fiscal responsibility for costs, that might be born by Court, by parents or deferred for payment by juveniles themselves. Requires Court to recess for adequate rest. Defines standards for education of juveniles in the justice system.

Article 37. Requires World Juvenile Court Judges to adopt to adopt Regulations of Juvenile Court to adapt specifically to needs of juveniles.

Part 5. Investigation and Prosecution

Article 38. Recommends procedure for Investigation and Prosecution to be based on the procedures defined for adult cases, but tempered for juvenile defendants. Encourages recommendations from the Judicial Commission for following matters:

Duties and powers of the Prosecutor;

Rights of persons during an investigation;

Role of Pre-Trial Chamber;

Pre-Trial Chamber functions and powers;

Issuance by the Pre-Trial Chamber of a warrant of arrest or a summons to appear;

Arrest proceedings in the custodial state;

Initial proceedings;

Confirmation of charges before trial;

Sanctions for misconduct before the Court.

Part 6. Trial

Permits participation of juveniles in juvenile juries and Juvenile Court. Encourages juveniles to take active and orderly part in Juvenile Court process. However, prosecutor and presiding judges must meet qualifications as defined in *Earth Constitution*.

Part 7 Sentencing

Defines process for proposing applicable penalties, to be submitting to upcoming session of Provisional World Parliament.

Declares Non-Prejudice to national penalties and national laws, but only within limits of the Statute on the Rights of the Child.

Establishes Trust Fund for benefit of victims of crimes within jurisdiction of Juvenile Court, and of families of victims.

Permits Court to order money and other property collected through fines or forfeiture to be transferred, by order of Juvenile Court, to Trust Fund. Permits Assembly of States Parties to submit a proposal to the World Parliament for consideration.

Part 8. Provides for Appeal and Revision

Part 9. Provides for International Cooperation and Judicial Assistance

Part 10. Permits Judicial Commission to elaborate Enforcement procedures in conformance with the Statute on the Rights of the Child and other world law.

Part 11. Permits Civil Cases involving juveniles to be handled by the Juvenile Bench: Cases of family custody;

Cases of custodial dispute involving public agencies;

Other civil cases involving juveniles.

Part 12. Financing

Recognizes need to support families of juveniles and the need for juvenile residential facilities.

Part 13. Final clauses
Permits format of Juvenile Code legislation to be presented in three forms, until second operational stage of world government begins, as defined in *Earth Constitution*:

- Legislative Summary;
- Short form, with reference to World Legislative Act #20 (Criminal Court) in redundant articles and provisions.
- Long form (engrossed form), including all redundant provisions from World Legislative Act #20 (Criminal Court).

Directs World Judicial Commission to examine and recommend improvements to Statute.

Includes Addendum with two lists and table of correlations of Criminal Bench to Juvenile Bench:

- Provisions of World Bench for Criminal Cases that are operative or substantially similar for Juvenile Court;
- Provisions of World Bench for Criminal Cases that are not operative, or that are substantially different for Juvenile Court:
- Table of corresponding differences between Criminal Court and Juvenile Court Statutes, by Article numbers or parts.

⊕⊕⊕⊕⊕⊕⊕⊕⊕⊕

The eighth session of the Provisional World Parliament adopted the World Juvenile Bench as World Legislative Act #28, August 2004, in Lucknow, Uttar Pradesh, India.

World Legislative Act #29
Summary

To inaugurate enabling legislation for the World Boundaries and Elections Administration, including provisions for a Global Peoples Assembly

Short title: **World Elections Act**

The Provisional World Parliament adopts this Act to inaugurate the World Boundaries and Elections Administration (WBEA), including provisions for a Global Peoples Assembly.

1. Assigns basic administrative structure of World Boundaries and Elections Administration, as per Article 8, Section C. of the *Earth Constitution.*

2. Defines administrative functions of World Boundaries and Elections Administration in conformance with Article 8, Section C. of the *Earth Constitution*, but also in additional terms not in conflict with the *Earth Constitution.*

3. Sets Boundaries; adopts the Ian Hackett / Hanna Newcombe Plan for World Districts and Regions, with adjustments as necessary to bring plan up to date and within constitutional limits. Recommends immediate public review of districting plan.

4. Establishes Voter Registry.

5. Defines process for nomination and election of World Parliament Members. Requires solemn undertaking from World candidates.

6. Enables conducting of world elections. Authorizes World Boundaries and Elections Commission to allocate funds.

7. Establishes Voter Information Office.

8. Requires political parties to ratify *Earth Constitution* to participate in world elections.

9. Establishes campaign limits.

10. Defines world legislative initiatives and process.

11. Defines world legislative referendum and process.

12. Defines world plebiscites and process.

13. Permits census process.

14. Establishes Global Peoples Assembly (GPA) as global para-governmental agency and process, comprising both non-governmental and governmental functions.
14.1. Defines Functions of Global Peoples Assembly, its subsidiary and partner organizations.
14.2. Defines Membership and Partner Organizations, including Participating members, Contributing members and Partner Organizations.
14.3. Defines Delegates Council, initial arrangements, Liaisons and Delegates. Encourages broad participation in Global Peoples Assembly. Recommends Voting Delegates Council and other groups of the Global Peoples Assembly to seek consensus, with 2/3 of those present required for decisions on resolutions, initiatives, policy, Charter and Bylaws. Defines and qualifies voting procedures. Declares Robert's Rules of Order Newly Revised, latest edition as basic manual for procedure of the Global Peoples Assembly and Delegates Council, unless Delegates Council or Global Peoples Assembly decides otherwise. Sets quorum of Delegates Council. Defines basic structure and terms of Delegates Council to include President, Vice-President, Secretary, and Treasurer. Requires Delegates Council to form Credentials Committee for world elections. Permits candidate for World Parliament to run for office without endorsement from Credentials Committee of Global Peoples Assembly, if all qualifications are met, as defined in *Earth Constitution.* Defines Internal Initiatives.
14.4. Defines Global Peoples Assembly Movement (GPAM) Plenary Sessions. Sets simple majority to vote on policy. Defines Voting for Candidates and Borda Count. Subjects other procedural issues not addressed in Bylaws to *Robert's Rules of Order Newly Revised*, latest edition.
14.5. Defines Financial Arrangements. Permits fiscal agents.

15. Declares intention to eventually provide dedicated facilities for Global Peoples Assemblies.

16. Promotes development of Internet programs and projects to create better and stronger world democratic process.

17. Authorizes Agency for Research and Planning to assign public radio and television frequencies for each District, Region and other jurisdictional levels of Earth Federation, to include dedicated frequencies for broadcast of each

District, Region and other jurisdictional level of Global Peoples Assembly.

18. Allows Low Technology systems to supplement participation.

19. Directs budgetary allocations for youth participation and parliamentary training in annual budget of the WBEA.

20. Incorporates World Syntegrity Project for advisory function.

21. Assigns World Boundaries and Elections Commission to prepare annual Budget.

22. Requires World Boundaries and Elections Administration annual report to World Parliament and to Presidium.

23. Claims to further provisions.

⊕⊕⊕⊕⊕⊕⊕⊕⊕⊕

The eighth session of the Provisional World Parliament adopted the World Elections Act as World Legislative Act #29, on 12 August 2004, in Lucknow, Uttar Pradesh, India.

World Legislative Act #30
Summary

The Water Act

- Draws directly from the Water Act of World Youth Parliament for Water, meeting at Assemblée Nationale, Quebec, 22nd November 2002.
- Conforms with call of World Youth Parliament, for parliaments of world to deliberate and adopt Water Act.

Recognizes 5 Principles related to water:

1. Water is part of world heritage.
2. Water, like air, is part of public domain.
3. Easy access to potable water and sanitation is human right. Clean water is fundamental right of all living beings.
4. No one should waste or pollute water.
5. Water is limited natural resources that is fundamental to life in all its forms and essential to health and prosperity of all peoples and to political stability in world: water must not be considered as merchandise in its natural state unless it is transported.

Actions

1. Requires World Parliament and national parliaments, in conformance with World Law, to enact legislation to ensure that use of water resources procures to all human beings.

2. Lists 33 measures related to water use and water regulation to be elaborated in upcoming world legislation.

3. Requires nomination of Water Commission of 10 members; to manage and attempt to solve water problems. Requires Water Commission or Ministry to coordinate with Global Ministry on Environment, and other agencies of Earth Federation. Expects Water Ministry to be responsive to citizen committees addressing water problems.

4. Requires World Parliament to entrust appropriate agencies collecting, producing and disseminating most rigorous and accurate information pertaining to easy access to water from standpoint of individual and collective needs; and water supply, use, conservation, protection and sustainable fair management of water resources for measures that relate to protection of water as world heritage.

5. Commends World Parliament of Youth for caring and foresight to initiateWater Act to protect Earth and humanity.

⊕⊕⊕⊕⊕⊕⊕⊕⊕⊕

The eighth session of the Provisional World Parliament adopted the Water Act as World Legislative Act #30, August 2004, convened at City Montessori School, Lucknow, Uttar Pradesh, India.

Ninth Session of the Provisional World Parliament, El Kabir Grand Hotel, Tripoli, Libya, April 2006

adopted World Legislative Acts #31 through #38.

World Legislative Act #31 Summary

Enabling Legislation for the World Ombudsmus

Short Title: **World Ombudsmus Act**

1. Empowers World Ombudsmus to hire persons to perform work of World Ombudsmus.

2. Requires World Ombudsmus to develop detailed proposal for accomplishment of work.

3. Conditionally names UN High Commission for Human Rights as ex-officio member of World Ombudsmus.

4. Directs World Police to cooperate and coordinate with World Ombudsmus to protect human rights. Specifies and directs World Ombudsmus to publicly observe World Police.

5. Grants access by World Ombudsmus to information of other branches of Earth Federation.

6. Establishes offices of World Ombudsmus, including liaison offices with certain other departments and branches of the Earth Federation. Directs World Ombudsmus to select from civil service lists to employ staff.

Permits Provisional placement before civil service lists are created.

7. Establishes system of elected World District Ombudsen and elected Deputy District Ombudsen to provide World Ombudsmus service within each World District of Earth Federation. Defines eligibility of World District Ombudsen and Deputy District Ombudsen, including conditions for removal from office.

8. Defines responsibility, powers, and duties of World District Ombudsen and Deputy District Ombudsen.

9. Gives directive, mandate and caveat to World Ombudsmus.

10. Allocates funds and defines Provisional budget for five years' function of World Ombudsmus.

⊕⊕⊕⊕⊕⊕⊕⊕⊕⊕

The ninth session of the Provisional World Parliament adopted the World Ombudsmus Act as World Legislative Act #31, on 12 April 2006, at Tripoli, Libya.

World Legislative Act #32
Summary

Enabling Legislation for the Department for Conflict Resolution within the Federation of Earth

Short Title: **Conflict Resolution**

1. Defines Department for Conflict Resolution, including internal governing structure of department.

2. Integrates Department for Conflict Resolution (DCR) with twenty regional world offices in relation to regional offices of World Attorney General and World Police. Requires regional DCR Commissioner to head each regional world DCR office.

3. Requires World Police under supervision of World Parliament to staff regional offices of Department for Conflict Resolution. Permits regions to have unequal number of personnel, based upon relative conflict resolution need.

4. Requires World Ombudsmus to have staff in each regional office of the Department for Conflict Resolution as liaison and to facilitate coordination with offices of World Ombudsmus.

5. Requires Department for Conflict Resolution to establish local offices on campuses of World University System. Permits qualified local professors to staff local campus offices.

6. Requires Department for Conflict Resolution to maintain liaison offices with World Commission on Terrorism (WCT). Prohibits liaison offices from surveillance, apprehension, arrest, or prosecution of violators of world law.

7. Prohibits World Attorneys General Office and World Police from using offices and staff of Department for Conflict Resolution for other world police or attorney general functions. Cites penal provision for violation. Establishes confidentiality between DCR staff and parties of conflict. Maintains mandated reporter status (WLA 14.10) for regarding suspected

cases of DCR corruption. Excludes powers of arrest from DCR personnel. Prohibits DCR officers and staff from carrying instruments of defense while on duty.

8. Requires Department for Conflict Resolution to make use of existing resources and expertise. Requires DCR to coordinate supportively with pre-existing programs established for conflict resolution.

9. Requires Department for Conflict Resolution to rely and build upon, if possible, local knowledge and existing efforts, mobilizing both mid-level leaders and ordinary citizens. Defines conditions under which DCR may bypass or interfere with local programs or efforts at conflict resolution.

10. Requires Department for Conflict Resolution to submit annual report to World Police and World Parliament detailing DCR conflict resolution activities, and work of local and community conflict resolution activities, in each world regions and extent of continuing violence or danger of violence in each region.
Requires World Attorney General and World Police to submit annual DCR budget to World Parliament as separate part of general Enforcement System budget request. Reserves World Parliament power to fund DCR budget separately from general request of Enforcement System budget based upon reports of World Ombudsmus and agencies of Integrative Complex.

11. Permits World Office of World Attorney General or World Office of World Police to remove for cause, under conditions of due process any officer or employee of World Department for Conflict Resolution.

⊕⊕⊕⊕⊕⊕⊕⊕⊕⊕⊕

The ninth session of the Provisional World Parliament adopted the Conflict Resolution Department as World Legislative Act #32, on 12 April 2006, at Tripoli, Libya.

World Legislative Act #33
Summary

Banning the Production of Fissile Materials for Nuclear Weapons and other Nuclear Explosive Devices

Short Title: **Fissile Materials Ban**
(Adopted at Ninth Session of the Provisional World Parliament, April 2006)

Enacts, as People of Earth, represented by Provisional World Parliament, World Statute banning production of fissile materials for nuclear weapons and other nuclear explosive devices.

1. Defines technical and legal terms related to fissile materials production ban.

2. Defines general prohibitions and obligations related to fissile materials production and processing, including prohibition of separation, production and processing of highly-enriched plutonium and uranium.

3. Requires disclosure, tracking, security, closure, and reporting. Requires World

Disarmament Agency verification and control. Requires access to facilities for application of verification system to ensure that facilities remain closed and decommissioned.

4. Fissile Materials Department
Establishes Fissile Materials Department (FM Department) to implement Statute. Declares seat, functions and responsibility of FM Department. Requires FM Department to verify closure operations of Fissile Materials facilities. Permits full range of civil enforcement by World Disarmament Agency and Enforcement System.
Assigns World Financial Administration to arrange payment for costs of FM Department's activities. Defines responsibilities of States and general terms of State Party credit arrangements with Earth Financial Credit Corporation. Requires separate appropriation sections for EFCC extension of credit for fissile materials costs. Reconfirms or establishes organs of FM Department: World Disarmament Agency Board of Trustees, Fissile Materials Council (FM Council), Fissile Materials Technical Secretariat (FM Technical Secretariat), and Fissile Materials Data Centre. Defines process for rules of procedure. Defines further powers and responsibilities of Fissile Materials Department.

5. Defines further powers and responsibilities of World Disarmament Agency Board of Trustees. (WDA Board).

6. Fissile Materials Council
Defines Fissile Materials Council (FM Council) as executive organ of FM Department. Declares FM Council accountable to WDA Board. Defines powers and responsibilities.

7. Establishes, and defines composition and responsibilities of Fissile Materials Technical Secretariat to perform verification, including Fissile Materials Director. Establishes, and defines composition and responsibilities of International Data Centre to manage, process, analyze and report data on fissile materials and facilities.

8. National Implementing Measures
Requires each State Party to *Earth Constitution* to adopt measures to implement Statute. Requires, in particular, State Party to: 8.1. Report to Enforcement System if natural and legal persons anywhere violate Statute; 8.2. Refrain from permitting Statute violation anywhere under State Party jurisdiction or control; 8.3 Enact cooperative law enforcement legislation with respect to all activities prohibited by Statute, to facilitate trans-jurisdictional due process to world federal level; and 8.4. Extend cooperative law enforcement legislation beyond geographic borders.

9. Settlement of Disputes
Defines process for dispute settlement under Statute.

10. Duration
Declares Statute to be of unlimited duration.

11. Status of Annexes
Requires World Disarmament Agency to make list of facilities and materials that are to be inspected, graded and verified, based upon reports of FM Department, FM Council and FM Technical Secretariat. Declares WDA Board-adopted Annex as integral to Statute.

12. Signature
Permits direct approval by Assembly of States Parties, but neither veto by Assembly nor statutory accession by nations. Permits Assembly of States Parties to recommend item amendments to House of Counsellors.

13. Ratification
Declares Statute not subject to ratification or veto by national States. Encourages about 25 national states to simultaneously give preliminary ratification to *Earth Constitution.*

14. Accession - Defines accession to constitutive document, not as process direct to Statute.

15. Declares timing of entry into force.

16. Reservations - Prohibits national or international reservations.

17. Depository
Declares responsibilities of Presidium of Earth Federation or Standing Executive Cabinet of Provisional World Parliament as Statute depository.

18. Authentic texts
Requires Commission for Legislative Review to submit authenticated language versions to Presidium.

⊕⊕⊕⊕⊕⊕⊕⊕⊕⊕

ANNEX 1 - Details additional verification requirements, including lists: fissile materials and facilities, methods of monitoring compliance, types of inspections, inspection schedules, inspection reports, and conditions for warrant service applications.

⊕⊕⊕⊕⊕⊕⊕⊕⊕⊕

The ninth session of the Provisional World Parliament adopted the Fissile Materials Ban as World Legislative Act #33, on 12 April 2006, at Tripoli, Libya.

World Legislative Act #34
Summary

Protocol for Nuclear Weapons Elimination

The Provisional World Parliament originally derived the base text for the Elimination Protocol from the Model Nuclear Weapons Convention of United Nations General Assembly Official Document A/C.1/52/7, produced by the International Association of Lawyers Against Nuclear Arms in association with Costa Rica. (http://www.ialana.net) Since the adoption of this Act, Costa Rica and Malaysia have updated and re-submitted in January of 2008 their version response as The Model Nuclear Weapons Convention, United Nations Official Document A/62/650. Therefore, the Provisional World Parliamen deliberated this Act further in July 2009 to help implement the operative nuclear dismantlement system. Adopted amendments of 2009 are not yet reflected in this version.)

Short Title: **Elimination Protocol**

Enacts protocol for nuclear weapons elimination together with elimination of all weapons of mass destruction and conveyances.

1. Defines General Obligations. Recognizes prior prohibition of development, testing, production, stockpiling, transfer, other use and threat of use of nuclear weapons. Requires states possessing nuclear weapons to dismantle and eliminate their respective arsenals according to series of phases. Integrates with weapons usable fissile materials production ban. Requires dismantlement or conversion of delivery vehicles to be destroyed or converted. Defines Terms.

2. Assigns to World Disarmament Agency responsibility for verification, ensuring compliance, and decision making. Further defines structure of Agency including Board of Trustees (Conference of Peoples and States Parties), Executive Council and Technical Secretariat.

3. Requires states to declare all nuclear weapons, nuclear material, nuclear facilities and nuclear weapons delivery vehicles they possess or control, and respective locations. Declares universal applicability and jurisdiction of World law to all citizens of Earth, not only citizens of nations giving preliminary or final ratification to *Earth Constitution*.

4. Outlines a series of five phases for the elimination of nuclear weapons beginning with taking nuclear weapons off alert, removing weapons from deployment, removing nuclear warheads from their delivery vehicles, disabling warheads, removing and disfiguring pits and placing fissile material under Earth Federation control. Prohibits nuclear weapons unconditionally.

5. Defines verification to include declarations and reports from States, routine inspections, challenge inspections, fixed on-site sensors, satellite photography, radionuclide sampling and other remote sensors, information sharing with other organizations, and citizen reporting. Protects citizens reporting suspected violations of law.

6. Requires national implementation measures to provide subjurisdictional law enforcement cooperation for prosecution of persons committing crimes, and for protection for persons reporting violations. Requires states to establish national authority to be responsible for national tasks in implementation.

7. Reaffirms individual responsibility. Applies obligations to individuals as well as States. Refers to applicable world legislation.

8. Defines further structure of World Disarmament Agency.

9. Defines nuclear materials prohibitions and protocol. Requires compliance to protocol regarding nuclear materials.

10. Defines nuclear weapons dismantlement protocol. Requires compliance to nuclear weapons dismantlement protocol.

11. Defines nuclear weapons delivery vehicle dismantlement and conversion protocol. Requires compliance to nuclear weapons delivery vehicle dismantlement and conversion protocol.

12. Defines nuclear facilities dismantlement protocol. Requires compliance to nuclear facilities dismantlement protocol.

13. Allows use of appropriate nuclear materials and appropriate nuclear research, such as for nuclear medicine, nuclear forensics, calibration of nuclear verification tools, etc.

14. Permits consultation, cooperation and fact-finding to clarify and resolve questions of interpretation with respect to compliance and other matters. Permits Agency to refer legal dispute to the International Court of Justice by mutual consent of States Parties. Requires International Court of Justice to respond to any request for advisory opinion from Agency on legal disputes. Requires conditional submission of warrant service application forms to World Attorneys General.

15. Permits conditional graduated responses for suspected non-compliance beginning with consultation and clarification, negotiation within legal limits, and, if required, permits civil penalties, recourse to U.N. General Assembly and Security Council for action or issuance of warrants for search and arrest by Enforcement System. Defines timing of entry into force.

16. Obliges nuclear weapons states to pay costs. Assists insolvent nuclear weapons states with financing payment of costs. Defines assistance conditions and requirements. Assigns world federal decommissioning fund to Earth Financial Credit Corporation to provide finance assistance.

17. Reserves amendments to World Parliament. Permits States Parties to *Earth Constitution* to introduce amendments through respective delegate Members to Parliament, through world parliamentary procedure.

18. Relates Protocol to prior existing international and world law. Defines Scope and application of Protocol to have no permission of withdrawal and no reservations by national governments or international bodies.

Refers to Fissile Materials Production Ban.

Defines optional program of energy assistance for States Parties not developing nuclear energy or planning to phase out existing nuclear energy programs.

⊕⊕⊕⊕⊕⊕⊕⊕⊕⊕

Universal amendments in memorandum by Provisional World Parliament:
Replaces word "Convention" and word "treaty" universally with word "Protocol".

Replaces word "use" universally with word "detonation", if reference is to the causing or allowing fissile materials to reach radiologically critical mass.

Replaces term "Conference of States Parties" universally with "World Disarmament Agency Board of Trustees", except in Article 2, where "Conference of Peoples and States Parties" is listed as alternate designation.

Replaces word "destroy" universally with word "dismantle".

Replaces word "destruction" universally with word "dismantlement".

Places Protocol into full numeric codification.

⊕⊕⊕⊕⊕⊕⊕⊕⊕⊕

Following annexes are under development or in process of completion and dissemination:

Annex on the Verification and Implementation

Annex on Nuclear Activities, Components and Equipment

Annex on Delivery Vehicles.

⊕⊕⊕⊕⊕⊕⊕⊕⊕⊕⊕

The ninth session of the Provisional World Parliament adopted the Elimination Protocol as World Legislative Act #34, on 12 April 2006, at Tripoli, Libya.
Amendments adopted in 2009 at the eleventh session of the Provisional World Parliament will be reflected in volumes 2 & 3 of *Emerging World Law.*

World Legislative Act #35
Summary

An Act including initial provisions for transfer, reconstitution and integration of the World Health Organization and (International) Atomic Energy Agency:

Nuclear Contamination Risk and Cost Assessment

Short title: **Nuclear Contamination**

1. Mandates World Health Organization (WHO) to initiate, analyze, report and review all radiation research and recommend health based safety regulations. Requires health professionals who are not linked to nuclear industry to perform review, rather than other scientists.

2. Withdraws International Atomic Energy Association (IAEA) mandate to promote so-called "peaceful nuclear technologies". Prohibits conditionally nuclear technology promotion. Annuls 1959 agreement between IAEA and WHO that prohibits WHO from warning global public of radiological dangers. Reserves to Provisional World Parliament at 11th session further review of 1959 letter of understanding. Prohibits international agencies and national authorities from interfering with work of health officials in measurement of deleterious effects of radiation and contamination (class 3 felony.) Authorizes WHO to send health professionals onto any nuclear facilities to make both clinical and radiological measurements. Requires WHO health professional display of identification.
Disclaims International Commission on Radiological Protection (ICRP) as viable agency. Warns public against pronouncements made by ICRP.

3. Expands IAEA mandate to include monitoring reduction and abolition of all nuclear weapons in nuclear nations in cooperation with World Disarmament Agency and Enforcement System. Requires IAEA to assist World Disarmament Agency in all nuclear related activities. Requires World Disarmament Agency to include IAEA budgetary itemization in annual budget.

4. Amends mandate of United Nations Scientific Committee on the Effects of Atomic Radiation (UNSCEAR) mandate to include monitoring of increasing levels of background radiation and nuclear emissions from reactors and nuclear accidents. Requires UNSCEAR budgetary reports. Assigns to

World Health Organization responsibility to estimate risk. Requires World Health Organization to estimate costs.

5. Entrusts WHO for decisions, including projected cost estimation, relative to safety of farm land, food and water ingestion and refugee relocation.

6. Assigns World Ombudsus to investigate imprisonment of scientists and physicians who have spoken out on behalf of public health relative to radiation exposure. Requires Human Rights Commission to establish special raporteur to work with World Ombudsmus and to project costs.

7. Requires Provisional Executive Cabinet to inform respective agencies of this Act .

8. Requires ongoing review of Act by Commission for Legislative Review, until Agency for Technological and Environmental Assessment together with World Health Organization certify safe resolution of nuclear contamination risk crisis.

9. Declares immediate entry into force.

⊕⊕⊕⊕⊕⊕⊕⊕⊕⊕⊕

The ninth session of the Provisional World Parliament adopted the Nuclear Contamination Act as World Legislative Act #35, in April 2006, at Tripoli, Libya.
The Parliament amended the act and slated the WHO/IAEA letter for review at the tenth session of Provisional World Parliament, meeting June 2007 at Kara, Togo, West Africa.
The Parliament reviewed the letter in Nainital, Uttarakhand, July 2009.

World Legislative Act #36
Summary

Directive for Mundialization of Guantánamo Bay

Short title: **Guantánamo Bay Directive**

Gives reasons for invoking eminent domain, including globally stategic location of Guantánamo Bay at vital strait, and impossibility of reasonable national ownership and administration of Guantánamo Base, as well as for protection of human rights.
Cites respective clauses from *Earth Constitution* that give power (Article 4, Item 26) and authority (Article 16. Section A) of eminent domain to People of Earth.

Mundializes Guantánamo Base, all vessels and all properties within 5 kilometers of Guantamano Base ramparts or outer fences, whichever is greater, and all waters of bay, out unto generally recognized waters of Earth Federation. Declares World City of Guantánamo Bay. On at least Provisional basis, Guantánamo Bay is declared World Federal Zone.

1. Defines geographic limits of Guantánamo Bay. Defines "Guantánamo Base". Prohibits departure of any vessel from Guantánamo Bay that is equipped with weapons of mass destruction. Declares violation of this provision as unauthorized misappropriation, theft or transfer of world federal property - Class 3 felony, in addition to any other charges that may generate from type possession or use of misappropriated weapons, or other violation.

2. Directs beginning of conversion of vessels (air and sea) of Guantánamo Base to civil police capacity, or for Emergency Earth Rescue Administration operations, or if not possible, to disable vessels. Requires clean-up. Permits law-abiding officers and servicemembers of Guantánamo Base to conditionally relieve and arrest any recalcitrant commanding officer.

3. Absolves all officers and Service Personnel from liability by supposedly higher authorities within United States military, NATO Alliance or United Nations security system, for refusal to obey national or international orders to violate this Act. Permits World Court to find that inappropriate subjurisdictional legal charges constitute impeding activities of agents of Provisional Earth Federation or Earth Federation. - Class 3 felony.
Recognizes and reminds regarding nationality rights.

4. Denies jurisdiction of United States and Cuba within Guantánamo Bay. Declares detainees world kidnap victims. Requires Guantánamo Base Commanding Officer to release detainees. Reminds World Court to observe also principle of habeas corpus. Quotes applicable law and penalty classifications. Permits law-abiding officers of Guantánamo Base to conditionally relieve and arrest any recalcitrant commanding officer.

5. Declares conditions for partial or full amnesty for officers, service members and veterans of Guantánamo Base. Excludes amnesty regarding civil charges of torture for civil cases. Guarantees travel freedom.

6. Declares and defines further protections, benefits and conditions, including conditional retention of instruments of defense. Creates salary accounts for residents of Guantánamo Bay.

7. Defines conditions for Habitat and Settlement Ministry together with Ministry of Revenue to receive Guantánamo Bay rents. Assigns interim revenue arrangements. Declares mundialization to operate by value tax assessment for land and harbor space usage based on Earth Federation assessed appreciation values, as well as for assessed value of mundialized marine vessels.

8. Requires Earth Federation to arrange and pay fair remuneration to Cuban government for mundialization of Guantánamo Bay, which may include perpetual portion of income from land rent tax collected by Earth Federation for lease of Guantánamo Bay land and harborage. Conditionally permits Cuba Government to sue through World Court if agreed terms are not met or kept by World Parliament. Subjects status of World Federal Zone to plebiscite by people of Cuba after final ratification of *Earth Constitution* by people of Cuba.

9. Requires Commanding Officer of Guantánamo Base to preserve dock works intact to Earth Federation. Reserves dock works together with additional 40% of lands circumscribed by mundialization, including up to 40% of beachfront in excess of docks and 40% of lands of Guantánamo Bay for administrative offices, residences, parks and shipyards of Earth Federation.

10. Grants conditionally to Cuban civilians first option to lease land. Requires lessees to ratify *Earth Constitution*, agree to abide by world legislation, including system of land value taxation. Permits conditionally civilians to apply for and receive land rent tax exemption.

11. Defines terms for Non-governmental Organizations and civil society organizations to lease land, vessels and harbor space.

12. Defines terms to permit Government of Cuba to lease land, vessels and harbor space.

13. Defines terms for lease of Guantánamo Bay land and harbor space to general public, including veterans.

14. Requires de-militarization of all vessels before leaving port of Guantánamo Bay. Subjects vessels to inspection by Earth Federation authorities. Requires prior vessel clearance for leaving port.

15. Establishes Guantánamo Bay Governing Board of up to 47 Members, to include municipal council and mayor. Defines sources of directors of Governing Board. Defines qualifications, terms, duties, conditions and replacements of Governing Board members. Permits Interim Municipal Council and Interim Mayor. Permits initial Board Meetings to begin.

16. Creates posts of Guantánamo Bay Harbor Master and Assistant Harbor Masters, including qualifications, manner of appointment and duties. Requires vessel compliance to Harbor Master team and generally-recognized international rules for harbor operation, not in conflict with Earth Federation and world legislation. Directs Harbor Master team to propose rules and penalties for violation.

17. Protects freedom of expression and recommends courteous expression, particularly regarding display of colors.

18. Declares and defines provisions for amnesty windows.

19. Declares grounds for demanding compliance and defines framework objectives for establishing compliance.

20. Requires Presidium to establish exterior relations. Welcomes managed immigration and visits to Guantánamo Bay. Encourages protection of Guantánamo Bay by residents and visitors.

21. Assumes all further costs and responsibility for general administration, clean-up, development and protection of harbor and lands at Guantánamo Bay.

⊕⊕⊕⊕⊕⊕⊕⊕⊕⊕

The ninth session of the Provisional World Parliament adopted the Guantánamo Bay Directive as World Legislative Act #36, in April 2006, at Tripoli, Libya.
The tenth session of the Parliament amended the act, meeting June 2007 at Kara, Togo, West Africa.

Summary Memorandum
[Derived from the International Criminal Court's Assembly of States Parties' *Agreement on the Privileges and Immunities of the International Criminal Court* (*APIC*)]

World Legislative Act #37
Summary

Act for Agreement on the World Federal Privileges and Immunities

Short title: **Privileges and Immunities**

Article 1. Defines use of terms. Adds term "Representatives of People" for delegate Members of Provisional World Parliament, World Parliament, and participating representatives of respective intergovernmental organizations. Adds term "Appointees of People" for committee designated Members of the Peoples Assemblies.

Article 2. Recognizes world legal status and juridical personality of the Court .

Article 3. Grants general necessary provision of privileges and immunities to Court.

Article 4. Declares inviolability of premises of Court.

Article 5. Permits to Court Flag, emblem and markings.

Article 6. Declares immunity of Court, Court property, funds and assets.

Article 7. Declares inviolability of archives and documents.

Article 8. Grants to Court exemption from taxes, customs duties and import or export restrictions.

Article 9. Defines exceptions and conditions for reimbursement of duties and/or taxes.

Article 10. Declares freedom from currency restrictions within world federal limits.

Article 11. Protects facilities in respect of communications.

Article 12. Protects exercise of functions of Court outside Court headquarters.

Article 13. Defines immunities and privileges for representatives of States participating in Assembly and subsidiary organs, for representatives of People, for Appointees of People and for officers of the Enforcement System and World Ombudsmus.

Article 14. Declares immunities and privileges for Representatives of States, Representatives of People, Appointees of People and for officers and personnel of the Enforcement System and World Ombudsmus. participating in proceedings of Court.

Article 15. Defines immunities and privileges of Judges, Prosecutor, Deputy Prosecutors and Registrar.

Article 16. Defines immunities and privileges of Deputy Registrar, staff of the Office of Prosecutor and staff of Registry.

Article 17. Defines immunities and privileges of personnel recruited locally and not otherwise covered by present Agreement.

Article 18. Defines immunities and privileges of counsel and persons assisting defence counsel.

Article 19. Defines immunities and privileges of witnesses.

Article 20. Defines immunities and privileges of victims.

Article 21. Defines immunities and privileges of experts.

Article 22. Defines immunities and privileges of other persons required to be present at seat of Court.

Article 23. Declares and defines limits on privilege and immunity for nationals and permanent residents.

Article 24. Requires respect and conditional cooperation with the authorities of States Parties.

Article 25. Declares duty of Court to waive privileges and immunities in case of impedance of world law. Declares duty of States Parties and intergovernmental organizations to recognize Court waivers of privilege and immunity provided for in articles 13 and 14.

Article 26. Declares duty of Court to waive privileges and immunities in case of impedance of world law. Declares duty of Court officials to recognize Court waivers of privilege and immunity provided for in articles 15 to 22.

Article 27. Grants conditional exemption to Court officials regarding national social security payments.

Article 28. Requires Registrar to issue periodic notification of lists of persons to whom Court privilege and immunity apply.

Article 29. Requires States Parties' acceptance of *laissez-passer* documents from United Nations, the Court or any agency of Earth Federation, yet does not require *laissez-passer.*

Article 30. Requires States Parties' expedition of visa or waiver of visa requirements for persons on Court business, yet does not require visas or recognize requirement of visas.

Article 31. Requires Court provision for settlement of disputes with third parties.

Article 32. Defines procedure for settlement of differences on interpretation or application of present Agreement.

Article 33. Declares applicability of the present Agreement as without prejudice to relevant rules of international and world law.

Article 34. As parliamentary legislation, waives requirement for signature, ratification, acceptance, approval or accession to the Statute. Recommends accession to *Earth Constitution.*

Article 35. Declares entry into force thirty days after 10th instrument of ratification of *Earth Constitution.* Permits States Parties' version to remain in force until that time, insofar as States Parties' version does not violate *Earth Constitution.*

Article 36. Defines conditions for amendment to Agreement.

Article 37. UDHR Article 21.3 applies. Reserves denunciation on an item-by-item basis through measured universal and equal suffrage by People of Earth.

Article 38. Assigns depositaries of Agreement.

Article 39. Requires deposition of authentic texts in Arabic, Chinese, English, Esperanto, French, Russian and Spanish as soon as feasible.

⊕⊕⊕⊕⊕⊕⊕⊕⊕⊕

The ninth session of the Provisional World Parliament adopted the World Federal Privileges and Immunities as World Legislative Act #37, in April 2006, at Tripoli, Libya.

World Legislative Act #38
Summary

Public Utilities

1. Creates annual public utilities fund.

2. Allocates annual budgets in Earth Hours:

2.1.1. World Court Children's Education Fund.

2.1.2. World Court General Adult Education Fund.

2.2. World Chief Justice Conference Fund.

2.3. Children's World Parliament Fund.

2.4. Diseases Fund.

2.5. Provisional World Parliament Fund.

3. Resolves unspent monies to accrue in the respective accounts, until one year after commencement of first operative stage of Earth Federation.

⊕⊕⊕⊕⊕⊕⊕⊕⊕⊕

The ninth session of the Provisional World Parliament adopted the Public Utilities as World Legislative Act #38, in April 2006, at Tripoli, Libya. The tenth session of the Parliament amended the act, meeting June 2007 at Kara, Togo, West Africa.

Tenth Session of the Provisional World Parliament, Palais des Peuples, Kara, Togo, June 2007

World Legislative Act #39 Summary

Prohibition of Unauthorized Destruction of Illegal Financial Instruments

Stock Record Destruction Ban

To assure accountable retirement of illegal stocks (divestment), prohibits unauthorized destruction of illegal financial instruments (bomb corporation stock certificates, holding certificates and related documents. Refer to WLA#13.1.2.1.).

1. Requires appropriate accounting, disposition and retirement of illegal securities.

2. Requires declaration and assignment of proceeds and records of illegal securities to World Disarmament Agency office of Earth Federation Funding Corporation.

3. Exempts brokers from prosecution conditional upon legal brokerage for retirement of illegal securities.

4. Defines conditional amnesty.

5. Defines compliance. Declares conditional amnesty for compliance.

6. Requires payment of retirement (redemption) of illegal financial instruments.

7. Includes bank stock liens against illegal financial instruments as documents for which unauthorized destruction is illegal.

⊕⊕⊕⊕⊕⊕⊕⊕⊕⊕⊕

The 10th session of the Provisional World Parliament adopted the Prohibition of unauthorized destruction of illegal financial instruments as World Legislative Act #39, in June 2007, at Kara, Togo, West Africa.

World Legislative Act #40
Summary

Indemnity Bonds

Creates Indemnity Bonds to catalyze rapid divestment from bomb corporation stock.

1. Assigns conditions for issuance of indemnity bonds, including conditions for plea bargaining and conditional amnesties with general public. Assigns value of indemnity bonds as up to twice retirement value that Earth Federation Funding Corporation receives.

2. Assigns additional conditions for issuance of indemnity bonds for brokers retiring illegal instruments and for illegal corporation financial officers who are cooperative with the Earth Federation.

3. Assigns conditions for issuance of indemnity bonds for bank stock liens against illegal financial instruments.

4. Assigns conditions for issuance of indemnity bonds for illegal financial instruments acquired by testament.

5. Assigns conditions for issuance of indemnity bonds for illegal financial instruments held in probate or trust.

6. Declares indemnity bonds to survive and to be transferable.

7. Requires delivery of retirement documents for illegal financial instruments to the Investigations Department of the Enforcement System. Requires payment of retirement proceeds to the World Disarmament Agency's Earth Federation Funding Corporation for eligibility to obtain the indemnity bonds.

8. Requires conditional confidentiality.

9. Reminds of penalties for unlawful activities.

10. Declares amnesties, plea bargains and indemnity bonds as catalytic precipitators for illegal arms stock divestment. Disclaims amnesties, plea bargains and indemnity bonds as permanent right in exchange for discontinuing illegal activities.

11. Allows reduction of issuance value after declaration of first operative stage of Earth Federation. Allows further reduction of issuance value after declaration of second operative stage of Earth Federation.

12. Prohibits issuance of indemnity bonds after second operative stage of Earth Federation.

13. Assigns limit in Earth Hour credits for Earth Federation Indemnity Bond initial issue.

⊕⊕⊕⊕⊕⊕⊕⊕⊕⊕⊕

The 10th session of the Provisional World Parliament adopted the Earth Federation Indemnity Bonds as World Legislative Act #40, in June 2007, at Kara, Togo, West Africa.

World Legislative Act #41
Summary

Posting the Stock Law

Requires public posting at stock markets worldwide of world law regarding brokerage and trade of illegal financial instruments.

1. Defines general procedure and content of primary postings.

2. Encourages international cooperation.

3. Assigns responsibility for exterior and interior postings. Designates compliance timings and fines for non-compliance.

4. Allows Enforcement System to list corporations being investigated, under indictment or convicted of violation of world law.

5. Restricts location of postings.

6. Requires Officers of Enforcement System on-duty to carry identification papers.

7. Requires warrant or invitation for Enforcement System entry to restricted access areas.

8. Permits unwarranted Enforcement System surveillance in public trading floors.

9. Requires posting in customary working language and in Esperanto.

10. Permits municipal and subsidiary government cooperation for postings.

11. Declares immediate entry into force.

⊕⊕⊕⊕⊕⊕⊕⊕⊕⊕

The 10th session of the Provisional World Parliament adopted the Posting the Earth Federation Stock Law as World Legislative Act #41, in June 2007, at Kara, Togo, West Africa.

World Legislative Act #42
Summary

Guaranteed Annual Income

Creates a guaranteed annual income for all citizens of the Earth Federation

1. Measures guaranteed annual income (GAI) in Earth Currency and Credit.

2. Specifies criteria for calculating a minimum income covering basic necessities.

3. Guarantees rapid, reliable procedures for applying for GAI supplemental assistance.

4. Entitles people with intermediate incomes to proportion of GAI entitlement assistance.

5. Defines the relationship of a person's total income to the right to receive GAI payments.

6. Guarantees GAI payments upon job loss, illness, or other calamities.

7. (Reserved).

8. (Reserved).

9. Enters effect during the first operative stage of world government as defined in Article 17 of the *Earth Constitution.*

The 10th session of the Provisional World Parliament adopted the Guaranteed Annual Income as World Legislative Act #42, in June 2007, at Kara, Togo, West Africa.

⊕⊕⊕⊕⊕⊕⊕⊕⊕⊕

Conclusion to the World Legislative Summaries

When designing and implementing a comprehensive program for constitutional Earth Federation, both a constitutional and legislative basis is necessary for practical operation. The world legislative summaries give a fair idea of how the entire body of world legislation has begun to reconstitute and integrate the prior systems of international convention law within the context of the *Earth Constitution*. The summaries provide guidelines for implementation of the Earth Federation as global self-government in conformance with the provisions of the *Constitution*. The general concept of how a systemic body of legislation functions in conformance with a constitution is an important step toward understanding an overall civil governing system.

However, general guidelines are not enough for a full understanding. Chapters of the following volumes include the full texts of most of the world legislative acts of the Provisional World Parliament. The following volumes include summary memorandums in the case of a few lengthy world statutes that are based on previously established, widely recognized international laws that are too long for inclusion in this 3 volume set.

As Secretary of the Provisional World Parliament, I hereby attest that to the best of my knowledge the world legislative summaries given in this book are accurate and complete. With very few exceptions, for demonstrative purposes only, the summaries herein were fully engrossed. Finally, the summaries are up-to-date as of spring 2009, using the most recent versions, to include all changes through the 10th session of Provisional World Parliament, which duly met at Kara, Togo, in June 2007, convened in conformance with Article 19 of the *Constitution for the Federation of Earth*.

Summaries Attested:

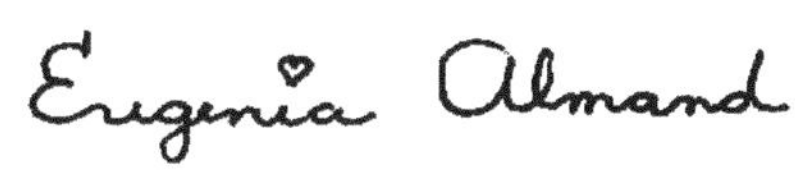

Eugenia Almand, JD, Secretary, Provisional World Parliament

The 10th session authorized the Call to the 11th Session of the Provisional World Parliament which convened in Nainital, Uttarakhand, India, in July 2009. The Provisional World Parliament there amended world legislative Act #34 for the Eliminarion Protocol, now entitled "Dismantling Procedure" (incorporating updates largely from United Nations Official Document #A/62/650), as well as adopted five new world legislative acts, to address human trafficking, civil disobedience, bureaucratic efficiency, prohibition of clandestine activities and integration of consulates, embassies and international agencies within the Earth Federation. At this time, it is not possible to incorporate these into this edition and volume of Emerging World Law, but these changes will be reflected in the upcoming volumes.

Chapter Ten

The *Earth Constitution* and Acts of the Provisional World Parliament as Legitimate World Law

"In practical terms, the judiciaries of the world need the support and cooperation of the legislative and executive organs whose respective spheres are to promulgate and to implement legislative measures."

Namibia High Court Senior Justice A. M. Silungwe (Also former Chief Justice of Zambia)

"We'll have a World Parliament; we'll have an International Court, we'll have the nations big or small respecting the laws made by the World Parliament and the decisions handed out by the International Court. The world would become a better place to live in."

Justice Vishnu Kant Sahai, Former Judge,
Allahabad High Court and Chairman, Law Commission of Uttar Pradesh

Eugenia Almand

Many people see the *Earth Constitution* as a mere model carrying no force of law until after it is officially ratified by the majority of the world electorate and by the majority of national governments or by all the nuclear-powered governments. Therefore, one must ask what is genuine law? What are the sources of law? Is genuine law tied to the illegitimate nation-state system? Is genuine law tied to military power? Is it tied to enforceability? We will see that the *Earth Constitution* and the legislation of the Provisional World Parliament acting under its authority are indeed manifestations of genuine world law.

In addition to what humans call immutable laws of physics and mathematics, humans have conceived of a principle of natural law of human society. In considering the sources of genuine law, we begin with that principle of natural law, that is, the idea that there is a moral law, prior to positive laws, to which both human actions and positive laws should conform.

This has sometimes been simplified to various versions of the golden rule. However, through the ages in philosophy and religion there have been descriptions of the natural law that are far more comprehensive. Under principles of natural law, if person *A* does something that is harmful to person *B*, person *B* is within rights to respond to prevent the harm, and we say the response is morally justified. Within natural law, there is for instance the concept of property right, such that if *B* laboured to produce a result, the results are the property of *B*, and if *A* tries to take the results without *B*'s permission, *B* may respond to prevent the taking or to retrieve the property.

From natural law, we proceed to the distinctly human principle of Institution of Law – For instance, in the realm of religion, sages and prophets have proclaimed divine revelations that together with the judgments of priests have emerged as institution of ecclesiastical law. In other words, the ecclesiastical law is part of the institution of law beyond the mere natural law of human society.

In addition to this, within non-sectarian societies around the world, there have been the gathering of persons, often either considered among the wisest or most powerful within respective tribes, to decide upon rules, often with some form of sanction for violating the rules, and some sort of deciding tribunal or judge to decide cases in which violation of the rules was accused. When a tribe decided upon a rule, that rule in effect became the law. When writing was invented, the scribes for the cases began writing the laws. This process of law development emerged with tribes and kingdoms, city-states and nations, until today we have the current systems of national, international, and world law in place, filling huge libraries. The institution of law is somewhat different from the natural law in that under natural law there are only moral consequences that might include the natural reaction of the persons involved in any case. However, in the institution of law, there come to be numerous elements that do not pre-exist in natural law of human society: (1) the lawgiver, (2) the written form, which may include a prescribed sanction in case of violation, (3) the enforcers, (4) the courts, including the judges, (5) the judicial decision, (6) the court record and so forth.

Regarding the institution of law, an argument is sometimes made that there is no genuine law without all of the above numbered elements in operation. However, this cannot necessarily be the case, because genuine law has to start somewhere and all of the elements do not emerge exactly at once. We can say that, upon the action of the lawgiver, genuine law takes form as the other above-numbered elements are conceptualized and eventually implemented.

The lawgiver might be the chief of a tribe, a council of elders, a king, a dictatorial junta or a parliament. The written form might be a constitution, a transcript of a presidential edict, or a parliamentary statute. The enforcers will be the members of the tribe or society directly, and/or the state, that is, groups of persons specially-armed and trained for the purpose of enforcing the social laws. In modern society, the judges tend to be persons formally trained in the law of the respective society, and appointed to the position. Also, in modern society, we accept principles of *stare decisis* and *res judicata*, meaning that the judges will consider not only constitutional and statutory laws, but also the case law of prior sittings of the courts, including the common law that has emerged through centuries of civilization with established court systems. With regard to the *Earth Constitution* and the Earth Federation, we have the lawgivers, which were the World Constituent Assemblies and sessions of the Provisional World Parliament, together with the heritage of international legal convention that is currently being deliberated for integration within world law.

As for the written form, the *Earth Constitution* itself embodies that, but also the Provisional World Parliament has elaborated parliamentary statutes, including criminal law statutes, that give further significance to the *Earth Constitution* itself. This is because the integrating body of world parliamentary statutes incorporates previously existing, viable international law provisions within the *Earth Constitution* framework for a vital world federal structure that far exceeds the strength of the prior con-federal structure of the United Nations system. The United Nations could not claim ultimate enforcement capacity other than war sanctions and economic sanctions of the United Nations Charter Chapters 6 and 7. Furthermore, the sanctions of Chapters 6 and 7 were not laws in any genuine sense, but merely the description of conditions under which the United Nations would resort to war or economic punishment of an entire society without the elements of lawgiver, courts, judicial decision, or court record. The principles of individual accountability and due process of law are not considered in the United Nations Charter Chapters 6 and 7 or anywhere else in the Charter.

With the work of the Assembly of States Parties, the Provisional World Parliament and the International Criminal Court, we are initiating due process with court cases and judges. The Provisional World Parliament has integrated the Rome Statute (by which the Assembly of States Parties operates) so thoroughly that the Court actually has more legitimate power within the paradigm of the *Earth Constitution*. So this is a live and growing world legal structure.

We must consider enforcement, which is often thought of as one expression of genuine law. Effective enforcement is not necessarily an element of genuine law, in that criminals might for some time evade the law enforcement. However, genuine law will consider and prescribe just means for effective enforcement. This consideration is already addressed in the law enforcement articles of the *Earth Constitution*. In conformance with these basic constitutional provisions, the world legislation of the Provisional World Parliament has elaborated just means and procedures of enforcement in great detail.

Justice A. M. Silungwe's address at the 2006 World Judicial Summit in Lucknow, India, from which the quote for this chapter was taken, can be interpreted as a world judicial mandate from the World Judicial Summit for the enforcement of world law. The enforcement itself is a slightly different function from that of adjudication. A primary function of the World Judicial Summit is for responsible judges to consider humanity's world legal predicament regarding the world problem of war and nuclear weapons and to respond judiciously. Ample world law and international law has very certainly posited the illegality of nuclear weapons, for instance in the International Court of Justice advisory judgment, 1996.

However, the illegality of the nuclear weapons (among other illegalities) is not so much a political or judicial issue now, but rather is more an enforcement issue. This was made clear in the numerous universal conventions on arms, by the Provisional World Parliament first session in Brighton, England, 1982, by World Court decisions in the 1980's and 1990's, and, in 1996 particularly, by the International Court of Justice (ICJ). Illegality of nuclear arms is not a political issue in any of the major parties promoting the continuing violation of these laws. The illegality of nuclear weapons was not a political issue at the World Judicial Summit, but rather was assumed as established world law. This was especially clear at the World Judicial Summit in the huge, commandeering posters quoting the rulings from the 1996 ICJ case and quoting former ICJ Vice-President Justice C. G. Weeramantry:

> My considered opinion is that the use or threat of use of nuclear weapons is illegal in any circumstances whatsoever. It violates the fundamental principles of international law, and represents the very negation of the humanitarian concerns which underlie the structure of humanitarian law. It offends conventional law and, in particular, the Geneva Gas Protocol of 1925, and Article 23(a) of the Hague Regulations of 1907. It contradicts the fundamental principle of the dignity and worth of the human person on which all law depends. It endangers the human environment in a manner which threatens the entirety of life on the planet.
>
> I regret that the Court has not held directly and categorically that the use or threat of use of the weapon is unlawful in all circumstances without exception. The Court should have so stated in a vigorous and forthright manner which would have settled this legal question now and forever.
>
> Instead, the Court has moved in the direction of illegality with some far-reaching pronouncements that strongly point in that direction, while making other pronouncements that are both less than clear and clearly wrong.
>
> I have therefore been obliged to title this a Dissenting Opinion, although there are some parts of the Court's Opinion with which I agree, and which may still afford a substantial basis for a conclusion of illegality. Those aspects of the Court's Opinion are discussed below. They do take the law far on the road towards total prohibition. In this sense, the Court's Opinion contains positive pronouncements of significant value.

Justice A. M. Silungwe, Senior Judge of the High Court of Namibia and former Chief Justice of Zambia, referred to Federation. Justice Silungwe is quoted as saying, "In practical terms, the judiciaries of the world need the support and cooperation of the legislative and executive organs whose respective spheres are to promulgate and to implement legislative measures." To take Justice Silungwe's quoted words at face value, the provisional Earth Federation now has a legal enforcement responsibility. This enforcement responsibility is also clear in the world legislation, particularly world legislative act #14 for the Enforcement System, but also in other subsequent legislation of the Provisional World Parliament.

This logically relates to the world legislatures and the world enforcement system, not to the UN, NATO, the UN Security Council, or national governments, none of which are mandated with regard to these respective spheres under their respective charters. There is a gaping hole in the national and international legal systems of the world, a gigantic legal vacuum, that is only filled by the legislative, judicial, and enforcement mechanisms provided by the *Earth Constitution* and the statutes of the Provisional World Parliament.

Not everyone working with Earth Federation should participate directly in the enforcement process. Furthermore, most of the persons participating even in the Enforcement System itself have no need to take up arms. (For instance, the officers of the Conflict Resolution Department, perhaps to be the largest branch of the Enforcement System, are prohibited from carrying firearms). The raw coercive power of world police force needs to be limited to trained officers in parts of the other four departments, especially the Apprehension & Arrest Department.

Therefore, the Enforcement System has a responsibility to try to work together immediately with other agencies for world law enforcement. Specifically, the Enforcement System offices have a responsibility to engage in continuing communication and integration with the various established law enforcement offices around the world, including the Office of the Prosecutor of the ICC, as well as with Interpol and other meta-national law enforcement agencies. The Enforcement System is neither subordinate nor advisory to these agencies. The Enforcement System has to give support to the World Judiciary.

One might say that not only the time has come for enforceable world law, but that now we have that enforceable law on the books. Moreover, the time has now come for appropriate and able world law enforcement. Every legal system has a beginning, an origin, outside of established procedures for lawmaking. Philosophers sometimes refer to this as *jurisgenesis*. Legitimate systems of law necessarily originate from social arrangements prior to these systems. They begin in Constituent Assemblies like the four that created the *Earth Constitution* in 1968, 1977, 1979, and 1991.

They begin in judicial decisions like those of the International Court of Justice or in common law systems that adjucate on the basis of principles of civilized living. They begin when citizens delineate enforcement mechanisms to arrest those (such as the present-day nuclear weapons criminals) who operate in rogue fashion outside of civilized norms and principles.

On this planet, meta-national criminals wield tremendous power. Recognizing the ICJ decision, nuclear power is seen to be primarily in the hands of criminals, except in some medical and non-military research applications. With an understanding of the law—international convention law, ICJ case law, ASP-ICC *Elements of Crimes*, and Provisional World Parliament legislation, it is logical, realistic, and practical to recognize that these real owners of nuclear weapons are criminals. In conformance with these bodies of world law, there is no national or international status of legality even for the possession of these weapons, much less the blatant overt threats that are and have been cast around at supposed high levels. Furthermore, provisional Earth Federation does not seek approval or consensus from world criminals as any basis for the world law.

Criminals will not willingly abandon criminal power and violent means. Therefore, the responsibility rests with world law enforcement now. We world citizens need not whine and claim that someone else needs to take the responsibility before us. It would be irresponsible, for instance, to depend upon a Security Council decision to "proscribe" these weapons. We live in a world disorder largely run by criminals whose national systems lack legitimacy. As world citizens we, and no one else, are responsible for recognizing that this criminal system is not legitimate and that the *Earth Constitution* fills the moral and legal vacuum with legitimate world law.

We are not concerned with retention of national powers. As Emery Reves clearly pointed out in the *Anatomy of Peace*, and as numerous world federal leaders reconfirmed, this is not a matter of someone else giving up power—of "giving up" sovereignty. That old argument is a shirking of responsibility from world citizenship. The nation-states can be sources of legitimate subsidiary laws only after they have federated under the *Earth Constitution*. World citizens alone can practice the jurisgenesis of recognizing world law, thereby leading to founding ratification conventions in which the nations can follow.

There has to be a federal World State, a World Legislature, a World Executive, and a World Court based upon a World Constitution. That world constitution cannot possibly come about from an abandonment of power. It has been developing through the ardent retention of power by world citizens who understand what this means. Those people who operate as world citizens with a world constitution hold the key. Though there have been hundreds of suggestions for world constitutions, nearly all world constitutions currently circulating share about 95% of their salient features and about 90% of their organic features. (Salient features, example: "Non-military, federal, democratic, parliamentary Earth Government." Organic features, examples: "Congress of Peoples, directly and proportionally elected by world citizens, House of Counsellors, Assembly of States Parties, Enforcement, World Court System, Human Rights Organ separate from both court and enforcement, Executive.") Among leading world federalists polled, there was 94% concurrence on salient features (Gaunt, 2003).

Though it will eventually be necessary for the people to directly confirm some world constitution, it is incorrect to assume that the national representatives must ratify before the system will begin operation. This is because the legal right remains with the participants of the system. In federation, the citizens are the primary participants—the nations are secondary. With initial support from some indefinite critical number of world citizens who claim the world constitution as the highest law, those citizens can legally act at the world level of jurisdiction. National governments or other lesser governments might attempt to interfere, but under the well-founded principles of subsidiarity, and of the right to establish with others one's own government, interference is not legal, and is a violation of rights already guaranteed by all the national governments through the *Universal Declaration of Human Rights* (*UDHR*, particularly by *UDHR* Articles 7 – for equal protection, 21.3 – for universal suffrage, and 28 - for guaranteed social order) and other nationally-guaranteed human rights conventions. There are also numerous world statutes with provisions prohibiting such interference.

The *Universal Declaration of Human Rights* Article 21.3. states, "The will of the people is the basis of the authority of government; Universal and equal suffrage shall express this will in periodic and genuine elections held by secret vote or by equivalent free voting procedures." This electoral process is required by the *Earth Constitution*, but it is not allowed by the *United Nations Charter* (*UNCH*) itself, because of the exclusion of world citizens under *UNCH* Articles 3 and 4, in which it is established that, "Membership is open to … States." This has always been taken to mean that the world citizens are to be excluded from voice in the United Nations, and in practice generally taken to mean that universal suffrage is to be suppressed from the United Nations (with very few exceptions, such as with the acquiescence to the *UDHR* in 1948).

Secondly, it behoves world citizens to examine the basis of nationhood. The *United Nations Charter* incorrectly assumes that nationhood comes from participation in the United Nations system in conformance with the *U.N. Charter*. However, that is an assumption of the basis of nationhood. The *Universal Declaration of Human Rights* (*UDHR*) does not define nationhood, but it does define the authority of government (largely by *UDHR* 21.3). The United Nations, as well as the United Nations Charter, do not even closely approach the requirements under *UDHR* as having any authority of government. A large bat, or a nuclear bomb, is not the legal authority. Likewise, the 192 U.N. Member "Nations" have no legal authority to do anything significant on their own at the global level (other than give preliminary ratification to an adequate democratic world constitution), and it would be an abdication of world citizenship to snivel that the ball is in their court, because it is not in their court.

The General Assembly of the United Nations Organization has never promulgated any law—no legislation whatsoever in 61 years—and the General Assembly is prohibited from attempting to do so by the *UN Charter* itself. That the General Assembly has pronounced a limited number of important global resolutions does not invalidate this assertion. Any delegate stepping out of line will promptly be disciplined by loss of a cozy $140,000 per year (or thereabouts) salary plus emoluments, so it would be in vain to expect the General Assembly to begin any legislative or constitutive process.

However, there is an Assembly of States Parties, with 108 official national governments participating and 139 national signatories. This Assembly of States Parties (ASP) is not the General Assembly of the United Nations Organization. The 108-state Assembly of States Parties has been busying itself with world legislation since before

1998, when it officially began formation. (There are several Conventions of States Parties, but the Assembly currently referred is the Assembly of States Parties that has been developing the *Rome Statute* family of world legislation.) The Assembly of States Parties was not originally federally constituted. Initially, the plenipotentiaries met in loose association with the United Nations, but that was distanced somewhat in 2003, and the ASP Secretariat itself shifted from New York City to The Hague.

Since 2003, there have been overtures for constitutive collaboration between the ASP and the provisional World Parliament. Among other items, the provisional World Parliament, meeting in Chennai in December 2003, adopted a version of the *Rome Statute for the International Criminal Court (Rome Statute)* that is very closely in line with the original. The parliamentary version is a legal requirement under UDHR 21.3 in that the provisional World Parliament is operating under the *Earth Constitution*, which requires and accepts the authority of the people through measured elections under conditions of universal suffrage. Additionally, the parliamentary version puts the statute into plainer language via standard professional legislative drafting guidelines that were not utilized in the original *Rome Statute.*

The parliamentary version also adequately answers objections of non-participating states, while at the same time granting much stronger power to the World Court itself. The conventional dissent by national governments also forms part of the basis for genuine law, just as the dissenting judicial opinions in court cases form part of the basis of case law. This is to say, valid reasons for India, China, United States and Russian Federation not signing and ratifying the *Rome Statute* (ratified by most nations) include the following: lack of provision for jury trial, lack of penal code, lack of *mandamus* (court order), lack of compulsory jurisdiction, allowance for military overrule, and disregard of state weighting from most continental federations for Assembly delegates and Judicial appointments. Under the original ICC Rome Statute, China, India and US combined, with half of the world's population, was permitted only 3 of 60 world supreme court judges and only 3 votes total. These three lands with half of the world's population are allowed only 3 votes of a total of over a hundred delegates in the Assembly of States Parties.

The people cannot permit these faults in a World Court, so the Provisional World Parliament made the minimal adjustments to require the International Criminal Court (ICC) to function as a true Criminal Case Bench within an integrating World Judicial System. The people, via the Provisional World Parliament assigned to the ICC the authority to begin provisional operations without waiting for the further national acceptance of the new version, as a proof of intention to get the World Court System operating strongly and effectively as soon as possible.

Who are the people, if not you and me? The United States was founded by a group of 55 men at a series of *ad hoc* meetings in Philadelphia in 1787. They began their Constitution with "We the people" even though most of the people in the thirteen former colonies at the time did not even know that they were meeting.

Because the Provisional World Parliament considered and responded adequately to the objections of national dissents regarding the International Criminal Court, it is not necessary for the remaining national governments, such as India and United States, to sign, ratify or otherwise accede to the original *Rome Statute* in order to consolidate and further the world judicial system. The World Criminal Court can embrace the objections within its world federal structure. *We the people* are directly participating in the development of world law.

The parliamentary version authorizes the Court to operate provisionally under ASP standards while consolidating the stronger version through working for the first operative stage of world government under the *Earth Constitution*. To understand this meaning, the Court is fully authorized already by the people. The people also urge, at the same time, the world elections and the accession to the *Earth Constitution* by secure joint action of approximately 25 national governments or more as specified in Article 17 of the *Constitution*. However, by world law the International Criminal Court may operate now either under the original *Rome Statute* or under the improved, stronger world statute that answered and answers the objections of the recalcitrant non-participating national states. The people's provisional authorization of the World Court helps prevent or reduce criminals from claiming the no *ex post facto* defense.

So the conventional dissent of national governments drove the people to world federal legal response that synthesized the correct and legitimate response to the objections within the Provisional World Parliament version of the World Court Statute, rather than just ignoring the objections. The objections were accommodated in the peoples' version without compromising the Criminal Bench. Indeed, the World Court is strengthened.

A significant part of the ICJ 1996 advisory opinion on the illegality of nuclear weapons was the ICJ 1996 advisory opinion dissent itself. The dissent is also part of the case law. In the ICJ 1996 advisory case there were two judges, Justice C. G. Weeramantry, and Justice Abdul Koroma, who dissented in favor of an even stronger opinion of the illegality of nuclear weapons (Nuclear weapons are illegal in absolutely all circumstances.) Their strong dissent is actually part of the advisory opinion and therefore part of the law. (To well understand the importance of the dissenting view, it should be noted that Justice Abdul Koroma was also head of the International Law Commission drafting the *ICC Rome Statute*.)

In a similar sense, the dissent of India, China, the United States and other nations regarding the *Rome Statute* can be viewed as part of the law governing the International Criminal Court. From the dissenting opinions, the Provisional World Parliament was able to draft, deliberate, and adopt an improved legal version of the *Rome Statute* that considers and incorporates the objections, the dissenting opinions against the original Statute, while strengthening the World Court from the original Statute.

Since 1998, the Assembly of States Parties has been promulgating good to excellent world legislative code. It has been doing so at a rate with which the Provisional World Parliament and the *Congrès des Peuples* have not been able to keep up. Coordination of these assemblies is extremely desirable. It is customary for the houses or chambers of national assemblies to draft or adopt versions of legislative code and to then consolidate power by negotiating the difference between the various versions to be the statement of the combined legislatures. This is a great power of multi-cameral legislature. If world citizens act strongly in support of such collaboration, world federal power could emerge as the primary state player in less than one or two years.

Here are examples of possible avenues of collaboration: in 2004, the Provisional World Parliament officially granted/assigned electoral functions to the *Registre des Citoyens du Monde* and to the World Service Authority. UNESCO recently acknowledged the function of the *Registre des Citoyens du Monde*. By building this power forward we would be able to bring more directly-elected representatives into the legislative deliberation process. These are the grounds of state power, and these directly supersede the national powers, because significant numbers of national governments (108 in case of *Rome Statute* family of world legislation) have already assigned certain pooling of sovereignty. The energy and law is there, if we world citizens will simply coordinate our actions strongly.

We urge all world citizens to be familiar with the world legislatures, to be supportive, and to build the strengths of these legislatures. Please do not give these assemblies and their functions short shrift! This support by world citizens is independent from national governments, but it is the key to world constitutional success and world federation success. Jurisgenesis arises from *we the people* who act to fill a moral and legal vacuum with legitimate emerging world law.

Rightfully, the world citizens are standing and coordinating to protect the Earth and all its peoples—Especially the better-off world citizens have a responsibility to protect those in oppressed/repressed regions of our Earth where there is already long-accelerating catastrophic turmoil and suffering. Realistic, practical and just world law enforcement emerges from the integration and convergence of the world legislatures acting in concert with the nascent world court system.

The *Earth Constitution* is a model, but not merely a model world constitution. We do claim already existent legality. The *Earth Constitution* is inherently legal and legitimate world law, not because it has already been ratified according to its provisions, but rather because it rightfully asserts that it can be so ratified. This assertion within the institution of law embraces the spirit of the *Universal Declaration of Human Rights* Article 21.3, as well as the *UDHR* provisions for equal protection (*UDHR* Article 7) and guaranteed social and international order (*UDHR* Article 28), and other provisions.

With this assertion for world constitutional ratification and for universal suffrage under conditions of free election, the world citizens who have ratified or otherwise affirmed the *Earth Constitution* are fully within their rights to volunteer implementation of the Earth Federation state, as defined in the *Earth Constitution*. This state apparatus is non-military, but is actually more forceful than the militaries, even more forceful than combined militaries, or regional blocks. This is because the essence of the world federal state is forensic with application of due process, rather than mere military coercion. Forensic application of due process against individual suspects is extremely difficult to resist and inspires popular support. On the other hand, military imposition incites reasonable, just, free, law-abiding human beings to militant non-cooperation and even, under duress, to civil insurgence.

Under the provisions of the *Earth Constitution*, the Provisional World Parliament has adopted a statutory code for an Enforcement System (World Legislative Act #14), including a tightly regulated World Police Department and related departments. The Enforcement System reinforces the Criminal Bench of the World Court by acting at the world jurisdiction to ensure both equal protection as well as social and international order, as guaranteed by the *Universal Declaration of Human Rights*. Neither of these two fundamental human rights can be protected by merely placing requests to national states. The World Court rightfully has compulsory jurisdiction. The Enforcement System, as a world federal state apparatus, confirms the compulsory jurisdiction of the World Court.

There are further constitutional grounds for the claim to legitimacy and the assertion of the *Earth Constitution* as a basis of genuine world law. The *Earth Constitution*, under its own terms is subject to final direct ratification by the people of Earth, and subject to periodic review (every 20 years). Failing direct ratification in measured elections by the people of Earth, the constitutive process would have to go back to drafting and deliberation. This does not necessarily mean that the world federal state power accumulated is sacrificed, but would only indicate that the world constitution needed further development for continuing legitimacy. There would still be world constituent deliberation, and world federal power accrued is not relinquished. The people of Earth are not voting against world constituent deliberation. This has long been a basic principle of law: that people can deliberate and adopt governing constitutions as well as establish government to protect their common interests and to protect themselves from one another.

The *Earth Constitution* itself provisionally recognizes national armies of participating nations, provided those armies do not use the defined and listed weapons of mass destruction and provided those armies do not take up arms against other Earth Federation member nations. Legally, the national armies may continue in this fashion until the second operative stage of Earth Federation, defined in the *Earth Constitution* as acceding to power when 50% or more of nations have ratified, which include 50% or more of total Earth population from the participating nations and world districts.

At the second operative stage, the Earth Federation's Enforcement System of world police, world investigators, world attorneys, penal personnel, and conflict resolution personnel will be operating in concert with the World Court System and the human rights system of the Earth Federation. These employees of the Earth Federation respect *habeas corpus*, use due process of law, warrant procedures, forensic discipline, and will be using other standard, non-military law enforcement processes, including the most advanced technology in less lethal munitions and law enforcement tools.

Strong world federal law enforcement by well-established non-military state principles can prevail over back-stabbing, self-destructive, and poorly coordinated military operations. Currently military operations around the world have been proving themselves to attack villages and neighbourhoods, and to use destructive, illegal equipment that even eventually kills the soldiers deploying the military system, such as with the depleted-uranium munitions. For it seems many persons, most or all of the soldiers themselves, will be slowing dying from the extremely toxic uranium oxide fumes that lodge in the lungs when firing the munitions. Military governments routinely neglect their own civilian populations and even their own troops.

We are moving ahead to the world federal law enforcement, instead of begging permission from illegal organizations that wield military powers. The world federal law enforcement is not starting over from a so-called "clean slate" devoid of legal precedent. Instead, federal law is basing its action upon not only the *Earth Constitution*, but also the pre-existing judicial decisions of the world court and pre-existing world convention laws regarding armaments, as well as more recent and currently developing world laws such as the *Elements of Crimes* (initially developed by the Assembly of States Parties). The Provisional World Parliament has been deliberating additional world legislation to integrate and empower the law enforcement function by which the World Court System will be secured and defended, and by which the human rights protection system is further initiated. There is no legal way to interfere with this development.

The Provisional World Parliament and the Assembly of States Parties are operating without any army and without a military apparatus. This is not to say that we disregard the necessity of irrepressible state power. We do not consider this necessity for irrepressible state power to be any misfortune. The world federal state is simply a practical requirement of survivability for protection of the Earth and humanity. Therefore, the world federal state is not a matter for shame but rather for pride in this advancement of human civilization.

The world federal state operates with enforcement power and tools including armaments that are appropriate for law enforcement purposes. We are not ashamed, but legitimately and moderately proud. In fact, there is no defined upper limit on the quantity of appropriate armaments and armed world federal state officers, and probably should not be any such limit. We believe that there will be long-term reductions in global violence when there is an increase in properly equipped civil law enforcement personnel for the global level of jurisdiction.

Furthermore, the world legislation of the Provisional World Parliament has taken strong legislative measures to empower the citizenry vis-a-vis the official world law enforcement system. Under the provisions of the world legislation of the Provisional World Parliament, the world police may have only those instruments of defence that are not prohibited to the world citizens, without requirement for world citizen license, registration, or display. There are even world legislative provisions (in World Legislative Act #14) for subsidy of munitions corporations that are supportive in our efforts for extending less lethal munitions and empowering the world federal state. These provisions work hand-in-hand.

Therefore, in conclusion, the *Earth Constitution* operates as legitimate world law already. Its roots are in the ancient principle that the people establish their own government. The *Earth Constitution* demands universal suffrage and allows the people to participate within its principles. However, persons that transgress the *Earth Constitution*, or the world laws as these emerge in conformance with the *Earth Constitution*, are liable now for legal prosecution within the World Court System, since adequate and operating World Court and Enforcement System statutes are already in effect. There is no specification in the *Earth Constitution* which states that world criminals must deliver their consensual permission before the Enforcement System can begin apprehension or prosecution. The current caseload is almost negligible, but this is bound to increase as the provisional Earth Federation gathers strength and establishes the district world courts.

The legitimacy of the *Earth Constitution* and other world law is not bound by the illegitimate nation-state system, because the institutions of law and enforcements of law originate from agreements among human beings, not from institutions that act against the interests of humanity. The *Earth Constitution* does not dissolve the nation states (as does the nation-state system itself in some cases), but instead embraces the national governments within a protective world federal regime, where the persons within the participating national government hierarchies are required to comply with the higher laws of humanity.

Military power is not a source of legitimacy. However, in conformance with the *Earth Constitution*, military powers have to accept human limits. Military powers that comply with the world law under the *Earth Constitution* have to internally re-organize for transition to comply with civilian law enforcement procedures, with respect to *habeas corpus*, due process, warrants and forensic investigation. Military organizations that do not comply with the World Law have an internal compulsion to become desperate and fearful. They restrict human freedom and endanger the Earth, bombing villages, schools, and hospitals. Outside the Earth Federation, both military officers and enlisted personnel feel alienation and de-personalization, because their consciousness is distanced and isolated from the world federal state. The commands they receive from national level are cruel, demeaning, and outside the law.

Genuine law and the legitimacy of the *Earth Constitution* emerge from the free and caring, intelligent, and comprehensive interaction of human beings. The justice of the institution of humane law at a global level, the justice of provisions for world due process— these are legitimacy in themselves. The *Earth Constitution* embraces self-government at a global level, world due process of law, and universal suffrage. Because the *Earth Constitution* does these, it is legitimate and genuine law, even before the ratification process completes. World institutions for the enforcement of law may begin formation, and human beings may train to enforce the world law in conformance with the *Earth Constitution*. This formative process that is the initiation of world federal state enforcement activities emerges from that pre-existing genuine law embodied in the *Earth Constitution*.

Recognition is a separate issue from the genuine law itself. Recognition of the genuine nature of the law of the *Earth Constitution* might come early for those persons who consider the moral imperative of the global level institution of law. It might come early to persons who are somehow intellectually initiated to the *Earth Constitution* and world laws. However, in accordance with our personal moral development, recognition of the genuine nature of the *Earth Constitution* as world law for some of us will only come upon learning of the effectiveness of prosecution from the Enforcement System defined by the *Earth Constitution*, or upon media report of some numbers of electorate in the *Earth Constitution*'s favour, or upon participation by some critical number of national governments, etc.

Since the question is not a question of whether the genuine law is recognized, but rather a question of the actual existence of genuine law, we can say that the *Earth Constitution* carries inherently the genuine force of law. The world law elaboration, adjudication, and enforcement in conformance with the *Earth Constitution* are manifestations of formative world federal state process. The world state is an expression of that genuine democratic emerging world law. The resolutions, memorials and legislative summaries of the Provisional World Parliament as integral parts of the world state are presented here for the first time in a single bound volume.

Chapter Eleven

Conclusion:

The Problem of Origins and the Birth of World Law

"When we survey our lives and endeavours we soon observe that almost the whole of our actions and desires are bound up with the existence of other human beings. We see that our whole nature resembles that of the social animals.... The greater part of our knowledge and beliefs has been communicated to us by other people through the medium of a language which others have created.... Only the individual can think, and thereby create new values for society – nay, even set up new moral standards to which the life of the community conforms. Without creative, independently thinking and judging personalities the upward development of society is unthinkable as the development of the individual personality without the nourishing soil of community."

Albert Einstein

"*Our main sin today is that we do not ultimately accept our human destiny.... This demand made upon Man seems to be superhuman, and yet is must be accepted. It is what the great philosopher Kant called: the dignity of Man. We are looking for something petty, something practical, something to give us shelter. We must realize that our present situation is very advanced and by no means petty. It brings us to the awareness that Man is greater than he thinks.*"

Eric Gutkind

Glen T. Martin

In the above quotation, Albert Einstein expressess a fundamental truth about our human situation. Each of us arises from the nourishing soil of community, and our lives represent and internalize these communities. However, not only our local communities but our planetary civilization absolutely need creative, independently thinking and judging personalities to lead humankind toward the realization of its immense inner potential for a democratic world order living in peace, justice, and ecological sustainability upon our precious planet Earth. According to Einstein, such creative and independently thinking persons today reach the following conclusion: "A world government must be created which is able to solve conflicts between nations by judicial decision. This government must be based on a clear cut constitution which is approved by the governments and the nations."

Perhaps our most fundamental failure in this regard is expressed by Eric Gutkind. Our smallness of vision, our satisfaction with tiny, inadequate advances, our Stoic acceptance of the immense evils and corruption of the present undemocratic world order all constitute, for Gutkind, "our main sin today." Our vision remains petty, practical, looking for shelter, while our moral obligation in the face of the immense suffering of the majority of human beings today, and the immense on-going destruction of the world's other living creatures, arises an absolute imperative: a gigantic demand that we create a decent world order of peace with justice in the here and now. Our central failure involves our smallness, pettiness, unwillingness to affirm human dignity, our lack of vision.

The extraordinary work of many world citizens over the past half century in connection with the World Constitution and Parliament Association (WCPA) in developing of the *Earth Constitution* and in holding sessions of the Provisional World Parliament (PWP) emerges from this sense of absolute moral obligation and the demand of human dignity. This half-century of creative work emanates from a sense of the greatness and real possibility of our humanity – democratic world law resulting in a transformed world order. Humankind is immeasurably greater than most persons think, and that is our chief sin today – to expect little, to be "realistic," to reduce everything to a so-called "common sense," to the point of denying the greatness of our human possibilities and our human destiny.

We do not have to wait until the Earth is an uninhabitable desert. We do not have to wait for the coming nuclear holocaust. We do not have to wait until the chains of global dictatorship under a superpower have solidified around our necks. We do not have to wait for 100 years or 1000 years to activate our destiny to live in a world where all persons are protected by law and all persons live under conditions in which their human potential can be realized. It can and must be done now, today, and that is the immense potential of the emerging world law collected in this volume.

1. The Problem of Origins

The problem faced by every creative and independent idea that can move civilization forward toward its true destiny has sometimes been called the "problem of origins." What is truly new has not yet been institutionalized, established, and sanctioned by existing customs or procedures. New truths or civilizing ideas usually find themselves at first ignored in human history, as Arthur Schopenhauer declared. They lie outside the limited "common sense" framework of the day. When they can no longer be ignored, ridicule and laughter become the fundamental response. Finally, however, these civilizing ideas achieve wide acceptance as plain, common sense truth. The origins of what is both truly new and overwhelmingly valid in history are encountered as problematic by the entrenched forces of every historical era as well as by those who minimize the greatness and dignity of our human destiny.

Ancient "common sense" ideas of human civilization under universal empires involving human slavery were not morally legitimate, yet advanced thinkers advocating human dignity were ridiculed at the time. Medieval ideas of human civilization involving serfs bound to the land under an eternal destiny administered by a universal church were not morally legitimate, yet those advocating freedom of thought and religion were ridiculed at the time. Modern ideas of autonomous, militarized sovereign nation-states competing with one another under U.N. structures of unenforceable international laws and undemocratic trade rules are not morally legitimate, yet today those advocating a single *Earth Constitution* with a World Parliament legislating enforceable world laws are either ignored or evoke laughter and ridicule.

In The Concept of Law, philosopher of law H.L.A. Hart identifies the source of legitimate law as a "rule of recognition" commonly accepted within a society that allows citizens to recognize when an authoritative and legally binding law or edict has been issued. This rule may involve a founding document, a set of recognized customs, the functioning of certain institutions, or other sources for recognizing legitimate laws. A central problem that world federalists face today, of course, is the problem of origins. Every rule of recognition must begin from a situation in which it is not yet recognized. A revolution occurs, an old order crumbles and must be replaced through the spontaneous action of a few leaders, a coup takes power and abolishes the legislature, a monarchy is seen as no longer legitimate and must be replaced by democracy. In all these instances and more, a constitution must be written or an institution constructed that provides a rule of recognition for future laws, but in the absence of democratic procedures for writing or constructing such authoritative sources of law, something must simply be begun.

On the planetary level, the problem is similar but clearly more difficult. Since the world has no institutions that can create binding world structures beyond the level of nations, from whence will appear a rule of recognition for world law? The currently accepted macro unit of government is the nation-state. Its self-definition of national sovereignty implies both internal and external autonomy, that is, the recognition of no binding authority beyond its borders. In a revolutionary situation within nation-states, different factions may vie for general recognition by the population and for their rule or institutions to function as a rule of recognition for authoritative laws. But there can be no such situation on the planetary level given the fragmentation of the world into approximately 193 autonomous units called nation-states.

Sovereignty today is indeed being eroded by multinational corporations (often with greater wealth and power than poverty stricken nation-states that host them), and by the World Trade Organization's imposition of binding trade rules capable of economically punishing uncooperative nations, by the impunity of superpowers free to violate weaker nations with invasions, assassinations, or economic blackmail, and by the emerging U.N. doctrine that the Security Council can authorize action against a nation with major violations of human rights within its borders. But none of this brings the world closer to democratic world law. Just the opposite, since all four of these global forces tend to be undemocratic in the extreme, more often than not violating many of the principles set forth in the U.N. Universal Declaration of Human

Rights. If the world is left to evolve toward different forms of governance through the actions of those who now wield tremendous undemocratic power, then the result will be anything but planetary democracy, peace, freedom, or prosperity.

While some federalist movements have debated for decades over the possibilities of calling a world constitutional convention or other means to overcome the problem of origins, the World Constitution and Parliament Association (WCPA) simply went ahead and did this, and has continued to do this from its founding in 1958 to the present in 2008. For the first time in an official publication, this volume collected some of the large body of quality work that resulted from the creative work dedicated to overcoming the problem of origins and founding a new world of peace with justice and prosperity. At the center of this body of work shines the *Earth Constitution* created through the continual efforts of thousands of world citizens and a process of four Constituent Assemblies culminating in 1991. This *Constitution*, we have seen, lays the foundation of genuinely democratic world law to replace the profoundly undemocratic and globally destructive modes of "governance" that have evolved from the U.N. treaty system: the multinational corporations, the WTO, the IMF, the World Bank, and superpower domination. The Provisional World Parliament (PWP) has continued the development of genuinely democratic world law through its ten sessions to date from 1982 to 2007.

We have also seen that Article 17 of the *Earth Constitution* gives the democratic requirements for official ratification and the activation of three operative stages of democratic world government. This democratic ratification process gives the Earth Federation is final legitimacy and authority. It is unlikely that any constitution in history was developed through truly democratic processes, since constitutions often replace an older order that has institutionalized legitimacy differently. The U.S. Constitution, for example, was developed by a few elite federalists who were part of that fateful meeting of a mere 55 persons in Philadelphia in 1787. It found its legitimacy and its binding force through its subsequent ratification by the states who would become members of that federation. As Professor Errol E. Harris puts the matter with regard to the *Earth Constitution*: "There are some who object to the *Constitution* because the body that drafted it was not democratically elected, but what makes a constitution democratic is not how, or by whom, it was drafted but whether it is freely accepted by those who are to become subject to its provisions." Article 17 spells out these democratic procedures in detail.

With regard to the problem of origins, no origin is ever legitimate within the older system when it is first initiated because no rule of recognition exists in those circumstances for legislating binding laws. There always must be a beginning outside the accepted system. After the American Revolution had been won in 1776, the former thirteen colonies loosely affiliated under the Articles of Confederation. Each former colony remained substantially a sovereign nation able to make its own foreign policy, etc. Because this system led to economic chaos among the former colonies and to squabbles that nearly led to wars between them, a group of leaders assembled in Philadelphia in 1787 to amend the Articles of Confederation, just as today large groups of people meet concerned to amend the unworkable U.N. System.

At the meeting there were a few visionaries, known as federalists, and the delegation from South Carolina came to the meeting with a draft of a federal constitution that became the basis of the U.S. Constitution. Their situation, as Harris points out was "similar to that in which the world as a whole finds itself today." They affirmed a federal constitution binding all the former colonies into one, while preserving a reasonable autonomy of internal government for each. There was no precedent and no mechanism by which this new constitution could be considered legitimate. Nevertheless the problem of origins was dealt with simply by going ahead and doing it, while building into the new constitution the criteria for its ratification by the member states.

In a similar vein, contemporary German philosopher Jürgen Habermas addresses the difficult problem of what he calls "jurisgenesis" in which human beings act collectively and morally to bring new institutions into existence. In *Between Facts and Norms: Contributions to a Discourse Theory of Law and Democracy*, he connects his own thought concerning the primacy of "communicative action" with that of American political philosopher Hannah Arendt:

> Arendt conceives political power neither as a potential for asserting one's own interests or for realizing collective goals, nor as the administrative power to implement collectively binding decisions, but rather as an authorizing force expressed in "jurisgenesis" – the creation of legitimate law – and in the founding of institutions. It manifests itself in orders that protect political liberty; in resistance against the forms of repression that threaten political liberty internally or externally; and above all in the freedom-founding acts that bring new laws and institutions "into existence." It emerges in its purest form in those moments when revolutionaries seize the power scattered through the streets; when a population committed to passive resistance opposes foreign tanks with their bare hands; when convinced minorities dispute the legitimacy of existing laws and engage in civil disobedience; when the sheer "joy of action" breaks through in protest movements. Again and again, it is the same phenomenon, the close kinship of communicative action with the production of legitimate law, that Arendt tracks down in different historic events and whose exemplar she found in the constitution-making force of the American Revolution.

This is precisely what the framers of the *Earth Constitution* did but with one substantial difference. As a minority of world citizens convinced that existing laws of nation-states and the U.N. were illegitimate, they acted magnificently to create a legitimate system for the Earth. The U.S. Constitution had come into existence primarily within the space of a single year (1787). Given the proportionally greater difficulty of uniting a planet of differing languages, cultures, religions, and nation-states under a single constitution, the framers spent more than 31 years of intensive communicative dialogue and debate with thousands of world citizens through four Constitutive Assemblies culminating in 1991. It is not power, violence, utility, slow reform, or "common sense" that will bring the transformed world order into existence. It is the power of communicative action exhibited in the creation of the *Earth Constitution* that can overcome the problem of origins and lift civilization to a higher level of existence. This courageous stance of doing what is right because it is right and expressing the right through communicative action and dialogue can transform the awareness of the people of Earth to see that there is a way out of their present suicidal trap: the ascent to a higher, more legitimate world order, the simple step that overcomes the problem of origins by uniting the nations under a non-military civilian democratic *Earth Constitution.*

The framers also wisely allowed for the development of provisional world government while the Constitution was being promoted for ratification under Article 17. The central way that provisional world government has been developed to date has been through sessions of the Provisional World Parliament (PWP). Rather than engage in civil disobedience or violent action, the revolutionaries of the WCPA engaged in morally grounded communicative dialogue demonstrating "the close kinship of communicative action with the production of legitimate law." They began demonstrating through the Provisional World Parliament, and through the Earth Federation Movement (EFM) with its "campaign for ratification," the justification and necessity of a world revolution through world law.

This volume has reproduced the 42 World Legislative Acts (WLAs) passed by these sessions of Parliament covering disarmament, nuclear issues, environment, economics, water resources, peacekeeping, intellectual property rights, etc. These acts do not address the problem of origins by attempting to impose any of this on the world. By an official decision of the Parliament, this provisional world legislation is not considered binding on the final world parliament that will be activated with the official ratification of the *Earth Constitution*. However, it serves as a guide, a beacon, and a model for emerging world law. It can be adopted, rewritten, or discarded by the final world parliament once activated, but the characteristics and spirit of the transformed world order of peace with justice are amply reflected in the provisional world legislation adopted to date, making clear to all that another world is possible.

2. Declaration of the Rights of Peoples and the Necessity Defense

The problem of origins confronts those who would create a democratic world order with the customs and institutions of an older, undemocratic world system that lacks institutions within which to develop this new order. There are no institutional mechanisms whatsoever in place for citizens to develop a global democratic world order. The evolution of the democratic idea to its logical conclusion in world democracy is actively blocked and defeated by the dominant global institutions that have colonized the word "democracy" in the service of a profoundly undemocratic world disorder. As we saw in the Introduction, the present global institutions maintaining the nation-state system and global monopoly capitalism are both self-defeating and self-contradictory. Human rights (including economic rights) are universal. They apply to every human being equally. They cannot be limited to national territories as if human rights stopped magically at some invisible political border. Nor can the rights to a life of minimum economic dignity possessed by all persons be prostituted to a global "marketplace" where human beings are sacrificed as chattel slaves to institutionalized greed in the service of private profit.

The closest we have come today to institutional mechanisms for developing a new world order that are really premised on the universality of human rights and dignity has been the World Constituent Assemblies organized by the WCPA in conjunction with thousands of world citizens. For only these institutions effectively address the problem of origins through a foundation of true universality. These Assemblies, and the Provisional World Parliament that subsequently developed under the authority of the *Constitution*, form the tender shoots of an institutional rebirth for the Earth. As such, they deserve our profound respect and support.

Many other international non-governmental organizations (NGOs) such as Greenpeace, Amnesty International, Oxfam, the collection of organizations allied under the U.N.'s "Millennium Development Goals," or the Simultaneous Policy Project (SIMPOL) have, of course, developed institutional structures. However, these structures explicitly call themselves "non-governmental" and by and large do not seriously question the dominant planetary institutions of the nation-state and global capitalism. They attempt to work within this profoundly undemocratic system and its self-defeating premises to "reform" it in the direction of peace, justice, or environmental sustainability. But a system whose very premises contradict democratic peace with justice cannot be reformed without changing the very premises of the system.

The Earth Federation Movement alone has set up fledgling institutions on entirely new and more legitimate premises – planetary democratic government under an *Earth Constitution* with a parliament legislating enforceable world laws protecting every human being. Unlike the institutions set up by international NGOs, these fledgling institutions are governmental, precisely because it is democratic government that the world lacks, precisely because the chaos of the present world disorder stems from lack of government over the "sovereign" nation-states and global multinational corporations. It is not arrogance or presumptuousness that has led the members of the Provisional World Parliament to claim that they are legislating "provisional world law" under constitutional (and hence governmental) authority. It is the fact that they are confronting the problem of origins in the only way legitimately possible: to originate what is needed.

They have summoned the courage and wisdom to act for precisely what is needed on Earth: enforceable democratic world law legislated by a world parliament. They are justified by necessity, a necessity stemming from the disasters and massive violations of human rights under the current world disorder lacking the rule of law. Just as the laws of most nations recognize the "necessity defense" when people take the law into their own hands to prevent disasters or other tragedies, so this same necessity applies to the problem of origins. Steps taken for moral reasons and without criminal intent are necessary to stop the present catastrophes taking place worldwide. Democratic world government is absolutely necessary and, since there are no viable existing mechanisms for its development, it must be begun. It must be initiated here and now, for catastrophe rages all around us and will clearly only worsen without such law.

The present world disorder confronts conscientious world citizens with an old order that is profoundly immoral, profoundly undemocratic, and deeply in violation of human rights and dignity. These violations of human decency and dignity, that we saw in the introduction to this volume, involve the dominant institutions of the present world: the system of sovereign nations and the global economic system. According to international legal scholar Francis A. Boyle, in his book *Protesting Power: War, Resistance, and Law* (2008), not only the government of the United States but many nations of the world operate according to the "realist view of international relations" as defined, for example by Hans Morgenthau in his classic political treatise Politics among Nations (1948). Boyle writes:

> In the realist view of international relations, international law is devoid of any intrinsic significance within the utilitarian calculus of international political decision making. International law, morality, ethics, and even knowledge itself become mere components in the power equation, devoid of noninstrumental significance or prescriptive worth, and subject to compulsory service as tools of power when deemed necessary for the national interest of a state. There are no barriers to the acquisitive nature of the nation-state beyond its domestic limitations and constraints imposed by the international political milieu. Consequently, the analysis and conduct of international relations must concentrate exclusively on the dynamics of power politics and national interest.

According to Boyle, those committing "civil resistance" by breaking U.S. domestic laws in response to the violations of human rights, destruction of life and property, and violations of international law caused by U.S. foreign policy are legally justified in doing so and have ample legal justification for acquittal in the courts. For example, the readiness of the U.S. nuclear arsenal alone, which includes such weapons of mass destruction its Minuteman III nuclear missile, already stands in violation of international law in any number of ways. U.S. citizens are fully justified in breaking domestic laws in the attempt to derail a U.S. military and foreign policy that is deeply destructive, deeply immoral, and in gross violation of human rights and international laws.

Boyle outlines the various defenses that could be mounted in the courts with regard to civil resistance intended to protect people, property, and human rights around the world: "People who engage in civil resistance have a constitutional right to rely on whatever statutory and common-law defenses are generally made available to every other criminal defendant in the jurisdiction concerned, for example, defense of self, defense of others, necessity, choice of evils, prevention of crime, execution of public duty, citizen's arrest, prevention of a public catastrophe, measures otherwise authorized by law, absence of criminal intent." All of these several defenses apply equally to those not committing civil resistance within nations but who confront the problem of origins in their attempt to create a democratic world order.

Under the laws of many countries, breaking the law with the absence of criminal intent (hence for some moral purpose) is justifiable to protect others in immanent danger of harm, to prevent a crime, or to prevent a public catastrophe. How much more, therefore, do these defense arguments justify those who are trying to establish a world order that prevents these lawless and criminal arrangements from happening in the first place? The criminal consequences of the present world order provide ample justification for citizens of the Earth to take active steps to found a democratic world order free of such consequences. The Eighth Session of the Provisional World Parliament, meeting in Lucknow, India in 2004, unanimously ratified the "Declaration of the Rights of People of Earth to create and ratify a World Constitution and hold sessions of the Provisional World Parliament." This document states that:

> The present institutions of the world are failed institutions. The global economic system has not led to prosperity for most of the Earth's citizens, but to starvation, poverty, disease, and misery for the majority. The present global political systems of the world, called territorial nation-states, have not led to a just or peaceful world order, but to endless wars, destruction of peoples and cultures, imperial domination and conquest, and global systems of exploitation of the weaker by the stronger. The United Nations has not led to a world where the many rights listed in its Universal Declaration of Human Rights have been extended to the Earth's citizens, but to denial of those rights for the majority and continuous increase in war, poverty, social chaos, and environmental destruction.

I recently made a similar point in *Ascent to Freedom: Practical and Philosophical Foundations of Democratic World Law*:

> When the framework of a democratically legislated body of enforceable law is missing (as in the international arena), the consequences are precisely those that we find all round us in the world today. The strong prey upon the weak, international child prostitution flourishes, slavery and trafficking in human beings or human organs is rampant, international drug smuggling is unstoppable, hit squads of assassins travel the globe looking for their targets designated by national governments or their counterparts in terrorist organizations, currency manipulation and financial fraud is commonplace. Imperialism destroys entire countries with its military and economic warfare, international exploitation of the poor by the rich worldwide flourishes, militarism and worldwide legal and illegal sales in weapons expands annually, unstoppable poverty grows nearly everywhere, and multi-faceted environmental destruction continues unabated. These horrors are not something yet to be dealt with through an evolution or tinkering with the system of international law. Rather, they follow directly from the absurd premises on which international law is based.

It is precisely this criminally based, inherently undemocratic world order that forms the grounds for the "necessity" of all persons of conscience to act for defense of the peoples of Earth and the collapsing planetary environment that sustains us all. Just as the domestic laws of many nations protect the necessity of persons to act to prevent catastrophe, to protect lives, or to prevent criminal activity so persons of conscience are faced with the necessity to create a democratic world order where these catastrophes are substantially reduced if not altogether eliminated. This clearly cannot be done within the framework of the present world order. As we saw in the introduction to this volume, the present institutions dominating our world disorder (global capitalism and sovereign nation-states) reflect failed institutions that we must understand as profoundly illegitimate. The people of Earth have the right to live in peace and freedom under legitimate democratic institutions premised on the common good and the equality of all.

Even the U.N. Universal Declaration of Human Rights specifies this fundamental human right: "Everyone is entitled to a social and international order in which the rights and freedoms set forth in this Declaration can be fully realized" (Article 28). Every person on Earth is entitled to an international order in which all thirty of the human rights listed in the Universal Declaration can be fully realized. These universal rights include Article 25, number 1: "Everyone has the right to a standard of living adequate for the health and well-being of himself and of his family, including food, clothing, housing and medical care and necessary social services, and the right to security in the event of unemployment, sickness, disability, widowhood, old age or other lack of livelihood in circumstances beyond his control." Very few nations on Earth satisfy Article 25 and no nation on Earth satisfies Article 28 precisely because there is no democratic world social order that can even begin to make this possible. It is the right and duty of every citizen of Earth, therefore, to create such an order, and the most practical and effective way of doing so is through ratification of the *Constitution for the Federation of Earth*.

The problem of origins involves the fact that there are no democratic institutions in place for creating world democracy. The U.N. Charter is premised on inherently undemocratic assumptions, despite some of its internal rhetoric. Article 2, Number 1, states that "The Organization is based on the principle of the sovereign equality of all its Members." This principle alone makes the rule of enforceable democratically legislated law on Earth impossible. It means that there is no enforceable law above the nations, because they are "sovereign." In addition, the General Assembly represents all nations equally, regardless of vast disparities of population, and regardless of the fact that many member states are not democracies and ambassadors do not represent their peoples in any significant way. The Security Council gives an absolute veto power to the five most powerful victors in World War Two and makes the U.N., in effect, a dictatorship under these five. The United Nations itself is in substantial violation of its own Universal Declaration of Human Rights (for example, Article 25) and its very structure massively violates Article 28 since under this "social and international order" it is manifestly impossible to protect the human rights of the Earth's citizens.

3. Interfacing with the United Nations and Existing International Law

Nevertheless, the Earth Federation Movement does not wish to abolish the U.N., which has a global infrastructure and many valuable agencies in place such as the World Health Organization (WHO), the High Commission on Human Rights (UNHCHR), the International Labor Organization (ILO) or the Educational, Scientific and Cultural Organization (UNESCO), the International Court of Justice (ICJ), and the International Criminal Court (ICC), to name but a few. These organizations perform real service to the people of Earth. These agencies and their infrastructure can and must be preserved, expanded, empowered, and made truly effective on a global scale.

The failure of the U.N. lies with its Charter, which remains a mere treaty among the sovereign states, and does not empower a democratic parliament to legislate binding world laws. This Charter must be replaced with the *Constitution for the Federation of Earth*. If the *Constitution* is ratified under the criteria specified in Article 17, the first immediate steps of the new Earth Federation in addition to activating the World Parliament will be to invite all viable U.N agencies to integrate into the ministries specified under the *Constitution*. The High Commission on Human Rights can integrate into the World Ombudsmus, the ICJ and ICC can integrate into the World Supreme Court System, etc.

Doing so will empower these agencies immeasurably. Their funding base will no longer be dependent on the voluntary contributions of nations but will be vastly expanded to make them effective on a planetary scale. Their office infrastructure will be expanded to provide what is needed for all the people of Earth. Their agencies will no longer be subject to the power politics of nations or the whims of imperial powers. The existing accomplishments of the U.N. will be magnified to serve as a basis for a real transformation of the world order. Only under a democratic constitution can this happen, for the present undemocratic structure of the world and the U.N. itself currently defeats the very goals that are articulated in the U.N. Charter "to promote social progress and better standards of life in larger freedom" for all human beings.

In addition to advocating replacement of the U.N. Charter with the *Earth Constitution*, the Provisional World Parliament has already taken steps to interface with existing U.N. movements for the development of world law, themselves facing the same problem of origins. Specifically, it has adopted a variety of world statutes developed by the Assembly of States Parties (ASP) who have been signatories to the treaty for an International Criminal Court (ICC). The Parliament has reconstituted and integrated the Rome Statute for the International Criminal Court as World Legislative Act #20 for a World Court Bench for Criminal Cases. It has also adopted and modified *The Rules of Procedure and Evidence* developed by the Assembly of States Parties for the ICC as World Legislative Act #24. In addition, the Parliament has adopted the Statute on the Rights of the Child, reconstituting with greater strength the original U.N. Convention on the Rights of the Child, as a necessary legal basis for creating a World Juvenile Bench that recognizes the generally accepted principles of juvenile law.

The problem facing the Convention on the Rights of the Child as well as the Assembly of States Parties in developing an International Criminal Court is that these have been so far developed within the framework of sovereign nation-states and hence can function as no more than voluntary treaties from which nations may withdraw if they please. The Rome Statute of the ICC was written under this assumption. The original ICC statutes, therefore, rather than empowering the Court for issuing *subpoenas* and requiring witnesses and evidence as commanded by enforceable law, could only "*request*" such things, since the ICC is dealing with possible crimes committed within sovereign nation-states who may be party to the ICC treaty. The ICC is a major step forward towards world law applied to individuals (as opposed to most "international law" that applies to nation-states), but it still faces the problem of origins in taking the leap to real law, enforceable over individuals.

The Provisional World Parliament (PWP) has changed only that wording that degrades the statutes of the ICC to compromise with the treaty system of sovereign states. Instead, it assumes the power of *mandamus*, the real power of a legitimate court to summon witnesses, order arrests, and compel testimony. The World Constitution and Parliament Association, from its interim offices at the New Humanity Centre in Kalamata, Greece, continued work during the 2006-2007 years to integrate the statutes of the ICC with the work of the PWP that would substantially strengthen both initiatives. This work continues with regard to a number of excellent statutes of international law that can easily be transformed into genuine world law.

Neither the WCPA nor the PWP command the significant resources and connections possessed by the ICC (which has a 90 million Euro internal budget for 2008). Yet the ICC lacks an institutional framework transcending the system of nation-states that can provide a rule of recognition for world law enforceable over individuals. If the ICC were to draw on the *Earth Constitution* and the work of the PWP for its authority and legitimacy, the cause of legitimate, enforceable world law would be advanced immeasurably, which appears to be the precise goal of both movements.

Both initiatives can further contribute to their legitimacy and mitigate the problem of origins by drawing on the Universal Declaration of Human Rights: Articles 7 (for equal protection under law), 21.3 (for the voice of people via universal suffrage as the authority of government) and 28 (for a guaranteed universal social order that makes effective protection of human rights possible). One can reasonably argue that multi-cameral world parliament is urgently required and already legal, since enforceable world law is recognized as a human right in this Declaration. However, the problem of origins can be more effectively dealt with through cooperation of the ICC and the PWP, for the PWP is actually doing precisely what is necessary if the ICC is to be ultimately legitimate and successful.

4. A Powerful Global Democracy

There are some world federalists who object to the *Earth Constitution* because it creates a powerful Earth Federation government with authority over many areas of world order. These thinkers believe that the world should create a much weaker federation giving more latitude to nations, global trade organizations, and local communities. They fear putting too much power into the hands of a centralized world bureaucracy. In 1950, before the information that we have today about the devastation of our world across the spectrum of human activities, this argument may have been cogent. And thinking exclusively in terms of the flawed, limited, and militarized institutions of "governance" now in place in the world, this argument might also be considered cogent. But in the light of the advanced condition of destruction throughout the spectrum of human activities that we are aware of today, and in the light of the carefully constructed democratic checks and balances embedded in an *Earth Constitution* that will be free of militarism, secrecy, and fear, both of these arguments appear deeply flawed.

Hannah Arendt distinguishes between power and violence in ways that may illuminate why powerful global democracy is not only legitimate but necessary and desirable:

> Power needs no justification, being inherent in the very existence of political communities; what it does need is legitimacy.... Violence can be justifiable, but it never will be legitimate.... We saw that the current equation of violence with power rests on government's being understood as domination of man over man by means of violence.... To substitute violence for power can bring victory, but the price is very high: for it is not only paid by the vanquished, it is also paid by the victor in terms of his own power.... Power and violence are opposites; where the one rules absolutely, the other is absent. Violence appears where power is in jeopardy, but left to its own course it ends in power's disappearance. This implies that it is not correct to think of the opposite of violence as nonviolence; to speak of non-violent power is actually redundant. Violence can destroy power; it is utterly incapable of creating it.

The *Earth Constitution* sets up a government with authority to regulate many aspects of our world order for the common good of the people of Earth including legal regulation of major globally necessary resources such as oil, global financial institutions, global corporations, and nation-states insofar as they must conform to the human rights specified in Articles 12 and 13. It also sets up a network of nonviolent mechanisms of governance that eliminate all need for a military, that promote conflict resolution and open dialogue world wide, that institutionalize world courts in the service of the rule of law and fairness, that strictly limit the prerogatives of the World Executive and World Police, and that institutionalize a World Ombudsmus devoted to protecting the people of Earth from all sources of harm, including the Earth Federation itself.

All these mechanisms maximize non-violence in human affairs. For this very reason, as Arendt points out, they also maximize authentic, legitimate power. The Earth Federation's real power to promote the common good and create a world of peace, justice, and sustainability will be activated to the extent that the political community of Earth recognizes, legitimates, and supports these mechanisms and methods of governance. It will lose power and legitimacy precisely to the extent that violence is used to protect arbitrary forms of domination. As Mahatma Gandhi expressed this in *Socialism of my Conception*, when exploitation and domination are absent, a government has no need of deception, lies, secrecy manipulation of information, or a military apparatus. Its operations will be transparent to the people and its power will be proportionate to their support. What we want and need is a powerful global democratic government capable of dealing with the immense catastrophes faced by human kind, from global poverty and disease to massive human rights abuses to planetary climate collapse.

In the Introduction, we reviewed Article 1 of the *Earth Constitution* that outlines the basic functions of the Earth Federation. Each of these six functions deals with a set of major global crises that plague humanity beyond the scope of any sovereign nation or treaty of such nations. Each of these crises already causes immense suffering and human rights violations among the peoples of Earth. And each can only be dealt with effectively by a powerful democratic government with sufficient authority to make and enforce laws everywhere on the planet. There is no other way to turn around climate collapse and restore the Earth to ecological health. There is no other way to eliminate all militaries and weapons of war from the Earth. There is no other way to create reasonable economic equality and prosperity for the peoples of Earth. There is no other way to effectively protect the human rights of every person on Earth. Powerful democratic government is utterly needed and those who claim otherwise are simply naïve or disingenuous.

Genuinely democratic government should be powerful, for it clearly must effectively protect human rights, the environment, the economic prosperity of all people, and end militarism and war. The real issue is not the power of government; the real issue is the design of government to ensure that genuine democracy is preserved and protected and how to authentically empower it on behalf of the common interests of the people of Earth. Close examination of the *Earth Constitution* reveals that it is brilliantly conceived to protect democratic processes and prevent tyranny. The analyses presented by Dr. Eugenia Almand in this volume demonstrate this careful design at great length. The Earth Federation will have no military. Its Executive Branch (always the most dangerous branch of any government) will not even have police powers. The Executive has no power to declare a state of emergency and suspend the Constitution, no power to refuse to implement the budget, and its members may be removed for cause through carefully defined procedures of the World Parliament.

It is also important to realize that under the Earth Federation the power of democratic government will be substantially transformed from what we presently think of as "powerful government" under the nation-state system. Powerful government today is associated with violent military and police powers that are used all over the world for surveillance, intimidation, and repression of populations. Hans Morgenthau's Politics among Nations stresses that nation states and their ruling elites are concerned with "power," which really means violent imposition of special interests at the expense of the majority. Like its forerunner, Machiavelli's *The Prince* (1532), political "realism" of leaders directs itself to violent "power" most basically, emphasizing militarism and coercion when necessary while at the same time using moral concepts (the rhetoric of democracy, peace, or popular goals like "protecting the environment") only as a means for political control and domination in the interests of the state and its ruling elites – whatever it takes in a world of scarcity built around absolute winners and losers.

It is precisely this pursuit of "power" so feared by those who believe in freedom today that will largely disappear from the authentic democratic system of the Earth Federation. When the non-democratic aspects of the world disappear, including the foreign policy of all "sovereign nations" with their militaries, their secrecy, and their espionage, then things will look very different. When the scarcity of goods and resources disappears through a rational and moral economic policy in the service of all persons, then the incentive to control what is available will largely evaporate. And when a media in the service of a ruling class and powerful governmental interests disappears (and all these will explicitly disappear under the *Earth Constitution*), then politics, leadership, police powers, and the uses of governmental bureaucracy will all be substantially transformed. We need powerful democracy, for genuine power is always "power of the people." But such democracy under the *Earth Constitution* will be substantially and demonstrably different from today's arbitrary big government insensitive to the public, using secrecy and security to cover up its real agenda, while actually destroying democracy and violating human rights everywhere on Earth.

5. The Roadmap

When I was in Japan in 2005, I met with many members of the Japanese World Federalist Movement (WFM) and other supporters of the democratic world government. World federalism in Japan has flourished more vibrantly than in many other parts of the world in part because the Japanese have kept alive their memory of the horror of nuclear weapons. I met a number of Japanese world federalists or WCPA supporters also devoted to preserving the memory of what happened in Hiroshima and Nagasaki. Yet world federalists there told me that the younger generation is asking for a "road map." They are not content with organizations advocating world government or educating people on the need for world government, they want to know how this can be accomplished.

The answer to that question is embodied in Articles 17 and 19 of the *Earth Constitution* that deal with ratification of the *Constitution* and the development of provisional world government respectively. Unlike some NGOs working for "global solutions," it is not necessary to spend vast amounts of time and energy fighting with the world's dominant institutions and their power structures over incremental modifications of the absurd and immoral world system. Article 17 wisely lays out three progressive levels of activation for the Earth Federation. Actions directed to achieving each of these three levels provide a specific roadmap for citizens of Earth to follow in order to liberate themselves from the trap of the present contradictory world disorder that uses the rhetoric of democracy and human rights to actively militate against transformation to genuine global democracy.

Ratification by political units

Section A specifies procedures for ratification that can include referendums for any defined political unit or referendums of electoral districts as these are worked out by the Provisional World Government. These include "local communities, cities, countries, states, provinces, cantons, prefectures, tribal jurisdictions, or other defined political units." All such referendums must include a minimum of all eligible voters over the age of 18. A simple majority vote of the voters shall determine ratification. Section A also specifies that "the universities, colleges and scientific communities and institutes in any country may ratify the *Constitution*." The roadmap becomes clear for those in each community of the world. The campaign for ratification can operate in any venue and at any level. The goal is to get as many defined political or educational units of the world as possible to ratify the *Constitution*.

Ratification by individuals and organizations

As we saw in the Introduction, individuals may also ratify the *Constitution* and take themselves out of the immoral condition of *de facto* war that now perverts human relationships worldwide. All such individuals can now discern this feature of the roadmap: through grassroots activism for worldwide referendums on the *Earth Constitution*, the ground swell will grow into the overwhelming demand for authentic global democracy and the dawn of a new era for humanity. At the same time the Earth Federation Movement also encourages organizations to affirm the ratification of the *Earth Constitution* as part of their organizational goals. It has been developing a network of organizations that work for the environment, to end poverty, to secure nuclear disarmament, or to protect human rights while at the same time affirming the *Constitution*. None such organizations can succeed in their goals unless the *Constitution* is ratified and enforceable world law is developed. As Professor Errol Harris expresses this:

> Greenpeace.... will not attain its ends unless it joins forces with other non-governmental organizations and with the World Constitution and Parliament Association in a campaign for the ratification of the World Constitution.... The goals of Oxfam are already included among the Directive Principles set out in the *Constitution for the Federation of Earth*, and only an authority with global jurisdiction could effectively legislate to attain them.... The human rights that Amnesty espouses...are all embodied in the World Constitution.
>
> To achieve its aims, therefore, Amnesty International must join the campaign to ratify the *Constitution for the Federation of Earth* and apply its skills and its energies as much to advertising that as to detecting violations of Human Rights.

Ratification by the minimum number of nations.

Article 17, Section C, provides for "preliminary or final ratification by a minimum of twenty-five nations, each having a population of more than 100,000." It provides for several combinations of ratification by nations with ratification by direct referendum of world electoral districts. (The WCPA has already done noteworthy work in defining these districts for the Earth Federation.) However, this minimum requirement makes the first operative stage of world government a practical and realizable goal. No other world federalist organization offers anything resembling this practical arrangement that can happen in the relatively near future and which is legitimated by the *Earth Constitution* itself. Concerned citizens of the Earth and the network of organizations described above should all be working for a founding ratification convention scheduled to meet at a specific time and place, convening at least the minimum number of nations who will simultaneously ratify the *Constitution*.

The Protocol of procedures for ratification at this founding ratification convention has already been developed by the Provisional World Parliament. Here is something specific, doable, and Earth-transforming that concerned individuals and organizations can incorporate into their goals. We are not lost in the maelstrom of struggling against endlessly resistant forces attempting to prevent the U.N. from becoming effective. We are not lost as private citizens or NGOs struggling against the overwhelming odds posed by multinational corporations. The most practical steps we can be taking involve establishing this founding ratification convention and bringing the minimum of twenty-five governments to the table, governments who realize that there is no way out of their present nightmare of poverty, disease, exploitation, and manipulation by the dominant world forces unless they act to found a new, democratic world system. As world-famous anthropologist Margaret Mead declared: "Never doubt that a small group of thoughtful, committed citizens can change the world. Indeed, it is the only thing that ever has."

Provisional world government

Article 19 empowers citizens of Earth to set up provisional world government in lieu of the failure of the governments of the world to cease in their criminal neglect of the global environment, global poverty, global militarism, or global human rights abuses. We saw the Declaration of the Rights of Peoples affirm that citizens of Earth have both a right and duty to live under the legitimate rule of democratically legislated world laws. This article provides criteria for initiating the Provisional World Executive, for financing the provisional world government, for setting up the provisional World Court system, and the Provisional World Parliament. All these are concrete tasks that citizens can be working on now to move the world rapidly forward to real transformation of its present self-defeating and self-contradictory premises.

We have seen that the aspect of Provisional World Government most developed to date has been the Provisional World Parliament, which as met ten times from 1982 to 2007 with an eleventh session scheduled for Kolkata, India in January 2009. The Parliament addresses the problem of origins head-on. It is not merely "provisional." It is also governmental representing, as no other organization does, all the people who live upon the Earth. Legitimate government for the Earth must begin somewhere, someplace before it is too late. Indeed, it is already a half century overdue. It begins under Article 19, here and now.

This article provides another dimension of the roadmap for people to build the foundations of a legitimate world order. While we have seen that these foundations are not binding on the final World Parliament activated with the First Operative Stage of the Earth Federation, its structures, institutions, decisions, financing systems, and laws will profoundly impact the future of Earth, and the newly ratified Earth Federation will have resources to draw upon (trained leaders, documents, organizational infrastructures, finances, etc.) that are ever more urgently needed as the Earth continues to descend into social chaos under its present illegitimate world disorder. As Eric Gutkind declares: "Man is greater than he thinks." We are capable of rising to the challenge.

The people of Earth have a concrete program available to them for a decent future. Present NGOs not affirming the *Earth Constitution* push on blindly in the face of ever-growing social chaos and destruction on the Earth. Most present world federalist organizations endlessly talk about "global democracy" in the face of ever-growing dictatorship and domination from the world's superpowers or hopelessly try to work within the present self-defeating system without confronting the problem of origins. Present national governments are either trapped into the endless cycle of poverty and domination through exploitation of their cheap labor and resources or caught in the competitive power struggle of weapons and greed that flushes down the toilet of militarism alone more than a trillion U.S. dollars per year. The only viable option is ratification of the *Earth Constitution* before it is too late. The *Earth Constitution* itself provides a roadmap with specific, achievable goals adequate to address our multifaceted planetary crises. Professor Harris eloquently describes what is at stake if we fail:

> The fruits of culture will be lost forever; the light of knowledge will be extinguished, and the discoveries of science will have been in vain; the illumination of consciousness will vanish from the Earth, abandoning it to oblivion as it becomes a dead planet, like Mars or Venus. Federalists of the Earth unite; we have everything to lose if you fail!

The three volumes of *Emerging World Law* together constitute an immense source of hope in the face of our chaotic world order. The monumental work by thousands of world citizens over half a century collected in them not only envisions a truly transformed world premised on peace, justice, and sustainable prosperity. It also confronts the problem of origins in ways that provide a genuine course of action for freeing ourselves from the self-contradictory premises of our present failed world system. For the first time, this astonishing synthesis of vision, integrity and hope will be available to humankind in a mere three volumes. We do not have to reinvent the wheel. Our task is to make it happen, to effectively address the immense suffering of the people of Earth, future generations, and the other life-forms on our precious planet by courageously facing, rather than avoiding, the problem of origins. We have before us a practical, realistic set of options for the people of Earth, a set of options that all those of vision, wisdom, and courage may embrace without compromise.

Emerging World Law - Volume One

Sources of the Epigraphs

Chapter One: Introduction

World Constituent Assemblies, (1977 and 1991), H. Philip Isely, Syed Md. Hussain, Terence P. Amerasinghe, D.M. Spencer and Max Habicht, principal authors, *A Constitution for the Federation of Earth*, p.2.

Chapter Two: Conceptualizing the Earth Federation

Antoine de Saint-Exupery, (1900 - 1944) *Columbia World of Quotations*, Columbia University Press, p. . In bartleby.com (Accessed June 2008)

Daniel H. Burnham, (1846 - 1912) *Columbia World of Quotations*, Columbia University Press. In bartleby.com (Accessed June 2008)

Chapter Three: A History of Emerging World Law

Alfred Lord Tennyson (1834) "Locksley Hall"

Chapter Three Addendum: Recent History of the Provisional World Parliament

Hermann Hesse (1877–1962) *Columbia World of Quotations*, Columbia University Press. In bartleby.com (Accessed June 2008)

Chapter Four: Manifesto of the Earth Federation

Calvin Coolidge (1872–1933) *Columbia World of Quotations*, Columbia University Press. In bartleby.com (Accessed June 2008)

Photo Plates from the historical roots and from the World Constituent Assemblies

Chapter Five: Analytical Commentary on World Constitution Concepts

Anna Elizabeth Dickenson, US Abolitionist and Suffragist (1842-1932) *Columbia World of Quotations*, Columbia University Press. In bartleby.com (Accessed June 2008)

Chapter Six: *The Constitution for the Federation of Earth*

Aristotle (384–323 B.C.) *Columbia World of Quotations*, Columbia University Press. In bartleby.com (Accessed June 2008)

Chapter Six Addendum: Signatories to the *Earth Constitution*

Anna Howard Shaw (1847–1919), U.S. minister, suffragist, and speaker.

April 19, 1910, before a hearing of the United States Senate Judiciary Committee *Columbia World of Quotations*, Columbia University Press. In bartleby.com (Accessed June 2008)

Chapter Seven: Clarification of the *Earth Constitution*

Quote from Benjamin Franklin at the close of the U.S. Constitutional Convention in 1787,

Chapter Eight: Resolutions and Memorials of the Provisional World Parliament

Henry David Thoreau (1817–1862) *Columbia World of Quotations*, Columbia University Press. In bartleby.com (Accessed June 2008)

Chapter Nine: Legislative Summaries of World Legislative Acts 1 through 42

Legislative Administration Committee, (1997), *Oregon Form and Style Manual for Legislative Measures* . (accessed August 2008): http://www.leg.state.or.us/lc/formstyle.html

Chapter Ten: Legitimate World Law

Namibia High Court Senior Justice A. M. Silungwe (Also former Chief Justice of Zambia) at International Conference of Chief Justices of the World on Article 51 of India Constitution (World Judicial Summit)

Justice Vishnu Kant Sahai, Former Judge, Allahabad High Court and Chairman, Law Commission of Uttar Pradesh at International Conference of Chief Justices of the World on Article 51 of India Constitution (World Judicial Summit) On-line. Available. (accessed August 2008):
http://www.cmseducation.org/article51/brief_rep.htm

Chapter Eleven: Conclusion – Volume 1

Einstein, Albert (1949). *The World As I See It.* Alan Harris, trans.

New York: Philosophical Library.

Einstein, Albert (1950). *Out of My Later Years.* New York: Philosophical Library.
Gutkind, Eric (1969). *The Body of God: First Steps Toward an Anti-Theology -- The Collected Papers of Eric Gutkind.* Lucie B. Gutkind and Henry LeRoy Finch, eds.
New York: Horizon Press.

Works Cited and Bibliography for Volume 1

Chapter One: Introduction

Agenda 21. [On-line.] Available. (accessed August 2008): http://www.un.org/esa/sustdev/documents/agenda21/english/agenda21toc.htm

Churchill, Ward, in Sterba, James (1994), *Social and Political Philosophy*, p. 266) Florence, Kentucky : Wadsworth

Engels, Friedrich (1882). *Socialism: Utopian and Scientific*. [On-line.] Available. (accessed August 2008): http://www.marxists.org/archive/marx/works/1880/soc-utop/index.htm

Mill, John Stuart. (1859) *On Liberty.* [On-line.] Available. (accessed August 2008): *http://www.constitution.org/jsm/liberty.htm*

Joint Vision 2020. [On-line.] Available. (accessed August 2008): http://www.dtic.mil/jointvision/jvpub2.htm

Kant, Immanuel (1964). *Groundwork of the Metaphysic of Morals*. H. J. Paton, trans. New York: Harper & Row. [Also On-line.] Available. (accessed August 2008): http://philosophy.eserver.org/kant/metaphys-of-morals.txt

Korten, David C. (2001). *When Corporations Rule the World.* Second Edition. Bloomfield, CT: Kumarian Press.

Kyoto Protocol. On-line. Available. (accessed August 2008): http://unfccc.int/resource/docs/convkp/kpeng.html

Locke, John (1965). John Locke: Two Treatises of Government. Revised Edition. Peter Laslett, ed. New York: Mentor Books. [Also On-line.] Available. (accessed August 2008): http://en.wikipedia.org/wiki/Two_Treatises_of_Government

Machiavelli, Niccolo (1532. English language reprint 1980) *The Prince*. New York: New American Library. [Also On-line.] Available. (accessed August 2008): http://www.constitution.org/mac/prince00.htm

Martin, Glen T. (2005) References to U.S. Supreme Court Justice John Marshall and Marshall Doctrine, "Twelve Political Editorials 12. Torture and the Illusions of Empire." [On-line.] Available. (accessed August 2008): http://www.runet.edu/~gmartin/Political%20Editorials.htm

Marx, Karl and Engels, Friedrich (1978). The Marx-Engels Reader. Second Edition. Robert C. Tucker, Ed. New York: W. W. Norton & Co.

Mill, John Stuart (1922). *Utilitarianism; On Liberty; Representative Government.* New York: E. P. Dutton & Co.

Peace of Westphalia (1648), [On-line.] Available. (accessed July 2008): The Avalon Project at Yale Law School: http://www.yale.edu/lawweb/avalon/westphal.htm

Perelman, Michael. *Railroading Economics: The Creation of the Free Market Mythology*, New York: Monthly Review Press, 2006, p. 199

"Project for the New American Century" [On-line.] Suspended. http://www.newamericancentury.org . "Project for the New American Century." [Also On-line.] Available. (accessed August 2008): http://en.wikipedia.org/wiki/Project_for_the_New_American_Century

Smith, Adam (1776, 1789. *Wealth of Nations: Selections* (Derived 1955) Chicago: The Great Books Foundation.

Thoreau, Henry David. (1845). On Civil Disobedience. In *Thoreau Civil Disobedience* & *Walden: Selections*. Number 15. (1955) Chicago: The Great Books Foundation.

Thurow, Lester C. (1975) *Generating Inequality.* New York: Basic Books, 1975, p. 149

United Nations Charter (1945) [On-line]. Available. (accessed July 2008): http://www.un.org/aboutun/charter/index.html

United States Declaration of Independence (1776). [On-line.] Available. (accessed August 2008): http://www.constitution.org/cs_found.htm

Universal Declaration of Human Rights. [On-line.] Available. (accessed August 2008): http://www.unhchr.ch/udhr/lang/eng.htm

World Constituent Assemblies, (1977 and 1991), H. Philip Isely, Syed Md. Husain, Terence P. Amerasinghe, D.M. Spencer and Max Habicht, principal authors, *A Constitution for the Federation of Earth*, in Harris, E. (2005), *Earth Federation Now!* Institute for Economic Democracy Press, Sun City, AZ.

Chapter Two: Conceptualizing the Earth Federation

CIA Factbook. On-line. Available. (accessed August 2008): https://www.cia.gov/library/publications/the-world-factbook/index.html

Galeros, E & Kaestle, K. Nations Online Project. [On-line.] Available. (accessed August 2008): http://www.nationsonline.org/

Hackett, Ian (1973). "The Spring of Civilization", Aylesbury, U.K. : Hunt Barnard

Newcombe, H., (>1977). "World Districts and Regions" white paper. Institute On World Problems archives.

Chapter Three: A History of Emerging World Law

Alam, H.M. (2001). World Constitution & Parliament Association Youth Commission [report. World Constitution and Parliament Association Archives. Lakewood, Colorado].

St. Augustine, "*De Civitatis Dei*". [English version on-line.] Available. (accessed August 2008): http://www.wischik.com/lu/senses/city-of-god.html

Einstein, Albert (1949). *The World As I See It.* Alan Harris, trans. New York: Philosophical Library.

Einstein, Albert (1950). *Out of My Later Years.* New York: Philosophical Library.

Emergency Council of World Trustees. (1973). "First Decree for the Protection of Life" [World Constitution and Parliament Association Archives. Lakewood, Colorado.]

First Preparatory Congress. Orr, B .& Orr B. (1963) [World Constitution and Parliament Association Archives. Lakewood, Colorado.]

Second Preparatory Congress. (1965) [World Constitution and Parliament Association Archives. Lakewood, Colorado.]

Third Preparatory Congress. (1967) [World Constitution and Parliament Association Archives. Lakewood, Colorado.]

Harris, E. (1993) *One World or None. : Prescription for Survival.* Atlantic Highlands, NJ.

Harris, Errol E. and Yunker, James A., eds. (1999). *Toward Genuine Global Governance: Critical Reactions to "Our Global Neighborhood."* Westport, CT: Praeger.

Isely, H.P. "The People Must Write the Peace" (1950). [World Constitution and Parliament Association Archives. Lakewood, Colorado.]

Isely, H.P. "Manifesto for a Peoples World Convention." [World Constitution and Parliament Association Archives. Lakewood, Colorado.]

"Call to all Peoples and all National Governments of the Earth" (1958) [World Constitution and Parliament Association Archives. Lakewood, Colorado.]

Isely, H.P. "Reclaiming Planet Earth for Humanity" (1966) [World Constitution and Parliament Association Archives. Lakewood, Colorado.]

Isely, H.P. (1968) "Declaration of Wolfach." [World Constitution and Parliament Association Archives. Lakewood, Colorado.]

Isely, H.P., Read, T. & Oaxley, L. (1971). "Proposal for Immediate Action by an Emergency Council of World Trustees". [World Constitution and Parliament Association Archives. Lakewood, Colorado.]

Isely, H.P. (1979). "The Rationale for a World Constitutent Assembly." [World Constitution and Parliament Association Archives. Lakewood, Colorado.]

Isely, H.P. (1994). "A Bill of Particulars: Why the U.N. Must Be Replaced". [World Constitution and Parliament Association Archives. Lakewood, Colorado.]

Isely, H.P. (1999). *Across Frontiers.* [bulletin]."Move over U.N.–N.A.T.O. is, now in command."

Isely, H.P. (2001). *Across Frontiers.* [bulletin]. "Crash!"

Martin, G.T. (2001). *Across Frontiers.* [bulletin]. "Open Letter to the Group of 77."

McNamara, R. S.,[attributed quote] Unavailable. However, See McNamara et al.

(accessed August 2008) [On-line]. Available: http://choo.fis.utoronto.ca/FIS/Courses/LIS2149/cuban/McNamara.html

Provisional World Parliament (1982). World Legislative Acts "Design & Action for a New World"

Provisional World Parliament (1985). World Legislative Acts 6 through 8.

Provisional World Parliament (1987). World Legislative Acts 9through 11.

Isely, H.P. & Amerasinghe, T.P. (1992) Global Ratification & Election Network Charter. [World Constitution and Parliament Association Archives. Lakewood, Colorado.]

Provisional World Parliament (1996). "Manifesto".
(accessed August 2008) [On-line]. Available: http://www.worldproblems.net english/legislation/full_texts_en_htm/wla_12_manifest_of_1996.html

Provisional World Parliament (2000). World Legislative Act 12.

Ramphal, S. & Carlsson, I. (1995), *Our Global Neighbourhood.* Oxford: Oxford University Press.

Reves, E. (1945) *The Anatomy of Peace.* New York: Harper & Brothers.

Rig Veda (1500 BCE) On-line. Available. (accessed August 2008): http://en.wikipedia.org/wiki/Rig_Veda

Shakespeare, W. (1623) *Julius Caesar.* First Folio.

United Nations Charter (1945) On-line. Available. (accessed July 2008): http://www.un.org/aboutun/charter/index.html

Wordsworth, W. (1843) "Ode Intimations of Immortality" in *Recollections of Early Childhood.* On-line. Available. (accessed July 2008): http://www.bartleby.com/101/536.html

World Constituent Assemblies, (1977 and 1991), H. Philip Isely, Syed Md. Husain, Terence P. Amerasinghe, D.M. Spencer and Max Habicht, principal authors, *A Constitution for the Federation of Earth*, in Harris, E. (2005), *Earth Federation Now!* Institute for Economic Democracy Press, Sun City, AZ.

World Constitution & Parliament Association (1981) "Call to the Provisional World Parliament) [World Constitution and Parliament Association Archives. Lakewood, Colorado.]

World Constitution & Parliament Association. (1999). *Across Frontiers*. [bulletin]

World Constitution & Parliament Association. (1999). "Immediate Economic Benefits of World Government". [World Constitution and Parliament Association Archives. Lakewood, Colorado.]

Chapter Three Addendum: Recent History of the Provisional World Parliament

Provisional World Parliament. (2003) World Legislative Acts 13 through 19. (accessed August 2008) [On-line]. Available: http://www.worldproblems.net

Provisional World Parliament. (2003) World Legislative Acts 20 through 24. (accessed August 2008) [On-line]. Available: http://www.worldproblems.net

Provisional World Parliament. (2003) "Memorial to the Assembly of States Parties". [memorial] (accessed August 2008) [On-line]. Available: http://www.worldproblems.net

Universal Declaration of Human Rights (1948). (1948). On-line. Available. (accessed August 2008): http://www.unhchr.ch/udhr/lang/eng.htm

Assembly of States Parties (2002). *Rules of Procedure and Evidence.* On-line. Available. (accessed July 2008): http://www.icc-cpi.int/library/about/officialjournal/Rules_of_procedure_and_Evidence_English.pdf

International Accounting Standards Board. *International Financial Reporting Standards.* (accessed August 2008) On-line. Available. : http://www.iasb.org

Koroma, I. et al., World Judicial Commission. (1998) *Rome Statute of the International Criminal Court.* On-line. Available. (accessed August 2008): http://www.icc-cpi.int/library/about/officialjournal/Rome_Statute_English.pdf

Provisional World Parliament. (2004) World Legislative Acts 25 through 30. (accessed August 2008) [On-line]. Available: http://www.worldproblems.net

International Chamber of Commerce. (2003) "Tax Policy Statement." [memorial. Extinct from web] See http://www.iccwbo.org/policy/taxation/.

Provisional World Parliament. (2003) "Tax Policy Statement". (accessed August 2008) [On-line]. Available: http://www.worldproblems.net

Provisional World Parliament. (2006) World Legislative Acts 31 through 38. (accessed August 2008) [On-line]. Available: http://www.worldproblems.net

Provisional World Parliament. (2007) World Legislative Acts 39 through 42. (accessed August 2008) [On-line]. Available: http://www.worldproblems.net

Weeramantry, C. et al., International Association of Lawyers Against Nuclear Weapons. General Assembly of the United Nations. (2008). Model Nuclear Weapons Convention (Revised) [UNGA document #A/62/650.]

Chapter Four: Manifesto of the Earth Federation

Ahmed, Nafeez Mosaddeq (2002). *The War On Freedom: How and Why America was Attacked, September 11, 2001*. Joshua Tree: California: Tree of Life Publications.

Amin, Samir (1997). Capitalism in the Age of Globalization. New York & London: Zed Books.

Blum, William (2000). Rogue State. A Guide to the World's Only Superpower. Monroe, Maine: Common Courage Press.

Blum, William (1995). *Killing Hope: U.S. Military and CIA Interventions Since World War II*. Monroe, Maine: Common Courage Press.

Boswell and Chase-Dunn (2000). *The Spiral of Capitalism and Socialism: Toward Global Democracy*. Boulder, CO: Lynne Rienner Publishers.

Boucher, Douglas H. (1999). *The Paradox of Plenty: Hunger in a Bountiful World*. Oakland, CA: Food First Books.

Brecher, Jeremy and Costello, Tim (1994). *Global Village or Global Pillage: Economic Reconstruction from the Bottom Up*. Boston: South End Press.

Brown, Lester R. (2001). *Eco-Economy: Building an Economy for the Earth*. New York: W. W. Norton & Co.

Burbach, Roger and Clarke, Ben, eds. (2002). *September 11 and the U.S. War: Beyond the Curtain of Smoke*. San Francisco: City Light Books.

Caldicott, Helen (1992). *If You Love This Planet*. New York: W.W. Norton & Co.

Caldicott, Helen (1994), *Nuclear Madness*. Revised Edition. New York: W. W. Norton & Co.

Caufield, Catherine (1996). *Masters of Illusion. The World Bank and the Poverty of Nations.* New York: Henry Holt and Company.

Chomsky, Noam (1996). *What Uncle Sam Really Wants.* Berkeley: Odonian Press.

Chomsky, Noam (1993). *Year 501: The Conquest Continues.* Boston: South End Press.

Chossudovsky, Michel (1999). *The Globalization of Poverty: Impacts of IMF and World Bank Reforms.* London: Zed Books LTD.

Commission on Global Governance. (1995). Report of the Commission on Global Governance. Oxford: Oxford University Press.

Daly, Herman E. (1996). *Beyond Growth: The Economics of Sustainable Development.* Boston: Beacon Press.

Daly, Herman E. and Cobb, John B. (1994). *For the Common Good. Redirecting the Economy toward Community, the Environment, and a Sustainable Future.* Boston: Beacon Press.

Flavin, Christopher, et al. (2002). *State of the World 2002.* New York: W. W. Norton & Co.

Galeano, Edwardo (1973). *The Open Veins of Latin America – Five Centuries of the Pillage of a Continent.* Cedric Belfrage, trans. New York: Monthly Review Press.

Harris, Errol E. (1993). *One World or None: Prescription for Survival.* Atlantic Highlands, NJ.

Harris, Errol E. (2000). *Apocalypse and Paradigm: Science and Everyday Thinking.* Westport, CT: Praeger.

Isely, Philip (2000). *Immediate Economic Benefits of World Government.* Lakewood, Colorado: Emergency Earth Rescue Administration of the World Constitution and Parliament Association.

Korten, David C. (1999). *The Post-Corporate World: Life After Capitalism.* West Hartford, CT: Kumarian Press, Inc.

Korten, David C. (2001) *When Corporations Rule the World.* Second Edition. Bloomfield, CT: Kumarian Press.

Mander, Jerry and Goldsmith, Edward (1996). *The Case Against the Global Economy: And for a Turn Toward the Local.* San Francisco: Sierra Club Books.

Martin, Glen T. (1999). "A Planetary Paradigm for Global Government." *Toward Genuine Global Governance: Critical Reactions to "Our Global Neighborhood,"* Errol E. Harris and James A. Yunker, eds. London: Praeger, pp. 1-18.

Martin, Glen T. (1999). "Three Stages in the Dialectical Realization of Democracy and the Constitution for the Federation of Earth," Part One. Across Frontiers - A WCPA/GREN Publication for Humanity, March-April, 1999, pp. 19-20. Part Two, Across Frontiers, May-June, 1999, pp. 20-22.

Martin, Glen T. (2002). "Unity in Diversity as the Foundation for World Peace." *Community, Diversity, and Difference: Implications for Peace.* Alison Bailey and Paula J. Smithka, eds. Amsterdam: Rodopi Press, pp. 309-325.

Marx, Karl and Engels, Friedrich (1978). *The Marx-Engels Reader.* Second Edition. Robert C. Tucker, ed. New York: W. W. Norton & Co.

Mayur, Rashmi (2002). *Beyond Johannesburg: Where Do We Go From Here?* Mumbai: International Institute for Sustainable Future.

Palast, Greg (2003). *The Best Democracy Money Can Buy.* New York: Plume Books of Penguin Publishers.

Renner, Michael. (1996). *Fighting for Survival: Environmental Decline, Social Conflict, and the New Age of Insecurity.* New York: W. W. Norton & Co.

Rich, Bruce (1994). *Mortgaging the Earth.* The World Bank, Environmental Impoverishment, and the Crisis of Development. Boston: Beacon Press.

Seligson, Mitchell A. and Passe-Smith, John T. (1993). *Development and Underdevelopment: The Political Economy of Inequality.* Boulder, CO: Lynne Rienner Publishers.

Shiva, Vandana (1997). *Biopiracy: The Plunder of Nature and Knowledge.* Boston: South End Press.

Shiva, Vandana (2000). *Stolen Harvest: The Hijacking of the Global Food Supply.* Boston: South End Press.

Shiva, Vandana (2002). *Water Wars: Privatization, Pollution, and Profit.* Boston: South End Press.

Singer, Peter (2002). *One World: the Ethics of Globalization.* New Haven: Yale University Press.

Smith, J. W. (1994). *The World's Wasted Wealth* 2. Cambria, CA: Institute for Economic Democracy.

Smith, J. W. (2002). *Economic Democracy – The Political Struggle of the Twenty-first Century.* Sun City, Arizona: Institute for Economic Democracy.

Smith, J. W. (2002). *Why? The Deeper History Behind the September 11, 2001, Terrorist Attack on America.* Sun City, Arizona: Institute for Economic Democracy.

Smith, J. W. (2003). *Cooperative Capitalism: A Blueprint for Global Peace and Prosperity*. Sun City, Arizona: Institute for Economic Democracy & Institute for Cooperative Capitalism.

Stiglitz, Joseph E. (2002). *Globalization and its Discontents*. New York: W. W. Norton & Co.

Tokar, Brian (1997). *Earth for Sale: Reclaiming Ecology in the Age of Corporate Greenwash*. Boston: South End Press.

Photo Plates from the Pictorial History (in order of presentation)

City Montessori School, Lucknow. 2006 "Dr. Terence Amerasinghe receives the World Visionary Award".

Nash, John. ""Royal Pavilion East Front from Nash's Views". 1826. Brighton & Hove City Council, U.K.

Almand, Eugenia. 1985. "2nd Session Provisional World Parliament Plenary." Courtesy of the Terence Amerasinghe Estate.

Almand, Al. 1987. "3rd Session Provisional World Parliament Plenary."

Almand, Al. 1987. "3rd Session Provisional World Parliament Committee."

Martin, Glen T. 1996. "4th Session Provisional World Parliament. Partial group photo."

Almand, Eugenia. 2000. "5th Session Provisional World Parliament. Partial group photo."

Almand, Eugenia. 2000. "5th Session Provisional World Parliament. Environment Committee."

Almand, Eugenia. 2000. "5th Session Provisional World Parliament. Middle East Committee."

Almand, Eugenia. 2001. "City Montessori School, Lucknow, Students dance for World Parliament at the 2nd World Judiciary Summit."

City Montessori School, Lucknow. 2001 "City Montessori School, Lucknow. 2006 "2nd World Judiciary Summit Panel."

Martin, Glen T., 2002. "Institute On World Problems Seminar, Takoradi, Ghana."

Government of Republique Togolaise. 2002. "Almand, Martin & Balouki in Cabinet Meeting with Togolese President & Cabinet."

Government of Republique Togolaise. 2002. “Late President Gnassingbe Eyadema & Cabinet in Meeting with Almand, Martin & Balouki.”

Almand, Eugenia, 2002. “Institute On World Problems seminar preparation. Photo of students and teachers of INSAK, Kara, Togo.”

City Montessori School, Lucknow. 2002. “Institute On World Problems Seminar.”

City Montessori School, Lucknow. 2002. “Institute On World Problems Seminar.”

Almand, Eugenia, 2003. “Sixth Session Provisional World Parliament.” (3 photos)

Almand, Eugenia, 2003. “Seventh Session Provisional World Parliament, Honourable Justice Sawant Lighting Lamp.”

Almand, Eugenia, 2004. “Eighth Session Provisional World Parliament, Honourable Dr. L. M. Singhvi, Lighting Lamp.”

City Montessori School, Lucknow. 2004. “Eighth Session Provisional World Parliament Voting.”

Almand, Eugenia. 2004. “Japanese Delegates in Full Assembly Hall. Eighth Session Provisional World Parliament.”

City Montessori School, Lucknow. 2006 “Seventh World Judiciary Summit Group Photo.”

Martin, Glen T. 2006. “ Libya Foreign Secretary Suleiman Shahumi on Dais with Others at 9th Session Provisional World Parliament.”

Almand, Eugenia. 2007. “Tenth Session Provisional World Parliament.”

Almand, Eugenia. 2007. “Cultural Festivities at Tenth Session Provisional World Parliament.

Chapter Five: Analytical Commentary on World Constitution Concepts

Beck, Sanderson. Commentary by Sanderson Beck. (Accessed February 2008). [On-line] Available: http://www.san.beck.org/GPJ27-Clark-SohnPlan.html#4

Borgese, G. A. et. al. of Chicago Committee to Frame a World Constitution. (1948) ***Constitution for the World.*** Chicago: University of Chicago Press, 1953

Center for UN Reform Education. (Accessed 2008, February). [On-line] Available: http://www.centerforunreform.org

Center for War/Peace Studies. (Accessed 2008, February). [On-line] Available: http://www.cwps.org

Clark, Grenville & Sohn, Lewis. ***World Peace through World Law.*** (Accessed February 2008). [On-line] Available: finding aid. http://oasis.harvard.edu/html/law00084.html [Search by title in quotes "World Peace through World Law"]

Constitution for the Federation of Earth. Institute On World Problems: (Accessed August 2008, August). [On-line] Available: http://www.worldproblems.net. Also, see entry in this bibliographic section below: World Constituent Assemblies, (1977 and 1991).

Davis, Garry. World Syntegrity Project. (Accessed February 2008). [On-line] Available: http://www.worldservice.org/synhis.html

Global Policy Forum. Security Council Reform: General Articles. (Accessed February 2008). [On-line] Available: http://www.globalpolicy.org/security/reform/generalindex.htm .

Habicht, Max. (1987) *The Abolition of War: Autobiographical Notes of a World Federalist and Collected Papers on Peace and World Federalism.* Paris: Club Humaniste

Musselwhite, Benton. *New United Nations Charter*: (Accessed August 2008). [On-line] Available: http://www.one-world-now.org/index.html

Office of the United Nations High Commissioner for Human Rights link page to conventional bills of rights, including the Universal Declaration of Human Rights, nine core international conventional human rights instruments and a compendium of links to about 101 supplemental conventional human rights declarations and treaties. (Accessed February 2008). [On-line] Available: http://www2.ohchr.org/english/law/index.htm

Provisional Peoples' Assembly. (Accessed February 2008). [On-line] Available: http://www.peoplesassembly.org/pa1/Main.aspx

Rauscher, Scott. *Constitution of the Earth Federation*: (Accessed Februaery 2008). [On-line] Available: http://www.markfoster.net/jcc/rs/constitution.html

Revolutionary Committees Movement (R.C.M.) (2000) "A Proposed Amendment to the Constitution of the World Federation." Pamphlet distributed at Qawra Malta, during the Fifth Session of the Provisional World Parliament.

Schwartzberg, Joseph. *Revitalizing the United Nations: Reform through Weighted Voting*. (Accessed February 2008). [On-line] Available: http://www/globalpolicy.org/security/reform/cluster1/2004/schwartzberg_weighted_voting.pdf

Strong, Maurice & Gorbachev, Mikhail et al. ***Earth Charter.*** **(Accessed February 2008). [On-line] Available: http://www.earthcharter.org http://www.earthcharterusa.org/earth_charter.html**

United Nations Charter: (Accessed February 2008). [On-line] Available: http://www.un.org/aboutun/charter/index.html
United Nations Charter Article 22. Go to above link, then in left frame, click on Chapter XIII.
United Nations Charter Article 109. Go to above link, then in left frame, click on Chapter XVIII.

United States Constitution Bill of Rights. (Amendments 2, 6, 7, 9 & 11. (Accessed February 2008). [On-line] Available: http://memory.loc.gov/ammem/help/constRedir.html

World Constituent Assemblies, (1977 and 1991), H. Philip Isely, Syed Md. Husain, Terence P. Amerasinghe, D.M. Spencer and Max Habicht, principal authors, *A Constitution for the Federation of Earth*, in Harris, E. (2005), *Earth Federation Now!* Institute for Economic Democracy Press, Sun City, AZ.

World Constitution & Parliament Association. (Accessed 2008, February). On-line] Available: http://www.wcpa.biz

World Government of World Citizens. Index to Collated Statements from the Syntegrations. (Accessed February 2008). [On-line] Available: http://www.worldservice.org/topics.html

Chapter Six: *The Constitution for the Federation of Earth*

State of Arizona Legislative Council. **(2007)** *The Arizona Bill Drafting Manual, 2007.* On-line. Available. (accessed August 2008): http://www.azleg.state.az.us/alisPDFs/council/bdmwog2007.pdf

World Constituent Assemblies, (1977 and 1991), H. Philip Isely, Syed Md. Husain, Terence P. Amerasinghe, D.M. Spencer and Max Habicht, principal authors, *A Constitution for the Federation of Earth*, in Harris, E. (2005), *Earth Federation Now!* Institute for Economic Democracy Press, Sun City, AZ.

Chapter Seven: Clarification of the *Earth Constitution*

Assembly of States Parties (2002) *Agreement on the Privileges and Immunities of the International Criminal Court (APIC)*] On-line. Available.(accessed July 2008): http://untreaty.un.org/cod/icc/apic/apic(e).pdf

Assembly of States Parties (2002). *Rules of Procedure and Evidence.* On-line. Available. (accessed July 2008): http://www.icc-cpi.int/library/about/officialjournal/Rules_of_procedure_and_Evidence_English.pdf

Ecimovic, Timi (2006). *The Information Theory of Nature.* Medosi, Korte, Slovenia: SEM Institute for Climate Change. On-line. Available (accessed August 2008): http://www.institut-climatechange.si/

Koroma, I. et al., World Judicial Commission. (1998) *Rome Statute of the International Criminal Court.* On-line. Available. (accessed August 2008): http://www.icc-cpi.int/library/about/officialjournal/Rome_Statute_English.pdf

Provisional World Parliament (1982). World Legislative Acts. On-line. Available (accessed August 2008): http://www.worldproblems.net

United Nations Charter. (1945) On-line. Available. (accessed August 2008): http://www.un.org/aboutun/charter/index.html

World Constituent Assemblies, (1977 and 1991), H. Philip Isely, Syed Md. Husain, Terence P. Amerasinghe, D.M. Spencer and Max Habicht, principal authors, *A Constitution for the Federation of Earth,* in Harris, E. (2005), *Earth Federation Now!* Institute for Economic Democracy Press, Sun City, AZ.

Chapter Eight: Resolutions and Memorials of the Provisional World Parliament

Assembly of States Parties (2002). *Rules of Procedure and Evidence.* On-line. Available. (accessed July 2008): http://www.icc-cpi.int/library/about/officialjournal/Rules_of_procedure_and_Evidence_English.pdf

Barney, Gerald O. (1980) *Global 2000 Report to the President of the United States.* New York: Pergamon. Washington, D.C.: Supt. of Docs. U.S. Government Printing Office

Declaration of the Rights of Man. "The Avalon Project at Yale Law School: The Nuremberg War Crimes Trials." On-line. Available. (accessed August 2008): http://www.yale.edu/lawweb/avalon/rightsof.htm

Koroma, I. et al., World Judicial Commission. (1998) *Rome Statute of the International Criminal Court.* On-line. Available. (accessed August 2008): http://www.icc-cpi.int/library/about/officialjournal/Rome_Statute_English.pdf

Nuremburg Accords. "The Avalon Project at Yale Law School: The Nuremberg War Crimes Trials." On-line. Available. (accessed August 2008): http://www.yale.edu/lawweb/avalon/imt/imt.htm

Security Council. Resolution 242 (1967) of 22 November 1967. On-line. Available. (accessed August 2008): http://domino.un.org/UNISPAL.NSF/361eea1cc08301c485256cf600606959/7d35e1f729df491c85256ee700686136!OpenDocument

Security Council. Resolution 338 (1973) of 22 October 1973. On-line. Available. (accessed August 2008): http://domino.un.org/unispal.nsf/dcb71e2bf9f2dca585256cef0073ed5d/7fb7c26fcbe80a31852560c50065f878!OpenDocument

Security Council. 194 (III). Palestine -- Progress Report of the United Nations Mediator. On-line. Available. (accessed August 2008): http://domino.un.org/unispal.nsf/9a798adbf322aff38525617b006d88d7/c758572b78d1cd0085256bcf0077e51a!OpenDocument

Provisional World Parliament (2003). World Legislative Act 19. *Criminal Code Penalty Classification (World Penal Code).*

Provisional World Parliament (2003). World Legislative Act 22. *World Equity Act.*

Provisional World Parliament (2004). World Legislative Act 29. World Boundaries and Elections Administration with a Global Peoples Assembly (*World Elections Act).*

Universal Declaration of Human Rights (1948). On-line. Available. (accessed August 2008): http://www.unhchr.ch/udhr/lang/eng.htm

World Constituent Assemblies, (1977 and 1991), H. Philip Isely, Syed Md. Husain, Terence P. Amerasinghe, D.M. Spencer and Max Habicht, principal authors, *A Constitution for the Federation of Earth*, in Harris, E. (2005), *Earth Federation Now!* Institute for Economic Democracy Press, Sun City, AZ.

Chapter Nine: Legislative Summaries of World Legislative Acts 1 through 42

Assembly of States Parties (2002). *Rules of Procedure and Evidence.* On-line. Available. (accessed July 2008): http://www.icc-cpi.int/library/about/officialjournal/Rules_of_procedure_and_Evidence_English.pdf

Assembly of States Parties (2002) *Agreement on the Privileges and Immunities of the International Criminal Court (APIC)*] On-line. Available. (accessed July 2008): http://untreaty.un.org/cod/icc/apic/apic(e).pdf

Cole, S. & Dorolle, P. (1959) Agreement Between the International Atomic Energy Agency and the World Health Organization. [Letter of Understanding] On-line. Available. (accessed July 2008): http://www.iaea.org/Publications/Documents/Infcircs/Others/inf20.shtml

Greenpeace International (2004). "Draft Treaty: Banning the Production of Fissile Materials for Nuclear Weapons and other Nuclear Explosive Devices," Extinct from Web. (accessed November 2005). Related reference: http://www.reachingcriticalwill.org/legal/fmct.html

International Accounting Standards Board (2008) *International Financial Reporting Standards*. Available. (accessed July 2008)): http://www.iasb.org

International Association of Lawyers Against Nuclear Arms (IALANA) and United Nations General Assembly (2008). *Model Nuclear Weapons Convention Convention on the Prohibition of the Development, Testing, Production, Stockpiling, Transfer, Use and Threat of Use of Nuclear Weapons and on Their Elimination. On-line.* Available (accessed July 2008): http://www.worldproblems.net/multilingual_legislative_docs/UNGA-off-A-62-650_disarmament.pdf

Koroma, I. et al., World Judicial Commission. (1998) *Rome Statute of the International Criminal Court.* On-line. Available. (accessed August 2008): http://www.icc-cpi.int/library/about/officialjournal/Rome_Statute_English.pdf

Kutner, L. World Judicial Commission (1974) *Statute of the World Court of Human Rights.* On-line. Available. (accessed July 2008): http://www.worldservice.org/wsalstat.html

Law of the Sea. (1982) On-line. Available. (accessed July 2008): http://www.un.org/Depts/los/convention_agreements/texts/unclos/closindx.htm

Legislative Administration Committee. (1997). *Oregon Form and Style Manual for Legislative Measures* . On-line. Available. (accessed August 2008): http://www.leg.state.or.us/lc/formstyle.html

Ricardo, R. (translated Todd, M.) (1994) *Guantánamo: The Bay of Discord.* Melbourne: Ocean Press

Robert, H. M. (2000). *Robert's Rules of Order Newly Revised*, tenth edition. On-line. Available. (accessed July 2008): http://www.robertsrules.com/book.html

United Nations General Assembly. (1989) *Rights of the Child.* On-line. Available. (accessed July 2008): http://www2.ohchr.org/english/law/crc.htm

World Constituent Assemblies, (1977 and 1991), H. Philip Isely, Syed Md. Husain, Terence P. Amerasinghe, D.M. Spencer and Max Habicht, principal authors, *A Constitution for the Federation of Earth*, in Harris, E. (2005), *Earth Federation Now!* Institute for Economic Democracy Press, Sun City, AZ.

World Youth Parliament for Water (2002) Water Act. Available. (accessed July 2008): http://www.i-s-w.org/en/PDF/PMJ_loi_sie_ang.pdf

Chapter Ten: Legitimate World Law

Gomez-Sorzano, G. (2006) _www.criminologyprize.com/dynamaster/file_archive/060608/4a4cc8237febc0b989d4564b430c0a45/abstracts.pdf

Kant Sahai, V. (2006) Address at the 6th International Conference of Chief Justices of the World on Article 51 of India Constitution (World Judiciary Summit).

Koroma, A, D. Thiam. D. , J. Crawford, J.et. al. Rome Statute of the International Criminal Court, 1998. International Law Commission. Rome Convention for the International Criminal Court.

Reves, Emery. (1937). *The Anatomy of Peace.* New York: Harper and Brothers.

Silungwe, A.W. (2006) Address at the 6th International Conference of Chief Justices of the World on Article 51 of India Constitution (World Judiciary Summit).

United Nations Charter (1945). Available. Accessed 17 June 2008. http://www.un.org/aboutun/charter/index.html

Weeramantry, C. G. (1996) Dissenting Opinion of Judge Weeramantry. International Criminal Court. Available: Accessed 17 June 2008. http://www.fas.org/nuke/control/icj/text/iunan_ijudgment_19960708_Dissenting_Weeramantry.htm

Chapter Eleven: Conclusion – Volume 1

Amnesty International. On-line. Available. (accessed August 2008): http://www.amnesty.org/

Arendt, Hannah (1958). *The Human Condition.* Second Edition. Chicago: University of Chicago Press.

Arendt, Hannah (1970). *On Violence.* New York: Harcourt Brace & Co.

Articles of Confederation. (1777). On-line. Available. (accessed August 2008): http://www.constitution.org/cons/usa-conf.htm

Assembly of States Parties, 14 December 2007. Resolution: Programme budget for 2008, the Working Capital Fund for 2008, scale of assessments for the apportionment of expenses of the International Criminal Court and financing appropriations for the year 2008PDF (323 KB). (accessed September 2008): http://www.icc-cpi.int/library/asp/ICC-ASP-6-20_Vol.I_Part_III_English.pdf , linked from http://en.wikipedia.org/wiki/International_Criminal_Court#cite_note-budget_resolution-79

Boyle, Francis A. (2008). *Protesting Power: War, Resistance, and Law.* Lanham, MD: Rowman & Littlefield Publishers.

Convention on the Rights of the Child. On-line. Available. (accessed August 2008): http://www2.ohchr.org/english/law/crc.htm

Davis, Garry (2004). *Letters to World Citizens.* Burlington, Vermont: World Government House.

Davis, Garry (2003). *World Government, ready or not!* Burlington, Vermont: World Government House.

Davis, Garry, with Guma, Greg (1992). *Passport to Freedom: A Guide for World Citizens.* Cabin John, Maryland: Seven Locks Press.

Einstein, Albert (1949). *The World As I See It.* Alan Harris, trans. New York: Philosophical Library.

Einstein, Albert (1950). *Out of My Later Years.* New York: Philosophical Library.

Gandhi, M. K. (1987). *The Mind of Mahatma Gandhi.* R.K. Prabhu and U.R. Rao, eds. Ahmedabad: Navajivan Publishing House.

Gandhi, M. K. (1972). *All Men Are Brothers.* Life and Thoughts of Mahatma Gandhi. Krishna Kripalani, ed. New York: World Without War Publications.

Gandhi, M. K. (1957). *Socialism of My Conception.* Anand T. Hingorani, ed. Bombay: Bharatiya Vidya Bhavan.

Gandhi, M. K. (1929). *An Autobiography or My Experiments With Truth.* Mahadev Desai, trans. Ahmedabad: Navajivan Publishing House.

Gutkind, Eric (1969). *The Body of God: First Steps Toward an Anti-Theology -- The Collected Papers of Eric Gutkind.* Lucie B. Gutkind and Henry LeRoy Finch, eds. New York: Horizon Press.

Habermas, Jürgen (1971). *Knowledge and Human Interests.* Jeremy J. Shapiro, trans. Boston: Beacon Press.

Habermas, Jürgen (1975). *Legitimation Crisis.* Thomas McCarthy, trans. Boston: Beacon Press.

Habermas, Jürgen (1998c). *Between Facts and Norms: Contributions to a Discourse Theory of Law and Democracy*. Cambridge: MIT Press.

Habermas, Jürgen (2001). *The Postnational Constellation: Political Essays.* Cambridge, MA: MIT Press.

Harris, Errol E. (1993). *One World or None: Prescription for Survival.* Atlantic Highlands, NJ.

Harris, Errol E. (2000). *Apocalypse and Paradigm: Science and Everyday Thinking.* Westport, CT: Praeger.

Harris, Errol E. (2005). *Earth Federation Now! Tomorrow is Too Late.* Sun City, Arizona, Institute for Economic Democracy Press.

Harris, Errol E. (2008). *Twenty-first Century Democratic Renaissance: From Plato to Neoliberalism to Planetary Democracy*. Sun City, AZ: Institute for Economic Democracy Press.

Harris, Errol E. and Yunker, James A., eds. (1999). *Toward Genuine Global Governance: Critical Reactions to "Our Global Neighborhood."* Westport, CT: Praeger.

Hart, H. L. A. (1994). *The Concept of Law*. Second Edition. Oxford: Oxford University Press.

International Court of Justice. On-line. Available. (accessed August 2008): http://www.icj-cij.org/

International Criminal Court. On-line. Available. (accessed August 2008): http://www.icc-cpi.int

International Criminal Court. Report of the Committee on Budget and Finance on the work of its tenth session. On-line. Available. (accessed August 2008): http://commons.wikimedia.org/wiki/Image:International_Criminal_Court_contributions,_2008.png . http://www.icc-cpi.int/library/asp/ICC-ASP-7-3_English.pdf

International Labor Organization. On-line. Available. (accessed August 2008): http://www.ilo.org/global/lang--en/index.htm

Koroma, A. et al., World Judicial Commission. (1998) *Rome Statute of the International Criminal Court.* On-line. Available. (accessed August 2008): http://www.icc-cpi.int/library/about/officialjournal/Rome_Statute_English.pdf

Martin, Glen T. (2005a). *Millennium Dawn. The Philosophy of Planetary Crisis and Human Liberation.* Sun City, Arizona: Institute for Economic Democracy Press.

Martin, Glen T., ed. (2005b). *World Revolution Through World Law: Basic Documents of the Emerging Earth Federation.* Sun City, AZ: Institute for Economic Democracy Press.

Martin, Glen T. (2008). *Ascent to Freedom: Practical and Philosophical Foundations of Democratic World Law.* Sun City, AZ: Institute for Economic Democracy Press.

Machiavelli, Niccolo (1532. English language reprint 1980) *The Prince.* New York: New American Library. Also On-line. Available. (accessed August 2008): http://www.constitution.org/mac/prince00.htm

Mahlon Marr. (2006). Schopenhauer quote cited in *Truth : Resuming the Age of Reason.* On-line. Available. (accessed August 2008): http://www.lulu.com/content/404157

Mead, Margaret. On-line. Available. (accessed August 2008): http://en.wikiquote.org/wiki/Margaret_Mead

Statute on the Rights of the Child. On-line. Available. (accessed August 2008): http://www.worldproblems.net

United Nations Charter. On-line. Available. (accessed August 2008): http://www.un.org/aboutun/charter/index.html

Universal Declaration of Human Rights. On-line. Available. (accessed August 2008): http://www.unhchr.ch/udhr/lang/eng.htm

United Nations Educational, Scientific and Cultural Organization. On-line. Available. (accessed August 2008): http://portal.unesco.org/en/ev.php-URL_ID=29008&URL_DO=DO_TOPIC&URL_SECTION=201.html

United Nations Office of the High Commission for Human Rights. On-line. Available. (accessed August 2008): http://www.ohchr.org/EN/Pages/WelcomePage.aspx

United States Constitution. (1787). On-line. Available. (accessed August 2008): http://www.constitution.org/cons/constitu.txt http://www.constitution.org/constit_.htm

Weeramantry, C.G. (1988). *Islamic Jurisprudence: An International Perspective.* New York: St. Martin's Press.

World Bench for Criminal Cases. On-line. Available. (accessed August 2008): http://www.worldproblems.net

World Constituent Assemblies, (1977 and 1991), H. Philip Isely, Syed Md. Husain, Terence P. Amerasinghe, D.M. Spencer and Max Habicht, principal authors, *A Constitution for the Federation of Earth*, in Harris, E. (2005), *Earth Federation Now!* Institute for Economic Democracy Press, Sun City, AZ.

World Constitution and Parliament Association. On-line. Available. (accessed January 2009): http://www.wcpa.biz

World Legislative Acts. On-line. Available. (accessed January 2009): http://www.worldproblems.net

World Trade Organization. On-line. Available. (accessed August 2008): http://www.wto.org/

Yunker, James (2007). *Political Globalization: A New Vision of Federal World Government*. Lanham, Georgia: University Press of America.

Index

Pages for Symbols, Numeric Entries, Selected Article & Section Numbers

#A/62/650 120
⊕ 44, 118, 264, 265, 266, 271, 273, 274, 276, 277, 278, 279, 283, 287, 289, 294, 295, 296, 297, 299, 300, 301, 302, 303, 304, 306, 308, 309, 312, 313, 314, 315, 316, 321, 322, 323, 325, 328, 329, 331, 333, 337, 339, 340, 341, 342, 344, 346, 347, 348, 350, 353, 352, 353, 354
1.3. 31, 247, 254, 293, 314, 315, 326, 334
1.4. 254, 293, 314, 316, 334
10.1.5. 249
10.2.08. 249
10.4.1. 249, 250
10.4.2.6. 250
10.4.4. 250
1000 5, 6, 51, 167, 248, 283, 372
106 113, 262, 320, 328, 363, 366
11.1.09. 250
11.2. 178, 250, 329
12.13. 250
12.14. 251
12.15. 250
12.17. 251
13.19. 251
14.2. 33, 252, 338
14.4.2. 247, 249
16.1.1. 247
16.1.2. 247
16.2. 34, 251
17.1.01 251, 254
17.1.04 251, 254
17.1.05. 252
17.1.07 251, 254
17.1.08. 252
17.1.09. 252
17.1.11. 252
17.3. 178, 252
17.3.02. 253
17.3.08. 249, 253, 255, 257, 258
17.3.09. 254, 255
17.3.10.08. 254
17.3.12.01. 254
17.3.12.04. 254
17.3.12.10. 254
17.4.06. 253, 254
17.4.07. 254
17.4.08. 254
17.5.2.07. 253, 255
17.5.2.08. 255
17.6. 178, 247, 254, 255
19.2.06. 249, 257
19.5.3. 249, 257
19.5.5. 258
2.6. 177, 246, 250, 322, 324
2.9. 246
226 specific rules 326
25 countries 34, 55, 57, 61, 78, 81, 255, 256, 306
25th instrument of national ratification 321. *See also* 25 countries
4.14. 254
4.16. 247, 254
4.17. 247, 254
4.19 254
4.23. 247
4.28. 247
4.30. 247
4.33. 254
4.40. 254
4.5. 246, 326
5.4.1. 246
5.5.3. 247
5.6.17. 247
6.3.1. 247
6.4.1. 246
6.4.3. 246
8.1.2. 247
8.1.3. 247
8.3. 252, 327
8.7.1.6. 247, 257
9.1. 178, 248
9.1.1. 248, 249
9.2.04 258
9.2.09. 248
9.4.02. 249
9.4.03. 249
9.4.04. 249
9.4.12. 249

A

abolition 23, 62, 347
Abrika, Dr. Belaïd 86
absolute private property rights 4, 14
absolute rights 151
Abubakar, Dr. Atiku 72
acceptance 59, 66, 69, 113, 321, 323, 352, 364, 372
accession 321, 344, 352, 365
accredited delegates 77, 267, 271
Across Frontiers 51, 80, 108
Act #1 250, 252, 254, 293, 305
Act #12 251, 305
Act #13 110, 248, 252, 254, 255, 307, 308
Act #14 30, 111, 248, 249, 250, 251, 255, 309, 367, 368
Act #15 111, 248, 249, 312, 316
Act #19 112, 251, 315, 316
Act #2 254, 295
Act #20 112, 248, 249, 317, 325, 326, 337, 381
Act #22 112, 247, 322
Act #24 112, 248, 325, 328, 381
Act #28 115, 248, 249, 334, 337
Act #29 115, 168, 246, 247, 249, 252, 253, 337, 339
Act #31 117, 250, 340, 341
Act #33 117, 255, 342, 344
Act #34 117, 250, 252, 254, 344, 347
Act #36 117, 252, 256, 348, 350
Act #37 117, 248, 351, 353
Act #39 119, 248, 252, 352
Act #40 110, 119, 252, 256, 352, 353
Act #5 248, 255, 299
Act #6 254, 300
Act #7 30, 44, 115, 247, 254, 256, 301
Addendum 107, 300, 316, 337, 389, 395
ad hoc tribunals 317
administration of justice 319, 327
Admissibility 334
adoption 57, 87, 103, 111, 120, 260, 263, 269, 271, 278, 294, 296, 317, 321, 328, 332, 333, 334, 344
Advisory Bench 32
Advisory Board 44, 301, 313
advisory world parliament 109
advocate 310
African Children's Parliament 117
African Union 156
agencies 4, 9, 30, 32, 34, 42, 43, 44, 59, 120, 122, 133, 134, 163, 170, 247, 252, 253, 255, 256, 259, 268, 273, 295, 299, 300, 302, 306, 313, 314, 322, 323, 324, 325, 329, 330, 333, 336, 339, 342, 347, 348, 361, 381
Agency for Research and Planning 32, 42, 44, 177, 338
Agency for Technological and Environmental Assessment 32, 42, 177, 322, 348
Agenda 21 4, 131, 132
aggravating circumstances 315, 316
Agreement 49, 351, 352, 353, 402, 404, 405
AIDS 138, 139, 140, 141, 148
Aiyar, Subramaniam 82
Al-Quadaffi, Muammar 82
Alam, Sarwar 82, 85, 86, 108
All India House Wives Association 60
Almand, Eugenia 29, 83, 84, 90, 107, 108, 118, 159, 245, 259, 289, 291, 355, 357, 384
Al Quds Al Sherif 264
alternative media 273
Alva, Hon. Smt. Margaret 60
Ameer, Abdul W. M. 72
Amendment 77, 161, 174
amendment 59, 63, 65, 115, 118, 164, 165, 166, 168, 169, 173, 252, 262, 268, 269, 270, 292, 318, 325, 333, 353. *See also* amendments
amendments 57, 71, 72, 76, 112, 115, 118, 119, 267, 268, 269, 270, 292, 294, 295, 296, 297, 299, 301, 302, 303, 305, 306, 308, 314, 315, 316, 321, 322, 323, 325, 326, 344, 346. *See also* amendment
Amer, Dr. Salem Bedi 82
Amerasinghe 49, 53, 54, 55, 56, 57, 58, 60, 61, 67, 68, 71, 76, 82
Amerasinghe, Dr. T. P. 60
American Revolution 374, 375
amnesty 349, 350, 352, 406
Amnesty International 377, 386, 406
Ananthanarayanan, Ramajunam 112

animal rights 264
Annex 343, 347
annual report 339, 342
Antarctica 246, 251, 305
appeal 80, 81, 257, 266, 298, 311, 319, 327
Appeals Division 318
Appelate Bench 32
Applicable Law 334
Appointees of People 351
approval 300, 304, 321, 328, 344, 352, 362
aquifer 135
Arabic 68, 318, 353
Arafat, Yasser 265
archives 91, 351, 392
Arendt 383
Arendt, Hannah 375, 383
Argentina 21, 54, 143
Arizona 55, 114
arms race 6, 53, 77
arrest 111, 315, 319, 320, 327, 332, 336, 341, 342, 346, 349, 361, 378
Article 109 116, 159, 162, 167, 168, 169, 170, 171, 173, 251, 278, 402
Article 12 14, 163, 178, 209, 247, 250, 251, 304, 309, 310, 316, 331, 334, 351
Article 22 159, 160, 161, 168, 169, 174, 332, 402. *See also* Second Assembly
Articles of Confederation 374, 406
Assembly of States Parties 43, 112, 113, 114, 120, 163, 260, 261, 262, 273, 274, 319, 321, 325, 326, 328, 336, 344, 351, 359, 362, 363, 364, 365, 368, 381, 382
Associate Justices 310
Atlee, Lord 82
audit 269, 301, 321
Augustine, St. 52
authentic global democracy 386
authentic texts 321, 326, 353
authority 5, 7, 8, 9, 10, 14, 15, 24, 26, 28, 50, 59, 75, 110, 112, 113, 122, 128, 133, 137, 138, 139, 140, 145, 146, 163, 166, 169, 173, 247, 252, 260, 262, 265, 266, 267, 273, 280, 296, 299, 313, 318, 332, 345, 348, 357, 363, 364, 373, 374, 377, 382, 383, 384, 386
Authority of License 313
autonomy 5, 164, 272, 273, 280, 281, 282, 283, 287, 373, 375
auxiliary languages 116, 261, 279
Awami League 288
Awwad, Dr. Hanan 84
Azad, Puran Singh 58
Azad, Shri Puran Singh 65, 68

B

Bahini, Mukti 288
Baker, Lord Philip Noel 61
Balouki, Dr. Simfei 105, 109, 117
Balram Jakhar 61, 65, 66
Bangkok 9, 60, 108, 109, 111, 126, 261, 266, 271, 272, 273, 294, 295, 296, 297, 300, 301, 303, 304, 306, 307, 308, 309, 312, 313, 314
Bangkok Centre Hotel 109
Bangladesh 55, 56, 119, 135, 275, 287, 288, 289
Barcelona 9, 71, 74, 77, 78, 94, 300, 304, 306
Basic Structure 177, 180
Beggs, Keith 74
Benches 32, 33, 42, 43, 44, 178, 328
Benn, Tony 61
Bestazzi, Dr. Edvige 68
bill of attainder 251
Bill of Particulars 76
Bill of Rights 33, 163, 164, 168, 178, 209, 268, 402
Binding Triad 159, 161, 166, 172, 174
biological weapons 143
birth rate 139
blockade 26
blockades 25, 85, 155, 307
Board of Directors 44, 295, 301, 304
Board of Trustees 264, 293, 297, 299, 300, 308, 343, 345, 346
Bolivia 21, 143
bomb corporation stock certificates 352
bombs 81, 110, 274, 275, 308

Borda count 249
border of 1967 264
Borgese, Elizabeth Mann 54, 161
Bose, Subhas Chandra 58
Boyle, Francis A. 378
Boyle, Professor Francis A. 64
brain drain 141
Breki, Dr. Ramadan 82, 116
Brighton iv, 9, 58, 61, 63, 66, 90, 92, 261, 264, 293, 294, 360
broad function 6, 7, 8
Broad Functions 6, 177, 180
brokerage 307, 352, 353
brokers 352
budget 109, 270, 294, 297, 308, 328, 330, 339, 341, 342, 347, 382, 384
bureaucracy 272, 280, 383, 385

C

campaign limits 338
cantons 386
capital 3, 12, 14, 15, 16, 69, 136, 146, 147, 264, 294, 298, 332
capitalism 2, 3, 11, 12, 13, 14, 15, 16, 19, 27, 28, 122, 127, 128, 133, 154, 286, 376, 377, 380
Carlsson, Ingvar 74
Carreras, José 117
Casely-Hayford, Archie 55
Castro, Dr. Josué de 50, 53, 71
Castro, Fidel 88
catalytic precipitators for illegal arms stock divestment 353
census 338
Center for War / Peace Studies 166
Central Bank 44, 66, 301
Chair 73, 109, 112, 114, 116, 120, 267, 268, 313
chairpersons 267
challenge inspections 345
Challenges 334
Chambers 318, 335
Chandola, Raj 114
Chattopadhyay, Dr. Santi Nath 120
Chennai 9, 76, 82, 90, 109, 112, 113, 121, 126, 261, 274, 276, 277, 294, 315, 316, 317, 322, 323, 325, 328, 364
Chennai Declaration 113, 274, 276
Chicago Committee to Frame a World Constitution 160, 400
Chief Justice 24, 310, 318, 326, 353, 357, 360, 390
Children's World Parliament Fund 353
China 25, 39, 40, 156, 162, 246, 364, 365
Chinese 318, 353
Chossudovsky, Michael 147
Circuit Tribunals 310, 311, 312
circulation 52, 136
cities 66, 82, 386
citizens 1, 6, 7, 9, 10, 13, 14, 16, 17, 18, 19, 20, 21, 22, 23, 26, 27, 29, 48, 49, 55, 59, 67, 82, 83, 86, 113, 169, 172, 247, 250, 253, 255, 259, 272, 275, 276, 279, 280, 281, 282, 283, 284, 285, 286, 319, 322, 342, 345, 354, 361, 362, 363, 366, 368, 372, 373, 374, 375, 376, 377, 378, 379, 380, 385, 387, 388
City Montessori School 92, 100, 102, 103, 104, 114, 251, 283, 287, 297, 328, 340
Civil Cases 32, 273, 336
civil disobedience 273, 375, 376
civilians 4, 117, 265, 307, 350
civil obedience 22, 23, 28
civil resistance 378
civil society organizations 350
Clark, Hon. Ramsey 61
Cleveland, Harlan 74
climate change 2, 4, 7, 21, 22, 23, 27, 254
climate collapse 384
Coalition for Democratic World Government 74, 253
codification 115, 175, 176, 260, 302, 313, 326, 346
Cold War 10, 52, 143
collapse of fisheries 133
colleges 386
Collegium of World Judges 33, 178, 249
commanding officer 349
Commission 30, 32, 33, 42, 43, 44, 45, 56, 67, 68, 71, 75, 111, 114, 115, 116, 117, 120, 121, 126, 177, 253, 270, 294, 295, 296, 299, 300, 301, 302, 306, 312,

313, 314, 316, 328, 330, 334, 336, 337, 338, 339, 340, 341, 344, 347, 348, 357, 365, 381
Commission for Legislative Review 32, 42, 44, 111, 115, 117, 126, 177, 296, 302, 312, 313, 314, 316, 344, 348
Commission on Global Governance 75, 121
common sense 19, 47, 372, 375
communications spectrum 141
communicative action 375, 376
communities 371, 383, 386
compensation 14, 119, 265, 320, 327, 328
competing requests 327
compliance 293, 294, 308, 323, 329, 344, 345, 346, 350, 352, 353
composting 152
compulsory jurisdiction 113, 273, 321, 364, 367
concentrations of wealth 14
concept of democratic law 11
conditional rights 151
Conference of Peoples and States Parties 345, 346. *See also* Board of Trustees
confidentiality 341, 353
consensus 81, 338, 362
Constitutional Cases 32, 258
constitutional mandate 6
Constitution for the World 160
Consultation 320
contamination 347, 348
continent 40, 140, 247
Control Commission of Elections to the Peoples Congress 253
Convention 48, 49, 50, 51, 52, 53, 54, 56, 67, 81, 82, 89, 120, 271, 307, 309, 333, 344, 346, 381, 382, 390, 393, 405, 406, 407
convergence of standards 277
conviction 319, 320, 327
cooperation 5, 54, 86, 281, 320, 327, 345, 346, 347, 352, 353, 354, 357, 360, 367, 382
corporations 3, 6, 7, 11, 13, 14, 15, 16, 17, 26, 66, 77, 373, 374, 377, 383, 387
corruption 8, 12, 124, 125, 150, 154, 155, 248, 249, 309, 317, 334, 342, 372
cost accounting 320
costs for juror selection and juror compensation 328
Costs of Ratification 178
councils 162, 163, 245
countries 49, 50, 51, 52, 53, 55, 57, 58, 61, 66, 68, 69, 71, 72, 73, 74, 77, 78, 80, 81, 82, 83, 87, 88, 89, 379, 386
Court 112, 113, 114, 115, 118, 119, 248, 249, 258, 260, 274, 292, 298, 307, 309, 310, 311, 312, 314, 316, 317, 318, 319, 320, 321, 325, 326, 327, 328, 334, 335, 336, 337, 346, 349, 351, 352, 353, 357, 359, 360, 361, 362, 364, 365, 367, 368, 369, 381, 382, 387, 390, 391, 395, 402, 403, 404, 405, 406, 408
court costs 320
Court Flag 351
Court of Human Rights 76
court order 113, 326, 364. *See also* mandamus
Court Reporter 312
courts 5, 7, 9, 11, 18, 20, 21, 22, 49, 248, 249, 294, 298, 317, 358, 359, 369, 378, 383
Court Seat 319
Covenant of the League of Nations 171
credit 17, 33, 44, 45, 69, 70, 77, 78, 80, 87, 90, 115, 118, 146, 147, 253, 256, 257, 294, 295, 300, 303, 304, 305, 306, 307, 321, 324, 325, 330, 343. *See also* credits
credits 87, 88, 294, 300, 303, 304, 315, 321, 353. *See also* credit
Crimes Against Humanity 119, 261, 287
crimes against humanity 110, 248, 287, 288, 317, 318
criminal 9, 11, 60, 114, 126, 132, 133, 164, 165, 249, 251, 273, 274, 307, 315, 316, 317, 318, 334, 335, 359, 362, 377, 378, 379, 380, 387
Criminal Cases 32, 113, 292, 317,

322, 325, 337, 381
Criminal Code Penalty Classification 112, 114, 274, 315, 319. *See also* World Penal Code
crop rotation 152
cruel sport 264
Cuba 84, 86, 89, 349, 350
currency 7, 9, 15, 17, 44, 66, 77, 90, 115, 118, 166, 254, 257, 280, 294, 295, 300, 303, 304, 315, 321, 323, 325, 351
currency restrictions 351
Currency transactions 314

D

Darwin 263
de-militarization 306, 350
death penalty 251
death squads 2, 6
decision 2, 4, 7, 8, 9, 10, 11, 22, 28, 51, 53, 108, 110, 111, 116, 120, 246, 259, 260, 265, 269, 271, 272, 280, 283, 310, 319, 327, 345, 348, 358, 359, 361, 362, 371, 376, 378
Declaration of Independence 8, 23, 26
Declaration of the Independence of the Earth Constitution 261
Declaration of the Rights of Man 8, 284
definitive signature 252
deforestation 3
Deguchi, Onisaburo 278
Delegates Council 338
demilitarization 143, 306
democracy 5, 6, 13, 14, 15, 16, 17, 19, 20, 21, 22, 23, 25, 26, 27, 62, 73, 109, 123, 125, 127, 150, 170, 246, 272, 285, 286, 330, 373, 374, 376, 380, 383, 384, 385, 386, 388
democratic 2, 4, 5, 6, 7, 8, 9, 10, 11, 14, 15, 16, 17, 18, 19, 20, 21, 22, 23, 24, 25, 26, 27, 31, 49, 52, 53, 59, 61, 67, 71, 75, 77, 80, 86, 87, 89, 90, 109, 123, 124, 126, 127, 128, 133, 134, 135, 139, 140, 145, 146, 149, 150, 151, 159, 165, 166, 169, 173, 179, 264, 268, 269, 270, 272, 273, 275, 276, 279, 283, 287, 300, 338, 362, 370, 371, 372, 373, 374, 376, 377, 378, 379, 380, 381, 383, 384, 385, 387
Democratic Social Forum of Bangladesh 119
Department for Conflict Resolution 117, 308, 341, 342
Departments 177, 308, 309
depleted uranium 143
Deputy District Ombudsen 341
detainees 349
detonation 346
development vi, vii, 2, 3, 7, 23, 25, 27, 58, 62, 63, 64, 68, 73, 78, 108, 112, 120, 128, 131, 133, 134, 135, 136, 137, 140, 141, 142, 143, 144, 146, 147, 148, 149, 151, 152, 153, 160, 165, 170, 248, 249, 261, 273, 275, 280, 281, 282, 283, 294, 295, 296, 317, 322, 330, 331, 338, 344, 346, 350, 358, 365, 367, 368, 370, 371, 374, 376, 378, 381, 385
Diagram of the Earth Federation 30, 252
directive 60, 77, 251, 255, 320, 341
Directive Principles 33, 163, 164, 178, 211, 386
directives 120, 251, 255, 259, 260, 302, 325
Directorate 44, 301
disarmament 5, 6, 49, 62, 66, 73, 110, 120, 293, 308, 376, 386
disclosure 311, 327, 342
disease 12, 27, 89, 122, 123, 126, 139, 140, 142, 153, 275, 282, 285, 318, 379, 384, 387
Diseases Fund 353
dismantle 345, 346
dismantlement 293, 344, 345, 346
dispersions of records 289
Dissanayake, Hon. Gamini 58
District Ombudsen 250, 341
District World Courts 32, 63, 164, 248, 298
divestment 110, 119, 257, 352, 353
dock works 349
dollars 66, 70, 88, 130, 137, 143,

144, 145, 150, 388
domination 2, 7, 10, 15, 25, 26, 126, 127, 129, 130, 143, 144, 146, 150, 152, 153, 154, 157, 274, 275, 285, 374, 379, 383, 384, 385, 388
double jeopardy 317
Dr. T. P. Amerasinghe 49, 53, 54, 55, 56, 57, 58, 60, 61, 67, 68, 71, 76, 82
drug trafficking 6
Dubcek, Alexander 61, 73
Dubcek, Dr. Alexander 61
due process 13, 26, 33, 119, 164, 281, 288, 289, 309, 342, 343, 359, 366, 367, 369

E

Earth Charter 125, 160
Earth Constitution 2, 5, 6, 7, 9, 10, 11, 13, 14, 15, 17, 18, 19, 23, 24, 26, 27, 28, 29, 30, 31, 32, 33, 34, 45, 57, 60, 61, 68, 73, 74, 78, 80, 82, 109, 110, 111, 115, 116, 125, 126, 128, 129, 133, 134, 135, 140, 141, 142, 144, 145, 150, 154, 159, 161, 162, 163, 164, 165, 170, 171, 172, 173, 174, 175, 227, 245, 246, 247, 248, 249, 250, 251, 252, 253, 254, 255, 256, 257, 258, 260, 261, 262, 265, 266, 268, 273, 274, 275, 276, 281, 282, 288, 294, 295, 296, 298, 299, 300, 303, 306, 307, 309, 311, 313, 314, 316, 318, 320, 321, 326, 330, 336, 337, 338, 343, 344, 345, 346, 348, 349, 350, 352, 353, 354, 355, 357, 359, 361, 362, 363, 364, 365, 366, 367, 368, 369, 370, 372, 373, 374, 375, 376, 377, 381, 382, 383, 384, 385, 386, 387, 388
Earth currency 44, 77, 294, 295, 300, 303, 304, 315, 323
Earth Dollar 70, 325
Earth Federation Educational Advisory Councils 330
Earth Federation Funding Corporation 29, 30, 44, 66, 110, 115, 256, 257, 294, 295, 300, 301, 352, 353. *See also* World Government Funding Corporation
Earth Federation Movement 5, 10, 74, 80, 376, 377, 381, 386
Earth Financial Credit Corporation 45, 69, 70, 110, 303, 304, 305, 314, 330, 343, 346
Earth Hour 44, 70, 90, 118, 257, 304, 321, 323, 325, 353
Earth Summit 131
East Jerusalem 264, 265
Ecimovic, T. 254
ecological sustainability 371
Economic Equality 280
economic rights 376
economics 2, 13, 17, 18, 19, 21, 23, 24, 25, 27, 121, 122, 123, 127, 134, 142, 145, 146, 150, 153, 376
Editors' interpretation 247, 250, 251, 252, 253
education 13, 17, 31, 73, 115, 122, 130, 131, 133, 134, 136, 137, 139, 140, 141, 142, 148, 153, 272, 280, 282, 303, 330, 332, 336
Educational, Scientific and Cultural Organization 381, 409
Education Commission Chairperson 330
Education Ministry 330
Einstein 47, 123, 124, 371
election 57, 72, 247, 249, 267, 288, 300, 306, 318, 330, 335, 337, 366
electoral districts 5, 6, 125, 283, 386
electorate 357, 370
Electromagnetic spectrum 314
electronic parliament 168
Elements of Crimes 110, 115, 316, 317, 334, 361, 368
Elias, Dr. Taslim 61
Elzubedi, Dr. Salem 81
emblem 351
Emergency Council of World Trustees 55
Emerging World Law 9, 10, 27, 47, 91, 115, 260, 289, 292, 326, 388
emerging world law 4, 10, 28, 366,

370, 372, 376
emissions trading 132
emoluments 310, 363
enforceable law 379, 380, 382
Engels, Friedrich 16
English 52, 68, 79, 120, 318, 353, 391, 393, 395, 403, 404, 405, 408, 409
entry into force 294, 317, 321, 334, 344, 346, 348, 353, 354
environmental crimes 248, 317
environmental destruction 3, 8, 21, 23, 121, 144, 275, 285, 379
environmental protection 263
Equador 143
equal pay for equal work 150, 151
equal protection 13, 33, 112, 163, 363, 366, 367, 382
Erskine May Code 271
escape 321, 328
Esperanto 103, 116, 252, 278, 279, 282, 318, 353, 353
evidence 77, 119, 312, 319, 327, 382
exceptions and conditions for reimbursement 351
exclusive private property rights 3
exclusive titles to nature's wealth 3
Executive 25, 29, 31, 32, 42, 43, 44, 45, 50, 56, 60, 83, 84, 90, 108, 109, 118, 120, 125, 177, 178, 189, 246, 252, 253, 267, 268, 300, 301, 304, 313, 344, 345, 348, 362, 383, 384, 387
Executive Cabinet 32, 42, 44, 45, 50, 108, 109, 118, 177, 246, 267, 304, 344, 348
Executive Committee 44, 300, 301
Executive Summary 29, 252, 253
exemption 350, 351, 352
expedition of visa 352
expiry of terms 249
exploitation 2, 3, 6, 7, 10, 12, 26, 58, 89, 90, 126, 127, 129, 131, 143, 144, 145, 146, 150, 151, 152, 153, 154, 156, 275, 285, 286, 295, 332, 379, 384, 387, 388
ex post facto 288, 365
extenuating circumstances 316
external relations 34
Extradition 320

F

factory farming 264
fair hearing 250
family custody 336
family planning 251
FAO 43
Federal Wage and Price Standard 323
Federation of Earth 1, 4, 5, 6, 8, 10, 13, 14, 17, 18, 22, 23, 27, 28, 30, 31, 34, 38, 43, 45, 48, 51, 54, 55, 56, 57, 60, 62, 63, 68, 69, 70, 71, 72, 73, 75, 76, 77, 78, 80, 81, 82, 83, 84, 86, 87, 113, 116, 120, 121, 122, 123, 124, 129, 133, 134, 143, 146, 155, 156, 159, 161, 162, 168, 172, 173, 175, 179, 255, 256, 261, 263, 264, 265, 266, 267, 268, 269, 270, 271, 272, 273, 274, 276, 278, 279, 280, 283, 285, 286, 287, 298, 341, 355, 380, 381, 386
felony 293, 296, 302, 304, 305, 315, 317, 320, 329, 331, 332, 333, 347, 348, 349
fertilizers 152
fines 313, 316, 319, 321, 328, 336, 353
First Decree for the Protection of Life 55
First Operative Stage 34, 178, 270, 388
first operative stage 34, 119, 171, 256, 307, 313, 319, 353, 353, 354, 365, 387
fisheries 2, 3, 122, 131, 133, 136, 137, 153, 284
fissile materials 342, 343, 344, 345, 346
Fissile Materials Production Ban 346
Fissile Production Prohibition 117, 255
fixed on-site sensors 345
forensic 111, 366, 367, 369
forests 2, 3, 19, 66, 131, 135, 136, 137, 138, 152, 153
formatting amendments 294, 295, 296, 297, 299, 301, 302, 303, 306, 308, 316, 322
Foster,, Mark 167

founded document 159, 165, 166, 167, 168, 169, 173, 252
Founding Ratification Convention 81, 120, 171, 271
founding ratification convention 387
fragmentation 2, 4, 6, 7, 8, 10, 11, 12, 14, 18, 19, 22, 23, 27, 28, 121, 124, 126, 155, 156, 281, 283, 373
fragmentation of humanity 2
framers 5, 8, 9, 11, 253, 257, 375, 376
free speech 13, 275
French 8, 58, 68, 77, 120, 278, 284, 318, 353
full faith and credit 33
full numeric codification 115, 175, 260, 346
Full Operative Stage 34, 178
full operative stage 249, 256, 308

G

G-8 7
GAI supplemental assistance 354
Gandhi, Mahatma 384
Gandhi, Mr. Jagdish 114
Gandhi, Rajiv 68
Gandhi, Shrimati Indira 60
GATT 129
gender equity 115, 167, 172, 174
General Assembly 5, 43, 57, 61, 71, 73, 115, 116, 120, 133, 166, 168, 169, 251, 254, 255, 260, 261, 262, 278, 344, 346, 363, 380
general election 288
General Review Conference 116, 167, 168, 169, 170, 171, 172, 173, 174, 278
genetic engineering 322
Genocide 119, 261, 287
George, Henry 151
Glen T. Martin 1, 114, 118, 121, 266, 371
Global 2000 Report 263, 403
Global Accounting Standards 112, 114, 324, 325
global climate 2, 4, 8, 21, 22
global democracy 383, 385, 386, 388
Global Education 330
global emissions trading 132
Global Energy Administration 306
Global Expositions 83, 89
Global Ministry of Environment 68, 302. *See also* World Environmental Protection Agency
Global Peoples Assembly 112, 162, 163, 168, 170, 172, 253, 283, 337, 338, 339, 404
Global Peoples Assembly Movement 112, 338
global problems 6, 8, 76, 86, 90, 274
Global Ratification and Elections Network 72, 74, 80, 83, 88, 89
global solutions 59, 71, 385
global trade organizations 383
Glossop, Professor Ronald J. 74
Godban, Dr. Ali 82
good government 17, 18, 151, 273, 279, 280, 281, 283, 330. *See also* Resolution on Good Government
Gorbachev, Mikhail 160
governance 76, 374, 383
Governing Board 350
governing units 251, 252, 256, 293
GPA 43, 338
GPAM 338
Graduate School of World Problems 63, 84, 89, 90, 91, 100, 297. *See also* Institute on Governmental Procedures and World Problems, *See also* Institute On World Problems
Great Depression 11
Greece 382
Green, Dr. Lucile 55, 61
Greenpeace 377, 386, 405
GREN 72, 73, 80, 81, 82, 83, 84, 86, 89, 90
Grima, Paula 83
gross domestic product 322
groundwater 135
group accounts 256
Guantánamo 117, 119, 348, 349, 350
Guantánamo Base 119, 348, 349
Guantánamo Bay 119, 348, 349, 350
Guantánamo Bay Governing Board 350
Guantánamo Bay Harbor Master 350
Guantánamo Directive 117

Guaranteed Annual Income 119
guaranteed annual income 354
Gupta, Dr. Dauji 108, 117
Gutkind 371, 372, 388, 390, 407
Gutkind, Eric 372

H

habeas corpus 33, 111, 248, 311, 349, 367, 369
Habermas, Jürgen 375
Habicht, Dr. Max 54, 61
harbor 349, 350
Harbor Master 350
Harris 388
Harris, Professor Errol 74, 386
Hart, H.L.A. 373
health care 130, 133, 136, 139, 140, 141, 151, 152, 332
hearing 250, 311, 312, 331, 390
Hegel, G. W. F. 128
Hesse, Herman 107
High Commission on Human Rights 381
Hiroshima 10, 385
His Honour Christopher Weeramantry 118
Hobbes, Thomas 128
Honorary Sponsors 268
Hoopha Sawan Religious Land 60
house arrest 315
House of Counsellors 5, 6, 32, 33, 42, 43, 172, 177, 247, 249, 344, 362
House of Nations 5, 24, 32, 42, 43, 56, 57, 125, 162, 172, 177, 246, 262
House of Peoples 5, 32, 42, 43, 56, 57, 125, 162, 177, 283
human beings 2, 4, 14, 18, 19, 20, 21, 23, 24, 27, 121, 138, 142, 153, 154, 155, 166, 250, 265, 274, 278, 284, 339, 367, 369, 371, 372, 375, 377, 379, 381
Humanist 56
humankind 1, 2, 4, 5, 7, 8, 9, 11, 26, 27, 69, 81, 89, 124, 126, 148, 263, 276, 287, 371, 388
human nature 12, 28, 154
Human Rights 14, 26, 32, 43, 60, 70, 76, 163, 164, 166, 169, 194, 250, 284, 285, 309, 310, 312, 316, 340, 348, 362, 363, 366, 367, 373, 379, 380, 381, 382, 386
human rights 5, 6, 7, 8, 14, 15, 19, 21, 22, 23, 24, 26, 31, 33, 67, 73, 123, 125, 127, 140, 144, 145, 150, 151, 163, 164, 166, 179, 250, 272, 279, 280, 281, 285, 286, 309, 311, 315, 340, 348, 363, 367, 368, 373, 376, 377, 378, 380, 382, 383, 384, 385, 386, 387
Human Rights Bench 164, 250, 309
Husain, Hon. Syed Mohamed 55
Hussain, Saddam 72
Hydrocarbon Resource Board 111
hydrogen 69, 138, 152, 303, 306
hydrogen power 306

I

ICC 381, 382, 408. *See also* International Criminal Court, *See also* World Bench for Criminal Cases
ICJ 381
ideology 12, 13, 14, 15, 16, 17, 24, 25, 148, 151, 279
illegal financial instruments 352, 353
illegal financial instruments acquired by testament 352
illegal financial instruments held in probate or trust 353
illegal securities 352
illness 3, 354
IMF 3, 142, 374
immigration 350
Immunities 117, 248, 335, 351, 353, 402, 404
Immunities and Privileges of the World Court 248
immunity 320, 351, 352. *See also* Immunities
imperial 12, 13, 25, 26, 126, 129, 132, 143, 145, 146, 150, 151, 152, 153, 155, 156, 285, 379, 381
imperialist 10
imprisonment 307, 312, 315, 316, 319, 320, 327, 332, 348
incompetence 8

Indemnity Bonds 119, 256, 352, 353
indemnity bonds 119, 257, 352, 353
independence of judges 318
Independence of the Ratification of the Constitution for the Federation of Earth 261, 266
India 9, 49, 54, 55, 58, 60, 61, 65, 68, 76, 82, 83, 90, 92, 93, 102, 103, 107, 108, 111, 112, 114, 115, 117, 120, 246, 274, 276, 277, 278, 279, 283, 287, 288, 294, 295, 296, 297, 299, 301, 302, 303, 306, 308, 315, 316, 317, 322, 323, 325, 328, 330, 331, 333, 337, 339, 340, 359, 364, 365, 379, 387, 390, 406
Indira Gandhi 60, 67
individuals 4, 14, 15, 16, 17, 20, 24, 66, 67, 73, 75, 110, 113, 124, 143, 145, 146, 147, 150, 151, 155, 256, 257, 272, 273, 280, 284, 307, 309, 311, 314, 318, 321, 324, 345, 382, 386, 387
Indonesia 21, 57, 143
inefficacy of international conventions 110
inhabitants 66, 77, 78, 248, 250, 255
initiation 262, 318, 327, 369
initiative 9, 29, 32, 57, 59, 61, 74, 251
initiatives 8, 9, 265, 338, 382. *See also* initiative
installments 255, 256, 320
Institute on Governmental Procedures and World Problems 32, 42, 177, 329. *See also* Graduate School of World Problems, *See also* Institute On World Problems
Institute On World Problems 89, 90, 252, 401. *See also* Graduate School of World Problems, *See also* Institute on Governmental Procedures and World Problems
institutes 386
institutionalized fragmentation 7, 27
instruments of defense 342, 349
insurgence 367
Integrative Complex 31, 32, 162, 177, 194, 247, 268, 302, 314, 330, 342
Intellectual Property Rights 322
intercontinental missiles 143
interest rates 3, 69, 146, 147
interests of other species 263
interference in world government 317
Interim Mayor 350
Interim Municipal Council 350
Interlaken 54
internal affairs 2, 5, 33
internal exile 315
Internal Initiatives 338
International Accounting Standards 114, 324, 325, 395, 405
International Accounting Standards Board 114, 324, 325
International Atomic Energy Agency 120, 255
International Bench 321
International Commission on Radiological Protection 347
International Conflicts 32
International cooperation 327
international cooperation 353
International Court of Justice 381, 408
International Criminal Court 9, 43, 112, 113, 248, 249, 260, 292, 317, 325, 326, 351, 359, 364, 365, 381, 382. *See also* Rome Statute
International Labor Organization 381, 408
international law 4, 5, 9, 63, 165, 248, 286, 287, 288, 292, 316, 359, 360, 378, 379, 382
international rules for harbor operation 350
International Seabed Authority 296
Interpol 43, 45, 361
interpretation 162, 172, 246, 247, 250, 251, 252, 253, 255, 257, 258, 319, 346, 352
interpretative clarification 245
interruption 249
intimidation 384
investigation 111, 318, 319, 320, 327, 336, 369
Investigations Department 301, 353
inviolability of premises 351

invitation 117, 254, 255, 353
Iraq 72, 81, 145, 274, 275, 284
irrigation 135
Isely, Philip 1, 48, 49, 50, 51, 52, 53, 55, 56, 58, 60, 61, 66, 69, 71, 74, 75, 82, 88, 93, 107, 108, 109, 175
Isely, Margaret 48, 49, 52, 57, 68, 78, 93, 107
Isely, Philip 48, 49, 52, 57, 61, 66, 68, 78, 93, 107
Israel 54, 55, 265

J

J. W. Smith 147, 150
Jakhar, Hon. Balram 61, 65
Japan 10, 54, 60, 63, 86, 116, 156, 297, 385
Japanese World Federalist 76, 385
Jayawardene, President J. R. 58
job loss 354
Johannesburg 4, 122, 130, 131, 132, 134, 398
joint session 314, 321
Joint Vision 2020 10
Judge 33, 56, 61, 63, 310, 312, 326, 357, 360
Judiciary 31, 32, 33, 125, 163, 178, 201, 250, 268, 328, 361
juridical personality 351
Juris-Consults 310
Jurisdiction 255, 326, 334
jurisdiction 25, 31, 32, 33, 34, 41, 56, 63, 113, 164, 251, 252, 253, 254, 258, 262, 273, 291, 294, 295, 307, 310, 311, 314, 317, 318, 321, 326, 328, 333, 334, 335, 336, 343, 345, 349, 362, 364, 367, 368, 378
Jurisgenesis 366
jurisgenesis 361, 362, 366, 375
juristic force 11
jury 114, 120, 326, 328, 364
Jury Development Commission 328
justice 1, 5, 11, 19, 27, 56, 59, 103, 114, 249, 272, 276, 279, 284, 285, 286, 288, 289, 312, 315, 319, 327, 336, 369, 371, 372, 374, 376, 377, 383, 388
Juvenile Bench 381
Juvenile Cases 113, 115, 273, 334
Juvenile Court 334, 335, 336, 337
juvenile jurisdiction 318
juvenile law 381
juvenile penal code 334

K

Kaiser, Dr. S. 57
Kalamata 382
Kamath, Hari Vishnu 61
Kamath, Indian M. P. Hari Vishnu 58
Kant 16, 18, 128, 357, 371
Kant, Immanuel 16
Kara 9, 105, 109, 118, 287, 289, 292, 297, 304, 323, 325, 348, 350, 353, 352, 353, 354, 355
keep and bear arms 174, 255
Khan, Muhammad Zafrulla 263
Khan, Sir Chaudhry Mohammad Zafrullah 61
kidnap 119, 349
Kirby, Hon. Justice Michael 61
Kolkata 387
Komo, Kenneth 57
Korten, David 15, 147
Kosokitiworg, Dr. Suchart 60
Kosolkitiwong, Suchart 60, 100, 108, 111
Kruliak, Mrs. Murial 52
Kuan Yin Inter-religious Park 111
Kungulovska, Eli 107
Kussman, Dr. Carmel 57
Kussman, Dr. Karmel 61
Kyoto Protocol 4, 122, 132

L

L. M. Singhvi 102, 114, 400
laissez-passer documents 352
Land rents 314
land rent tax 349, 350
Latin American Union 156
law enforcement 111, 248, 249, 253, 255, 307, 309, 343, 345, 359, 361, 362, 366, 367, 368, 369
Law of the Sea 58, 63, 296, 405
League of Nations 48, 171
lease 349, 350
legitimacy 23, 110, 165, 173, 261, 284, 285, 286, 362, 367, 369, 374, 375, 382, 383

legitimate 372, 374, 375, 376, 377, 380, 382, 383, 387, 388
less lethal munitions 249, 308, 367, 368
Liberation 274, 288, 289, 408
liberation 274, 276, 287, 288
liberty 6, 14, 15, 16, 18, 19, 20, 21, 22, 23, 327, 375
Libya 9, 81, 82, 90, 104, 340, 341, 342, 344, 347, 348, 350, 353
liens 352
Lillich, Justice Professor Richard B. 64
Limitations 177
line 3, 24, 27, 41, 52, 70, 130, 253, 303, 363, 364
lines of credit 70, 294, 303, 330
living wage 307, 323
loan 146, 300, 301
loans 3, 66, 74, 80, 81, 86, 87, 117, 146, 147, 300, 330
local communities 371, 383, 386
Local Economic Trading Systems 315
Locke 14, 15, 18, 19
Locke, John 15
Lord, Mrs. Mia 57
Lucknow 9, 90, 92, 100, 102, 103, 104, 107, 114, 116, 126, 251, 261, 278, 279, 283, 287, 294, 295, 296, 297, 299, 300, 301, 302, 303, 304, 306, 308, 316, 318, 322, 323, 328, 330, 331, 333, 337, 339, 340, 359, 379

M

M'Baye, Hon. Kéba 61
Machiavelli 2
Machiavelli's 384
Magna Carta 8
magnetic power 306
majority 3, 12, 14, 15, 17, 18, 20, 21, 25, 34, 42, 50, 87, 123, 126, 127, 129, 141, 142, 153, 156, 253, 267, 268, 269, 270, 271, 284, 285, 287, 288, 314, 328, 338, 357, 372, 379, 384, 386
majority vote 34, 42, 267, 268, 269, 270, 271, 314, 386
Makasa, Kapasa 61
Malta 9, 55, 80, 82, 83, 84, 85, 90, 107, 265, 305, 306
mandamus 113, 326, 364, 382
mandated reporter 341
Markar, Hon. Mohammed Bakeer 58
market 12, 13, 21, 86, 88, 132, 150, 277
market valuation 277
Marshall, Chief Justice John 24
Marshall Doctrine 25
Martin, Glen 74, 88, 89, 90, 105, 108, 116
Martin, Glen T. 1, 114, 118, 121, 266, 371
Martin, Glen 90
Martin, Glen T. 1
Marx 13, 16
Marx, Karl 13
matrix 16, 17, 18
Max Habicht 1, 51, 54, 61, 175
maximum wage 118, 304, 323
May, Erskine 271
Mayur, Rashmi 71, 108
Mazi, Bernard Shaw 72
McNamara, Secretary of Defence Robert S. 52
Mead, Margaret 387
Members of World Parliament 32, 313
memorial 113, 115, 118, 251, 259, 278, 395
Memorial to the Assembly of States Parties 113, 114, 261, 395
mental element 318, 335
Mercieca, Dr. Charles 55
Miami Beach 9, 65, 68, 70, 94, 302
militant 367
militarism 3, 19, 20, 23, 84, 122, 130, 131, 133, 137, 140, 142, 143, 144, 145, 275, 383, 384, 387, 388
military 2, 4, 5, 6, 10, 16, 19, 20, 22, 24, 25, 26, 27, 31, 32, 33, 43, 56, 63, 66, 70, 81, 85, 101, 111, 113, 125, 127, 130, 143, 144, 145, 152, 154, 156, 161, 163, 166, 167, 168, 169, 175, 179, 252, 253, 255, 265, 268, 269, 270, 274, 279, 285, 286, 293, 294, 300, 302, 306, 307, 308, 349, 357, 361, 362, 364, 366, 367, 368, 369, 376, 378, 379, 383, 384

Mill, John Stuart 3, 16
Millennium Assembly 85
Millennium Declaration 132
Millennium Development Goals 377
minimum income 354
minimum wage 118, 304, 323
Mining surcharges 314
Minuteman III nuclear missile 378
misconduct 318, 319, 327, 336
misdemeanour 314, 315, 329
mistake of fact 318
mistake of law 318, 335
mitigating and aggravating circumstances 316
Miyake, Rev. Dr. Toshio 60
Monguno, Ali 72
monopoly 13, 14, 15, 19, 27, 28, 73, 84, 122, 128, 130, 147, 148, 151, 286, 376
moral imperative 370
Morgenthau, Hans 378
motion to dismiss 311
multinational corporations 6, 7, 26, 373, 374, 377, 387
mundialization 349
Murahari, Goday 55, 65
Murahari, Hon. Goday 58
Musslewhite, Benton 167

N

Nagasaki 10, 385
Nath, Onkar 54
nation-state 12, 19, 20, 24, 26, 27, 286, 357, 369, 373, 376, 377, 378, 384
nation-states 2, 3, 4, 6, 19, 22, 23, 24, 25, 27, 28, 266, 272, 273, 285, 286, 305, 362, 373, 375, 377, 380, 382, 383
national boundaries 7, 31
nationality rights 349
national level ratification 115, 262
national security 319
national social security payments 352
native habitat 264
NATO 83, 85, 349, 361
natural resources 3, 6, 44, 58, 142, 146, 147, 148, 150, 151, 339
Nazis 26
Ne bis in idem 317, 334
Nehru, R. K. 54
Netherlands 49, 54, 57, 160
Newcombe, Dr. Hanna 57
Newcombe Plan 29, 40, 337
New Delhi 9, 58, 60, 61, 63, 65, 66, 67, 68, 76, 82, 299
New Humanity Centre 382
Newman, Hon. Justice Professor Frank 63
NGO 88, 89. *See also* NGOs
NGOs 377, 385, 387, 388
Niemoller, Dr. Martin 54
Nigam, Brij 65
Nigam, Shri B. P. 60
Nigam, Smt. Savitri 60
Non-Aligned Movement 260
non-compliance 329, 346, 353
Non-governmental Organizations 350
non-military 4, 16, 24, 31, 33, 111, 169, 175, 252, 268, 269, 270, 279, 300, 361, 366, 367, 368, 376
North Atlantic Treaty Organization 85
notification of lists of persons 352
Nuclear Contamination Act 117, 348
nuclear disarmament 62, 386
nuclear energy 306, 346
nuclear holocaust 7, 20, 284, 372
nuclear material 345
nuclear weapons 62, 64, 265, 284, 308, 342, 344, 345, 347, 359, 360, 361, 362, 365, 385
Nuclear Weapons Elimination Protocol 117, 120
Nujoma, Sam 74
Nulla poena sine lege 317, 335
Nullum crimen sine lege 317
numeric codification 115, 175, 176, 260, 346
Nuremburg Accords 287, 403

O

"Outline for the Debate and Drafting of a World Constitution" 56
observers 101, 270
officers 20, 109, 260, 267, 289, 297, 304, 324, 342, 349, 351, 352, 361, 368, 369
official capacity 318
Oliver, Justice Professor Covey 63

Ombudsmus 31, 33, 42, 43, 56, 75, 117, 125, 145, 163, 164, 178, 250, 260, 268, 272, 311, 315, 317, 321, 328, 340, 341, 342, 348, 351, 381, 383
One World Now 167
Operative Stage 34, 178, 270, 388
opposition parties 125
order 9, 10, 11, 12, 17, 19, 25, 26, 51, 71, 78, 81, 89, 90, 113, 119, 260, 268, 269, 274, 275, 276, 277, 284, 285, 288, 289, 311, 320, 326, 336, 363, 364, 365, 366, 367, 371, 372, 373, 374, 375, 376, 377, 378, 379, 380, 381, 382, 383, 385, 388. *See also* orders
orders 318, 320, 327, 328, 349, 375. *See also* order
Ording, Aake Anker 54
organic farming 152
organizations 73, 74, 80, 85, 86, 377, 379, 381, 383, 385, 386, 387, 388
organizing agent 267, 268, 269, 270
Organs 31, 177, 181, 335
Oxfam 377, 386
Oxley, Lloyd 55
ozone depletion 133
ozone layer 7, 137, 138, 284
ozonosphere 308

P

Pabhassarakul, Dhanabhumi 109
paired ratification 45
Pakistan 50, 54, 61, 287, 288
Palestine 84, 264, 265, 404
Parker, Ms. Jean 117
Parmalee, Foster 57
parties 67, 73, 125, 252, 310, 311, 338, 341, 352, 360
partition 41
Patel, A. B. 57
Pauling, Dr. Linus 61
peace 1, 5, 6, 13, 16, 19, 20, 21, 27, 28, 50, 51, 52, 56, 60, 71, 73, 85, 89, 102, 111, 122, 123, 125, 126, 128, 129, 133, 134, 137, 141, 142, 145, 151, 154, 156, 157, 172, 179, 265, 272, 275, 276, 278, 280, 281, 283, 330, 371, 372, 374, 376, 377, 380, 383, 385, 388
peacekeeping 43, 145, 376
Peace of Westphalia 2, 24
peace studies 330
pedagogies 330
penal slavery 250
penalties 7, 274, 307, 313, 316, 319, 327, 336, 346, 350, 353
Pentagon 10, 26
people of Earth 2, 3, 5, 10, 23, 24, 25, 26, 29, 31, 33, 34, 50, 57, 59, 122, 125, 128, 133, 134, 136, 137, 139, 151, 157, 171, 266, 269, 280, 285, 286, 309, 322, 367, 376, 380, 381, 383, 384, 388
peoples' assembly 133
Peoples Congress 253
Peter, Emil E. O. 68
petitions 251, 255, 268, 273, 309
Philadelphia 374
Philip Isely 1, 48, 49, 50, 51, 52, 53, 55, 56, 58, 60, 61, 66, 69, 71, 74, 75, 82, 88, 93, 107, 108, 109, 175
Piere, Abbe 54
Ping, President Jean 251
plea bargains 353
plebiscites 29, 40, 246, 338
Pledge of Allegiance 113, 261, 276
plenipotentiary 252
police 9, 11, 18, 21, 22, 31, 83, 145, 167, 171, 275, 341, 349, 361, 367, 368, 384, 385
Polio 140
political parties 252, 338
politicians 11, 12, 61, 154, 287
pollution 2, 3, 7, 68, 69, 131, 132, 137, 138, 139, 140, 152
pollution credits 132
Pontzen, Prof. Theo 54
population 2, 3, 4, 5, 7, 15, 19, 21, 23, 26, 31, 34, 40, 58, 122, 130, 131, 132, 133, 135, 137, 138, 139, 140, 141, 146, 148, 149, 152, 153, 166, 248, 254, 265, 281, 283, 364, 367, 373, 375, 380, 386
postings 353, 354

postponement 320
poverty 3, 6, 7, 12, 13, 15, 17, 27, 31, 81, 88, 89, 121, 122, 123, 127, 130, 131, 132, 133, 135, 136, 137, 138, 139, 140, 141, 143, 144, 148, 150, 151, 153, 275, 281, 284, 285, 286, 330, 373, 379, 384, 386, 387, 388
power 2, 3, 6, 11, 12, 14, 15, 16, 17, 19, 20, 25, 31, 32, 49, 51, 59, 71, 72, 73, 74, 75, 77, 82, 83, 88, 107, 113, 124, 125, 127, 138, 142, 144, 154, 155, 156, 162, 163, 166, 168, 170, 171, 174, 246, 250, 252, 262, 269, 273, 275, 277, 281, 285, 298, 306, 307, 317, 326, 329, 334, 342, 348, 357, 359, 361, 362, 364, 365, 366, 367, 368, 369, 373, 374, 375, 378, 380, 381, 382, 383, 384, 385, 388
power block 156
Powers 17, 31, 177, 178, 182, 334
powers of arrest 342
Pre-Trial Division 318
Preamble 4, 134, 177, 263, 272, 281
prefectures 386
Preliminary ratification 34
Preparatory Commissions 51, 178
Presidency 72, 318
Presiding Council 310, 318, 335
Presiding Judge 310, 312
Presidium 32, 34, 42, 44, 56, 177, 247, 255, 306, 317, 321, 339, 344, 350
prima facie 311
Principles 19, 33, 163, 164, 172, 178, 211, 335, 339, 386
prison 316
prisons 22
Privileges 117, 248, 335, 351, 353, 402, 404
probate 353
Procedures 32, 42, 44, 56, 112, 177, 194, 329
proceedings 114, 250, 271, 319, 326, 327, 329, 336, 351
production of body 311
professors 12, 13, 73, 341
profits 3, 6, 17, 70, 277
prohibitions 33, 112, 332, 342, 345
property 3, 4, 6, 7, 11, 13, 14, 15, 16, 17, 18, 19, 33, 41, 67, 147, 148, 149, 151, 301, 304, 307, 322, 329, 336, 348, 351, 358, 376, 378
proposal 114, 116, 160, 161, 162, 165, 166, 167, 168, 169, 170, 171, 172, 251, 268, 269, 328, 336, 340
prosecution 111, 317, 318, 320, 327, 328, 335, 341, 345, 352, 369, 370
Prosecutor 318, 319, 326, 327, 334, 335, 336, 351, 361. *See also* World Attorneys General
prostitution 6, 130, 331, 332, 379
Protocol 4, 117, 120, 344, 346, 360, 387, 391
protocol 344, 345
provinces 386
Provisional District World Court 63
Provisional Earth Federation 34, 178, 224, 257, 306, 325, 349
Provisional Education Minister 330
Provisional Office of World Revenue 111, 115, 314, 315
provisional world ministries 9
Provisional World Parliament iv, 9, 10, 29, 34, 44, 45, 47, 58, 61, 62, 63, 65, 66, 68, 69, 70, 71, 72, 73, 74, 76, 78, 80, 81, 82, 83, 84, 85, 89, 90, 91, 92, 93, 94, 100, 101, 103, 104, 105, 107, 108, 109, 110, 111, 112, 113, 114, 115, 116, 117, 118, 120, 121, 124, 126, 134, 162, 163, 164, 165, 170, 172, 173, 178, 245, 246, 247, 248, 249, 250, 251, 252, 253, 254, 255, 257, 259, 260, 261, 262, 263, 264, 265, 266, 267, 270, 271, 272, 273, 274, 276, 277, 278, 279, 283, 284, 286, 287, 289, 291, 292, 293, 294, 295, 296, 297, 298, 299, 300, 301, 302, 303, 304, 305, 306, 307, 308, 309, 312, 313, 314, 315, 316, 317, 321, 322, 323, 325, 328, 330, 331, 333, 334, 336, 337, 339, 340, 341, 342, 344, 346, 347, 348, 350, 351, 353, 352, 353,

354, 355, 357, 359, 360, 361, 364, 365, 366, 367, 368, 370, 372, 374, 376, 377, 379, 381, 382, 387
Provisional World Parliament Fund 353
provisions 19, 29, 63, 109, 110, 112, 113, 114, 115, 116, 119, 120, 165, 168, 169, 170, 171, 172, 173, 227, 245, 246, 247, 250, 259, 262, 296, 299, 303, 305, 306, 311, 316, 320, 321, 326, 327, 328, 332, 334, 337, 339, 347, 350, 355, 359, 363, 366, 367, 368, 369, 374
Proxy 271
public agencies 336
Public Cases 32
public trading floors 353
Public Utilities 117, 353

Q

Quainson-Sackey, Dr. Alex 61
quorum 51, 108, 171, 268, 271, 338

R

R.C.M. 81, 82, 162. *See also* Revolutionary Committees Movement
Radio for Peace International. 117
radiological dangers 118, 120, 347
radionuclide sampling 345
Rahman, Sheikh Mujibur 288
Rajda, Ratna Singh 65
Rajiv Gandhi 68
Ram, Justice S. K. 82
Ramajunam Ananthanarayanan 112
Raman, Shri Venkata 60
Rashtrapathi Bhawan 76
ratification 8, 9, 34, 45, 57, 58, 59, 60, 68, 70, 71, 72, 74, 75, 77, 78, 80, 81, 101, 109, 114, 115, 120, 126, 155, 162, 165, 173, 246, 247, 251, 252, 253, 255, 257, 262, 264, 265, 266, 267, 268, 269, 300, 303, 321, 344, 345, 349, 352, 353, 362, 366, 367, 369, 374, 375, 376, 380, 385, 386, 387, 388
Rationale 59
ratione personae 317, 335
Rausher, Scott 167
Read, Thane 55
recall of loans 146, 147
reduction of issuance value 353
referendum 57, 338, 386
Reform 71, 75, 76, 159
refugee relocation 348
Regional Courts 310
Regional Peoples' Assemblies 162
Regional World Courts 32, 63, 164, 248, 298
Regional World Police Captains 33, 45
Registrar 312, 318, 351, 352
Registre des Citoyens du Monde 366
Registry 253, 318, 326, 335, 337, 351
Registry of World Citizens 253
Regulations 318, 336, 360
Regulations of the Court 318
reimbursement 320, 321, 351
Reinhart Ruge 52, 53, 55, 60, 61, 68, 71, 82, 93, 100, 108, 112, 114, 175
reparations 319
replacements 295, 326, 350
representation 5, 82, 104, 125, 162, 167, 168, 271, 274, 283, 307
Representatives of People 351
repression 375, 384
Request 320
request 50, 71, 113, 251, 267, 293, 294, 329, 342, 346, 382
requests 320, 327, 367. *See also* request
reservation 252, 269. *See also* reservations
reservations 321, 344, 346. *See also* reservation
residents 349, 350, 352
resolution 61, 73, 81, 84, 111, 113, 116, 162, 259, 260, 262, 263, 264, 265, 266, 272, 273, 279, 282, 283, 289, 341, 342, 348, 367, 383
Resolution on Good Government 115, 261
resources 2, 3, 6, 7, 19, 20, 21, 22, 25, 44, 58, 62, 66, 67, 69, 72, 73, 103, 117, 119, 125, 126, 130, 131, 134, 136, 137, 138,

139, 140, 141, 142, 144, 146, 147, 148, 149, 150, 151, 179, 275, 276, 280, 282, 295, 296, 303, 313, 314, 339, 340, 342, 376, 382, 383, 385, 388
Resource utilization fees 314
respondent's return 312
retention of unnamed rights 164
retirement of illegal stocks 352
Review Conference 116, 159, 167, 168, 169, 170, 171, 172, 173, 174, 251, 261, 278
revision of conviction 320, 327
revolution 53, 59, 80, 123, 128, 165, 373, 376
Revolutionary Committees Movement 81, 116, 161, 162, 246, 253, 401. *See also* R.C.M.
Richie, Lionel 117
right of return 265
Rights of the Child 115, 331, 333, 336, 381, 382, 405, 407, 409
right to competent interpretation 319
right to fair trial 249
right to jury 164
right to own counsel 319
right to refuse jury 251
right to self protection 164, 167, 169, 174
right to testify 249
right to trial by jury 251
Rio Conference 4
Rio de Janeiro 122, 130, 131, 138
Risangkom, Colonel Dr. Somkid 109
roadmap 385, 386, 388
Robert's Rules 271, 338, 405
Rome Statute 110, 112, 113, 114, 120, 163, 249, 262, 274, 292, 317, 325, 326, 333, 359, 364, 365, 366, 381, 382. *See also* International Criminal Court
routine inspections 345
royalties 322
Ruge, Dr. Reinhart 53, 68, 93, 100, 108, 112, 114, 175
Ruge, Reinhart 61
rule of recognition 373, 374, 382
rules of procedure 247, 249, 258, 260, 299, 343
Rules of Procedure and Evidence 114, 249, 274, 298, 318, 325, 326, 328, 381
ruling class 11, 15, 16, 19, 385
ruling elites 4, 384, 385
Russian 86, 318, 353, 364
Rwanda 21, 143

S

S.Varadaraju, Professor 82
safety regulations 347
salaries 70, 247, 300, 318, 322, 323, 335
salary 323, 349, 363
salary accounts 349
sanctions 127, 146, 147, 155, 311, 319, 359
sanitation 18, 138, 139, 140, 141, 146, 149, 152, 153, 275, 282, 284, 339
satellite photography 345
Sawant, Justice P. B. 112
Schopenhauer, Arthur 372
Schwartzberg Weighting proposal 161, 171
Schweitzer, Albert 263
scientific communities 386
Second Assembly 169, 170. *See also* Article 22
Second Operative Stage 34, 178
second operative stage 256, 353, 367
secrecy 383, 384, 385
Secretary General 32, 51, 55, 56, 60, 61, 72, 74, 82, 93, 177
security 6, 7, 11, 14, 15, 16, 17, 18, 19, 21, 22, 23, 50, 80, 81, 85, 93, 101, 119, 169, 179, 249, 250, 275, 279, 281, 309, 319, 332, 342, 349, 352, 380, 385, 401
Security Council 43, 54, 59, 71, 85, 113, 129, 159, 165, 166, 167, 168, 169, 171, 173, 174, 307, 317, 346, 361, 362, 373, 380
self-defense 255
self-government 249, 355, 369
self-protection 166, 255
Senior Administrator 32, 330
sentence 319, 320, 321, 327
sentencing 110, 112, 294, 316, 318, 319, 334
servicemembers 349

Sette-Camar, Hon. Jose 61
sewage 139
Shahumi, Mr Suleiman 116
show cause 311
Shri Puran Singh Azad 60, 61, 65, 68
signatures 34, 57, 88
simple majority 267, 268, 269, 271, 314, 328, 338, 386
SIMPOL 377
Simultaneous Policy Project 377
simultaneous ratification 120, 155
Singh, His Excellency Zail 65
Singhvi, L. M. 114
single performance statement 277
Siva, Vandana 147
Smith, Adam 3
Smith, J.W. 147, 150
social contract 109, 252
social disintegration 143
Sohn, Louis 161
solar energy 306
solemn undertaking 318, 337. *See also* oath
Somalia 21, 143
South Carolina 375
sovereign 2, 3, 4, 6, 12, 18, 19, 22, 23, 24, 25, 27, 28, 43, 58, 59, 74, 75, 86, 110, 122, 127, 128, 129, 132, 133, 134, 137, 143, 145, 152, 153, 273, 275, 284, 286, 373, 374, 377, 378, 380, 381, 382, 384, 385
sovereign equality 380
sovereign nation-states 2, 3, 4, 6, 19, 27, 28, 122, 137, 145, 152, 153, 286, 373, 380, 382
sovereignty 4, 5, 23, 24, 25, 26, 27, 31, 48, 59, 63, 67, 75, 125, 128, 129, 132, 157, 265, 269, 272, 285, 325, 362, 366, 373
Spanish 318, 353
Special Drawing Rights 70
speciality 327
special raporteur 348
specialty of charges 320
spectrum 141, 148, 314, 383
Spencer, D. H. 55
Spinoza, Baruch 128
spiritual evolution 8
Sri Aurobindo Ashram 61
Stages of Implementation 178
standard of living 380
Standing Parliamentary Commission on Translations 120
state apparatus 366, 367
state terrorism 144
statute 259, 308, 318, 333, 358, 364, 365
statute of limitations 308, 318
Steering Committee 267, 268, 269, 270, 271, 295, 296
stewarding agency 328, 329
stock liens 352
Strasbourg Court 76
Strategy Committee 85, 88, 89
Strong, Maurice 160
Subandjo, Dr. Ahmed 57
subjurisdictional legal charges 349
subpoenas 382
subsidiary organs 351
subsistence use 264
subventions 330
Summary Memorandum 326, 351
summons 319, 336
Superior Tribunal 33, 178, 298
superpower 10, 25, 26, 284, 372, 374
supplemental assistance 354
Surrender 320
surrender 320, 327
surveillance 384
surveillance in public trading floors 353
sustainable 1, 4, 7, 18, 19, 62, 66, 123, 128, 131, 133, 134, 140, 141, 142, 143, 144, 146, 147, 148, 149, 151, 152, 153, 154, 274, 275, 282, 299, 322, 340, 388
sweat-shop labor 12
system 2, 3, 4, 5, 6, 7, 8, 9, 10, 11, 12, 13, 14, 17, 18, 19, 20, 21, 22, 23, 24, 26, 27, 28, 31, 43, 48, 58, 59, 63, 64, 69, 70, 77, 81, 86, 90, 103, 111, 114, 115, 119, 121, 122, 123, 124, 125, 126, 127, 128, 129, 130, 132, 133, 134, 136, 137, 138, 139, 140, 142, 143, 145, 146, 148, 149, 150, 151, 152, 153, 154, 156, 161, 162, 163, 164, 165, 166, 168, 169, 172, 173, 248, 249, 253, 254, 272, 273, 275,

280, 281, 282, 283, 285, 286, 294, 303, 305, 307, 315, 322, 323, 326, 328, 330, 336, 341, 343, 344, 349, 350, 355, 357, 359, 361, 362, 363, 365, 366, 367, 368, 369, 374, 375, 376, 377, 378, 379, 382, 384, 385, 387, 388
system of exclusive private property rights 3

T

Taj Coromandel Hotel 76
Takoradi 90
Tamil Nadu 82, 90, 277, 315, 316, 322, 323, 325, 328
Tanzania 21, 50, 143
tax 15, 261, 277, 313, 314, 315, 349, 350
tax collection 314, 315
taxes 16, 22, 66, 314, 315, 351
tax evasion 314
Technology rents 314
Tennyson 61
term of office 267, 310
territory 16, 24, 285, 287
terror 274
terrorism 66, 67, 121, 122, 132, 144
terrorist 10, 66, 67, 68, 144, 379
testament 352
testimony 382
Thant, U 55
The Rules 325, 326, 328, 381. *See also* Rules of Procedure and Evidence
Thongsima, Associate Professor Yandej 109
Thoreau, Henry David 17
threat of sanctions 147
threats to humanity 8
Thring, Dr. James B. 74
Thurow, Lester C. 11
Togo 9, 77, 105, 109, 116, 117, 118, 275, 287, 289, 292, 297, 323, 325, 348, 350, 353, 352, 353, 354, 355
topsoil 136
torture 287, 288, 332, 349
Tovivich, Dr. Phichai 109
toxic wastes 3, 137, 138
trading floors 353
transit 72, 77, 296, 327
transparency 5, 277
Treasurer 49, 50, 68, 108, 114, 270, 338
treasurer 267, 270
Treasury 44, 300, 328, 330
treatment of animals 263
Trial Division 318
tribal jurisdictions 386
tricameral 262
Tripoli 9, 104, 116, 261, 340, 341, 342, 344, 347, 348, 350, 353
trust 2, 353
Tucker, Dr. Helen 57
Tucker, Mrs. Helen 55
Tutu, Most Rev. Desmond M. B. 61
twenty-five nations 146, 147, 156, 386. *See also* 25 countries
two-thirds majority 269, 270

U

U.N. Charter 4, 48, 75, 77, 86, 129, 133, 134, 161, 167, 168, 172, 363, 380, 381
U. N. Reform 71
U.S. 8, 10, 11, 23, 24, 25, 26, 49, 52, 53, 61, 71, 72, 76, 81, 82, 85, 130, 135, 137, 143, 150, 153, 156, 162, 167, 168, 374, 375, 378, 388, 389, 390, 391, 396, 403
U.S. Constitution 374, 375
U.S. dollars 130, 137, 143, 388
UDHR 112, 164, 166, 171,174, 353, 363, 364, 366. *See also* Universal Declaration of Human Rights
UN 242 264
UN 338 264
undemocratic 6, 19, 20, 21, 22, 127, 129, 133, 272, 372, 373, 374, 376, 377, 378, 379, 380, 381
UNESCO 381
United Nations 4, 30, 34, 43, 48, 57, 59, 68, 71, 72, 74, 75, 76, 77, 83, 113, 115, 116, 120, 122, 127, 129, 130, 132, 134, 137, 159, 160, 161, 162, 164, 165, 166, 167, 168, 169, 170, 172, 173, 174, 251, 254, 255, 260,

261, 262, 265, 268, 278, 285, 286, 307, 308, 317, 333, 344, 347, 349, 352, 359, 363, 364, 379, 380, 381
United Nations Environmental Council. 160
United Nations Scientific Committee on the Effects of Atomic Radiation 347
United States 10, 11, 24, 26, 52, 88, 114, 117, 130, 135, 142, 148, 149, 152, 153, 164, 246, 263, 275, 349, 364, 365, 378
United States Constitution 164, 402
unity-in-diversity 124, 128, 151, 155
unity in diversity 5, 11, 14, 17, 18, 19, 27, 125, 134, 179, 272, 273, 276, 281, 283, 330
universal ballot 269
Universal Card System 77
Universal Declaration of Human Rights 14, 26, 163, 164, 166, 167, 168, 169, 284, 285, 363, 366, 367, 373, 379, 380, 382, 392, 395, 401, 404, 409. *See also* UDHR
Universal Guaranteed Annual Income 119
universal suffrage 382
universities 12, 43, 53, 57, 247, 386
UNSCEAR 347
unsustainable 2, 88, 135, 136, 139
uranium 143, 342, 368
utopia 156

V

Vaitha, Karikar 82, 112
valuation 277
Verification 347
vessels 348, 349, 350
veterans 308, 349, 350
Veziroglu, Dr. 69
Vickman, Leon 63
victims 6, 13, 119, 286, 319, 327, 336, 349, 352
Victims and Witnesses Unit 326
Vig, Jorgen Laursen 55
Vigyan Bhawan 65
vital resources 3, 22
voluntary contributions 321, 381
Voter Information Office 338
Voter Registry 337

W

waiver of visa 352
waivers 352
war crimes 110, 248, 287, 288, 317, 318
War of Liberation of 1971 289
War on Terror 10
warrants 33, 45, 307, 309, 319, 329, 346, 369
Water Act 115, 339, 340, 406
wealth 3, 6, 11, 12, 14, 15, 16, 17, 19, 26, 44, 52, 81, 89, 128, 137, 145, 146, 147, 150, 151, 154, 275, 282, 305, 322, 373
weapons 2, 3, 6, 14, 20, 22, 33, 55, 62, 63, 64, 78, 119, 127, 130, 141, 143, 145, 151, 152, 154, 250, 252, 253, 254, 255, 257, 265, 274, 275, 284, 293, 305, 308, 309, 342, 344, 345, 346, 347, 348, 360, 361, 362, 365, 367, 378, 379, 384, 385, 388
weapons of mass destruction 2, 6, 20, 22, 33, 55, 62, 63, 78, 127, 151, 250, 252, 253, 255, 257, 265, 275, 293, 305, 344, 348, 367, 378
Weeramantry, His Honour Christopher 118
Weston, Professor Burns H. 64
WHO 43, 118, 120, 347, 348, 381. *See also* World Health Organization
withdrawal of investments 146
witnesses 319, 327, 352, 382
Wolfach 53
World Administration 31, 32, 177, 192, 268, 305, 322
World Attorney 33, 45, 251, 301, 307, 318, 341, 342
World Attorneys General 308, 309, 317, 318, 326, 328, 334, 341, 346. *See also* Prosecutor
World Attorneys General Office 30, 308, 309, 328, 341
World Bank 3, 80, 88, 126, 129, 132, 141, 142, 147, 374

World Bench for Criminal Cases 113, 292, 317, 322, 325, 337. *See also* International Criminal Court. *See also* Rome Statute
World Bench for Human Rights 111, 312
World Bench for Juvenile Cases 113, 115, 334
World Boundaries and Elections Administration 32, 38, 42, 44, 177, 252, 253, 337, 339
world capitals 34
World Chief Justice Conference Fund 353
World Citizens Assembly 61, 75
World Civil Service Administration 32, 42, 44, 177, 256
World Co-ordinating Council 73, 89
World Commission on Terrorism 30, 45, 67, 301, 341
World Constituent Assembly 34, 44, 52, 55, 57, 58, 59, 71, 72, 75, 164, 170, 175, 178, 254, 260, 261, 267, 268, 269, 270, 271, 314
World Constitutional Convention 34, 48, 49, 50, 51, 52, 53, 54, 56, 82, 258
World Constitution and Parliament Association 1, 10, 47, 48, 51, 52, 53, 54, 55, 57, 58, 59, 60, 61, 65, 66, 70, 71, 72, 74, 76, 78, 80, 81, 82, 85, 86, 89, 91, 116, 155, 372, 374, 382, 386, 410
World Court Children's Education Fund 353
World Court General Adult Education Fund 353
World Disarmament Agency 30, 45, 62, 250, 253, 293, 294, 306, 308, 309, 342, 343, 345, 346, 347, 352, 353
World District Ombudsen 341
World Economic Development Organization 110, 294, 303, 324
World Electoral and Administrative Districts 32, 42, 268
World Environmental Protection Agency 264. *See also* Global Ministry of Environment
World Executive 31, 32, 43, 56, 125, 177, 178, 189, 246, 268, 313, 362, 383, 387
World Federal Authority 54
world federal corruption 317
World Federalist Movement 76, 253, 385
world federalist movement 10
World Federal Privileges & Immunities 117
World Federal Zone 348, 349
World Federal Zones 34, 178, 213, 306
World Financial Administration 29, 32, 42, 44, 177, 255, 256, 257, 324, 343
world government 4, 5, 6, 7, 8, 9, 10, 16, 18, 19, 20, 21, 23, 26, 27, 48, 49, 51, 52, 53, 56, 59, 61, 69, 71, 73, 74, 76, 77, 80, 81, 85, 86, 89, 90, 121, 122, 123, 124, 126, 128, 129, 133, 134, 135, 136, 139, 140, 141, 142, 143, 144, 145, 146, 149, 152, 160, 172, 268, 269, 270, 272, 273, 279, 280, 283, 284, 285, 286, 287, 295, 317, 328, 329, 334, 337, 354, 365, 371, 374, 376, 377, 385, 387
World Government Funding Corporation 30, 66, 110, 115, 255. *See also* Earth Federation Funding Corporation
World Government of World Citizens 160, 309, 402
world government records 329
World Health Organization 120, 255, 347, 348, 381. *See also* WHO
World Hydrocarbon Reserve Board 313
World Hydrogen Energy System Authority 303
World Judicial Commission 312, 334, 337, 395, 403, 405, 408
World Judiciary 31, 32, 33, 163, 178, 201, 250, 268, 328, 361, 406
World Jury Commission 114, 328
World Juvenile Bench 381. *See also* Juvenile Bench. *See also* Juvenile Court

World law 345
world law 4, 5, 6, 7, 9, 10, 15, 22, 23, 26, 28, 31, 63, 100, 102, 107, 109, 113, 119, 126, 143, 150, 165, 246, 248, 249, 266, 287, 301, 309, 317, 336, 341, 346, 352, 353, 357, 358, 359, 360, 361, 362, 365, 366, 367, 368, 369, 370, 372, 373, 374, 376, 377, 381, 382, 386
world legislation 31, 32, 34, 63, 101, 109, 110, 111, 113, 115, 118, 163, 164, 165, 168, 171, 173, 174, 247, 248, 250, 251, 254, 256, 257, 260, 261, 262, 270, 273, 274, 291, 292, 296, 298, 300, 301, 302, 305, 306, 314, 316, 318, 325, 329, 334, 339, 345, 350, 355, 359, 360, 363, 364, 366, 368, 376
World Legislative Act 30, 38, 44, 77, 78, 81, 110, 111, 112, 115, 117, 119, 164, 168, 247, 256, 257, 293, 294, 295, 296, 298, 299, 300, 301, 302, 303, 304, 305, 306, 307, 308, 309, 312, 313, 314, 315, 316, 322, 323, 325, 328, 330, 331, 333, 334, 337, 339, 340, 341, 342, 344, 347, 348, 350, 351, 353, 352, 353, 354, 367, 368, 381
World Legislative Bill 62, 63, 65, 66, 67, 69, 265
world ministries 9, 86
World Oceans and Seabeds Commission 296
World Ombudsmus 31, 33, 56, 75, 117, 125, 145, 163, 164, 178, 208, 250, 260, 268, 272, 311, 315, 317, 321, 328, 340, 341, 342, 348, 351, 381, 383
World Patents 112, 322
World Peace Act 110, 111, 307, 308
World Peace Envoy 60, 108, 109, 253
World Penal Code 110, 112, 315, 316. *See also* Criminal Code Penalty Classification
World Police 45, 206, 207, 383
World Police Supervisor 33, 44, 45, 207
World Region 29, 38
world regions 5, 342
World Revenue 111, 115, 314, 315
World Security Act 111, 308, 309
World Service Authority 253, 366
World Social Forum 127
world state 370
World Supreme Court 32, 42, 44, 63, 164, 178, 249, 258, 298, 381
World Syntegrity Project 160, 339, 401
world system 7, 17, 19, 22, 24, 27, 122, 127, 132, 138, 139, 140, 143, 145, 148, 149, 150, 152, 165, 376, 385, 387, 388
World Trade Organization 7, 126, 129, 142, 373
World Union 61
World Unity and Peace Education Department 114
World University System 45, 63, 70, 90, 297, 341
World Youth Parliament for Water 339, 406

Y

Yadav, His Excellency Singhe 115
Youngman, Ms. Althya 54
youth participation 339
Yugoslavia 85, 145, 275

Z

Zaidi, Dr. Husbafa 82
Zail Singh 65, 93
Zamenhof, Dr. Ludoviko 278

The Institute for Economic Democracy is dedicated to producing a philosophy for elimination of waste within the economy, that ends poverty, and that provides a quality life for each citizen of Earth. Toward that end we have published the books listed below. For later books, go to www.ied.info.

Triumph of Civilization: Democracy, Non-violence and the Piloting of Spaceship Earth 2010, Glen Martin.

Ascent to Freedom: Practical and Philosophical Foundations of Democratic World Law, 2008, Glen T. Martin.

Money: A Mirror Image of the Economy, 2nd edition, 2008, J.W. Smith.

The Earth Belongs to Everyone, 2008, Alanna Hartzok.

Millennium Dawn: The Philosophy of Planetary Crisis and Human Liberation, 2005, Glen T. Martin.

Earth Federation Now! Tomorrow is Too Late, 2005. Errol E. Harris.

Economic Democracy: The Political Struggle of the Twenty-First Century, 4th edition, 2005, J.W. Smith.

21st Century Democratic Renaissance, 2006. Errol E. Harris.

WHY: The Deeper History of the September 11th Terrorist Attack on America, 3rd edition, 2005, J.W. Smith.

The Emperor's God: Misunderstandings of Christianity, 2008, D. Michael Rivage-Seul.

A Constitution for the Federation of Earth in English, French, Spanish, and Esperanto Editor, Eugenia Almand, (forthcoming).

Cooperating Organizations

The Institute for Economic Democracy
Global peace and sustainable development equals peace and prosperity for all
www.ied.info

World Prout Assembly
Economy of the People, For the People and By the People!
www.worldproutassembly.org/

International Philosophers for Peace
Developing a just social, economic, & political basis for peace and human well-being
www.ippno.org/

Institute On World Problems
Creating a world order of peace, justice, and freedom
www.worldproblems.net

Earth Rights Institute
Dedicated to securing a culture of peace and justice by establishing dynamic worldwide networks of persons of goodwill and special skill, promoting policies and programs which further democratic rights to common heritage resources, and building ecological communities.
www.earthrights.net

Action Institute for Literacy and Human Resource Development
Education through Project Learning Communnities (PLC)
www.ailahhurd.org/

The Hour Money Institute for Global Harmony
Dedicated to establishing an hour of work as the money unit worldwide
www.hourmoney.org/

Network on Democracy Over Empire
Dedicated to egalitarian democracies replacing the global imperial system
www.waltedavis.info/

Global Issues
A very active supporter but does not take donations at this time
www.globalissues.org

Rights are available for publishing in your region, in English or translations, www.ied.info/. We are available to present these concepts to your class or group. ied@ied.info

www.ingramcontent.com/pod-product-compliance
Lightning Source LLC
Chambersburg PA
CBHW041320210926
51847CB00002B/7
9781933567167